PENGUIN ACADEMICS

CHANGING MINDS
ARGUMENTS ON CONTEMPORARY AND ENDURING ISSUES

Jon Ford

De Anza College

Marjorie Ford

Stanford University

Longman

New York Boston San Francisco
London Toronto Sydney Tokyo Singapore Madrid
Mexico City Munich Paris Cape Town Hong Kong Montreal

Executive Editor: Lynn M. Huddon
Senior Marketing Manager: Sandra McGuire
Senior Supplements Editor: Donna Campion
Production Manager: Stacey Kulig
Project Coordination, Text Design, and Electronic
   Page Makeup: Pre-Press PMG
Cover Designer/Manager: John Callahan
Cover Image: Getty Images
Senior Manufacturing Buyer: Alfred C. Dorsey
Printer and Binder: Courier/Westford
Cover Printer: Lehigh/Phoenix Color Corp.

For more information about the Penguin Academic series, please contact us by mail at Pearson Education, attn. Marketing Department, 51 Madison Avenue, 29th floor, New York, NY 10010 or by e-mail at pearsonhighered@pearson.com.

For permission to use copyrighted material, grateful acknowledgment is made to the copyright holders on pp. 535–541, which are hereby made part of this copyright page.

Library of Congress Cataloging-in-Publication Data
Ford, Jon (Jon M.)
   Changing minds: arguments on contemporary and enduring issues/
Jon Ford, Marjorie Ford.—1st ed.
       p. cm.
   ISBN-13: 978-0-205-56813-0
   ISBN-10: 0-205-56813-0
   1. English language—Rhetoric.   2. Persuasion (Rhetoric)   3. College readers.   4. Reasoning.   I. Ford, Jon.   II. Title.
   PE1431.F58 2009
   808'.042—dc22

                                                          2009018364

1 2 3 4 5 6 7 8 9 10—CRW—12 11 10 09

Longman
is an imprint of

www.pearsonhighered.com

ISBN-13: 978-0-205-56813-0
ISBN-10: 0-205-56813-0

contents

| CHAPTER 3 | Educating a Nation   93

| CHAPTER 4 | Revisioning Immigration   146

CHAPTER 5   Engaging Work   211

CHAPTER 6   Censoring Extreme Speech   261

preface

Changing Minds is a collection of classic and contemporary essays intended for the general reader as well as for college teachers and students of argument and critical thinking. The book is designed to acquaint readers with strategies for developing an effective and persuasive argument and to demonstrate the rich and complex nature of such writing by providing examples of essays on a number of subjects of controversy. The included texts were written for a variety of audiences and publications, including popular books, newspapers, newsmagazines and nontraditional weeklies, professional journals, opinion magazines, political publications, online journals, as well as speeches delivered before Congressional committees and other public forums.

Our book begins with a chapter on the art of argument that presents essential elements of argument as well as common strategies and misunderstandings in reading and writing arguments. We introduce the history of argument and the concept of the "rhetorical triangle" between the advocate of an issue, his or her audience, and the subject being argued. We also explain the use of claims and warrants, refutation strategies, deductive and inductive reasoning and fact-based support, as well as the proper role of emotion in argument. We consider logical fallacies related to logic, factual proofs, and emotions. The distinctions among definition, cause and effect, evaluative, and proposal arguments are made clear, and strategies for close analytical and evaluative reading are presented. The chapter ends with an annotated professional essay.

After this useful introduction to argument, nine chapters of readings on contemporary issues are included. Each chapter has a brief introduction and seven to eight readings, the final two of which focus on a narrower aspect of the chapter theme and illustrate differing positions. Every selection is introduced by a headnote that provides information about the author's background, education, related experiences, and publications. A set of three questions concludes each selected reading. These questions can be used to promote close reading, to develop class discussions, for practice in analyzing argumentative strategies and critical thinking, or as prompts for writing an argument. The topic chapters integrate opportunities for strengthening reading and critical thinking skills and for doing informal and formal writing about issues, while reflecting on how one's point of view has been re-enforced or changed by the arguments presented. Each of the chapters covers issues that have had an evolving and controversial history that each new generation faces—issues such as new definitions of the family, changing views of education, diversity and immigration, free speech and privacy issues, the impact of media and the Internet on communication and behavior, as well environmental concerns such as global warming and biologically engineered seeds and foods.

We hope the informational and formal organization of *Changing Minds* will open the way to serious and critical thinking about change and new ideas. Writing an effective argument, giving a persuasive speech, being discerning about persuasive claims that are illogical, debating an issue, or changing someone's mind feels satisfying once the work is complete. In the end, we must always remember that imagination, creativity, and honesty can help to touch other people's minds and hearts.

Additional Teaching Resources

The Instructor's Manual for *Changing Minds* (available to adopters) provides detailed answers to study questions for all reading selections in the book, as well as brief critiques of the reasoning and alternative positions on the core argument in many selections. Extra writing options and activites also are suggested, particularly for Chapter 1, which presents the key steps in constructing an argument and spotting logical fallacies, as well as critical reading tips.

The MyCompLab website integrates the market-leading instruction, multimedia tutorials, and exercises for writing, grammar, and research that users have come to identify with the program and includes a new online composing space and new assessment tools. The result is a revolutionary application that offers a seamless and flexible teaching and learning environment built specifically for writers. Created after years of extensive research and in partnership with composition faculty and students across the country, the new MyCompLab provides help for writers in the context of their writing, with instructor- and peer-commenting functionality, proven tutorials and exercises for writing, grammar and research, an e-portfolio, an assignment-builder, a bibliography tool, tutoring services, and a gradebook and course management organization created specifically for writing classes. Visit www.mycomplab.com for more information.

Acknowledgments

We acknowledge the following critics for their invaluable input in helping us to select particular essays and approaches to argument for *Changing Minds*: Alex E. Blazer, University of Louisville; Linda Borla, Cypress College; Jennifer Brezina, College of the Canyons; Kimberly Costino, California State University, San Bernardino; Shahara Drew, Tufts University; Kate Egerton, Indiana University South Bend; Conseula Francis, College of Charleston; Keith Haynes, Yavapai College; Sandra Kay Heck, Walters State Community College; Tobi Jacobi, Colorado State University; Tom Lovin, Southwestern Illinois College; Kathryn McCormick, Central Missouri State University; Robin Parent, Utah State University; Dan Schierenbeck, Central Missouri State University; Abby Spero, Montgomery College; William Thelin, The University of Akron.

Jon Ford
Marjorie Ford

Jon Ford was educated at the University of Texas-Austin and the University of Wisconsin-Madison. After moving to California in 1968, he wrote and translated poetry before studying education at San Francisco State University. He began teaching writing and critical thinking at the College of Alameda in 1970, working there until his retirement. Currently, he teaches classes in critical thinking and writing at De Anza College and co-authors textbooks in argumentation and critical thinking with his wife, Marjorie Ford.

Marjorie Ford was born in Los Angeles and educated at the University of California, Berkeley. She has taught in the writing program at Stanford University for twenty years, where she edited the nationally distributed program newsletter *Notes in the Margins*. She has travelled and lived abroad in Europe, Vietnam, Thailand, India, Japan, and Brazil; she has also co-authored textbooks and anthologies in writing, literature, argumentation, and community-service learning.

CHAPTER 1

Introduction to Writing and Reading Arguments

What Is Argument?

We often think that an argument is a verbal or written disagreement, sometimes one that escalates into a "battle of words" grounded in strong emotions which, if not subdued, could come to real blows. To calm things down, people may say, as Rodney King did during the Los Angeles riots, "Can't we all just get along?" However, since individuals have different perspectives on specific issues, disputes arise; therefore, the need to argue cases is inevitable. Miraculously, after a good argument, we may actually get along better with our antagonist, or at least feel better about presenting our case.

The problem is not really with argument itself; for if we were never allowed to disagree and argue, we would likely feel frustrated, deprived of a fundamental liberty: the opportunity to let our opinions be heard in the communities to which we belong and in public forums. In fact, the ability to solve our disputes through verbal or symbolic argument is an important part of what makes us advance the quality of our lives. Argument may have helped us to advance and to prosper in the evolutionary struggle for survival as we debated the usefulness of a new tool, a new way of performing a task, or a new idea. Today the advancements of technology have changed our lives radically. Our progress has been a process of vision and creativity as well as a result of finding solutions to problems. Solutions are developed out of discussion, debate, and argument.

Propaganda: Argument in the Marketplace

We live in a society that values competition almost absolutely. We must compete in order to get into the best pre-school, elementary school, high school, college, and job. Because of the prominence of competition in our society and in the marketplace, we may have come to view argument as a propaganda tool rather than as a form of dialogue that can lead to mutual understanding and advancement of knowledge. In today's world, types of one-sided, propagandistic "argument" might include written, oral, and/or visual arguments for an actual purchase—from a soft drink, to a dress, to a car, to an insurance policy, to a home. Other arguments may claim that we should be making a "purchase" of ideas, such as a political position or ballot proposition. Under the pressure of slogans and visual presentation in the media, in paying with the currency of our voting power or cash contribution to the candidate or cause presented, we may forget that there are larger consequences to our political choices. Thinking critically under such pressure can be difficult because sometimes we don't get all of the information and evidence needed to make an informed decision.

The common nature of propaganda arguments in our society produces negative assumptions and definitions that people may apply to all forms of argument: first, that argument is a win-or-lose, all-or-nothing proposition; therefore, an arguer must do whatever it takes (without absolutely lying) to establish an ultra-positive, near-flawless view of the "product" or issue at stake. Needless to say, such an arguer pays little attention to the arguments of opponents even if they seem truthful and reasonable. Propaganda is a manipulative form of communication and must not be confused with ethical argument.

Definition of Argument: A Positive Perspective

In contrast to the negative stereotype we have just presented, meaningful argument can be defined as a way of developing and sharing ideas on a significant and controversial topic through examining and evaluating alternative viewpoints. This view of argument may seem closer to a discussion; it is often termed "dialogic" after the "Socratic" philosophical dialogues of Socrates himself, Plato, Cicero, and other early philosophers, whose works resembled public forums of debate designed to lead readers to new perspectives through a guided discussion over seemingly contradictory choices and ideas. In addition, an argument cannot include the "opposition" unless the arguer knows the values and interests of his or her audience. For example, one would have to shape one's argument for one's audience on a controversial topic such as peer-to-peer file sharing. The argument to a student, the president of Atlantic records, or to a college dean of students would each be unique in techniques used to reach its audience.

Argument that tries to persuade rather than to bully is not always designed to win a debate but often to bring a curious audience of listeners into new territory, opening their minds to a new and different perspective. To be inclusive, we could place the different degrees of argument on a scale leading from those that seek to win absolute agreement from the audience, to those designed to change the thinking of neutral or skeptical listeners, to dialogic arguments designed to create compromise, to those that are more openly exploratory, designed to seek truth rather than a particular solution or goal.

The Rhetorical Triangle in Argument

Civic rhetoric was defined by the Greek philosopher Aristotle as a human skill (*techne*) involving strategies of arrangement (structure and sequence of ideas), invention, and style (sentence structure, word choice, figurative language), combined with three kinds of "proofs" (*ethos, pathos,* and *logos*). These proofs are what make an argument convincing—without them, the writing might seem witty and entertaining, like a good advertisement, but it would not be genuine and moving in a deeper sense. Logos, ethos, and pathos are the components of a rhetorical argumentative strategy directed to an audience that is open-minded and responsive to reason.

These three rhetorical strategies are often represented and explained in the form of what is known as the rhetorical triangle (see diagram on the following page).

The lines connecting the three points of this equilateral triangle signify the ideal relationship between the three "corners" of the image.

4

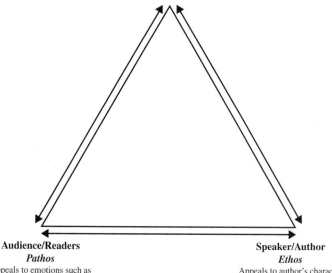

Subject/Message
Logos
Appeals to reason such as logic,
facts, statistics, case studies,
expert testimony.

Audience/Readers
Pathos
Appeals to emotions such as
love, loyalty, pity, fear, anger.

Speaker/Author
Ethos
Appeals to author's character
qualities of authority,
credibility, commonsense, fairness.

Examine the corners of the triangle: the *message* (i.e., what the argument asserts or claims to be true), the *speaker* (the person who holds the views expressed in the argument), and the *audience* (the person or group of people for whom the message is intended). The speaker must express his or her ideas so that the audience will understand and attend to them or accept them as true, or at least as worthy of consideration.

The triangle of rhetoric in argument is complicated by the interests, associations, and qualities of each of the three "corners." *Ethos*, or "character," is connected to the corner associated with the speaker and represents the efforts the advocate makes in the argument to gain the trust of the audience. Advocates establish their ethos by speaking truthfully and directly and sometimes by providing examples that help the audience to accept them as people with background and wisdom in the area under consideration.

Pathos ("experience" in Greek) is most closely connected to the audience corner of the triangle. Pathos refers to the audience's need to experience lived emotions in the argument and the speaker or writer connecting with the listener's or reader's values and concerns. Imaginative language, examples, and narratives all help to engage an audience's emotions. Thirdly, *logos* ("word" in Greek) is directly connected to the message corner at the apex of the triangle, and involves the presentation of consistent logical and factual proofs designed to clarify the subject and convince the audience intellectually of the writer's position.

If the "triangle" is unbalanced or if any "corner" is lacking in development, the structure of an argument collapses, failing to persuade or to change minds. For instance, a deceitful or propagandistic argument may convince some readers through its powerful language or emotional storytelling, but objective audiences may find that such an argument contains an excess of *pathos* (e.g., too much emotionality and "pulling on the heart strings"), and/or a lack of intellectually convincing *logos* (e.g., fallacies of reasoning, factual distortions, and manipulation). Excessive *pathos* and *logos*—or not enough—weaken the *ethos* or believability of the argument and may lead to a possible rejection of its overall position.

Selecting an Issue to Argue

An argument may consider a controversial subject such as gun ownership, AIDS, the war in Iraq, global warming, or censorship, using one such topic as the beginning of an issue question and statement of purpose. An issue question often begins with the word "should" followed by two or more posed action choices, or positions for or against. "Should we (the United States, Congress, or the courts) do X about Y?" A "should" query provides the possibility for a variety of reasons available on either side of the issue: Should AIDS be our number-one health care priority? Should public schools receive more funding? Before selecting, narrowing, and defining your issue, you should ask whether enough evidence and reasonable arguments exist both for a positive and a negative position on the chosen issue; in other words, is it "arguable"?

After choosing a topic and the specific issue you wish to argue, spend some time exploring various positions that can be taken on it, drawing general contrasts between viewpoints and pointing out the limits and logical pitfalls of each. Do a preliminary Internet search at home and in library databases to see what has been written on the topic, and collect some quotations reflecting a variety of approaches to the issue you have chosen. If too much has been written on the topic, narrow the original issue. For example, instead of writing about the skyrocketing cost of gas, you might write about a solution that encourages state government to fund more public transportation in large urban cities and encourages citizens to use the public transportation that already exists. Or you could argue that people need to carpool and that businesses need to create incentives for employees to carpool.

Clarifying and Focusing the Position Statement

Arguers must define key terms and ideas in their issue statements. When writing about euthanasia of terminally ill patients, clarify what type of euthanasia you accept or disapprove of. For example, in one form of "passive" euthanasia (legal in many states), a terminally ill patient is disconnected from a life-support system with the advice and consent of family members and physicians. "Active" euthanasia, on the other hand, such as administering drugs to help a patent die, is usually considered to be unethical and illegal. An issue statement that would clarify the limits of the proposition under debate might read as follows: "Euthanasia is a term with many emotional associations, and it is used in a variety of ways. In this paper, I will be arguing for what is known as _____ euthanasia; for example, _____." Avoid terms that are designed to manipulate your audience, such as expressions like "mercy killing" to describe the practice of euthanasia. Furthermore, the controversy around an issue can be channeled effectively in the form of constructive argumentation only if claims are qualified. It is not feasible to argue that "murderers should receive the death penalty," because the reader will find many exceptions to such a sweeping statement. On the other hand, a qualified statement such as "murder during an act of child molestation should result in the death penalty" is a more limited and arguable claim, although of course some readers would still disagree with it.

Considering the Opposition/Reaching Out to the Audience

What seems appropriate for one set of readers may not meet the demands of another. In effective argument, it is important to determine the characteristics of the audience. The following checklist helps to define the audience and to select strategies for communication:

1. How large and/or diverse is the audience? What are their genders, ages, economic, political, and social backgrounds?

2. What background knowledge does the audience need in order to understand the issues at hand? Will any technical or complex words or concepts need to be defined or explained?
3. How can I engage the audience's interest in the topic? How will the argument or solution benefit them?
4. What objections might the audience have to the information, approach, or point of view in the argument, and how can these objections be overcome?
5. What values do I share with my audience? How are my values different from theirs?

Creating a clear mental image of the audience will help in selecting appropriate arguments, effective examples, and a proper choice of language for the paper as a whole. The audience should be approached respectfully, taking into account their possible perceptions and sensitivities about the issue under discussion and acknowledging potential shared concerns. The following brief example is from an argument paper in favor of surrogate parenting directed to a conservative anti-technology audience. Notice how the author anticipates and acknowledges the feelings of her audience. What else could she do more to reassure them that surrogacy is a fair and ethical practice?

> Many people find surrogate parenthood an unnatural way to reproduce, potentially exploitive of the birth mother. I can fully understand these reservations and experience some of them myself. Nevertheless, I believe that the benefits of this practice outweigh the potential for abuse, and that people should have a right to make this choice based on their own needs and values.

Persuasive Warrants: Ethics, Logic, and Facts

A strong argument includes convincing "warrants," or reasons, to back up the claim of the paper. The warrant in argument is similar to a warrant in law: it gives a claim a sense of authority, making the audience consider that it might be credible. Warrants or reasons may include ethical statements: "I am against automatic drug testing [claim] *because it is an invasion of the right to privacy*" [warrant]; "I am opposed to late-term abortion *because it involves killing a viable human life*" [warrant]. Practical, factual considerations can also be convincing: "The exposure of children to materialistic values is difficult to avoid or reverse, *because toy companies, clothing brands, media advertising, peer pressure, and many parents' lifestyles increasingly reinforce such values*" [warrant].

How many and what kind of reasons and facts are needed to create a convincing argument? An over-zealous researcher might write a paper so full of facts and details that the reader could lose the main point of the argument. Although there is no absolute point at which a writer can say "that's enough," consider the projected length of the essay along with the needs and expectations of the audience. If space allows, consider using several types of reasonable or ethical supports, different kinds of factual supports or reasons, and emotional or feeling-based discussion, for a balanced approach. Always remember to develop each support fully to make a clear and convincing point.

Refutation

Refutation or rebuttal can be employed at any point in an argument to demonstrate mistaken ideas, concepts, or facts of a position or proposal. This is important both in examining the positions other arguers take as well one's own. If arguing against surrogacy, one could point out the emotional and financial problems involved, as well as the number of other options available to couples: fertility clinics, medications, adoption, or just enjoying interacting with other people's children. Another essay might be focused on a student arguing for the legalization of a certain recreational drug and show different ways that a campaign to outlaw the drug has failed. In addition to refuting the failed "solutions" of the opposition, the arguer must also defend his or her position against potential criticism, anticipating in advance such critiques and explaining, in a straightforward, honest manner, why they would not apply.

In the following refutation from an editorial in favor of the passage of an initiative that would make it illegal to manufacture or transport nuclear materials or nuclear weaponry within county lines, the author points out weaknesses in the reasoning and factual statements in the opposition argument as well as logical fallacies such as the "appeal to fear," the "slippery slope fallacy," and "false cause." (These logical fallacies are explained below.)

> The opposition to the initiative for a nuclear-free zone argues in its campaign brochure that the initiative will result in an increase in "standing in line" and "documents written in a language only bureaucrats can understand." This statement seems to be a case of questionable or false causal reasoning. It provides no evidence to demonstrate that the nuclear-free zone measure will result in any waiting in lines or filling out of difficult forms. In fact, most of the

arguments presented against the measure reflect a kind of slippery-slope reasoning and a related appeal to fear: "It'll be a nightmare," the opposition argues, presenting a specter of "numerous hearings . . . endless reporting requirements." This claim has no basis in the simple, direct language of the nuclear-free zone measure, and sounds like a groundless future prediction. The opposition also argues that the measure will cost taxpayers millions of dollars each year, as well as "lost jobs, lost businesses, and higher taxes." Since few if any jobs in the county, and little of the tax base, have any direct relationship to nuclear weapons production or the nuclear power industry, I can hardly see how this appeal to fear has any real basis in fact.

Deductive Reasoning In Argument

Deductive reasoning is a more formal way of what we do when we discuss a position or idea in daily life. To evaluate new ideas and experiences, we draw inferences, moving from a fact or idea that we believe to be true to evaluate new ideas and experiences in relationship to that which we already know or assume to be true. Similarly, deduction starts with a "premise," or statement, which has already been tested or that is accepted as law in an ethical, moral, or regulatory area and proceeds to apply the premise to specific cases in order to learn more about the world or to help make a decision or evaluation. For example, a prosecuting attorney might argue, reasoning deductively, that since stealing expensive items is against the law and should be punished, it follows that if Sam Wilson has stolen a new car, he should be jailed.

Although such deductively drawn conclusions seem logical, no argument, no matter how carefully constructed, will be accepted by everyone. In the case of Sam Wilson, his lawyer might attempt to reason deductively that Sam is a first offender, and that there is an element of fairness and forgiveness implicit in our legal system, and that we believe in giving people a "second chance" if they have a character that is redeemable.

The Syllogism

With major premises and conclusions drawn from known facts and beliefs, logicians have devised a three-part structure for the deductive argument: the syllogism. It is helpful to reword informal, condensed statements, such as the ones above about Sam Wilson and his trial, as syllogisms consisting of an initial general statement (known as the major premise) followed by a minor premise in which the major premise is applied or related to a specific situation. Finally, by drawing a concluding statement from the relation between the first two premises, we complete the syllogism:

> **Major Premise:** Stealing an expensive object ("grand theft") requires strict punishment.
> **Minor Premise:** Sam Wilson has stolen a new Lexus, an expensive object, thus committing grand theft.
> **Conclusion:** Therefore, due to his act of grand theft, Sam should receive strict punishment, serving jail time.

A syllogism should have a precisely worded and factually or ethically acceptable major premise, which in the example above is clearly worded and is a commonly held belief and legal fact. The minor premise is also factual and "fits" neatly within the boundaries of the major premise; therefore, it follows logically that the "conclusion" can be drawn from the first two premises. This syllogism is referred to as a "valid" syllogism, in that the three terms—major premise, minor premise, and conclusion—are correctly and logically related to one another. However, aspects of the syllogism—its facts and principles—can still be debated: Was it actually Sam who stole the Lexus? Does he have a clean record? Is he genuinely repentant?

Syllogisms that are free of unexamined assumptions and faulty core premises increase the *logos* of an argument, as audiences are likely to consider them to be valid (correctly reasoned), and many will feel the ideas to be "sound." Knowing how to investigate the deductive arguments of others for the criteria of validity and soundness is helpful both in reading and creating argumentative statements. We can improve the quality of our own thinking as well as point out more effectively the weak points in the arguments of our opposition, an essential part of the "refutation" or counterargument.

Avoiding Fallacies of Logic

Fallacies of logic are statements that appear to be logical but which actually conceal intentional or unintentional errors in the reasoning process. They may trick the reader through logical indicators or transitions such as "because" or "therefore," yet because of the illogical way that they are developed, and sometimes because of the deceptive intentions of the arguer, fallacies can be misleading and can obstruct critical thinking. It is important to be able to recognize fallacies, both in your own reasoning in order to become a more effective thinker and arguer, and to be able to notice fallacies in the arguments of others. When you can understand and effectively discredit fallacies, you will be more likely to convince others. At the same time, you need to be courteous and cautious in pointing out people's fallacious reasoning, for what you perceive as a fallacy may be the very foundation of another person's belief system.

Circular Reasoning or Begging the Question

In circular reasoning, a key premise or warrant is missing, but an arguer simply assumes a proposition as proven, often through repetition or rewording: "My candidate for city council is the best choice because she's far better than any of the others" or "Your solution is no good because it's simply wrong-headed." When confronted with what looks like circular reasoning, continue to ask the question "But why?"

Faulty Analogy

An analogy is sometimes used in argument and other forms of writing to make the unfamiliar clear, as we might do in comparing an echo to a ball bouncing off a wall and returning to the hands of the thrower. But analogies in argument can be ineffectual or deceptive. For an analogy to have force in an argument, enough similarities must be present to make it an appropriate comparison. For example, a person might make an analogy between students and professional politicians, arguing that if it is ethical for politicians to hire ghost writers to write their speeches, it should be acceptable to allow students to hire tutors to write their papers. However, students and politicians have few attributes in common: the student is in school to learn through writing, whereas the politician is a busy professional who is simply delegating responsibility; and therefore the comparison is not convincing. When confronted with an analogy in an argument, try making a list of similarities and differences between the items being compared. If you find a number of differences and very few similarities, the analogy is probably faulty.

Either/or, or the Faulty Dilemma

Propagandistic arguers often try to manipulate their opponents by allowing them to consider only two possibilities or choices, both perhaps undesirable. In some situations only two viable choices are available, such as an election in which only two candidates are running; and, if you want to have an impact, you need to vote for one or the other of them. However, an argument presented as a "dilemma" is usually a fallacy, because in any situation, there are usually several alternative standpoints. If one argues, for example, that people can only "love" their country or else "leave it," as was stated in a popular slogan in the 1960s, it is not a realistic choice, as it is certainly possible to imagine a position between such extremes. When confronted with either/or thinking, ask the question, "What other choices do I have?"

Induction In Argument

Unlike deductive reasoning, which moves from a generally accepted premise to a conclusion, induction begins with a preliminary "hypothesis," a thesis to be proved or disproved by further testing and factual analysis. Also known as the scientific method, induction is extensively used in argumentation, where solid facts, case histories, tests, and statistics help the arguer make points more convincingly. With most issues, emphasis on facts makes an argument more credible to an audience than an appeal based on purely deductive or ethical reasoning, which can seem overly abstract or subjective for audiences untrained in formal logic. However, an inductive thinker must think and observe carefully, refraining from drawing any conclusions until all of the evidence, facts, and examples have been checked for credibility. Taking the time to study, evaluate, and draw conclusions from surveys, polls, and sociological or psychological studies done by reputable professionals will surely be helpful.

Induction and Fact-based Fallacies

Following are some questions and fallacy definitions that will help you to evaluate both your own inductive results and the inductive research and arguments of others.

Hasty Generalization and Sweeping Generalization These errors in induction involve *generalizing* without enough evidence or ignoring exceptions to a hypothesis or general rule. The following questions are important to ask to avoid such problems.

1. **Is the initial hypothesis clearly stated?** What is it designed to prove or to disprove?
2. **What are the goals and purposes of the research?** Some research studies are produced or funded by corporations eager to make their

products look effective and also harmless, rather than by independent scientists and laboratories that do not have such agendas.

3. **Is the sample "known"?** Who or what did the research, and how many cases have been observed, under what conditions, and for how long? Is the study inadequately described making it impossible to draw meaningful conclusions? Watch for vague or unsubstantiated statements such as "Two out of three persons surveyed preferred Farm Fresh Produce"; "Countless cases of welfare fraud go unreported each year."

4. **Is the sample large enough?** Have conclusions been drawn after only a few observations, creating what is known as a "hasty generalization"?

5. **Is the sample representative and randomly drawn?** Has a careful, clearly described method been used for selecting a sample to be studied or surveyed? Are representatives present from all the different groups and areas included in the population being tested or surveyed?

6. **Does the sample contain a "control group," that is, a similar group studied that has not been subject to the same influences as the main group tested?** Without a control group for comparison, we might become involved in asking time-consuming "What if?" questions about an experiment.

7. **Are there obvious exceptions to the "rule" supposedly proved by testing?** If so, this may be a case of the sweeping generality, a sign of a serious weakness in the experimental data.

Card-Stacking   In a fact-based argument, sometimes the display of numerous facts in a particular area is used in order to create a "smoke screen" to disguise a hidden flaw in the argument. This fallacy is known as "card-stacking." For example, proponents of a new sports arena may show impressive plans about the beauty of the architecture and the business it will bring to the community while ignoring disturbing facts about environmental pollution on the proposed site or the lack of parking available in the lots provided.

Pointing to Another Wrong   This fallacy is related to card-stacking because an attempt may be made to distract the audience with an argument over facts that take the form of "Yes, but what about X?" Sponsors of a sports complex may be informed by opponents that they could better use their energies in focusing on social problems, such as the plight of the poor and homeless in the area. This tactic creates a distraction from the original issue of debate. Keep asking the question,

"But what does that have to do directly with what were discussing? Let's get back to the issue!"

Honest and Faulty Uses of Emotion in Argument

Strong emotional appeals are sometimes considered inappropriate in argumentative writing. A distinction can be made in the case of "persuasive" arguments, including sermons, eulogies, or closing arguments in a trial. In persuasive writing, strong emotional appeal is acceptable, because the main issue for the audience in such cases is emotional concern and engagement.

However, as the rhetorical triangle model implies, in most public arguments, the goal is to appeal to the audience's whole person in a balanced way, not simply to the rational mind. The left brain/right brain theory of human consciousness suggests that we are what we are as people because of the complex interaction between our emotive, intuitive side and our rational, sequential-thinking side. Emotions and experience play such a significant role in our lives that argumentative writing that tries to be altogether rational, presuming that emotional concerns are unimportant and that only facts count, is unrealistic, and will be dry and uninteresting.

Thus, emotions, both your own and those of the audience, are a central concern in argument. For example, in the sensitive issue of euthanasia, acknowledging your own feelings and those of the audience relative to the taking of human life or the needless prolongation of suffering is relevant to the position that you are taking and is a necessary step toward creating a rapport with the audience. Following is an example of a discussion of subject-related emotions from a student essay that makes a case for the "working mother." Notice how the student uses her own evolving relationship with her mother to argue that the positive example set by the self-sufficient working woman can have a beneficial long-term emotional impact on her daughter. What other, less subjective arguments and facts could she add here?

> As a child, I was scared and lonely when there was no one to take care of me. I felt as though I had been partially cheated out of my childhood; many times I could not lead a carefree existence. When I was younger, I resented my mother, for I believed she was selfish and enjoyed her work more than she did me. Why had most of the other mothers decided to stay home to fix bag lunches while mine didn't? Today, I understand and respect the reasons why she worked. Not only

was it for her own satisfaction, but also to provide a better life for my sister and me. Besides financial security, she set an example of a self-sufficient woman to show us that we can both be independent women. I look at my mother as a role model now, for she is a strong, resourceful woman capable of making her own decisions. Whether I will choose her path remains uncertain, but at least I will have the freedom of choice. I feel that this freedom is a legacy left to many daughters of working women, a legacy I would be proud to pass on to my own daughter.

Fallacies of Emotional Appeal

An important distinction should be made between acknowledging feelings and exploiting them in order to manipulate. Certainly some strong arguments have an emotional foundation, but feelings can be exaggerated in order to make a point, and can cause us to overlook important issues. Since emotions are "contagious," an arguer will often try to build up the feelings of an audience to make points that are questionable. Imbalance in the ratio between logos and pathos occurs when there is a great deal of feeling shown with a dishonest intent or with only a few facts to back up the emotions. Following are some of the most common types of positive and negative emotional appeals, often exaggerated and manipulative in intent.

Appeal to Pity If a lawyer is trying to get a client acquitted of a charge, he or she will often try to appeal to the sympathies of the judge and jury: "My client had an impoverished, unhappy childhood, a cruel parent, no job." Sometimes the appeal to pity is relevant, but it should not be used to excuse actions that have little to do with the client's early hardship and suffering.

Appeal to Guilt Often combined with the appeal to pity is an appeal to guilt, as seen in solicitations for charities that ask for donations based on an appeal to pity for the unfortunate along with appealing to the guilt of potential donors with prosperous, secure lives.

Appeal to the Common Person If a film company is promoting a new film, a media campaign is often built around a sense of community roots, the "average person" image, by inviting them to identify with the story. Although it is true that understanding the needs of average people is important, such appeals are often designed to distract the audience from looking too closely at the values or violence promoted in the new film or a new television program.

Appeal to the Masses, Popularity, and/or Patriotism   Variations on the appeal to the common include appeal to the masses, sometimes known as the fallacy of the patriotic appeal and/or the popularity bandwagon: "Vote for Mathew Marvin, a war veteran and an American patriot!"; "Join the many hard-working Californians who support Barbara Burke for Congress!"; "Buy Pepsi, the most popular soft drink in America!"

Appeal to Fear   Our fears can be easily manipulated by skillful propagandists. Since fear leads us to want to protect ourselves and our loved ones, we invest in products, from insurance to toothpaste to politicians, that are marketed as "keeping us safe." Similarly, an attack can be made against a certain group by suggesting that its members are "after your job," as is often the case in anti-immigration arguments. While some of our fears may have a basis in reality, many are exaggerated and "pumped up" by skillful political or advertising campaigns.

Slippery Slope   Closely related to the "appeal to fear," the slippery slope fallacy is designed to frighten an audience by suggesting that if one small change (for example, as in a ballot measure causing a slight reduction or increase in governmental spending) is allowed to happen, then a sequence of disturbing events will follow, leading to more and more devastating results, such as runaway inflation and economic devastation.

Appeal to Personal Attack   This particularly negative fallacy directs attacks on the activates from the distant past or personal habits of an opponent. A politician may imply or state directly that a rival has a bad marriage, is a religious fanatic, has criminal tendencies, or has previously used drugs or alcohol. Such allegations are often used to distract people from real environmental or gender issues or competency, for example.

Different Types of Arguments and Claims

Argument on a controversial issue can be seen in many of the examples above, which take either a "pro" or "con" stance; however, several other kinds of claims occur in arguments concerning definition, causes and/or effects, evaluation, or problem and solution. Longer, complex arguments often combine several of these approaches, especially if the author is examining and considering various sources with different positions on an issue.

The Argument of Definition: Does X Really Belong in the Same Category as Y?

Definitions, both short and expanded, can be used not only as a way of clarifying the denotative or dictionary meanings of the crucial words and abstract terminology used in argument but also as a way of exploring connotative definitions of terms based on feelings, values, and language. Definition includes clarifying a term's meaning through precise use of language and through distinguishing among several words that have overlapping meanings.

Found in philosophical, legal, psychological, and political writing, the extended argument over definition often begins by explaining why controversy about this term and its meaning exists, then moves on to a formal definition that places the term in a larger class or context: "An obsession is a strong emotional response." Placing a term in too large a class or failing to distinguish it from others in the class, will make it difficult to develop ideas clearly and may confuse the reader. Thus, the arguer must provide some key details or qualifying phrases to distinguish this term from others in the larger category of strong emotions: "An obsession is an emotional response or preoccupation that is compulsive and highly repetitive; a response over which a person often has little or no control and that can have destructive consequences."

Such a definition often implies a larger social or philosophical controversy that becomes the argumentive issue at stake in a definition essay: Can obsession be a positive drive as well as a destructive phenomenon? Where do we draw the line? Considering a political term to define, such as "freedom," we might ask the question whether the idea of freedom implies any bounds and responsibilities for our behavior, or whether true freedom is the absence of limits. How much of our freedom must we give away in order to live in a safe and secure society?

Sometimes a strong definition argument goes beyond any term presently found in the dictionary in order to name and clarify a new concept. This is common in the language of the ecological movement, which has given rise to specific terms such as "carbon offsets" and "greenwashing," as well as to the more general term "global warming," which is subject to debate and re-definition in several of the essays in this book.

Once you have created the initial definition and answer to your issue question, you can proceed to develop an essay using other analytical writing strategies such as example analysis, discussion of cause and effect, classification, or comparative relationships. For example, you could discuss several of the qualities of a typical free person, providing an ordered exploration of the stages we go through in our relationship to freedom at different stages of life. For clarity, reader interest, and concept development, examples and illustrations can be used effectively with any of the larger analytical strategies that you might wish to take advantage of in your essay, including references to personal experience, friends, or reading.

Contradiction   In developing a definition, be careful not to create a contradiction or equivocation by defining a term in one way and then shifting the definition to another level of meaning. A better strategy for acknowledging the real complexity of certain words is to concede in the introduction to an essay that this is an expression with seemingly contradictory or ironic shades of meaning; then explain its complexity in the definition and paper that follow.

The Argument of Evaluation: Is X Good or Bad, Sound or Unsound, Pleasing or Unpleasing?

Evaluation is an important thinking and argumentation skill because we need to be able to evaluate effectively in order to make good choices: What kind of school will we choose to attend, what kind of books do we want to read, how do we want to invest our money or our time? What kind of people do we want to associate with? For whom do we wish to vote? What kind of argument will we "entertain" or accept as valuable and sound? In argument, we share our evaluations to help others understand and accept why we think a particular way. A solid evaluation (as opposed to a simple statement of taste or preference such as "I like loud music and fast cars") creates a judgment or assessment of value about a particular item, text, person, issue, or situation, based on relevant, clearly expressed and defined standards or criteria, as in a law court where judge and attorneys spend time defining for the jury what it means in the court for someone to be found guilty "beyond a reasonable doubt," and how various kinds of evidence are to be evaluated.

Following are some of the common criteria for making an evaluation. They are similar to the criteria used for defining a word or concept, which is not surprising because evaluation is a kind of definition: we are defining a person, place, thing, idea, or a "work" as bad, good, beautiful, valuable, or lacking in worth. The subject of evaluation must

1) resemble or fit into a group with _____ ; 2) not resemble or fit into a group with _____ ; 3) have or demonstrate the following qualities: _____ 4) not have the following qualities: _____.

One important aspect of evaluation is the use of appropriate standards and proper application of criteria for judging. In evaluating an inexpensive automobile, you wouldn't use the type of criteria for evaluating an expensive luxury or sports car. Standards also need to be stated in clear, precise language, not in vague or ambiguous terms, and should be applied only when we are thoroughly informed and objective as possible about the subject at hand. Bias or prejudice results in premature evaluation.

Evaluations often need to be researched to obtain the background knowledge necessary to make an informed presentation. What facts are necessary to obtain depends on the subject being evaluated, but regardless of the evaluee, you should make a conscious effort to experience it directly—drive the car, read the book, watch the film, preferably more than once, and with close attention. You can also observe similar objects or works for comparison's sake, read reviews, and try to discover typical issues that arise in making judgments in this particular area.

After you have finished some background research, you are ready to make an evaluative claim and warrant statement; you might try using the following as a start:

> I would evaluate the following (idea, artwork, object, person, food, or essay) as (good, bad, inspiring, mediocre, excellent, competent, incompetent, guilty, innocent, immoral, uplifting, or degrading) because it meets my criteria for evaluating. My criteria are as follows: _____.

Your claim statement can then be developed with reasons and examples drawn from your research and experience. Remember to appeal to your audience level and needs, such as providing the right amount of descriptive and narrative detail drawn from your experience of the item evaluated, the correct amount of logical and fact-based reasons for your evaluation, and, if necessary, authorities who agree with your views.

Many of the "Differing Perspectives" essays in this book use evaluation as a step towards refutation or acceptance of new ideas or products. We see this in the essays debating the consequences of divorce in Chapter 2 of this book. Judith Wallerstein and Theodora Ooms evaluate a number of arguments for and against different solutions to the problem of maintaining a viable marriage before drawing their own conclusions about the "best" position on the issue. Both writers give a clear definition of their criteria and examples to support their evaluations.

At the end of this chapter under "Evaluation of an Argument" are a number of questions to ask oneself in evaluating a written argument or possible source for a research paper. These questions reveal the kind of considerations just examined for other types of evaluation and the importance of crafting your own types of evaluative questions for anything you need to evaluate in writing or in life.

The Argument for Cause and/or Effect Connections

Does X really cause Y to occur? How and why does X cause Y to occur? Are there multiple causes for Y? In what sequence do they occur?

Causal analysis is a fundamental part of both the thinking process and the subject of many arguments. Finding connections that exist between two or more events, understanding how one event led to or produced another event, and speculating about the consequences of earlier events all involve causal reasoning, as well as research.

Observing and Collecting Information   Observing and collecting information will increase your chances of making accurate causal connections and inferences. Keeping a journal of direct observations and newspaper clippings or stories downloaded from the Internet will help you become more alert to issues of cause and effect in the external world, both local and global: immediate and long-term causes for and effects of our country's attack on another nation, or the effects of a series of natural disasters on the rate of global pollution and the flow of refugees out of and into various countries.

Be careful to make sure that the causal connections you select are actual valid ones, because causality is difficult to perceive directly. Observe carefully and consider all possible causes, not simply the obvious, immediate ones. In writing a causal analysis, whether of a personal or a social issue, it is essential to provide adequate evidence, both factual and logical, for any conclusions drawn. An arguer must re-create for the reader, in clear and specific language, the mental process gone through to arrive at cause-effect conclusions, or find authoritative voices in research that explain the process. Methodically and carefully questioning your own thought process will help you clarify your insights, to generate new ideas and evidence that can be used to support your analysis, and to avoid logical fallacies relating to causality.

Fallacies of Causality

Although the fallacies involving causal relations are related to those of induction and fact-based argument, they are especially important in the type of claims and research necessary for this type of essay.

Post Hoc Fallacy (After this, therefore because of this) This fallacy of inadequate causal observation connects two events causally which simply happened in a temporal sequence, as when a person catches a cold and blames a particular person they recently came in contact with, despite the fact that they could have picked it up anywhere. If there is a train accident, for example, investigators will usually consider a faulty brake system as the cause. Instead of just presuming the brakes went out, they will look closely to see if the brakes were defective prior to the accident, and therefore may be the major cause of the wreck. Thus establishing true cause and effect sequence has much to do with ruling out false causes or assumptions, and testing the suspected causes with care.

Causal Oversimplification By singling out one cause and ignoring contributing causes, you can seriously distort causal reality. Be careful to explore all relevant causes. You might argue that that the time spent watching or playing video games is the reason why many children do poorly in school, but there are many other factors that influence childrens' school performance such as lack of parental supervision of homework or overcrowded classrooms.

Causal Over-Complication or Remote Cause You can also distort causal reality by pointing out too many causes, especially if you include insignificant contributors that happened at the same time. Sometimes this is done on purpose, as in legal or political card-stacking, to distract voters or jury from the truth by overcomplicating a situation in order to spread doubt and confusion. With remote cause, often used in historically oriented arguments, the advocate may maintain that a minor event that happened long ago is the true cause for a current conflict. On the other hand, some causes remote in time are powerful enough to influence current events, such as the way the harsh realities of slavery continue to influence the status of African-Americans in this country.

It is probably easier to refute false cause than it is to demonstrate actual cause. An excellent example can be seen in the essays in this book on the impact of the media on youth violence (Chapter 7). Despite the fact that some authors in the chapters notice a distinct behavioral and attitudinal response in children and youth to media violence; however, despite the studies that demonstrate scientifically observed correlations between violent video and gaming stimuli and violent thoughts and desires, there is considerable dispute over how convincing such data really is, since there is a difference between showing a correlation (something that is present along with another factor) and proving an actual cause. There are many societal influences that can lead youth to act out violently: the influence of parents, of peers, and of the violence that already exists in our society such as murder and war, both of which are reported frequently in the media. In order to develop a convincing argument in such an area, a writer must examine a variety of reputable, objective studies in order to build a convincing case.

Despite the difficulties involved in convincing skeptical readers, causal reasoning can lead you closer to understanding and developing theories and explanations for the multiple causes and effects of the issues you encounter in your reading and in your own life, and this can prepare the way for proposals for change and solutions to the problems caused by unfortunate chains of events. With an awareness of the complexities of causal thinking, you should be able to think and write more critically, clearly, and convincingly.

The Argument for a Solution to a Problem

What can be done about X? How might Y or Z improve the situation? Problem-solving can be an everyday activity that most of us do somewhat automatically, especially when involved with overcoming routine difficulties. With public issues, you are frequently invited to join in a problem-solving process through voting on ballot propositions that attempt to solve larger societal problems: What (if anything) should we do about the problem of illegal immigration? About world hunger? About environmental pollution in our nation, state, or community? About homelessness? Should we vote for a bond issue to raise more money for a socially beneficial project, or should we vote to repeal a certain law many citizens find oppressive?

After deciding on a general problem area to approach, begin making a preliminary definition of the problem, narrowing and focusing the exact area of study. Next, prepare a demonstration of some of its ill effects using an appropriate authority, citation of relevant scientific facts and studies that demonstrate a causal relationship between certain events and the ill effects in question. At this stage, you are making use of the kind of reasoning and evidence gathering done in the traditional causal argument described above. Here you should also be wary of the fallacies of causal reasoning. However, it is important also at this stage to be persuasive in communicating your conviction that the problem at hand is truly necessary to resolve, and that the audience must desire to act in order to be part of the solution: to vote for it, to write their representatives in government, or at least to talk to their friends about it and spread the word in the community.

The next stage of the solutions essay is to do some brainstorming and research to come up with alternatives—some new, some that have been tried before and that have worked on a limited scale, such as a neighborhood treatment center for drug or alcohol treatment, a particular charter school that has shown promising results for youth at risk, or successful methods of conflict resolution on a local scale. You might also feel that you could benefit from combining two or more solutions that have significant advantages in particular areas, as in the case of larger problems like revitalizing a rundown, impoverished community. Which of the possible solutions that you find desirable might work in a larger arena, such as an entire city or state? What kind of financial needs would your solution demand, and what kind of trained leaders would need to be attracted both for fundraising and work with the public? These and other concerns need to be anticipated and defined in order to convince an audience that the chosen solution or group of related solutions is both valuable and viable.

Defense and Rebuttal   At some point in your argument, you must engage in both defense of your proposal against potential attack as well as refutation or rebuttal of solutions you have reason to believe would not be as effective as the ones you have chosen to propose. Here it is helpful to try to put yourself in the position of the audience. What would audience members be most likely to object to about your proposal—increased taxes? Limitations on their freedoms? Potential job losses? Or just the fact that your proposal would bring change, which is in itself threatening to many people? Anticipating such objections and answering them one by one is the best way to keep readers with you as you present your ideas designed to "make a difference."

Another kind of "objection" the audience might have is other proposals they may have heard of, some of which may seem more desirable than yours, at least superficially. Therefore, you should do research in anticipation of such proposals in order to counter their appeal to the audience. Perhaps the proposal might seem desirable because it is cheaper and simpler than the one you endorse; therefore, look into its "hidden costs" and suggest some reasons why it might fail because of its simplistic approach. It may also have other hidden negative effects that you could point out, or you could suggest that its supporters may have a vested interest because the "solution" they endorse might make them wealthy.

Changing Minds contains several developed proposal arguments, such as Henry Jenkins's testimony before Congress, found in Chapter 7, concerning a strong rebuttal to what he saw as the falsely attributed influence of media mayhem and faulty, oppresive solutions for youth violence proposed in the wake of the 1999 Columbine killings. Jenkins proceeds in the final paragraphs of his essay to offer a number of solutions that he believes would work, supporting them with his own reading and research into how youth tend to interact with media and school life. Studying and outlining such arguments is helpful in planning successful proposals.

Reading and Critiquing Arguments

In reading and studying arguments such as the ones in this book, either as possible sources for your own research or as subjects for critique and refutation, you need to apply some of the basic principles of close critical reading, particularly if the text is difficult or remote from your own experience. The critical reading process can be divided into several stages: pre-reading, draft reading, study, analysis and interpretation, and evaluation.

Pre-Reading or Browsing

Browsing an argument selection is not an aimless process; closely scan and consider the headings and subheadings, overall structure, and the major claims and warrants of the argument before you begin to interpret and critique the text. Organizational indicators are created by the author to guide and frame your understanding of the text that you are reading. For example, the title often gives an insight into central issues and positions. An introduction or headnote will give you a summary of the text's topic and point of view as well as some information about the author, while the subheading sections define the basic parts of the work, often providing key words or phrases that will alert you to think seriously about their impact on the topic or idea being covered. Visual design features are yet another way to gain insight into the emphasis, structure, and concerns of the text. Finally, the footnotes, works cited references, and appendices provide information on the sources that the author has used in constructing the works that you are reading. Pre-reading will become an even more helpful process if you write down any questions that you have in this initial browsing stage.

Pre-Reading Questions

1. **Was the selection written within the last decade or in a more distant past?** If what you are planning to read is modern, you are more likely to be able to relate to the ideas and references used by the author; conversely, if the selection was written many years ago, you should realize that some words and expressions may be unfamiliar, as will many of the allusions to historical figures or works, and may require some Google searches, and perhaps Wikipedia, to understand the selection and its arguments.

2. **How similar is your background knowledge and experience to the writer's?** Where and when was the author born and where did he or she grow up and/or reside? Is the selection's subject matter familiar to you? The answers to such questions will determine how much of a "stretch" you will have to make to grasp the perspective of the reading and how much background you will have to fill in as you study the text.

3. **What kind of text are you reading?** Most selections will have a particular form or discipline-based vocabulary; therefore, try to identify the form, or "genre," of the argument and its "jargon" in order to understand, interpret, and evaluate its meaning, purpose, and worth. There are many representative forms of writing that use argument: sociological, historical, or psychological analysis such as that found in a professional journal; science writing; proposal or solution plans in various areas; brief calls to action such as an argument for a vote for or against a ballot proposition; newspaper or magazine editorials on issues of controversy; or journalistic accounts of a controversy with a point of view.

4. **What seems be the author's argumentative purpose?** An author may satirize the ideas of others or a current situation; argue or persuade in an editorial or letter to the editor; refute the arguments or proposals of others; examine causal relationships; evaluate a product, an idea, or an artistic work; or argue for a definition of a particular term or set of terms. Complex

argumentive writing is often divided into more than one of the above categories of purpose. You will be able more effectively to focus your reading of a text once you have an idea of an author's overall intentions.

   5. **Who was the intended audience for the selection?** Consider how the author of the argument shaped his or her work for a particular audience: local or national newspaper readers; a particular age, class, or gender magazine or newspaper readers; student readers; readers with a particular political perspective—liberal, progressive, conservative, libertarian—or technicians, scholars or professionals in a particular field. It is important to try to put yourself in the position of the intended audience to get a full understanding of the text.

Asking and answering such questions can help you to become more involved with the text and to put yourself into a frame of mind that is receptive and alert to what you are about to read.

Draft Reading and a Quick Response

After browsing a text, you can move onto the early or "draft" reading stage, in which, as in writing a first draft, you simply plunge in and read the work quickly to get an overall sense of its arguments and key supports. Here you can check off or star a few key passages or put a question mark by an idea, detail, or word that seems confusing. Don't be overly concerned about what you don't yet understand; at this stage of the reading process try to become engaged with the energy and issues in the text.

   An immediate and unstructured written response to what you have just read can help to develop your interest, to understand and clarify what you have just read, and to become engaged with the core argument. Later on, in rereading your response, you may find that your first impressions of the piece were the beginning of an interpretation; a quick response often contains a synthesis of what you think the author intended as well as the personal thoughts and experiences that you bring to the reading. Don't be afraid to talk back to the essay. If you disagree with one or more of the points the author is making, write him or her an imaginary letter expressing your point of view.

The "Study Stage"

In the study stage, read more slowly, taking note of particular sentences and passages that advance the argument or that you may disagree with. Read with a pencil in hand, ready to utilize the strategies explained below.

Marking the Text   Marking the text is an essential part of the process of studying a text closely and perceptively. Cultivate the habit of making marks in the margins as well as underlining passages you consider especially important, including topic sentences or key word phrases. You can also circle words and phrases you found hard to understand initially. Make marginal notes as well (refer to the sample annotated essay at the end of this chapter), pointing out essential facts, representative examples, central statements of cause or effect, comparisons, and thesis ideas. You may consider using some of these points useful when you write your first draft.

Paraphrasing: An Aid to Close Reading   Writing a paraphrase of a text will help you to pay close attention to what you are reading and to understand it more thoroughly. To paraphrase, you put the main concepts of the text into your own words and sentence structure without changing the fundamental meaning of the original material. Searching for synonyms and altering sentence structure will help you to rephrase the text while not changing its basic content. If you find yourself having difficulty putting the idea of your source into your own language, it may be because you do not understand a key word or phrase in the original. Keep a good dictionary and thesaurus nearby to use when paraphrasing.

Summarizing   Any text, from a paragraph to an entire book, can be summed up in a few well-chosen phrases or sentences. A summary is different from a paraphrase. In a summary you restate the source's main ideas and overall point of view. You need to capture the intention of the argument in as few words as possible; don't be restricted by the original language or structure of the source. The best summaries are written using your own voice, while also capturing the tone of the original. In writing your summary, even if it is only a few sentences long, you should come closer to identifying with the author and the key arguments he or she presents. This is an important step towards understanding the argument at hand; even if you disagree with the author's point of view, perhaps you will come to see some reason for what he or she is saying.

Outlining What You Have Read   Making an outline of the major ideas in an argument will give you a visual perspective on its major claims and warrants and can help you to better understand the selection's structure and development of thought. This strategy can also help to focus your thinking, enhance your understanding of key points and major supports in what you have read, and give you some critical distance.

Analysis and Interpretation   Once you have started to analyze a reading by breaking it down as a series of points and supports, it is helpful to write a brief analytic interpretation of the piece. Interpretation involves going beyond simply finding the main idea, which you did in your summary; this process involves looking for patterns of language and thought that support the dominant argument of the work. At this point you need to think about how logic and facts, emotional appeals, and metaphorical language strategies are helping to create the text's meaning and persuasive power.

In writing an interpretation, divide the work into a series of points, structural stages, idea or evidence groupings, and other strategies. In reading an argument, you will need to analyze crucial aspects of argumentative technique, particularly the logos—the series of points, ideas, or types of evidence used to support ideas. You can make a list of any logical fallacies you detect, as well as "holes" in the argument—what evidence did the author neglect to provide for a certain claim? Also, consider the use of pathos and ethos in the argument: Does the author use an honest, ethical approach to the audience? Is there a balance between pathos appeals and logos?

Examine the imaginative use of rhetoric in the selection (part of the *pathos* of an argument) in terms of how it supports and clarifies the argument as a whole. Ask yourself how much of the work is meant to be responded to literally, and how much is to be considered as either an ironic statement (meant to be seen as different in its meaning from the stated meaning, as in some forms of satire or humorous argument) or as symbolic or metaphorical (that is, meant to represent ideas). Repeated ideas and emphatic grammatical forms such as balanced sentences, key metaphors, and repeated images, deepen the impact of the work—but they may also distract readers from fundamental weaknesses of logic or factual support.

As you read over the written record of your reactions at this stage of reading, you will probably find that your ideas have deepened considerably, and that you will have a more comprehensive view of the argument and its presentation than you did initially. This kind of textual analysis will help you to arrive at a better understanding of the meaning of the work and the unique way that argument emerges from the written text itself. Through analysis, you can gain a greater appreciation for the technique of the argument, while at the same time developing and refining your ability to respond to and evaluate its ideas.

Evaluation of an Argument

Although in published works textual evaluation is done by professional reviewers, in college writing assignments students are often asked to evaluate arguments. To a certain extent we should, as good critical thinkers, evaluate everything we read for accuracy and reasonable perspective, and discriminate between fair and honest argument and propaganda. Analysis leads naturally to evaluation, and is in fact an essential part of it. By taking an essay apart and observing its components, we are better able to see how they work together to produce a powerful argument—or how they fail to do so, in part or in whole. Evaluation is an essential aspect at the heart of both argumentative and research writing, as it is necessary to evaluate both your arguments and those of others for sound or fallacious reasoning as well as to decide which sources of information are reliable.

Just as in other types of evaluation discussed previously, appropriate standards for evaluation of arguments are essential, as well as clarity about what those standards are. Apply your criteria in a fair and consistent way. For example, you wouldn't criticize an editorial in *Time* on job outsourcing using the same critical rigor with which you might evaluate a scholarly paper on the same subject in a professional journal; nor should you evaluate an argument negatively just because you don't like the subject, the political perspective of the publication it appears in, or the writer.

Questions for Evaluating an Argument or Choosing a Source for Research

1. **Was the article written recently?** Remember that contemporary issue sources can become dated quickly as court decisions go into effect or new laws are passed to solve disputes. However, older texts can be helpful to stress historical turning points or to show a slow process of change in public attitude on key issues.

2. **Was the place where the article originally appeared a reliable publication?** Many good arguments are published in advocacy periodicals or Internet blogs, but remember that such small, do-it-yourself publications often do not have workers who can check information that might be derived from potentially unreliable or inappropriate sources.

3. **Is the writing generally clear and reasonable, or is there a lot of emotional, "heated up" language present, including emotional fallacies?** See the above discussion of the place of emotions in argument.

4. **Is the deductive reasoning in the paper clear, with major steps clearly articulated and based on sound general principles and ethical values?** Are there obvious fallacies or defects of logic present? See the section above on fallacies of logic.

5. **Does the author rely on factual supports and use effective inductive reasoning, or does he or she simply provide a series of general fact claims or unsupported assertions?** See the sections above on fallacies of fact and fallacies of cause.

6. **If the author uses factual studies or statistics, are they documented or footnoted so that their sources are clear and seem legitimate?** Remember that facts, including accounts of experiments and tests, can be distorted if they are removed from their original context. Documentation lets us know if the source of the data is a reliable one, such as a primary source.

7. **If the author uses authorities and quotes them, do they seem legitimate experts or scholars or perhaps just members of the author's political or philosophical group?** If in doubt, you can look up authors or officials referred or quoted in the article in a database or on the Internet.

8. **Is your overall response to the claims, ideas, and emotions in the work primarily positive or negative?** Would you wish to act on the advice presented in the article? Would you recommend the work to other readers? Why or why not?

Annotated Professional Argument

Notice how the annotation in the following argument exemplifies the various stages of the reading process, and makes questioning and evaluative statements that could help the reader to decide whether this is an article helpful for research on the issue of excessive medical diagnoses and their effects. What other questions would you ask of this article? Would you agree with the annotator's marginal comments and conclusions about it? What would your own evaluation of it be?

H. GILBERT WELCH, LISA SCHWARTZ, AND STEVEN WOLOSHIN

"What's Making Us Sick Is an Epidemic of Diagnoses"

Gilbert Welch, a general internist, is Professor of Medicine and Community and Family Medicine, Dartmouth Medical School, and Co-Director of the White River Junction Outcomes Group in White River Junction, Vermont. He is the author of Should I Be Tested for Cancer? Maybe Not and Here's Why *(University of California Press, 2004). He has done most of his research work in the area of over-diagnosis on cancer screening. Dr. Schwartz and Dr. Woloshin are senior research associates at the White River Junction Outcomes Group who have collaborated with Dr. Welch on a number of articles in such publications as* The Journal of the American Medical Association, The British Medical Journal, *and* The Journal of the National Cancer Institute.

Title provides a key claim and thesis for entire essay. Place of original publication of essay in serious news publication suggests it will cover significant issues for a general, but well-educated audience.

Ethos: Positions, research experience, and prior publications on cancer research establish ethos of authors as authorities in the field essay covers.

31

For most Americans, the biggest health threat is not avian flu, West Nile or mad cow disease. It's our healthcare system.

You might think this is because doctors make mistakes (we do make mistakes). But you can't be a victim of medical error if you are not in the system. The larger threat posed by American medicine is that more and more of us are being drawn into the system not because of an epidemic of disease, but because of an epidemic of diagnoses.

Americans live longer than ever, yet more of us are told we are sick.

Attention getting first sentence: Rejected health threat causes and key causal claim— Dismisses the usual disease suspects dramatically. Claims excessive diagnosis leads to more people seeing themselves as part of the medical system and thus is a "health threat" in itself. Is this logical, or a play on words?

Attention-getting paradox, a fact, followed up by a leading question and an answer: we live longer, yet are constantly told we are ill. How? Why? Excessive medical resources cause more diagnoses, an "epidemic."

Defines "epidemic," a key word in the essay's title and thesis claim. The word has a strong pathos appeal, very disturbing in connotation.

Two ill effects of over-diagnosis:

1. Our health is threatened by ordinary experiences becoming diagnosed as "symptoms". Examples of experiences now considered "symptoms" provided.
2. Children over diagnosed, leading to ill-effects for those with only temporary or minor symptoms. (examples provided).

Claim of overly early diagnosis for those without symptoms: examples would be helpful here.

How can this be? One reason is that we devote more resources to medical care than any other country. Some of this investment is productive, curing disease and alleviating suffering. But it also leads to more diagnoses, a trend that has became an epidemic.

This epidemic is a threat to your health. It has two distinct sources. One is the medicalization of everyday life. Most of us experience physical or emotional sensations we don't like, and in the past, this was considered a part of life. Increasingly, however, such sensations are considered symptoms of disease. Everyday experiences like insomnia, sadness, twitchy legs and impaired sex drive now become diagnoses: sleep disorder, depression, restless leg syndrome and sexual dysfunction.

Perhaps most worrisome is the medicalization of childhood. If children cough after exercising, they have asthma; if they have trouble reading, they are dyslexic; if they are unhappy, they are depressed; and if they alternate between unhappiness and liveliness, they have bipolar disorder. While these diagnoses may benefit the few with severe symptoms, one has to wonder about the effect on the many whose symptoms are mild, intermittent or transient.

The other source is the drive to find disease early. While diagnoses used to be reserved for serious illness, we now diagnose illness in people who have no symptoms at all, those with so-called predisease or those "at risk."

Two developments accelerate this process. First, advanced technology allows doctors to look really hard for things to be wrong. We can detect trace molecules in the blood. We can direct fiber-optic devices into every orifice. And CT scans, ultrasounds, M.R.I. and PET scans let doctors define subtle structural defects deep inside the body. These technologies make it possible to give a diagnosis to just about everybody: arthritis in people without heartburn and prostate cancer in over a million people who, but for testing, would have lived as long without being a cancer patient.

Second, the rules are changing. Expert panels constantly expand what constitutes disease: thresholds for diagnosing diabetes, hypertension, osteoporosis and obesity have all fallen in the last few years. The criterion for normal cholesterol has dropped multiple times. With these changes, disease can now be diagnosed in more than half the population.

Most of us assume that all this additional diagnosis can only be beneficial. And some of it is. But at the extreme, the logic of early detection is absurd. If more than half of us are sick, what does it mean to be normal? Many more of us harbor "pre-disease" than will ever get disease, and all of us are "at risk." The medicalization of everyday life is no less problematic. Exactly what are we doing to our children when 40 percent of summer campers are on one or more chronic prescription medications?

No one should take the process of making people into patients lightly. There are real drawbacks. Simply labeling people as diseased can make them feel anxious and vulnerable—a particular concern in children.

But the real problem with the epidemic of diagnoses is that it leads to an epidemic of treatments. Not all treatments have important benefits, but almost all can have harms. Sometimes the harms are known, but often the harms of new therapies take years to

Lists causes for over-diagnosis and treatments: Examples of technological breakthroughs provided that make easy premature, unnecessary diagnosis. Actual hard evidence of misuse of the technology would strengthen this point.

Definition argument: The threshold of disease in several cases has been redefined several times by lowering the numbers on tests for what constitutes sickness. Good examples provided.

Negative psychological and physical effects of excessive diagnoses and prescriptions suggested, despite assumptions otherwise. No evidence provided, just deductive reasoning and pathos appeals.

Claim: Harms can come from excess treatment for those not severely ill. [Note—no examples of actual harms provided—some would strengthen the argument.]

Groups causing excessive diagnoses: doctor/hospital/pharmaceutical industries and advocacy groups blamed, yet authors don't establish a clear link between these "suspects" and unnecessary tests.

Conclusion, solution: a little vague and unconvincing: Would new goals provided by NIH for medical service reduction really be helpful? Aren't there many people who can't afford even basic medical services as it is?

Overall evaluation of the article: This argument appeals more to emotion (pathos) than to fact-based reasoning (logos). It might appeal to readers of the *New York Times* who have high-end medical insurance, but not as much to average people with minimal insurance. Still, the essay should shock some readers and make people want to read further to consider the need for large batteries of recommended tests when no real symptoms are present.

emerge—after many have been exposed. For the severely ill, these harms generally pale relative to the potential benefits. But for those experiencing mild symptoms, the harms become much more relevant. And for the many labeled as having predisease or as being "at risk" but destined to remain healthy, treatment can only cause harm.

The epidemic of diagnoses has many causes. More diagnoses mean more money for drug manufacturers, hospitals, physicians and disease advocacy groups. Researchers, and even the disease-based organization of the National Institutes of Health, secure their stature (and financing) by legal concerns also drive the epidemic. While failing to make a diagnosis can result in lawsuits, there are no corresponding penalties for over-diagnosis. Thus, the path of least resistance for clinicians is to diagnose liberally—even when we wonder if doing so really helps our patients.

As more of us are being told we are sick, fewer of us are being told we are well. People need to think hard about the benefits and risk of increased diagnosis: the fundamental question they face is whether or not to become a patient. And doctors need to remember the value of reassuring people that they are not sick. Perhaps someone should start monitoring a new health metric: the proportion of the population not requiring medical care. And the National Institutes of Health could propose a new goal for medical researchers: reduce the need for medical services, not increase it.

CHAPTER 2

Re-creating the Family

Introduction

The American family has changed greatly over the century and-a-half since Elizabeth Cady Stanton wrote her "Declaration of Sentiments" in 1848 arguing for full societal and familial rights for women. For many reasons—improvements in technology, birth control, the increasing legal ease of divorce, blended families, single mothers, fathers and mothers who have full-time careers or parents who work part-time and take care of their families part-time, and same sex marriage or domestic partnerships—the original narrow definition of a family and the molding of children through family guidance have evolved in new directions. Articles in this chapter by Mary Pipher and Juliet B. Schor make arguments and propose solutions related to the impact on children of intense pressures from peer and media culture. As adolescent girls step into a larger peer society they see themselves regarded as sexual objects, while the influence of media advertising encourages both boys and girls to desire products such as video games, cell phones, and brand name clothes. Their social world expects them to behave like the party-oriented youth seen on popular television shows, rather than youth who spend time with their parents and siblings engaging in family activities.

In contrast to media and peer pressures on the family, Rachel Lehmann-Haupt and Judith Warner write about practical concerns— the amount of time a husband and/or wife should work outside the home, who should take care of the children, and whether the government should step in and provide universal affordable childcare for all families. Jonathan Rauch argues for legalizing gay marriages at the individual state level, rather than at the federal level to preserve local values.

Finally, in our "Differing Perspectives" section of this chapter, the authors debate solutions to problems in nuclear family life that often lead to divorce. Judith Wallerstein presents some ways of helping the children of divorce to heal from the experience of family loss and re-grouping, while Theodora Ooms examines valuable solutions to help keep families together despite economic stress. The essays in this chapter suggest that marriage remains a desirable and resilient institution, despite its many transformations. Being a family member remains at the core of one's identity.

MARY PIPHER

"Saplings in the Storm"

Mary Pipher (b.1947) earned a B.A. in cultural anthropology at the University of California at Berkeley (1969) and her Ph.D. at the University of Nebraska–Lincoln, where she studied clinical psychology and went on to join the faculty. Her recent books include Another Country: Navigating the Emotional Terrain of our Elders *(1999) and* Letters to a Young Therapist *(2003). Pipher is best known for* Reviving Ophelia: Saving the Selves of Adolescent Girls *(1994, 1997), which was awarded the American Psychological Presidential Citation for excellence. In the selection from* Reviving Ophelia *that follows, Pipher argues that adolescence for girls has always been difficult, but that it is harder now because of recent social changes that have made the protected time of childhood increasingly shorter.*

When my cousin Polly was a girl, she was energy in motion. She danced, did cartwheels and splits, played football, basketball and baseball with the neighborhood boys, wrestled with my brothers, biked, climbed trees and rode horses. She was as lithe and as resilient as a willow branch and as un-restrained as a lion cub. Polly talked as much as she moved. She yelled out orders and advice, shrieked for joy when she won a bet or heard a good joke, laughed with her mouth wide open, argued with kids and grown-ups and insulted her foes in the language of a construction worker.

We formed the Marauders, a secret club that met over her garage. Polly was the Tom Sawyer of the club. She planned the initiations, led the spying expeditions and hikes to haunted houses. She showed us the rituals to become blood "brothers" and taught us card tricks and how to smoke.

Then Polly had her first period and started junior high. She tried to keep up her old ways, but she was called a tomboy and chided for not acting more ladylike. She was excluded by her boy pals and by the girls, who were moving into makeup and romances.

This left Polly confused and shaky. She had temper tantrums and withdrew from both the boys' and girls' groups. Later she quieted down and reentered as Becky Thatcher. She wore stylish clothes and watched from the sidelines as the boys acted and spoke. Once again she was accepted and popular. She glided smoothly through our small society. No one spoke of the changes or mourned the loss of our town's most dynamic citizen. I was the only one who felt that a tragedy had transpired.

Girls in what Freud called the latency period, roughly age six or seven through puberty, are anything but latent. I think of my daughter Sara during those years—performing chemistry experiments and magic tricks, playing her violin, starring in her own plays, rescuing wild animals and biking all over town. I think of her friend Tamara, who wrote a 300-page novel the summer of her sixth-grade year. I remember myself, reading every children's book in the library of my town. One week I planned to be a great doctor like Albert Schweitzer. The next week I wanted to write like Louisa May Alcott or dance in Paris like Isadora Duncan. I have never since had as much confidence or ambition.

Most preadolescent girls are marvelous company because they are interested in everything—sports, nature, people, music and books. Almost all the heroines of girls' literature come from this age group— Anne of Green Gables, Heidi, Pippi Longstocking and Caddie Woodlawn. Girls this age bake pies, solve mysteries and go on quests. They can take care of themselves and are not yet burdened with caring for others. They have a brief respite from the female role and can be tomboys, a word that conveys courage, competency and irreverence.

They can be androgynous, having the ability to act adaptively in any situation regardless of gender role constraints. An androgynous person can comfort a baby or change a tire, cook a meal or chair a meeting. Research has shown that, since they are free to act without worrying if their behavior is feminine or masculine, androgynous adults are the most well adjusted.

Girls between seven and eleven rarely come to therapy. They don't need it. I can count on my fingers the girls this age whom I have seen: Coreen, who was physically abused; Anna, whose parents were divorcing; and Brenda, whose father killed himself. These girls were courageous and resilient. Brenda said, "If my father didn't want to stick around, that's his loss." Coreen and Anna were angry, not at themselves, but rather at the grown-ups, who they felt were making mistakes. It's amazing how little help these girls needed from me to heal and move on.

A horticulturist told me a revealing story. She led a tour of junior-high girls who were attending a math and science fair on her campus. She showed them side oats grama, bluestem, Indian grass and trees—redbud, maple, walnut and willow. The younger girls interrupted each other with their questions and tumbled forward to see, touch and smell everything. The older girls, the ninth-graders, were different. They hung back. They didn't touch plants or shout out questions. They stood primly to the side, looking bored and even a little disgusted by the enthusiasm of their younger classmates. My friend asked herself, What's happened to these girls? What's gone wrong? She told me, "I wanted to shake them, to say, 'Wake up, come back. Is anybody home at your house?'"

Recently I sat sunning on a bench outside my favorite ice-cream store. A mother and her teenage daughter stopped in front of me and waited for the light to change. I heard the mother say, "You have got to stop blackmailing your father and me. Every time you don't get what you want, you tell us that you want to run away from home or kill yourself. What's happened to you? You used to be able to handle not getting your way."

The daughter stared straight ahead, barely acknowledging her mother's words. The light changed. I licked my ice-cream cone. Another mother approached the same light with her preadolescent daughter in tow. They were holding hands. The daughter said to her mother, "This is fun. Let's do this all afternoon."

Something dramatic happens to girls in early adolescence. Just as planes and ships disappear mysteriously into the Bermuda Triangle, so do the selves of girls go down in droves. They crash and burn in a social and developmental Bermuda Triangle. In early adolescence, studies show that girls' IQ scores drop and their math and science scores plummet. They lose their resiliency and optimism and become less curious and inclined to take risks. They lose their assertive, energetic and "tomboyish" personalities and become more deferential, self-critical and depressed. They report great unhappiness with their own bodies.

Psychology documents but does not explain the crashes. Girls who rushed to drink in experiences in enormous gulps sit quietly in the corner. Writers such as Sylvia Plath, Margaret Atwood and Olive Schreiner have described the wreckage. Diderot, in writing to his young friend Sophie Volland, described his observations harshly: "You all die at 15."

Fairy tales capture the essence of this phenomenon. Young women eat poisoned apples or prick their fingers with poisoned needles and fall asleep for a hundred years. They wander away from home, encounter great dangers, are rescued by princes and are transformed into passive and docile creatures.

The story of Ophelia, from Shakespeare's *Hamlet,* shows the destructive forces that affect young women. As a girl, Ophelia is happy and free, but with adolescence she loses herself. When she falls in love with Hamlet, she lives only for his approval. She has no inner direction; rather she struggles to meet the demands of Hamlet and her father. Her value is determined utterly by their approval. Ophelia is torn apart by her efforts to please. When Hamlet spurns her because she is an obedient daughter, she goes mad with grief. Dressed in elegant clothes that weigh her down, she drowns in a stream filled with flowers.

Girls know they are losing themselves. One girl said, "Everything good in me died in junior high." Wholeness is shattered by the chaos of adolescence. Girls become fragmented, their selves split into mysterious contradictions. They are sensitive and tenderhearted, mean and competitive, superficial and idealistic. They are confident in the morning and overwhelmed with anxiety by nightfall. They rush through their days with wild energy and then collapse into lethargy. They try on new roles every week—this week the good student, next week the delinquent and the next, the artist. And they expect their families to keep up with these changes.

My clients in early adolescence are elusive and slow to trust adults. They are easily offended by a glance, a clearing of the throat, a silence, a lack of sufficient enthusiasm or a sentence that doesn't meet their immediate needs. Their voices have gone underground—their speech is more tentative and less articulate. Their moods swing widely. One week they love their world and their families, the next they are critical of everyone. Much of their behavior is unreadable. Their problems are complicated and metaphorical—eating disorders, school phobias and self-inflicted injuries. I need to ask again and again in a dozen different ways, "What are you trying to tell me?"

Michelle, for example, was a beautiful, intelligent seventeen-year-old. Her mother brought her in after she became pregnant for the third time in three years. I tried to talk about why this was happening. She smiled a Mona Lisa smile to all my questions. "No, I don't care all that much for sex." "No, I didn't plan this. It just happened." When Michelle left a session, I felt like I'd been talking in the wrong language to someone far away.

Holly was another mystery. She was shy, soft-spoken and slow-moving, pretty under all her makeup and teased red hair. She was a Prince fan and wore only purple. Her father brought her in after a suicide attempt. She wouldn't study, do chores, join any school activities or find a job. Holly answered questions in patient, polite monosyllables. She really talked only when the topic was Prince. For several weeks we talked about him. She played me his tapes. Prince somehow spoke for her and to her.

Gail burned and cut herself when she was unhappy. Dressed in black, thin as a straw, she sat silently before me, her hair a mess, her ears, lips and nose all pierced with rings. She spoke about Bosnia and the hole in the ozone layer and asked me if I liked rave music. When I asked about her life, she fingered her earrings and sat silently.

My clients are not different from girls who are not seen in therapy. I teach at a small liberal arts college and the young women in my classes have essentially the same experiences as my therapy clients. One student worried about her best friend who'd been sexually assaulted. Another student missed class after being beaten by her boyfriend. Another asked what she should do about crank calls from a man threatening to rape her. When stressed, another student stabbed her hand with paper clips until she drew blood. Many students have wanted advice on eating disorders.

After I speak at high schools, girls approach me to say that they have been raped, or they want to run away from home, or that they have a friend who is anorexic or alcoholic. At first all this trauma surprised me. Now I expect it.

Psychology has a long history of ignoring girls this age. Until recently adolescent girls haven't been studied by academics, and they have long baffled therapists. Because they are secretive with adults and full of contradictions, they are difficult to study. So much is happening internally that's not communicated on the surface.

Simone de Beauvoir believed adolescence is when girls realize that men have the power and that their only power comes from consenting to become submissive adored objects. They do not suffer from the penis envy Freud postulated, but from power envy.

She described the Bermuda Triangle this way: Girls who were the subjects of their own lives become the objects of others' lives. "Young girls slowly bury their childhood, put away their independent and imperious selves and submissively enter adult existence." Adolescent girls experience a conflict between their autonomous selves and their need to be feminine, between their status as human beings and their vocation as females. De Beauvoir says, "Girls stop being and start seeming."

Girls become "female impersonators" who fit their whole selves into small, crowded spaces. Vibrant, confident girls become shy, doubting young women. Girls stop thinking, "Who am I? What do I want?" and start thinking, "What must I do to please others?"

This gap between girls' true selves and cultural prescriptions for what is properly female creates enormous problems. To paraphrase a Stevie Smith poem about swimming in the sea, "they are not waving, they are drowning." And just when they most need help, they are unable to take their parents' hands.

Olive Schreiner wrote of her experiences as a young girl in *The Story of an African Farm*. "The world tells us what we are to be and shapes us by the ends it sets before us. To men it says, work. To us, it says, seem. The less a woman has in her head the lighter she is for carrying." She described the finishing school that she attended in this way: "It was a machine for condensing the soul into the smallest possible area. I have seen some souls so compressed that they would have filled a small thimble."

Margaret Mead believed that the ideal culture is one in which there is a place for every human gift. By her standards, our Western culture is far from ideal for women. So many gifts are unused and unappreciated. So many voices are stilled. Stendhal wrote: "All geniuses born women are lost to the public good."

Alice Miller wrote of the pressures on some young children to deny their true selves and assume false selves to please their parents. *Reviving Ophelia* suggests that adolescent girls experience a similar pressure to split into true and false selves, but this time the pressure comes not from parents but from the culture. Adolescence is when girls experience social pressure to put aside their authentic selves and to display only a small portion of their gifts.

This pressure disorients and depresses most girls. They sense the pressure to be someone they are not. They fight back, but they are fighting a "problem with no name." One girl put it this way: "I'm a perfectly good carrot that everyone is trying to turn into a rose. As a carrot, I have good color and a nice leafy top. When I'm carved into a rose, I turn brown and wither."

Adolescent girls are saplings in a hurricane. They are young and vulnerable trees that the winds blow with gale strength. Three factors make young women vulnerable to the hurricane. One is their developmental level. Everything is changing—body shape, hormones, skin and hair. Calmness is replaced by anxiety. Their way of thinking is changing. Far below the surface they are struggling with the most basic of human question: What is my place in the universe, what is my meaning?

Second, American culture has always smacked girls on the head in early adolescence. This is when they move into a broader culture that is rife with girl-hurting "isms," such as sexism, capitalism and lookism, which is the evaluation of a person solely on the basis of appearance.

Third, American girls are expected to distance from parents just at the time when they most need their support. As they struggle with countless new pressures, they must relinquish the protection and closeness they've felt with their families in childhood. They turn to their none-too-constant peers for support.

Parents know only too well that something is happening to their daughters. Calm, considerate daughters grow moody, demanding and distant. Girls who loved to talk are sullen and secretive. Girls who liked to hug now bristle when touched. Mothers complain that they can do nothing right in the eyes of their daughters. Involved fathers bemoan their sudden banishment from their daughters' lives. But few parents realize how universal their experiences are. Their daughters are entering a new land, a dangerous place that parents can scarcely comprehend. Just when they most need a home base, they cut themselves loose without radio communications.

Most parents of adolescent girls have the goal of keeping their daughters safe while they grow up and explore the world. The parents' job is to protect. The daughters' job is to explore. Always these different tasks have created tension in parent-daughter relationships, but now it's even harder. Generally parents are more protective of their daughters than is corporate America. Parents aren't trying to make money off their daughters by selling them designer jeans or cigarettes, they just want them to be well adjusted. They don't see their daughters as sex objects or consumers but as real people with talents and interests. But daughters turn away from their parents as they enter the new land. They befriend their peers, who are their fellow inhabitants of the strange country and who share a common language and set of customers. They often embrace the junk values of mass culture.

This turning away from parents is partly for developmental reasons. Early adolescence is a time of physical and psychological change, self-absorption, preoccupation with peer approval and identity formation. It's a time when girls focus inward on their own fascinating changes.

It's partly for cultural reasons. In America we define adulthood as a moving away from families into broader culture. Adolescence is the time for cutting bonds and breaking free. Adolescents may claim great independence from parents, but they are aware and ashamed of their parents' smallest deviation from the norm. They don't like to be seen with them and find their imperfections upsetting. A mother's haircut or a father's joke can ruin their day. Teenagers are furious at parents who say the wrong things or do not respond with perfect answer. Adolescents claim not to hear their parents, but with their friends they discuss endlessly all parental attitudes. With amazing acuity, they sense nuances, doubt, shades of ambiguity, discrepancy and hypocrisy.

Adolescents still have some of the magical thinking of childhood and believe that parents have the power to keep them safe and happy. They blame their parents for their misery, yet they make a point of not telling their parents how they think and feel; they have secrets, so things can get crazy. For example, girls who are raped may not tell their parents. Instead, they become hostile and rebellious. Parents bring girls in because of their anger and out-of-control behavior. When I hear about this unexplainable anger, I ask about rape. Ironically, girls are often angrier at their parents than at the rapists. They feel their parents should have known about the danger and been more protective; afterward, they should have sensed the pain and helped.

Most parents feel like failures during this time. They feel shut out, impotent and misunderstood. They often attribute the difficulties of this time to their daughters and their own failings. They don't understand that these problems go with the developmental stage, the culture and the times.

Parents experience an enormous sense of loss when their girls enter this new land. They miss the daughters who sang in the kitchen, who read them school papers, who accompanied them on fishing trips and to ball games. They miss the daughters who liked to bake cookies, play Pictionary and be kissed goodnight. In place of their lively, affectionate daughters they have changelings—new girls who are sadder, angrier and more complicated. Everyone is grieving.

Fortunately adolescence is time-limited. By late high school most girls are stronger and the winds are dying down. Some of the worst problems—cliques, a total focus on looks and struggles with parents—are on the wane. But the way girls handle the problems of adolescence can have implications for their adult lives. Without some help, the loss of wholeness, self-confidence and self-direction can last well into adulthood. Many adult clients struggle with the same issues that overwhelmed them as adolescent girls. Thirty-year-old accountants and realtors, forty-year-old homemakers and doctors, and thirty-five-year-old nurses and schoolteachers ask the same questions and struggle with the same problems as their teenage daughters.

Even sadder are the women who are not struggling, who have forgotten that they have selves worth defending. They have repressed the pain of their adolescence, the betrayals of self in order to be pleasing. These women come to therapy with the goal of becoming even more pleasing to others. They come to lose weight, to save their marriages or to rescue their children. When I ask them about their own needs, they are confused by the question.

Most women struggled alone with the trauma of adolescence and have led decades of adult life with their adolescent experiences unexamined. The lessons learned in adolescence are forgotten and their memories of pain are minimized. They come into therapy because their marriage is in trouble, or they hate their job, or their own daughter is giving them fits. Maybe their daughter's pain awakens their own pain. Some are depressed or chemically addicted or have stress-related illnesses—ulcers, colitis, migraines or psoriasis. Many have tried to be perfect women and failed. Even though they followed the rules and did as they were told, the world has not rewarded them. They feel angry and betrayed. They feel miserable and taken for granted, used rather than loved.

Women often know how everyone in their family thinks and feels except themselves. They are great at balancing the needs of their coworkers, husbands, children and friends, but they forget to put themselves into the equation. They struggle with adolescent questions still unresolved: How important are looks and popularity? How do I care for myself and not be selfish? How can I be honest and still be loved? How can I achieve and not threaten others? How can I be sexual and not a sex object? How can I be responsive but not responsible for everyone?

As we talk, the years fall away. We are back in junior high with the cliques, the shame, the embarrassment about bodies, the desire to be accepted and the doubts about ability. So many adult women think they are stupid and ugly. Many feel guilty if they take time for themselves. They do not express anger or ask for help.

We talk about childhood—what the woman was like at ten and at fifteen. We piece together a picture of childhood lost. We review her own particular story, her own time in the hurricane. Memories flood in. Often there are tears, angry outbursts, sadness for what has been lost. So much time has been wasted pretending to be who others wanted. But also, there's a new energy that comes from making connections, from choosing awareness over denial and from the telling of secrets.

We work now, twenty years behind schedule. We reestablish each woman as the subject of her life, not as the object of others' lives. We answer Freud's patronizing question "What do women want?" Each woman wants something different and particular and yet each woman wants the same thing—to be who she truly is, to become who she can become.

Many women regain their preadolescent authenticity with menopause. Because they are no longer beautiful objects occupied primarily with caring for others, they are free once again to become the subjects of their own lives. They become more confident, self-directed and energetic. Margaret Mead noticed this phenomenon in cultures all over the world and called it "pmz," post-menopausal zest. She noted that some cultures revere these older women. Others burn them at the stake.

QUESTIONS

1. What are the conflicting choices that young girls face when they reach adolescence? What narrative evidence does Pipher provide of the troubled choices that young girls must make today as they move into adolescence? Would other kinds of fact-based evidence made her argument more persuasive? Why?
2. How does Pipher's use of quotations and paraphrase from prominent women writers and intellectuals deepen her analysis of the causes and effects of the "gap" between girls' true selves, cultural expectations, and peer pressure to act like a "female"?
3. Argue for or against Pipher's claim that girls entering adolescence today have greater pressures and difficulties than girls in previous generations. You might want to research the impact of the advantages that girls entering adolescence today have, such as class flexibility, career opportunities, and scholarships available to girls from poor and immigrant families.

JULIET B. SCHOR

"Decommercializing Childhood"

Juliet B. Schor earned her B.A. at Wesleyan University and her Ph.D. in economics from the University of Massachusetts. She taught at Harvard for nine years before joining the faculty at Boston College as a professor of sociology. She is best known for her research and writings abut family, women's issues, and economic justice. Schor has published articles in Business Week, *the* New York Times, *and the* Boston Globe. *Her books reflect her interest in overworked Americans and the effect of their materialism on family life and society.* The Overworked American *(1993), and* The Overspent American *(1999) are widely read. In the excerpt that follows from* Born to Buy *(2004), Schor argues that parents must help free their children from the culture of consumption.*

The Need for Social Cooperation

Today's most sophisticated children's marketers operate by insinuating themselves into existing social dynamics. They have nuanced understandings of how peer pressure operates; identify trendsetters, influencers, and followers; and target each group with tailored approaches. Fifty-eight percent of nine to fourteen year olds now say that they feel pressure to buy stuff in order to fit in. In addition to the onus of acquiring particular consumer items, social pressures surrounding media content and personal style are of great concern to parents. At what age should kids be permitted to see PG-13 or R movies, use instant messaging, surf the Internet, or get a tattoo? Industry helps popularize these activities.

The more that market-driven trends structure peer interactions, parental restrictions put kids at risk for social exclusion. But basing decisions about what to allow on the basis of other kids' or parents' choices may mean losing control altogether. It's one of the trickiest aspects of parenting today.

The cooperative solution entails adults' and kids' getting together to set limits jointly. This reduces the pressure on kids and keeps the standards from changing more than individuals want. Such collaboration is already occurring with drug and alcohol use, commodities most adults feel should be absolutely forbidden. Around the country, parents have formed Communities of Concern and signed the Safe Homes Pledge, promising that they will supervise gatherings at their home to prohibit minors from using alcohol, drugs, or firearms. The community comes together to create structures that ease the peer pressures on kids and protect them from danger.

A related approach is possible for other consumer practices that involve peer pressure. A first step is community dialogue. Schools and PTAs can sponsor conversations and workshops on topics such as movie ratings, media use, video games, school fashion, spending money—even the customs surrounding birthday parties. As communities come together to work through their attitudes, awareness is created, and common approaches can develop. Sometimes the simple fact of airing a topic contributes to changes in social practices and norms. If the dialogue progresses to the point where people feel more formal action is useful, analogues to the Safe Homes Pledge can be developed. Formalization helps socialize newcomers and maintains standards over time.

Smaller-scale cooperation can also be effective. In my research in Doxley, I found that mothers communicate to control consumption choices. Some call before sleepovers to find out what video the kids will be watching. Those who restrict certain types of content make their rules known. Mothers caucus about group dates to the movies. They confer about the acceptability of particular CDs. In some cases, they talk through options and take common responsibility. Occasionally one agrees to play bad cop. The larger point is that to raise children well, adults need to communicate and cooperate and establish safe and healthy environments for them. It's an old-fashioned value that's being lost as neighborhood interaction and community has declined. We owe it to our kids to get it back.

Decommercializing the Household: Evidence from Doxley

Many parents are uncomfortable with aspects of consumer culture. The parents I interviewed in Doxley certainly were, although their likes and dislikes, as well as their rationales, varied widely, from the aesthetic to the practical. Some hate television because its content is junky. Some feel that designer labels aren't good value, and others object to trendiness itself. They worry about sex on the Internet, media violence, adult themes in movies, and excessive attraction to video games. Their attitudes are rather typically middle class, an issue I discuss in some detail in the endnote to this paragraph.

Where the families may be less typical is in their success at controlling and limiting those parts of consumer culture that they object to. Granted, they were mostly financially secure and could afford high levels of maternal involvement. They didn't need television as a baby-sitter. But more than economics is at work. Those who were most successful were thoughtful and consistent in their rules and choices. They spent a lot of time with their children. And perhaps most important, these families' lives were full of engaging alternatives to the corporate offerings.

One perhaps unsurprising finding is the importance of restricting television viewing. My data showed that kids in Doxley watch relatively little television. Virtually every household I interviewed had rules about when, how much, and what kids could watch. Some allowed only minimal viewing. Many opted not to get cable. The restrictions appeared to be relatively effective, in contrast to other research findings with a less affluent sample, among whom there were fewer nonemployed mothers. (See the accompanying note for a fuller discussion of this issue.) In Doxley, the keys to success appeared to be consistency, rules tailored to the needs of individual children, and heavy time commitments to homework, sports, extracurricular activities, and outdoor play.

None of the parents I interviewed prohibited television altogether, but some came close. Their experiences are notable because they contradict widely held views that children need TV. One argument is that prohibiting television will backfire, and children will become avid viewers once parents relinquish control. A second is that children need television knowledge to prevent social exclusion. Some media scholars have also argued that the dominance of electronic media is so strong that prohibition deprives children of basic cultural literacy. The absence of these problems in the households I visited was notable, even allowing for the fact that Doxley is a low-viewing environment.

My own experience also supports this view. After our first child was born, we decided not to expose him to television, reasoning that he'd eventually become well versed in electronic media, but that love of reading and the dying print culture would be more difficult to instill. When people challenged me on this policy, as many did, I responded that we would let him watch television when he started asking for it. I agreed with the common view that we were at risk of forbidden-fruit syndrome if we were too rigid. But a funny thing happened: he never asked. We told him that we didn't think television was good for him, and he accepted that. When he entered first grade, we started watching videos sometimes. He's twelve now, and we do allow occasional viewing of sporting events. We've followed the same policies with our daughter. She doesn't ask either.

I include my story because things turned out so differently than I had expected. A decade ago, I put much more stock in the counterarguments, such as the view that kids need television knowledge to fit in socially and that only by allowing television can parents prevent children from wanting it too much. In my case, neither of these sentiments turned out to be correct. I believe my children have been much better off growing up TV free. I think it's enhanced their creativity, taught them how to amuse themselves, and given them many more hours of beneficial and more satisfying activities such as reading, writing poetry, doing art projects, and getting exercise. Of course, to be successful in restricting television for our kids, we had to stop watching it ourselves. So we put our set in a third-floor room, where the temperature is uncomfortable in both winter and summer. Instead of creating a special child-only deprivation, we changed the environment in which we all live. And we're all better for it.

My interview material also suggests that the families who are most successful in keeping the corporate culture at bay are involved with alternatives. Some of the most restrictive mothers are active in their churches. Some of the immigrant families, who tend to be rather strict about commercial influences, come together in each other's homes for regular worship and socializing. I encountered a variety of nonreligious activities as well. One woman started a mother-daughter book club, with discussion of the book and an activity. One household had family movie nights, with row seating, ushers, and popcorn. Another specialized in elaborate but low-budget theme parties—Greek mythology, insects, Peter Pan, and Eskimos (complete with a full-scale igloo). Other popular activities were wood-working, playing board games after school, and unorganized sports. The activities they described typically involved parents and kids together. One family makes a yearly pilgrimage to a mine to collect rocks, another took the kids out of school for nearly a year of travel, a third are avid canoeists and campers. These experiences jibe with anecdotal evidence from the downshifter movement, which suggests that many families are rediscovering simple, inexpensive pleasures. Eco-psychologists have also found that disconnection from nature erodes emotional and spiritual well-being. Fostering children's connection to the outdoors serves as a bulwark against excessive involvement with consumer culture.

These kinds of activities require time and energy. My earlier books addressed the inadequacy of free time and the mounting financial pressures on families. Scarcity of time and money is especially acute among low-income and single-parent households, whose members usually have long hours and inflexible jobs, ever-present financial worries, and high-stress lives. But reducing stress and finding time are crucial to engaging with kids in less commercial ways. National survey data suggest that children wish for more of that from their parents, and noncommercial activities remain popular. For example, in their 2003 poll of kids aged nine to fourteen, the Center for a New American Dream found that fewer than a third (32 percent) reported that they spend a lot of time with their parents. Sixty-nine percent of kids said they'd like to spend more time with them, and if granted one wish that would change their parents' job, 63 percent said it would be a job that gave them "more time to do fun things together." Only 13 percent wished their parents made more money. When asked what they would most like to do with their parents, 23 percent chose the three noncommercial outdoor activities offered: building a snowman or a tree house; riding bikes or doing something outside, and gardening. Twenty percent opted for a movie, 18 percent for a ball game, and 13 percent wanted a visit to a zoo or aquarium.

Reducing corporate influences does not entail exorcising money from children's lives. The ideology of childhood sacredness and innocence is frequently counterposed against the profane adult world of money and desire. The moral panic surrounding Pokémon trading cards, and to a lesser extent Beanie Babies and sport cards, revealed the pervasiveness of attitudes that children's play should be motivated by love of the objects themselves rather than acquisitive or speculative desires. Such an attitude pervades the position of the anticommercial Motherhood Project: "We face a conflict of values . . . between the values of the money world and the values of the 'motherworld'—the values of commerce and the values required to raise healthy children."

While restricting children from the profanity of the money world has a superficial appeal, such sacralization unduly deprives children of their right to be economic agents. Recent ethnographic research shows that children are typically engaged in a variety of productive practices—not only trading cards and toys but also participated in lunchtime food swaps, networks of reciprocal favors, and informal entrepreneurial activities. Indeed, children have far more sophisticated and extensive economic lives than many adults give them credit for. Why should they be deprived of these?

I do not raise this point merely for academic purposes. It is important because it makes a distinction between economic activity per se and the contemporary capitalist marketplace. Big businesses rather than a generic world of money are the forces that children need to be protected from.

In Doxley, I was impressed with how parents were teaching their children to handle money. Most families used allowance systems, and many required that children devote a portion of their allowances to charity or savings, or both. Allowances were also used to teach children the difference between needs and wants and to help them budget for things they wanted. Often kids could save up for items the parents didn't want to buy but wouldn't necessarily forbid, such as video game systems or expensive CD players. Parents developed thoughtful schemes about what they would and would not pay for. Many worried about excessive materialism and tried to teach the value of money by letting the kids manage it. Overall, attitudes toward these money matters were practical, respectful of children's skills and decision-making abilities, and founded on values of balance and prudence. At least among the families I interviewed, the kids were learning valuable lessons about the world of commerce rather than being excluded from it.

I end with an obvious but important point. Parents who are interested in reducing the influence of commercial culture on their children need to walk their talk, especially as children age. Preaching against expensive athletic shoes isn't credible with a closet full of Manolo Blahnik shoes. Restricting television is much harder in households where parents watch a lot. Surveys show that highly materialist kids are more likely to have highly materialist parents. And highly materialist parents are likely to have kids with similar priorities. To transmit values effectively, you need to live them. Parents who desire less commercial lifestyles for their children need to change with them.

Join the Movement to Oppose Corporate-Constructed Childhood

The legislative, cultural, and social changes I have been discussing will be realized only if enough people organize to make them happen. A growing number of groups have begun that work, among them Commercial Alert, Stop the Commercial Exploitation of Children, Obligation Inc., the Center for the Analysis of Commercialism in Education, the Center for Media Education, and the Center for a New American Dream. There are many others. National groups include Daughters and Dads, the Media Education Foundation, Teachers Resisting Unhealthy Children's Entertainment (TRUCE), the New Mexico Media Literacy Project, TV Turn-Off Network, the Alliance for Childhood, and the Motherhood Project. There are numerous local groups, many working on school-related commercialization. (I have put contact information for these organizations in Appendix B.)

Although these groups are vastly outmatched in terms of money and personnel, they have managed some impressive successes, especially recently. Daughters and Dads has taken action against offensive commercials, such as a Campbell's soup ad that promoted the product as a diet aid for young girls. The company pulled the ad. In 2002, Scholastic rescinded its sponsorship of the Golden Marble awards for the best children's commercials after a coalition of children's advocates questioned the very fact of targeting kids in its "Have you lost your marbles?" counter-awards. Thousands of communities around the country participate in TV Turn-Off Week. Anticommercialism efforts have made their way into state legislatures and in California led to the passage of two bills. As the public becomes educated about what's going on, it's easier to mobilize support for restricting corporate practices.

The worlds of adults and children are merging. In my mind, that's mainly a good thing. But the commercial aspects of that integration are not working for children. The prevalence of harmful and addictive products, the imperative to keep up, and the growth of materialist attitudes are harming kids. If we are honest with ourselves, adults will admit that we are suffering from many of the same influences. That means our task should be to make the world a safer and more life-affirming place for everyone. Reversing corporate-constructed childhood is a good first step.

QUESTIONS

1. Why is Schor concerned about how the media and materialism have infiltrated the homes and schools of young children all over the nation? Give examples of children and youth who are addicted to toys, clothes, and media games, to name a few products. How do these children get hooked?

2. According to Schor's research, what types of parents are most successful at limiting their children's dependence on consumption, the Internet, and computer games?

3. Do you think that Schor is being realistic in thinking that children and youth can be separated from our culture of consumption? Why or why not? Would the "solutions" suggested in the essay work in the long term?

RACHEL LEHMANN-HAUPT

"Multi-Tasking Man"

Rachel Lehmann-Haupt has a B.A. in English Literature from Kenyon College and an M.A. from the Graduate School of Journalism at the University of California, Berkeley. She currently lives in Manhattan's West Village where she writes essays and fiction about gender politics and media culture. Her articles have appered in the New York Times, Wired, Vogue, Business Week, *and* Folio, *where she is a regular columnist. She also is the author of an in-air stress-relief manual,* Airplane Yoga *(2003). In the article that follows, Lehmann-Haupt argues for the need to "multi-task" in order for both women and men to meet the complex, shifting needs of dual-career families.*

Feminism's first supermodel was an ancient goddess. As the story goes, Mahisa, a rebellious and greedy god, seized the celestial kingdom when his creator, Brahman, denied him immortality. The gods became so incensed by this tyrant that in order to win back their kingdom they combined their powers to produce a divine force in the form of a beautiful woman. Durga was a shapely siren with eight wild arms wielding deadly weapons.

Whirling her mighty arms, Durga sought Mahisa and seduced him. When he fell in love with her, she smiled, batted her wide eyes, and whispered that she could only marry a man who could defeat her in battle. Mahisa was charmed by her challenge, and so sure that he could beat a woman that he took her on.

Their battle was fierce. Mahisa, slick and focused, maneuvered in between and around the swipes of Durga's weapons. The goddess struggled, but didn't give up. When Mahisa was convinced that he had won, she suddenly overwhelmed him with the whisk of her arms and won the battle with a deadly blow to his heart.

In 1972 this multiarmed goddess appeared on the premiere issue of *Ms.* magazine. This time she juggled new weapons: a telephone, a steering wheel, an iron, a clock, a feather duster, a frying pan, a mirror, and a typewriter. There she was in high gloss, with her head tilted in a luring glance, dainty smirk, and demure eyes. She was no longer delivering blows to the ancients, but a modern media message to thousands of housewives and husbands of post–World War II America. A woman's ancient power to juggle multiple tasks, she declared, was the key to the economic power that would free her from cloistered suburbia, housebound ennui, and Freudian shackles that held that anatomy is destiny.

Helen Fisher, the feminist anthropologist, in her book *The First Sex*, says that a woman's skill to juggle multiple tasks evolved out of men and women's naturally separate worlds—and naturally different brain structures—that date back millions of years to the sunburnt plains of East Africa. The women of the tribal village were responsible for gathering more than half of the meal, taking care of the children, watching out for wild animals, and managing the social and marketing networks of the village. The village men were responsible for focusing on the hunt.

"As our male forebears tracked warthogs and wildebeests," Fisher writers, "they gradually evolved the brain architecture to screen out peripheral thought, focus their attention, and make step-by-step decisions." Women's brains, she argues, evolved to handle many tasks at the same time; what she calls "web thinking." There is even scientific evidence from studies that the corpus callosum, the bundle of millions of nerve fibers that connects the two hemispheres of the brain, is larger in women, and therefore allows for greater communication between each side.

By harnessing these ancient juggling powers, the second wave of feminism was supposed to wash away the wife's troubles and empower her from the bedroom to the boardroom. Rather than husbands and wives operating in separate fiefdoms, pulling their weight at the office and the home, respectively, women could liberate themselves by dominating both environments. Ms. Durga's many arms meant that the modern woman could have it all. She could be the working woman, the housemaid, and the sexy goddess, and her gallant god in shining gray flannel stability, unchanged, would still love her.

Thirty years later women have indeed come a long way. Women managers still make 76 cents for every dollar earned by their male counterparts, but women now account for almost half of the labor force. And that number is rising. The majority of men and women no longer live in separate and isolated worlds. Technology and the global economy have connected us together both at work and in our homes, and there are now ways for each sex to play more equal roles in each realm. Home offices and telecommuting options, on-line grocery shopping and home delivery services, high-speed breast milk pumps and web cams in day care centers allow us all to toggle more efficiently between the duties of work and home.

These profound cultural changes have created an opportunity for traditional gender roles to break down and evolve. Now that Ms. Durga has tipped the scales, for better or for worse, isn't it time for her to put down her weapons and take the focus off trying to hold it all? Isn't the next step a new and altogether different feminist supermodel? What about a multi-tasking man?

Despite feminist progess, the majority of modern men are still focused solely on the hunt. "My career, not my home life," as one young technology entrepreneur in his twenties, who works at home, put it. "The hunt is not the nest. It is the hunt."

Today American men are still only doing a fraction more of the work in the home than they were thirty years ago. A 2002 report by the Institute for Social Research at the University of Michigan found that American men are doing a mere four more hours of housework a week than they were in 1965. Women aren't doing as much housework, but they are still doing 27 hour more a week than men are. The nanny/housekeeper may act as a bejeweled arm for many upper-income goddesses, but then we must ask, how many of these appendages of privilege are men?

While the traditional corporate wife of the '50s has become all but obsolete, the corporate husband has yet to really define himself. There are now the few corporate superheroes such as Hewlett-Packard CEO Carlton Fiorino, who boasted in a 2002 *Fortune* magazine story that the stay-at-home husband is "The New Trophy Husband." The reality, however, is that most American women feel more overworked than men because the brunt of multi-tasking is not equally distributed.

It may simply be a communication problem. Women, in their quest to figure out how to have it all, may have lost track of the conversation with men. In the 1970s the ideal feminist woman became the tomboyish Charlie perfume girl. She didn't ask her man to change. She merely untied her apron strings and took long strides of bold suited confidence that told us that she bought her own seduction potion rather than waiting for that special gift from her man. In the 1980s she wore broad shoulder-padded suits, took the train to Wall Street, and competed with high-octane men, all without asking her man to make a similar conversion. He was still the head of the household, still the stoic Marlboro man at the center of every scene. He might have moved over a bit to share his office with the broad in the pants, but it was still his world. Despite a few sensitive moments, he was still focused mainly on the hunt. "We saw women as equals," said a lawyer in his forties. "But it was still about the boys' network and a female secretary who supported you."

As it turned out, women did not really resemble the cool and confident Charlie girl. They were exhausted, anxiety-ridden and overburdened. By the end of the 1980s women were suffering from what Arlie Hochschild, a sociology professor at the University of California-Berkeley, called "the stalled revolution." In her book *The Second Shift: Working Parents and the Revolution at Home,* she argued that men and the organizations that they worked for weren't helping take on the weight of domestic labor. "Workplaces have remained inflexible in the face of family demands of their workers," she wrote. "At home most men have yet to really adapt to the changes in women."

In the 1990s the "stalled revolution" in some ways got worse. Men and women became even more alienated from each other. Women gained more economic power and more confidence about their innate feminine powers. Many even argued that a woman's natural abilities to multi-task gave her an advantage over men in a new technology age where everyone was bombarded from all directions with the web, instant messages, and cell phone conference calls from offices around the globe in an ever-growing—and feminized—service economy.

Ms. Durga transformed from the shoulder-padded career woman to the post-feminist power girl who could gracefully toggle between work and home; talk of politics and nail polish; Madeleine Albright's weapons strategy and Monica's thongs. Men were suddenly "stiffed," as Susan Faludi observed. They may have learned that it was cool to tap into their more gentle side, carry the Baby Björn, and push the stroller with both hands. They may have traded the bachelor party entertainment of silicon-enhanced strippers for silicon-enhanced facials, manicures and massages at day spas. They also lost track of what it meant to be men.

Many men reacted by running away to pound their chests in the woods. They became cigar aficionados. They joined Promise Keepers meetings in baseball stadiums. They did everything to grasp the last hold on traditional manliness. "That means Russell Crowe. Someone who has steely clear, focused confidence. Someone linear and ballsy. A brute. A guy who can fix things," said a writer in his thirties.

At the turn of the twenty-first century American women are sill sent happy-ending messages through the media—and all the fairy tales that we read as kids—that we need a prince who will let us let down our hair and save us—both financially and emotionally. Many women still want this image, or at least are sexually attracted to it. They want "a man."

But rather than a half-liberated prince in a gray Armani suit, what women really need is Durga's twin brother. A multi-tasking mensch. A man who can take some of the weight off women's many arms by bringing home the bacon, frying it up in a pan, without ever letting us forget that he's "a man!" The problem with this vision is that anatomy may be destiny. Men might not have the neurological wherewithal to deliver. "I can see how it would make my relationship with a woman easier, but it's just not natural for me to multi-task," says a New York editor in his thirties. "I know women think I'm just being stubborn, but when I try I feel like the slow kid in the fast class."

In 2001, Alladi Vankatesh, a sociologist at the University of California at Irvine's Center for Research on Information Technology began studying this very issue by looking at how traditional gender roles are shifting in the information age. Vankatesh, a soft-spoken Indian man in his mid-forties, spent a year in the sprawling suburban home of Los Angeles observing the different ways men and women respond to computer technology. After interviewing close to seventy families, he discovered that not much has changed in a million years. When men use computers, they tend to focus on a single task or an immediate goal. Play game! Win game! Find information!

Women on the other hand, he says, think about how the computer integrates into the rest of their lives. How it can help them toggle between working at home and maintaining a connection with their children's school and other parents in their community, for example. "The good news is that because computer technology does seem to be saving women time, they are feeling less pressure about the work of home," he says. The fact remains, however, that men are overwhelmingly still focusing on the hunt.

The human brain has not changed significantly in twenty thousand years. As Helen Fisher explains, even if women in the nations with the highest birth rates, such as Africa and India, begin to select partners who are inclined toward more feminine behavior—including multitasking—it's going to take a long time before an actual hard-wiring evolution occurs. A new breed of super multi-tasking man is not arriving any time soon.

Maybe the optimal partnership will have to be more like the Wonder Twins, the characters in the '80s television cartoon *The Super Friends*. Zan and Jayna were from the planet Exxor. Zan, the boy, had the power to change spontaneously into any water-based form. Jayna, the girl, could become any animal. In order to activate their shape-shifting powers, the twins needed to touch hands. "Wonder Twin Powers, activate!" they would shout. When fighting a villain, Jayna would shout "Shape of the Sphinx!" and Zan would yell "Form of an Ice Shovel!" The Sphinx would then hit the villain over the head with the ice shovel. Their super powers worked only when they combined their different strengths.

Clinging to evolutionary determinism, however, could also thwart social progress. As women's salaries become necessities for survival of the modern family, men, despite ill-wiring, can no longer afford to focus solely on the hunt. Many modern men, especially those of the generation who were nurtured in Ms. Durga's multiple arms and grew up in the multi-tasking world of computer technology, have therefore begun to adapt.

Even in the most neo-traditional households, where the husband still takes the train to the organization and the wife has set up her office at home in order to manage the house and child care, a new multi-tasking masculinity is beginning to emerge. "Fathering is all about multi-tasking," said a writer in his thirties. "Just last night, in fact, I was swinging my daughter in the car seat to try to coax her to sleep, while at the same time I was downloading music into our computer, checking e-mail, reading a Philip Roth novel, and tinkering with an upcoming article. I only have two hands but sometimes I feel like an octopus. I have literally begun to undertake certain tasks with my feet.

"I also do almost all the cooking," he continued. "That said, my father was fairly shocked when he came to visit, because he saw me doing a lot of things that he never had to worry about—and I think he found that somewhat inappropriate." For men of generations X and Y, the social effects of feminism are slowly taking hold, but the pressures for more change are mounting. As women become more economically independent, they are staying single longer, choosing to rely on their social networks of friends for support rather than settling for a male partner who may not necessarily meet their standards of companionship. A higher divorce rate is forcing more men to live alone, care for themselves and develop the skills of the home front that traditionally have fallen to women. As liberated gay couples become more prominent, gay men, who either through biological or social wiring fall into more traditionally feminine roles, are becoming new social role modes.

Most major corporations still lack in-house day care. Most men are still not granted paternity leave. There are still strong cultural pressures on men that make them feel that if they scant their jobs in favor of the work of home and child care, they might appear wimpy or uncommitted. Despite these obstacles, men are progressing in the direction of Durga's twin. If the conversation continues, the balance of roles will improve even more.

There may even be the possibility for change in men's brain circuits. Eric Kandel, a neuroscientist at Columbia University, won the first Noble Prize in medicine of the twenty-first century for his seminal work with the sea slug aplysia. By studying the way the slug's nerve cells respond to chemical signals that produce changes in its behavior, Kandel and his colleagues discovered that learning can produce physical changes in the brain by strengthening connections between nerve cells.

Men aren't sea slugs, but it could be that the more they multi-task between the work of the home and their work, the more their brains will learn and change. It could be that once upon a time in the future, Durga's multi-tasking twin in shining armor could come to her rescue, overthrow the tyranny of the pressure for her to do it all, and prove that anatomy isn't destiny, experience is.

QUESTIONS

1. To what ancient historical development does Helen Fisher attribute women's superior ability to multi-task? What is meant by "web thinking"? How do studies of the *corpus callosium* help to support Fisher's theory? Do you agree with her that men are inherently different from women in their interest in or ability to multi-task, or is there some other reason why they don't like to help out with household chores and childcare?

2. What is the significance of the "stalled revolution"? What are its causes? How and why did the stalled revolution for women worsen in the 90s, according to the author?

3. How and why, according to Lehmenn-Haupt, is a "new multi-tasking masculinity" becoming more common today? What evidence does she present to support her claim? Do you agree with her? Why or why not?

"For a Politics of Quality of Life"

Judith Warner was a correspondent for Newsweek *in Paris and has reviewed books and written on politics and women's issues for the* New York Times, The Washington Post, *and* The New Republic. *She has written non-fiction books such as* Hillary Clinton: The Inside Story *(1999) and, with Howard Dean,* You Have the Power: How to Take Back Our Country and Restore Democracy in America *(2005). Her most recent book,* Perfect Madness: Motherhood in an Age of Anxiety *(2006), is part of a larger political debate about the changing family. In the selection that follows from* Perfect Madness, *Warner argues that the government must acknowledge the problems that today's families face and pass legislation that will support family values, such as flexible child care.*

THE DISUNITY [among mothers] is so bad that a much-touted October 2002 Barnard College symposium, described by its organizers as a "call

FOR A POLITICS OF QUALITY OF LIFE

to a Motherhood Movement," stalled entirely because its participants could not find common ground. One prominent feminist attacked a prominent antifeminist naysayer for supposedly misrepresenting data. Other feminists refused to endorse any statements of purpose that promoted the notion of easing the lives of mothers who leave the workforce. "Motherhood-movement" activists from the stay-at-home camp blocked the proceedings with their quasireligious pro-stay-at-home agenda. The only thing all the demoralized participants could agree on was a need for mothers' "validation."

And yet even that need tripped them up, because what they wanted to have validated was mutually contradictory. Validation for one group necessarily meant demonization of the other. It was politics as clique formation—junior high–style, one disgusted participant told me. "God forbid anyone is doing things differently from us," she said, describing the proceedings. "We can't unite, because if we do it's as though we're admitting that the way we do things isn't absolutely perfect."

The same ideological binding that has stymied the development of a real and practical politics of the family in America has limited the vision of the "motherhood movement." Way too much verbiage is spent on maintaining the illusion of mothers' "choices," too much energy is spent diverting attention from the fact that without help from the government, mothers have only the most paltry options to choose from. Too much energy is being expended on seeking validation—a recognition of mothers' "value" ("we count") and of motherhood as "the most important job in the world" through measures like including unpaid household labor in the GDP. Too much attention has been spent on trying to secure a tax subsidy for stay-at-home moms—an expensive measure whose pointlessness I saw illustrated clearly in France, where one stay-at-home mother of four I knew referred to her $468 monthly government allowance as "sweater money." The only women in France for whom the stay-at-home allowance can conceiveably make a meaningful difference are those who are unemployed or partially employed, or tenuously employed in minimum-wage work, earning close to nothing anyway. Earning a little bit less in those circumstances and being able to stay home with the children (with housing vouchers and the like helping make it possible) is certainly better for these mothers than leaving their children with strangers for the sake of an non-lucrative, non-life-enhancing job.

We used to have a program recognizing this in America, too. It was called welfare. That we would abolish that taxpayer-funded program for needy stay-at-home moms and replace it with another simply to provide "validation" for middle-class moms is utterly absurd, financially useless for families, and expensive for society. (In 1999, a $250 tax break for stay-at-home parents with children under the age of one floated around by the Clinton administration was projected to cost $1.3 billion over five years.)

It should not be the business of the government to provide validation for women who lack self-esteem. The needs of families are much too important for this.

A Politics of Quality of Life

If we were to desacralize the motherhood issue and drop all the narcissistic and ideological goals that now infuse it, what would families need?

Simply put: *institutions that can help us take care of our children so that we don't have to do everything on our own.* We need institutions made accessible and affordable and of guaranteed high quality by government funding, oversight, and standards.

We need a new set of profamily *entitlements*—standing programs that can outlast election-year campaign promises made by politicians and are more widespread and universally available than the "privileges" sometimes accorded to parents by private employers.

It's time to admit that the idea that businesses will "do the right thing" for American families is a lost hope. More than a decade into the era of "family-friendly policies," more than a third of all working parents in America have neither sick leave nor vacation leave. Many parents are creating their own "family-friendly" career path, and what this much-vaunted assertion of "free choice" implies is taking part-time jobs with few advancement opportunities and often no benefits.

During the late 1990s economic boom, more than five years after the passage of the Family and Medical Leave Act, only 46 percent of U.S workers were covered and eligible for unpaid leave. And, as the millennium turned, a large number of parents reported not taking advantage of the leave they did have because the culture of their workplace pressured them so strongly against it.

It could be said that making an argument for a set of middle-class entitlements is obscene when the conditions of working-class and poor families in this country are so dire. (And, indeed, they can be horrifying: you need only think of the news stories of working mothers with no child care who, fearing for their jobs, lock their children into their cars—and sometimes land in jail—to understand the impossible stresses of "balancing" the unbalanceable.)

But I believe that the kinds of quality-of-life measures I have out-lined are potentially helpful for everyone. I also believe, given the "compassion fatigue" that is, in the politest formulation, said to under-lie Americans' hostility toward programs for the poor, you cannot get Americans on board to provide *more* help for the needy until they feel they are getting help too. I think perhaps if so much of the American middle class feels so hostile to "handouts," it's because they themselves feel so beleaguered.

If there's any way to get people to sign on to and pay for a politics of quality of life, it has to come from the creation of a new kind of pro-family consensus of opinion—and in countries like France that con-sensus has been built through policies that bring something to everyone, to the fortunate as well as to the poor.

People commonly say there's no way you can make government ac-tivism on the part of the family palatable. For one thing, they say, in America, we consider the family to be people's private business, out of the reach of the long arm of government. But the truth is, we already have government programs that meddle in family life—and in very in-trusive ways.

The Welfare Reform Act of 1996 had as part of its stated purpose to prevent out-of-wedlock pregnancies and encourage the creation of two-parent families. The Bush administration's 2002 welfare reform reauthorization proposal included $300 million for "demonstration grants" to teach couples how to stay married and avoid having babies out of wedlock. The "pro-fatherhood movement" that took off in the late 1990s used government funds for the specific purpose of restoring men to their "God-given" roles as heads of families.

In truth, the opposition to government programs to help families isn't really about protecting people's private lives from government intru-sion. It's about ideology (some kinds of intrusion are bad; some kinds are good). It's also about money. That's why relatively cheap programs that "valorize" a certain form of family life can fly. (A National Fatherhood Initiative flyer once put it, succinctly, "What reduces crime, child poverty, teen pregnancy AND requires no new taxes?") It's also why other more substantive and meaningful initiatives—like the short-lived Clinton ad-ministration attempt to rally support for the idea of government-mandated day-care standards—are instantly, and consistently, tabled.

There's no rhyme or reason to this. It's paternalistic, condescend-ing, and, above all, hypocritical. After all, Americans do foot the bill for child care for some people: we spend hundreds of millions of dollars a year funding day care for the children of military personnel (as well we should, and the care is excellent). Many federal workers in Washington, too, have access to excellent on-site day care, some of it subsidized by the government. I think that's great. But why shouldn't the rest of us enjoy similar benefits of our tax money? Aren't we all *entitled?*

The cost of implementing the kind of public policies I advocate is daunting. According to economists Barbara R. Bergmann and Suzanne W. Helburn, authors of 2002's clear-eyed and comprehensive *America's Child Care Problem: The Way Out,* it would cost nearly $50 billion a year ($30 billion more than the federal government currently spends on subsidy programs) simply to solve the problem of caring for preschool-age children in America—chiefly through the form of vouchers to subsidize high-quality early-education programs.

And yet, when the political will is there, we can do seemingly impossible things. Political will brought about welfare reform in 1996. It brought about the New Deal. It brought about the Reagan Revolution. Things can change when the change presented fits the social values of the moment. And there are many indicators now showing that the time may be right for changes that will guarantee American families a better quality of life.

Polling conducted by the Center for Policy Alternatives in 1992, 1996, and 2000 has shown that quality-of-life issues are being rated higher and higher as areas of concern by the American public. Among women, the "time crunch" has surpassed reproductive rights as an area of acute concern.

Quality-of-life issues came to the fore most prominently in the 2000 campaign year, when polling found the "minivan moms" of the turn of the millennium to be considerably more *tired* than the soccer moms of the 1996 election year. And so, in the midst of unprecedented levels of wealth, candidates found themselves talking about the "time famine," and "livability" issues. Even suburban men with young children (minivan dads?) were saying they felt squeezed for time.

The spread of the "simplicity movement" also argues that people are hungry for a kind of slowing-down change. Indeed, 71 percent of people surveyed in 2000 said they would choose a job with more flexibility and benefits over one that offered more pay. Poll results have shown, too, that people are now open to government-directed solutions. In 1999, a *Business Week* poll showed that 74 percent of women and 70 percent of men thought that government should take a larger role to help working families. In 2000, a bipartisan polling team found that a plurality of both men and women said they believed that there should be a government solution to child care. In September 2002, California—a state often considered a bellwether for national political trends—passed the first paid parental-leave law in the country. Polling done nationally at the time showed that 82 percent of women and 75 percent of men said they would support a similar measure in their state. A ballot initiative prompted by Arnold Schwarzenegger to provide universal after-school care for children was also approved by 57 percent of California voters. This from a state that only eleven months later elected Schwarzenegger as governor on a platform of fiscal responsibility.

Clearly, if presented in the right way, quality-of-life policies can garner political support in the most unlikely of places. And the additional $30 billion needed to cover child care is nothing compared with the cost of the Bush tax cuts, which are said now to cost more than $200 billion annually. It's only slightly more (in the stratosphere of the billions) than the $27.2 billion that the tax exemption for Social Security benefits enjoyed by our nation's wealthy currently costs taxpayers. Even if America were, proportionally, to spend as much as France does on subsidized child care and paid leave—increasing our budget outlays by $85 billion a year—*it would still cost less than the Bush tax cuts.*

It isn't really a question of money, it's a question of priorities. And it's a question, too, for Americans, of how we conceive of quality of life.

After all, we already have a politics of quality of life in America. But it is quality of life defined as luxury spending. It is paid for by tax policies calibrated to permit the wealthy to keep most of their money and spend it on *stuff,* sending their material quality of life skyrocketing, while the middle class, bearing most of the impact of taxation, foots the bill. And it has brought about a culturewide impoverishment of the forms of quality of life that actually generate happiness, as in time with family, leisure time, relaxation, and peace of mind.

There is every reason to think that the kind of material quality of life that was so dramatically fostered by the tax policies and cultural values of the past quarter century are not conducive to happiness. The percentage of people who described themselves as "very happy" fell from 36 to 29 percent between 1970 and 1999. During the boom years, the demands of the 24/7 economy were such that, by 1999, fully two-fifths of all employed Americans were working mostly during evenings, nights, or weekends—and reporting sleep disturbances, stomach problems, perpetual fatigue, and depression. Couples working split shifts—one spouse at night and one during the day—as a way to avoid paying for child care were divorcing at up to five times the rate of other married couples. Even people with lives of relative ease were stressed to the gills: In 2002, a Gallup poll on stress and relaxation time found that families with household incomes of over $75,000 a year were among the "most stressed" households in America. Fourteen percent of Americans, the pollsters found, said they "never have time to relax."

Which form of quality of life our government policies espouse says a great deal about our national priorities. And strikes to the heart of what kind of society we want to be.

For which is more important: the ability to cruise around in ever-larger cars with ever-softer leather interiors and better drink holders? Or the ability to find parking spots and breathe cleaner air?

Which should we "choose": the ability to afford private school (which means buying into the soul-rending process of getting into these schools) or the relief of being able to sign up and show up for a neighborhood public school which is of truly high quality?

Which is more valuable: the ability to afford a $25,000 time share in the Hamptons, or to take an entire month off for vacation?

And which is a better form of parenting: to teach our children the single-minded selfishness they need to thrive in the winner-take-all society—or to change that society so that *everyone wins*?

Changing The Rules of the Game

At the end of *The Feminine Mystique,* Betty Friedan said, "If women were really *people*—no more, no less—then all the things that kept them from being full people in our society would have to be changed. . . . It would be necessary to change the rules of the game to restructure professions, marriage, the family, the home."

Seven years later, with the women's movement gaining steam, she said, "We have to break down the actual barriers that prevent women from being full people in society, and not only end explicit discrimination but build new institutions."

To do less, she concluded, would be to make the women's movement "all talk."

I would say now: If women are really to be *equal*, no more, no less, then all the things that still keep them from being equal in our society have to change.

Because there is a real gap today between the ideals of gender equality we as a society espouse and the ability of American women to make good on the promises of their freedom. They face compromises that men do not share. Their right to "choose"—to remain true to themselves, to make (and act upon) their own choices—is systematically curtailed when they become mothers. And that's because the structures of our society as they currently exist do not allow mothers to make meaningful choices.

Too many are forced to abdicate the dreams of a lifetime because the demands of the workplace are incompatible with family life.

Others, in the quest to support their families, must "choose" to consign their children to seriously substandard care.

Others must abdicate their dreams of homemaking because it is simply too costly—or the psychological demands of total-reality motherhood are too onerous. And all are, at least on a psychological level, denied that inalienable right of "the pursuit of happiness." Because for a mother to pursue her happiness is in many quarters these days called sheer selfishness.

And though many women can and do manage to accept (or at least adjust to) this situation for themselves, there's a twinge of real sadness that comes out when they talk about their daughters. As a forty-something mother mused one evening to me, "I look at my daughter and I just want to know: What happened? Because look at us: it's 2002 and nothing's changed. My mother expected my life to be very different from hers but now it's a lot more like hers than I expected, and from here I don't see where it will be different for my daughter. I don't want her to carry this crushing burden that's in our heads. . . . [But] what can make things different?"

The odd mix of 1970s feminism and Reaganomics that molded our minds and conditions our politics has not produced a world that is worthy of our daughters. And it has not given us the tools to imagine a world that could be different. After all, most of us in the middle and upper middle class are entirely complicit with the system of winners and losers that condemns us to mother like lunatics. We may, very often, complain about the maddening pace and pressures of our lives, but we rarely stop to question the values that make it all necessary. And I think that's because the very same values that impoverish the lives of so many women, and families, in our society—untrammeled self-interest, individualism, freedom from government intrusion—are those upon which most successful women's lives (whether working or at-home) are built.

But is the success of the few worth the mess of the many? Do we really need, any longer, to promote the prospects, values, and virtues of natural-born "winners"? And are they necessarily role models?

"The original idea of feminism as I first encountered it, in about 1969, was twofold," Barbara Ehrenreich has written: "that nothing short of equality will do and that in a society marred by injustice and cruelty, equality will never be good enough." Top-achieving women are the heroines of a winner-take-all society. But is the equality to compete, to climb over others to the top of the heap, the only kind of equality we want? What is much more challenging—and meaningful—is finding a way to let *most* women become the people they want to be as they move through the different stages of their lives.

I can imagine that, because I have not embraced the idea of women's work as tantamount to women's liberation, or the idea of women's work-place success as tantamount to success for the gender, that people will think I'm a reactionary. Or that because I have looked for ways more women can stay home or work part-time I will be interpreted as believing that women *should* stay home, or *should* work part-time. I do not think that at all. Indeed, I do not think that women *should* do anything—other than remain true to themselves so that they can be happy.

And I do not think most women can be happy in our current culture of motherhood. It is just too psychologically damaging.

I think the kinds of "choices" women must now make, the kinds of compromises, adjustments, and adaptations they must accept in the name of "balance" and Good Motherhood, the kinds of disappointments and even heartbreaks they must suck up for the sake of marital harmony, do them a kind of psychological violence. Too often, they end up anxious and depressed, running scared, becoming rigid, shutting down their horizons, and turning a deaf ear to their dreams.

And this is not just a problem of individual women and their privately managed psychological pain. It is a problem of society.

QUESTIONS

1. What factors does Warner believe have caused the "motherhood movement" to break apart into warring factions? What governmental action does Warner think needs to be taken to provide a better "quality of life" for mothers and children? Why does she hold this view? Do you agree that "governmental action" is the solution? Do mothers have other options?

2. Why does Warner believe that we are at a point in contemporary history when the government will provide funds through legislation that will make it possible for many more children to receive proper child care? What polls and previous government policies does

she cite? Is her use of evidence adequate and convincing? Why or why not?

3. How convincing is Warner's argument that all mothers today—those who work part time outside of the home, those who stay at home to raise their children, and those who work full time—are suffering from a lack of meaningful choices and "a kind of psychological violence"? What is the source of the violence, and could her solution help alleviate it? Do you think such "violence" exists to the extent that Warner believes it does?

"A More Perfect Union"

Jonathan Rauch graduated Summa Cum Laude with a B.A. in History from Yale University in 1982. Since then he has been contributing editor at the National Journal *and Writer in Residence at the Brookings Institution. He has appeared often on television and has written for publications such as the* Economist, Atlantic Monthly, Reason, *and* The New Republic. *His books include* Kindly Inquisitors: The New Attacks On Free Thought *(1993), and* Gay Marriage: Why It Is Good for Gays, Good for Straights, and Good for America *(2004). The following article from the* Atlantic Monthly *(2004) argues that states should be able to make their own decisions about the legality of gay marriage.*

Last November the Supreme Judicial Court of Massachusetts ruled that excluding gay couples from civil marriage violated the state constitution. The court gave the legislature six months—until May—to do something about it. Some legislators mounted efforts to amend the state constitution to ban same-sex marriage, but as of this writing they have failed (and even if passed, a ban would not take effect until at least 2006). With unexpected urgency the country faces the possibility that marriage licenses might soon be issued to homosexual couples. To hear the opposing sides talk, a national culture war is unavoidable.

But same-sex marriage neither must nor should be treated as an all-or-nothing national decision. Instead individual states should be left to try gay marriage if and when they choose—no national ban, no national mandate. Not only would a decentralized approach be in keeping with the country's most venerable legal traditions; it would also improve, in three ways, the odds of making same-sex marriage work for gay and straight Americans alike.

First, it would give the whole country a chance to learn. Nothing terrible—in fact, nothing even noticeable—seems to have happened to marriage since Vermont began allowing gay civil unions, in 2000. But civil unions are not marriages. The only way to find out what would happen if same-sex couples got marriage certificates is to let some of us do it. Turning marriage into a nationwide experiment might be rash, but trying it in a few states would provide test cases on a smaller scale. Would the divorce rate rise? Would the marriage rate fall? We should get some indications before long. Moreover, states are, as the saying goes, the laboratories of democracy. One state might opt for straight-forward legalization. Another might add some special provisions (for in-stance, regarding child custody or adoption). A third might combine same-sex marriage with counseling or other assistance (not out of line with a growing movement to offer social-service support to so-called fragile families). Variety would help answer some important questions: Where would gay marriage work best? What kind of community sup-port would it need? What would he the avoidable pitfalls? Either to for-bid same-sex marriage nationwide or to legalize it nationwide would be to throw away a wealth of potential information.

Just as important is the social benefit of letting the states find their own way. Law is only part of what gives marriage its binding power; com-munity support and social expectations are just as important. In a com-munity that looked on same-sex marriage with bafflement or hostility, a gay couple's marriage certificate, while providing legal benefits, would confer no social support from the heterosexual majority. Both the couple and the community would be shortchanged. Letting states choose gay marriage wouldn't guarantee that everyone in the state recognized such marriages as legitimate, but it would pretty well ensure that gay married couples could find some communities in their state that did.

Finally, the political benefit of a state-by-state approach is not to be underestimated. This is the benefit of avoiding a national culture war.

The United States is not (thank goodness) a culturally homoge-neous country. It consists of many distinct moral communities. On certain social issues, such as abortion and homosexuality, people don't agree and probably never will—and the signal political advantage of the federalist system is that they don't have to. Individuals and groups who find the values or laws of one state obnoxious have the right to live somewhere else.

The nationalization of abortion policy in the Supreme Court's 1973 Roe v. Wade decision created a textbook example of what can happen when this federalist principle is ignored. If the Supreme Court had not stepped in, abortion would today be legal in most states but not all; pro-lifers would have the comfort of knowing they could live in a state whose law was compatible with their views. Instead of endlessly confronting a cultural schism that affects every Supreme Court nomination, we would see occasional local flare-ups in state legislatures or courtrooms.

America is a stronger country for the moral diversity that federal-ism uniquely allows. Moral law and family law govern the most inti-mate and, often, the most controversial spheres of life. For the sake of domestic tranquility, domestic law is best left to a level of government that is close to home.

So well suited is the federalist system to the gay-marriage issue that it might almost have been set up to handle it. In a new land whose citi-zens followed different religious traditions, it would have made no sense to centralize marriage or family law. And so marriage has been the do-main of local law not just since the days of the Founders but since Colo-nial times, before the states were states. To my knowledge, the federal government has overruled the states on marriage only twice. The first time was when it required Utah to ban polygamy as a condition for join-ing the Union—and note that this ruling was issued before Utah became a state. The second time was in 1967, when the Supreme Court, in Loving v. Virginia, struck down sixteen states' bans on interracial marriage. Here the Court said not that marriage should be defined by the federal gov-ernment but only that states could not define marriage in ways that vio-lated core constitutional rights. On the one occasion when Congress directly addressed same-sex marriage, in the 1996 Defense of Marriage Act, it decreed that the federal government would not recognize same-sex marriages but took care not to impose that rule on the states.

Marriage laws (and, of course, divorce laws) continue to be estab-lished by the states. They differ on many points, from age of consent to who may marry whom. In Arizona, for example, first cousins are al-lowed to marry only if both are sixty-five or older or the couple can prove to a judge "that one of the cousins is unable to reproduce." (So much for the idea that marriage is about procreation) Conventional wis-dom notwithstanding, the Constitution does not require states to recognize one another's marriages. The Full Faith and Credit clause (Article IV, Section 1) does require states to honor one another's public acts and judgments. But in 1939 and again in 1988 the Supreme Court ruled that the clause does not compel a state "to substitute the statutes of other states for its own statutes dealing with a subject matter concerning which it is competent to legislate." Dale Carpenter, a law professor at the University of Minnesota, notes that the Full Faith and Credit clause "has never been interpreted to mean that every state must recognize every marriage performed in every other state." He writes, "Each state may refuse to recognize a marriage performed in another state if that marriage would violate the state's public policy." If Delaware, for example, decided to lower its age of consent to ten, no other state would be required to regard a ten-year-old as legally married. The public-policy exception, as it is called, is only common sense. If each state could legislate for all the rest, American-style federalism would be at an end.

Why, then, do the states all recognize one another's marriages? Because they choose to. Before the gay-marriage controversy arose, the country enjoyed a general consensus on the terms of marriage. Interstate differences were so small that states saw no need to split hairs, and mutual recognition was a big convenience. The issue of gay marriage, of course, changes the picture, by asking states to reconsider an accepted boundary of marriage. This is just the sort of controversy in which the Founders imagined that individual states could and often should go their separate ways.

Paradoxically, the gay left and the antigay right have found themselves working together against the center. They agree on little else, but where marriage is concerned, they both want the federal government to take over.

To many gay people, anything less than nationwide recognition of same-sex marriage seems both unjust and impractical. "Wait a minute," a gay person might protest. "How is this supposed to work? I get married in Maryland (say), but every time I cross the border into Virginia during my morning commute, I'm single? Am I married or not? Portability is one of the things that make marriage different from civil union. If it isn't portable, it isn't really marriage; it's second-class citizenship. Obviously, as soon as same-sex marriage is approved in any one state, we're going to sue in federal court to have it recognized in all the others."

"Exactly!" a conservative might reply. "Gay activists have no intention of settling for marriage in just one or two states. They will keep suing until they find some activist federal judge—and there are plenty—who agrees with them. Public-policy exception and Defense of Marriage Act notwithstanding, the courts, not least the Supreme Court, do as they please, and lately they have signed on to the gay cultural agenda. Besides, deciding on a state-by-state basis is impractical; the gay activists are right about that. The sheer inconvenience of dealing with couples who went in and out of matrimony every time they crossed state lines would drive states to the lowest common denominator, and gay marriages would wind up being recognized everywhere."

Neither of the arguments I have just sketched is without merit. But both sides are asking the country to presume that the Founders were wrong and to foreclose the possibility that seems the most likely to succeed. Both sides want something life doesn't usually offer—a guarantee. Gay-marriage supporters want a guarantee of full legal equality, and gay-marriage opponents want a guarantee that same-sex marriage will never happen at all. I can't offer any guarantees. But I can offer some reassurance.

Is a state-by-state approach impractical and unsustainable? Possibly, but the time to deal with any problems is if and when they arise. Going in, there is no reason to expect any great difficulty. There are many precedents for state-by-state action. The country currently operates under a tangle of different state banking laws. As any banker will tell you, the lack of uniformity has made interstate banking more difficult. But we do have interstate banks. Bankers long ago got used to meeting different requirements in different states. Similarly, car manufacturers have had to deal with zero-emission rules in California and a few other states. Contract law, property law, and criminal law all vary significantly from state to state. Variety is the point of federalism. Uniform national policies may be convenient, but they risk sticking us with the same wrong approach everywhere.

My guess is that if one or two states allowed gay marriage, a confusing transitional period, while state courts and legislatures worked out what to do, would quickly lead in all but a few places to routines that everyone would soon take for granted. If New Jersey adopted gay marriage, for instance, New York would have a number of options. It might refuse to recognize the marriages. It might recognize them. It might honor only certain aspects of them—say, medical power of attorney, or inheritance and tenancy rights. A state with a civil-union or domestic-partner law might automatically confer that law's benefits on any gay couple who got married in New Jersey. My fairly confident expectation is that initially most states would reject out-of-state gay marriages (as, indeed, most states have preemptively done), but a handful would fully accept them, and others would choose an intermediate option.

For married gay couples, this variation would be a real nuisance. If my partner and I got married in Maryland, we would need to be aware of differences in marriage laws and make arrangements—medical power of attorney, a will, and so on—for whenever we were out of state. Pesky and, yes, unfair (or at least unequal). And outside Maryland the line between being married and not being married would be blurred. In Virginia, people who saw my wedding band would be unsure whether I was "really married" or just "Maryland married."

Even so, people in Virginia who learned that I was "Maryland married" would know I had made the strongest possible commitment in my home state, and thus in the eyes of my community and its law. They would know I had gone beyond cohabitation or even domestic partnership. As a Jew, I may not recognize the spiritual authority of a Catholic priest, but I do recognize and respect the special commitment he has made to his faith and his community. In much the same way, even out-of-state gay marriages would command a significant degree of respect.

If you are starving, one or two slices of bread may not be as good as a loaf—but it is far better than no bread at all. The damage that exclusion from marriage has done to gay lives and gay culture comes not just from being unable to marry right now and right here but from knowing the law forbids us ever to marry at all. The first time a state adopted same-sex marriage, gay life would change forever. The full benefits would come only when same-sex marriage was legal everywhere. But gay people's lives would improve with the first state's announcement that in this community, marriage is open to everyone.

Building consensus takes time. The nationwide imposition of same-sex marriage by a federal court might discredit both gay marriage and the courts, and the public rancor it unleashed might be at least as intense as that surrounding abortion. My confidence in the public's decency and in its unfailing, if sometimes slow-acting, commitment to liberal principles is robust. For me personally, the pace set by a state-by-state approach would be too slow. It would be far from ideal. But it would be something much more important than ideal: it would be right.

Would a state-by-state approach inevitably lead to a nationwide court mandate anyway? Many conservatives fear that the answer is yes, and they want a federal constitutional amendment to head off the courts—an amendment banning gay marriage nationwide. These days it is a fact of life that someone will sue over anything, that some court will hear any lawsuit, and that there is no telling what a court might do. Still, I think that conservatives' fears on this score are unfounded.

Remember, all precedent leaves marriage to the states. All precedent supports the public-policy exception. The Constitution gives Congress a voice in determining which of one another's laws states must recognize, and Congress has spoken clearly: the Defense of Marriage Act explicitly decrees that no state must recognize any other state's same-sex marriages. In order to mandate interstate recognition of gay marriages, a court would thus need to burn through three different firewalls—a tall order, even for an activist court. The current Supreme Court, moreover, has proved particularly fierce in resisting federal incursions into states' rights. We typically reserve constitutional prohibitions for imminent threats to liberty, justice, or popular sovereignty. If we are going to get into the business of constitutionally banning anything that someone imagines the Supreme Court might one day mandate, we will need a Constitution the size of the Manhattan phone book.

Social conservatives have lost one cultural battle after another in the past five decades: over divorce, abortion, pornography, gambling, school prayer, homosexuality. They have seen that every federal takeover of state and local powers comes with strings attached. They have learned all too well the power of centralization to marginalize moral dissenters—including religious ones. And yet they are willing to risk federal intervention in matrimony. Why?

Not, I suspect, because they fear gay marriage would fail. Rather, because they fear it would succeed.

One of the conservative arguments against gay marriage is particularly revealing: the contention that even if federal courts don't decide the matter on a national level, convenience will cause gay marriage to spread from state to state. As noted, I don't believe questions of convenience would force the issue either way. But let me make a deeper point here.

States recognized one another's divorce reforms in the 1960s and 1970s without giving the matter much thought (which was too bad). But the likelihood that they would recognize another state's same-sex marriages without serious debate is just about zero, especially at first: the issue is simply too controversial. As time went on, states without gay marriage might get used to the idea. They might begin to wave through other states' same-sex marriages as a convenience for all concerned. If that happened, however, it could only be because gay marriage had not turned out to be a disaster. It might even be because gay marriage was working pretty well. This would not he contagion. It would be evolution—a sensible response to a successful experiment. Try something here or there. If it works, let it spread. If it fails, let it fade.

The opponents of gay marriage want to prevent the experiment altogether. If you care about finding the best way forward for gay people and for society in a changing world, that posture is hard to justify.

One rationale goes something like this: "Gay marriage is so certain to be a calamity that even the smallest trial anywhere should be banned." To me, that line of argument smacks more of hysteria than of rational thought. In the 1980s and early 1990s some liberals were sure that reforming the welfare system to emphasize work would put millions of children out on the street. Even trying welfare reform, they said, was irresponsible. Fortunately, the states didn't listen. They experimented—responsibly. The results were positive enough to spark a successful national reform.

Another objection cites not certain catastrophe but insidious decay. A conservative once said to me, "Changes in complicated institutions like marriage take years to work their way through society. They are often subtle. Social scientists will argue until the cows come home about the positive and negative effects of gay marriage. So states might adopt it before they fully understood the harm it did."

Actually, you can usually tell pretty quickly what effects a major policy change is having—at least you can get a general idea. States knew quite soon that welfare reforms were working better than the old program. That's why the idea caught on. If same-sex marriage is going to cause problems, some of them should be apparent within a few years of its legalization.

And notice how the terms of the discussion have shifted. Now the anticipated problem is not sudden, catastrophic social harm but subtle, slow damage. Well, there might be subtle and slow social benefits, too. But more important, there would be one large and immediate benefit: the benefit for gay people of being able to get married. If we are going to exclude a segment of the population from arguably the most important of all civic institutions, we need to be certain that the group's participation would cause severe disruptions. If we are going to put the burden on gay people to prove that same-sex marriage would never cause even any minor difficulty, then we are assuming that any cost to heterosexuals, however small, outweighs every benefit to homosexuals, however large. That gay people's welfare counts should, of course, be obvious and inarguable; but to some it is not.

I expect same-sex marriage to have many subtle ramifications— many of them good not just for gay people but for marriage. Same-sex marriage would dramatically reaffirm the country's preference for marriage as the gold standard for committed relationships. Of course there might be harmful and neutral effects as well. I don't expect that social science would be able to sort them all out. But the fact that the world is complicated is the very reason to run the experiment. We can never

know for sure what the effects of any public policy will be, so we conduct a limited experiment if possible, and then decide how to proceed
on the basis of necessarily imperfect information.

If conservatives genuinely oppose same-sex marriage because they
fear it would harm straight marriage, they should be willing to let states
that want to try gay marriage do so. If, on the other hand, conservatives
oppose same-sex marriage because they believe that it is immoral and
wrong by definition, fine—but let them have the honesty to acknowledge that they are not fighting for the good of marriage so much as
they are using marriage as a weapon in their fight against gays.

QUESTIONS

1. Why does Rauch argue that legislation about partners of the same sex
   should be left to the individual states, rather than to Congress or
   Constitutional amendment? What are the advantages and the
   drawbacks of his position? What rhetorical strategies does he use
   to make his point?
2. Do research to find out which states and countries have legalized civil
   marriages between partners of the same gender. After reading the
   article and considering your own research and values about the
   meaning and role of family life, write or outline a position paper on
   your point of view.
3. How do you think that the reality of partnerships of the same sex has
   had and will continue to have an impact on the definition and meaning
   of marriage in our culture?

Differing Perspectives: How Can Individuals and Social Institutions Help to Sustain Marriages and Reduce the Rate of Divorce?

Judith Wallerstein

"The Legacy of Divorce"

*In 1980, Judith Wallerstein established the Center for the Family in Transition,
which has become a nationally acclaimed resource for families going through
divorce. Wallerstein, a psychologist and researcher at the University of California
at Berkeley, has devoted 25 years to the study of the long-term effects of divorce.
She often lectures to professional and nonprofessional organizations that help
families go through divorce. She has written many books on the family, including
A Good Marriage (1995). In the selection that follows from* The Unexpected

Legacy of Divorce (2000), Wallerstein argues for greater social concern about the long-term impact of divorce on children and presents ideas for decreasing the negative social and psychological effects of divorce.

"What's done to children, they will do to society."

Karl A. Menninger

Around the time I was finishing this book, a very important judge on the family law bench in a large state I shall not name invited me to come see him. I was eager to meet with him because I wanted to discuss some ideas I have for educating parents under court auspices that go beyond the simple advice "don't fight." After we had talked for a half an hour or so, the judge leaned back in his chair and said he'd like my opinion about something important. He had just attended several scientific lectures in which researchers argued that children are shaped more by genes than by family environment. Case in point, studies of identical twins reared separately show that in adulthood such twins often like the same foods and clothing styles, belong to the same political parties, and even bestow identical names on their dogs. The judge looked perplexed. "Do you think that could mean divorce is in the genes?" he asked in all seriousness. "And if that's so, does it matter what a court decides when parents divorce?"

I was taken aback. Here was a key figure in the lives of thousands of children asking me whether what he and his colleagues do or say on the bench makes any difference. He seemed relieved by the notion that may be his actions are insignificant.

I told him that I personally doubt the existence of a "divorce gene." If such a biological trait had arisen in evolution, it would be of very recent vintage. But, I added, "What the court does matters enormously. You have the power to protect children from being hurt or to increase their suffering."

Now it was his turn to be taken aback. "You think we've increased children's suffering"?

"Yes, Your Honor, I do. With all respect, I have to say that the court along with the rest of society has increased the suffering of children."

"How so?" he asked.

We spent another half hour talking about how the courts, parents, attorneys, mental health workers—indeed most adults—have been reluctant to pay genuine attention to children during and after divorce. He listened respectfully to me but I must say I left the judge's chambers that day in a state of shock that soon turned to gloom. How can we be so utterly lost and confused that a leading judge would accept the notion of a "divorce gene" to explain our predicament? If he's confused about his role, what about the rest of us? What is it about the impact of divorce on our society and our children that's so hard to understand and accept?

Having spent the last thirty years of my life traveling here and abroad talking to professional, legal, and mental health groups plus working with thousands of parents and children in divorced families, it's clear that we've created a new kind of society never before seen in human culture. Silently and unconsciously, we have created a culture of divorce. It's hard to grasp what it means when we say that first marriages stand a 45 percent chance of breaking up and that second marriages have a 60 percent chance of ending in divorce. What are the consequences for all of us when 25 percent of people today between the ages of eighteen and forty-four have parents who divorced? What does it mean to a society when people wonder aloud if the family is about to disappear? What can we do when we learn that married couples with children represent a mere 26 percent of households in the 1990s and that the most common living arrangement nowadays is a household of unmarried people with no children? These numbers are terrifying. But like all massive social change, what's happening is affecting us in ways that we have yet to understand.

For people like me who work with divorcing families all the time, these abstract numbers have real faces. When I think about people I know so well, including the "children" you've met in this book, I can relate to the millions of children and adults who suffer with loneliness and to all the teenagers who say, "I don't want a life like either of my parents." I can empathize with the countless young men and women who despair of ever finding a lasting relationship and who, with a brave toss of the head, say, "Hey, if you don't get married then you can't get divorced." It's only later, or sometimes when they think I'm not listening, that they add softly, "but I don't want to grow old alone." I am especially worried about how our divorce culture has changed childhood itself. A million new children a year are added to our march of marital failure. As they explain so eloquently, they lose the carefree play of childhood as well as the comforting arms and lap of a loving parent who is always rushing off because life in the postdivorce family is so incredibly difficult to manage. We must take very seriously the complaint of children like Karen who declare, "The day my parents divorced is the day my childhood ended."

Many years ago the psychoanalyst Erik Erikson taught us that childhood and society are vitally connected. But we have not yet come to terms with the changes ushered in by our divorce culture. Childhood is different, adolescence is different, and adulthood is different. Without our noticing, we have created a new class of young children who take care of themselves, along with a whole generation of overburdened parents who have no time to enjoy the pleasures of parenting. So much has happened so fast, we cannot hold it all in our minds. It's simply overwhelming.

But we must not forget a very important other side to all these changes. Because of our divorce culture, adults today have a greater sense of freedom. The importance of sex and play in adult life is widely accepted. We are not locked into our early mistakes and forced to stay in wretched, lifelong relationships. The change in women—their very identity and freer role in society—is part of our divorce culture. Indeed, two-thirds of divorces are initiated by women despite the high price they pay in economic and parenting burdens afterward.

People want and expect a lot more out of marriage than did earlier generations. Although the divorce rate in second and third marriages is sky-high, many second marriages are much happier than the ones left behind. Children and adults are able to escape violence, abuse, and misery to create a better life. Clearly there is no road back.

The sobering truth is that we have created a new kind of society that offers greater freedom and more opportunities for many adults, but this welcome change carries a serious hidden cost. Many people, adults and children alike, are in fact not better off. We have created new kinds of families in which relationships are fragile and often unreliable. Children today receive far less nurturance, protection, and parenting that was their lot a few decades ago. Long-term marriages come apart at still surprising rates. And many in the older generation who started the divorce revolution find themselves estranged from their adult children. Is this the price we must pay for needed change? Can't we do better?

I'd like to say that we're at a crossroads but I'm afraid I can't be that optimistic. We can choose a new route only if we agree on where we are and where we want to be in the future. The outlook is cloudy. For every person who wants to sound an alarm, there's another who says don't worry. For everyone concerned about the economic and emotional deprivations inherited by children of divorce there are those who argue that those kids were "in trouble before" and that divorce is irrelevant, no big deal. People want to feel good about their choices. Doubtless many do. In actual fact, after most divorces, one member of the former couple feels much better while the other feels no better or even worse. Yet at any dinner party you will still hear the same myths: Divorce is a temporary crisis. So many children have experienced their parents' divorce that kids nowadays don't worry so much. It's easier. They almost expect it. It's a rite of passage. If I feel better, so will my children. And so on. As always, children are voiceless or unheard.

But family scholars who have not always seen eye to eye are converging on a number of findings that fly in the face of our cherished myths. We agree that the effects of divorce are long-term. We know that the family is in trouble. We have a consensus that children raised in divorced or remarried families are less well adjusted as adults than those raised in intact families.

The life histories of this first generation to grow up in a divorce culture tell us truths we dare not ignore. Their message is poignant, clear, and contrary to what so many want to believe. They have taught me the following:

From the viewpoint of the children, and counter to what happens to their parents, divorce is a cumulative experience. Its impact increases over time and rises to a crescendo in adulthood. At each developmental stage divorce is experienced anew in different ways. In adulthood it affects personality, the ability to trust, expectations about relationships, and ability to cope with change.

The first upheaval occurs at the breakup. Children are frightened and angry, terrified of being abandoned by both parents, and they feel responsible for the divorce. Most children are taken by surprise; few are relieved. As adults, they remember with sorrow and anger how little support they got from their parents when it happened. They recall how they were expected to adjust overnight to a terrifying number of changes that confounded them. Even children who had seen or heard violence at home made no connection between that violence and the decision to divorce. The children concluded early on, silently and sadly, that family relationships are fragile and that the tie between a man and woman can break capriciously, without warning. They worried ever after that parent-child relationships are also unreliable and can break at any time. These early experiences colored their later expectations.

As the postdivorce family took shape, their world increasingly resembled what they feared most. Home was a lonely place. The household was in disarray for years. Many children were forced to move, leaving behind familiar schools, close friends, and other supports. What they remember vividly as adults is the loss of the intact family and the safety net it provided, the difficulty of having two parents in two homes, and how going back and forth cut badly into playtime and friendships. Parents were busy with work, preoccupied with rebuilding their social lives. Both moms and dads had a lot less time to spend with their children and were less responsive to their children's needs or wishes. Little children especially felt that they had lost both parents and were unable to care for themselves. Children soon learned that the divorced family has porous walls that include new lovers, live-in partners, and stepparents. Not one of these relationships was easy for anyone. The mother's parenting was often cut into by the very heavy burdens of single parenthood and then by the demands of remarriage and stepchildren.

Relationships with fathers were heavily influenced by live-in lovers or stepmothers in second and third marriages. Some second wives were interested in the children while others wanted no part of them. Some fathers were able to maintain their love and interest in their children but few had time for two or sometimes three families. In some families both parents gradually stabilized their lives within happy remarriages or well-functioning, emotionally gratifying single parenthood. But these people were never a majority in any of my work.

Meanwhile, children who were able to draw support from school, sports teams, parents, stepparents, grandparents, teachers, or their own inner strengths, interests, and talents did better than those who could not muster such resources. By necessity, many of these so-called resilient children forfeited their own childhoods as they took responsibility for themselves; their troubled, overworked parents; and their siblings. Children who needed more than minimal parenting because they were little or had special vulnerabilities and problems with change were soon over-whelmed with sorrow and anger at their parents. Years later, when contemplating having their own children, most children in this study said hotly, "I never want a child of mine to experience a childhood like I had."

As the children told us, adolescence begins early in divorced homes and, compared with that of youngsters raised in intact families, is more likely to include more early sexual experiences for girls and higher alcohol and drug use for girls and boys. Adolescence is more prolonged in divorced families and extends well into the years of early adulthood. Throughout these years children of divorce worry about following in their parents' footsteps and struggle with a sinking sense that they, too, will fail in their relationships.

But it's in adulthood that children of divorce suffer the most. The impact of divorce hits them most cruelly as they go in search of love, sexual intimacy, and commitment. Their lack of inner images of a man and a woman in a stable relationship and their memories of their parents' failure to sustain the marriage badly hobbles their search, leading them to heartbreak and even despair. They cried, "No one taught me." They complain bitterly that they feel unprepared for adult relationships and that they have never seen a "man and woman on the same beam," that they have no good models on which to build their hopes. And indeed they have a very hard time formulating even simple ideas about the kind of person they're looking for. Many end up with unsuitable or very troubled partners in relationships that were doomed from the start.

The contrast between them and children from good intact homes, as both go in search of love and commitment, is striking. (As I explain in this book, children raised in extremely unhappy or violent intact homes face misery in childhood and tragic challenges in adulthood. But because their parents generally aren't interested in getting a divorce, divorce does not become part of their legacy.) Adults in their twenties from reasonably good or even moderately unhappy intact families had a fine understanding of the demands and sacrifices required in a close relationship. They had memories of how their parents struggled and overcame differences, how they cooperated in a crisis. They developed a general idea about the kind of person they wanted to marry. Most important, they did not expect to fail. The two groups differed after marriage as well. Those from intact families found the example of their parents' enduring marriage very re-assuring when they inevitably ran into marital problems. But in coping with the normal stresses in a marriage, adults from divorced families were at a grave disadvantage. Anxiety about relationships was at the bedrock of their personalities and endured even in very happy marriages. Their fears of disaster and sudden loss rose when they felt content. And their fear of abandonment, betrayal, and rejection mounted when they found themselves having to disagree with someone they loved. After all, marriage is a slippery slope and their parents fell off it. All had trouble dealing with differences or even moderate conflict in their close relationships. Typically their first response was panic, often followed by flight. They had a lot to undo and a lot to learn in a very short time.

Those who had two parents who rebuilt happy lives after divorce and included children in their orbits had a much easier time as adults. Those who had committed single parents also benefited from that parent's attention and responsiveness. But the more frequent response in adulthood was continuing anger at parents, more often at fathers, whom the children regarded as having been selfish and faithless.

Others felt deep compassion and pity toward mothers or fathers who failed to rebuild their lives after divorce. The ties between daughters and their mothers were especially close but at a cost. Some young women found it very difficult to separate from their moms and to lead their own lives. With some notable exceptions, fathers in divorced families were less likely to enjoy close bonds with their adult children, especially their sons. This stood in marked contrast to fathers and sons from intact families, who tended to grow closer as the years went by.

Fortunately for many children of divorce, their fears of loss and betrayal can be conquered by the time they reach their late twenties and thirties. But what a struggle that takes, what courage and persistence. Those who succeed overcome their difficulties the hard way—by learning from their own failed relationships and gradually rejecting the models they were raised with to create what they want from a love relationship. Those lucky enough to have found a loving partner are able to interrupt their self-destructive course with a lasting love affair or marriage.

In other realms of adult life—financial and security, for instance—some children were able to overcome difficulties through unexpected help from fathers who had vanished long before. Still others benefit from the constancy of parents or grandparents. Many men and women raised in divorced families establish successful careers. Their workplace performance is largely unaffected by the divorce. But no matter what their success in the world, they retain some serious residues—fear of loss, fear of change, and fear that disaster will strike, especially when things are going well. They're still terrified by the mundane differences and inevitable conflicts found in every close relationship.

I'm heartened by the hard-won success of these adults. But at the same time, I can't forget those who've failed to straighten out their lives. I'm especially troubled by how many divorced or remained in wretched marriages. Of those who have children and who are now divorced, many, to my dismay, are not protecting their children in ways we might expect. They go on to repeat the same mistakes their own parents made, perpetuating problems that have plagued them all their lives. I'm also concerned about many who, by their mid- and late thirties, are neither married nor cohabiting and who are leading lonely lives. They're afraid of getting involved in a relationship that they think is doomed to fail. After a divorce or breakup, they're afraid to try again. And I'm struck by continuing anger at parents and flat-out statements by many of these young adults that they have no intention of helping their moms and especially their dads or stepparents in old age. This may change. But if it doesn't, we'll be facing another unanticipated consequence of our divorce culture. Who will take care of an older generation estranged from its children?

What We Can and Cannot Do

Our efforts to improve our divorce culture have been spotty and the resources committed to the task are pitifully small. The courts have given the lion's share of attention to the 10 to 15 percent of families that continue to fight bitterly.

Caught between upholding the rights of parents and protecting the interests of children, they have tilted heavily toward parents. Such parents allegedly speak in the name of the child just as those who fight bloody holy wars allegedly speak in the name of religion. Thus, as I explained to the judge with whom I began this chapter, our court system has unintentionally contributed to the suffering of children. At the same time, most parents receive little guidance. Some courts offer educational lectures to families at the time of the breakup, but the emphasis is on preventing further litigation. Such courses are typically evaluated according to how much they reduce subsequent litigation and not on how they might improve parenting. Curricula to educate teachers, school personnel, pediatricians, and other professionals about child and parenting issues in divorce are rare. Few university or medical school programs in psychiatry, psychology, social work, or law include courses on how to understand or help children and parents after separation, divorce, and remarriage. This lack of training persists despite the fact that a disproportionate number of children and adolescents from divorced homes are admitted as patients for psychological treatment at clinics and family agencies. In many social agencies, close to three-quarters of the children in treatment are from divorced families. Some school districts have organized groups for children whose parents are divorcing. And some communities have established groups to help divorcing parents talk about their children's problems. A few centers such as ours have developed programs to help families cope with high conflict and domestic violence. But such efforts are not widespread. As a society, we have not set up services to help people relieve the stresses of divorce. We continue to foster the myth that divorce is a transient crisis and that as soon as adults restabilize their lives, the children will recover fully. When will the truth sink in?

Let's suppose for a moment that we had a consensus in our society. Suppose we could agree that we want to maintain the advantages of divorce but that we need to protect our children and help parents mute the long-term effects of divorce on future generations. Imagine we were willing to roll up our sleeves and really commit the enormous resources of our society toward supplementing the knowledge we have. Suppose we gave as much time, energy, and resources to protecting children as we give to protecting the environment. What might we try?

I would begin with an effort to strengthen marriage. Obviously, restoring confidence in marriage won't work if we naively call for a return to marriage as it used to be. To improve marriage, we need to fully understand the nature of contemporary man-woman relationships. We need to appreciate the difficulties modern couples confront in balancing work and family, separateness and togetherness, conflict and cooperation. It's no accident that 80 percent of divorces occur in the first nine years of marriage. These new families should be our target.

What threats to marriage can we change? First, there's a serious imbalance between the demands of the workplace and the needs of family life. The corporate world rarely considers the impact of its policies on parents and children.

Some companies recognize that parents need time to spend with their children but they don't understand that the workplace exerts a major influence on the quality and stability of marriage. Heavy work schedules and job insecurity erode married life. Families with young children especially postpone intimate talk, sex, and friendship. These are the ties that replenish a marriage. When the boss calls, we go to the office. When the baby cries, we pick up the child. But when a marriage is starving, we expect it to bumble along. Most Western European countries provide paid family leave. What about us? Why do we persist in offering unpaid leave and pretend that it addresses the young family's problem? One additional solution might be social security and tax benefits for a parent who wants to stay home and care for young children. That alone would lighten the burden on many marriages. Other suggestions for reducing the stresses on young families include more flex time, greater opportunities for part-time work, assurances that people who take family leave will not lose their place on the corporate ladder, tax advantages for families, and many other ideas that have been on the table for years. Public policy cannot create good marriages. But it can buffer some of the stresses people face, especially in those early, vulnerable years when couples need time to establish intimacy, a satisfying sex life, and a friendship that will hold them together through the inevitable challenges that lie ahead. Ultimately, if we're really interested in improving marriage so that people have time for each other and their children, we need to realign our priorities away from the business world and toward family life.

We might also try to help the legions of young adults who complain bitterly that they're unprepared for marriage. Having been raised in divorced or very troubled homes, they have no idea how to choose a partner or what to do to build the relationship. They regard their parents' divorce as a terrible failure and worry that they're doomed to follow in the same footsteps. Many adults stay in unhappy marriages just to avoid divorce. We don't know if we can help them with educational methods because we haven't tried. Our experience is too limited and our experimental models nonexistent. But when so many young people have never seen a good marriage, we have a moral obligation to try to intervene preventively. Most programs that give marital advice are aimed at engaged couples who belong to churches and synagogues. These are very good beginnings that should be expanded. But many offer too little and arrive too late to bring about changes in any individual's values or knowledge. Nor is the excitement that precedes a wedding the best time for reflection on how to choose a lifetime partner or what makes a marriage work. Academic courses on marriage mostly look at families from the lofty perch of the family scholar and not from the perspective of children of divorce who feel "no one ever taught me."

In my opinion, a better time to begin helping these youngsters is during mid-adolescence, when attitudes toward oneself and relationships with the opposite sex are beginning to gel. Adolescence is the time when worries about sex, love, betrayal, and morality take center stage. Education for and about relationships should begin at that time, since if we do it right, we'll have their full attention. It could be based in the health centers that have been established in many schools throughout the country. Churches and synagogues and social agencies might provide another launching place. Ideally, adolescents in a well-functioning society should have the opportunity to think and talk about a wide range of relationships, issues, and conflicts confronting them. As an opening gambit, think about asking the deceptively simple question: "How do you choose a friend?" A group of teenagers considering this problem could be drawn to the important question of how to choose a lover and life partner—and even more important, how not to choose one. Specific topics such as differences between boys and girls, cultural subgroups, and how people resolve tensions would follow based on the teenagers' interests and their willingness to discuss real issues. Colleges could also offer continuing and advanced courses on an expanded range of subjects, including many problems that young men and women now struggle with alone.

We are on the threshold of learning what we can and cannot do for these young people. Still one wonders, can an educational intervention replace the learning that occurs naturally over many years within the family? How do we create a corps of teachers who are qualified to lead meaningful courses on relationships? By this I mean courses that are true to life, honest, and respectful of students. I worry about the adult tendency to lecture or sermonize. In a society where the family has become a political issue, I'm concerned about attacks from the left and the right, about the many people who would attack such interventions the way they've attacked the Harry Potter books. Mostly I'm concerned about finding a constituency of adults who would rally behind an idea that has so many pitfalls. But I'm also convinced that doing nothing—leaving young people alone in their struggles—is more dangerous. We should not give up without a try.

QUESTIONS

1. Anti-divorce advocates have quoted Wallerstein to support their own views on making it more difficult to obtain a divorce. Based on this reading selection, do you think that they are distorting her perspective on divorce? In your opinion, what would her response be to advocates of strict divorce laws?

2. Some critics reject Wallerstein's conclusions because her writing is often anecdotal, with examples from a narrow and unrepresentative sample of the children of divorce. Based on this article, what would be your response to such criticism of her use of evidence?

3. Examine the proposals Wallerstein presents to help reduce the impact of divorce on young children. How do her proposals help to support her argument? Do some research on your own and write an argument that supports your point of view on reducing the negative impact of divorce on children.

"Marriage Plus"

Theodora Ooms is a senior analyst at the Center for Law and Social Policy (CLASP) in Washington D.C., where she works on couples and marriage policy with a special focus on low-income families. From 1981 to 1999, she was the executive director of the Family Impact Seminar, a nonpartisan policy research institute. Prior to 1976, she worked as a clinical social worker, family therapist, and program administrator in New Haven and Philadelphia. Ooms received her B.A. from Oxford University and her M.S.W. from the University of Connecticut. She has conducted studies and authored publications on teenage pregnancy, parenthood, unwed fathers, family involvement in schools, and marriage. She is also an independent scholar to the Oklahoma Marriage Initiative and the co-author of a new report on state efforts to strengthen marriage and two-parent families.

The public has been concerned about "family breakdown" for a long time, but it was not until the passage of welfare reform in 1996 that the federal government decided to get into the business of promoting marriage. Although it was little noticed at the time, three of the four purposes of the welfare legislation refer directly or indirectly to marriage and family formation. The law exhorts states to promote "job preparation, work and marriage," to "prevent and reduce the incidence of out-of-wedlock pregnancies," and to "encourage the formation and maintenance of two-parent families."

The Bush administration, as it contemplates this year's extension of welfare legislation, plans to make marriage even more central. The administration's reauthorization proposal, announced February 27, includes $300 million for demonstration grants to focus on promoting healthy marriages and reducing out-of-wedlock births. Meanwhile, Oklahoma Governor Frank Keating has launched a $10-million, multi-sector marriage initiative, and other smaller-scale government-sponsored initiatives have been enacted in Arizona, Florida, Louisiana, Michigan, and Utah. The federal government is primarily concerned with reducing out-of-wedlock births, which it views as a principal cause of welfare dependency and a host of other social problems. By contrast, state marriage initiatives are most concerned about the effects of high divorce rates and father absence on children.

This new emphasis on marriage as a panacea for social problems is troubling to many liberals. For one thing, it risks being dismissive of children who happen to find themselves in single-parent families. It also can be seen as disparaging single mothers and ignoring the fact that many women have left abusive marriages for good reasons.

That said, it's hard to dismiss an overwhelming consensus of social-science research findings that children tend to be better off, financially and emotionally, when their parents are married to each other. Around 50 percent of all first marriages are expected to end in divorce, and 60 percent of all divorces involve children. One-third of all births are out of wedlock, nearly 40 percent of children do not live with their biological fathers, and too many nonresident fathers neither support nor see their children on a regular basis.

Children living with single mothers are five times as likely to be poor as those in two-parent families. Growing up in a single-parent family also roughly doubles the risk that a child will drop out of school, have difficulty finding a job, or become a teen parent. About half of these effects appear to be attributable to the reduced income available to single parents, but the other half is due to non-economic factors. It's not just the presence of two adults in the home that helps children, as some argue. Children living with cohabiting partners and in stepfamilies generally do less well than those living with both married biological parents.

Marriage also brings benefits to husbands and wives. Married adults are more productive on the job, earn more, save more, have better physical and mental health, and live longer, according to an extensive review of research, conducted by scholar Linda Waite. Although Waite admits that these findings partly reflect the selection of better-adjusted people into marriage, she finds that when people marry, they act in more health-promoting and productive ways.

Conservatives are prone to exaggerate these research findings and underplay the importance of economics. If married people are more likely (other things being equal) to produce thriving children, other things are not, in fact, equal. It's not just the case that single mothers find themselves poor because they are unmarried; they find themselves unmarried because they are poor. Successful marriages are more difficult when husbands and wives are poorly educated, lack access to jobs that pay decently, and cannot afford decent child care. Economic hardship and other problems associated with poverty can wreak havoc on couples' relationships.

The controversy mostly isn't about research, however, but about values. Most people regard decisions to marry, divorce, and bear children as intensely private. Any policy proposals that hint at coercing people to marry, reinforcing Victorian conceptions of gender roles, or limiting the right to end bad marriages are viewed as counter to American values of individual autonomy and privacy. Some worry about the existence of hidden agendas that threaten to put women back into the kitchen, ignore domestic violence, and eliminate public assistance for low-income families. Others fear that holding out marriage as the ideal blames single parents, many of whom do a terrific job under difficult circumstances. Use of the term "illegitimate" is especially offensive because it stigmatizes children (and, in fact, is legally inaccurate, as children born outside of marriage now have virtually the same legal rights as those born within marriage).

And some worry that the pro-marriage agenda discriminates against ethnic and sexual minorities and their children, particularly gays and lesbians.

There are also more pragmatic concerns. Skeptics of the pro-marriage agenda observe that the decline in marriage is worldwide, a result of overwhelming social and economic forces that cannot be reversed. In their view, attempts to change family formation behavior are largely futile; we should instead just accept and help support the increasing diversity of family forms. For others, the concern is less about the value of promoting marriage and more about whether government, rather than individuals, communities, or faith institutions, should lead the charge.

Finally, marriage per se is too simplistic a solution to the complex problems of the poor. Marrying a low-income, unmarried mother to her child's father will not magically raise the family out of poverty when the parents often have no skills, no jobs, terrible housing, and may be struggling with depression, substance abuse, or domestic violence. Advocates also worry that funds spent on untested marriage-promotion activities will be taken away from programs that provide desperately needed services for single parents, such as child care.

In response to some of these concerns—as well as research showing that serious parental conflict harms children—some marriage advocates respond that marriage per se should not be the goal but rather voluntary, "healthy" marriages. They also agree that protections should be built into programs to guard against domestic violence. But this only raises doubts about how "healthy" will be defined, and by whom, and whether we even know how to help people create better relationships.

There also are some plainly foolish ideas in the marriage movement. West Virginia currently gives married families an extra $100 a month in welfare payments as a "marriage incentive." Robert Rector of the Heritage Foundation has proposed giving a $4,000 government bounty to welfare recipients who marry before they have a child and stay married for two years. Charles Murray wants to end public assistance altogether and has proposed eliminating all aid to *unmarried* mothers under 21 in one state to test the idea. This proposal is especially egregious and surely would harm children of single mothers.

Progressives and others thus are placed in a quandary. They don't want to oppose marriage—which most Americans still value highly—but are skeptical of many pro-marriage initiatives. Given that healthy marriage is plainly good for children, however, one can envision a reasonable agenda—one that would gain broad support—that we might call Marriage-Plus. This approach puts the well-being of children first by helping more of them grow up in married, healthy, two-parent families. However, for many children, the reality is that marriage is not a feasible or even a desirable option for their parents. Thus, a secondary goal is to help these parents—whether unmarried, separated, divorced, or remarried—cooperate better in raising their children. These are not alternative strategies. Children need us to do both.

A marriage-plus agenda does not promote marriage just for marriage's sake. It acknowledges that married and unmarried parents, mothers and fathers, may need both economic resources and non-economic supports to increase the likelihood of stable, healthy marriages and better co-parenting relationships. In addition, a marriage-plus agenda focuses more on the front end—making marriage better to be in—rather than the back end making marriage more difficult to get out of.

Here are some elements of this agenda.

Strengthen "fragile families" at the birth of a child. For many poor families, relationship-education programs may be helpful but not enough. A new national study finds that at the time of their child's birth, one-half of unmarried parents (so-called "fragile families") are living together, and another third are romantically attached but not cohabiting. The majorities of these parents are committed to each other and to their child and have high hopes of eventual marriage and a future together—although these hopes too often are not realized. We should reach out to young parents to help them achieve their desire to remain together as a family. A helpful package of services to offer these young families might include a combination of "soft" services—relationship-skills and marriage-education workshops, financial-management classes, and peer-support groups—and "hard" services, such as job training and placement, housing, medical coverage, and substance-abuse treatment, if necessary. At present, all we do is get the father to admit paternity and hound him for child support.

Reduce economic stress by reducing poverty. Poverty and unemployment can stress couples' relationships to their breaking point. Results of a welfare-to-work demonstration program in Minnesota suggest that enhancing the income of the working poor can indirectly promote marriage. The Minnesota Family Investment Program (MFIP), which subsidized the earnings of employed welfare families, found that marriage rates increased for both single-parent long-term recipients and two-parent families. Married two-parent families were significantly more likely to remain married. MFIP also reduced the reported incidence of domestic abuse.

Provide better-paying jobs and job assistance for the poor. The inability of low-skilled, unemployed men to provide income to their families is a major reason for their failure to marry the mothers of their children. Better employment opportunities help low-income fathers, and men in general, to become responsible fathers and, perhaps, more attractive and economically stable marriage partners. There is also growing support for making changes in the child-support system to ensure that more support paid by fathers goes to the children (rather than being used to recoup government program costs).

Invest more in proven programs that reduce out-of-wedlock childbearing. Teen pregnancy and birth rates have fallen by over 20 percent since the early 1990s, and there is now strong evidence that a number of prevention programs are effective. A related strategy is enforcement of child support. States that have tough, effective child support systems have been found to have lower nonmarital birth rates, presumably because men are beginning to understand there are serious costs associated with fathering a child.

Institute workplace policies to reduce work/family conflict and stress on couples. Stress in the workplace spills over into the home. Persistent overtime, frequent travel, and inflexible leave policies place great strain on couples at all income levels. Employers are increasingly demanding nonstandard work schedules. A recent study found that married couples with children who work night and rotating shifts are at higher risk of separation and divorce. The absence of affordable and reliable child care forces many parents who would prefer a normal workday to working split shifts solely to make sure that a parent is home with children.

Reduce tax penalties and other disincentives to marriage. There has always been strong support for reducing marriage tax penalties for many two-earner families. This is a complicated task because the majority of married couples, in fact, receive tax bonuses rather than penalties. A positive step was taken in 2001 to reduce significantly the marriage penalty affecting low-income working families in the Earned Income Tax Credit program. While there is uncertainty about the extent to which these tax-related marriage penalties affect marital behavior, there is broad general agreement that government has a responsibility to "first do no harm" when it comes to marriage. Similarly, there is near unanimous agreement that government should not make it harder for eligible two-parent families to receive welfare benefits and assistance. In the past, the old welfare program, Aid to Families with Dependent Children, was much criticized for offering incentives to break up families. At least 33 states already have removed the stricter eligibility rules placed on two-parent families, and the President's welfare reauthorization proposal encourages the other states to do the same. In addition, it proposes to end the higher work participation rate for two-parent families, a federal rule that has been criticized widely by the states. Another needed reform would forgive accumulated child-support debt owed by noncustodial fathers if they marry the mothers of their children. (Currently, such debt is owed to the state if the mothers and children are receiving welfare benefits.)

Educate those who *want* to marry and stay married about how to have healthy relationships and good marriages. A vast industry is devoted to helping couples plan a successful wedding day—wedding planners, 500-page bridal guides, specialty caterers, the list goes on. But where do young people go to learn about how to sustain good, lifelong marriages? In fact, we now know a lot about what makes contemporary marriages work. With the transformation of gender roles, there now are fewer fixed rules for couples to follow, meaning they have to negotiate daily about who does what and when. In the absence of the legal and social constraints that used to keep marriages together, there's now a premium on developing effective relationship skills. Building on three decades of research, there are a small but rapidly growing number of programs (both religious and secular) that help people from high school through adulthood understand the benefits of marriage for children and for themselves, develop realistic expectations for healthy relationships, understand the meaning of commitment, and learn the skills and attitudes needed to make marriage succeed. Other programs help married couples survive the inevitable ups and downs that occur in most marriages, and remarried couples with the additional challenges of step-parenting. Oklahoma, Utah, and Michigan have begun using government funds to make these relationship- and marriage-education programs accessible to low-income couples. The Greater Grand Rapids Community Marriage Policy initiative is urging area businesses to include marriage education as an Employee Assistance Program benefit, arguing that it's more cost-effective to prevent marital distress than incur the costs of counseling and lost productivity involved when employees' marriages break up.

A marriage-plus agenda that includes activities such as these is not just the responsibility of government. Some of the strategies proposed here are being implemented by private and religious groups, some by governments, and some by partnerships between these sectors. The approach adopted in Oklahoma, Greater Grand Rapids, and Chattanooga, for example, mobilizes the resources of many sectors of the community—government, education, legal, faith, business, and media—in a comprehensive effort to create a more marriage-supportive culture and to provide new services to promote, support, and strengthen couples and marriage and reduce out-of-wedlock childbearing and divorce. This "saturation model" seems particularly promising because it takes into account the many factors that influence individuals' decisions to marry, to divorce, or to remain unmarried. We should proceed cautiously, trying out and evaluating new ideas before applying them widely.

Ironically, in the midst of this furor about government's role in marriage, it's worth noting that the federal government recently has begun to shirk a basic responsibility: counting the numbers of marriages and divorces in the United States. Since budget cuts in 1995, the government has been unable to report on marriage and divorce rates in the states or for the nation as a whole. And, for the first time in the history of the Census, Americans were not asked to give their marital status in the 2000 survey. What kind of pro-marriage message from the government is that?

If liberals and conservatives are serious about strengthening families for the sake of helping children, liberals ought to acknowledge that noncoercive and egalitarian approaches to bolstering marriage are sound policy. Conservatives, meanwhile, should admit that much of what it takes to make marriage work for the benefit of spouses and children is not just moral but economic.

QUESTIONS

1. Why is Ooms opposed to federal legislation that will "encourage the formation and maintenance of two-parent families" as morally and culturally superior to other types of family units?

2. How does Ooms define Marriage Plus? What kinds of solutions to the problems of maintaining families does she propose for her program? How would these solutions be financed?
3. Do you agree or disagree with the federal favoritism for and maintenance of the two-parent family? Do some research on both points of view and then argue for or against the encouragement of two-parent families by government interference.

CHAPTER 3

Educating a Nation

Introduction

John Dewey, a prominent thinker and writer on education in the early years of the twentieth century, argued for learning through experience and application of knowledge in real-life situations. However, many modern educators, like Linda Darling-Hammond, whose essay begins this chapter, stress the importance of formal education and raise the issue of disparity in educational opportunity and quality of teaching in affluent communities as opposed to those with low teacher salaries and high levels of unemployment and poverty.

Technology and the Internet bring with them new expenses for cash-strapped schools and many controversies for modern educators. Some, like Robert Kubey, believe that computers and media analysis have become essential to a strong education, while technology critics like Lowell Monke argue, in the tradition of John Dewey, that younger students need to learn through doing, emphasizing contacts with nature and useful projects in the community. In a similar mode, college honor society sponsor Dacia Charlesworth wishes to replace the utilitarian approach to the student as a consumer in search of a job with a view of the student as an individual who is socially engaged and wishes to be of service to the community and to democracy.

The "Differing Perspectives" that close this chapter contrast two conflicting views of high-stakes testing in grade school as required under the No Child Left Behind Act, one by former Secretary of Education Rod Paige, who believes that such testing promotes continued high educational attainment by students, the other by education professors David C. Berliner and Sharon L. Nichols, who argue that such testing causes damage to "teachers, students, and schools."

LINDA DARLING-HAMMOND

"Unequal Opportunity: Race and Education"

Currently a professor of education at Stanford University, Darling-Hammond earned her B.A. at Yale University in 1973 and her Ph.D. from Temple College in 1978. She began her career as a public school teacher and has always been deeply engaged in an effort to redesign schools to focus more effectively on teaching and learning. Her book, The Right to Learn *(1997), was awarded the American Educational Research Associations Outstanding Book Award in 1998. She has also worked as an advisor for education research at the White House. The excerpt that follows first appeared in the* Brookings Review *(1998). Darling-Hammond argues that minority children have unequal access to key educational resources, including skilled teachers and quality curricula, making it difficult for them to succeed in school.*

W. E. B. Du Bois was right about the problem of the 21st century. The color line divides us still. In recent years, the most visible evidence of this in the public policy arena has been the persistent attack on affirmative action in higher education and employment. From the perspective of many Americans who believe that the vestiges of discrimination have disappeared, affirmative action now provides an unfair advantage to minorities.

From the perspective of others who daily experience the consequences of ongoing discrimination affirmative action is needed to protect opportunities likely to evaporate if an affirmative obligation to act fairly does not exist. And for Americans of all backgrounds, the allocation of opportunity in a society that is becoming ever more dependent on knowledge and education is a source of great anxiety and concern.

At the center of these debates are interpretations of the gaps in educational achievement between white and non-Asian minority students as measured by standardized test scores. The presumption that guides much of the conversation is that equal opportunity now exists; therefore, continued low levels of achievement on the part of minority students must be a function of genes, culture, or a lack of effort and will (see, for example, Richard Herrnstein and Charles Murray's *The Bell Curve* and Stephan and Abigail Thernstrom's *America in Black and White*).

The assumptions that undergird this debate miss an important reality: educational outcomes for minority children are much more a function of their unequal access to key educational resources, including skilled teachers and quality curriculum, than they are a function of race. In fact, the U.S. educational system is one of the most unequal in the industrialized world, and students routinely receive dramatically different learning opportunities based on their social status. In contrast to European and Asian nations that fund schools centrally and equally, the wealthiest 10 percent of U.S. school districts spend nearly 10 times more than the poorest 10 percent, and spending ratios of 3 to 1 are common within states. Despite stark differences in funding, teacher quality, curriculum, and class sizes, the prevailing view is that if students do not achieve, it is their own fault. If we are ever to get beyond the problem of the color line, we must confront and address these inequalities.

The Nature of Educational Inequality

Americans often forget that as late as the 1960s most African-American, Latino, and Native American students were educated in wholly segregated schools funded at rates many times lower than those serving whites and were excluded from many higher education institutions entirely. The end of legal segregation followed by efforts to equalize spending since 1970 has made a substantial difference for student achievement. On every major national test, including the National Assessment of Educational Progress, the gap in minority and white students' test scores narrowed substantially between 1970 and 1990, especially for elementary school students. On the Scholastic Aptitude Test (SAT), the scores of African-American students climbed 54 points between 1976 and 1994, while those of white students remained stable.

Even so, educational experiences for minority students have continued to be substantially separate and unequal. Two-thirds of minority students still attend schools that are predominantly minority, most of them located in central cities and funded well below those in neighboring suburban districts. Recent analyses of data prepared for school finance cases in Alabama, New Jersey, New York, Louisiana, and Texas have found that on every tangible measure—from qualified teachers to curriculum offering—schools serving greater numbers of students of color had significantly fewer resources than schools serving mostly white students. As William L. Taylor and Dianne Piche noted in a 1991 report to Congress:

> Inequitable systems of school finance inflict disproportionate harm on minority and economically disadvantaged students. On an interstate basis, such students are concentrated in states, primarily in the South, that have the lowest capacities to finance public education. On an intra-state basis, many of the states with the widest disparities in educational expenditures are large industrial states. In these states, many minorities and economically disadvantaged students are located in property-poor urban districts which fare the worst in educational expenditures . . . (or) in rural districts which suffer from fiscal inequity.

Jonathan Kozol's 1991 *Savage Inequalities* described the striking differences between public schools serving students of color in urban settings and their suburban counterparts, which typically spend twice as much per student for populations with many fewer special needs. Contrast MacKenzie High School in Detroit, where word processing courses are taught without word processors because the school cannot afford them, or East St. Louis Senior High School, whose biology lab has no laboratory tables or usable dissecting kits, with nearby suburban schools where children enjoy a computer hookup to Dow Jones to study stock transactions and science laboratories that rival those in some industries. Or contrast Paterson, New Jersey, which could not afford the qualified teachers needed to offer foreign language courses to most high school students, with Princeton, where foreign languages begin in elementary school.

Even within urban school districts, schools with high concentrations of low-income and minority students receive fewer instructional resources than others. And tracking systems exacerbate these inequalities by segregating many low-income and minority students within schools. In combination, these policies leave minority students with fewer and lower-quality books, curriculum materials, laboratories, and computers; significantly larger class sizes; less qualified and experienced teachers; and less access to high-quality curriculum. Many schools serving low-income and minority students do not even offer the math and science courses needed for college, and they provide lower-quality teaching in the classes they do offer. It all adds up.

What Difference Does It Make?

Since the 1966 Coleman report, *Equality of Educational Opportunity*, another debate has raged as to whether money makes a difference to educational outcomes. It is certainly possible to spend money ineffectively; however, studies that have developed more sophisticated measures of schooling show how money, properly spent, makes a difference. Over the past 30 years, a large body of research has shown that four factors consistently influence student achievement: all else equal, students perform better if they are educated in smaller schools where they are well known (300 to 500 students is optimal), have smaller class sizes (especially at the elementary level), receive a challenging curriculum, and have more highly qualified teachers.

Minority students are much less likely than white children to have any of these resources. In predominantly minority schools, which most students of color attend, schools are large (on average, more than twice as large as predominantly white schools and reaching 3,000 students or more in most cities); on average, class sizes are 15 percent larger overall (80 percent larger for nonspecial education classes); curriculum offerings and materials are lower in quality; and teachers are much less qualified in terms of levels of education, certification, and training in the fields they teach. And in integrated schools, as UCLA professor Jeannie Oakes described in the 1980s and Harvard professor Gary Orfield's research has recently confirmed, most minority students are segregated in lower-track classes with larger class sizes, less qualified teachers, and lower-quality curriculum.

Research shows that teachers' preparation makes a tremendous difference to children's learning. In an analysis of 900 Texas school districts, Harvard economist Ronald Ferguson found that teachers' expertise—as measured by scores on a licensing examination, master's degrees, and experience—was the single most important determinant of student achievement, accounting for roughly 40 percent of the measured variance in students' reading and math achievement gains in grades 1–12. After controlling for socioeconomic status, the large disparities in achievement between black and white students were almost entirely due to differences in the qualifications of their teachers. In combinations, differences in teacher expertise and class sizes accounted for as much of the measured variance in achievement as did student and family background.

Ferguson and Duke economist Helen Ladd repeated this analysis in Alabama and again found sizable influences of teacher qualifications and smaller class sizes on achievement gains in math and reading. They found that more of the difference between the high- and low-scoring districts was explained by teacher qualifications and class sizes than by poverty, race, and parent education.

Meanwhile, a Tennessee study found that elementary school students who are assigned to ineffective teachers for three years in a row score nearly 50 percentile points lower on achievement tests than those assigned to highly effective teachers over the same period. Strikingly, minority students are about half as likely to be assigned to the most effective teachers and twice as likely to be assigned to the least effective.

Minority students are put at greatest risk by the American tradition of allowing enormous variation in the qualifications of teachers. The National Commission on Teaching and America's Future found that new teachers hired without meeting certification standards (25 percent of all new teachers) are usually assigned to teach the most disadvantaged students in low-income and high-minority schools, while the most highly educated new teachers are hired largely by wealthier schools. Students in poor or predominantly minority schools are much less likely to have teachers who are fully qualified or hold higher-level degrees. In schools with the highest minority enrollments, for example, students have less than a 50 percent chance of getting a math or science teacher with a license and a degree in the field. In 1994, fully one-third of teachers in high-poverty schools taught without a minor in their main field and nearly 70 percent taught without a minor in their secondary teaching field.

Studies of underprepared teachers consistently find that they are less effective with students and that they have difficulty with curriculum development, classroom management, student motivation, and teaching strategies. With little knowledge about how children grow, learn, and develop, or about what to do to support their learning, these teachers are less likely to understand students' learning styles and differences, to anticipate students' knowledge and potential difficulties, or to plan and redirect instruction to meet students' needs. Nor are they likely to see it as their job to do so, often blaming the students if their teaching is not successful.

Teacher expertise and curriculum quality are interrelated, because a challenging curriculum requires an expert teacher. Research has found that both students and teachers are tracked: that is, the most expert teachers teach the most demanding courses to the most advantaged students, while lower-track students assigned to less able teachers received lower-quality teaching and less demanding material. Assignment to tracks is also related to race: even when grades and test scores are comparable, black students are more likely to be assigned to lower-track, nonacademic classes.

When Opportunity is More Equal

What happens when students of color do get access to more equal opportunities? Studies find that curriculum quality and teacher skill make more difference to educational outcomes than the initial test scores or racial backgrounds of students. Analyses of national data from both the High School and Beyond Surveys and the National Educational Longitudinal Surveys have demonstrated that, while there are dramatic differences among students of various racial and ethnic groups in course-taking in such areas as math, science, and foreign language, for students with similar course-taking records, achievement test score differences by race or ethnicity narrow substantially.

Robert Dreeben and colleagues at the University of Chicago conducted a long line of studies documenting both the relationship between educational opportunities and student performance and minority students' access to those opportunities. In a comparative study of 300 Chicago first graders, for example, Dreeben found that African-American and white students who had comparable instruction achieved comparable levels of reading skill. But he also found that the quality of instruction given African-American students was, on average, much lower than that given white students, thus creating a racial gap in aggregate achievement at the end of first grade. In fact, the highest-ability group in Dreeben's sample was in a school in a low-income African-American neighborhood. These children, though, learned less during first grade than their white counterparts because their teacher was unable to provide the challenging instruction they deserved.

When schools have radically different teaching forces, the effects can be profound. For example, when Eleanor Armour-Thomas and colleagues compared a group of exceptionally effective elementary schools with a group of low-achieving schools with similar demographic characteristics in New York City, roughly 90 percent of the variance in student reading and mathematics scores at grades 3, 6, and 8 was a function of differences in teacher qualifications. The schools with highly qualified teachers serving large numbers of minority and low-income students performed as well as much more advantaged schools.

Most studies have estimated effects statistically. However, an experiment that randomly assigned seventh grade "at-risk" students to remedial, average, and honors mathematics classes found that the at-risk students who took the honors class offering a pre-algebra curriculum ultimately outperformed all other students of similar backgrounds. Another study compared African-American high school youth randomly placed in public housing in the Chicago suburbs with city-placed peers of equivalent income and initial academic attainment and found that the suburban students, who attended largely white and better-funded schools, were substantially more likely to take challenging courses, perform well academically, graduate on time, attend college, and find good jobs.

What Can be Done?

. . . Last year the National Commission on Teaching and America's Future issued a blueprint for a comprehensive set of policies to ensure a "caring, competent, and qualified teacher for every child," as well as schools organized to support student success. Twelve states are now working directly with the commission on this agenda, and others are set to join this year. Several pending bills to overhaul the federal Higher Education Act would ensure that highly qualified teachers are recruited and prepared for students in all schools. Federal policymakers can develop incentives, as they have in medicine, to guarantee well-prepared teachers in shortage fields and high-need locations. States can equalize education spending, enforce higher teaching standards, and reduce teacher shortages, as Connecticut, Kentucky, Minnesota, and North Carolina have already done. School districts can reallocate resources from administrative super-structures and special add-on programs to support better-educated teachers who offer a challenging curriculum in smaller schools and classes, as restructured schools as far apart as New York and San Diego have done. These schools, in communities where children are normally written off to lives of poverty, welfare dependency, or incarceration, already produce much higher levels of achievement for students of color, sending more than 90 percent of their students to college. Focusing on what matters most can make a real difference in what children have the opportunity to learn. This, in turn, makes a difference in what communities can accomplish.

An Entitlement to Good Teaching

The common presumption about educational inequality—that it resides primarily in those students who come to school with inadequate capacities to benefit from what the school has to offer—continues to hold wide currency because the extent of inequality in opportunities to learn is largely unknown. We do not currently operate schools on the presumption that students might be entitled to decent teaching and schooling as a matter of course. In fact, some state and local defendants have countered school finance and desegregation cases with assertions that such remedies are not required unless it can be proven that they will produce equal outcomes. Such arguments against equalizing opportunities to learn have made good on Du Bois's prediction that the problem of the 21st century would be the problem of the color line.

But education resources do make a difference, particularly when funds are used to purchase well-qualified teachers and high-quality curriculum and to create communities in which children are well known. In all of the current sturm und drang about affirmative action, "special treatment," and the other high-volatility buzzwords for race and class politics in this nation, I would offer a simple starting point for the next century's efforts: no special programs, just equal educational opportunity.

QUESTIONS

1. Darling-Hammond makes the point that the quality of education in the United States is more linked to social status than it is in Asian or European countries, where funding for schools is centralized and equal. What changes do you think would help to bring more equal access to education for all children in the United States regardless of their social class, ethnicity, or culture?

2. If, as the author argues, it is especially crucial to have excellent teachers in poorer school districts that are underfunded, what do you think would be the best way to encourage highly qualified teachers to work in inner-city schools with predominantly minority students from low-income backgrounds? What special skills does a teacher need to be effective at teaching underprivileged children?

3. Do you agree with Darling-Hammond that affirmative action would benefit schools in poorer school districts? Explain your position, and, if you disagree, consider other ways to improve the educational outlook for children from poor and minority families.

"How Media Education Can Promote Democracy"

Robert Kubey is director of the Center for Media Studies in the School of Communication, Information and Library Studies at Rutgers University in New Jersey. The Center is dedicated to understanding media literacy and the impact of media on modern society. Faculty and students from a range of departments, including all of Rutgers' campuses, come together to work with citizens, educators, foundations, government agencies, and media professionals. Kubey's books include Television and the Quality of Life: How Viewing Shapes Everyday Experience *(1990),* Media Literacy in the Information Age: Current Perspectives *(1996), and* Creating Television: Conversations With the People Behind 50 Years of American TV *(2003). The essay that follows argues for an ambitious national effort to promote media-literacy education in the schools.*

Media-literacy education is much more developed around the world than many readers in the United States might know. Indeed, numerous societies are at a watershed moment as we make inevitable and gradual changes in what we do in classrooms, homes and youth groups to make education more student-centered and responsive to young people's and society's real-world needs.

Indeed, in 1998–99, the 29th General Conference of the United Nations Educational and Scientific and Cultural Organization (UNESCO) approved support for media education. Forty-one invited representatives from 33 countries met in Vienna and made the following statement and recommendations:

Media education is the entitlement of every citizen, in every country in the world, to freedom of expression and the right to information and is instrumental in building and sustaining democracy. . . . Media education should be introduced wherever possible within national curricula as well as in tertiary, non-formal and lifelong education. Australia and Canada now require media education nationwide. Media education is increasingly well developed in England, Scotland and New Zealand. It is on the rise in Russia, China, Taiwan, Japan, Korea, through nearly all of Western Europe and in an increasing number of countries in South America and Africa.

But while media education is spreading rapidly elsewhere, formal media education in the United States lags behind every other major English speaking country in the world. At the same time, there are many positive and noteworthy media literacy developments in the United States. In addition to new national organizations, a growing number of states have added media literacy goals to their state education standards and new national organizations have been established. In a 1999 study with Frank Baker, then the president of the Alliance for a Media Literate America, we documented that 48 of the 50 states in the United States (50 of 50 as of the year 2000) now have one or more elements of media education in their Core Curricular Frameworks. These frameworks constitute an important and growing legitimacy for media education in the U.S. Each state's media education standards can be viewed at http://edstandards.org/StSu/Health.html.

The considerable presence of media-analysis goals among the state educational frameworks in the subject areas of health and consumer skills surprised us. Seventy-four percent of states (37 of 50) now have media-education elements in their health and consumer education frameworks. Ninety-four percent (47 states) have media education elements in English and language and communication arts frameworks, but only 60% (30 states) call for media elements in social studies, history, and civics.

Though I believe media education will eventually come fully on line in the United States, it is not going to be achieved simply. There are still too few graduate education programs that teach teachers how to implement media education. To move things along, we need committed teachers, parents, school administrators and members of media industries to push for media curricula in the schools.

Over the years, the National Television Academy, among other professional groups, has been active in fostering media literacy through workshops and programs in schools. The Television Academy's current effort is called National Student Television, a program designed to enhance media literacy by doing rather than preaching-educating high-school students in the practice of real-life broadcast journalism.

Media professionals should support media education. One such key supporter is veteran television producer Norman Felton (Dr. Kildare, The Man from U.N.C.L.E.), whose generous funding has made it possible to develop the innovative media literacy curriculum that we are currently piloting at a local charter school here in New Jersey. It will be described shortly. Indeed, it can be argued that a better educated audience will create more opportunity to create more complex and sophisticated material. As Walt Whitman wrote, "To have great poets, there must be great audiences, too." Second, as the Free Expression Policy Project has recognized, media literacy education can provide an antidote to the wish of some groups to censor the media. The Project was established four years ago to examine censorship issues.

Most fundamentally, and particularly in the United States, we need more educational leaders to come to recognize that the way we communicate as a society has changed enough in this century that traditional training in literature and print communication is no longer sufficient by itself.

What is Media Literacy Education and Why Is It Important?

What is media literacy?

Media literacy involves critically analyzing media messages, evaluating sources of information for bias and credibility, raising awareness about how media messages influence people's beliefs, attitudes and behaviors and producing messages using different forms of media.

Why is it so important? Let's start with the fact that children throughout the United States, and an ever-growing proportion of countries around the world, spend an average of three hours each day watching television. At this rate, by the time they reach age 75 they will have spent nine full years watching TV. In the U. S., two of those nine years will have been spent watching television ads.

When we add the number of hours young people spend watching movies, listening to music, playing videogames, and surfing the Internet, they (and we) easily devote one-third to one-half of our waking lives to the electronic media. Yet many schools still treat poetry, short stories and the novel as the only forms of English expression worthy of study. As a result, most children are still not becoming media literate, and they are poorly equipped to actively engage and think critically about the very media that most impact their lives.

The Rutgers University-based Center for Media Studies, which I direct, has been piloting media-literacy curricula at a local charter school. What we do gives you a sense of what media-literacy education can cover. Using techniques and materials from journalism (print and broadcast), scriptwriting, and advertising, students in grades 5-8 further develop their language-arts skills. Students learn how information is organized and presented and how persuasive strategies in written and other media work; they learn how to differentiate between fiction and nonfiction, fact and opinion; and they learn to identify story elements, story structure and such literary devices as point of view and metaphor. The students put these skills to use, creating ads, scripts and news reports of their own. Students are also using media characters found in film, television, advertising, video games and comic books to discuss and analyze the difference between heroes and celebrities, and to examine stereotyping, gender representation, popular depictions of various age, ethnic and racial groups, and how young people form images of self.

Older students are exploring, through journalism, advertising and the Internet, the concepts of fact vs. opinion, the constructed nature of media messages, freedom of speech and the press, democracy and civic responsibility. Students are being taught elements of visual literacy, including composition, form, scale, light, color, and subject and camera movement. Students analyze and create their own storyboards and create their own media products.

Critical Thinking

School systems throughout the United States are mandated to deliver an education that promotes critical thinking. But if a school is teaching critical thinking and not linking critical thinking to the media world that many students spend upwards of six hours a day with, then they are leaving a potential gold mine unexplored.

Those who have engaged in media literacy instruction have observed that before long, parents report that their children are no longer watching television in the same way they did before media literacy education. Indeed, parents often remark that after instruction in media literacy, their children begin to point out all manner of things while they watch television. They identify production techniques, such as jump cuts, fades, and voiceovers. They detect bias and the power of words in narration to shift meaning in news, and the power of music to alter the viewer's mood.

What's happening is that an activity-television viewing that normally involved three hours of relatively passive reception has now become much more mentally active. Willingly, and without knowing it, the student is now spending a bigger chunk of those three hours of daily television viewing engaged in critical thinking than would have been the case if it had not been for media-literacy training. And the same can happen when they are surfing the net, listening to radio, watching movies, reading the newspaper, or playing videogames. This is not to say that they will be critically analyzing every moment, but they will be using their higher critical faculties much more if they have been given some of the basic tools of media literacy, of media analysis, than if they have not.

And we know of no evidence that more critical appraisal depreciates one's enjoyment of television or film. To the contrary, understanding how television and film are made enhances one's enjoyment. In some cases, one's tastes may eventually run to less obvious or more sophisticated material, but there is no reason to expect that a media literate person can not still enjoy media and derive pleasure and information simultaneously.

Media Literacy Education Teaches Critical-Thinking Skills for Citizens and Future Voters

The Jeffersonian ideal of an informed electorate also necessitates media literacy education precisely because it teaches critical-thinking skills for citizens and future voters. And research has shown that media literacy in social studies classes significantly promotes civic participation and increases regular newspaper readership among teenagers. With the incredible rise of the Internet and the unedited nature of many websites, students need to learn, more than ever, how to assess the validity and credibility of the information sources.

Our political life began to become largely mediated in the middle of the last century and now—certainly in campaigns and elections, and in day-to-day governance—media could hardly be more critical to how we view politicians, our leaders, and how we think about the critical issues of the day. Should we go to war? How will we protect the environment? Will we be taxed more or less? These and every other vital question in our democracy are raised and debated, often superficially, in the nation's media. Politicians have become extraordinarily adept at using media to their advantage. When politicians' interests are in line with the public's, this can result in effective government. But as often as not, well intended or not, there are distortions that take place in our public life, and these distortions are partly a function of how our media systems operate.

To the degree that media are used to propagandize or manipulate and interfere with the public being well informed, is the degree to which we need media education to be part of our school's civics and social studies classes. No student should leave high school without knowing the classic techniques of persuasion and propaganda, many of which have been taught for decades, but not to all students. Students should be able to recognize "name-calling," "bandwagon" and "glittering generalities" in the arguments they hear and read. But this is only the most basic of beginnings.

Media Literacy Can Promote Health Awareness and Reduce Violence

Media literacy techniques are also being used increasingly in programs designed to promote health and prevent substance abuse among young people. A particularly useful health-education assignment involves having groups of middle-school students in a class produce a five-minute videotape on a health topic of their choosing. The topic might have to do with nutrition, exercise, safe sex; or alcohol, drug, or tobacco abuse; and the final production is shown to the whole class, if not the whole school, or to the public via public access cable.

Here is what often happens. First, interest in the research aspects of the project are greatly increased because the students have been given the responsibility of making a health public service message for their peers and for the larger community. Compared to doing a written report that only the teacher will see, students become very motivated and concerned that they have researched the topic well so that the information they convey is accurate. The students learn organizational, research, writing, editing and production skills. And guess whose public-service announcement other students are more likely to pay attention to and learn from: the government's, the advertising council's, or the ones made by their peers? Such peer-driven media-literacy health projects can really bring students alive and make schoolwork more relevant.

Media-literacy approaches can also be used in programs focused on conflict resolution and the reduction of aggression and violence. Middle or high school students can be asked, for example, to view part of a television program depicting a growing conflict between two rival gangs in a school. The program is stopped and the students are then put in groups and assigned to write the next scene wherein the characters resolve the conflict through words and talk, rather than with fists, knives or guns. The assignment gives rise to students thinking through how a conflict might be peaceably resolved, and then, in sharing their solutions, the class has the opportunity to hear a variety of solutions. Research indicates that doing so increases the likelihood that some of these solutions will be mentally available should students become involved in a similar conflict.

Access, Analyze, Evaluate, and Produce

One of the significant developments in the history of U.S. media education occurred in 1992 when the Aspen Institute brought 25 educators and activists together for a National Leadership Conference. At the meeting, the group established a definition and vision for developing media education stating that a media literate person should be able to access, analyze, evaluate, and produce both print and electronic media. Why those four verbs?

Access

With the rise of the Internet, access is more important than ever. And not only should students be able to access the World Wide Web, they should also receive instruction in how to assess the value and validity of websites, whether they be medical, political, or educational. Now that most anyone can create their own website, a great deal of freedom has been accorded citizens who choose to use the technology. But with the freedom of the Internet comes a new and increasing demand on our educational systems and on caregivers, to help young people use the Internet, and all other media, critically and thoughtfully.

Analyze

Analysis involves being able to pick out persuasive techniques employed in media messages, to understand that there are always people involved-behind the scenes-in the construction of media messages, and that nearly all media messages are deliberately designed to do something, whether it is to inform, entertain, or persuade. Young people, and adults alike, need to learn how media construct our understandings of issues, of products, of people, of gender and race, of whole nation states. Indeed, one of the few laws of communication is that people are most impressionable and most easily persuaded, on any issue, when they know very little about the topic.

Evaluate

Evaluating media is different than analyzing it. By evaluation, we mean that people will learn to appraise the value of media products for themselves, for others, and for their society. This is arguably an even more subjective process than is analysis, but it is no less important. Media literacy education ought to contribute to an individual's ability to appraise for themselves the value of any given television program, film, videogame, website, magazine or newspaper article.

Most especially, we want to encourage students to become autonomous in their assessment of media and to develop their own modes of criticism, interpretation and evaluation. With young children, we often must choose and supervise their media exposure, but eventually as parents and teachers we have to let go and expect young people to negotiate the increasingly complex media worlds they inhabit on their own. And just as there is no single, correct way to interpret all of literature, there is no single, correct way to interpret all of television or film. The goal of media education should be to provide a grounding upon which students can better develop their own idiosyncratic responses.

As important as are the matters of critical thinking, health, and democracy, we ought not to forget that television and media are aesthetic forms. We also want students to become more sophisticated in their appreciation of art forms across all media. The educational establishment must come to recognize that there are television and film classics that are works of substantial artistry, subtlety, and power.

Let me be clear. I am not suggesting that we jettison Twain and Dickens. I am saying that other important modes of storytelling have developed and that they also deserve formal study in our schools. Reading and writing remain fundamental. One way to integrate media literacy with traditional literacy is to emphasize writing skills in students' scripts, storyboards, and in their critical analysis and review of films, TV programs, news, advertising, and websites.

One of the ways to increase students' interest in literature is to help them recognize that many of the same storytelling techniques used in the classics are also used in the popular television programs and films with which they are already familiar. Students already respond to foreshadowing in a television series like *Malcolm in the Middle* but are often simply unaware that foreshadowing is a deliberate technique used to heighten suspense, drama and irony. Knowing the terms and being able to apply them is more important than some might think. Knowing about foreshadowing, symbolism, character development and other techniques used in literature and in film and television permit greater appreciation and understanding of the art form.

Produce

Students should also be able to produce media. First, being able to create one's own media messages is extraordinarily empowering. Sometimes, for the first time in their lives, students see that they, too, can participate in making art or news, a film, a television program, or a website that affects other people. Many students involved in a media production in middle or high school will report that it was among the most exciting and motivating experience of their years in school. Second, by producing media, students learn in a more personal and profound way that media messages are "constructed."

One can show students how the most simple edits in television can substantially change the meaning and emotional impact of a scene or of an entire story. Students can be shown how easy it is to include or edit out a particular shot, or how pairing a shot with one kind of music or another can make a huge difference in how the audience experiences a character, a moment in a story, or a whole group of people. Showing students these things is an important and necessary part of media literacy instruction, but even better is for the students to become involved in making editorial decisions of their own, deciding themselves what to leave in or leave out, and what order to present material. Once they have edited their own material, they become much more aware of how virtually everything they see in the media has been edited.

Toward the Future

One of the obstacles to more rapid acceptance of media education is that some educators remain convinced that the only area appropriate for formal study in English and language arts classes is literature. But there can be little question that as the electronic media age, the patina of time alone will make their formal study increasingly acceptable to educational traditionalists. This is why I believe that we can expect media education to become commonplace by the middle of this century, if not before.

Over 2,300 years ago, Plato wrote that a "sound education consists in training people to find pleasure and pain in the right objects." But though most Americans now spend half their leisure time watching television and film, too few schools have yet to devote formal attention to helping students become more sophisticated media consumers. Let us hope that the picture continues to improve.

Most fundamentally, we need to encourage our nation's future voters and leaders to take media seriously, to understand where media messages come from, and why messages are presented as they are and to what effect. As the author Charles Brightbill wrote in 1960, "The future will belong not only to the educated, but to those who have been educated to use leisure wisely."

QUESTIONS

1. How does Kubey define media-literacy education? Why does he think that we need media literacy so much? What facts and statistics does he present to support his view? Do you agree with his position?
2. What does Kubey believe needs to be done to overcome the lack of effective media education in the United States? What effective and creative activities does he detail? In his opinion, what is the relationship between media education and critical thinking?
3. How effectively does Kubey refute objections to his program for media education, study, and creative production, such as the argument that media education might lead to the neglect of classical literature and the art of writing generally?

LOWELL MONKE

"Unplugged Schools"

Lowell Monke, who received his Ph.D. from Iowa State in 1999, is assistant professor of education at Wittenberg University in Springfield, Ohio, where he teaches Philosophical and Sociological Perspectives in Education. His research and writing interests include alternative education, diversity, and the social and psychological impact of high technology on children's development. Monke's essays have appeared in numerous publications, including Orion, Teacher Magazine, *and* Netfuture. *He is coauthor of the forthcoming book,* Breaking Down the Digital Walls: Learning to Teach in a Post-Modem World *(SUNY Press), which critically examines his experiences working with high school students on telecollaborative projects. Monke taught for 20 years in K–12 schools, not just in the United States but also in South America and Europe. In the following essay from* Orion *(2007), Monke presents his vision of schools and activities that promote a sense of being "unplugged."*

Educators say the darndest things. Consider this from a high school social studies teacher who told me, "Kids don't read anymore. The only way I can teach them anything is by showing them videos." Or this from a middle school principal who defended serving children junk food every day by telling me, "That's what they're used to eating. They won't eat it if it doesn't taste like fast food."

Aside from their stunning capitulation of adult responsibility, these comments illustrate what has become a common disregard for one of schooling's most important tasks: to compensate for, rather than intensify, society's excesses.

I first encountered the idea of the compensatory role of schools in 1970, while preparing to become a teacher. In *Teaching as a Subversive Activity*, Neil Postman and Charles Weingartner argued that one of the roles of schools in a free society is to serve as a cultural thermostat—to take the temperature of the culture, determine where the culture is over- and underheated, and then gear instruction to compensate for those extremes. If a culture becomes too enamored with competition, schools would emphasize cooperation; if it overemphasizes individuality, schools would emphasize community responsibility; if it allows poor children to go hungry, schools would (and do) develop lunch and breakfast programs to feed them; and so on.

Postman and Weingartner recognized that there are limits to this role. Schools can't be expected to solve all of our social ills. But one place where we would do well to employ this thermostatic approach is in our relationship to technology and the fundamental ways that a vast number of electronic tools mediate and shape our children's experiences.

Let me give an example. Several years ago a study found that young people actually prefer ATMs and automated phone systems to bank tellers and clerks. I presented the study, with unconcealed scorn, to a graduate class I was teaching at the time. The next day a student sent me an e-mail that included the following:

> I do feel deeply disturbed when I can run errand after errand, and complete one task after another with the help of bank clerks, cashiers, postal employees, and hairstylists without ANY eye contact at all! After a wicked morning of that, I am ready to conduct all business online.

In a society in which adults so commonly treat each other mechanically, perhaps we shouldn't be surprised that our youth are more attracted to machines. It seems to me that in such a society one task of schools would be to stress the kind of deeply caring, fully present, and wholly human interaction that long ago disappeared from ordinary public life and is now rapidly evaporating from private experience as well. By helping our youth become good at and appreciate the value of profound human engagement, we may help cool the attraction to mediated experiences expressed by my student.

To be sure, this effort would represent a radical reversal of schools' traditional relationship with media. To a large degree, American schools were invented out of a need to heat up children's access to media. From the seventeenth century through the first half of the twentieth, schools were places children went to gain entry into the world of symbols. The abstract character of the texts and numbers found in schools complemented the intensely physical character of life outside. Rarely, however, was it allowed to supercede it. Those children who spent an inordinate amount of time in the world of abstractions were typically chastised for being "bookworms" and pushed outside to get some fresh air.

All of this changed with television, which threw iconic rather than textual representations at children (and adults) at a mind-numbing pace. A few observers quickly recognized the significance of this inundation. Marshall McLuhan, for example, proposed that schools would have to serve as "civil defense against media fallout." That didn't happen, of course. Even as city streets became unsafe for exploration, as a mostly rural environment gave way to a relatively sterile suburban one, and as physical labor gave way to the information age, schools never responded to the cultural shift toward abstraction by moving in the opposite direction. Indeed, by the time television's brawnier, more powerful symbol-manipulating cousin, the computer, came along, schools were fully committed to reinforcing rather than compensating for the symbol-saturated world in which children lived.

Of course, symbol manipulation—reading, writing, mathematics—is the unavoidable nuts and bolts of schooling. But it is not the sole purpose of education. Education must help children come to know themselves, become good citizens, and (with increasing urgency) come to terms with the natural world around them. It is possible that a school system wholly devoted to developing technical skills would not be particularly damaging if other institutions compensated for children's severely mediated lives. Unfortunately, the institutions that could serve that function—church, family, community—have been diminished by technology's cultural dominance. School is about the only institution left that has the extensive claim on children's attention needed to offset that dominance.

The health of our children's inner lives, their civic engagement, and their relationship with nature all would be improved if schools turned down the thermostat on that technologically overheated aspect of American culture. Schools dedicated to that task—we might call them "unplugged schools"—would identify the values associated with technological culture and design curricula and an environment focused on strengthening the human values at the other end of the scale.

The most obvious thing schools can do in this regard is give children experiences with the real things toward which symbols are only dim pointers. Unless emotionally connected to some direct experience with the world, symbols reach kids as merely arbitrary bits of data. A picture may be worth a thousand words, but to a second grader who has held a squiggly nightcrawler in her hand, even the printed symbol "worm" resonates with far deeper meaning than a thousand pictures or a dozen Discovery Channel videos.

Nature is, of course, the richest resource for firsthand experience. Individual teachers have long tried to provide some contact with the natural world by bringing plants and small animals into their classrooms—a limited approach yielding limited results. Many schools are beginning to think on a larger scale. They have torn up the asphalt surrounding the schools, planted trees and flowers indigenous to the area, and even established ponds and waterways that quickly attract a remarkably diverse number of critters. In 1997, for instance, Lewis and Clark Elementary School in Missoula, Montana, began creating the state's first schoolyard habitat. Working under the guidance of Kent Watson, a local landscape architect, the school turned a large section of its playground into a habitat that included a native-grasses mound, a waterfall, stream, and pool, a plot of plants "discovered" by Lewis and Clark, a rock garden, a variety of native trees and shrubs, and a butterfly garden. Not only do students at the school use the area for environmental studies, they were directly involved in the original design and development process: mapping the soil, surveying existing plants and animals, studying the history and culture of the region, determining what seeds to plant, designing and building benches and pathways.

A different type of habitat project is currently getting under way where I live, in Springfield, Ohio. It involves creating "curricular gardens" in front of the newly built high school as an alternative to the vast grass lawn planned by the original architects. A colleague of mine at Wittenberg University, Stefan Broidy, is working with teachers at the high school and nearby elementary and middle schools to connect the curricula of various departments, ranging from art to science, with corresponding gardening projects. This is the first step in a long-term effort to eventually revitalize a long-neglected fifty-acre land lab that lies adjacent to the schools.

These are just a couple examples of thousands of innovative local nature habitat programs being developed by schools all over the country. (A number of other examples can be found in *Richard Louv's article* in the March/April 2007 issue of this magazine.) As one reads about these programs, it becomes clear just how important it is that we help children get beyond the environment we have built to fit humans and experience the larger environment within which humans must learn to fit. Only nature can suffice for that, of course, but more specifically, the wild—that which has not been entirely tamed and domesticated by human intervention—is vital. By helping children understand the limitations of human power, the wild provides some inoculation against the day-to-day charm of a technological milieu that seduces us into believing that those limitations do not exist.

In Europe, recognition of the benefits of being in the wild is behind one of its fastest-growing educational movements: forest kindergartens. They originated in Denmark in the 1950s but only recently began to attract attention because of their rapid expansion throughout Germany in the 1990s. These multi-age, year-round outdoor classrooms are designed to foster a love and knowledge of nature, while using the forest to encourage children to imaginatively create fantasy play worlds. Few full-blown forest kindergartens have been created in the U.S., but they have inspired a number of schools to establish forest weeks or weekly forest days. And, of course, where there are no forests, prairie weeks, pond months, or desert days can serve as well.

A second important compensation would move in the opposite direction of nature—toward the conscious investigation of the tools that mediate our lives. With "magical" black boxes so integrated into our lives that they have become nearly invisible, unplugged schools would disintegrate technology, first by surrounding young children with only those tools whose working principles are visible and understandable and then by gradually bringing more complex, opaque technologies, from radios to eventually computers, into the educational arena—not just as study aids but objects of study.

Montessori schools are noted for their reliance on devices that make learning very much a hands-on activity. However, I know of no schools that incorporate into their curricula the kind of systematic, progressive study of tools I have described above. The trend has been in the opposite direction, as even rural schools eliminate the middle school shop and home ec classes that once gave students at least some experience with simple tools. Children now have to go to "children's museums" to get hands-on experience with common hand tools. The fact that these places are called museums perhaps explains why good models of this kind of learning in schools are hard to come by. Our society seems to have decided that in the age of powerful mental tools, working with and understanding physical tools is a thing of the past.

Of course, computers are physical tools of a sort. But their physical workings are so concealed from view that mainstream schooling has simply defaulted on helping youth dispel this quite consequential ignorance. Education is hardly improved by revealing the world to kids through the use of tools whose workings cannot themselves be revealed. It doesn't have to be this way. Learning the fundamental principles of computer operations is not beyond the capabilities of most high school students if approached appropriately. For years, Valdemar Setzer at the University of São Paulo has taught high school seniors the principles of computer operations by first having the students as a class act out physically what takes place inside the computer during a simple computation. The idea is not to make everyone a computer programmer—it is to help youth comprehend why our increasingly computerized environment functions the way it does. Only if they possess that understanding will they be able to decide which human powers are appropriate to hand off to computer calculation and which should be reserved for our own judgment.

So much daily communication is now mediated by machines that the *U.S. News & World Report* has estimated that youth graduating from schools today have had about one-third fewer face-to-face conversations than their parents had when they came out of school. Unplugged schools would compensate for this by creating an environment teeming with adults and older students conversing with, telling stories to, and working directly with younger students. Resources and time spent by other schools to integrate technology into the classroom would be spent integrating community members.

This is just what Ron Berger and his colleagues did for over two decades at Shutesbury Elementary School, in western Massachusetts. In *An Ethic of Excellence*, Berger writes, "Town citizens of all ages are in the school every day as mentors and tutors for children. Senior citizens are guests at concerts and annual Valentine and Thanksgiving meals hosted by the Kindergarten and Pre-Kindergarten. We invite town citizens to our work exhibitions, to be panelists at formal portfolio presentations, and as experts, helping our classes in their learning."

Berger notes that senior citizens have also suffered from the effects of a technological culture that favors mobility and individuality over stability and continuity. They have become so isolated from the rest of the community that children rarely see and hear the wisdom and dignity encased in creaky joints and weathered skin. Bringing these elders into schools would benefit both generations. Salt Lake City is one of a number of communities that has worked at this intergenerational integration. It instituted its Senior Motivators in Learning and Educational Services program in 1977 with 15 volunteers. Today there are over 250 seniors in the district schools involved with tutoring, story reading, field trips, sports, art, and music. They are encouraged to share with children the vast variety of skills, knowledge, history, and traditions accumulated during their lives.

Combined with the emphasis on direct contact with the physical world, forging connections with older generations can help unplugged schools offset a glorification of constant change by fostering an appreciation for what is enduring and mature. It would help balance our hard-charging, future-obsessed culture with an environment that fosters compassion, reverence, and a sense of obligation toward those who have come before.

As much as they need direct contact with caring adults, children also need quiet places that give them a respite from the din of adult-generated electronic media constantly assaulting their eyes and ears. In past generations, playhouses, treehouses, forts, or even a sheet thrown over a card table served as places to escape adult intervention for a time. Children's studies author Elizabeth Goodenough calls these places "secret spaces," where children retreat for undirected fantasy play, security, and quiet contemplation. With ubiquitous media making these places harder to come by, enlightened schools are creating their own quiet (if not secret) spaces for their students. I have visited a preschool and kindergarten in West Des Moines, Iowa, that has a loft with an adult-unfriendly five-foot ceiling. Children go there to rest, play, or just withdraw for a while. The imaginative powers of children being what they are, these quiet spaces don't always have to be physical. In Goodenough's book *Secret Spaces of Childhood*, Harvard professor John Stilgoe recalls putting the leaves of sweet fern in his math books when he was in junior high so he could take a whiff of it during school, which would transport him back to the gravel bank where he spent so much idle time in summer. Evidently, the concern for keeping students "on task" had not yet reached the point that it prevented his teacher from giving him some space for daydreaming. This and the kindergarten loft are just two ways that schools can, in remarkably simple ways, give children the opportunity to withdraw from the ceaseless noise of high-tech life and do the kinds of things that their childish nature calls to them to do.

It should be clear by now that all of the compensatory activities of unplugged schools have ideological implications. For example, our plugged-in society values the Internet for its capacity to overcome time and space—to allow us to "go anywhere at anytime." Unplugged schools would recognize that this benefit has been accompanied by increased difficulty among children in feeling that they belong to any place at any time. According to educator R.W. Burniske, belonging is just what kids need to survive a media-saturated environment. "When you are drowning in a river of information," he once wrote me, "the last thing you need to know is the temperature of the water. What you need is a rock to stand on." One way to find that rock is through what has come to be called place-based education. By using the local community as a primary means of learning, place-based learning counteracts the alienation generated by too much of what Postman called "information from nowhere."

Berger gives a good sense of the expansive character of place-based education, along with its impact on school-community relations:

> Students clean town roads every year, raise money for town efforts, and engage in other serious projects to benefit the community: testing homes for radon, testing streams for pollution, testing wells for water quality, conducting research to contribute to town historical records, taking a census of local animals for state officials. It's not by chance that we've earned trust and support for the school.

This is not just the fairly widespread practice of community service, done in the students' spare time. This is the day-to-day work of the school, integrated into the very core of the curriculum and evaluated by the quality of the results. Schoolwork takes on deep meaning as students recognize themselves as valuable community members.

Technological culture promotes a doggedly instrumental orientation to life in which every act is calculated as a means to something else. Even something as intrinsically rewarding as childhood play now must be considered useful in order to be scheduled into children's frenetic lives. Adults intent on teaching techniques of dancing, sports, music, art, drama, etc., squeeze free play at one end while video games and television—both ultimately adult directed—squeeze it from the other end. Children, and their teachers, have so lost their intuitive sense of imaginative free play, undertaken just for the sheer joy of playing, that for the past two summers Penny Wilson, a "playworker" from London, has toured the U.S. under sponsorship from the Alliance for Childhood, training recreation personnel in major cities on how to help children recover their natural capacity for unstructured play. Providing opportunities for that kind of play is yet another way unplugged schools would compensate for what our culture leaves out of childhood.

Yet compensation for an overheated technological culture should not be mistaken for rejection of it. With years of unplugged experiences anchoring youth against the current of technological overindulgence, high school students should be capable of making much richer connections between the symbols encountered on computer screens and the real things those symbols represent. Learning with and about high technology then becomes a very different experience.

Ten years ago Burniske and I designed and coordinated a telecomputing project we called Media Matters. We enlisted high school students from various parts of the world to analyze how different media told the stories of several global events. While the students were figuring out how the character of radio, TV, newspapers, magazines, and a new form of communication called the World Wide Web shaped how information was conveyed, we were discovering that even though these students were sophisticated in putting media to work for them, they were naïve about how it worked *on* them. Today, in the age of cell phones, instant messaging, MySpace, and YouTube, this naïveté is even more consequential. Thus, not only should schools help students understand how these media work, they should also help them understand how such tools shape their appetites, relationships, and very conceptions of the world in which they live.

There are many other specific things that schools could do to compensate for the lack of balance children experience in our overmediated culture. But one thing they must do is provide an alternative to the current penchant for viewing children as little biological machines whose knowledge and skills can be "constructed," assessed, and labeled in schools according to the same cold logic of the spreadsheet that businesses use in producing commodities. This intensely mechanistic view of children is central to the belief that a very meager set of numbers can determine their abilities (and future opportunities), to the confidence that a single curriculum can serve children just as well whether they live in Jackson Hole or Brooklyn, and to the conviction that a child's failure to adapt to the inhospitable clockwork machinery of school operations can be "fixed" by applying a little chemical grease (like Ritalin) to a malfunctioning gear inside her head.

The efforts to label and sort children while constantly seeking technical means to accelerate, enhance, and otherwise tinker with their intellectual, emotional, and physical development are acts of mechanistic abuse (there is really no other name for it) committed against children's nature. There is no more critical task for schools than to counter this unfolding tragedy. Schools can make headway simply by patiently honoring and nurturing each child's internally timed, naturally unfolding developmental growth, by abandoning anxious efforts to hurry children toward adulthood, and by giving these young souls time to heal from the wounds inflicted by a culture that shows no respect for childhood innocence. As Richard Louv and others have argued, nature is a particularly effective antidote for this condition. Eliminating the clock as the means of governing everything is another more modest but important move. However it is undertaken, what is important to recognize is that compensating for the dominant view of children-as-mechanisms is, at its core, spiritual work. It acknowledges that some facet of a child's inner life must remain sacred—off-limits to our machinations—to be viewed not as new territory for scientific investigation and technical manipulation but simply with awe and reverence and our own best, most human, expressions of support. To grant the dignity of that inner core is perhaps the most important gift unplugged schools can give children in the technological age. And, in turn, to foster within children those once universal but now nearly extinct childhood qualities of awe and reverence is spiritual education in its most elemental sense.

The list of schools that have directly and comprehensively tied children's overmediated lives to spiritual health is a very short one, I'm afraid, limited mostly to a number of Waldorf schools, whose philosophy has long coupled spiritual development with a critical stance toward the use of electronic media by young children. The Washington [D.C.] Waldorf School just completed a year-long series of public seminars and staff meetings investigating how best to bring computers and other high-tech devices into the high school curriculum so that students not only have the skills they need to go on to college or work, but understand the full impact of technology on human culture, the environment, and their own inner lives. The faculty has discovered that an effective program requires paying attention to the curriculum and methods not only at the high school level but at the elementary level as well (where children do not use computers). They understand that there is much inner preparation that young children need to do if they are one day to give mature direction to the enormous power these external tools provide.

If one stitched together all of these examples and concerns, one might be able to imagine at least the contours of an unplugged school. Certainly, unplugged schools would get children deeply involved with nature and community; they would give a prominent place to the expressive arts; they would determine tool use according to developmental readiness; they would study technology explicitly; they would give children time and space to look inward; and they would rely on assessments that are rigorous and multifaceted rather than reductionist and multiple choice. But there are a vast number of ways all of this could be done. The compensatory activities of any particular unplugged school could not be standardized. They would have to depend heavily on the specific children, educators, parents, geography, and culture of the communities they serve.

Of course, right now there is no escaping, at least in public schools, a whole host of technocratic fetters, such as standardized curricula and testing, that are turning teaching as well as learning into intellectual factory work. Still, educators and parents can always find some wiggle room within technocratic structures, and it is in these gaps that a wide variety of subversive unplugging can gain a foothold.

Ultimately, though, if schools were to throw off those fetters and restore balance to children's lives, they would have to establish goals that reflect our best sense of what it means to be human. Producing workers adapted to the demands of a high-tech economy would no longer drive what these schools do. Schools would establish life as the measure of value, not machines. They would be dedicated to showing young people how to live as dignified members of an increasingly mediated and fragile world. And they would consciously work to cool down society's infatuation with technology while heating up our concern for those we live with and the Earth we live on.

QUESTIONS

1. What do Monke's metaphors of "unplugged schools" and "turning down the thermostat of technology" mean? How do these ideas relate to earlier concepts of "compensation" as an educational goal, as opposed to simply following cultural and technological trends using a mechanistic model of the student learner?

2. Why does Monke believe that education must provide students with a connection to the natural world, to the wild? What examples of such efforts, his own and those of schools around the world, does he provide?

3. Why does Monke attribute so much importance to student projects in the community? How would he make such projects more integrated with school learning than typical "community service projects" that students do? Does his distinction here seem clear to you?

4. Monke attempts to refute the criticism that his idea of school learning would altogether ignore the significance of technology, computers, and the Internet. How would he integrate computers into the learning process in a less mechanistic, more humanistic manner than is typically seen in schools? Do his ideas on this type of project seem clear and convincing to you? Why or why not?

DACIA CHARLESWORTH

"Which Number Will You Be?"

Dacia Charlesworth earned a Ph.D. from Southern Illinois University and currently is Associate Professor in the Department of Communication at Indiana University–Purdue University at Fort Wayne. She has lectured and published papers on speech, gender, and AIDS-related topics. The following speech was delivered at the students' induction ceremony into the National Society of Collegiate Scholars, an honors and service-related organization for students at Robert Morris University. In a society that often views students as "just numbers," Charlesworth's 2004 address is a definition argument that challenges students to re-evaluate the meaning of a college education and to make a difference in their communities.

2.4 million. This is the number of college degrees that the U.S. Census projects will be conferred this year. Since all of today's inductees are well on their way to being one of the 27% of our nation's adults 25 and over who have a least a bachelor's degree, I am wondering which of the following numbers you will choose to be: Will you be like one of the 106 million who voted in the 2000 Presidential election? Or will you be like one of the 100 million who did not? Will you be line one of the 83.9 million people who volunteered their time in 2003? Or will you be like one of the 106.8 million who did not? The reason I ask which number you will be is because the number you are shapes who you will become.

This year marks a significant anniversary for me as an educator. Ten years ago, in 1994, I first entered the college classroom as a teacher. As a graduate teaching assistant, I was young and naïve. So much so in fact, that I began every class the same way for five years: I began by asking students to tell me why they were pursuing a college degree. The answers I received varied and included: "To further my education," "To become more well-rounded," "Because I want to study more about my major," and "To get a job and make money." You probably noticed that I said I only asked this question for the first five years of my life as a teacher. The reason I quit beginning my classes this way is because although the question was the same, the answers, initially, were not. Then one semester, I began to notice that one answer began appearing more and more until it was heard above all others, and that answer was "To get a job and make money." Today, it is my hope that you, the members of the National Society of Collegiate Scholars, will once again offer different answers so that I might dare ask that question again.

As NSCS inductees you have already demonstrated your ability to succeed in the classroom; (through my remarks today, I hope that you come to recognize your obligation to succeed in ways that transcend a grade point average, both inside and outside the classroom). NSCS was founded on the principle that with scholarship comes a responsibility to obtain leadership and a duty to perform service. One primary way for you to fulfill these obligations is for you to become defenders of education. In order to do so, you must first understand the link between education and citizenry and the current state of higher education. Finally, I will offer you four tenets by which I hope you strive to live your lives, not only as scholars but also as citizens.

Education, while still relatively valued, was once prized above all else. Turning first to the bedrock of Western civilization, Ancient Greece, we encounter Isocrates, a some-time Sophist. While philosophers including Socrates, Plato and Aristotle have managed to be kindly remembered by history, Sophists have not been as fortunate. Though you may have never heard of the Sophists, I am sure that you are aware of the word that today still designates one as knowledgeable and worldly: Sophisticated. Isocrates was Athenian-born, a noble, and devoted his life to developing good citizens through education. Isocrates's students studied debate, speaking, writing, philosophy, prose and poetry, math, science and history. They studied these subjects so that they could fulfill their duties as citizens and be actively engaged in the political process. Does this Ancient Greek curriculum seem familiar? It should, for it is upon Isocrates's instruction that we have based our conceptualization of liberal education. Now, what exactly is a liberal education supposed to do? The answer to this is simple; look to the root of the word. A liberal education is intended to liberate the learner so that he or she may live a questioning, fulfilling life.

The Romans, as they were like to do, took the Greek notion of liberal education and amended it. In the Institutes of Oratory, Quintilian posits that citizens should be taught rhetoric from "the cradle to the grave." Here we see the ideals of a civilized culture, one in which its citizens desire to be life-long learners. In that same text, Quintilian, echoing the claims of Isocrates and many others, defines a rhetorician as "a good man speaking well." Here we see the inextricable link between education and citizenry. To be a good speaker and, in turn a good leader, one must also be a good person.

During the Renaissance, education was also viewed as a way to improve one's status as well as one's nation. Citizens were expected to live vita activa. In this "active life," citizens were expected to place the needs of their country first, then consider the needs of other citizens, then consider the needs of their family and friends, and then finally consider their own needs. Contemporary U.S. culture, being as individualistic as it is, does not easily lend itself to vita activa.

What the U.S culture does lend itself to, however, is the belief that education has an intrinsic value. We only need to consider the social movements that have occurred during our nation's history to understand the relationship between education and civil rights. For example, this year marks the 50th anniversary of the Brown vs. Board of Education decision. Who can forget the images of the African-American students being escorted by armed men into the hallowed halls of various schools? Certainly, education is equivalent to civil rights.

Despite the historic link between education and citizenry, we have somehow lost sight of it and the current state of higher education worries me at times. When I am advising a student, listening to class discussion, or just talking informally to students, it breaks my heart when I hear students report that they do not understand why it is that they have to take an Arts and Humanities class, a History class, or an Intercultural communication class. These statements break my heart because they make me realize how we, educators within the humanities, have failed our students. For whatever reasons, those who have come before me and those of us who teach now have been content to allow student's discontent to rise. We have failed to inform students of their obligations once they leave our classrooms and our colleges. We have failed to persuade students that a myopic education is not the goal of a university degree. We have failed, quite simply, to teach students about the value of a degree—a value that transcends money, a job, and a career.

As evidence, of our failure, consider the common distinction between the "real-world" and the college experience. Few things raise my ire more than hearing someone refer to their world as "real" as if what I am doing in the college classroom is not real. What I teach my students is not only real, but it matters. Consider this: Would members of our culture so readily distinguish between the "real-world" and the experiences within my classroom if they truly believed that we were developing good citizens? Would students be so quick to draw this distinction if they themselves believed that we were truly preparing them for life within a nation, within a state, within a community?

Perhaps most students do not consider their college experience as a "real-world" experience because of the student-as-consumer metaphor that some individuals in higher education are so fond of using. William Lowe Bryan once said, "Education is one of the few things a person is willing to pay for and not get." When individuals in higher education refer to students as consumers, we encourage students to enter the classroom with a sense of entitlement and watch them develop a sense of apathy. For if students are encouraged to view themselves as consumers, how can we be surprised when the only commodity they want is a final grade rather than the knowledge that accompanies it? The continual use of this metaphor detracts from the noble goals of education and categorizes education as nothing more than a commodity that can be bought and sold just as easily as one purchases fast food: The end result is expected immediately and the lasting effect is negligible.

If we are to reclaim the link between education and citizenry, we must help others understand the value of a liberal education, that a college experience is a "real" experience, and that we only harm students when we encourage them to view themselves as consumers.

To reclaim this link between education and citizenry, I offer you the following four tenets for you to live by. In an attempt to convince you to consider these and actually remember them, I have developed these tenets in the form of a mnemonic device: NSCS.

My first goal of you: N. Never forget the power of education.

bell hooks, an English professor and extraordinary writer, explains how she viewed herself as a student: "I entered the classroom with the conviction that it was crucial for me and every other student to be an active participant, not a passive consumer. . . . Education connects the will to know with the will to become. Learning is a place where paradise can be created."

My second goal for you: S. Seek out knowledge; not because you have to, but because you want to.

Voltaire once said "Judge a man by his questions, rather than by his answers."

My third goal for you: C. Cultivate yourself as a person of good character, extreme intelligence, and as an excellent citizen.

On July 1, 1776, our beloved Robert Morris voted against the Declaration of Independence because he wished to hold out for reconciliation. On July 4, he declined to vote. On August 2, however, he signed the Declaration pronouncing "I am not one of those politicians that run testy when my own plans are not adopted. I think it is the duty of a good citizen to follow when he cannot lead."

My final goal for you: S. Support others in their desire to learn by teaching and modeling.

Gwendolyn Brooks, a noted poet, wrote, "We are each other's harvest; we are each other's business; we are each other's magnitude and bond."

Albert Einstein once said "People like us, who believe in physics, know that the distinction between past, present, and future is only a stubborn, persistent illusion." Break that illusion and let the past beliefs about the importance of education and citizenry intermingle with your present pursuit of scholarship and your future actions as a good citizen.

For those of you who know me, you know that my personal role model is the Rev. Dr. Anna Howard Shaw who, despite tremendous obstacles, was able to earn degrees in theology and medicine from Boston University during a time when women were not even expected to complete elementary school. Shaw went on to become an instrumental figure in our nation's temperance and suffrage movements. Later in her life, she was addressing a group of college students and she offered them the following advice: "There always have been and always will be eager runners who bear the torch of life's ideals ahead of the multitude, but that which inspires and leads them on comes from a great love of humanity, a love which nothing can quench. [This love] can endure all things and still trust with such an abiding faith that it saves, if not others, at least oneself." It is up to you to be the torchbearers at Robert Morris University: Lead the way in the classroom, lead the way in our community, and do so, if not for the respect of others, then for the love of yourselves.

I would like to thank the officers and the membership of NSCS for not only bestowing upon me this great honor, but for also allowing me the privilege to share my vision of my ideal world with you. Students, please remember, as is stated in Luke 12:48, "For unto whomsoever much is given, of him shall be much required." We are giving you much and are expecting more: we want you to never forget the power of education, to seek out knowledge, to cultivate your desire to be a good citizen, and to support others in their desire to learn. Fulfill these obligations as members of NSCS. Fulfill these obligations so that, as 27% of our nation's adults who have at least a bachelor's degree, you will be like one of the 106 million who voted in the 2000 Presidential election and will you be like one of the 83.9 million people who volunteered their time in 2003. When you consider which number you will be, be a number that matters and makes a positive difference.

QUESTIONS

1. How does Charlesworth use the concept of a number to emphasize and counterpoint her central critique of American values and her argument about what the inductees should do with their college educations?
2. How does Charlesworth contrast the educational values of the Greeks, the Romans, and the Renaissance with those of modern Americans? How does her example from the place of education in the civil rights struggle help to advance her argument?
3. In her final pages, what key expressions, mnemonic devices, and metaphors does Charlesworth present to replace the modern definition of the student as a consumer in search of a job? Argue for or against Charlesworth's definition of education and its purpose.

BRITA BELLI

"Cleaner, Greener U"

Brita Belli began her writing career as the Arts & Entertainment editor of the Fairfield County Weekly in Bridgeport, Connecticut. Currently, she is managing editor of E / The Environmental Magazine and writes for Alternet. Her articles have covered many aspects of environmental awareness and green work, education, childrearing, and lifestyle choices. In the following article from E Magazine, Belli focuses her interests on the increasing number of environmental and anti-global-warming initiatives written by students, both on campus and in the community, and she argues for teaching college students how to protect our environment.

"Climate change is our generation's civil rights movement," says Brianna Cayo Cotter, communications director for the Energy Action Coalition, swilling from a tall cup of coffee. Cotter talked fast and raked her fingers through her thick, wavy hair, staring intently, as though she'd been on a steady diet of nothing but caffeine for the last few days. This was PowerShift 2007, held at the University of Maryland, the largest gathering of college students ever assembled to fight climate change, a weekend of non-stop workshops and speakers and rallies brought together by Energy Action staff. The previous week, the group's server had crashed as college students across the nation logged on to register. On Halloween night, they hit 5,500 registrants, sending up a cheer in Energy Action offices. Cotter was literally buzzing with enthusiasm. "We're at a crucial moment in history," she said. "Climate change is an issue that's already impacting us, from the destruction of the Appalachian Mountains to the wildfires in California. We get that the resource wars and super storms are connected. And we get that the steps taken today will end up being the future for tomorrow."

Shifting the Power

Surrounded by foldout tables topped with organic T-shirts, cloth bags, environmental magazines and activist pamphlets, the Energy Action crew had created its own environmental how-to Mecca. Students roamed the halls clutching containers of coffee and complementary tote bags, migrating to one of hundreds of workshops that happened simultaneously and around the clock across the UM campus, on everything from radical lobbying to art and activism to communicating a winning message and running an energy-efficiency campaign in your house of worship.

The workshops were followed by the largest youth lobbying effort ever assembled in Washington to stop global warming. In addition to more than 300 individual meetings with Congressional leaders, youth climate spokesperson Billy Parish, cofounder of the Energy Action Coalition, was one of several environmentalists who testified before the House Select Committee on Energy Independence and Global Warming. The hearing had some 2,000 people in attendance. It was followed by a boisterous rally outside on the lawn.

"We're saying to these leaders, 'You've got a year to show action, to give us a climate bill,'" says Sean Miller, an Energy Action Coalition representative and director of education for Earth Day Network. "We're targeting members of Congress who don't meet our needs."

By all accounts, the youth voices were heard over that long weekend, strategically timed a year before the 2008 Presidential elections. Congressman Edward Markey (D-MA), chair of the House Select Committee, and Speaker of the House Nancy Pelosi (D-CA) gave the students a platform and spoke before the Saturday night conference. Congresswoman Lucille Roybal-Allard (C-CA) spent the better part of an hour talking about pollution issues with Los Angeles teacher Andrew Stephens and his "Mean Green Team" high school students, many of whom had just flown in on the first plane rides of their lives.

And the momentum, fanned in large part by college students, is carrying global warming from the sleeper issue it was in the 2006 midterm elections to a defining campaign talking point. In May, energy independence and global warming trailed only health care as America's most important domestic challenge, according to Democratic pollster Stan Greenberg. And by last October, the only issue appearing more than global warming in campaign ads was the Iraq war.

Back in Maryland, the Public Interest Research Group (PIRG) New Voters Project set up shop in a Powershift lobby, with life-sized cardboard cutouts of the candidates so young voters could take digital pictures while holding aloft word balloons reading, "What's Your Plan?" in reference to global warming solutions.

"This is how democracy works," says New Voters Project Director Ellynne Bannon, who says PIRG advocates a non-partisan, peer-to-peer method of civic engagement. In 2004, a year after the program's launch, the group registered more than a half million new voters, and those numbers have grown with each election year. "We hope it makes candidates realize it's worth it to go to campuses and not just appear on [online social networking site] Facebook," Bannon says.

Campus sustainability initiatives—from local food in cafeterias (see sidebar), to renewable energy courses, to wind and solar installations—are multiplying fast. Schools are polishing their green credentials in an effort to outshine other schools, and they are swapping success stories online and in person.

At press time, 458 school presidents had signed the American College and University President's Climate Commitment, which requires schools to have a plan to go carbon neutral within two years of signing. Nina Rizzo, the California Freedom from Oil campus organizer for Global Exchange, is encouraged by the progress students are making, and the university system in California is a leader in environmental initiatives from LEED-certified buildings to bicycle lanes, but she has yet to see "radical action" that parallels the civil rights struggles of the 1960s. "The movement is potent, but we're not there yet," Rizzo says. "I don't think people are angry enough yet."

Michael M'Gonigle, author of Planet U, a professor of environmental law and policy at the University of Victoria and a co-founder of Greenpeace International, agrees that the incremental changes he's seeing on campuses have yet to resemble the sustained force of 1960s radicalism.

"Certainly in the states, it's not in the public consciousness that there is this movement," says M'Gonigle. "But the anxiety about climate change is really palpable—students feel it. And there's an overarching social anxiety, something we have to act on. It's not like stopping the deployment of anti-ballistic missiles in Europe. It's local. We can do something right here and right now at this institution."

Remaking a Campus

Outside the stately brick UM building that served as the conference's main hub, three students from Florida Atlantic University relaxed on the grass, passing time between workshops. As students at a beachfront school, they see the realities of global warming outside their dorm windows in the eroding sand and freakish storms. Nicole Henken, a freshman, says, "Beaches around us are having to ship in sand because it's so washed out from rain and storm activity."

"They dredge it from the ocean and put it on the beach," adds Veronica LaFranchise, another freshman, who hopes to major in marine biology and work on removing trash from the nation's waterways.

The three say that although Al Gore's documentary, An Inconvenient Truth, didn't inspire them to fight climate change, it reinforced their understanding of an environment gone wrong. "Al Gore made it accessible to people," says sophomore Jen Cohen, who showed the film to her less environmentally aware mom. "You're not a crazy hippie if you believe in global warming."

Students are beginning to feel their collective power, and they are pushing for immediate changes in the way their colleges and universities operate. They see their campuses as perfect microcosms for society at large, places where they can change everything from basic policies to education directions to how energy is purchased and recycling handled. They can then take these lessons out into the world at large.

"All the power dynamics are there on a campus," says 26-year-old Matt Stern, campus organizer with the Chesapeake Climate Action Network. "The constituencies and organizing potential are concentrated. It's a great learning ground for students."

Stern's group deals with a regional coalition of 10 schools in Virginia and Maryland, focusing on specific campaigns. Last year, they rallied hundreds of students to pressure administrators at Johns Hopkins University to sign the president's climate commitment. While many larger schools are shying away from the agreement and opting to write their own policies, says Stern, the formal commitment has teeth. "We focus on institutional policies," he says, "for buses to run on biodiesel or for zero-percent carbon emissions."

Judy Walton, acting executive director of the Association for the Advancement of Sustainability in Higher Education (AASHE), says student activism has been critical in getting schools to look at their greenhouse gas emissions and find solutions. "Student action is one of the driving forces on many campuses," Walton says. "There are a few cases where the administration took the lead, but that's rare."

Beyond the Campus Confines

"I was a student at Penn State," says Maura Cowley, now the national campaign director for the Sierra Student Coalition. "And when [the college] bought five percent wind energy, we changed the market price in Pennsylvania. . . . We changed the price of wind power and changed the whole dynamic and evolution of the state's energy."

According to the Environmental Protection Agency (EPA) "Green Power Partnership" rankings, Penn State now ranks third among schools for green power purchasing, with 20 percent of its total electricity use coming from wind power. Its fellow state school, the University of Pennsylvania, has seen the light on green energy, too, and is now second, at 29 percent. New York University is number one, with an incredible 100 percent of its electricity use coming from wind power.

"It's surprising how important colleges and universities are as regional players," says M'Gonigle. "Any town of 50,000 or more has a college. Take out the college and it's like cutting off a limb. They are big corporations with economic clout."

When students decide to get active on regional issues, they have the power to force attention on environmental issues, and even change the course of local policy. A coalition of students in Virginia has teamed up to fight a new Dominion "clean coal" plant in Wise County, Virginia. The plant is slated for construction on a former surface coal mine site, and the students are arguing for clean energy instead. "No new coal" has become a battle cry among college greens, particularly those in the Southeast confronted with the devastation of mountaintop removal mining, which leads to polluted water, filthy air and land stripped of life.

"We are working together with many other individuals and grass-roots organizations to send a message to the energy corporations that we don't want any new coal plants," says Ryan Hasty, a junior at Emory and Henry College in southwestern Virginia, who became president of The Greens on his campus last year. "It's an old technology, it's very dirty and it isn't worth sacrificing the health and well-being of those who live near the mine sites and the power plants. Not to mention the destruction of some of the cleanest and most biodiverse waterways in the world."

While some of the students involved in the anti-coal campaign live in Virginia, they hadn't confronted the realities of mountaintop removal mining: the eerie, denuded landscape interrupted only by polluted headwater streams. "Before I got to James Madison University," says sophomore Vicente Rosa, "I didn't know much about environmental issues." Once there, he joined the Earth Club, which together with such local groups as Appalachian Voices, is educating people about coal's effects and working to stop new plants before they're built. "Coal is one of the top polluters," says Rosa. "We're telling Dominion we want clean energy."

As research sites, colleges bring innovation and expertise to those expanding clean technologies. Ten Texas universities joined forces with government agencies and corporate partners as the Lone Star Wind Alliance, which last June won a $2 million Department of Energy grant for a large-scale wind-turbine and blade-testing facility. Oil giant BP donated 22 acres just north of Corpus Christi for the effort. Texas beat California to become the leading national producer of wind power in 2006, and researchers at the University of Texas in Austin are developing ways to overcome the variability and intermittent nature of wind power to make it truly competitive with fossil fuels.

Arizona State University's clean cities vision comes from the top down. ASU President Michael Crow came to the campus from Columbia University committed to making the university a leader in sustainability. Five years later, the university's Global Institute for Sustainability pushes students and faculty to find solutions to resource depletion in water-deprived, population-dense cities like Phoenix, which is a stand-in for many cities worldwide coping with desertification (a threat to some 20 percent of the world's population). "We see campuses as living labs," says Bonny Bentzin of ASU's Global Institute of Sustainability. "In Phoenix, we're on the frontline as one the fastest-growing communities in the U.S. We have to figure out how not only how to have a sustainable water supply, but how to manage air quality."

Book Learning

There are changes underway inside the classrooms, too. Duke University has a new Energy and Environment track (combining business and environmental management) that prepares students to remake their worlds in concrete ways. Erika Lovelace of Duke's Office of Enrollment says, "The degree prepares you to come up with sustainable ideas to assist local communities."

At the University of Colorado in Boulder, 22-year-old environmental studies major Paul Chase says working environmental education into the broader curriculum is a major campus goal. He's the only student undergrad represented on the Chancellor's Committee on Energy, Environment and Sustainability. Making the sprawling university the first of its size to go climate neutral (tentatively scheduled for 2060) is only one of many of the committee's goals.

Chase talks about changing the core curriculum at Boulder, calling it "a huge undertaking, which involves expanding environmental education into all aspects of the university and to every student."

For some students, reforming the course offerings isn't splashy enough. Whether launching a recycling program or passing out petitions for clean energy purchases, they want to see changes made now. "It's a challenge to balance long-term goals with the students that want to see immediate returns," says Bentzin.

Students are looking for the kind of impact made by the University of California's solar energy commitment in 2003, which involved installing 10 megawatts of renewable energy (equivalent to power used by 5,000 homes) across UC's 10 campuses. The schools also pledged to purchase 20 percent of their electricity from clean energy sources by 2017 (enough to power 26,000 homes). UC Santa Cruz is going far beyond that, pledging to purchase 100 percent renewable energy for its campus.

Such strides helped motivate students at other colleges, such as the University of Colorado in Denver, which was inspired to build the fifth-largest campus solar project. Corey Nadler, a campus organizer with the Colorado Public Interest Research Group (CoPIRG), spoke before a rapt audience in one Powershift workshop, describing his school's solar victory. The activists gathered 2,000 student signatures, gained administrative support, and then, says the curly-haired spokesperson, "The public utilities commission threatened to veto the project." So students got the media involved and won their case. It was a huge effort just to offset three and half percent of the school's energy output to solar. But the students had made visible strides, with rooftop solar panels as proof of their victory.

Greener than U.

This is a race not only against the inevitable march of climate change, but against other colleges and universities eager to tout their green accomplishments. A school without a sustainability office seems hopelessly outdated, a passive part of the old economy instead of a vital part of the new. Signing climate commitments, university presidents are bestowed an immediate badge of honor, one that shows they know the importance of their place in the new world.

"We're really pushing to become a leader, a model, of how a large university becomes carbon neutral," says Chase at the University of Colorado, Boulder. "It's vital to have that competition. And it's a great thing when you're competing for the right reasons, to be the cleanest, not the richest, school."

Some schools have already attained "green cred" through their single-minded focus on sustainability, an easier feat at a small, liberal arts school. Middlebury College in Vermont offers the complete package, from its natural landscape design to its fully composted dining hall waste to its "yellow bike" borrowing system for on-campus commutes. The school's $11 million biomass facility is scheduled to open in late fall, with the capacity to burn enough wood chips to displace the use of $1 million gallons of fuel oil, cutting the school's fuel needs in half. And it's a gasification system, turning wood to gas that's then burned, reducing the amount of sulphur oxide and nitrous oxide in the emissions. The school's existing power plant is already a cogeneration system, heating the campus with steam, but the biomass facility will take Middlebury's sustainability commitment to the next level. Jack

Byrne, Middlebury's campus sustainability coordinator, says the bio-mass facility is one part of the big picture vision at the college.

"More than likely, wood and biomass will become an increasingly sought-after source of energy," says Byrne. In years to come, Middlebury may be able to bypass wood altogether in favor of growing its own willow shrubs. School officials traveled to the State University of New York's School of Forestry to learn about how willow (a hardy perennial that requires minimal fertilizer and pesticides to grow) can be used as a fuel source. The school has a 10-acre test plot underway.

All of this is helping Middlebury reach one of the most ambitious goals any college has set: carbon neutrality by 2016. "It's not an easy goal," Byrne admits, but students have been relentless on the issue. "The general approach is renewables, conservation and efficiency," Byrne says, "and, as a last resort, carbon offsets."

Minnesota's Carleton College is another small liberal arts school with green might, installing its own wind turbine on campus, engaging in "dorm wars" to encourage low energy use, and committing to green building retrofits and composting all food waste. The college's 1.65-megawatt wind turbine is the first utility-grade installation by a college. Mathias Bell, an environmental associate, says the turbine has become a powerful force on campus. "It's a looming presence," Bell says, "and it's an incredible educational tool."

A similarly focused school, Maine's College of the Atlantic, has achieved near perfection in its student-led green pursuits, eliminating or offsetting all its greenhouse gas emissions, supporting on-campus watershed preservation and following the highest standards of green building in all new campus structures.

Really the Best?

Not surprisingly, the media is surfing the wave with lists of "10 Coolest Schools" (Sierra Magazine) or "15 Green Colleges and Universities" (Grist) and "50 Green Colleges" (Kiwi Magazine). Most attempt to rank schools based on a nebulous collection of green attributes, including food served, classes taught, buildings built and transportation supported. Rather than pointing out the positive heights colleges and universities are reaching, these lists tend to create a furor among schools that were left out.

AASHE has developed the Sustainability, Tracking, Assessment and Rating System (STARS) to serve as a guideline for measuring schools based on a wide range of green credentials. "People are angry about those lists," says Walton, "They're often meaningless and there's a lack of transparency."

The STARS assessment will function like the LEED rating system for buildings, relying on schools to submit documentation proving their "green" merits. That information will be made available to the public online. Initially, STARS will not be third-party verified.

For the past two years, the Sustainable Endowments Institute has had a separate rating system, looking at the 200 public and private universities with the highest endowments, and giving them grades based on shareholder engagement and endowment transparency as well as on food and recycling, green building and other typical green benchmarks. While their statistics show that campus initiatives are growing, with nearly 45 percent of schools committed to fight climate change, endowments to sustainable causes have not kept pace.

But it is not only in making physical retrofits, purchasing wind power and adding bike lanes that these schools do the essential work of curing the nation's fossil-fuel dependency. It is in educating students about the importance of creating and supporting a new green economy and turning out leaders. In that respect, the campus sustainability movement has been a resounding success.

"We really see our futures at stake," says Stern. "We have to nail this problem. Everything else is negated."

QUESTIONS

1. What rhetorical strategies that open the selection are effective and why? Why does the Earth Network want to change the policies of Congress? According to the Network, which particular issues are the most detrimental to our nation's sustainability?

2. Why does Belli compare the civil rights movement with the environmental movement? What are the differences in the motivational strategies of each? Do you think her comparison makes sense?

3. Belli claims that Middlebury College in Vermont has the most eco-sustainable campus in the country. What have they done to create their sustainability? How has and will Middlebury's enactment of sustainability affect other schools, according to the author? Does she provide enough evidence to support her claims about Middlebury?

DIFFERING PERSPECTIVES: DOES HIGH STAKES UNIFORM ACHIEVEMENT TESTING DO MORE HARM THAN GOOD?

Roderick Paige

"Testing Makes for Progress in Learning"

Roderick "Rod" Paige (b. 1933) grew up in a home of educators and dedicated his life to the belief that education equalizes opportunity. He earned a bachelor's degree from Jackson State University in Mississippi and a master's degree and an Ed.D. from Indiana University Bloomington. After working for many years in educational administration positions, he was the first African-American to be chosen to serve as the United States secretary of education (2001–2005). Paige continues to be involved in educational curricula and writes and speaks about his beliefs. The article that follows presents his point of view on the impact on student progress of the achievement testing required under the No Child Left Behind Act.

Q: Are the tests required by No Child Left Behind making schools more accountable? Yes: Testing has raised students' expectations, and progress in learning is evident nationwide

Testing is a part of life. In fact, testing starts at the beginning stages of life: The moment we are born, neonatologists measure our reflexes and responses and give us what is called an Apgar score on a scale of one to 10. As we grow up, our teachers test us in school and we take other standardized tests that compare us with the rest of the nation's students. We are tested if we want to practice a trade whether it is to get a cosmetology license, a driver's permit or pilot training. And often we are retested and retested again to show that our skills remain at peak level.

In short, tests exist for a reason. In the case of a doctor, they certify that he or she is capable of practicing medicine. In the case of a teacher, they show that he or she has the knowledge to help children learn a given subject. And in the case of a student, they demonstrate whether a child has indeed learned and understood the lesson or the subject.

At their core, tests are simply tools they subjectively measure things. In education, they are particularly important because they pinpoint where students are doing well and where they need help. In fact, testing has been a part of education since the first child sat behind the first desk. Assessments are an important component of educational accountability; in other words, they tell us whether the system is performing as it should. They diagnose, for the teacher, the parent and the student, any problems so that they can be fixed.

Educational accountability is the cornerstone of the No Child Left Behind Act, President George W. Bush's historic initiative that is designed to raise student performance across America. The law embraces a number of commonsense ways to reach that goal: accountability for results, empowering parents with information about school performance and giving them options, more local control, and flexibility to tailor the law to local circumstances.

No Child Left Behind is a revolutionary change, challenging the current educational system and helping it to improve. It aims to challenge the status quo by pushing the educational system into the 21st century so that American students leave school better prepared for higher education or the workforce.

Educational accountability is not a new concept several states have been instituting accountability reforms for years. No Child Left Behind builds on the good work of some of these states that were at the forefront of the reform movement. The truth is that this law has one goal: to get all children reading and doing math at grade level. It's that simple. The law itself is a federal law, but it is nothing more than a framework. Elementary and secondary education are the traditional province of state and local governments, which is why the specific standards, tests and most of the other major tenets of the law are designed and implemented by the state departments of education, because they are in the best position to assess local expectations and parental demands.

The federal role in education also is not a new concept. There is a compelling national interest in education, which is why the federal government is involved and has been for some time. The federal government has stepped in to correct overt unfairness or inequality, starting with measures to enforce civil rights and dismantle segregation in the wake of the Brown v. Board of Education case (a Supreme Court decision that is now 50 years old). The federal government's first major legislative involvement in education goes back to 1965 with the Elementary and Secondary Education Act, which marked the first federal aid given to school districts with large percentages of children living in poverty. In 2001 the law was reauthorized as the No Child Left Behind Act (NCLB), which preserves the states' traditional role but asks them to set standards for accountability and teacher quality, thereby improving the quality, inclusively, fairness and justice of American education.

NCLB focuses on facts, not just feelings and hunches. It is no longer acceptable simply to believe schools are improving without knowing for certain whether they are. As Robert F. Kennedy asked back in 1965 when this federal education law was first debated, "What happened to the children? [How do we know] whether they can read or not?" With new state-accountability systems and tests we will have the full picture.

Let's examine what we do know. According to the nation's report card (the National Assessment of Educational Progress, or NAEP), only one in six African-Americans and one in five Hispanics are proficient in reading by the time they are high-school seniors. NAEP math scores are even worse: Only 3 percent of blacks and 4 percent of Hispanics are testing at the proficient level. This is the status quo result of a decades-old education system before the NCLB.

Of the 10 fastest-growing occupations in the United States, the top five are computer-related, which are jobs that require high-level skills. High-school dropouts need not apply. We are all concerned about outsourcing jobs overseas, and we should note that the unemployment rate for high-school dropouts is almost twice that of those with high-school diplomas (7.3 percent compared with 4.2 percent) and nearly four times that of college graduates (7.3 percent vs. 2.3 percent). For young black men the unemployment rate is a staggering 26 percent. Even a high-school diploma isn't the cure: A vast majority of employers sadly expect that a high-school graduate will not write clearly or have even fair math skills. No wonder a recent study claimed a high-school diploma has become nothing more than a "certificate of attendance." For millions of children, they were given a seat in the school but not an education of the mind.

It is clear that our system as a whole is not preparing the next generation of workers for the global economy ahead of them. As Federal Reserve Chairman Alan Greenspan noted recently: "We need to be forward looking in order to adapt our educational system to the evolving needs of the economy and the realities of our changing society. It is an effort that should not be postponed." That's why I am so passionate about making these historic reforms and drawing attention to the issue.

The old system the status quo is one that we must fight to change. That's why the president and both parties in Congress understood the urgency of the situation and put NCLB into law. They also ensured that the money would be there to get the job done, providing the means to states fully to implement the law; indeed, there's been 41 percent more federal support for education since President Bush took office.

But some defenders of the status quo have aired complaints about the law, saying its requirements are unreasonable and the tests are arbitrary. The bottom line is, these cynics do not believe in the worth of all children they have written some of them off. You can guess which ones fall into that category. This pessimism relegates these children to failure. The president aptly refers to this phenomenon as the "soft bigotry of low expectations." But NCLB says the excuses must stop all children must be given a chance.

NCLB helps us zero in on student needs. With little information about individual students' abilities with different skills, most teachers must rely on a "buckshot" approach to teaching their classes, aiming for the middle and hoping to produce a decent average. With an emphasis on scientifically based research techniques and effective use of information, NCLB helps fund programs that teachers can use to identify specific areas of weakness among their students.

For example, the Granite School District in Utah used Title I funds (support for economically disadvantaged students) to procure the "Yearly

Progress Pro" computer program. Now a fourth-grade class at Stansbury Elementary School visits the computer lab for a quick 15-minute test each week; the teacher walks out with a printout identifying changes in performance in specific skill areas over the week.

Child by child, the improvements add up. For example, a study by the Council of Great City Schools examined the recent gains in large metropolitan school systems. The Beating the Odds IV report showed that since NCLB has been implemented; public-school students across the country have shown a marked improvement in reading. The report found that the achievement gap in reading and math between African-Americans and whites, and Hispanics and whites in large cities, is narrowing for fourth- and eighth-grade students. And it appears, according to the report, that our big-city schools are closing the gap at a faster rate than the statewide rate. Not only are the achievement gaps closing, the report states, but also math and reading achievement are improving.

For a concrete example of how the law is working, look at the Cheltenham School District in Pennsylvania, where leaders are disaggregating data to find the cracks they must fill. Drawing on test results, the district provides schools with specific information about each student's abilities and weaknesses in specific academic areas. Schools receive this data in easily accessible electronic formats in July, before the students arrive, giving them time to plan for the year. Now teachers can account for the effectiveness of their strategies and, if they are not working for some students, adapt to alternatives.

These findings are especially significant because research shows that it is often the students in the large-city schools who need the most help and face the greatest odds. Clearly, this report demonstrates that if you challenge students, they will rise to the occasion. This concept is at the fundamental core of NCLB because we can no longer mask our challenges in the aggregate of our successes. We must make sure that all children, regardless of their skin color and Zip codes, have the opportunity to receive a high-quality education.

While the press focuses on the complaints of the unwilling, whole communities are taking on the challenge of accountability and achieving great results. Perhaps my favorite example is in the Peck School in rural Michigan, where I visited in late March and found that the school culture had embraced the accountability treatment. A huge poster hangs in the hallway of the school emblazoned with No Child Left Behind! Showing creativity and commitment, the school launched a tutoring program, began intervening sooner with low-performing students, and even created a peer-counseling program to address the conflicts that often spill into the classroom and distract from learning. Everyone in the Peck School is taking responsibility for the students' education, truly fostering the character of good citizenship.

It is time to think of the children and to give them what they need. It is time to work to make the law successful. We need to create an American public educational system that matches the vision of this law, where we strive for excellence without exclusion, where our children achieve greatness rather than greatly underachieving, and where 10 or 20 years from now a new generation of adults realize that we gave them a better life because we had courage and conviction now.

QUESTIONS

1. Although Paige argues for the value and validity of testing, do you think that he leaves out any important aspects of learning—some of which may have already been mentioned in this chapter? Why does Paige think that education must be controlled on a national level? What do his statistics about the least advanced students suggest to you?
2. Do you think that the No Children Left Behind program really worked? Use examples and evidence to support your point of view. Your values will help you to shape a position.
3. Have a class debate that focuses on the best ways to educate children and youth. Use the two articles that are juxtaposed here, as well as research and evidence from your own experiences and those of friends and family, to support your point of view.

David C. Berliner and Sharon L. Nichols

"High-Stakes Testing is Putting the Nation at Risk"

David C. Berliner is the Regents' professor of education at Arizona State University, in Tempe, and a past president of the American Educational Research Association. Sharon L. Nichols is an assistant professor of educational psychology at the University of Texas at San Antonio. They are the co-authors of Collateral Damage: How High-Stakes Testing Corrupts America's Schools, *published by Harvard Education Press. In the article that follows, they argue against the "No Child Left Behind" federal act that enforces national standards for testing children and the effectiveness of schools.*

In his 2007 State of the Union address, President Bush claimed success for the federal No Child Left Behind Act. "Students are performing better in reading and math, and minority students are closing the achievement gap," he said, calling on Congress to reauthorize this "good law." Apparently, the president sees in No Child Left Behind what he sees in Iraq: evidence that his programs are working. But, as with Iraq, a substantial body of evidence challenges his claim.

We believe that this federal law, now in its sixth year, puts American public school students in serious jeopardy. Extensive reviews of empirical and theoretical work, along with conversations with hundreds of educators across the country, have convinced us that if Congress does not act in this session to fundamentally transform the law's accountability provision, young people and their educators will suffer serious and longterm consequences. If the title were not already taken, our thoughts on this subject could be headlined "A Nation at Risk."

We note in passing that only people who have no contact with children could write legislation demanding that every child reach a high level of performance in three subjects, thereby denying that individual differences exist. Only those same people could also believe that all children would reach high levels of proficiency at precisely the same rate of speed.

Validity problems in the testing of English-language learners and special education students also abound, but we limit our concerns in this essay to the No Child Left Behind law's reliance on high-stakes testing. The stakes are high when students' standardized-test performance results in grade retention or failure to graduate from high school. The stakes are high when teachers and administrators can lose their jobs or, conversely, receive large bonuses for student scores, or when humiliation or praise for teachers and schools occurs in the press as a result of test scores. This federal law requires such high-stakes testing in all states.

More than 30 years ago, the eminent social scientist Donald T. Campbell warned about the perils of measuring effectiveness via a single, highly consequential indicator: "The more any quantitative social indicator is used for social decision-making," he said, "the more subject it will be to corruption pressures and the more apt it will be to distort and corrupt the social processes it is intended to monitor." High-stakes testing is exactly the kind of process Campbell worried about, since important judgments about student, teacher, and school effectiveness often are based on a single test score. This exaggerated reliance on scores for making judgments creates conditions that promote corruption and distortion. In fact, the overvaluation of this single indicator of school success often compromises the validity of the test scores themselves. Thus, the scores we end up praising and condemning in the press and our legislatures are actually untrustworthy, perhaps even worthless.

Campbell's law is ubiquitous, and shows up in many human endeavors. Businesses, for example, regularly become corrupt as particular indicators are deemed important in judging success or failure. If stock prices are the indicator of a company's success, for example, then companies like Enron, Qwest, Adelphia, and WorldCom manipulate that indicator to make sure they look good. Lives and companies are destroyed as a result. That particular indicator of business success became untrustworthy as both it and the people who worked with it were corrupted.

Similarly, when the number of criminal cases closed is the indicator chosen to judge the success of a police department, two things generally happen: More trials are brought against people who may be innocent or, with a promise of lighter sentences, deals are made with accused criminals to get them to confess to crimes they didn't commit.

When the indicators of success and failure in a profession take on too much value, they invariably are corrupted. Those of us in the academic world know that when researchers are judged primarily by their publication records, they have occasionally fabricated or manipulated data. This is just another instance of Campbell's law in action.

We have documented hundreds of examples of the ways in which high-stakes testing corrupts American education in a new book, *Collateral Damage*. Using Campbell's law as a framework, we found examples of administrators and teachers who have cheated on standardized tests. Educators, acting just like other humans do, manipulate the indicators used to judge their success or failure when their reputations, employment, or significant salary bonuses are related to those indicators.

The law makes all who engage in compliance activities traitors to their own profession. It forces education professionals to ignore the testing standards that they have worked so hard to develop.

We found examples of administrators who would falsify school test data or force low-scoring students out of school in their quest to avoid public humiliation. We documented the distortion of instructional values when teachers focused on "bubble" kids—those on the cusp of passing the test—at the expense of the education of very low or very high scorers. We found instances where callous disregard for student welfare had replaced compassion and humanity, as when special education students were forced to take a test they had failed five times, or when a student who had recently suffered a death in the family was forced to take the test anyway.

Because so much depends on how students perform on tests, it should not be surprising that, as one Florida superintendent noted, "When a low-performing child walks into a classroom, instead of being seen as a challenge, or an opportunity for improvement, for the first time since I've been in education, teachers are seeing [that child] as a liability." Shouldn't we be concerned about a law that turns too many of the country's most morally admired citizens into morally compromised individuals?

We also documented the narrowing of the curriculum to just what is tested, and found a huge increase in time spent in test preparation instead of genuine instruction. We found teachers concerned about their loss of morale, the undercutting of their professionalism, and the problem of disillusionment among their students. Teachers and administrators told us repeatedly how they were not against accountability, but that they were being held responsible for their students' performance regardless of other factors that may affect it. Dentists aren't held responsible for cavities and physicians for the onset of diabetes when youngsters don't brush their teeth, or eat too much junk food, they argue.

Teachers know they stand a better chance of being successful where neighborhoods and families are healthy and communicate a sense of efficacy, where incomes are both steady and adequate, and where health-care and child-care programs exist. So the best of them soon move to schools with easier-to-teach students. This is no way to close the achievement gap.

Dozens of assessment experts have argued eloquently and vehemently that the high-stakes tests accompanying the implementation of the No Child Left Behind Act are psychometrically inadequate for the decisions that must be made about students, teachers, and schools. Furthermore, the testing standards of the American Educational Research Association are being violated in numerous ways by the use of high-stakes tests to comply with the law. The law, therefore, makes all who engage in compliance activities traitors to their own profession. It forces education professionals to ignore the testing standards that they have worked so hard to develop. We wonder, would the federal government treat members of the American Medical Association or the National Academy of Sciences with such disdain?

In reauthorization hearings for the law, members of Congress should abandon high-stakes testing and replace it with an accountability system that is more reasonable and fair.

What might such a system look like?

A move to more "formative" assessments and an abandonment of our heavy commitment to "summative" assessments would be welcome. Assessment for learning, as opposed to assessment of learning, has produced some impressive gains in student achievement in other countries, and ought to be tried here. Likewise, the use of an inspectorate—an agency that sends expert observers into schools—has proved itself useful in other countries, and could also help improve schools in the United States.

End-of-course exams designed by teachers, as some states are now offering, increase teachers' commitment to the testing program and, if the teachers get to score the tests, can also be a great professional-development opportunity. There are other alternatives to high-stakes testing, as well.

Our research informs us that high-stakes testing is hurting students, teachers, and schools. It is putting the nation at risk. By restricting the education of our young people and substituting for it training for performing well on high-stakes examinations, we are turning America into a nation of test-takers, abandoning our heritage as a nation of thinkers, dreamers, and doers.

QUESTIONS

1. Explain how the authors' use the expertise of Donald T. Campbell to support the article's argument. How does Campbell add ethos and credibility to the argument?

2. Why do Berliner and Nichols oppose testing and evaluation of students as indicators of their success or failure? Why do they believe that

testing and evaluation corrupt academic institutions, businesses, and professional corporations? To what extent do you agree with them and why? Use examples to support your point of view.

3. What solutions to relieve the negative affects of testing on students, teachers, and administrators do Berliner and Nichols suggest? What solutions do you think would help?

Revisioning Immigration

Introduction

Our fourth chapter examines the controversial issue of Americans' attitudes towards and attempts to shape patterns of immigration, beginning with reporter Carolyn Hochhead's study of the unpredictable results of so-called "immigration reform" from the early years of our nation to the present. By the twentieth century, the dominant concept of American immigrant identity was one of assimilation, as implied by the metaphor of the melting pot, in which, as Crevecoeur put it, "individuals of all nations are melted into a new race of man," becoming uniquely American. However, by the latter decades of the century, the argument over American identity was transformed into a desire for recognition of each unique culture. A new sense of diversity began to be honored, one that even liberal writers like Arthur Schlesinger resisted, thinking that the new multiculturalism could create disunity and strife between ethnic groups and communities.

With the turn of the twenty-first century, the idea of the multicultural nation has become more accepted, although the older concept of assimilation continues to be honored, along with what sociologist Herbert Gans terms "the American kaleidoscope," whose constantly shifting patterns of intermarriage and new migrations vary from decade to decade. Like a kaleidoscope, each new pattern of immigration changes the overall picture of America.

Representing the voices of new immigrants from radically different ends of the ladder of affluence and prior education are East Indians, a small but highly successful group of skilled immigrants; in contrast, Mexican-Americans may or may not possess the skills necessary for a job with a future. In his essay in this chapter, Dinesh D'Sousa, originally from Bombay, India, writes idealistically of the advantages of freedom for middle-class immigrants who accept traditional American values. Conservative columnist Linda Chavez, however, notes that recent Mexican-American immigrants with little education or job skills have encountered difficulties in making the transition to becoming successful citizens in this country, although they have been aided by their strong sense of family values. Alejandro Portes, in contrast to these two more optimistic authors, notes in his essay in this chapter that the children of new, uneducated immigrants have a harder job today of achieving a good education and ascendancy to good jobs than those of previous generations of "assimilated" immigrants.

Our "Differing Perspectives" essays in this chapter comment on a movement for noncitizen immigrant voting that has arisen because of the long waits encountered by many recent immigrants attempting to attain citizenship status even though they have lived for a number of years in the same community and are raising families there. CUNY professor and author Ron Hayduk argues in favor of such voting rights in order to give noncitizen immigrants a voice in their communities, as was the case until the 1920s in many municipalities. In contrast, CUNY professor Stanley Renshon argues that such voting rights laws would unfairly blur the line between citizens' rights and those of noncitizens, and thereby provide less motivation to become a full citizen.

CAROLYN LOCHHEAD

"A Legacy of the Unforeseen"

Carolyn Lochhead graduated from the University of California at Berkeley and received an M.A. in journalism at Columbia University. She has written for Reason and Insight Magazine and has been the Washington bureau correspondent for the San Francisco Chronicle since 1991, reporting on Congress, political campaigns, economic, energy, and high tech issues, as well as immigration concerns in feature stories and in her Politics Blog at sfgate.com. In the following article, Lochhead provides a short history of U.S. immigration "reform" programs that have attempted to create strict limits on numbers for some immigrants and preferences for others— efforts which, Lochhead argues, have often produced totally unanticipated effects that have given rise to continual dissent and debate while also helping to create the diverse nation we have today.

Many of the most radical changes in the origins and numbers of America's vast flow of immigrants were unintentionally set in motion, experts say, by politicians who expected an entirely different result. As for the complex immigration overhaul now before Congress, they say history's lesson from a century of immigration reform is: Fasten your seat belts.

Unlike goods that move across borders, immigrants are people. An estimated 12 million are living illegally in the United States now. Another 1 million gain legal residence each year. Millions more are expected to seek entry in coming decades. No one can accurately predict how they might respond to the harsh border crackdown offered by the House or the Senate's plan to offer a path to citizenship for those here illegally and a guest worker program for new arrivals. "Human behavior has often defied the best-laid plans," said Daniel Tichenor, an immigration expert at Rutgers University.

The past is seldom consulted during today's debates, but previous attempts at reform provide a roadmap of how quickly things can go off course. It was a freshly minted young Massachusetts senator named Edward Kennedy who 40 years ago, in what he called "my maiden effort in the Senate," managed the landmark Immigration Act of 1965— at the time a minor coda to the Civil Rights Act. Today, Kennedy is the lead Democratic sponsor of the Senate's bipartisan bill.

The 1965 act eliminated the national origins quotas of the 1920s that favored northern Europe. It established visa preferences, still in place today, based on family unification and labor skills. It imposed the first numeric limits on Latin American immigration. And it forever changed the face of the United States. "Arguments against the bill were chiefly based on unsubstantiated fears that the bill would greatly increase annual immigration" and permit "excessive entry" of Asians and Africans, Kennedy wrote in 1966. The administration declared that "immigration will not be predominantly from Asia and Africa . . . indeed very few people from certain areas could even pay the cost of tickets to come here."

New migrants were expected to come from Italy, Greece and elsewhere in southern and eastern Europe that had been restricted by the national origins quotas, in addition to the British, Germans and Scandinavians who had dominated the quotas. Members of Congress asserted that hordes from other, darker continents would be unable to use family unification because they had no relatives in the United States. Oddly, the national origins quotas had ignored Mexico, leaving the Southern border all but open before 1965. By blocking southern and eastern Europeans, the quotas allowed Mexican laborers—and black farmers migrating from the South—to fill their shoes. Lawmakers considered Mexicans, unlike Poles or Italians, to be "returnable," Tichenor said. "If you want to look at the very early origins of illegal immigration as an issue in America, there it is."

"This bill that we will sign today is not a revolutionary bill," President Lyndon Johnson said on Liberty Island, Oct. 3, 1965. "It does not affect the lives of millions." Within five years, Asian immigration had quadrupled. The first new entrants came through occupational visas, then brought their families, beginning unanticipated network migrations, said New York University historian David Reimers. Within a decade, the proportion of European to Asian and Latin American immigrants had reversed.

"The way we teach students is we say, in general, the unintended consequences of immigration reforms are more important than the intended consequences," said Philip Martin, a farm immigration expert at UC Davis.

Two decades later, on Nov. 7, 1986, President Ronald Reagan signed another major immigration reform. It was intended to stop illegal immigration, then seen as a burgeoning problem, by providing a one-time amnesty and banning employers from knowingly hiring illegal workers. "Future generations of Americans will be thankful for our efforts to humanely regain control of our borders and thereby preserve the value of one of the most sacred possessions of our people, American citizenship," Reagan said.

Sen. Alan Simpson, R-Wyo., a chief sponsor of the bill, predicted employers would voluntarily comply with the new sanctions. Employer sanctions quickly collapsed under widespread document fraud. Enforcement, never vigorous, has dropped to negligible levels. "People following it at the time knew that employer sanctions would be a joke without secure means of identification," said Peter Skerry, a political scientist at Boston College. "Everyone was sort of holding their nose, blocking their eyes, doing the best that could get cobbled together."

Many experts believe that the current pattern of illegal immigration from Mexico and Central America was a consequence of the 1986 law's border tightening—followed by a tougher crackdown in 1996 that built fences in San Diego and El Paso. "The perverse effect has been to dramatically lower return migration out of the country," said Douglas S. Massey, a Princeton University sociologist and co-director of the Mexican Migration Project, a longitudinal survey of more than 18,000 migrants, the largest of its kind. "So we've transformed what was before 1986 a circular flow of workers into an increasingly settled population of families. We have actually accelerated the rate of undocumented population growth in the United States and shifted it from a relatively less costly population of male workers into a much more costly population of families."

The problem, he said, is that by making border crossing "very risky and unpleasant and increasingly expensive, you prolong the length of the trips, you reduce the probability of return migration, and you make it more likely that migrants . . . just hunker down and stay."

The rate of migration from Mexico has actually stayed constant for the last two decades, Massey found. But the rate of return has fallen by half, from 50 percent to 25 percent.

Ever since Ben Franklin expressed alarm that growing enclaves of Germans in Pennsylvania showed no signs of learning English, Americans have feared new immigrants and waxed sentimental about the previous stock.

"One lesson from the past is that Americans have tended to celebrate their immigrant past but dread the immigrant present," Tichenor said. "They have often viewed the newest arrivals as menacing or as threats to the national identity or economy. What's intriguing is they've usually made snap judgments in very short time horizons."

U.S. policy has lurched between bouts of expansion and restriction, often accompanied by strong racial animus. Borders were open until the late-1800s, when Congress passed the Chinese Exclusion Act in 1882. The 1907 "Gentlemen's Agreement" barred Japanese laborers—a deal made after the San Francisco school board ordered Japanese children to segregated Chinese schools. The Chronicle warned of an invasion of vagrant Japanese workers it deemed "bumptious, disagreeable and unreliable."

The government conducted mass deportations of Mexicans during the Great Depression and in a program labeled Operation Wetback in 1954, deporting an estimated 1.4 million people in all. Bad economic times, backlashes against new immigrants, or worries about national security often brought new restrictions. The national origins quotas of 1924 and 1928 followed the Great Migration at the turn of the century and the isolationism and fear of Bolshevik influences that followed World War I. Not even the Holocaust moved Congress to ease the restrictions.

Immigration often expanded after wars. The 1954 War Brides Act admitted 100,000 spouses after World War II and the Korean War. After the Vietnam War, more than 1 million Vietnamese, Laotians and Cambodians were admitted.

Expansions of immigration were often made over public objection. "I don't know a single poll going back to the 1930s that's indicated the public wants more immigrants to come in as opposed to fewer," said Reimers, the historian. Defiance of public opinion is a striking constant of immigration policy, long fascinating political scientists. Major expansions were often achieved through unorthodox alliances joining business, ethnic groups, free-market think tanks and churches.

Because immigration has often divided both political parties, interest groups wield extraordinary influence in the debates, said Stanford University political scientist Carolyn Wong, author of "Lobbying for Inclusion." Business lobbies wanting more labor visas, and ethnic groups wanting more family visas, often join powerful alliances.

California growers have long been key players. Congress created its first major guest worker plan in 1942, the Bracero ("strong-armed one") program for unskilled Mexicans to relieve temporary labor shortages during World War II. The program lasted 22 years, admitting 4.5 million workers. Rife with abuses, it was dropped around passage of the Civil Rights Act in 1964.

Many scholars believe the Bracero program laid the groundwork for today's illegal immigration by setting up labor networks in Mexico and distorting the U.S. farm economy. The program was plagued by red tape and graft on both sides of the border, inducing many Mexicans to cross illegally. By providing an ample labor force of often-abused workers, it induced growers to plant high-profit, labor-intensive crops. California growers were able to undercut Southern growers—producing California's vibrant fruit and vegetable industry which to this day relies on illegal migrants.

Because wages for migrant farm workers hardly rose, those who could leave for better paying jobs in cities fled the farms, requiring a constant flow of workers.

Growers warned that California's canned tomato industry would die and food prices would rise if the Bracero program ended. At its height in 1960, 45,000 farm workers harvested 2.2 million tons of processing tomatoes, said Martin of UC Davis. Six years after the program ended, a new oblong tomato was developed that could be machine harvested. By 1999, just 5,000 farm workers harvested 12 million tons of tomatoes and costs fell 54 percent, Martin found. The United Farm Workers union soon won a wage increase.

"I think they honestly didn't think change could happen near as quickly as it actually happened," Martin said.

Another expansion came in the 1990 immigration reform, including an obscure provision known as the "diversity visa" to fix perceived problems created by the 1965 act, then referred to by some as the "Irish Exclusion Act," according to a study by DePaul University political scientist Anna O. Law. Sponsored by Kennedy, the diversity visa was to redress the unforeseen problems of the 1965 law that had accidentally restricted immigration from "old seed sources of our heritage." But the diversity visa today admits 50,000 a year and is used heavily by Egyptians, Moroccans, Nigerians and other Africans.

"My own ballpark estimate is that in about 10 years, the country may not be so hysterical about Hispanics and may be more hysterical about Africans," Reimers said.

Evolution of Immigration Standards

The United States has always attracted large numbers of immigrants, often driven by economic and political events at home and abroad. Large expansions are usually followed by restrictions and retrenchment. U.S. laws have often led to unanticipated changes in the nature and composition of immigration flows.

Open borders: From the founding until the 1880s, borders were open under the Naturalization Act of 1790 that said, "Any alien, being a free white person, may be admitted to become a citizen of the United States." The Irish Potato Famine of the 1840s and 1850s and the California Gold Rush in 1849 drew many. From 1820 to 1880, Germany sent 3 million, Ireland 2.8 million and Britain 2 million. Chinese laborers began to arrive through San Francisco in the 1850s to build the railroads. The Great Wave of European migration peaked from 1900 to 1910, before the outbreak of World War I. From 1880 to 1930, 4.6 million arrived from Italy, 4 million from the Austro-Hungarian Empire, 3.3 million from Russia, 2.8 million from Germany, 2.3 million each from Canada and Britain, and 1.1 million from Sweden.

Chinese Exclusion Act 1882: Along with the 1907 "Gentlemen's Agreement" with Japan and the Alien Contract Labor laws of 1885 and 1887, this law banned Asian laborers from the United States. Congress also enacted a 50-cent head tax on all immigrants and banned entry of idiots, lunatics, convicts and persons likely to become a public charge.

National Origins Quotas 1924–1964: Enacted during an isolationist period after World War I and a backlash to the Great Wave of southern and eastern European migration. Quotas for each nationality were set at 2 percent of the number of foreign-born persons of that nationality residing in the United States in 1890, at attempt to lock in the ethnic makeup of the nation three decades earlier. All but 14 percent of the quotas went to northern and western Europe. The Western Hemisphere was exempt. Many Mexican laborers entered during this time to expand and maintain the railroads. The ban on immigrants from the "Asia-Pacific Triangle" continued until China became a U.S. ally in World War II. In 1952, many countries in Asia and Africa were given token allotments of 100 visas.

Bracero Program 1942–1964: Intended to meet farm labor shortages during World War II, the program lasted 22 years and brought in 4.5 million workers. It was little used during the war. It reached an annual peak of 450,000 workers in 1956. It proved unwieldy as well as harsh, and is widely believed to have laid the foundation for illegal Mexican immigration. It also gave birth to Cesar Chavez's United Farm Workers of America.

Immigration Act of 1965: Enacted shortly after the 1964 Civil Rights Act and 1965 Voting Rights Act in an era of liberalization, it abolished the national origins quotas. The Civil Rights Act includes the phrase "national origin" as a prohibited class of discrimination. Initiated by President John Kennedy, who wrote the pamphlet, "A Nation of Immigrants," it was carried to enactment after his assassination by his younger brother, Massachusetts Sen. Edward Kennedy. The act created the structure of today's immigration system based on preferences for family reunification and to a lesser extent job skills. It also established the first quotas on Western Hemisphere immigration. Sponsors expected the measure's family unification provisions to open immigration to Italians, Poles and other Europeans excluded by the national origins system. Instead, immigration shifted to Asia and Latin America.

Refugees: Used as a foreign policy tool during the Cold War and in response to wars. President Dwight Eisenhower used his parole power to admit 30,000 Hungarian refugees in 1956. President Lyndon Johnson welcomed Cubans upon signing the 1965 act, the same day he said, "The days of unlimited immigration are over." President Ronald

Reagan spurned refugees from El Salvador and Guatemala, where Marxist rebels were battling pro-U.S. governments, but welcomed Iranians. After the Vietnam War, more than 1 million Vietnamese, Laotians and Cambodians were admitted.

Immigration Reform and Control Act of 1986: Backed by President Ronald Reagan, this law aimed to reduce the number of illegal immigrants, whose population had reached 5 million, through a combination of amnesty and sanctions against employers who hired illegal aliens. Debate extended over a decade and was eerily parallel to today's. Employer sanctions soon failed because of rampant document fraud and a general unwillingness to enforce them. A special, looser amnesty for agriculture provided five times the number of legalizations anticipated. Many of the farm worker applications were believed to be fraudulent but immigration agents were too overwhelmed to check. No allowance was made for future flows, leading to further illegal entries. Many families remained in a "mixed status," partly legal and partly illegal. Congress extended the amnesty in 1990 to include immigrants' family members.

Diversity Lottery: Enacted in 1990 as an obscure provision of a wider bill addressing legal immigration, the "diversity visa" was intended to correct the exclusion of Irish and Italians by the 1965 act. By the time the law passed, however, Italians had lost interest in emigrating. The day it took effect, the Merrifield Post Office in Virginia, where applications were sent, received 1 million applications for 55,000 slots. A few years later, the Irish also lost interest as their economy boomed. Now used mainly by immigrants from Africa and the Middle East, the program works on a random lottery limited to countries that do not send large numbers of immigrants through other programs.

Illegal Immigration Reform and Immigrant Responsibility Act of 1996: A tough border crackdown initiated by the Republican-led Congress and signed by Democratic President Bill Clinton, the 1996 law was a backlash to the amnesty enacted 10 years earlier. Spending on border enforcement soared. Combined with 1986 border measures, border enforcement spending rose from $1 billion to nearly $5 billion a year. Spending for detention and removal grew more than 750 percent. Barriers were erected in San Diego and El Paso. The law had the unanticipated result of interrupting circular migration patterns and trapping Mexican immigrants in the United States. Illegal immigration continued to rise from the late 1990s to today.

—*Sources:* Statue of Liberty-Ellis Island Foundation; U.S. Citizenship and Immigration Services; David Reimers, "Unwelcome Strangers: American Identity and the Turn against Immigration;" Philip Martin, UC Davis; Migration Policy Institute.

QUESTIONS

1. What conclusions can you draw from Lochhead's historical analysis of the unanticipated consequences of changing immigration reforms? Why have those consequences been so different from the intended ones, in your view?
2. How have the changing reforms exploited and made life harder for immigrants? Give two examples from Lochhead's analysis that support the fact that immigrants are being exploited. How have the reforms, often stemming from prejudice against certain groups, magnified certain forms of ethnic isolation and racism?
3. Would you agree that the diverse population growth created by immigration has helped this nation? Give specific examples for your perspective from the way the nation as a whole, your state in particular, and your own life have or have not benefited.

ARTHUR SCHLESINGER, JR.

"The Return of the Melting Pot"

Arthur M. Schlesinger, Jr. (1917–2007) was a prominent political historian who attended Harvard University and became a professor of history there (1946–1961). He also taught at the Graduate Center of City University of New York, where he was appointed Albert Schweitzer Professor of Humanities in 1966. A special assistant and advisor to the Kennedy Administration, Schlesinger was a strong advocate of Kennedy's approach to government, writing speeches for several Democratic presidential candidates and writing a book about the Kennedy administration in A Thousand Days: John F. Kennedy in the White House *(1965). Schlesinger criticized the emerging politics of multiculturalism in* The Disuniting of America: Reflections on a Multicultural Society *(1991). His last book was* War and the American Presidency *(2004). The following essay, "The Return of the Melting Pot" (1990), argues that the multicultural movement contradicts the* e pluribus unum *(out of many, one) or "melting pot" philosophy of immigration that America was founded upon.*

"What then is the American, this new man?" a French immigrant asked two centuries ago. Hector St. John de Crevecoeur gave the classic answer to his own question. "He is an American, who, leaving behind him all his ancient prejudices and manners, receives new ones from the new mode of life he has embraced, the new government he obeys, and the new rank he holds. . . . Here individuals of all nations are melted into a new race of man."

The conception of America as a transforming nation, banishing old identities and creating a new one, prevailed through most of American history. It was famously reformulated by Israel Zangwill, an English writer of Russian Jewish origin, when he called America "God's crucible, the great melting pot where all the faces of Europe are melting and re-forming." Most people who came to America expected to become Americans. They wanted to escape a horrid past and to embrace a hopeful future. Their goals were deliverance and assimilation.

Thus Crevecoeur wrote his "Letters from an American Farmer" in his acquired English, not in his native French. Thus immigrants reared in other tongues urged their children to learn English as speedily as possible. German immigrants tried for a moment to gain status for their language, but the effort got nowhere. The dominant culture was Anglo-Saxon and, with modification and enrichment, remained Anglo-Saxon.

Repudiation of the Melting Pot

The melting pot was one of those metaphors that turned out only to be partly true, and recent years have seen an astonishing repudiation of the whole conception. Many Americans today righteously reject the historic goal of "a new race of man." The contemporary ideal is not assimilation but ethnicity. The escape from origins has given way to the search for "roots." "Ancient prejudices and manners"—the old-time religion, the old-time diet—have made a surprising comeback.

These developments portend a new turn in American life. Instead of a transformative nation with a new and distinctive identity, America increasingly sees itself as preservative of old identities. We used to say e pluribus unum. Now we glorify *pluribus* and belittle *unum*. The melting pot yields to the Tower of Babel.

The new turn has had marked impact on the universities. Very little agitates academia more these days than the demands of passionate minorities for revision of the curriculum: in history, the denunciation of Western civilization courses as cultural imperialism; in literature, the denunciation of the "canon," the list of essential books, as an instrumentality of the existing power structure.

A recent report by the New York State Commissioner of Education's task force on "Minorities: Equity and Excellence" luridly describes "African Americans, Asian Americans, Puerto Ricans/Latinos and Native Americans" as "victims of an intellectual and educational oppression." The "systematic bias toward European culture and its derivatives," the report claims, has "a terribly damaging effect on the psyche of young people of African, Asian, Latino and Native American descent"—a doubtful assertion for which no proof is vouchsafed.

Of course teachers of history and literature should give due recognition to women, black Americans, Indians, Hispanics and other groups who were subordinated and ignored in the high noon of male Anglo-Saxon dominance. In recent years they have begun belatedly to do so. But the *cult of ethnicity*, pressed too far, exacts costs—as, for example, the current pressure to teach history and literature not as intellectual challenges but as psychological therapy.

There is nothing new, of course, about the yearnings of excluded groups for affirmations of their own historical and cultural dignity. When Irish-Americans were thought beyond the pale, their spokesmen responded much as spokesmen for blacks, Hispanics and others respond today. Professor John V. Kelleher, for many years Harvard's distinguished Irish scholar, once recalled his first exposure to Irish-American history—"turgid little essays on the fact that the Continental Army was 76 percent Irish, or that many of George Washington's closest friends were nuns and priests, or that Lincoln got the major ideas for the Second Inaugural Address from the Hon. Francis P. Mageghegan of Alpaca, New York, a pioneer manufacturer of cast-iron rosary beads." John Kelleher called this "the there's-always-an-Irishman-at-the-bottom-of-it-doing-the-real-work approach to American history."

Fortunately most Irish-Americans disregarded their spokesmen and absorbed the American tradition. About 1930, Kelleher said, those "turgid little essays began to vanish from Irish-American papers." He added, "I wonder whose is the major component in the Continental Army these days?" The answer, one fears, is getting to be blacks, Jews and Hispanics.

There is often artificiality about the attempts to use history to minister to psychological needs. When I encounter black insistence on inserting Africa into mainstream curricula, I recall the 1956 presidential campaign. Adlai Stevenson, for whom I was working, had a weak record on civil rights in America but was a champion of African nationalism. I suggested to a group of sympathetic black leaders that maybe if Stevenson talked to black audiences about Africa, he could make up for his deficiencies on civil rights. My friends laughed and said that American blacks couldn't care less about Africa: That is no longer the case; but one can't escape the feeling that present emotions are more manufactured than organic.

Let us by all means teach women's history, black history, Hispanic history. But let us teach them as *history*, not as a means of *promoting group self-esteem*. I don't often agree with Gore Vidal, but I liked his remark the other day: "What I hate is good citizenship history. That has wrecked every history book. Now we're getting 'The Hispanics are warm and joyous and have brought such wonder into our lives,' you know, and before them the Jews, and before them the blacks. And the women. I mean, cut it out!"

Novelists, moralists, politicians, fabulators can go beyond the historical evidence to tell inspiring stories. But historians are custodians of professional standards. Their objective is critical analysis, accuracy and objectivity, not making people feel better about themselves.

Heaven knows how dismally historians fall short of their ideals; how sadly our interpretations are dominated and distorted by unconscious preconceptions; how obsessions of race and nation blind us to our own bias. All historians may in one way or another mythologize history. But the answer to bad history is not "good citizenship history"—more bad history written from a different viewpoint. The answer to bad history is better history.

The ideological assault in English departments on the "canon" as an instrument of political oppression implies the existence of a monolithic body of work designed to enforce the "hegemony" of a class or race or sex. In fact, most great literature and much good history are deeply subversive in their impact on orthodoxies. Consider the American canon: Emerson, Whitman, Melville, Hawthorne, Thoreau, Mark Twain, Henry Adams, William and Henry James, Holmes, Dreiser, Faulkner. Lackeys of the ruling class? Agents of American imperialism?

Let us by all means learn about other continents and other cultures. But, lamentable as some may think it, we inherit an American experience, as America inherits a European experience. To deny the essentially European origins of American culture is to falsify history.

We should take pride in our distinctive inheritance as other nations take pride in their distinctive inheritance. Certainly there is no need for Western civilization, the source of the ideas of individual freedom and political democracy to which most of the world now aspires, to apologize to cultures based on despotism, superstition, tribalism, and fanaticism. Let us abjure what Bertrand Russell called the fallacy of "the superior virtue of the oppressed."

Of course we must teach the Western democratic tradition in its true proportions—not as a fixed, final and complacent orthodoxy, intolerant of deviation and dissent, but as an ever-evolving creed fulfilling its ideals through debate, self-criticism, protest, disrespect and irreverence, a tradition in which all groups have rights of heterodoxy and opportunities for self-assertion. It is a tradition that has empowered people of all nations and races. Little can have a more "terribly damaging effect on the psyche" than for educators to tell young blacks and Hispanics and Asians that it is not for them.

One Step at a Time

Belief in one's own culture does not mean disdain for other cultures. But one step at a time: No culture can hope to ingest other cultures all at once, certainly not before it ingests its own. After we have mastered our own culture, we can explore the world.

If we repudiate the quite marvelous inheritance that history has bestowed on us, we invite the fragmentation of our own culture into a quarrelsome spatter of enclaves, ghettos and tribes. The bonds of cohesion in our society are sufficiently fragile, or so it seems to me, that it makes no sense to strain them by encouraging and exalting cultural and linguistic apartheid. The rejection of the melting pot points the republic in the direction of incoherence and chaos.

In the 21st century, if present trends hold, non-whites in the U.S. will begin to outnumber whites. This will bring inevitable changes in the national ethos but not, one must hope, at the expense of national cohesion. Let the new Americans foreswear the cult of ghettoization and agree with Crevecoeur, as with most immigrants in the two centuries since, that in America "individuals of all nations are melted into a new race of man."

QUESTIONS

1. According to Schlesinger, what motivated most of the people who originally came to America to make the journey? Why were the original immigrants eager to learn English and to rapidly acquire "American" culture? How have the values of the new immigrants changed, in Schlesinger's view, and how have these new values influenced the universities?

2. Schlesinger uses a number of negatively connotative phrases such as "Tower of Babel," "cult of ethnicity," "psychological therapy," and "the cult of ghettoization" to characterize the proponents of multi-culturalism and ethnic studies. Does his use of such phrases seem helpful, or does it inject a feeling of bias and ridicule into his argument?

3. In his final paragraphs, Schlesinger argues for several potential ill effects of rejecting the melting-pot theory of "a new race of man." What are the ill effects he mentions, and do you think he provides sufficient evidence to convince us of his belief? Could you think of ill effects of the melting-pot theory that he neglects to mention? If so, what are they?

HERBERT J. GANS

"The American Kaleidoscope, Then and Now"

Herbert J. Gans (b.1927) has taught at Columbia University since 1971, where he is currently Lynd Professor of Sociology. In 2006, Gans was given the Career of Distinguished Scholarship Award of the American Sociological Association. He is an influential sociologist who has published over 170 articles and 12 books. He has been a long-time critic of urban renewal and high-rise construction of inner city housing, which has often wiped out the complex, lively immigrant communities that preceded large housing complexes. In contrast, he has been a proponent of planned subdivisions structured to create a complex web of social interactions. In recent years he has turned to media criticism, becoming involved with the sociological study of television and its impact. His more recent books include The War Against The Poor *(1995),* Making Sense of America *(1999), and* Democracy and the News *(2003). In the following essay, "The American Kaleidoscope," Gans argues for a new term to describe both the blending and the distinctions that remain among different cultural and ethnic groups in America.*

It was at the start of the twentieth century, in the midst of the last great wave of immigration to America, that the English playwright Israel Zangwill produced his signature work, *The Melting Pot*. The play presented a utopian vision of America as a crucible that blended all nationalities and races into a new American people, interethnic and interracial, who would build "the Republic of Man" and "the Kingdom of God." It is an appealing vision, hopeful that the New World might bring about the total ethnic, racial and even religious blending that was impossible in Europe. Yet even in Zangwill's time, there was no single

American culture into which immigrants could blend. Long before Southern and Eastern European immigrants started arriving in the 1880s, America was already remarkably diverse, as Alexis de Tocqueville had noticed as early as the 1830s.

But while immigrants to America never really "melted," losing all trace of their origins, they did and still do undergo assimilation. This is a slower and more complex process than Zangwill imagined, and it takes several forms. For all newcomers, economic assimilation has to begin almost at once: immigrants must find work and make their first move into the mainstream American economy, or one of its ethnic enclaves. This kind of assimilation is made easier by the fact that immigrants are resigned to working longer hours at lower wages than the native-born.

Cultural assimilation has to begin almost as quickly, for newcomers have to learn enough about American ways and institutions to send their children to school, cope with landlords and bureaucracies and maneuver around their new communities. American popular culture has always been a force for assimilation, perhaps because much of it was created by immigrants. However, cultural assimilation really takes place almost automatically as newcomers learn that the habits of everyday life brought from the old country often do not work here.

But social assimilation occurs much more slowly. It does not happen until immigrants, or more likely their descendants, are comfortable enough to join nonimmigrant groups, such as neighborhood organizations, civic associations, women's clubs and mainstream churches. More important, they have to be accepted by native-born Americans; otherwise, they cannot move away from their immigrant moorings.

Today, as in the past, the factors that most influence assimilation are class and race. Middle-class newcomers have a far easier time than poor ones, since they bring along their own financial, cultural and social resources, or "capital." Among the past European immigrant group, for example, Eastern European Jews and Northern Italians, who already came with job skills demanded in the urban economy, assimilated more easily than groups who were mainly peasants or farm laborers. This differential, or segmented, assimilation has also been taking place among the "new," post-1965 immigrants, although far fewer of them were peasants.

The most important obstacle to speed and ease of assimilation, however, is race. In the nineteenth century, swarthy Jews, "black" Irish, and Italian "guineas"—a not so subtle euphemism borrowed from the

African country of Guinea—were all seen as what we today call "people of color." These immigrants terrified lighter-skinned native-born Americans, who accepted the newcomers as "white" only when they—actually, their descendants—began to earn middle-class incomes. Of course, skin color does not affect an immigrant's ability to absorb American culture. But color can play a large part in hindering economic and social assimilation: today's black newcomers, from the Caribbean and elsewhere, are often treated as part of the African-American population, with all the associated disadvantages.

"Asians"—the term Americans use for immigrants from all the countries of the Far East—are in a very different situation. Because so many are middle-class professionals, and because their children often excel in school, native-born white Americans sometimes classify Asians as a "model minority." Still, being considered a model minority does not mean automatic acceptance in white America. On-the-job glass ceilings remain in place, and when Asians, like other immigrants, compete for jobs, housing and other resources in limited supply, discrimination can rear its head very quickly.

"South Asians" are a special case, and one that demonstrates the importance of social class. Indians, for example, are currently the most highly educated of the new arrivals—over half come with college degrees—and though they are often darker-skinned than African immigrants, they are frequently welcomed as if they were whites. Whether Indians would be able to marry whites at the same high rates as lighter-skinned Asians or Hispanics is still a moot issue because Indian parents strongly discourage their children from intermarrying, but the question will surely come up before too long.

"Hispanics"—a language group that has now been redefined as a quasi-race—and solidly in the racial middle. Lighter-skinned Hispanics are treated just about like Asians. Those with darker skin and other traces of their Indian ancestors have a harder time; and black Hispanics, notably Dominicans and other West Indians, suffer from the same discrimination and segregation as other black immigrants.

Matters are complicated by the fact that immigrants quickly pick up the discriminatory practices of their new country. Regardless of where they come from, immigrants learn that, in America, lighter is always better, darker is always worse and black is worst. Little time passes before immigrants become prejudiced against African-Americans. This, too, is a kind of assimilation, and one that Israel Zangwill's idealistic vision never anticipated.

It has taken the American mainstream—including scholars—a long time to understand assimilation. A century ago, it took native-born observers a good many years to understand how the new European immigrants were slowly being absorbed into their adopted country. The journalists, social workers and amateur social scientists, almost all of them WASPs, who first wrote about these newcomers generally had a very low opinion of their manners, morals, intelligence and sanitary habits. Because the new arrivals were packed into terrible slums, many with outhouses and shared wash-stands, WASP observers thought they were opposed to bathing. (One of the more widespread stereotypes of the time had new immigrants using their bathtubs as coal bins.) Unlike Zangwill, such observers were convinced that this uncivilized mass could never be Americanized. Some of them argued for an immediate end to all immigration; others joined with advocates of eugenics in proposing that the newcomers be sterilized or sent to communities that would today be described as concentration camps.

Then, during the first decade of the twentieth century, a handful of American universities graduated the first professional sociologists trained to undertake empirical research. Some of these scholars headed for the immigrant slums. The problem was that most spoke only English, and as a result they did much of their research among English-speaking young adults of the second generation. These researchers were often no less prejudiced against immigrants than earlier writers, but as a result of their generational "sampling bias" they spoke to far more Americanizing young people than first-generation immigrants maintaining their old culture. As a consequence, these scholars portrayed a second generation that was moving away from its parents' culture and escaping from immigrant poverty. The scholars were generally pleased by the Americanization they uncovered, and the term they used to describe it was *assimilation*.

Later, other researchers posited a theory of assimilation that suggested it was happening, in effect, in a "straight line." Essentially, these thinkers believed, cultural, social and other kinds of assimilation would continue uninterrupted, without slowing, over several generations. With assimilation would come speedier upward mobility, which in turn would generate still more assimilation. Immigrant institutions would erode further and further, and immigrant culture would eventually disappear, until finally the newcomers—at least the light-skinned ones— would be indistinguishable from other Americans.

Because this process was thought to be roughly the same for all immigrants, the theory could indeed be pictured on a graph as a straight line: it began with the immigrants' arrival and ended when they had become fully American. What's more, because the theory was formulated around the time Congress outlawed further immigration to America, in 1924, it was thought that the straight line would eventually end with the Americanization of all the immigrants then in the country. In fact, the straight-line argument was a more gradual version of Zangwill's melting pot metaphor—and like Zangwill, it envisioned a single kind of new American.

Only in the quarter-century after World War II did some scholars begin to recognize that the straight-line theory was too simple. In fact, assimilation moved in many and sometimes mysterious ways, and was influenced by a number of factors. Economic assimilation, for instance, was slower among ethnic groups that dominated an occupational niche, as the Poles and other Slavs that then dominated the steel and automobile industries. Different groups' ethnic cultures and ethnic institutions also declined at different speeds: more slowly, for example, if ethnic traditionalists or ethnic churches were influential enough to hold back change. And working-class communities were generally slower to give up on their ethnic institutions than middleclass groups, which were by then sending their young people directly into the new and quintessentially American postwar suburbs.

In fact, it turned out there was no single pattern. Given their different speeds of assimilation, different ethnic groups needed their own "lines" on the chart of assimilation. In most cases, these trajectories were not straight at all, but rather wavy or bumpy, and each in a somewhat different way. Even as people were assimilating, they were reworking rather than just dropping ethnic traditions, and often they created new ethnic practices and traditions to fit present needs. As women began to demand more equality, for example, the bar mitzvah celebrating the religious adulthood of thirteen-year-old Jewish boys was complemented by the newly invented bat mitzvah ceremony for girls.

Nor could anyone say for sure where, when and how the various bumpy lines would end—if indeed they did end. For one thing, journalists and researchers periodically discovered seventh- and eighth-generation descendants of nineteenth-century immigrants who still identified with their ancestors, calling themselves Swedish, German, or Scotch-Irish, even though in all other respects they were entirely American. At the same time, however, significant numbers of third- and even second-generation descendants of later European im-migrants were already intermarrying. Then the intermarried couple had to choose which of their ethnic backgrounds, if any, they would try to pass on to their children. In sociologist Mary Waters's now classic phrase, people found that they had "ethnic options."

The picture was complicated further still when social scientists realized that, contrary to the classic model, the descendants of immi-grants were not assimilating into a single American culture—they were not turning into WASPs. In fact, this was not a new development. The Scandinavians and many of the Germans who came to America in the early to mid-nineteenth century were white Protestants, but even they did not adopt much of the WASP culture of Puritan America. Indeed, there was great diversity among WASPs themselves. The dirt-poor Appalachian "hillbillies" were WASPs too, after all, and just as "Anglo-Saxon" as the elite who controlled the economy, politics and culture.

The more social scientists looked at assimilation, and at America, the more complex, and in some ways contradictory, the process turned out to be. Although the straight-line theory was clearly too simple, its under-lying thesis remains accurate: the institutions and cultures that immi-grants bring from the old country erode further with each generation. Eventually, most of them will probably disappear, except among small groups of traditionalists and scholars working to keep them alive through ethnic festivals and in museums. At the same time, bits and pieces from these cultures persist, albeit transformed from generation to generation, modernized and supplemented by new versions of old tradi-tions. Meanwhile, as long as the American economy needs new infu-sions of cheap labor, and as long as people around the world see the prospect of a better life in America, immigration will continue. And each wave of new arrivals will add its culture to the country's evolving diver-sity. Were Zangwill to come back and see what had happened in the hun-dred years since he wrote, he might agree that the best metaphor for America is not a melting pot but rather a kaleidoscope. Only that image really captures the constant flux, the persistent but changing populations and cultures, that make up the overall pattern of the nation.

Will the immigrants who have been arriving on these shores since about 1965 assimilate in the same way as those who came from Europe a century ago? Certainly the straight-line theory will become less and less apt. Unlike the old European immigration, which was all white and all poor, the new wave of immigrants consists of people from many dif-ferent social classes and skin colors; and by now researchers understand how much those differences can affect the speed and characteristics of assimilation. Still, though it will take new and different forms, it's a sure bet that assimilation will continue.

Unlike their predecessors, today's researchers are able to study first-generation immigrants, not just their English-speaking children. We are learning that assimilation begins much earlier than originally thought, and perhaps earlier than it did in the past. Immigrants who arrive with professional schooling and middle-class habits can assimilate almost as quickly as they choose—that is, if their skin is light enough. They can also move faster into the higher ranks of the economy, previously open only to the best-schooled children and grandchildren of immigrants. Glass ceilings remain, but they are much higher than they once were. Italian, Polish, Greek and other European Americans had to wait a century to gain entry to the top echelon of American business, but today's immigrants will be allowed in earlier—and this time, not just the men.

However, despite the Americanization that today's immigrants are already undergoing, some of their children reject what is happening and question the very idea of assimilation. They proudly proclaim the virtues of their ethnic or racial backgrounds and celebrate the distinctiveness of their identities. Determined to be loyal to the communities they come from, they want to avoid being transformed into what they perceive to be mass-produced, homogenized Americans. As for straight-line theory, if it ever was accurate, they are convinced it does not apply to them.

To be sure, these reactions are not shared by all members of the second generation. Most of them are busy with everyday pursuits and practical problems; few of them use words such as "assimilation" or "identity." Concern about one's ethnic or racial allegiances—what some sociologists call "identity work"—is more likely to be undertaken by young people who do not yet have parental and other responsibilities, and by political activists. Those seeking to protect what they see as their community's cultural integrity seem to be found mostly among second-generation ethnic and racial groups who are the first in their families to attend college or to work in public agencies and other large institutions. It is particularly common when they constitute numerical minorities in the midst of not-always-friendly native-born white Americans.

What this suggests is that the public expression of ethnic or racial culture and loyalty is in part a reaction to the discrimination and subordinate status often imposed on these second-generation pioneers. "Hyphenated" Americans discover that they are still considered foreigners; students have to learn from reading lists filled entirely with the writings of those they scorn as "dead white males." Even third- and fourth-generation Asian-Americans may be asked where they learned to speak accent-free English. No wonder many of them feel insulted and respond with a stronger pride in their origins.

Of course, this movement has a political side too. Students expressing their ethnic or racial identity as a way of coping with slights and rejections may found or join a campus organization or national movement extolling community pride and group identity. Like all organizations that pursue cultural objectives and advocate ideological positions, these groups also seek power and resources. Leaders press for decisionmaking positions and jobs in public agencies, and they lobby for legislation to benefit their members and supporters. Likewise, campus activists demand ethnic and racial studies departments with faculties, courses and scholarships for their constituents.

Many people, including those whose ancestors came here so long ago that they have forgotten their own immigrant roots, are put off by such activity, now commonly called "identity politics." Although we are all supposedly multiculturalists now—most Americans are sympathetic to the ideal of diversity—identity politics can still make some people nervous. It should not be surprising that both the right and the left are sometimes unhappy with the politics of difference, particularly when its advocates fail to support public policies that could benefit all Americans.

Right and left opponents have different reasons for questioning identity politics. Some on the right worry that ethnically or racially targeted policies, and ethnic militancy in general, will threaten what they see as an already fragile nation. In some parts of the country, identity politics is being fought with opposition to bilingual education or "English only" policies that ban the official use of immigrant languages, and some even want to close the door to further immigration. What these opponents do not mention, and perhaps do not even realize, is how much they worry about losing their dominant role in American society.

Meanwhile, those on the left believe that identity politics can only get in the way of attempts to revitalize antipoverty programs and revive the welfare state. An economically and politically more egalitarian society, they believe, would benefit ethnic and racial minorities more than successful public assertions of their identities. In his classic critique of identity politics, sociologist and critic Todd Gitlin rightly accused identity movements of wasting their time by marching on college English departments to demand ethnic studies courses and politically correct language while conservatives were taking over the White House.

My own opinion is that both right and left overestimate the political power of identity politics. The world's only current superpower is not as fragile as some political pessimists believe. And even if identity politicians were to march on the White House instead of on English departments—even if they were to join the liberal struggle to build a new, more egalitarian welfare state—they still would not win that struggle, sad to say.

At the same time, it is important to recognize that whites, being the dominant American racial group, do not always realize when they are themselves engaged in racial identity politics. They believe their own intentions and goals to be free of racial underpinnings. Actually, most whites don't even realize that they are also a race, and that most practitioners of identity politics are pursuing the same American Dream as everyone else. Policies that call for African-Americans and other racial minorities to support a race-blind country are often a disguised attempt to keep whites firmly in control—in effect, white identity politics. And when white America appoints Asians as a model minority, in fact the real model, implied if not stated, is a white one. Accordingly, the appeal to other racial groups to model themselves on Asians becomes white identity politics, no matter its intent.

But whatever one's political viewpoint, today's struggles over multiculturalism need to be understood in historical context. While identity politics appears to be a new idea, in fact it was already alive and well among the European immigrants of the late nineteenth and early twentieth centuries. Concerned as they were with economic survival and better living conditions, these newcomers were also caught up in identity politics, except that it was then called ethnic politics. The big urban political machines of the day lost no time in seeking the votes of the new immigrants, and in return offered them free coal, Thanksgiving turkeys and jobs. Patronage jobs in city agencies were dealt out by ethnic group. In New York City, for example, the Irish often got the police and fire departments, Eastern European Jews dominated public school teaching, and Italians took over sanitation. As the number of ethnic votes grew, the machines presented voters with so-called "balanced" slates that included candidates from each major white ethnic group. Later, Democratic candidates for big-city mayoralties, and even for the presidency, made sure to travel to Ireland, Italy, Poland and, after 1948, Israel. Meanwhile, Republicans campaigned among Anglo-Saxons, Scandinavians and other Northern Europeans, but these were not defined as ethnic groups.

One major difference is that, for European immigrants, there was no campus-based identity politics, for the simple reason that before World War II only a tiny proportion of the population attended college. Second-generation Jews were among the first "white ethnics" to arrive on the campuses of private colleges, and they were more segregated and self-segregated than today's nonwhite students. But by the time the descendants of other European immigrants made it to college, assimilation had sufficiently eroded their ethnic identities that they had no interest in Polish, or Italian, or Irish studies.

Eventually, assimilation will also undermine today's identity politics. Some of the current activists will graduate into local and perhaps even national politics, but many of their erstwhile constituents will think more about families and mortgages than about identity. Some will vote with their racial and ethnic blocs, some will not, though most are likely to support continuing immigration. And the next generation, the grand-children of the post-1965 immigrants, will probably behave more like the grandchildren of the European immigrants, voting in accord with their personal and national interests rather than in terms of their ethnic origins. These interests will also determine their choice of political party. Depending on the economic and social conditions of the moment, some could even become vocal opponents of further immigration.

Still, whatever the pace of political assimilation, individual ethnic identity and ethnic pride will not necessarily disappear. Ethnicity is a hearty plant, and it can easily coexist with assimilation. In fact, some people may nourish pride in their ethnic origins precisely to compensate for their continuing assimilation. After all, identifying with one's heritage does not require knowing much about it. Pride and a sense of belonging can be evoked by attending an ethnic folk festival, visiting an ethnic restaurant or merely seeing a film made in the old country. "Symbolic" activities of this kind have become one of the main ways in which white ethnicity persists, and there is no reason to think it will not also persist among the later generations of today's immigrants. Eventually, however, even such symbolic ethnicity may well prove transitory, as intermarriage creates a population so multiethnic that its ethnic options run out. After all, no one can identify with four or more ethnic cultures at the same time.

The more durable challenge to assimilation is race. Racial identity, grounded on harsher realities than ethnic identity, will persist for a good deal longer, since skin color has consequences for economic and social assimilation. Race also has consequences for intermarriage rates. About half of all Asian-Americans and light-skinned Hispanics now marry whites, and at that rate, they may be defined as near whites in a few decades. When it comes to African-Americans, however, less than 10 percent marry whites. Until they are able and willing to intermarry at the same rates as lighter-skinned people, blacks will remain a separate and segregated population. Racial intermarriage requires equal partners, and a significant increase in black-white marriage must await much greater racial equality than exists today. As a result, black identity movements may survive longer and remain stronger than others.

Still, in the longer run, and if all goes well racially, all Americans may have brown skins one day—just the right color to survive global warming. Such an outcome would prove Israel Zangwill's dream of the melting pot to have been right, though not quite in the way he thought. Once assimilation results in across-the-board intermarriage, and generations of intermarriage erase differences in skin color, eye shape, and the other visible bodily features from which we construct "race," the interracial American that Zangwill dreamed of could actually come into being. But with one qualification. The melting pot was a utopian vision, and like all utopias, it was unrealistically static. For the foreseeable future, in the real America, immigration is likely to continue bringing new racial groups and new ethnic cultures to our shores all the time. Assimilation will continue, but so will the shifting patterns of the American kaleidoscope, which will remain the quintessential image of what it means to be American.

QUESTIONS

1. Why does Gans believe that the "melting pot" idea of immigration was never more than an "appealing vision"? What have been, and remain, the traditional obstacles to full assimilation, in Gans's view? What historical examples does he give of such obstacles?

2. How does Gans differentiate between the melting-pot ideal, "straight line" assimilation, and its complications in the modern age? What has led to the controversy over the emerging "identity politics" and multiculturalism, and why do both liberals and conservatives question such positions? What is Gans's position on "white identity politics"? Do you agree with him? Why or why not?

3. How does Gans compare today's identity politics to the "ethnic politics" of the past? What lesson does the fate of ethnic politics have for our current multicultural concerns? Why does Gans believe that, despite the eventual disappearance of distinct races through intermarriage, America will continue to be a cultural "kaleidoscope"? Do you agree?

DINESH D'SOUZA

"Becoming American"

Dinesh D'Souza (b. 1961) came to the United States in 1978 from India and attended Dartmouth College, graduating Phi Beta Kappa in 1983. He has been an editor for the Policy Review *in Washington, D.C. and a policy advisor under Ronald Reagan, as well as a member of the conservative American Enterprise Institute. He is currently a fellow at the Hoover Institution at Stanford University. His idea of conservatism combines the idea of universal moral standards along with "classical liberalism," which he defines as "the principles of the American Revolution." However, D'Souza rejects ideas such as social welfare programs, gay rights, feminism, affirmative action, and the hegemony of the United Nations, attributing them to the "cultural left and its allies." His books include* Illiberal Education *(1991) and* Letters to a Young Conservative *(2002). The following selection is taken from D'Souza's* What's So Great About America *(2002), in which he argues that America offers great opportunities for today's immigrants, so long as they accept its cultural values.*

Critics of America, both at home and abroad, have an easy explanation for why the American idea is so captivating, and why immigrants want to come here. The reason, they say, is money. America represents "the bitch goddess of success." That is why poor people reach out for the American idea: they want to touch some of that lucre. As for immigrants, they allegedly flock to the United States for the sole purpose of getting rich. This view, which represents the appeal of America as the appeal of the almighty dollar, is disseminated on Arab streets and in multicultural textbooks taught in U.S. schools. It is a way of demeaning the United States by associating it with what is selfish, base, and crass: an unquenchable appetite for gain.

It is not hard to see why this view of America has gained a wide currency. When people in foreign countries turn on American TV shows, they are stupefied by the lavish displays of affluence: the sumptuous homes, the bejeweled women, the fountains and pools, and so on. Whether reruns of *Dallas* and *Dynasty* are true to the American experience is irrelevant here; the point is that this is how the United States appears to outsiders who have not had the chance to come here. And even for those who do, it is hard to deny that America represents the chance to live better, even to become fantastically wealthy. For instance, there are several people of Indian descent on the *Forbes* 400 list. And over the years I have heard many Indians now living in the United States say, "We want to live an Indian lifestyle, but at an American standard of living."

If this seems like a crass motive for immigration, it must be evaluated in the context of the harsh fate that poor people endure in much of the Third World. The lives of many of these people are defined by an ongoing struggle to exist. It is not that they don't work hard. On the contrary, they labor incessantly and endure hardships that are almost unimaginable to people in the West. In the villages of Asia and Africa, for example, a common sight is a farmer beating a pickax into the ground, women wobbling under heavy loads, children carrying stones. These people are performing very hard labor, but they are getting nowhere. The best they can hope for is to survive for another day. Their clothes are tattered, their teeth are rotted, and disease and death constantly loom over their horizon. For the poor of the Third World, life is characterized by squalor, indignity, and brevity.

I emphasize the plight of the poor, but I recognize, of course, that there are substantial middle classes even in the underdeveloped world. For these people basic survival may not be an issue, but still, they endure hardships that make everyday life a strain. One problem is that the basic infrastructure of the Third World is abysmal: the roads are not properly paved, the water is not safe to drink, pollution in the cities has reached hazardous levels, public transportation is overcrowded and unreliable, and there is a two-year waiting period to get a telephone. Government officials, who are very poorly paid, are inevitably corrupt, which means that you must pay bribes on a regular basis to get things done. Most important, there are limited prospects for the children's future.

In America, the immigrant immediately recognizes, things are different. The newcomer who sees America for the first time typically experiences emotions that alternate between wonder and delight. Here is a country where *everything works*: the roads are clean and paper smooth, the highway signs are clear and accurate, the public toilets function properly, when you pick up the telephone you get a dial tone, you can even buy things from the store and then take them back. For the Third World visitor, the American supermarket is a thing to behold: endless aisles of every imaginable product, fifty different types of cereal, multiple flavors of ice cream. The place is full of countless unappreciated inventions: quilted toilet paper, fabric softener, cordless telephones, disposable diapers, roll-on luggage, deodorant. Most countries even today do not have these benefits: deodorant, for example, is unavailable in much of the Third World and unused in much of Europe.

What the immigrant cannot help noticing is that America is a country where the poor live comparatively well. This fact was dramatized in the 1980s, when CBS television broadcast an anti-Reagan documentary, "People Like Us," which was intended to show the miseries of the poor during an American recession. The Soviet Union also broadcast the documentary, with a view to embarrassing the Reagan administration. But by the testimony of former Soviet leaders, it had the opposite effect. Ordinary people across the Soviet Union saw that the poorest Americans have television sets and microwave ovens and cars. They arrived at the same perception of America that I witnessed in a friend of mine from Bombay who has been unsuccessfully trying to move to the United States for nearly a decade. Finally I asked him, "Why are you so eager to come to America?" He replied, "Because I really want to live in a country where the poor people are fat."

The point is that the United States is a country where the ordinary guy has a good life. This is what distinguishes America from so many other countries. Everywhere in the world, the rich person lives well. Indeed, a good case can be made that if you are rich, you live better in countries other than America. The reason is that you enjoy the pleasures of aristocracy. This is the pleasure of being treated as a superior person. Its gratification derives from subservience: in India, for example, the wealthy enjoy the satisfaction of seeing innumerable servants and toadies grovel before them and attend to their every need.

In the United States the social ethic is egalitarian, and this is unaffected by the inequalities of wealth in the country. Tocqueville noticed this egalitarianism a century and a half ago, but it is, if anything, more prevalent today. For all his riches, Bill Gates could not approach a homeless person and say, "Here's a $100 bill. I'll give it to you if you kiss my feet." Most likely the homeless guy would tell Gates to go to hell! The American view is that the rich guy may have more money, but he isn't in any fundamental sense better than you are. The American janitor or waiter sees himself as performing a service, but he doesn't see himself as inferior to those he serves. And neither do the customers see him that way: they are generally happy to show him respect and appreciation on a plane of equality. America is the only country in the world where we call the waiter "Sir," as if he were a knight.

The moral triumph of America is that it has extended the benefits of comfort and affluence, traditionally enjoyed by very few, to a large segment of society. Very few people in America have to wonder where their next meal is coming from. Even sick people who don't have proper insurance can receive medical care at hospital emergency rooms. The poorest American girls are not humiliated by having to wear torn clothes. Every child is given an education, and most have the chance to go on to college. The common man can expect to live long enough and have free time to play with his grandchildren.

Ordinary Americans enjoy not only security and dignity, but also comforts that other societies reserve for the elite. We now live in a country where construction workers regularly pay $4 for a nonfat latte, where maids drive very nice cars, where plumbers take their families on vacation to Europe. As Irving Kristol once observed, there is virtually no restaurant in America to which a CEO can go to lunch with the absolute assurance that he will not find his secretary also dining there. Given the standard of living of the ordinary American, it is no wonder that socialist or revolutionary schemes have never found a wide constituency in the United States. As sociologist Werner Sombart observed, all socialist utopias in America have come to grief on roast beef and apple pie.*

Thus it is entirely understandable that people would associate the idea of America with a better life. For them, money is not an end in itself; money is the means to a longer, healthier, and fuller life. Money allows them to purchase a level of security, dignity, and comfort that they could not have hoped to enjoy in their native countries. Money also frees up time for family life, community involvement, and spiritual pursuits: thus it produces not just material, but also moral, gains. All of this is true, and yet in my view it offers an incomplete picture of why America is so appealing to so many. Let me illustrate with the example of my own life.

Not long ago, I asked myself: what would my life have been like if I had never come to the United States, if I had stayed in India? Materially, my life has improved, but not in a fundamental sense. I grew up in a middle-class family in Bombay. My father was a chemical engineer; my mother, an office secretary. I was raised without great luxury, but neither did I lack for anything. My standard of living in America is higher, but it is not a radical difference. My life has changed far more dramatically in other ways.

If I had remained in India, I would probably have lived my entire existence within a one-mile radius of where I was born. I would undoubtedly have married a woman of my identical religious, socioeconomic, and cultural background. I would almost certainly have become

DINESH D'SOUZA

174

* Werner Sombart, *Why Is There No Socialism in the United States?* (White Plains: International Arts and Sciences Press, 1976), 109–10.

a medical doctor, an engineer, or a software programmer. I would have socialized within my ethnic community and had cordial relations, but few friends, outside that group. I would have a whole set of opinions that could be predicted in advance; indeed, they would not be very different from what my father believed, or his father before him. In sum, my destiny would to a large degree have been given to me.

This is not to say that I would have no choice; I would have choice, but within narrowly confined parameters. Let me illustrate with the example of my sister, who got married several years ago. My parents began the process by conducting a comprehensive survey of all the eligible families in our neighborhood. First they examined primary criteria, such as religion, socioeconomic position, and educational background. Then my parents investigated subtler issues: the social reputation of the family, reports of a lunatic uncle, the character of the son, and so on. Finally my parents were down to a dozen or so eligible families, and they were invited to our house for dinner with suspicious regularity. My sister was, in the words of Milton Friedman, "free to choose." My sister knew about, and accepted, the arrangement; she is now happily married with two children. I am not quarreling with the outcome, but clearly my sister's destiny was, to a considerable extent, choreographed by my parents.

By coming to America, I have seen my life break free of these traditional confines. I came to Arizona as an exchange student, but a year later I was enrolled at Dartmouth College. There I fell in with a group of students who were actively involved in politics; soon I had switched my major from economics to English literature. My reading included books like Plutarch's *Moralia*; Hamilton, Madison, and Jay's *Federalist Papers*; and Evelyn Waugh's *Brideshead Revisited*. They transported me to places a long way from home and implanted in my mind ideas that I had never previously considered. By the time I graduated, I decided that I should become a writer, which is something you can do in this country. America permits many strange careers: this is a place where you can become, say, a comedian. I would not like to go to my father and tell him that I was thinking of becoming a comedian. I do not think he would have found it funny.

Soon after graduation I became the managing editor of a policy magazine and began to write freelance articles in the *Washington Post*. Someone in the Reagan White House was apparently impressed by my work, because I was called in for an interview and promptly hired as a senior domestic policy analyst. I found it strange to be working at the

White House, because at the time I was not a United States citizen. I am sure that such a thing would not happen in India or anywhere else in the world. But Reagan and his people didn't seem to mind; for them, ideology counted more than nationality. I also met my future wife in the Reagan administration, where she was at the time a White House intern. (She has since deleted it from her résumé.) My wife was born in Louisiana and grew up in San Diego; her ancestry is English, French, Scotch-Irish, German, and American Indian.

I notice that Americans marry in a rather peculiar way: by falling in love. You may think that I am being ironic, or putting you on, so let me hasten to inform you that in many parts of the world, romantic love is considered a mild form of insanity. Consider a typical situation: Anjali is in love with Arjun. She considers Arjun the best-looking man in the world, the most intelligent, virtually without fault, a paragon of humanity! But everybody else can see that Arjun is none of these things. What, then, persuades Anjali that Arjun possesses qualities that are nowhere in evidence? There is only one explanation: Anjali is deeply deluded. It does not follow that her romantic impulses should be ruthlessly crushed. But, in the view of many people and many traditions around the world, they should be steered and directed and prevented from ruining Anjali's life. This is the job of parents and the community, to help Anjali see beyond her delusions and to make decisions that are based on practical considerations and common sense.

If there is a single phrase that encapsulates life in the Third World, it is that "birth is destiny." I remember an incident years ago when my grandfather called in my brother, my sister, and me, and asked us if we knew how lucky we were. We asked him why he felt this way: was it because we were intelligent, or had lots of friends, or were blessed with a loving family? Each time he shook his head and said, "No." Finally we pressed him: why did he consider us so lucky? Then he revealed the answer: "Because you are Brahmins!"

The Brahmin, who is the highest ranking in the Hindu caste system, is traditionally a member of the priestly class. As a matter of fact, my family had nothing to do with the priesthood. Nor are we Hindu: my ancestors converted to Christianity many generations ago. Even so, my grandfather's point was that before we converted, hundreds of years ago, our family used to be Brahmins. How he knew this remains a mystery. But he was serious in his insistence that nothing that the three of us achieved in life could possibly mean more than the fact that we were Brahmins.

This may seem like an extreme example, revealing my grandfather to be a very narrow fellow indeed, but the broader point is that traditional cultures attach a great deal of importance to data such as what tribe you come from, whether you are male or female, and whether you are the eldest son. Your destiny and your happiness hinge on these things. If you are a Bengali, you can count on other Bengalis to help you, and on others to discriminate against you; if you are female, then certain forms of society and several professions are closed to you; and if you are the eldest son, you inherit the family house and your siblings are expected to follow your direction. What this means is that once your tribe, caste, sex, and family position have been established at birth, your life takes a course that is largely determined for you.

In America, by contrast, you get to write the script of your own life. When your parents say to you, "What do you want to be when you grow up?" the question is open-ended; it is you who supply the answer. Your parents can advise you: "Have you considered law school?" "Why not become the first doctor in the family?" It is considered very improper, however, for them to try and force your decision. Indeed, American parents typically send their teenage children away to college, where they live on their own and learn independence. This is part of the process of forming your mind and choosing a field of interest for yourself and developing your identity. It is not uncommon in the United States for two brothers who come from the same gene pool and were raised in similar circumstances to do quite different things: the eldest becomes a gas station attendant, the younger moves up to be vice president at Oracle; the eldest marries his high-school sweetheart and raises four kids, the youngest refuses to settle down, or comes out of the closet as a homosexual; one is the Methodist that he was raised to be, the other becomes a Christian Scientist or a Buddhist. What to be, where to live, whom to love, whom to marry, what to believe, what religion to practice—these are all decisions that Americans make for themselves.

In most parts of the world your identity and your fate are to a large extent handed to you; in America, you determine them for yourself. In America your destiny is not prescribed; it is constructed. Your life is like a blank sheet of paper, and you are the artist. This notion of you being the architect of your own destiny is the incredibly powerful idea that is behind the worldwide appeal of America. Young people especially find irresistible the prospect of being in the driver's seat, of authoring the narrative of their own lives. So too the immigrant discovers that America permits him to break free of the constraints that have held him captive, so that the future becomes a landscape of his own choosing.

QUESTIONS

1. What is D'Souza's perspective on the view that people come to the United States primarily to become wealthy? What reasons does D'Souza believe make the United States a superior place to live?
2. What does D'Souza consider the "social ethic," "moral triumph," and "better life" of the United States? What examples does he provide for his beliefs about this country? Do his examples (including his own life experiences) seem convincing? Why or why not?
3. In the final paragraphs, D'Souza introduces the advantages of being able to "write the script of your own life" as the unique advantage of being an American. Do you agree with him that the choice of what one is to do with one's life is actually that widely available in the United States, and if so, is this freedom necessarily beneficial for most people? Is it unique to the United States? Explain your perspective.

LINDA CHAVEZ

"Hispanics and the American Dream"

Linda Chavez (b. 1947) earned a bachelor of arts degree from the University of Colorado in 1970. She is a conservative author and commentator of Hispanic-American background who served as chair of the National Commission on Migrant Education (1988–1992) and as staff director of the U.S. Commission on Civil Rights (1983–1985) during the Reagan presidency. In 1992 she was elected as U.S. Expert to the U.N. Sub-commission on the Prevention of Discrimination and Protection of Minorities. Currently Linda Chavez is a syndicated columnist and a Fox News political commentator; she is also chair of the Center for Equal Opportunity, an organization that opposes both bilingual education and affirmative action. Chavez has written several books, including Out Of The Barrio: Toward A New Politics Of Hispanic Assimilation *(1991) and* An Unlikely Conservative *(2002). In the following essay from* Imprimis *Magazine (1996), Chavez refutes what she regards as negative stereotypes of Mexican-Americans, seeing them as models of immigrant assimilation with a strong sense of family.*

The more than 21 million Hispanics now living in the United States are fast becoming the nation's largest minority group. Some demographers can already see the day when one of three Americans will be of Hispanic descent. Will this mean a divided nation with millions of unassimilated, Spanish-speaking, poor, uneducated Hispanics living in the barrios? Well, here is one reply:

Each decade offered us hope, but our hopes evaporated into smoke. We became the poorest of the poor, the most segregated minority in schools, the lowest paid group in America and the least educated minority in this nation.

This pessimistic view of Hispanics' progress—offered in 1990 by the president of the National Council of La Raza, one of the country's leading Hispanic civil rights groups—is the prevalent one among Hispanic leaders and is shared by many outside the Hispanic community as well. Hispanics are widely perceived as the dregs of society with little hope of participating in the American Dream.

The trouble with this perception is that it is wrong. The success of Hispanics in the United States has been tremendous. They represent an emerging middle class that is a valuable addition to our culture and our economy. However, their story has been effectively suppressed by Hispanic advocates whose only apparent interest is in spreading the notion that Latinos cannot make it in this society. This has been an easy task since the Hispanic poor, who, although they only constitute about one-fourth of the Hispanic population, are visible to all. These are the Hispanics most likely to be studied, analyzed, and reported on, and certainly they are the ones most likely to be read about. A recent computer search of stories about Hispanics in major newspapers and magazines over a twelve-month period turned up more than 1,800 stories in which the words *Hispanic* or *Latino* occurred in close connection with the word *poverty*. In most people's minds, the expression "poor Hispanic" is almost redundant.

Has Hispanics' Progress Stalled?

Most Hispanics, rather than being poor, lead solidly lower middle- or middleclass lives, but finding evidence to support this thesis is sometimes difficult. Of course, Hispanic groups vary one from another, as do individuals within any group. Most analysts acknowledge, for example, that Cubans are highly successful. Within one generation, they have virtually closed the earnings and education gap with other Americans.

Although some analysts claim their success is due exclusively to their higher socioeconomic status when they arrived, many Cuban refugees—especially those who came after the first wave in the 1960s—were in fact skilled or semi-skilled workers with relatively little education. Their accomplishments in the United States mainly are attributable to diligence and hard work.

Cubans have tended to establish enclave economies, in the traditional immigrant mode, opening restaurants, stores, and other emigre-oriented services. Some Cubans have even formed banks, specializing in international transactions attuned to Latin American as well as local customers, and others have made major investments in real estate development in south Florida. These ventures have provided not only big profits for a few Cubans but jobs for many more. By 1980, there were 18,000 Cuban-owned businesses in Miami, and about 70 percent of all Cubans there owned their own homes.

But Cubans are, as a rule, dismissed as the exception among Hispanics. What about other Hispanic groups? Why has there been no "progress" among them? The largest and most important group is the Mexican-American population. Its leaders have driven much of the policy agenda affecting all Hispanics, but the importance of Mexican Americans also stems from the fact that they have had a longer history in the United States than any other Hispanic group. If Mexican Americans whose families have lived in the United States for generations are not yet making it in this society, they may have a legitimate claim to consider themselves a more or less permanently disadvantaged group.

That is precisely what Mexican-American leaders suggest is happening. Their "proof" is that statistical measures of Mexican American achievement in education, earnings, poverty rates, and other social and economic indicators have remained largely unchanged for decades. If Mexican Americans had made progress, it would show up in these areas, so the argument goes. Since it doesn't, progress must be stalled. In the post-civil rights era, it is also assumed that the failure of a minority to close the social and economic gap with whites is the result of persistent discrimination. Progress is perceived not in absolute but in relative terms. The poor may become less poor over time, but so long as those on the upper rungs of the economic ladder are climbing even faster, the poor are believed to have suffered some harm, even if they have made absolute gains and their lives are much improved. But in order for Hispanics (or any group on the lower rungs) to close the gap, they would have to progress at an even greater rate than non-Hispanic whites.

Is this a fair way to judge Hispanics' progress? No. It makes almost no sense to apply this test today (if it ever did) because the Hispanic population itself is changing so rapidly. In 1959, 85 percent of all persons of Mexican origin living in the United States were native-born. Today, only about two-thirds of the people of Mexican origin were born in the United States, and among adults barely one in two was born here. Increasingly, the Hispanic population, including that of Mexican origin, is made up of new immigrants, who, like immigrants of every era, start off at the bottom of the economic ladder. This infusion of new immigrants is bound to distort our image of progress in the Hispanic population if, each time we measure the group, we include people who have just arrived and have yet to make their way in this society.

In 1980, there were about 14.6 million Hispanics living in the United States; in 1990, there were nearly 21 million, representing an increase of 44 percent in one decade. At least one-half of this increase was the result of immigration, legal and illegal. Not surprisingly, when these Hispanics—often poorly educated with minimal or no ability to speak English—are added to the pool being measured, the achievement level of the whole group falls. Yet no major Hispanic organization will acknowledge the validity of this reasonable assumption. Instead, Hispanic leaders complain, "Hispanics are the population that has benefited least from the American economy."

In fact, a careful examination of the voluminous data on the Hispanic population gathered by the Census Bureau and other federal agencies shows that, as a group, Hispanics have made significant progress and that most of them have moved into the social and economic mainstream. In most respects, Hispanics—particularly those born here—are very much like other Americans: They work hard, support their own families without outside assistance, have more education and higher earnings than their parents, and own their own homes. In short, they are pursuing the American Dream with increasing success.

The Hispanic Family

No institution is more important to the success of Hispanics (or any group) than the family. Studies published in the early 1990s reported that 73 percent of all Mexican-origin families and 77 percent of all Cuban-origin families consist of married couples. Only 20 percent of the Mexican-origin and 19 percent of the Cuban-origin families are headed by women with no husband present. While out-of-wedlock births to Mexican-origin women are higher than those to white women generally, they fall considerably short of the number of such births to black women, and Hispanic children born out of wedlock are still likely to grow up in families with two parents.

The babies of Mexican-origin women, even those who have received little or no prenatal care, are generally quite healthy. There is also a lower infant mortality rate and smaller incidence of low birth weight, a common predictor of health problems, than among blacks and whites. While researchers are not sure what accounts for the apparent health of even poor Mexican babies, one reason may be that their mothers are less likely to drink, smoke, or use drugs, and they place special emphasis on good nutrition while pregnant.

In general, Hispanic families are somewhat more traditional than non-Hispanic families: Men are expected to work to support their families and women to care for children. Hispanic families tend to be child-centered, which increases the importance of women's role as child bearers. Hispanics are also more likely than other Americans to believe that the demands and needs of the family should take precedence over those of the individual. In an earlier age this attitude was common among other ethnic groups—Italians, for example. Today, however, it runs counter to the dominant culture of individualism characteristic of American life and may even impede individual success. This perhaps explains why so many young Hispanics are starting to drop out of school to take jobs, a decision that has some immediate financial benefits for the family but is detrimental to the individual in the long run. Nonetheless, Hispanics' attachment to family is one of their most positive cultural attributes. Family members are expected to help each other in times of financial or other need, which some analysts believe explains why so many Mexican-origin families shun welfare even when their poverty makes them eligible for assistance.

Hispanics and Public Policy

For most Hispanics, especially those born in the United States, the last few decades have brought greater economic opportunity and social mobility. They are building solid lower middle- and middle-class lives that include two-parent households, with a male head who works full-time and earns a wage commensurate with his education and training. Their educational level has been steadily rising, their earnings no longer reflect wide disparities with those of non-Hispanics, and their occupational distribution is coming to resemble more closely that of the general population. They are buying homes—42 percent of all Hispanics owned or were purchasing their homes in 1989, including 47 percent of all Mexican Americans—and moving away from inner cities. Even in areas with very high concentrations of Hispanics, like Los Angeles, the sociologist Douglas Massey reports, "segregation [is] low or moderate on all dimensions." And, in what is perhaps the ultimate test of assimilation, about one-third of all U.S.-born Hispanics under the age of thirty-five are marrying non-Hispanics.

In light of these facts, the policy prescriptions offered by many Hispanic advocacy organizations and by most politicians seem oddly out of sync. They rely too much on government programs of doubtful efficacy like affirmative action, welfare, and bilingual public education. And they perpetuate demeaning stereotypes of the very people they claim they are championing. What they should be doing instead is promoting tax reform, deregulation, enterprise zones, English instruction, and private education—all of which will help Hispanics help themselves.

Groups do not all advance at precisely the same rate in this society—sometimes because of discrimination, sometimes because of other factors. As Thomas Sowell and others have pointed out, no multi-ethnic society in the world exhibits utopian equality of income, education, and occupational status for every one of its ethnic groups. What is important is that opportunities be made available to all persons, regardless of race or ethnicity. Ultimately, however, it will be up to individuals to take advantage of those opportunities. Increasing numbers of Hispanics are doing just that. And no government action can replace the motivation and will to succeed that propels genuine individual achievement.

QUESTIONS

1. According to Chavez, why does a negative stereotype of the Hispanic, and particularly the Mexican, exist in this culture? What does she believe has perpetuated this inaccurate stereotype? Can you think of other reasons for it?

2. Why does Chavez argue that their traditional family structure has helped Hispanics succeed and is one of their "most positive cultural attributes"? Has this continued to be true in recent years? Examine some statistics on single-parent families in Mexican-American immigrant communities.

3. Examine the policy solutions that Chavez rejects to problems Hispanics have in assimilating and prospering in the United States, as well as those she endorses in her final paragraphs. Do you agree with her selection of policies, pro and con? Why or why not?

"Immigration's Aftermath"

Alejandro Portes, originally from Havana, Cuba, earned his Ph.D. in sociology from the University of Wisconsin, Madison in 1970. He is a professor of sociology at Princeton University, where he is currently director of the Center for Migration and Development. He works and teaches in areas such as immigration and economic sociology, with a special focus on Third World urbanization. He has lectured at universities and conferences around the world on the topic of international immigration. His books include, with Rubén G. Rumbaut, Legacies: The Story of the Immigrant Second Generation (2001) and Immigrant America: Portrait (2006); and, with Josh Dewind, Rethinking Migration: New Theoretical and Empirical Perspectives (2008). "Immigration's Aftermath" argues that the children of immigrants whose families came to the United States with limited education to work at unskilled labor often have difficulty achieving a position in society that offers stable employment and a promising future.

It is well known by now that immigration is changing the face of America. The U.S. Census Bureau reports that the number of foreign-born persons in the United States surged to 28 million in 2000 and now represents 12 percent of the total population, the highest figures in a century. In New York City, 54 percent of the population is of foreign stock—that is, immigrants and children of immigrants. The figure increases to 62 percent in the Los Angeles metropolitan area and to an amazing 72 percent in Miami. All around us, in these cities and elsewhere, the sounds of foreign languages and the sights of a kaleidoscope of cultures are readily apparent. But the long-term consequences are much less well known.

A driving force behind today's immigrant wave is the labor needs of the American economy. While those needs encompass a substantial demand for immigrant engineers and computer programmers in high-tech industries, the vast majority of today's immigrants are employed in menial, low-paying jobs. The reasons why employers in agribusiness, construction, landscaping, restaurants, hotels, and many other sectors want this foreign labor are quite understandable. Immigrants provide an abundant, diligent, docile, vulnerable, and low-cost labor pool where native workers willing to toil at the same harsh jobs for minimum pay have all but disappeared.

The same agribusiness, industrial, and service firms that profit from this labor have extracted from Congress ingenious loopholes to ensure the continued immigrant flow, both legal and undocumented.

Most notable is the requirement, created by the Immigration Reform and Control Act of 1986, that employers must certify that their employees have proper documents without having to establish their validity. Predictably, an entire industry of fraudulent papers has emerged. Would-be workers at construction sites and similar places often are told to go get "their papers" and return the following day. Through such subterfuges, firms demanding low-wage labor have continued to receive a steady supply, thus guaranteeing their profitability.

Defenders of this free flow portray it as a win-win process: Immigrants seeking a better life and the businesses that need their labor both gain. Opponents denounce it as a kind of invasion, as if employers did not welcome these workers. But this debate sidesteps a more consequential one: What becomes of the children of these immigrants? Business may think of them as nothing but cheap labor—indeed, that's why many business groups support pure bracero programs of temporary "guestworkers." But the vast majority of these immigrants want what everyone else wants: families.

So the short-term benefits of migration must be balanced against what happens next. The human consequences of immigration come in the form of children born to today's immigrants. Immigrant children and children of immigrants already number 14.1 million—one in five of all Americans aged 18 and under—and that figure is growing fast. A large proportion of this new second generation is growing up under conditions of severe disadvantage. The low wages that make foreign workers so attractive to employers translate into poverty and inferior schooling for their children. If these youngsters were growing up just to replace their parents as the next generation of low-paid manual workers, the present situation could go on forever. But this is not how things happen.

Children of immigrants do not grow up to be low-paid foreign workers but U.S. citizens, with English as their primary language and American-style aspirations. In my study with Rubén G. Rumbaut of more than 5,200 second-generation children in the Miami and San Diego school systems, we found that 99 percent spoke fluent English and that by age 17 less than a third maintained any fluency in their parents' tongues. Two-thirds of these youths had aspirations for a college degree and a professional-level occupation. The proportion aspiring to a postgraduate education varied significantly by nationality, but even among the most impoverished groups the figures were high.

The trouble is that poor schools, tough neighborhoods, and the lack of role models to which their parents' poverty condemns them make these lofty aspirations an unreachable dream for many. Among Mexican parents, the largest group in our survey as well as in the total immigrant population, just 2.6 percent had a college education. Even after controlling for their paltry human capital, Mexican immigrants' incomes are significantly lower than those of workers with comparable education and work experience. Similar conditions were found among other sizable immigrant groups such as Haitians, Laotians, Nicaraguans, and Cambodians. Children born to these immigrants are caught between the pitiful jobs held by their parents and an American future blocked by a lack of resources and suitable training. Add to this the effects of race discrimination—because the majority of today's second generation is nonwhite by present U.S. standards—and the stage is set for serious trouble.

The future of children growing up under these conditions is not entirely unknown, for there are several telling precedents. Journalistic and scholarly writings concerning the nearly five million young inner-city Americans who are not only unemployed but unemployables—and the more than 300,000 young men of color who crowd the American prison system—commonly neglect to mention that this underclass population did not materialize out of thin air but is the human aftermath of earlier waves of labor migration. The forebears of today's urban underclass were the southern-black and Puerto Rican migrants who moved to the industrializing cities of the Northeast and Midwest in the mid-twentieth century in search of unskilled factory employment. They too willingly performed the poorly paid menial jobs of the time and were, for that reason, preferred by industrial employers. Yet when their children and grandchildren grew up, they found the road into the American middle class blocked by poverty, lack of training, and discrimination. The entrapment of this redundant population in American inner cities is the direct source of the urban underclass and the nightmarish world of drugs, gangs, and violence that these cities battle every day.

Children of poor immigrants are encountering similar and even more difficult conditions of blocked opportunity and external discrimination. In the postindustrial era, the American labor market has come to resemble a metaphoric hourglass, with job opportunities concentrated at the top (in professional and technical fields requiring an advanced education) and at the bottom (in low-paid menial services and agriculture). New migrants respond by crowding into the bottom of the hourglass, but their children, imbued with American-style aspirations, resist accepting the same jobs. This means that they must bridge in the course of a single generation the gap between their parents' low education and the college-level training required to access well-paid nonmenial jobs. Those who fail, and there are likely to be many, are just a step short of the same labormarket redundancy that has trapped descendants of earlier black and Puerto Rican migrants.

Assimilation under these conditions does not lead upward into the U.S. middle class but downward into poverty and permanent disadvantage. This outcome is not the fault of immigrant parents or their children but of the objective conditions with which they must cope. All immigrants are imbued with a strong success drive—otherwise they wouldn't have made the uncertain journey to a new land—and all have high ambitions for their children. But family values and a strong work ethic do not compensate for the social conditions that these children face.

Parents' educational expectations are quite high, even higher than their children's. Expectations vary significantly by nationality, but among all groups, 50 percent or more of parents believe that their offspring will attain a college degree. Yet the resources required to achieve this lofty goal—parental education, family income, quality of schools attended—often are not there. The differences found among immigrant nationalities . . . show the wide disparities in parents' income and education and in their children's attendance at poor inner-city schools. Groups that comprise the largest and fastest-growing components of contemporary immigration, primarily Mexicans, have the lowest human-capital endowments and incomes, and their children end up attending mostly inner-city schools.

Effects of these disparities do not take long to manifest themselves in the form of school achievement and the probability of dropping out of school. Parental education and occupation are consistently strong predictors of children's school achievement. Each additional point in parental socioeconomic status (a composite of parents' education, occupation, and home ownership) increases math-test scores by 8 percentile points and reading by 9 points in early adolescence (after controlling for other variables). Living in a family with both parents present also increases performance significantly and reduces the chances of leaving school. Growing up in an intact family and attending a suburban school in early adolescence cuts down the probability of dropping out by high school by a net 11 percent, or approximately half the average dropout rate (again controlling for other variables).

. . . While the correlation is not perfect, the groups with the lowest family incomes and educational endowments—and highest probability of attending inner-city schools—also tend to produce the most disadvantaged children, both in terms of test scores and the probability of achieving a high-school diploma.

At San Diego's Hoover High, there's a group that calls itself the Crazy Brown Ladies. They wear heavy makeup, or "ghetto paint" and reserve derision for classmates striving for grades ("schoolgirls" is the Ladies' label for these lesser beings). Petite Guatemalan-born Iris de la Puente never joined the Ladies, but neither did she make it through high school. The daughter of a gardener and a seamstress, she has lived alone with her mother for several years, since her father was deported and did not return. Mrs. de la Puente repeatedly exhorted Iris to stay in school, but her message was empty. The pressure of work kept the mother away from home for many hours, and her own modest education and lack of English fluency did not give her a clue how to help Iris. By ninth grade, the girl's grade-point average had fallen to a C and she was just hanging in there, hoping for a high-school diploma. When junior year rolled around, it was all over. "Going to college would be nice, but it was clear that it was not for me," Iris said. Getting a job, no matter how poorly paid, became the only option. As far as the immigrant second generation is concerned, it simply is not true that "where there's a will, there's a way." No matter how ambitious parents and children are, no matter how strong their family values and dreams of making it in America, the realities of poverty, discrimination, and poor schools become impassable barriers for many. Like Iris de la Puente, these youths find that the dream of a college education is just that. The same children growing up in inner cities encounter a ready alternative to education in the drug gangs and street culture that already saturate their environment. The emergence of a "rainbow underclass" that includes the offspring of many of today's immigrants is an ominous but distinct possibility.

The short-term economic benefits of immigration are easy to understand and equally easy to appropriate by the urban firms, ranches, and farms that employ this labor, ensuring their profitability. Absent heroic social supports, the long-term consequences are borne by children growing up under conditions of severe disadvantage and by society at large. If the United States wants to keep indulging its addiction to cheap foreign workers, it had better do so with full awareness of what comes next. For immigrants and their children are people, not just labor, and they cannot be dismissed so easily when their work is done. The aftermath of immigration depends on what happens to these children. The prospects for many, given the obstacles at hand, appear dim.

QUESTIONS

1. What rhetorical strategies make the introduction to Portes's article informative, engaging, and thought provoking? In what sense is this article a call for change?

2. Why do immigrants work in low-paying jobs that natives would never accept? What reform bill ensured the vulnerability of these immigrants? Why do employers profit from the reform bill and the reality that immigrants can be deported without notice?

3. In spite of their intentions to have better lives than their parents, what blocks many of the children of immigrants from countries such as Mexico, Cambodia, and Haiti from becoming successful in today's labor market? How well does Portes use examples and statistics to clarify and support their "dim" futures?

DIFFERING PERSPECTIVES: SHOULD DOCUMENTED NON-CITIZEN IMMIGRANTS BE GIVEN THE RIGHT TO VOTE ?

Ronald Hayduk

"Non-Citizen Voting: Pipe Dream or Possibility"

Ron Hayduk , a former social worker, is currently professor of political science at CUNY in Manhattan and the co-founder of the Immigrant Voting Project, which is dedicated to changing current voting laws to allow and assist immigrants in voting in local elections. He is the author, with Kevin Mattson, of Democracy's Moment: Reforming the American Political System for the 21st Century *(2002), co-author with Benjamin Shepard of* From ACT UP to the WTO: Urban Protest and Community Building in the Era of Globalization *(2002), and author of* Democracy for All: Restoring Immigrant Voting Rights in the United States *(2006). The following article provides a brief history of legal noncitizen immigrant voting rights in the United States and argues for the need, fairness, and feasibility of such rights.*

Introduction

The acquisition of political rights—including voting rights—has been a vital tool for every disempowered group in American's history to achieve economic, social and civil rights and equality (Williamson, 1960; Porter, 1971). Because legislative bodies confer rights and make public policy, it is critical to possess the capacity to influence and/or select representatives. Legal barriers to political participation, however, have hampered the attainment of such rights by distinct classes of citizens, including African-Americans, women, and youth.

Previously excluded groups have gained access to the franchise principally through political struggle. They fought their way into the polity through political agitation, sometimes using the courts as a tool. Ultimately they needed the support of other sectors in society to win political rights. The agitation of the property-less encouraged sectors of the propertied to extend the franchise; the abolitionist movement and civil rights movements led whites to enfranchise blacks; the suffragettes compelled men to include women among the voting citizenry; and younger adults, whose participation in the social movements of the 1960s and 1970s, were granted voting rights by older adults.

Why not for immigrants too?

Although noncitizen immigrants behave in much the same ways as citizens, they possess fewer rights and benefits. Immigrants are subject to all laws and pay taxes, work in and/or own businesses, send their children to schools, serve in the military and can be drafted, and participate in all aspects of daily social life. Nevertheless, noncitizen immigrants are precluded from selecting those who fashion public policy and represent them at every level of governance. As Salvador Hernandez, a 40-year-old immigrant from El Salvador who works for an organization called Centro Presente that promotes and supports immigrant civic activism, argued, "My children attend the public schools, so I should have a say in choosing those people who oversee how the [sic] school system is run. Similarly, I have the responsibility to pay taxes, so why can't I have the privilege of contributing to how those taxes are spent?" (McNaught, 1999.) Increasingly, we hear countless similar voices across the country.

It is undeniable that immigrants have re-emerged as pivotal players in American politics. The last three decades of mass migration have produced the largest immigrant population in the United States since the turn of the century. One in ten individuals is foreign born, the highest level since 1910 when over 14% were foreign-born. Moreover, most of the new arrivals have come from Latin America, Asia and the Caribbean, changing the ethnic and racial composition of the U.S. population. Since 1965, the number of immigrants living in the U.S. has tripled. Nearly one in ten families in the U.S. currently is a "mixed" family, having one or more parent that is a noncitizen and one or more child that is a citizen (Fix and Zimmerman, 1999). The U.S. Census reports that several states and locales now have a majority minority population, led by Hispanics who have surpassed African Americans as the single largest "minority" group in the U.S.

These demographic changes hold significant political implications, especially in the states and metropolitan areas where immigrants are concentrated. Six states are home for the overwhelming majority of new immigrants—California, New York, Florida, Texas, Illinois and New Jersey (in that order)—and within these states they are concentrated in eight metropolitan regions: Los Angeles, New York City, Miami, Anaheim, Chicago, Washington D.C., Houston and San Francisco. These immigrant-receiving states play an important role in choosing representatives for Congress—affecting the apportionment of seats in the House of Representatives—and hold critical electoral votes for the presidency. At the state and local level, where they make up a larger proportion of the potential electorate, immigrants can have an even greater impact.

Yet, of the nearly thirty million foreign-born people that currently live in the U.S., there are over twelve million legal permanent residents who remain noncitizens and are barred from voting, over one third! In the 1996 elections, for example, 15.5% of the people who did not vote said they were noncitizens (The U.S. Bureau of the Census, http://www.census.gov). Of those individuals, 53% were Hispanic; 13.5% were white; 9% were black (there was no category for Asians). Despite the recent increase in the number of immigrants who naturalize—largely due to a host of anti-immigrant legislation—the average time it takes to obtain citizenship is nearly ten years. Moreover, many legal immigrants never become U.S. citizens—not wanting to lose ties to their home country—but remain full time U.S. residents.

Available evidence reveals immigrant political participation lags behind their numerical strength, especially compared to native born citizens. Consider voting. Studies show that immigrants register and vote at slightly lower rates than native born citizens, though wide variation exists among different immigrant groups (Mollenkopf, Olsen and Ross, forthcoming; Minnite, Holdaway and Hayduk, 2001; DeSipio, 2001). Variations exist, for example, among Latino immigrants who tend to take longer to naturalize than Asian immigrants, but who register and vote at higher rates than Asians. Foreign-born whites and Asians voted at lower rates than their native stock counterparts in the 1996 presidential elections, but foreign-born naturalized black and Latino citizens voted at higher rates than native-born counterparts (Mollenkopf, Olsen, and Ross, forthcoming; DeSipio, 2001). In the 2000 elections in New York City, nearly 40% of all the 2.2 million votes cast were by immigrants who have naturalized and are now citizens. (The New York Immigration Coalition http://www.thenyic.org/nyicpublishing/nyic.html).

Drawing upon the work of other scholars and immigrant rights advocates, this article argues for the reinstatement of noncitizen voting rights. Given the significant anti-immigrant sentiment in the U.S., the notion of allowing noncitizens to vote might appear outlandish upon initial exploration. But once examined, a compelling case can be made for noncitizen voting.

It's legal. The Constitution does not preclude it and the courts have upheld voting by noncitizens. In fact, noncitizens enjoyed voting rights for most of our country's history—from the founding until the 1920s—in much of the country.

It's rational. There are good reasons for the enfranchisement of immigrants—both moral and practical—including notions of equal rights and treatment (as articulated in the American Revolution, the abolitionist movement, the suffrage movement, and the civil rights tradition).

It's feasible. Recently, noncitizen voting has been re-established in several municipalities in the U.S. New York and Chicago permit noncitizen voting in school board elections; several municipalities in Maryland and Massachusetts have extended the right to vote for local offices to noncitizens; and a nearly another dozen other jurisdictions have recently considered or are currently moving to establish noncitizen voting rights.

The Appearance and Disappearance of Noncitizen Voting Rights

Even though federal law does not preclude voting by noncitizens, its elimination from American political practice has eviscerated national memory. "Aliens" voted in local, state and even national elections in twenty-two states and federal territories from the founding until the 1920s and noncitizen immigrants held public offices, such as alderman, coroner and school board member (Raskin, 1993).

Early in our country's history, emerging republicanism and liberalism embodied in slogans such as "no taxation with out representation" made noncitizen voting a logical democratic practice tied to notions of "inhabitants" and difficult to challenge. Voting rights were predominantly tied to race and property. In fact, alien suffrage was compatible with exclusion of other categories of residents (women, men without property, and blacks/slaves), and actually buttressed the privileging of propertied white male Christians (Raskin, 1993:1401, citing Collier, 1992).

During the antebellum period and westward expansion, however, the issue increasingly became more contentious. Although the War of 1812 slowed and even reversed the spread of alien suffrage—in part by raising the specter of foreign "enemies"—Northern states generally held that alien suffrage fell in line with basic rights of the Republic while Southern states saw immigrants as a threat because of the newcomers' general hostility to slavery. Alien suffrage was a major issue in the Civil War (Raskin, 1993). Alien suffrage, nevertheless, spread in the South and West with the growing need for new labor, particularly after the Civil War and during Reconstruction. Many new states and territories used alien suffrage as an incentive to attract settlers and as a pathway to citizenship (though not as a substitute). The general practice was to require residency from six months to one year before voting rights were granted. At least thirteen new states adopted alien suffrage. Noncitizen voting was practiced to its greatest extent by about 1875. By the close of the nineteenth century, nearly one-half of all the states and territories had some experience with voting by aliens, most of them lasting for more than half a century (Alysworth, 1931).

But with the massive increase of darker Mediterranean and politically suspect immigrants at the turn of the century, however, anti-alien passions flourished that halted and reversed these practices. The loss of noncitizen voting rights during the first decades of this century—coupled with the malaportionment of cities—came at the same time when the population of urban America rivaled the populations in much of the rural and suburban parts of the country (Hayduk, 2000). In fact, by 1920, 51% of the population in the U.S. resided in cities (Judd and Swanstrom, 2002). Moreover, 70% of total government spending was done at the state and local levels before 1929 (Ethington, 1993:307).

Interestingly, the timing of immigrant disenfranchisement—and other poor and minority groups through means such as literacy tests, poll taxes, restrictive voter registration procedures and the like—may not have been coincidental. Such disenfranchising measures were promoted and enacted by powerful economic and political elites just when the electoral potential for working class constituencies and powerful third party movements was growing (Keyssar, 2000; Piven and Cloward, 2000; Burnham, 1970; Schattschneider, 1960; and Hayduk, 2002). Additional legislation drastically reduced the flow of immigrants into the U.S., and limited the proportion of non-Western European immigrants.

Arguments for Noncitizen Voting

Aside from legal arguments mentioned above, there are moral and political claims that immigrant rights organizations utilize to advocate for non-citizen voting rights in state and local elections. Generally, advocates employ many of the same arguments used in past struggles to expand the franchise to previously excluded groups, including blacks, women, and youth. There are three primary arguments (Raskin, 1993; Shimmelman, 1992; Gordon, 1999; Harper-Ho, 2000; Brozovich, 2002).

First, a basic tenet of democratic theory is found in the notion of the social contract. The legitimacy of government rests on the consent of the governed. Members of legitimate democratic communities are rightfully obliged to obey the laws they are subject to if they possess a means to participate in governance, such as by voting. Citizens consent to be governed by possessing power to select their representatives and hold them accountable. The founding fathers enshrined this notion in the phrase "no taxation without representation," which provided a rallying cry for the American Revolution. This argument emphasizes the rights of immigrants themselves as members of democratic communities. In fact, federal, state and local governments already treat noncitizens—both legal permanent residents and undocumented people—like other community members. The most obvious example is that all residents must pay income taxes regardless of their immigration status. In fact, the overwhelming proportion of immigrants pay more in taxes than they receive in benefits, and more than the average American (except refugees), while contributing positively to the nation's economy on the whole (Fix and Passel, 1994; Foner, et. Als, 2001).

The argument is that noncitizens have the same stake and interest in a community's political decisions as that of any citizen. Like other citizens, immigrants tend to become involved and invested in their communities and the nation when given a voice and means of participating in social and political processes. Indeed, voting is an important means of becoming incorporated and engaged in a polity, not merely the outcome of becoming assimilated. According to this line of reasoning, the proper measure of membership in democratic communities is residency, not nationality per se. The main point—one that runs through all three arguments—is fairness. Vladimir Morales, a member of the local governing body in Amherst, Massachusetts and who led the campaign for noncitizen voting rights there, argued that "Resident aliens own houses and businesses in Amherst, pay property taxes and send their children to school, but they cannot participate in the democratic process. We have a lot of citizens who pay taxes who make decisions for other people who pay taxes . . . It's about expanding democracy." Similar arguments made in Cambridge Massachusetts led its City Council to extend voting rights to resident aliens in 2000 for School Committee Elections. These same kinds of issues are currently being articulated in other jurisdictions in Massachusetts and elsewhere, which are considering following suit.

A second argument refers to issues of discrimination and bias. Noncitizens are at risk of bias in majoritarian electoral systems because they lack voting rights and politicians can ignore their interests. Discriminatory districting schemes as well as a broad range of legislation and practices (in employment, housing, education, healthcare, and criminal justice) are inevitable by-products of their political exclusion, not to mention xenophobic political campaigning and racial profiling. Again, advocates of immigrant enfranchisement marshal standard democratic and civil rights principles. Noncitizens have legitimate interests in a community's political processes and need protections within it. As Jamin Raskin, a law professor at American University who led the successful campaign for noncitizen voting rights in Tacoma Park, Maryland stated, "If you can't vote, you tend to be disregarded politically. It [noncitizen voting rights] has extended real visibility to a formerly invisible population" (Donn, 1998).

A third argument stresses the benefits that would accrue to other community members who have common interests. Working class individuals and people of color—particularly in metropolitan regions—face many of the same problems that immigrants do, including discrimination in employment, housing, education and the like. Common interests can forge common ground, reduce competition and strife, and enhance mutual understanding and cooperation. On the other hand, the struggle for scarce economic resources, cultural differences and prejudice can breed intergroup conflict. Universal voting rights can provide a buffer against strife, segmented assimilation, or incorporation/assimilation on basis of race, education level, income, and ideology (i.e. skewed/biased incorporation).

Alliances among competing minority groups in struggles for fair employment practices, living wage campaigns, access to affordable housing and education and so on, have formed the basis of such effective coalitions. Noncitizen political participation could help strengthen potential alliances in electoral contests and public policy formation. Indeed, an enlarged electorate might have changed the outcome of close elections.

Arguments Against Noncitizen Voting and Counter Arguments

Oppponents to this line of reasoning raise several objections (Geyer, 1998). Some argue that immigrants already have a means of obtaining voting rights: by becoming citizens. Another counter argument is that since noncitizens have not sworn a loyalty oath to the U.S., they cannot be trusted to vote in the best interests of this country, as opposed to their own interests or those of their country of origin. Yet, proponents of this argument, critics contend, ignore the fact that people born in the United States are not required to swear allegiance to the Constitution (Gordon, 1999). Ostensible proof of noncitizen commitment and loyalty to the U.S. would be their naturalization. Not only is it flawed to assume that native born residents are "loyal," but it is equally untrue that noncitizens are not "loyal." In addition, this argument overlooks that immigrants are, in fact, already community members. A measure of noncitizen commitment and loyalty is evident in their choice of coming to the United States, and perhaps more tellingly, in their continued presence here. Noncitizens demonstrate their commitment and loyalty daily, such as in participating in voluntary organizations or opening a small business. In fact, during earlier periods of American history, it was widely believed that noncitizen immigrants who declared their intent to naturalize should be allowed voting rights because it would encourage acquisition of knowledge about the U.S. and hasten integration and assimilation. To make their right to participate in the management of public affairs dependent upon renouncing citizenship to their home country—which might preclude their right to return or to hold property in their country of origin—amounts to denial of the latter rights. Given the magnitude of such consequences, including not seeing family and loved ones, many immigrants don't naturalize yet live in the U.S. for decades.

Another counter argument is that noncitizens lack sufficient knowledge of and feeling for American political institutions and issues to make informed voting decisions. Immigrant rights advocates note that specific knowledge is not a prerequisite for political participation. If it were, many native born citizens would fail tests of even basic political knowledge, as survey research has consistently shown. Moreover, such notions come dangerously close to those previously used to impose literacy tests, or to exclude or expel people on the basis of ideological beliefs. In addition, most "education" on campaign issues often occurs in the few weeks and months before an election, not years prior, and is all too often done by the media and candidates anyway. Even conceding that political education has long-term components it is not safe to assume that large differences would exist between the two populations. In fact, because noncitizens have chosen this country rather than being born into it, and are in the process of learning about its language and culture, they often pay more attention to the events around them than many disaffected citizens do. Foreign-language television, radio, and newspapers in many immigrant communities keep people up to date on politics here as well as abroad. If it is the politics of immigrants that opponents dislike or fear, that issue must be exposed as such and publicly debated.

Opponents of noncitizen voting also argue that noncitizens would tip the political balance in a state or community by voting in their own interest. For example, noncitizens could vote to grant state public assistance to undocumented people, or permit bilingual instruction in the public schools.

While it may be true that many noncitizen immigrants might vote for such policies, native born citizens also vote their own interests. Both groups, however, are not homogeneous. It is not exactly clear how noncitizens would actually vote and what impacts they would actually have on the political balance of power. Indeed, this is an area that requires more research. There is some evidence that what little is known about the voting patterns of newly naturalized U.S. citizens—as well as noncitizen voting in Europe—suggests only modest shifts, if any, would occur (DeSipio, 2001; Minnite, Holdaway, Hayduk, 2001). Newly naturalized immigrants do tend to be more sympathetic toward other noncitizen immigrants than native born citizens (Minnite, Holdaway, Hayduk, 2001). Moreover, the enfranchisement of immigrant voters could invigorate electoral dynamics and produce a general increase in democratic participation of all classes of voters. Indeed, social and political conflicts might be able to be worked out at the ballot box instead of the streets.

Another counter argument is that allowing noncitizen voting would increase electoral fraud. Unethical immigrants or dishonest politicians might use corrupt voting practices to compromise the integrity of the ballot. But logically immigrants are no more likely to be bought or sold than citizens. There is little hard evidence of voter fraud, both historically and contemporarily, contrary to some popular misconceptions (Hayduk, 2002). Furthermore, strong anti-fraud measures are already in place that can detect and deter fraud. To be sure, there are practical problems of managing the simultaneous voting of different classes of electors while preventing potential double voting and the like, which need to be solved. Decisions will need to be made about whether, for example, to restrict voting to legally admitted noncitizens who have been residing in a jurisdiction for a certain period of time (i.e. how many months or years?), and whether to require voters to prove this at poll sites or during the registration process with appropriate identification papers. In order to reduce potential for erecting other cumbersome barriers as well as costs and confusion, the fewer the distinctions between classes of voters and procedures that are required, the better. Finally, existing systems that allow noncitizens to vote illustrate the viability of such reform. Maryland's board of elections, for example, keeps two separate lists of citizens and noncitizen voters for local elections and for state and national elections.

Conclusion: Expand the Franchise

Emerging patterns of immigration are challenging current political alignments and creating new fault lines with the potential to alter the balance of social and political power. Immigration is changing the political arithmetic, propelling parties and politicians who jockey for advantage to adjust campaign strategies to reflect evolving electoral conditions. Some interest groups and politicians actively court immigrant allegiance and forge new political alliances, while others attack or distance themselves from immigrant groups. The case of California—particularly evident in the passage of Proposition 187, and the shifting fortunes of Democrats and Republicans in electoral contests for key offices—and the recent "anti-terrorist" legislation are perhaps the most dramatic but not unique examples. Controversy swirls about the impacts immigrants have on labor markets and public spending to the merits of bi-lingual education and how we define what it means to be an "American." We see proposals that restrict immigration, hear debates about where the lines should be drawn between aliens and citizens in social policies, and witness explosive tensions among immigrants and the native born.

These developments, among others, have shown signs of a growing immigrant consciousness. Even while anti-immigrant sentiments have reigned in public discourse and policy, a mobilization among immigrant groups and their political allies is evident. Immigrant rights organizations have proliferated and engage in a broad range of activism and advocacy. Immigrants walk picket lines and lobby legislatures with greater frequency and force. Such activity reveals a growing sense among new immigrants that they possess legitimate claims on the American polity, and they are commanding greater attention. These issues cut to the heart of democratic participation and citizenship.

A growing number of immigrant rights advocates, politicians and candidates, and scholars argue for the reinstatement of noncitizen voting rights in the aforementioned locales in the United States. Europe also provides a compelling case for noncitizen voting rights. The Maastricht Treaty granted all Europeans the right to vote in European countries other than their own, expanding what has been practiced for years in Sweden (1975), Ireland (1975), the Netherlands (1975), Denmark (1977), and Norway (1978); several Swiss cantons (Neufchatel and Jura) permit noncitizen voting and Finland and Iceland allow Nordic citizens voting rights; and Estonia allows noncitizen voting at the local level.

A campaign based upon democratic and moral claims can mobilize noncitizens and likely allies. Such a campaign could provide immigrants with an important means to defend against nativist attacks, and also give other minority groups greater means to forge winning voting blocks that can advance their mutual interests. Immigrant's taxation without representation not only challenges the legitimacy of America's mantle of democratic governance, it also provides a rationale and opportunity for organizing a progressive political majority. Historically, immigrant votes often accounted for the difference between the winners and the losers in elections. Noncitizen political participation could help strengthen potential progressive alliances in electoral contests and public policy formation.

Just as the civil rights movement sought to extend the franchise to African-Americans and others who had been barred from voting to attain equitable representation, a renewed movement for human rights would further extend the franchise to new Americans. The dominant political parties and candidates are increasingly turning their attention towards immigrants. It would be wise for today's progressives to lead the way.

QUESTIONS

1. Evaluate Hayduk's historical overview of immigrant voting—how does it prepare the way for his following arguments for allowing legal noncitizen immigrants the right to vote?
2. Examine Hayduk's arguments for voting rights for noncitizen immigrants. Which are most persuasive? How well does he support them with evidence and examples?
3. How effectively does Hayduk refute the possible arguments against immigrant voting rights? Could you think of other such arguments?

Stanley A. Renshon

"The Debate Over Non-Citizen Voting"

Stanley A. Renshon, who earned a PhD. in political science from the University of Pennsylvania in 1972, is a professor of political science and coordinator of the Interdisciplinary Program in the Psychology of Social and Political behavior at the City University of New York Graduate Center, as well as a certified psychoanalyst. He has published articles in many professional journals; among his 14 books are One America?: Political Leadership, National Identity, and the Dilemmas of Diversity *(2001) and* The 50% American: Immigration and National Identity in an Age of Terrorism *(2005). In the following article*

Renshon takes the opposite position from Hayduk on immigrant voting rights, arguing that the vast numbers of uneducated and unknowledgeable new noncitizen voters would have a grave effect on future decisions and policies in many urban areas throughout the country and reduce the need and desire for actual citizenship.

There is no more iconic feature of American democracy and citizenship than the right to vote. Men and women have marched for it, fought for it, and died for it. Historically, those without property, women, and African-Americans have all legitimately counted their progress toward full citizenship by their ability to vote. And they have correctly judged America's progress toward living up to its ideals by the extension of the vote to all of the country's citizens.

Given these facts, it is understandable that the average American might well ask: What debate?

A Debate Gaining Momentum

The answer to that question is that this debate has been slowly gathering momentum out of the public view for some time. While most Americans have been understandably preoccupied with terrorism, Iraq, the economy, illegal immigration, and other issues, a steady drumbeat of advocacy has been gathering force trying to legitimize and implement the idea that the United States should allow new immigrants to vote without becoming citizens.

Advocates of this position use many arguments—about fairness, representation, teaching democracy, increasing participation, expanding democracy, being welcoming to immigrants, the large number of Hispanics who are not yet citizens, and so on. They buttress their claims with the fact that several foreign counties now allow immigrants to vote in local elections, that some American states and territories once allowed it, and that some localities allow it now.

This last fact, that there are several municipalities in the United States that currently allow non-citizens to vote in local elections, may come as somewhat of a surprise. The best known of these is Takoma Park, Md., which introduced the practice in 1992, although its legality has never been tested in the courts. In addition, legislation has been formally introduced in a number of cities, including New York City and Washington, D.C., and in at least two states—New York and Minnesota—to allow non-citizens to vote in local elections. In Massachusetts, the cities of Amherst, Cambridge, and Newton have approved measures to allow non-citizens to vote in local elections, but the ordinances require approval by the state legislature, which has not yet acted favorably on these proposals. A number of other cities are in the initial stages of considering such schemes.

Chicago allows non-citizens to vote in school board elections, and New York did until elected school boards were abolished in 2003. Boulder, Colo., recently introduced a measure to allow non-citizens to serve on city boards and commissions. And in City Heights, Calif., all residents, regardless of citizenship, are able to vote for members of the Planning Committee.

Iconic Words, Prosaic Motivations

Anyone who delves into the arguments put forward in favor of giving non-citizens the right to vote soon encounters iconic terms like "justice," "fairness," and "democracy." A great deal of the advocacy for non-citizen voting makes extensive use of what Mary Ann Glendon refers to as "rights talk," the tendency to turn every policy debate into a clash of rights. From the advocate's perspective this is a winning strategy. One of the chief advocates of the non-citizen voting movement, Ron Hayduk, is quite direct about this strategy: "The use of democratic and moral claims on the polity has often been an effective tool used by social justice advocates in struggles for equality." In their view, advocates are simply pressing for what they believe many would agree in theory would be a good thing—more democracy, higher morality, more social justice, and more equality, to name all four iconic terms used in that single sentence.

The problem with these iconic words is that they have many meanings. Their incantation is not necessarily synonymous with persuasive argument. Advocates use expansive definitions of these terms to further their goals, and rarely address the political, cultural, and policy implications of their proposals. Moreover, while advocacy rhetoric emphasizes lofty theoretical sentiments, there often are much more prosaic motives at work. Many supporters of non-citizen voting are seeking what they feel will be a large and reliable source of votes for their progressive political agenda. Hayduk, for instance, writes that for allies it is important to drive "home the potential benefits of non-citizens to forge progressive political majorities."

Others are more interested in furthering the political fortunes of the ethnic groups they favor. Louis DeSipio and Rodolfo de la Garza argue that non-citizens should be given the right to vote, although their focus is on the Spanish-speaking community. Mr. DeSipio details in a separate book "the low level of citizenship among Latino immigrants," but argues that "Latino permanent residents offer a new pool of citizens and new voters. Sufficient numbers could naturalize to have influence in the next election." And some proponents are simply interested, as one would expect from incumbents who wish to remain in office, in having what they envision as a large pool of reliable voters for their reelection.

It would be a tempting to dismiss calls for non-citizen voting as an idea that is not likely to get very far. That however, would be a mistake. There is now a concerted campaign by a vocal group of liberal (or progressive, if you prefer) academics, law professors, elected public officials, and community activists, working in tandem, to decouple voting from American citizenship. Their odds are long, but the stakes are high.

These activists are trying to erase the distinction between citizen and alien, or between national and foreigner . . . [speaking] directly to the nature of state sovereignty itself." This sounds like a somewhat abstract argument, but it is a debate with the most immediate, direct and profound consequences.

Some Non-Citizen Voting Proposals

Advocates for non-citizen voting have put forward a variety of proposals. Some focus on gaining non-citizens the vote in local school board elections. Others see granting voting rights at the local level, in less-threatening venues like school board elections, as a bridge to a wider expansion of voting rights for non-citizens. Others focus on gaining voting rights for non-citizens at the local level, even though as one advocate has written, "it is admittedly hard to think of any principled way to justify the inclusion of aliens in local elections, but exclude them from state elections. The problem is that the U.S. constitution categorically makes all persons enfranchised in state legislative elections into federal electors, and *alien participation in national elections presents a far more troubling proposition.*"

Some want non-citizens to have voting rights at the state as well as the local level. They advocate this despite, or perhaps because of, the fact is that, as noted, given the structure of constitutional law this would inevitably involve granting voting rights at the national level as well. Some want the Supreme Court to declare non-citizen voting a federal right, thereby nullifying the overwhelming number of state constitutions that specifically state that voting is a right reserved for citizens. And some see no reason why non-citizens should not be allowed to run and serve in public office, as well as vote.

The New York City Proposal

In the spring of 2005, William Perkins, then the New York City Council's Deputy Majority Leader, introduced a bill that defines a municipal voter as, "a person who is not a United States citizen, but is lawfully present in the United States, and has been a resident of New York City, as defined herein, for six months or longer by the date of the next election, and who meets all qualifications for registering to vote under the New York State election law, except U.S. citizenship, and has registered to vote with the New York City Board of Elections under this provision." This proposed bill would allow non-citizens to vote for "any municipal officer, including, but not limited to, the mayor, the comptroller, the public advocate, members of the council, borough presidents, and any other future elected municipal official." These new voters may vote in, "without limitations, primary elections, and on municipal ballot questions."

This proposal effectively bypasses all the requirements for learning about the immigrant's new country that are built into the nationalization process. It does not require a demonstrated familiarity with the English language. It does not require a demonstration of any knowledge of American civics and history. And it does not require any knowledge of the issues on which the person would be voting, since the person need only have been in the country for six months.

The most immediate (but not the only) drawbacks to such a proposal are obvious. The new non-citizen voters would be unfamiliar with the United States, its politics, its history, its culture, its language, and the issues on which they are being allowed to vote. Further, having been granted a green card simply acknowledges that a person has applied for and been granted permanent residence. Allowing non-citizens to vote before they have gone through the naturalization process is likely to diminish immigrants' interest in undertaking that process. And this in turn is likely to marginalize a process through which many immigrants increase their emotional and psychological attachment to their new American community. Proposals to allow non-citizens to vote fail to recognize that attachment is an important part of integrating immigrants into the American national community, and that the naturalization process has an important role to play in this regard.

The DeSipio/de la Garza Hispanic Non-citizen Voting Proposal

As noted, some proposals for non-citizen voting have come from ethnic advocates interested in furthering the political clout of their favored ethnic groups. Louis DeSipio, now at the University of California, Irvine, and Rodolfo de la Garza, at the University of Texas, first put forward such a proposal in 1993. Their proposal "is a modified form of the current effort to make non-citizens eligible to vote." They, however, "add two twists":

"First, we would allow noncitizens to vote for the five-year period during which they are statutorily ineligible to naturalize. Under this system, recently immigrated permanent residents would be able to obtain a five-year voter registration card (transferable across jurisdictions, but not extendable). After five years, they would no longer be eligible for permanent resident voting privileges, but would be able to naturalize. Recognizing that the INS suffers from frequent backlogs, *we would allow some provision for extending the temporary privileges while the application is on file*."

The proposal's authors disagree on the range of elections to which their proposal would apply. "Because of their ability to shape national policy," de la Garza, would extend this limited non-citizen voting *only* for state and local elections." His co-author, DeSipio, "however fears the administrative burdens to local election officials of having to create two sets of voting lists and two ballots would allow permanent residents to vote in all elections during the first five years of residence."

This proposal, like that of New York Councilman William Perkins noted above, raises the same set of voting readiness issues. Here too, new non-citizen voters would not have to be familiar with or knowledgeable of any aspect of the country's history, language, politics, or culture. Yet what is truly unique about this proposal is the authors' highly unusual reassurance as to why it should be adopted: Hispanics won't make use of it.

In surely one of the oddest underlying arguments put forward in favor of non-citizen voting, the authors note, "We think that regardless of one's philosophical attitudes toward noncitizen voting in the contemporary political environment it has one serious flaw: Few noncitizens would use the right." A few pages later, they remind their readers thusly: "Again, it is important to make note that neither one of us thinks that many noncitizens would vote in large numbers under this proposal."

The question immediately arises then: Why bother? Well, it seems that the authors are really of two minds about their proposal. On one hand, their view is that most of those for whom it is intended won't use it. On the other hand, they think it might have a "great impact" on cities where there is a sizable non-citizen population." One reviewer of a book authored by Mr. DeSipio notes that he calls for "a massive, national citizenship campaign targeting these noncitizens [because it] would foster a sense of Latino unity and purpose, and translate into a serious political movement. The momentum created by hundreds of thousands of immigrants joining the polity would spur all Latinos toward greater political participation, culminating in a Latino electorate taking its place among the major new electorates of this century." Allowing non-citizens to vote for a five-year period that could be renewable for some further period would be very consistent with that aim.

The professors also point out that there could be national implications to such a policy. They write that "it must be noted that the only national race—the campaign for the presidency—is in fact just fifty state races in which the winner takes all of the states' electoral votes. Thus in a very close race that is determined by the votes of the larger states (most of which are immigrant receiving states), an empowered noncitizen electorate could swing the election." These advocates try to be reassuring by noting that, "The scenarios vary from the possible—influence in local elections—to the highly unlikely, that is, national or state level influence."

So, their point seems to be that non-citizens are unlikely to use the vote if it is given to them. On the other hand, if they do use it, they may be able to tip elections. This raises a very basic and direct question: Why should the United States have to take any chance that persons who have literally just arrived in the country and are very unlikely to know anything about its politics—much less the complex issues that citizens are called upon to address—have the opportunity to hold the fate of public decisions in their hands?

In Lieu of Naturalization?

The DeSipio/de la Garza proposal, like others that would allow an immigrant to vote within a short time of arrival, would substantially downgrade the importance of naturalization. That is because the second of their "two twists" involves allowing non-citizen voters to substitute evidence that they have voted for having to take the naturalization test. In their words, "naturalization applicants who can show that they voted in most primary and general elections would be exempt from the naturalization examination. The examination is designed to test good citizenship through indirect measures such as knowledge of American history and civics. We propose that voting is an equally good measure of commitment to and understanding of the American system."

The authors make a number of basic mistakes in this statement. They err in equating the knowledge of American history and citizenship with "commitment." Such knowledge can be part of the basis for forming an emotional attachment, and that attachment in turn can grow into a commitment over time, but it is a mistake to equate abstract knowledge with the emotional attachments that go into developing a commitment.

The authors also err in failing to see that knowledge of American history and citizenship, as well as knowledge of English (that the authors belatedly added to their list of items tested by the citizenship test) are not so much measures of good citizenship, indirect or otherwise, as they are a *foundation* for it. Knowledge of the English language and American history and civics does not automatically make you a good citizen, but it does provide a starting point for becoming one.

It is hard to see how immigrants who know little of American history or American politics and its debates and who do not speak the language will develop that foundation by just pressing a lever three or four times over a five-year period. In practice this would mean that they have voted in "most" of the five elections that take place in any five-year period. In a later publication, they change the requirement of voting in "most" elections to a requirement that such immigrants vote "regularly." It is unclear what this term means.

Perhaps this would require new immigrants to vote in a minimum of three or maybe four elections. In return for this, the authors would "grant citizenship automatically upon application." No civics test. No American history test. No test of minimum English language facility. And no further mechanism for encouraging new immigrants to get that important basic knowledge. On all these matters, the proposal is very ill advised. Proposals that would grant non-citizens the right to vote will severely curtail the importance of the naturalization process, and that process plays an important role in the integration of new citizens into the American national community.

Potential Impact

Whether or not non-citizens would make use of the vote is one question. How many would be eligible to do so is another question. Those numbers give us some indication of the potential impact of such proposals. It is useful to begin framing the issues that underlie the debate by first asking a deceptively easy question: What is the number of non-citizens in this country that would be potentially be affected by allowing non-citizens to vote? That is not an easy number to ascertain. Some studies include persons residing in the country illegally. Some count those "recently naturalized," while others count all naturalized citizens, whenever they were naturalized. And finally, different studies rely on different data sets that add variations to the figures. With those caveats in mind, we can at least attempt to narrow the range of estimates of the numbers of legal non-citizen residents who would be affected by the proposals to allow non-citizens to vote.

The Eligible Pool of Non-citizen Voters

The March 2007 Current Population Survey, conducted by the Census Bureau, reported that there were about 20.2 million adult non-citizens in the country, about half of whom are believed (based on other research) to be illegal immigrants. Adding to this figure are two important factors. The first is the number of legal immigrants admitted to the country every year. These constitute the pool of potential non-citizen voters for any given five-year period before they begin the naturalization process and become citizens (if they do so). Let us stipulate that the whole process from entry to oath takes six years to complete. So, to take the previous six-year period the numbers would be 1,058,902 for 2001; 1,059,356 for 2002; 703,542 for 2003; 957,883 for 2004; 1,122,373 for 2005; and 1,226,264 for 2006. Thus, in 2006, the pool of non-citizen voters would be the number of new immigrants for the preceding five years, which totals 4,902,056 minus the number that were below voting age (18) in any single year. So, in 2006, the country admitted 1,226,254 immigrants of whom 78 percent were over 18 and thus immediately eligible to vote under most of the non-citizen voting proposals. This figure would need to be added to the number of immigrants from previous years over 18 who had not naturalized.

A number of new immigrants will become naturalized citizens, thus reducing the pool of potential non-citizen voters, but how many? Here again, numbers and the means by which they are calculated vary. A 2007 study by the Pew Hispanic Center estimated that naturalization rates among those eligible were 52 percent for the year 2005. These rates, however, have varied over time depending on levels of immigration and political circumstances. In 1970, the naturalization rate was 64 percent but it dropped over time until in 1996 it stood at 39 percent.

Assuming a continuing robust naturalization of 50 percent, we can then estimate that the pool of non-citizen voters will increase somewhere between 400,000 and 500,000 each year. *So a prudent working assumption would be that there are today about 10.5 million legally resident non-citizens, with that number is growing at the rate of 400,000 to 500,000 each year.*

State and Local Impact

The numbers above are figures for the United States as a whole, but given immigrant settlement patterns it is clear that some localities and elections would be affected more than others. One way to look at this impact is to begin to look at the state distributions of new immigrant settlement. The Passel study of naturalization lists six states as major destinations. They are (with the number of persons eligible but not yet naturalized): California (2.6 million), New York (1.1 million), Texas (766,000), Florida (607,000), New Jersey (373,000), and Illinois (340,000). In addition, each of the major destination states has a pool of soon-to-be eligible immigrants ranging from a high of 717,000 (California) to 142,000 (Illinois).

Seen from a slightly different perspective, a U.S. Census report from 2003 found that non-citizens accounted for about 10 percent or more of the populations of six major states plus the District of Columbia: California (15.5 percent), D.C. (10.4 percent), Florida (9.5 percent), Nevada (11.3 percent), New Jersey (10.3 percent), New York (10.2 percent), and Texas (10.2 percent).

Within states, some cities and metropolitan areas are magnets for new immigrants. Within New York City's foreign-born population of 2.87 million foreign-born residents in 2000, 65.5 percent or 1.59 million were non-citizens. When introducing his non-citizen voting bill into the New York City Council, Mr. Perkins used a figure of 1,361,007 noncitizens of voting age living in New York as of 2005.

Hayduk provides us with some further information on the number of non-citizens in various kinds of local geographical areas. Twenty-nine states contain cities with a non-citizen voting population of more than 10 percent. In immigrant-rich states, the figures can be dramatic. In California, 19 percent of the state population is made up of non-citizens. In at least 85 cities, 25 percent of the population consists of non-citizens. Eighteen percent of municipalities have non-citizen populations of between 40 and 49 percent. In 12 other municipalities, non-citizens comprise a majority of the adult population—between 50 and 63 percent.

However, the potential political impact of allowing non-citizens to vote is unlikely to be felt only in California. Across the United States, 874 cities have an adult non-citizen populations of more than 10 percent; 193 cities have a non-citizen population of more than 25 percent. And 21 cities have an adult non-citizen population of 50 percent or more.

The 10 most populous cities in the United States have a large percentage of adult non-citizens. These range from a high of 32.2 percent (Los Angeles) to a low of 13.8 percent (Austin). Other major cities with substantial adult non-citizen populations include New York City (22.9 percent), Chicago (16.4 percent), Houston (22.9 percent), Phoenix (17.5 percent), San Diego (16.6 percent), Dallas (22.27 percent), San Francisco (16.7 percent), and San Jose (24.9 percent).

The Consequences of Non-citizen Voting on American Political Culture

For many advocates, non-citizen voting represents the so-far unachieved holy grail of liberal politics, the creation of a major and sustainable progressive voting majority. Commenting on the possibilities of non-citizen voting, Hayduk writes that the "Creation of a truly universal suffrage would create conditions conducive to forming progressive coalitions." He then immediately goes on to exalt: "Imagine the progressive political possibilities in jurisdictions of high numbers of immigrants such as New York City; Los Angeles; Washington D.C.; and Chicago—as well as in such states—if non citizens were re-enfranchised."

Hayduk and many of his allies nurture high hopes for the impact of these initiatives. He writes, "noncitizen adults already comprise over 10 percent of the voting-age population in seven states and the District of Columbia, and 19 percent of all California voters. If these noncitizens were enfranchised, they could yield decisive power in state races." And one might add here, a number of cities, towns, and municipalities.

There is, however, one question that advocates of non-citizen voting do not address: What would happen to America's politics and political culture were advocates to get their wish? What would happen if they were able to successfully accomplish their goals and non-citizens nationwide were given the right to vote? How would American citizens in any state, city, or county feel about having an election decided by people who had not yet joined the community of citizenship and might never do so?

What if the political center of gravity in those places shifted decisively to the left because of the influx of these new voters as advocates hope? How would most Americans who, on repeated national surveys, see themselves as moderate, react to having their city, town, and state policies determined by a surging influx of progressive voters who have not become citizens?

These thought experiments lead easily to the conclusion that such occurrences would be profoundly upsetting to many, if not most, Americans. And it is easy to develop scenarios based on the overwhelming rejection of illegal immigration in this country by Americans in general that the responses to these circumstances would be emotionally vivid and strong.

One legitimate question, as yet unanswered by advocates, is whether such political trauma is really necessary. The United States is not a country that keeps immigration to a minimum. It takes in for permanent settlement more people from more countries every year than any other country on earth.

It does not base its citizenship on blood or lineage as other countries do, keeping its immigrants in a perpetual state of limbo. Instead, it offers citizenship to almost every legal immigrant after a modest waiting period and after the satisfaction of several other relatively simple requirements. And it offers immigrants, before they become citizens, many ways to take part in politics other than voting.

Non-citizen voting is a potentially politically traumatic and clearly unnecessary answer to a problem that is not very pressing.

Arguments for Non-Citizen Voting

Advocates of non-citizen voting make many arguments for what would be a radical historic change. In just one article, one author claimed 30 separate benefits. It is only fair, advocates say, since non-citizens already pay taxes and can serve in the military. It provides an ideal way for new immigrants to learn about citizenship, they assert. It helps new immigrants feel more welcomed and included, they argue. It ensures that those who are not yet citizens will be represented, they suggest. And, it will help to increase declining rates of political participation, they promise.

These arguments seem reasonable. To advocates they are compelling. Yet, a closer look at each suggests they are neither.

Voting has always been a critical element of full citizenship; courts have called it the essential element. It is true that over 80 years ago, some states allowed resident non-citizens to vote. However, this was always an exception to a more general rule that preserved voting for citizens. By the 1920s, non-citizen voting had been ended by legislation, duly debated and passed by the people's representatives and signed into law by their governors, and with good reason.

Voting is one of the few, and doubtlessly the major, difference between citizens and non-citizens. Citizenship itself, and open access to it, is one of the major unifying mechanisms of E Pluribus Unum. When citizenship loses its value—and it would if voting were not an earned privilege—a critical tie that helps bind this diverse country together will be lost. Given the challenges that face us, this should not be done lightly.

What of fairness? Don't non-citizens pay taxes, and therefore isn't it unfair to not allow them to vote? That argument assumes that non-citizens get nothing for their taxes, and need the vote to compensate for that. However, the truth is that immigrants from most countries enjoy an immediate rise in their standard of living because of this country's advanced infrastructure—for example, hospitals, electricity, communications. They also get many services for their taxes—like public transportation, police, trash collection, and so on. Most importantly and immediately they get what they came for: freedom and opportunity.

What of serving in the armed forces? If they can serve, why can't they vote? The difference here is between *can* and *must*. Non-citizens can serve if they volunteer, but they are not required to serve as part of the citizenship process. When they do volunteer, they earn this country's gratitude and, by presidential order, a shortening of the time period before they can become citizens.

Doesn't voting help immigrants learn about their new country? Yes, but the fallacy of that argument is the assumption that there are not other, less damaging ways, to do so. No law bars non-citizens from learning democracy in civic organizations or political parties. No law keeps them from joining unions or speaking out in public forums. Indeed, no law bars them from holding responsible positions within all these groups. In all of these many ways, legal residents can learn about their new country and its civic traditions. Voting is not the only means to do so, and may not even be the best since it can be done from start to finish with the pull of a lever.

What of representation? Isn't it bad for democracy and against democratic principles to have so many people unrepresented? The first problem with this argument is that the condition is temporary and easily remedied by time and patience. Second, the very fact that advocates push non-citizenship voting undercuts the argument that this group's interests are not represented. This country is a republic, not a democracy. We depend on our representatives to consider diverse views. The views of legal non-citizen residents are no exception. The more such persons take advantage of the many opportunities to participate in our civic and political life, the more likely it is that their voices will be heard.

Well, what about participation? Won't giving non-citizens the vote increase participation, and isn't that good for democracy? The answers to those two questions are no and maybe. The record of non-citizen voters should lead all of us to pause and reflect. When New York City allowed non-citizens to vote in local school-board elections, presumably something in which they had a direct, personal, and immediate stake, less that 5 percent of that group did so. Takoma Park, Md., often cited as a model by advocates, refuses to ascertain whether non-citizen voters are in the country legally. Even so, their participation went from a high point of 25 percent in 1997, to 12 percent in the next election, and 9 percent in the election thereafter. In November 2007, only 10 non-citizens voted. In a special election held that year, "officials took extra steps to get the word out. They mailed a notice, in Spanish and English, to every home. They sent a second notice to every registered voter," yet not a single non-citizen voted. In the end, the touted benefits of non-citizen voting participation turn out to be very small and in some cases non-existent—very small gain upon which to sacrifice such a core element of American citizenship.

There are many things this country could and should do to make new immigrants feel welcomed. We could, and should, provide free English classes to all those who want them—and that want is great. We could set up classes to help immigrants learn about the nuts and bolts of our country's life—how do you get insurance, why do you raise your hand in class. We take these things for granted, but new immigrants cannot. If elected officials really want to help new immigrants, these initiatives would be of direct and immediate benefit and won't have the downside of destroying citizenship.

Every effort should be made to integrate legal immigrants into our national community. Yet, isn't it fair to ask that they know something about that community before they fully take up the responsibilities, and not just the advantages, of what has been the core of citizenship? Some non-citizen voting proposals would require three years as a legal resident—saving a mere two years before naturalization and the vote. Others suggest a period of only one year or less, allowing people practically just off the plane to help make complex public decisions.

Advocates of non-citizen voting do not discus whether these new voters would need to demonstrate language proficiency or knowledge of this country, as they must now do for naturalization. Would that requirement be waived? Nor have they said what they would do if many decided there was no longer a need to become a citizen—since they already can vote.

In the end, we do immigrants, and this country, no favor—indeed, we likely to do damage—by giving in to demands for erasing the distinction between immigrants and citizens.

QUESTIONS

1. Referring back to the comments made in Hayduk's essay earlier in this chapter, how accurately does Renshon seem to present the objectives of those who favor noncitizen immigrant voting? Is it fair for him to accuse these proponents of hypocrisy in using "iconic words" such as "justice," "fairness," and "democracy" to defend their voting reform views? What does Renshon believe their true motivation to be?

2. Renshon uses complex statistics to show how many potential new immigrant voters there potentially would be in urban areas across the country, and how they might change previous election patterns. Would you consider this an appeal to facts and reason or an appeal to fear?

3. In the final part of his essay Renshon refutes one by one the "iconic words" and other arguments used by the proponents of noncitizen voting, including the argument that noncitizens learn about democracy through voting and the argument that they once had such voting rights in many states. Evaluate Renshon's refutation approach used in this section, as well as the "alternative solutions" to welcoming immigrants that he uses at the end. How thorough and convincing are both the refutation and the alternatives, and how would an advocate like Hayduk respond to them?

CHAPTER 5

Engaging Work

Introduction

Work is a topic about which people often disagree. Critics of salaried labor find work itself at best a necessary evil—as Bertrand Russell argues—holding that, with advancements in technology and automation, people should be working less and thinking more about how to use their leisure time. Many sociologists and economists writing today see the American workplace as both unkind and unstable. Stuart Tannock questions why young unskilled workers in service jobs receive so little respect and often become the scapegoats of both customers and bosses, while Jyoti Thottam points out that many Americans with respected, skilled jobs face the possibility of losing them through outsourcing. In contrast, other writers such as Lisa Takeuchi Cullen argue more positively about how first-generation immigrants are being helped by their college-educated children, who have learned about business in college, to open and maintain successful family businesses. Columnist Steven Greenhouse presents an example of enjoyable local and socially worthwhile job creation in his recent essay on "green jobs," which represent a step up, a chance for retraining, and a sense of being involved in improving the environment for many workers. In another essay on better work environments, author William Greider maintains that people can work harder and achieve more if they are included as co-owners in the community of their business organization.

The "Differing Perspectives" debate in this chapter focuses on the value and meaning of work. While philosopher Alain de Botton argues, as does Bertrand Russell, that work can never be truly a source of meaning and happiness, in our final essay, cultural critic bell hooks demonstrates how finding the right kind of work that helps improve the lives of others can truly "make life sweet."

BERTRAND RUSSELL

"In Praise of Idleness"

Bertrand Russell (1872–1970), a mathematical theorist, philosopher, and social activist, received degrees in mathematics and moral sciences from Trinity College, Cambridge, where he taught before being dismissed and imprisoned for his World War I pacifist writings. His Introduction to Mathematical Philosophy *(1919) was written from a prison cell. Although he is considered one of the greatest twentieth century logicians, he won the Nobel Prize for literature in 1950 largely because of his social and moral philosophy and his work for peace. In 1955, he and Albert Einstein produced the Russell-Einstein manifesto, which argued for nuclear disarmament; Russell remained active as a leader for peace until his death. His nonmathematical writings include* The Conquest of Happiness *(1930),* Power: A New Social Introduction to its Study *(1938), and* In Praise of Idleness *(1935), from which the following argument on the need for a shorter work day is excerpted.*

Like most of my generation, I was brought up on the saying: 'Satan finds some mischief for idle hands to do.' Being a highly virtuous child, I believed all that I was told, and acquired a conscience which has kept me working hard down to the present moment. But although my conscience has controlled my actions, my opinions have undergone a revolution. I think that there is far too much work done in the world, that immense harm is caused by the belief that work is virtuous, and that what needs to be preached in modern industrial countries is quite different from what always has been preached. Everyone knows the story of the traveler in Naples who saw twelve beggars lying in the sun (it was before the days of Mussolini), and offered a lira to the laziest of them. Eleven of them jumped up to claim it, so he gave it to the twelfth. This traveler was on the right lines. But in countries which do not enjoy Mediterranean sunshine idleness is more difficult, and a great public propaganda will be required to inaugurate it. I hope that, after reading the following pages, the leaders of the YMCA will start a campaign to induce good young men to do nothing. If so, I shall not have lived in vain. . . . All this is only preliminary. I want to say, in all seriousness, that a great deal of harm is being done in the modern world by belief in the virtuousness of work, and that the road to happiness and prosperity lies in an organized diminution of work.

First of all: what is work? Work is of two kinds: first, altering the position of matter at or near the earth's surface relatively to other such matter; second, telling other people to do so. The first kind is unpleasant and ill paid; the second is pleasant and highly paid. The second kind is capable of indefinite extension: there are not only those who give orders, but those who give advice as to what orders should be given. Usually two opposite kinds of advice are given simultaneously by two organized bodies of men; this is called politics. The skill required for this kind of work is not knowledge of the subjects as to which advice is given, but knowledge of the art of persuasive speaking and writing, i.e. of advertising.

Modern technique has made it possible to diminish enormously the amount of labor required to secure the necessaries of life for everyone. This was made obvious during the war. At that time all the men in the armed forces, and all the men and women engaged in the production of munitions, all the men and women engaged in spying, war propaganda, or Government offices connected with the war, were withdrawn from productive occupations. In spite of this, the general level of well-being among unskilled wage-earners on the side of the Allies was higher than before or since. The significance of this fact was concealed by finance: borrowing made it appear as if the future was nourishing the present. But that, of course, would have been impossible; a man cannot eat a loaf of bread that does not yet exist. The war showed conclusively that, by the scientific organization of production, it is possible to keep modern populations in fair comfort on a small part of the working capacity of the modern world. If, at the end of the war, the scientific organization, which had been created in order to liberate men for fighting and munition work, had been preserved, and the hours of the week had been cut down to four, all would have been well. Instead of that the old chaos was restored, those whose work was demanded were made to work long hours, and the rest were left to starve as unemployed. Why? Because work is a duty, and a man should not receive wages in proportion to what he has produced, but in proportion to his virtue as exemplified by his industry.

This is the morality of the Slave State, applied in circumstances totally unlike those in which it arose. No wonder the result has been disastrous. Let us take an illustration. Suppose that, at a given moment, a certain number of people are engaged in the manufacture of pins. They make as many pins as the world needs, working (say) eight hours a day. Someone makes an invention by which the same number of men can make twice as many pins: pins are already so cheap that hardly any more will be bought at a lower price. In a sensible world, everybody concerned in the manufacturing of pins would take to working four hours instead of eight, and everything else would go on as before. But in the actual world this would be thought demoralizing. The men still work eight hours, there are too many pins, some employers go bankrupt, and half the men previously concerned in making pins are thrown out of work. There is, in the end, just as much leisure as on the other plan, but half the men are totally idle while half are still overworked. In this way, it is insured that the unavoidable leisure shall cause misery all round instead of being a universal source of happiness. Can anything more insane be imagined?

The idea that the poor should have leisure has always been shocking to the rich. In England, in the early nineteenth century, fifteen hours was the ordinary day's work for a man; children sometimes did as much, and very commonly did twelve hours a day. When meddlesome busybodies suggested that perhaps these hours were rather long, they were told that work kept adults from drink and children from mischief. When I was a child, shortly after urban working men had acquired the vote, certain public holidays were established by law, to the great indignation of the upper classes. I remember hearing an old Duchess say: 'What do the poor want with holidays? They ought to work.' People nowadays are less frank, but the sentiment persists, and is the source of much of our economic confusion.

Let us, for a moment, consider the ethics of work frankly, without superstition. Every human being, of necessity, consumes, in the course of his life, a certain amount of the produce of human labor. Assuming, as we may, that labor is on the whole disagreeable, it is unjust that a man should consume more than he produces. Of course he may provide services rather than commodities, like a medical man, for example; but he should provide something in return for his board and lodging. To this extent, the duty of work must be admitted, but to this extent only. . . .

If the ordinary wage-earner worked four hours a day, there would be enough for everybody and no unemployment—assuming a certain very moderate amount of sensible organization. This idea shocks the well-to-do, because they are convinced that the poor would not know how to use so much leisure. . . . The wise use of leisure, it must be conceded, is a product of civilization and education. A man who has worked long hours all his life will become bored if he becomes suddenly idle.

But without a considerable amount of leisure a man is cut off from many of the best things. There is no longer any reason why the bulk of the population should suffer this deprivation; only a foolish asceticism, usually vicarious, makes us continue to insist on work in excessive quantities now that the need no longer exists. . . . What will happen when the point has been reached where everybody could be comfortable without working long hours?

In the West, we have various ways of dealing with this problem. We have no attempt at economic justice, so that a large proportion of the total produce goes to a small minority of the population, many of whom do no work at all. Owing to the absence of any central control over production, we produce hosts of things that are not wanted. We keep a large percentage of the working population idle, because we can dispense with their labor by making the others overwork. When all these methods prove inadequate, we have a war: we cause a number of people to manufacture high explosives, and a number of others to explode them, as if we were children who had just discovered fireworks. By a combination of all these devices we manage, though with difficulty, to keep alive the notion that a great deal of severe manual work must be the lot of the average man. . . .

The fact is that moving matter about, while a certain amount of it is necessary to our existence, is emphatically not one of the ends of human life. If it were, we should have to consider every navvy superior to Shakespeare. We have been misled in this matter by two causes. One is the necessity of keeping the poor contented, which has led the rich, for thousands of years, to preach the dignity of labor, while taking care themselves to remain undignified in this respect. The other is the new pleasure in mechanism, which makes us delight in the astonishingly clever changes that we can produce on the earth's surface. Neither of these motives makes any great appeal to the actual worker. If you ask him what he thinks the best part of his life, he is not likely to say: "I enjoy manual work because it makes me feel that I am fulfilling man's noblest task, and because I like to think how much man can transform his planet. It is true that my body demands periods of rest, which I have to fill in as best I may, but I am never so happy as when the morning comes and I can return to the toil from which my contentment springs." I have never heard working men say this sort of thing. They consider work, as it should be considered, a necessary means to a livelihood, and it is from their leisure that they derive whatever happiness they may enjoy.

It will be said that, while a little leisure is pleasant, men would not know how to fill their days if they had only four hours of work out of the twenty-four. In so far as this is true in the modern world, it is a condemnation of our civilization; it would not have been true at any earlier period. There was formerly a capacity for light-heartedness and play which has been to some extent inhibited by the cult of efficiency. The modern man thinks that everything ought to be done for the sake of something else, and never for its own sake. Serious-minded persons, for example, are continually condemning the habit of going to the cinema, and telling us that it leads the young into crime. But all the work that goes to producing a cinema is respectable, because it is work, and because it brings a money profit. The notion that the desirable activities are those that bring a profit has made everything topsy-turvy. The butcher who provides you with meat and the baker who provides you with bread are praiseworthy, because they are making money; but when you enjoy the food they have provided, you are merely frivolous, unless you eat only to get strength for your work. Broadly speaking, it is held that getting money is good and spending money is bad. Seeing that they are two sides of one transaction, this is absurd; one might as well maintain that keys are good, but keyholes are bad. Whatever merit there may be in the production of goods must be entirely derivative from the advantage to be obtained by consuming them. The individual, in our society, works for profit; but the social purpose of his work lies in the consumption of what he produces. It is this divorce between the individual and the social purpose of production that makes it so difficult for men to think clearly in a world in which profit-making is the incentive to industry. We think too much of production, and too little of consumption. One result is that we attach too little importance to enjoyment and simple happiness, and that we do not judge production by the pleasure that it gives to the consumer.

When I suggest that working hours should be reduced to four, I am not meaning to imply that all the remaining time should necessarily be spent in pure frivolity. I mean that four hours' work a day should entitle a man to the necessities and elementary comforts of life, and that the rest of his time should be his to use as he might see fit. It is an essential part of any such social system that education should be carried further than it usually is at present, and should aim, in part, at providing tastes which would enable a man to use leisure intelligently. I am not thinking mainly of the sort of things that would be considered "highbrow." Peasant dances have died out except in remote rural areas, but the impulses which caused them to be cultivated must still exist in human nature. The pleasures of urban populations have become mainly passive: seeing cinemas, watching football matches, listening to the radio, and so on. This results from the fact that their active energies are fully taken up with work; if they had more leisure, they would again enjoy pleasures in which they took an active part.

In a world where no one is compelled to work more than four hours a day, every person possessed of scientific curiosity will be able to indulge it, and every painter will be able to paint without starving, however excellent his pictures may be. Young writers will not be obliged to draw attention to themselves by sensational pot-boilers, with a view to acquiring the economic independence needed for monumental works, for which, when the time at last comes, they will have lost the taste and capacity. Men, who, in their professional work, have become interested in some phase of economics or government, will be able to develop their ideas without the academic detachment that makes the work of university economists often seem lacking in reality. Medical men will have the time to learn about the progress of medicine, teachers will not be exasperatedly struggling to teach by routine methods things which they learnt in their youth, which may, in the interval, have been proved to be untrue.

Above all, there will be happiness and joy of life, instead of frayed nerves, weariness, and dyspepsia. The work exacted will be enough to make leisure delightful, but not enough to produce exhaustion. Since men will not be tired in their spare time, they will not demand only such amusements as are passive and vapid. At least one per cent will probably devote the time not spent in professional work to pursuits of some public importance, and, since they will not depend upon these pursuits for their livelihood, their originality will be unhampered, and there will be no need to conform to the standards set by elderly pundits. But it is not only in these exceptional cases that the advantages of leisure will appear. Ordinary men and women, having the opportunity of a happy life, will become more kindly and less persecuting and less inclined to view others with suspicion. The taste for war will die out, partly for this reason, and partly because it will involve long and severe work for all. Good nature is, of all moral qualities, the one that the world needs most, and good nature is the result of ease and security, not of a life of arduous struggle. Modern methods of production have given us the possibility of ease and security for all; we have chosen, instead, to have overwork for some and starvation for others. Hitherto we have continued to be as energetic as we were before there were machines; in this we have been foolish, but there is no reason to go on being foolish forever.

QUESTIONS

1. What are Russell's major arguments and evidence for shortening the working day to four hours? How effective are his historical examples of the World War I and post-war employment situations?

2. How does Russell attempt to refute the "leisure" problem of the four-hour day? Why and how does he believe that workers will eventually learn to use their extra time?

3. When Russell wrote this essay, the average work week was long. Today, many Europeans and some Americans have flexible hours, considerably more vacation time, and shorter work weeks than they did in the 1930s. With all this time off, do modern workers use their spare time as productively as Russell imagines? Why or why not?

STUART TANNOCK

"On the Front Lines of the Service Sector"

Stuart Tannock (b. 1969) is a lecturer in the Social and Cultural Studies program in the Graduate School of Education at the University of California, Berkeley. He has written extensively on the subject of young workers, who often take the lowest-paying and lowest-status jobs in the retail, food, and entertainment service sectors. He has published several articles on youth and work, including "Why Do Working Youth Work Where They Do?" and "I Know What It's Like to Struggle: The Working Lives of Young Students in an Urban Community College" (2003). The selection below is excerpted from Tannock's book, Youth at Work: The Unionized Fast Food and Grocery Workplace *(2001), which is based on a study of 95 interviews with young fast-food and grocery workers. The article describes the exploitive nature of the stress of their jobs and the abusive on-the-job interactions among service workers, managers, and customers.*

High Stress, Low Status, Low Wages

"I would say the stress is the worst thing about it," a young Fry House cashier says of her fast-food job. "Sometimes I get so stressed out, 'cause some days you're in a bad mood yourself, you know, having to deal with people, you just don't want to, you'd rather be somewhere else, anywhere except work." High stress levels are the most widespread complaint young workers in Box Hill and Glenwood have about their grocery and fast-food employment. Stress can be caused by many aspects of grocery and fast-food work: difficult relations with customers and managers; repetitive work tasks; low occupational status and small pay-checks; continual workplace surveillance; and hot, greasy, and often dangerous work environments. But the number-one factor young workers point to as the cause of workplace stress is the lack of time to do the work they are expected to do. Either there are not enough workers on shift to cover customer rushes and necessary preparation and cleaning work, or workers are not given long enough shifts to get their work stations ready for lunch and evening rushes and clean up after such rushes are through.

Lack of time lies behind almost all other causes of workplace stress. Young workers regularly endure abuse from their customers. Workers are yelled at, sworn at, and insulted by customers; they are frowned at, glared at, and sneered at; they are ignored, treated as social inferiors, and assumed to be servants whose role in life is to cater to and anticipate a customer's every whim and fancy. There are different reasons for such abusiveness. Young grocery and fast-food workers make easy targets for the displacement of hostility. "Often people come into Fry House," a cashier in Glenwood says, "because they've been yelled at by their bosses, they don't have anybody they can yell at, so they yell at us 'cause they think they can." "Customers go off on some grocery employee," says a stocker in Box Hill, "'cause it makes 'em feel powerful."

Grocery and fast-food workers also incite abuse when their job responsibilities put them in conflict with customers' interests. Checkers in Box Hill, for example, become the target of customers' anger when they are put in the position of having to police company rules on accepting checks or enforce government laws for using food stamps or selling alcohol. In one supermarket, I witnessed a checker politely decline to sell alcohol to a young couple who were clearly intoxicated—as she was required to do by law, under penalty of losing her job. The couple stalked out of the store, and on their way out turned to yell at the checker, "Fuck you! Fuck you, you fucking bitch!" while giving her the finger.

Beyond these various motivations, however, many young workers feel that grocery and fast-food customers are abusive primarily because they fail to appreciate the time pressure under which workers labor:

> That's the worst aspect of it for me, having to explain to people [customers] that, well, this is how it works, because they don't know. . . . I've said, you're welcome to come back here, take a tour, sit here for an

*hour, watch us when it's busy, please. Actually, a lady who worked here
for about a month, and then she got another job . . . she said, "You
know, I used to get really mad when I had to wait for stuff, but I have a
total new respect for people that work in fast-food. I know what you
have to do. I know what it's like. I feel so bad for any time I ever blew
up at anybody." She says, "I don't know how you guys do it; how you
can handle it. I really, really, really admire you guys for that, for keeping your cool the way you do, 'cause it's hard to do."*

"They think we're dumb and slow," a Fry House cashier complains
of his customers, "but they don't understand. If they came in here and
tried to do what we're doing, they'll be about three times as slow as we
are." Young workers are often caught in difficult situations in their relations with customers: On the one hand, they are not given enough
time or staff support by their employers to perform at the speed and
quality levels their customers would prefer; on the other, they lack the
status to be able to persuade customers to respect them for the work
that they do manage to do under what are often difficult and stressful
working conditions.

Managers are another primary source of workplace stress. Like customers, some managers yell and swear at their young employees, talk
down to them, and call them "stupid," "incompetent," and "lazy." Many
workers believe that the younger the worker, the more latitude managers feel they have in verbally attacking and belittling that worker.
Managers in fast-food and grocery, young workers say, often "go on
power trips," order workers around, and "tell you every little thing you
do wrong"—all the while, failing to provide encouragement or acknowledgment of jobs well done. Managers criticize workers behind
their backs; worse, they dress employees down to their faces, in front
of coworkers and customers. Young workers in both Box Hill
and Glenwood complain widely of the stress caused by managerial
favoritism—by managers picking on workers they dislike and confer-
ring favors on workers they prefer. Many feel that managers will abuse
their power by trying to get rid of employees they don't want working
in their stores. "When a manager doesn't want you to work there," explains a cook in Glenwood, "they look for things, they kind a set you up
so they can give you something bad."

As it does with customer-caused stress, time pressure often stands
behind manager-caused workplace stress. Workers, for example, sometimes encounter what they refer to as "office managers"—managers who

hide in their offices (claiming to be doing needed paperwork) and avoid helping with rushes. Because stores' labor budgets generally assume that managers will work on the floor when needed, "office managers" put increased stress on already overloaded workers. Workers have to deal with "cheap" managers—managers who (in efforts to keep costs low and earn year-end bonuses) skimp on allocating labor hours. Workers have to deal with managerial error—with managers who regularly screw up when submitting hours to company payroll, so that workers' checks are late or incorrect, or with managers who screw up scheduling, ordering, or inventory tasks. "I notice our managers forget a lot," one Fry House worker complained, "so we have to explain to our customers, 'We have no fried chicken tonight.' 'How can you have no fried chicken when it's Fry House?' 'Well, our manager forgot to order chicken.' It's crazy!"

Managers in the grocery and (especially) fast-food industries come and go with great frequency. Fry House store managers change over about every six months, while area managers change over every couple of years. Store managers in Box Hill chain supermarkets change over less frequently, but assistant managers come and go every few months. Workers find that they can develop a relationship and system of doing things with one manager, then that manager will quit or be fired, transferred, or promoted. They will then have to start over, building up a new relationship and new system with a new manager. Over time, management instability can be as stressful and wearing as bad or abusive management. "Every time a new manager comes in, they change everything," complains a Fry House cashier. "It's just like being hired. They have to retrain you on everything. It's pretty hard, because once you get into something, you just keep with it. Then somebody else comes in, and they're like, 'No, no! You're doing it wrong; you have to do it this way.'"

Grocery and fast-food work is low-status work. Fast-food work especially carries a stigma, and fast-food workers are stereotyped as being stupid, lazy, slow, and lacking in life goals and initiative. . . . Fast-food and grocery "youth" jobs (baggers, stockers) are also low in status simply because they are seen as typically being held by young workers. "What's the image of a fast-food job?" a Fry House cashier asks rhetorically. "You get the image of some kid with about a hundred pimples on his face trying to take an order for somebody, and he doesn't understand what to do." Young workers in Box Hill and Glenwood are well aware that if the work they perform were considered glamorous and important, it would be adults and not youths who would be taking on these jobs.

For many young workers, grocery and fast-food work lacks real or intrinsic meaning, interest, and value. "You can't be very proud of yourself as a grocery worker," says a young stocker in Box Hill. "What is your gift to the world [if] you work at Good Grocers your whole life?" The problem with grocery and fast-food work, for many young workers, is that it is difficult to feel a sense of accomplishment or progress. A grocery bagger, for example, explains why she would never want a grocery career:

> It's tough to have a job where it's just a constant flow of people and nothing ever ends or begins, where you're always just providing a service, the same service over and over again. . . . It seems like, to be a checker, to always be saying hello, how are you, have a good day, to always be doing the same thing, I would like a job better where I started and finished something.

In grocery and fast-food work, tasks tend to repeat themselves almost without end. The work is repetitive, mundane, and often boring. Workers may find getting up to and maintaining speed in what are very fast-paced workplaces initially challenging, but once the basic set of tasks has been mastered, workplace learning plateaus, and workers are left with the drudgery of simply executing tasks that long ago became second nature.

Grocery and fast-food work is often said to be "low-skill" work—and, indeed, many young workers in Box Hill and Glenwood slam their jobs by saying that anyone "with half a brain" could do the work they do. Attributions of skill are notoriously tricky, however: They tend to involve assessments of the social standing of a particular job and the kinds of people who hold that job as much as they refer to any absolute and objective measurement of cognitive demands inherent in a given set of work tasks. Young grocery and fast-food workers develop considerable local expertise in their jobs: knowledge of how best to handle individual customers and managers; of how to bend official work rules to get work done effectively and efficiently on the ground; how to make ad hoc repairs and improvisations in the workplace when machines break down, work tools go missing, or the maddening rush of customer demand overwhelms normal working procedures. What can be said of grocery and fast-food work is that such local expertise emerges within jobs that are seen overall—by workers, customers, and managers—as repetitive and low in status, meaning, challenge, and value.

QUESTIONS

1. What is particularly stressful about work in the service sector? What skills are required?
2. What major causes for the negative work environment of fast-food workers are presented in the essay? What effects on workers' attitudes and examples from the workplace does Tannock examine?
3. Observe a local fast-food restaurant and then write a proposal for the management, describing the problems you found and proposing ways to improve the morale and working conditions of the staff. Develop solutions that would help to make the working lives of service workers less stressful and more rewarding.

JYOTI THOTTAM

"Is Your Job Going Abroad?"

Jyotti Thottam graduated from Yale and Columbia universities. She has worked as a journalist in India and Thailand, and in the United States she has written articles for publications such as Time Magazine, *the* Village Voice, *and the* Wall Street Journal. *Her articles often focus on complex issues related to the advances in technology. In the article below, "Is Your Job Going Abroad?", Thottam argues that outsourcing, a strategy that American companies are increasingly depending on to increase their profits, exploits Third World workers, who can be paid much less than American workers, and causes many American workers to lose jobs that their families depend on to survive.*

Rosen Sharma is sure about one thing. His nine-month-old company, Solidcore, a start-up that makes backup security systems for computers, could not survive without outsourcing. By lowering his development costs, the 18 engineers who work for him in India for as little as one-fourth the salary of their American counterparts allow him to spend money on 13 senior managers, engineers and marketing people in Silicon Valley. If he doesn't outsource, in fact, the venture capitalists who fund start-ups like his won't give him a nickel. Sharma's Indian-American team, tethered by a broadband connection, gets his product in front of customers faster and cheaper. "As a business, you have to stay competitive," he says. "If we don't do it, our competitors will, and they're going to blow us away."

But Sharma's sharp analysis loses its edge when he thinks about what decisions like his will mean someday for his children, a 2-year-old daughter and another on the way. "As a father, my reaction is different than my reaction as a CEO," he says. He believes that companies like his will always need senior people in the U.S., like the systems architects who design new products and the experienced salespeople who close deals. "But if you're graduating from college today, where are the entry-level jobs?" Sharma asks quietly. How do you get to that secure, skilled job when the path that leads you there has disappeared?

That's an issue that economists, politicians and workers are struggling with as the U.S. finds itself in the middle of a structural shift in the economy that no one quite expected. There must be a mix-up here. We ordered a recovery, heavy on the jobs, please. What we're getting is a new kind of homeland insecurity powered by the rise of outsourcing, a bland yet ominous piece of business jargon that seems to imply that every call center, insurance-claims processor, programming department and Wall Street back office is being moved to India, Ireland or some other place thousands of miles away.

To be sure, public anxiety and election-year finger pointing have blurred some important distinctions. To set them straight: most of the jobs that have shifted to places like Mexico and China in the past several decades have been in manufacturing, which is being done with ever increasing sophistication in low-wage countries. Some have also blamed trade-liberalization deals like the North American Free Trade Agreement (NAFTA), which the Labor Department estimates was responsible for the loss of more than 500,000 U.S. jobs between 1994 and 2002. That's a significant number but modest in comparison with the millions of jobs that are created and lost annually in the constant churn of the U.S. economy. Indeed, much of the job loss during the recent U.S. recession was cyclical in nature. But in recent years, one noteworthy segment of the economy began suffering from the permanent change of outsourcing (or off shoring), particularly the movement of service-industry, technology-oriented jobs to overseas locations with lower salaries. What puts teeth into the buzz word is the sense that getting outsourced could happen to almost anyone.

Outsourcing, primarily to India, accounts for less than 10% of the 2.3 million jobs lost in the U.S. over the past three years. But the trend is speeding up, and it is quickly becoming the defining economic issue of the election campaign. The Administration learned that the hard way a few weeks ago, when President Bush's chief economic adviser suddenly found himself on the wrong side of the issue. In a casually imperious tone worthy of Martha Stewart, Gregory Mankiw declared, "Outsourcing is just a new way of doing international trade . . . More things are tradable than were tradable in the past, and that's a good thing."

Many economists agree with him. Anything that makes an economy more efficient tends to help in the long run. But in reducing job losses to macroeconomic landfill, Mankiw handed Democrats an issue. His words, accompanied by an ominous drumbeat, are now immortalized on the AFL-CIO's website . . .

Unfortunately for Bush, outsourcing has become Exhibit A in any gripe session about why the economic recovery has been weak in creating new jobs. To some extent, he succeeded in making a plausible connection between his tax cuts and the robust pace of economic growth. "People have more money in their pocket to spend, to save, to invest," he has said. "[Tax relief] is helping the economy recover from tough times." But his efforts to sell a pastiche of programs to help the unemployed have had a tougher time punching through. When it comes to jobs, the numbers fail him. On the basis of previous recoveries, Bush was promising to add 2.6 million new jobs this year. That pledge is starting to look like fantasy, and the Administration has distanced itself from its own predictions. . . .

From Mexico to India: How Did We Get There?

Before acquiring its current incendiary meaning, outsourcing referred to the practice of turning over non-critical parts of a business to a company that specialized in that activity. At first it was ancillary functions like running the cafeteria or cleaning the offices. Then it started moving up to corporate-service functions. Why operate a call center if what you really do, your core competence, is run a credit-card business? So credit-card companies hired independent call centers to take over the phones, and that industry put down roots in places like Omaha, Neb., which early on had a fiber-optic hub. But as the price of information technology fell and the Internet exploded, capacity began popping up around the world. Which meant that all you needed to run a call center, or a customer-service center, was information technology (IT) and employees who spoke English. Hello, India.

From there, multinational companies began moving up the food chain. Silicon Valley, which for years had been importing highly educated Indian code writers—driving up wage and real estate costs— discovered it was a lot cheaper to export the work to the same highly educated folks over there. So did Wall Street, which employs an army of accountants, analysts and bankers to pore over documents, do deal analysis and maintain databases. The potential list gets longer: medical technicians to read your x rays, accountants to prepare your taxes, even business journalists to interpret companies' financial statements.

Jared Bernstein, senior economist at the Economic Policy Institute, says the frustration of these educated workers is what gives the debate over outsourcing such intensity. "There is no safety net for $80,000-a-year programmers," he says, and perhaps there shouldn't be. Their education is supposed to provide that. Bernstein says that after the factory closings of the 1980s and the emergence of the "knowledge economy," many liberals and conservatives alike had reached a consensus that manufacturing jobs could not be saved but the "lab coat" jobs would always stay here. "Now that vision is under siege," Bernstein says. And the white-collar middle class is feeling the sting of insecurity that manufacturing workers know so well.

Why So Fast?

It's doubly difficult for people to watch outsourcing accelerate as the economy improves. The stock market had a strong 2003, and corporate profits in many industries exceeded expectations, so why haven't companies that started outsourcing as a way to cut costs reversed course and brought the jobs back home? That might have happened after other recessions, but this shift is different. To some extent, companies are gun-shy about committing to full-time workers and the attendant fringe benefits. Instead of rushing to expand their computer systems and hiring people to maintain them, firms are keeping their outsourcing companies on speed dial.

That's why outsourcing to India has exploded during the recovery. It jumped 60% in 2003 compared with the year before, according to the research magazine Dataquest, as corporations used some of their profits (not to mention tax breaks) to expand overseas hiring. That translates to 140,000 jobs outsourced to India last year. Vivek Paul, president of Wipro, one of India's leading outsourcing companies (it handles voice and data processing for Delta Airlines, for instance), says its service business grew 50% in the last quarter of 2003. "Companies that are emerging from the slowdown are beginning to invest some of that in India," he says. John McCarthy, author of the Forrester Research landmark study that predicted 3.3 million jobs would move overseas by 2015 (there are about 130 million jobs in the U.S. today), says last year's gains in outsourcing didn't come from new companies jumping on the bandwagon. The most dramatic changes came from outsourcing dabblers who finally made a commitment and now allocate as much as 30% of their IT budgets offshore.

Another factor speeding things up is the development of an industry devoted to making outsourcing happen, thanks to entrepreneurs like Randy Altschuler and Joe Sigelman. Just five years ago, they were junior investment bankers at the Blackstone Group and Goldman Sachs, one in New York City, the other in London. During one particularly long night of proofreading PowerPoint slides and commiserating by phone about finding yet another error courtesy of their companies' in-house document service, they had an epiphany. They would find a better way of doing that work. This was at the height of the dotcom boom, and everyone they knew was trying to figure out a way to Silicon Valley. These two had a different idea. They would go to India, set up a team of accountants and desktop-publishing experts and persuade investment banks in New York to outsource their confidential financial documents and client presentations halfway around the world.

The entrepreneurs' families, not to mention Silicon Valley's venture capitalists, "were looking at us in a crazy way," Sigelman says, especially when he relocated to Madras. Five years later, as it moves into more complex work, OfficeTiger, with $18 million from British investors, plans to increase the number of its employees in India this year from 1,500 to 2,500 and more than triple its U.S. work force, from 30 to 100.

Getting Left Behind

Billy Johnson of Altamonte Springs, Fla., is convinced that one of the tens of thousands of new jobs in India should be his. Johnson, 41, was a programmer for WorldCom when the company imploded in the wake of a massive accounting scandal. After six months of looking for a programming job, Johnson realized that the work he knows is exactly what outsourcing companies do best. "I spent $5,000 of my own money to become an Oracle [enterprise software] developer," he says. "Nobody's hiring Oracle developers." For a while, he believed it was just the economy. A lifelong Republican, he believed that when the Bush tax cuts kicked in, the jobs would follow. "I feel like I've been betrayed," he says. "I keep hearing about jobs being created, but I don't see them."

Vince Kosmac of Orlando, Fla., has lived both sad chapters of outsourcing—the blue-collar and white-collar versions. He was a trucker in the 1970s and '80s, delivering steel to plants in Johnstown, Pa. When steel melted down to lower-cost competitors in Brazil and China, he used the G.I. Bill to get a degree in computer science. "The conventional wisdom was, 'Nobody can take your education away from you,'" he says bitterly. "Guess what? They took my education away." For nearly 20 years, he worked as a programmer and saved enough for a comfortable life. But programming jobs went missing two years ago, and he is impatient with anyone who suggests that he "retrain" again. "Here I am, 47 years old. I've got a house. I've got a child with cerebral palsy. I've got two cars. What do I do—push the pause button on my life? I'm not a statistic."

Neither is Scott Kirwin, 37, of Wilmington, Del., who represents another trend. A career contract worker, he is under constant threat from outsourcing. He is the breadwinner in his family—his wife is a medical student, and they have a 7-year-old son—and he has twice lost his job to outsourcing. In both cases, he had been hired as a contractor, and he sees little opportunity for anything else. "It's really nasty if you're looking for stability," he says. During unemployment spells, his family accumulates debt and reverts to making minimum credit-card payments. Vague talk about retraining leaves Kirwin cold. "Tell me which other industry I should train for," he says. A few people have suggested his father's trade, plumbing. His father had an eighth-grade education and expected better options for his college-educated son. "My father would be outraged," Kirwin says.

Whom Will Outsourcing Affect Next?

As it proves its value to more companies, outsourcing will change the way they hire. San Francisco-based DFS Group, a division of luxury-goods maker LVMH that runs duty-free shops in airports around the world, reduced operating expenses about 40% after hiring the outsourcing firm Cognizant, based in Teaneck, N.J., to take over most of its 265-person internal IT operations in 2002. Today those jobs are being done in India. DFS reinvested the savings primarily in better software. "They can add more stores efficiently. They know more about the products in the store," says Ron Glickman, DFS's former chief information officer. DFS continues to hire in the U.S. but only for certain key functions. When it needs more IT support at peak times or for special projects, DFS is more likely to turn to Cognizant. "We're going to go to them first," Glickman says.

That shift marks another fundamental change in the way companies do business. "Intrinsic to outsourcing is the replacement of the employer-employee function with a third party," says Gregg Kirchhoefer, a partner with the law firm Kirkland & Ellis in Chicago. Kirchhoefer, who has been handling outsourcing transactions with Indian companies since the early 1990s, sees outsourcing as the logical extension of the evolutionary process that began with contract manufacturing and continued into corporate services. Thanks to technology, more kinds of work can now be spun off into contracts rather than tied to employees. Once a person's labor can be reduced to a contract, it matters little whether the contract is filled in India or Indiana; the only relevant issue is cost. And the speed of technological change accelerates the process. As soon as a job becomes routine enough to describe in a spec sheet, it becomes vulnerable to outsourcing. Jobs like data entry, which are routine by nature, were the first among obvious candidates for outsourcing. But with today's advanced engineering, design and financial-analysis skills can, with time, become well-enough understood to be spelled out in a contract and signed away.

Without a "social contract" binding employer and employee, long-term jobs are an illusion. For the past two years, the Department of Labor has reported that household employment is much stronger than payroll numbers—indicating that workers are getting by with freelance or contract work, whether or not they want to. In January, for example, there were 2.8 million more people employed than in January 2002, according to the household survey, while the payroll numbers were almost flat at 130 million.

Can Americans Learn To Love Outsourcing?

While it's small consolation to workers who lose their jobs, outsourcing has become an essential element of corporate strategy, even for small companies. "Any start-up today, particularly a software company, that does not have an outsourcing strategy is at a competitive disadvantage," says Robin Vasan, managing director of Mayfield, a venture-capital firm based in Menlo Park, Calif. He felt so strongly about "global sourcing" that Mayfield organized a daylong session for the firms it invests in to meet with outsourcing companies and experts. About 60% of them now have an outsourcing plan. "That's a good start," Vasan says.

The move to outsourcing forces a company to use its resources where they count most, like product development. "For some of them, it's almost a question of survival. If they don't develop new products, they'll fail," says Laxmi Narayanan, CEO of Cognizant. Nielsen Media

Research, which rates television shows, used Cognizant's programmers in India to develop NetRatings for websites. That new line of business allowed the company to hire sales staff and analysts in the U.S. to interpret the ratings for clients and eventually to start selling the product in Asia. Light Pointe, an optical-networking firm based in San Diego, will add about 10 people to its 75-person staff this year thanks to an arrangement with a company in China. That firm will handle Light Pointe's sales and marketing there as the company expands into a huge new market. Without the local help, says Light Pointe CEO John Griffin, he could not have entered the Chinese market and would have been limited to the flailing U.S. telecom market. "Some of my competitors were not as flexible," Griffin says. "They're dead. All those employees are gone."

Should Outsourcing Be Controlled?

As the rhetoric of the campaign heats up, so does populist sentiment that there ought to be a law against outsourcing—or at least something to slow it down. Various schemes have been proposed, such as tax initiatives or trade barriers to keep jobs from moving. Some companies may feel political pressure. Dell has moved some call-center support for business-enterprise customers back to the U.S., but the company cited poor service as the reason.

Analysts doubt that any protectionist strategy will slow what appears to be a permanent shift in the way the U.S. does business. As Mankiw tried to explain before he was shouted down by fellow Republicans, structural change like this is inevitable and recurring. It's just that the transition can be ugly. New England was a textile center until that business went south, to the Carolinas, then east, to China. Software supplanted steel in Pittsburgh, Pa. In both places, high-tech companies later occupied some of the old mill buildings. Now some of those companies' programmers have gone the way of loom operators and steel rollers.

The Economic Policy Institute's Bernstein says businesses ought to find a way to "share some winnings with those who lose" by creating funds for wage insurance or retraining. Otherwise there is a risk that the benefits of outsourcing will widen the gap between the rich and everyone else. The McKinsey Global Institute, a think tank run by McKinsey & Co., recommends that companies sending jobs abroad contribute about 5% of their savings to an insurance fund that would compensate displaced workers for part of the difference in wages paid by their old and new jobs. During the 1980s and '90s, most workers displaced by trade found only lower-paying jobs. Those displaced by outsourcing are likely to share the same fate.

As demand for Indian workers increases, their prices are rising, just like anything else. Wipro's Paul says that even though his sales soared 50% last fall, his margins are shrinking, mostly because of rising labor costs. "India has been discovered," he says. "It's something that is as susceptible to global competition as anything else." Wipro, in an effort to rein in expenses, is pushing workers to be more productive. But at some point in the future, the trend that is pulling jobs out of America will catch up with India. Somewhere a lower-wage alternative will develop—Central Asia, the Philippines or Thailand—and Indian politicians and workers will be clamoring about foreigners taking their jobs. It's not pretty wherever it happens, but it's just the way the business world turns.

—With reporting by Barbara Kiviat/New York, Sara Rajan/ New Delhi, Cathy Booth Thomas/Dallas and Karen Tumulty/Washington

QUESTIONS

1. What causes of outsourcing are presented in the essay? How has outsourcing evolved over the past few years? What economic benefits does it provide for American companies and foreign workers? What evidence does Thottam present for the causes she presents?

2. What negative effects of outsourcing does Thottham discuss? For example, how does she see outsourcing as a way of undermining the "social contract" between employer and employee? Do you agree with her, or do you think that the effects are greater (or lesser) on the economy and the U.S. workforce than she implies?

3. What methods of controlling or softening the impact of outsourcing on U.S. workers does Thottham present in her final paragraphs? Which of these ideas seem most promising to you, and why is the practice of outsourcing so difficult to control?

LISA TAKEUCHI CULLEN

"The Legacy of Dreams"

Lisa Takeuchi Cullen, formerly a Tokyo correspondent from Kobe, Japan, became a reporter for Time Magazine *after immigrating to the United States. She has written a book on modern funeral rituals,* Remember Me: A Lively Tour of the New American Way of Death *(2006). In the* Time *essay that follows, "The Legacy of*

Dreams" (2004), Cullen argues that immigrant and minority family businesses have thrived because of the creative insights and knowledge of business practices that second-generation youth who had previously looked for employment as professionals in large corporations have learned.

For Peter Kim, the call to join the family business came as a rude awakening. Snoring away a spring-break morning at the University of Southern California in 1994, Kim picked up the phone to hear his father Sang Hoon Kim shouting at him in Korean. "He goes, 'The company's got problems. Everybody's got to help out,'" recalls the younger Kim. The son did a lot more than that. At the time, office workers were no longer buying the polyester blouses the family company, Protrend, churned out. Sales were tumbling 50% every year. What's more, the father had invested in real estate during a market peak, and as a result the company shouldered $10 million in debt. Today Peter Kim, 33, is CEO of a debt-free, $15 million-a-year business. In 1999 he launched Drunknmunky, an Asian-influenced men's street-wear line that pulls in the bulk of the company's revenue. Battling low-cost production from competitors in China and elsewhere, Kim decided to pursue the higher profit margins in design and retail. "That's where I believe the industry is going: either you're a brand or you're dirt cheap," he says.

The Kims are part of a phenomenon sociologists call ethnic niche business, in which an immigrant group comes to dominate an industry, often with no discernible connection to its original culture. Think Chinese and laundry services, Arabs and gas stations, Koreans and groceries. And garments too. Experts estimate that more than half the 144,000 garment workers in Southern California are of Korean origin and up to half the companies are Korean owned. Entrepreneurs of Indian origin today own 38% of all hotels in the U.S. and more than half of budget motels. Mexican Americans whose forebears worked California's vineyards are becoming owners. Once, immigrant business owners were reluctant to pass the torch to their kids, hoping their labor would hoist the younger generation into more prestigious professions. That's changing. As the businesses grow, American-born heirs are increasingly willing to follow in their immigrant parents' footsteps. Armed with native English, advanced education and a comfort with change, the new generation is modernizing the family businesses in ways their parents never dreamed possible.

This generation's business strategies and goals far outpace their parents'. Drunknmunky, for instance, publicizes its popularity with hip-hop acts like Cypress Hill and Linkin Park and sponsors raves and rap concerts. Kim's ambitions include music and video-game production, accessories, bags and shoes. "I'd like to be more of a household brand, not just a clothing company—like [Ralph Lauren's] Polo," he says. Unlike their parents, Kim and his peers pursue deals outside their immigrant communities; Drunknmunky works with partners in FUBU, the African-American-owned clothing line. Instead of hewing to production, most Korean-owned companies are now full package, offering everything from fabric to manufacturing to export for major American labels, says Bruce Berton of Los Angeles' Fashion Institute of Design and Merchandise (where half the students are second- or third-generation Korean Americans).

Changing attitudes toward money have allowed the next generations to update and expand their companies. Early immigrants, suspicious of and unable to secure standard loans, turned to community loan clubs, in which relatives and friends put up money to help start businesses. This financing method is common but limited. What Koreans call kye is a hui for the Chinese, ekub for Ethiopians, san for Dominicans. Today, says Steven Gold, a sociologist at Michigan State University, immigrant businesses have access to loans from other ethnic sources, including banks or investors that cater to their community. The younger generation is also far savvier about landing tax-advantaged loans from the Small Business Administration and various minority-business-development funds. Some companies, including the Korean-owned clothing retailer Forever 21, are planning to go public.

Koreans arriving in the 1970s specialized in apparel manufacturing for some of the same reasons Indian immigrants gravitated toward the hotel industry: those businesses let them use family members as staff, conduct transactions in cash and get by with minimal English or experience. The Patel family's entry into the hotel business is exceedingly typical, right down to their surname. Natu Patel, a banana farmer in the Gujarat region of India—where most of the U.S.'s Indian hoteliers have roots and the majority of residents are named Patel—arrived in San Francisco nearly three decades ago with his family and $10. He learned the business working for motels owned by wife Hansa's relatives and then sought out affordable properties in remote regions before settling on a small inn in Cleveland, Tenn., later adding motels in Waco, Texas, and Kennesaw, Ga.

Priti Patel, 33, hardly remembers another life. At 8, she was counting change and working the front desk. "I used to hate it," she says. "Everybody else gets to go home after school and get a snack. I had to help at the hotel. On weekends I had to cut grass." When friends drove by and saw her working, she would feel embarrassed. Still, the industry intrigued her enough to pursue a business degree at the University of Tennessee, and afterward she worked for the Small Business Administration. She returned to the family's HNP Enterprises to take over as manager of the Kennesaw motel in 1997.

Patel's management style differs from that of her parents. For one thing, she refuses to live on property, choosing instead to separate her work life from her family. Unlike her parents, who prefer to do the work themselves, she employs a housekeeping manager, a desk manager and a sales manager to oversee the property in her place. "I let go a lot more than my dad does," she says. Patel and her brother Hitesh, 25, plan to expand into restaurant franchises. Though their methods and goals may differ, says Patel, their father is proud of their achievements. "That's why he sent us to school."

Education is proving a key tool in grooming the second generation of Indian hoteliers. Unlike, say, the construction business, hospitality is an immigrant-heavy industry with a ready infrastructure of formal training. Over the past five years or so, as a new generation has come of age, students of Indian background have flooded hotel schools like the one at Cornell University. There they learn how to broker acquisitions, arrange complicated financing, set up room-booking technology and modernize marketing. Many take internships and first jobs in related fields like real estate or investment banking. The training helps "prepare them to take on an industry vastly more competitive and complex than when their parents entered it," says Cornell professor Chekitan Dev.

The new generation of Indian-American hotel owners is also learning, sometimes the hard way, how to play politics. After Sept. 11, ethnic-Indian proprietors suffered a wave of xenophobia, exhibited by signs outside competing hotels that claimed AMERICAN OWNED AND OPERATED. The bias cut into bookings, hurting business in an already devastating climate for travel. Yet while major hotel corporations lobbied for and received relief from Washington, the Asian American Hotel Owners Association had no presence or influence there to follow suit. "We learned from that," says Naresh (Nash) Patel, 38, current chairman of the association and a second-generation hotel owner. The group swiftly launched lobbying efforts and invited politicians like Newt Gingrich to speak at its gatherings. It set up a nationwide program to provide free hotel rooms for families of active military members on leave. Nash Patel called the owner of a Florida hotel with an offending sign. The owner took it down.

In some cases, the children of immigrants, thanks to education and experience, are leaving hard labor behind for good. Mexican workers in California's wine country have been preparing for generations to face their unique challenge: trading grape-stained work gloves for ownership papers. Since the 1940s, millions of Mexicans have traveled across the border to work the California vineyards. Those economics haven't changed in what is now the $33 billion U.S. wine capital. During harvest, Napa County is home to up to 2,700 migrant workers, most from Mexico. For as much as $15 an hour, the workers endure 18-hour days of backbreaking labor, often with no benefits or job security. "Without the Mexican labor force, there wouldn't be a wine industry," says Amelia Ceja, 48. Her children were to the vineyard born, all right—to migrant workers. Their grandparents toiled in the fields for $1 a day. Amelia met her husband Pedro while picking grapes at age 12. The family bought its first 15 acres, outside Napa, in 1983. By 1999, it owned 113 acres. Today Ceja Vineyards provides grapes for well-known brands in addition to its own labels. The company now produces 5,000 cases of wine annually, compared with just 750 in 2001. The Ceja children study at local universities and will inherit vineyards, not dreams.

Salvador Renteria traveled illegally across the border in the early 1960s to work in Napa. He moved up from driving stakes in the vineyards as a laborer for $20 a day to being a salaried foreman and supervisor. His son Oscar earned a college degree while learning all his father knew about vineyard management. In 1987 Salvador opened Renteria Vineyard Management, which oversees 1,500 acres of vineyard for 27 high-profile clients, employs 130 people and hauls in revenues of $8 million a year. Recently Oscar, 36, who took over the company in 1993, launched the company's own wine. "By growing grapes, there's not a lot of exposure," he says. "By making wine, you tell a story."

Sometimes the ambitions of business heirs fly far beyond anything the founders imagined. When he was rolling penny cigars on a sidewalk in early-1900s Cuba, Teorifio Perez-Carillo could not have dreamed that someday his handiwork would be legendary among Hollywood stars and other aficionados. Or that his son Ernesto would buy the building behind his sidewalk stake and turn it into a tobacco warehouse. Or that his grandson, also named Ernesto, would take over the operation in Miami and become a multimillionaire.

Ernesto Perez-Carillo Jr., 52, considers that improbable journey as he strolls among the dozen men and women sorting and rolling molasses-colored leaves in El Credito Cigars' pungent storefront in Miami's Little Havana. His father expanded production to 140,000 cigars a day, at one point supplying troops during World War II. They fled to Miami after Fidel Castro's takeover in 1959. In 1968, finally convinced the exile was permanent, the elder Ernesto paid $5,000 for a cigarmaking factory in Miami. To find a niche among the 30 or so other cigar factories, Ernesto Sr. began testing some signature brands. He developed a mail-order business to reach markets in Chicago and the Northeast, leafing through the Yellow Pages to find doctors, lawyers and other potential cigar smokers.

Though he had set out for New York City to make it as a jazz drummer, Ernesto Perez-Carillo Jr. returned to Miami when his father came down with Lou Gehrig's disease. In the midst of negotiations to sell the business, "something came over me," says Perez-Carillo. He persuaded his father to decline the offer and turn the business over to him. Ernesto Sr. died in 1980. El Credito's focus on premium lines paid off in the early '90s, gaining the company notice during the cigar boom. An article in Cigar Aficionado magazine sparked a flood of orders, causing a six-month backlog. Bill Cosby, Sharon Stone and Arnold Schwarzenegger became loyal clients, says Perez-Carillo.

The trickiest decision for immigrant business owners is often the exit strategy. Though both have worked in the business, Perez-Carillo's son Ernesto III, 22, is a recent Stanford grad and consultant, and his daughter Lissette McPhillips, 30, is a lawyer. So Perez-Carillo knew he faced a choice in 1999 when tobacco company Swedish Match offered to buy El Credito for a reported $20 million. He sold. "Most people would have thought, Millions and millions of dollars—this is my dream, my dream has come true," says McPhillips. But for her father, "there was a sadness there." Perez-Carillo now works for General Cigar, a subsidiary of Swedish Match, and still runs El Credito in Miami.

In part because of such potential rewards, these days many immigrant children no longer view following their parents' path as a jail sentence. All the second-generation members of the Rama family, whose Greenville, S.C., JHM Group owns a string of more than 40 hotels, have worked in the family business since they could fold towels. Three are pursuing degrees in architecture, business or hotel management—by choice. "I knew I wanted to make the hotel business my career. My head was always in it," says D.J. Rama, 36, a Cornell M.B.A. and vice president of operations for JHM. "Work is the fabric that weaves the wealth the first generation built together with the next."

Others take more convincing. When he was called back to work for the family company, Peter Kim was less than thrilled. But one day he had an epiphany while driving down the freeway. "I was feeling sorry for myself," he says. "Then it hit me: You are such a coward. My parents and that whole generation come to this country with nothing—like, a suitcase and maybe, what, a couple hundred bucks?" His father, seated beside him, says, "Thirty-eight dollars."

"They don't know the language," Peter Kim continues. "They don't know the culture. They can't even find a bathroom. They know nothing but can build this. It was almost like somebody took a frying pan and smacked me on the head. I am born in this country. I am educated in this country. We can make a go of this." The American Dream, after all, is worth fighting for.

—With reporting by Anne Berryman/Kennesaw, Laura A. Locke/ Napa, Siobhan Morrissey/Miami, Constance E. Richards/Greenville and Sean Scully/Los Angeles

QUESTIONS

1. Takeuchi Cullen relies on many examples from first and second generations of immigrants in the United States to make her point. Are these examples effective and persuasive? Would her essay have been more effective if she had used other types of evidence? What kind of evidence?

2. What factors have drawn immigrant youth back to family businesses after working in the corporate world, according to the author? What flaws in corporate work culture are suggested by these returns?

3. After considering Cullen's argument and your experiences with similar types of businesses, do you think that family-owned businesses will continue to grow and flourish in this county? What obstacles do such businesses face?

STEVEN GREENHOUSE

"Millions of Jobs of a Different Collar"

Steven Greenhouse received a B.A. from Wesleyan University, an M.A. from the Columbia University Graduate School of Journalism, and a law degree from New York University. Greenhouse has worked at the New York Times since 1983, covering business news as well as investigating labor and workplace concerns. He has spent several years as a business and economics correspondent for the Times *in Chicago, Paris, and Washington, D.C., where he also reported on state department and foreign affairs issues. He is the author of a new book,* The Big Squeeze: Tough Times for the American Worker *(2008). In the article that follows, Greenhouse argues for creating new jobs that will help to create a sustainable future.*

Everyone knows what blue-collar and white-collar jobs are, but now a job of another hue — green — has entered the lexicon.

Presidential candidates talk about the promise of "green collar" jobs — an economy with millions of workers installing solar panels, weatherizing homes, brewing biofuels, building hybrid cars and erecting giant wind turbines. Labor unions view these new jobs as replacements for positions lost to overseas manufacturing and outsourcing. Urban groups view training in green jobs as a route out of poverty. And environmentalists say they are crucial to combating climate change.

No doubt that the number of green-collar jobs is growing, as homeowners, business and industry shift toward conservation and renewable energy. And the numbers are expected to increase greatly in the next few decades, because state governments have mandated that even more energy come from alternative sources.

But some skeptics argue that the phrase "green jobs" is little more than a trendy term for politicians and others to bandy about. Some say they are not sure that these jobs will have the staying power to help solve the problems of the nation's job market, and others note that green jobs often pay less than the old manufacturing jobs they are replacing.

Indeed, such is the novelty of the green-job concept that no one is certain how many such jobs there are, and even advocates don't always agree on what makes a job green.

"A green-collar job is in essence a blue-collar job that has been upgraded to address the environmental challenges of our country," said Lucy Blake, chief executive of the Apollo Alliance, a coalition of environmental groups, labor unions and politicians seeking to transform the economy into one based on renewable energy.

Carl Pope, executive director of the Sierra Club, said: "A green job has to do something useful for people, and it has to be helpful to, or at least not damaging to, the environment."

It can be difficult to parse the difference between green- and blue-collar jobs. Dave Foster, executive director of the Blue Green Alliance, a partnership between the United Steelworkers and the Sierra Club, pointed to workers who mine iron ore in Minnesota and ship it to steel mills in Indiana. "Ten years ago, that steel was used for making low-efficiency automobiles, so those jobs were part of the dirty economy," he said. "But now that steel is being used to build wind turbines. So now you can call them green jobs."

But to Andrew W. Hannah, chief executive of Plextronics, a start-up in Pittsburgh, green-collar jobs often have little relation to their blue-collar counterparts. His company produces high-tech polymer inks that are used to make electronic circuitry for solar panels. Of the company's 51 employees, 20 have Ph.D.'s in fields like physics, chemistry and material science.

It is hard to gauge the number of green-collar jobs nationwide. Welders at a wind-turbine factory are viewed as having green jobs, but what about the factory's accountant or its janitors? Workers with Sustainable South Bronx, a nonprofit group that plants vegetation to keep the area cooler and reduce air-conditioning demands, would seem to fit the bill. But so would the employees of Tesla Motors, south of San Francisco, who are producing an all-electric Roadster that sells for $98,000.

In the most-often-cited estimate, a report commissioned by the American Solar Energy Society said that the nation had 8.5 million jobs in renewable energy or energy efficient industries. And Jerome Ringo, president of the Apollo Alliance, predicted that the nation could generate three million to five million more green jobs over the next 10 years.

Green jobs are especially good "because they cannot be easily outsourced, say, to Asia," said Van Jones, president of Green for All, an organization based in Oakland, Calif., whose goal is promoting renewable energy and lifting workers out of poverty. "If we are going to weatherize buildings, they have to be weatherized here," he said. "If you put up solar panels, you can't ship a building to Asia and have them put the solar panels on and ship it back. These jobs have to be done in the United States."

Many advocates of green employment say the jobs should be good for the workers as well as the environment. Two weeks ago in Pittsburgh, more than 800 people attended a national green-jobs conference, where much of the talk was about ensuring that green jobs provided living wages. Many speakers anticipated that the jobs would do so, because they often required special skills, like the technical ability to maintain a giant wind turbine (and the physical ability to climb a 20-story ladder to work on it).

"These jobs will be better for the workers' future, for their job security," said Ms. Blake of the Apollo Alliance. "These green technologies are making products that the world wants, like energy-efficient buildings and light fixtures."

Not everyone, however, is enamored with green jobs. Take the Competitive Enterprise Institute, a Washington group that opposes state mandates requiring that a certain percentage of power come from renewable sources. Myron Ebell, the institute's director of energy and global warming policy, argues that creating green jobs often does not create jobs on a net basis.

"If you create jobs in wind power or ethanol," he said, "that will take away jobs in other industries," like building and operating conventional gas turbine power plants.

Mr. Ebell suggested that green jobs might not prove to be so great. "There will undoubtedly be a lot of jobs created in industries that are considered green or fashionable," he said. "Some will last a long time, and some will go like the dot-coms."

Twenty-eight states have mandates generally requiring that 10 to 25 percent of their energy be obtained through renewable sources in a decade or two. In response, many companies have rushed to build wind- and solar-power systems, and some are researching how to transform prairie grass into biofuel.

Joy Clark-Holmes, director of public sector markets for Johnson Controls, which manages heating and cooling systems in buildings nationwide, sees strong job growth in the green economy. Her company's building efficiency business, she said, expects to hire 60,000 workers worldwide over the next decade.

"We see the market for greening our customers as growing," Ms. Clark-Holmes said. She talked of demand for technicians who install and maintain heating and cooling systems, managers who oversee those functions and engineers who develop and design such systems.

With scientists voicing increased concern about climate change, some highly talented people have left other fields to help build the green economy. For instance, Lois Quam, who helped create and run a $30 billion division of United Health Group, a health insurer, has joined the renewable energy cause, becoming managing director for alternative investments at Piper Jaffray, an investment bank based in Minneapolis. She is setting up investment funds that focus on renewable energy and clean energy.

"The development of a green economy creates a broad new set of opportunities," Ms. Quam said. "When I first started looking at this area, many people commented on how this will be as big as the Internet. But this is so much bigger than the Internet. The only comparable example we can find is the Industrial Revolution. It will affect every business and every industry."

Mr. Jones, the head of Green for All, joined the green economy after graduating from Yale Law School. He became executive director of the Ella Baker Center for Human Rights in Oakland, using that position to start a program that trains low-income workers in how to weatherize homes and install solar panels.

Mr. Jones calls such jobs green pathways out of poverty. "The green economy needs Ph.D.'s and Ph.-do's," he said. "We need people who are highly educated at the theoretical level, and we need people who are highly educated at the level of skilled labor."

He sees green jobs as providing a career ladder. Some workers might start at $10 an hour inspecting homes for energy-efficient light bulbs. Then they might become $18-an-hour workers installing solar panels and eventually $25-an-hour solar-team managers. Eventually they might become $40-an-hour electricians or carpenters who do energy-minded renovations.

"Right now we don't have the infrastructure to train a sufficient number of green-collar workers," Mr. Jones said.

As the green economy grows, states are vying for green investments— and green jobs. Pennsylvania has been especially successful, attracting German and Taiwanese companies that are building solar equipment factories, as well as attracting Gamesa, a Spanish wind turbine company. Gamesa has two factories in the state, employing 1,300 workers. Facing pressure from the United Steelworkers, which views the greening of the economy as a way to increase union membership, Gamesa agreed not to fight an organizing drive, and now many workers are unionized.

Pennsylvania's efforts have been helped by the presence of many skilled manufacturing workers in the state and its commitment to having 18.5 percent of its power come from renewable sources by 2020.

"We have gone after this sector first and foremost because the green of the sector is important, because it is the green that goes into the pocketbooks and wallets of workers," said Kathleen McGinty, the state's environmental secretary. "They are good-paying jobs, jobs that often require advanced skills."

Jim Bauer, 55, is delighted to work for Gamesa. There he leads a team that assembles parts for wind turbines, earning slightly less than he did at United States Steel, which laid him off from his crane operator's job after 25 years. Now he earns $17 an hour in his job, while many assembly workers earn $13.50 an hour.

"It feels good working for a company that is bringing jobs into the country instead of taking jobs out of the country," Mr. Bauer said.

He admits to feeling noble doing a green job. "We have to get away from fossil fuels and oil so we can tell the Saudis to take a hike," he said.

QUESTIONS

1. What is Greenhouse's definition of a "green job"? What rhetorical strategies does he use to create his definition?
2. What reasons and evidence in the essay support the importance of green jobs? Why are some institutions and corporations skeptical of the value of green jobs and their ability to alleviate some of the economic and environmental problems in our society? In contrast, why do many scientists and investment brokers think that creating green jobs that will make our environment more sustainable is more important than the development of the Internet? Which position makes most sense to you and why?
3. Do some research into the impact of green jobs on the economy and the environment. Do your findings support the significance of such jobs that Greenhouse argues for in his essay? Also, think about how your community has created green jobs.

WILLIAM GREIDER

"Work Rules"

William Greider has been a reporter for more than 35 years for U.S. newspapers, magazines, and television. Greider was also the former assistant managing editor for national news at the Washington Post, *where he worked for nearly 15 years as a national correspondent, editor, and columnist. He has served as the on-air correspondent for six television documentaries, including* Frontline, *the documentary film series of the Public Broadcasting System. His books include* One World Ready or Not: the Manic Logic of Global Capitalism *(1997). The following excerpt from his* The Soul of Capitalism *(2003) argues for worker-controlled companies.*

Thorstein Veblen, whose corrosive critiques of American capitalism in the early twentieth century remain relevant and wickedly entertaining today, had one tender spot in his thinking. Veblen believed in engineers. The engineer, he wrote, is not captive to the money compulsion and other malignant illusions associated with capitalism. Engineers gain their satisfaction and status mainly from figuring out how to make things work better. Veblen's romantic notion was that someday engineers and the other dedicated technicians in business would rise up and take control from the absentee owners. Then they would redesign the production system so that it works better for humanity. I share Veblen's soft spot for engineers and similar types. My father, Harold W. Greider, was a research chemist and chemical engineer in a midsize manufacturing company, a prolific inventor and practical-minded optimist of twentieth-century industry who believed problems could be solved if people applied their minds rigorously (at the end of his long life, his mind was working on the ecological crisis).

I was reminded of Veblen's vision when I talked with Joseph Cabral, the CEO of Chatsworth Products Inc., a small and very successful California manufacturer owned 100 percent by its employees. Joe Cabral was schooled in accounting—"I'm one of the bean counter guys," he says—but became an executive whose business sensibilities harmonize with Veblen's. Cabral's manner is can-do practicality and rigor with the facts, yet he also nurtures a big-think understanding of how the system should be reformed. Experience tells him that making capitalist enterprise more equitable and human scale—more like "family"—actually makes it more productive and enduring.

"We have a wonderful capitalistic society that makes the United States really inventive, but as with anything, you find some flaws in it," he told me. "The way our society has rolled out, the wealth that's created through that vehicle called capitalism ends up in too few hands. The entrepreneur who's fortunate enough to be there at the start ends up really receiving a disproportionate amount of the wealth. And all the working folks who enabled that success to take place share in little of that wealth. So we end up in a society with a wealth structure where the top of one percent owns 90 percent or something like that. It's so disproportionate that, in my heart, I'd say that kind of ownership structure is not sustainable. At some point, capitalism is going to burst because we haven't done right for the folks who have actually created that wealth."

Cabral discovered the alternative of self-ownership in 1990. The Chatsworth operation in the San Fernando Valley, where he was comptroller in division management, was discarded by the conglomerate that had acquired it only a few years before. The plants would be closed down, since the only interested buyers simply wanted to purchase the machinery and other hard assets for pennies on the dollar. Chatsworth was small and low-tech—it fabricates the metal frames for stacking computers in data-storage centers—while the Harris Corporation wished to be known as high-tech. The faddish practice of "rationalizing" product lines and balance sheets (better known to workers as downsizing) is popular with large corporations because it typically boosts the stock price and provides tax write-offs. It also destroys a vast, unmeasurable volume of viable production, not to mention jobs and careers. The destruction is what often motivates the preventive takeovers by employees. They know what is being lost.

"We valued ourselves higher than any outsiders would value us," Cabral said. "I must tell you, we had all the confidence this would work." After Harris stripped away some elements it wanted to retain, only one hundred or so employees remained but, led by eight top managers, they organized an employee stock ownership plan (ESOP). The ESOP's trust arrangement enables workers to borrow the money to buy all or a portion of their firm, then pay off the debt from the company's future earnings. The ESOP device was invented nearly half a century ago by Louis Kelso, a San Francisco investment banker who elaborated his own seminal critique of capitalism's maldistribution between capital and labor. His idea did not really take off until the 1970s, when Senator Russell Long of Louisiana, chairman of the Senate Finance Committee, pushed through a series of tax breaks to sweeten the deal for owners and bankers. Long was a conservative Democrat with a deep understanding of how the American system really works. His father was Huey Long, the inflammatory 1930s populist whose "Share the Wealth" crusade deeply frightened the American establishment during the Great Depression. Russell Long used to say: "Remember, it was my father who was the revolutionary—I'm a reformer."

"When I read about ESOPs in CFO magazine, I thought, yeah, this really makes sense," Joe Cabral says. "Everybody is sharing in the wealth that they're creating. There's a fundamental philosophy of, We're all in this together. We're not just doing this for some outside shareholder, we're doing it because we are the shareholders. In most companies you want to do well in order to have a job or career advancement, but you're basically in it for the paycheck. In CPI we created this wonderful foundation of ownership and people were totally aligned with the success of the company."

The bonding of interests between Chatworth's managers and assembly-line workers was tested up front. Under the two-year purchase option Harris agreed to reduce the $2.5 million sale price if Chatsworth employees could cut operating costs and boost profits in the meantime (in effect, sharing the income gains with the workers). "We did some amazing things, making old equipment work for us and learning to operate with a lot less inventory," Cabral says. "It was kind of a neat period in that way, seeing how creative people can be when they're put in a situation, how they work their way through it." The employees managed in one year to knock $1 million off the purchase price. They raised some money from personal savings, borrowed the rest, and bought total control.

Through the nineties, Chatsworth Products flourished spectacularly, riding the Internet boom because its equipment supplied the celebrated Silicon Valley firms building the huge data-storage centers. CPI's employment grew more than sixfold. All six hundred became owners (a majority of the workforce is composed of minorities, Hispanic and Asian). Their privately held stock rose in value from $4 a share to $121. When the Internet bubble burst at the end of the decade, CPI hung on for a year and a half, treading water and furiously cutting costs, before it too was compelled to shrink its workforce. "We lost 150 owners," Cabral says. "It was traumatic, painful, but nobody was surprised or shocked. They knew how hard we tried to avoid this, that we pulled out all the stops. They created the wealth and, when they leave the company, their wealth goes with them. That's what it's all about."

People who started with Chatsworth in 1991 (and most who came in afterward) departed with six-figure checks or considerably more. Some of those who invested personal savings ten years before have accrued balances of more than a million dollars. "These folks could never have accumulated that kind of wealth in any other way," Cabral says. "Nobody ever got rich on a paycheck."

Chatsworth's success is not typical, of course, since most employee-owned companies have less glamorous stories and less spectacular wealth accumulations: Nor is Joe Cabral a typical ESOP manager. Many of them are flinty, old-fashioned bottom-line guys, bemused or even irritated by his lofty talk about the just distribution of wealth. Cabral represents a hybrid type not widely recognized in the American business culture but that would have fascinated Veblen. "Humanist-populist-capitalists," ESOP consultant Christopher Mackin of Ownership Associates has dubbed them. His oxymoron mixes hard-nosed and idealistic, savvy accounting and human-scale vision.

Among the ones I've met, the social values seem fused with their practical business instincts, so comfortably integrated it is difficult to know which came first. Did they engineer the sale of a family-owned company to faithful, long-term employees because it seemed the "right thing" to do? Or to save the enterprise from failure and corporate predators? Or was the ESOP simply a "smart money" move to harvest the tax breaks? The deal, they would say, "made sense" for lots of reasons. Perhaps these "humanists" are an unintended by-product of American abundance, business people who know how to make lots of money but look around and ask: Is this all there is to life? In any case, their presence is story enough among ESOP managers that Joe Cabral was elected board chair of the ESOP Association and speaks for thousands of them.

Louis Kelso's vision for achieving broadened, even universal ownership of the nation's capital assets is sometimes compared to the homesteading movement in the nineteenth century, when the federal government have away millions of western acres to the families who settled the land if they made it productive. In the modern industrial economy stock shares are roughly equivalent to land as the principal income-producing asset. The ESOP process is not "free," however. The new owners must "work off" the loan by producing profitably. The transaction may also dilute share value for other stockholders, though they will be well rewarded if the new worker-owners make the firm successful and more profitable. A better comparison may be with the New Deal credit reforms in the 1930s that enabled ordinary families to buy their own homes through liberalized mortgage terms. Two generations of broadening home ownership brought stability and a long-term time horizon to people's lives. Ownership anchors the "American dream" of middle-class prosperity that now feels threatened for so many families.

In the best of circumstances, an economy functioning with broadly shared ownership of enterprises would not eliminate the stark inequalities that already exist. But, over several generations, spreading wealth laterally through the society would generate profound social consequences, including greater family security, time, and satisfaction, as well as more deeply rooted connections with others. In time, the dominating political influence of concentrated wealth, both corporate and individual, on democracy would be greatly diluted, if not entirely extinguished. In time, if families accumulate substantial nest eggs, Kelso envisioned the financial assets generating a second stream of income that would make people less dependent on the "wage slavery" that early labor leaders decried and still exists for many Americans.

Essentially, there are three main arguments on behalf of a system of self-ownership that would replace employment as we know it. The first is David Ellerman's argument that the natural rights of people are inescapably violated by the enduring master-servant relationship, illegitimately separating them from self, from the personal accountability one never escapes in human existence. As a result, lives are stunted, confined, commanded, and dominated. People need democratic governance in the system of production in order to realize their full capacities as human beings.

The second argument, grounded in the economic theories of Louis Kelso, holds that universal ownership—and thus broad distribution of capitalism's returns—is not only more just, but is necessary to prevent an eventual economic and political crisis for the present system. As technology increasingly displaces labor in production processes, Kelso argued, the depressing pressures on wage incomes intensify while the wealthy minority accumulates a still greater imbalance of power. The economic danger, he suggested, is an eventual failure of available demand when workers lack the incomes to purchase what the economic system can produce. . . . When these conditions develop, Kelso warned, the government will face unbearable pressures to enlarge the welfare state and to intervene more profoundly in the free-running economy. As a libertarian conservative he dreaded that outcome, yet he saw it as inevitable unless workers accumulate the income-producing assets—that is, shares of ownership—that can complement their wage incomes.

The third argument, which draws on both of the others, simply observes that businesses perform better when the employees share a stake in the ownership. That is, the companies are more efficient because workers contribute more readily to the processes and signal managers when something is amiss. The emerging academic research on employee-owned companies supports this claim. ESOP companies, compared with similar firms where employees have no ownership, generate greater annual sales and faster employment growth. They are also more likely to survive profitably, pay higher wages, and provide benefits like diversified pensions.

Chris Mackin, whose Ownership Associates counsels both labor and management on employee ownership initiatives, summarized the research results from Joseph Blasi and Douglas Kruse of Rutgers University, as well as other scholars: "The combination of a substantial employee ownership stake and an effective program to communicate it and thereby realize the previously untapped imagination and enthusiasm of employees leads to competitive advantages of between 8–11 percent over the conventionally structured competition."

1. Who is Joseph Cabral and why does he think that "at some point, capitalism is going to burst"? Do you agree or disagree with this argument? How does Greider use Cabral's ideas to deepen his own argument?
2. What are the three arguments for employee-owned companies discussed in this article? Do you believe these points are realistic? How well does Greider use facts and case histories to support his solutions?
3. Argue for or against the employee-run organization. What are the advantages and disadvantages of this type of business model? How could these types of companies better the economy and the working conditions of the employees? Could the employee-owned companies compete against conventional corporations?

DIFFERING PERSPECTIVES: SHOULD WORK MAKE US HAPPY?

Alain de Botton

"Workers of the World, Relax"

Alain de Botton (b. 1969) earned his B.A. at Cambridge University and his M.A. at Oxford University; he went on to Harvard to work on a Ph.D., but dropped out as he became increasingly interested in writing. He currently lives in London and contributes to many magazine and journals. Botton also writes nonfiction, film scripts, and novels. His latest works include The Consolations of Philosophy *(2000),* Status Anxiety *(2004), and* The Architecture of Happiness *(2006). Botton argues with wit on serious topics as he gives advice to his readers. In the selection that follows from the* New York Times *(2004), Botton looks back at the history of work and considers why modern society has a mistaken idea about the purpose and benefits of life on the job.*

All societies throughout history have had work right at their center; but ours—particularly America's—is the first to suggest that it could be something other than a punishment or penance. Ours is the first to imply that a sane human being would want to work even if he wasn't under financial pressure to do so. We are unique, too, in allowing our choice of work to define who we are, so that the central question we ask of new acquaintances is not where they come from or who their parents are but, rather, what it is they do—as though only this could effectively reveal what gives a human life its distinctive timbre.

It wasn't always like this. Greco-Roman civilization tended to view work as a chore best left to slaves. For both Plato and Aristotle, fulfillment could be reached only when one had the command of a private income and could escape day-to-day obligations and freely devote oneself to the contemplation of ethical and moral questions. The entrepreneur and merchant may have had a nice villa and a heaping larder, but they played no role in the antique vision of the good life.

Early Christianity took a similarly bleak view of labor, adding the even darker thought that man was condemned to toil in order to make up for the sin of Adam. Working conditions, however abusive, could not be improved. Work wasn't accidentally miserable—it was one of the planks upon which earthly suffering was irrevocably founded. St. Augustine reminded slaves to obey their masters and accept their pain as part of what he termed, in "The City of God," the "wretchedness of man's condition."

The first signs of the modern, more cheerful attitude toward work can be detected in the city-states of Italy during the Renaissance, and in particular, in the biographies of the artists of the time. In descriptions of the lives of men like Michelangelo and Leonardo, we find some now familiar-sounding ideas about what our labors could ideally mean for us: a path to authenticity and glory. Rather than a burden and punishment, artistic work could allow us to rise above our ordinary limitations. We could express our talents on a page or on a canvas in a way we never could in our everyday lives. Of course, this new vision applied only to creative elite (no one yet thought to tell a servant that work could develop his true self: that was a claim waiting for modern management theory), but it proved to be the model for all successive definitions of happiness earned through work.

It was not until the late 18th century that the model was extended beyond the artistic realm. In the writings of bourgeois thinkers like Benjamin Franklin, Diderot and Rousseau, we see work recategorized not only as a means to earn money, but also as a way to become more fully ourselves. It is worth noting that this reconciliation of necessity and happiness exactly mirrored the contemporary re-evaluation of marriage: just as marriage was rethought as an institution that could deliver both practical benefits and sexual and emotional fulfillment (a handy conjunction once thought impossible by aristocrats, who saw a need for a mistress and a wife), so too work was now alleged to be capable of delivering both the money necessary for survival and the stimulation and self-expression that had once been seen as the exclusive preserve of the leisured.

Simultaneously, people began to experience a new kind of pride in their work, in large part because the way that jobs were handed out took on a semblance of justice. In his autobiography, Thomas Jefferson explained that his proudest achievement had been to create a meritocratic United States, where "a new aristocracy of virtue and talent" replaced the old aristocracy of unfair privilege and, in many cases, brute stupidity. Meritocracy endowed jobs with a new, quasi-moral quality. Now that prestigious and well-paid posts seemed to be available on the basis of actual intelligence and ability, your job title could perhaps say something directly meaningful about you.

Over the 19th century, many Christian thinkers, especially in the United States, changed their views of money accordingly. American Protestant denominations suggested that God required his followers to lead a life that was successful both temporally and spiritually. Fortunes in this world were evidence that one deserved a good place in the next—an attitude reflected in the Rev. Thomas P. Hunt's 1836 bestseller "The Book of Wealth: In Which It Is Proved From the Bible That It Is the Duty of Every Man to Become Rich." John D. Rockefeller was not shy to say that it was the Lord who had made him rich, while William Lawrence, the Episcopal bishop of Massachusetts, writing in 1892, argued, "We, like the Psalmist, occasionally see the wicked prosper, but only occasionally," adding, "Godliness is in league with riches."

As meritocracy came of age, demeaning jobs came to seem not merely regrettable, but, just like their more exciting counterparts, also deserved. No wonder people started asking each other what they did—and listening very carefully to the answers.

Though all this may seem like progress, in truth, modern attitudes toward work have unwittingly caused us problems. Today, claims are made on behalf of almost all kinds of work that are patently out of sync with what reality can provide. Yes, a few jobs are certainly fulfilling, but the majority are not and never can be. We would therefore be wise to listen to some of the pessimistic voices of the pre-modern period, if only to stop torturing ourselves for not being as happy in our work as we were told we could be.

William James once made an acute point about the relationship between happiness and expectation. He argued that satisfaction with ourselves does not require us to succeed in every endeavor. We are not always humiliated by failing; we are humiliated only if we first invest our pride and sense of worth in a given achievement, and then do not reach it. Our goals determine what we will interpret as a triumph and what must count as a failure: "With no attempt there can be no failure; with no failure no humiliation." So our self-esteem in this world is determined by the ratio of our actualities to our supposed potentialities. Thus:

$$\text{Self-esteem} = \text{Success/Pretensions}$$

If happiness at work is now so hard to earn, perhaps it is because our pretensions have so substantially outstripped reality. We expect every job to deliver some of the satisfaction available to Sigmund Freud or Franklin Roosevelt. Perhaps we should be reading Marx instead. Of course, Marx was a poor historian and wrong in all his prescriptions for a better world, but he was rather acute at diagnosing why work is so often miserable. In this respect, he drew on Immanuel Kant, who wrote in his "Groundwork of the Metaphysics of Morals" that behaving morally toward other people required that one respect them "for themselves" instead of using them as a "means"

ALAIN DE BOTTON

for one's enrichment or glory. Thus Marx, famously accused the bourgeoisie, and its new science, economics, of practicing "immorality" on a grand scale: "Political economy knows the worker only as a working animal—as a beast reduced to strictest bodily needs." The wages paid to employees were, said Marx, just "like the oil which is applied to wheels to keep them turning," adding, "The true purpose of work is no longer man, but money."

Marx may have been erratically idealizing the pre-industrial past and unduly castigating the bourgeoisie, but he ably captured the inescapable degree of conflict between employer and employee. Every commercial organization will try to gather raw materials, labor and machinery at the lowest possible price to combine them into a product that can be sold at the highest possible price.

And yet, troublingly, there is one difference between "labor" and other elements that conventional economics does not have a means to represent, or give weight to, but which is nevertheless unavoidably present: labor feels pain and pleasure. When production lines grow prohibitively expensive, they may be switched off and will not cry at the seeming injustice of their fate. A business can move from using coal to natural gas without the neglected energy source walking off a cliff.

But labor has a habit of meeting attempts to reduce its price or presence with emotion. It sobs in toilet stalls, it gets drunk to ease its fears of under-achievement, and it may choose death over redundancy.

These emotional responses point us to two, perhaps conflicting, imperatives coexisting in the workplace: an economic imperative that dictates that the primary task of business is to realize a profit, and a human imperative that leads employees to hunger for financial security, respect, tenure and even, on a good day, fun. Though the two imperatives may for long periods coexist without apparent friction, all wage-dependent workers live under an awareness that should there ever have to be a serious choice between the two, it is the economic one that must always prevail. These pressures are no less absent from the lives of the self-employed—whether they own the corner laundry or the town real-estate brokerage—for in their cases, the economy as a whole (local, national and global) acts as the employer.

Struggles between labor and capital may no longer, in the developed world at least, be as bare-knuckled as in Marx's day. Yet, despite advances in working conditions and employee protections, workers remain in essence tools in a process in which their own happiness or economic well-being is necessarily incidental. Whatever camaraderie may build up between employer and employed, whatever goodwill workers may display and however many years they may have devoted to a task, they must live with the knowledge and attendant anxiety that their status is not guaranteed—that it remains dependent on their own performance and the economic well-being of their organizations; that they are hence a means to profit, and never ends in themselves.

This is all sad, but not half as sad as it can be if we blind ourselves to the reality and raise our expectations of our work to extreme levels. A firm belief in the necessary misery of life was for centuries one of mankind's most important assets, a bulwark against bitterness, a defense against dashed hopes. Now it has been cruelly undermined by the expectations incubated by the modern worldview.

Now perhaps, as many of us return from summer vacations, we can temper their sadness by remembering that work is often more bearable when we don't, in addition to money, expect it always to deliver happiness.

QUESTIONS

1. Why do you think that de Botton begins his essay with the ideas about work in the Greco-Roman civilization and early Christianity? How do these "classical" attitudes toward work contrast with those in modern society? What socioeconomic factors, according to the author, have caused these changes in attitude?

2. In his historical analysis, what points does de Botton make about the futility of finding satisfaction and joy in work? Why does he end his analysis with the ideas of Karl Marx? Are there more recent thinkers he could have mentioned?

3. Argue for or against de Botton's point of view on work. If you agree with him, propose some solutions that would help to alleviate the stress caused by modern attitudes and economic issues involving work.

bell hooks

"Work Makes Life Sweet"

Bell hooks (b. 1952) is the pen name for Gloria Watkins, a pen name that honors her grandmother. Hooks was born into a family with six girls in Hopkinsville, Kentucky, a small, segregated community. She graduated from Stanford University with a B.A. in English (1973), earned her M.A. at the University of Wisconsin (1976) and her Ph.D. at the University of California at Santa Cruz in 1983. She has taught at many universities and is currently Distinguished Professor in Residence at Berea College in Kentucky. Her writings focus on gender, race, and class—issues that she sees as continuing markers of oppression for black women today. Hooks is the author of more than thirty books, including the essay collections Talking Back: Thinking Feminist, Thinking Black *(1989);* Yearning: Race, Gender, and Cultural Politics *(1990); and* Where We Stand: Class Matters *(2000). In her writing, hooks reflects deeply upon her own experiences while her ideas continue to lead readers to think critically about important social issues. In the following selection from* Sisters of *the Yam: Black Women and Self-Recovery (1993), hooks examines with vivid examples the changing attitudes of black women toward work, from acceptance of dead-end jobs to survive to a more recent quest for meaningful work, or "right livelihood."*

"Work makes life sweet!" I often heard this phrase growing up, mainly from old black folks who did not have jobs in the traditional sense of the word. They were usually self-employed, living off the land, selling fishing worms, picking up an odd job here and there. They were people who had a passion for work. They took pride in a job done well. My Aunt Margaret took in ironing. Folks brought her clothes from miles around because she was such an expert. That was in the days when using starch was common and she knew how to do an excellent job. Watching her iron with skill and grace was like watching a ballerina dance. Like all the other black girls raised in the fifties that I knew, it was clear to me that I would be a working woman. Even though our mother stayed home, raising her seven children, we saw her constantly at work, washing, ironing, cleaning, and cooking (she is an incredible cook). And she never allowed her six girls to imagine we would not be working women. No, she let us know that we would work and be proud to work.

The vast majority of black women in the United States know in girlhood that we will be workers. Despite sexist and racist stereotypes about black women living off welfare, most black women who receive welfare have been in the workforce. In *Hard Times Cotton Mill Girls*,[1] one can read about black women who went to work in the cotton mills, usually leaving farm labor or domestic service. Katie Geneva Cannon[2] remembers: "It was always assumed that we would work. Work was a given in life, almost like breathing and sleeping. I'm always surprised when I hear people talking about somebody taking care of them, because we always knew that we were going to work." Like older generations of southern black women, we were taught not only that we would be workers, but that there was no "shame" in doing any honest job. The black women around us who worked as maids, who stripped tobacco when it was the season, were accorded dignity and respect. We learned in our black churches and in our schools that it "was not what you did, but how you did it" that mattered.

A philosophy of work that emphasizes commitment to any task was useful to black people living in a racist society that for so many years made only certain jobs (usually service work or other labor deemed "undesirable") available to us. Just as many Buddhist traditions teach that any task becomes sacred when we do it mindfully and with care, southern black work traditions taught us the importance of working with integrity irrespective of the task. Yet these attitudes towards work did not blind anyone to the reality that racism made it difficult to work for white people. It took "gumption" to work with integrity in settings where white folks were disrespectful and downright hateful. And it was obvious to me as a child that the black people who were saying "work makes life sweet" were the folks who did not work for whites, who did what they wanted to do. For example, those who sold fishing worms were usually folks who loved to fish. Clearly there was a meaningful connection between positive thinking about work and those who did the work that they had chosen.

Most of us did not enter the workforce thinking of work in terms of finding a "calling" or a vocation. Instead, we thought of work as a way to make money. Many of us started our work lives early and we worked to acquire money to buy necessities. Some of us worked to buy school books or needed or desired clothing. Despite the emphasis on "right livelihood" that was present in our life growing up, my sisters and I were more inclined to think of work in relation to doing what you needed to do to get money to buy what you wanted. In general, we have had unsatisfying work lives. Ironically, Mama entered the paid workforce very late, after we were all raised, working for the school system and at times in domestic service, yet there are ways in which she has found work outside the home more rewarding than any of her children. The black women I talked with about work tended to see jobs primarily as a means to an end, as a way to make money to provide for material needs. Since so many working black women often have dependents, whether children or other relatives, they enter the workforce with the realistic conviction that they need to make money for survival purposes. This attitude coupled with the reality of a job market that remains deeply shaped by racism and sexism means that as black women we often end up working jobs that we do not like. Many of us feel that we do not have a lot of options. Of the women I interviewed, the ones who saw themselves as having options tended to have the highest levels of education. Yet nearly all the black women I spoke with agreed that they would always choose to work, even if they did not need to. It was only a very few young black females, teenagers and folks in their early twenties, who talked with me about fantasy lives where they would be taken care of by someone else.

Speaking with young black women who rely on welfare benefits to survive economically, I found that overall they wanted to work. However, they are acutely aware of the difference between a job and a fulfilling vocation. Most of them felt that it would not be a sign of progress for them to "get off welfare" and work low-paying jobs, in situations that could be stressful or dehumanizing. Individuals receiving welfare who are trying to develop skills, to attend school or college, often find that they are treated with much greater hostility by social-service workers than if they were just sitting at home watching television. One woman seeking assistance was told by an angry white woman worker, "welfare is not going to pay for you to get your B.A." This young woman had been making many personal sacrifices to try and develop skills and educational resources that would enable her to be gainfully employed and she was constantly disappointed by the level of resentment toward her whenever she needed to deal with social services.

Through the years, in my own working life, I have noticed that many black women do not like or enjoy their work. The vast majority of women I talked to. . . . agreed that they were not satisfied with their working lives even though they see themselves as performing well on the job. That is why I talk so much about work-related stress in [*Remembered Rapture*]. It is practically impossible to maintain a spirit of emotional well-being if one is daily doing work that is unsatisfying, that causes intense stress, and that gives little satisfaction. Again and again, I found that many black women I interviewed had far superior skills than the jobs they were performing called for but were held back because of their "lack of education," or in some cases, "necessary experience." This routinely prevented them from moving upward. While they performed their jobs well, they felt added tension generated in the work environment by supervisors who often saw them as "too uppity" or by their own struggle to maintain interest in their assigned tasks. One white-woman administrator shared that the clearly overly skilled black woman who works as an administrative assistant in her office was resented by white male "bosses" who felt that she did not have the proper attitude of a "subordinate." When I spoke to this woman she acknowledged not liking her job, stating that her lack of education and the urgent need to raise children and send them to college had prevented her from working towards a chosen career. She holds to the dream that she will return to school and someday gain the necessary education that will give her access to the career she desires and deserves. Work is so often a source of pain a frustration.

Learning how to think about work and our job choices from the standpoint of "right livelihood" enhances black female well-being. Our self-recovery is fundamentally linked to experiencing that quality of "work that makes life sweet." In one of my favorite self-help books, Marsha Sinetar's *Do What You Love, the Money Will Follow*, the author defines right livelihood as a concept initially coming from the teaching of Buddha which emphasized "work consciously chosen, done with full awareness and care, and leading to enlightenment." This is an attitude toward work that our society does not promote, and it especially does not encourage black females to think of work in this way. As Sinetar notes:

> *Right Livelihood, in both its ancient and its contemporary sense, embodies self-expression, commitment, mindfulness, and conscious choice. Finding and doing work of this sort is predicated upon high self-esteem and self-trust, since only those who like themselves, who subjectively feel they are trustworthy and deserving dare to choose on behalf of what is right and true for them. When the powerful quality of conscious choice is present in our work, we can be enormously productive. When we consciously choose to do work we enjoy, not only can we get things done, we can get them done well and be intrinsically rewarded for our effort.*

Black women need to learn about "right livelihood." Even though I had been raised in a world where elderly black people had this wisdom, I was more socialized by the get-ahead generation that felt how much money you were making was more important than what you did to make that money. We have difficult choices ahead.

As black females collectively develop greater self-esteem, a greater sense of entitlement, we will learn from one another's example how to practice right livelihood. Of the black women I interviewed the individuals who enjoyed their work the most felt they were realizing a particular vocation or calling. C.J. (now almost forty) recalls that generations of her family were college-educated. She was taught to choose work that would be linked with the political desire to enhance the overall well-being of black people. C.J. says, "I went to college with a mission and a passion to have my work be about African-Americans. The spirit of mission came to me from my family, who taught us that you don't just work to get money, you work to create meaning for yourself and other people." With this philosophy as a guiding standpoint, she has always had a satisfying work life.

When one of my sisters, a welfare recipient, decided to return to college, I encouraged her to try and recall her childhood vocational dreams and to allow herself adult dreams, so that she would not be pushed into preparing for a job that holds no interest for her. Many of us must work hard to unlearn the socialization that teaches us that we should just be lucky to get any old job. We can begin to think about our work lives in terms of vocation and calling. One black woman I interviewed, who has worked as a house-wife for many years, began to experience agoraphobia. Struggling to regain her emotional well-being, she saw a therapist, against the will of her family. In this therapeutic setting, she received affirmation for her desire to finish her undergraduate degree and continue in a graduate program. She found that finishing a master's and becoming a college teacher gave her enormous satisfaction. Yet this achievement was not fully appreciated by her husband. A worker in a factory, whose job is long and tedious, he was jealous of her newfound excitement about work. Since her work brings her in touch with the public, it yields rewards unlike any he can hope to receive from his job. Although she has encouraged him to go back to school (one of his unfulfilled goals), he is reluctant. Despite these relational tensions, she has found that "loving" her work has helped her attend to and transform previous feeling of low self-esteem.

A few of the black woman I interviewed claimed to be doing work they liked but complained bitterly about their jobs, particularly where they must make decisions that affect the work lives of other people. One woman had been involved in a decision-making process that required her to take a stance that would leave another person jobless. Though many of her peers were proud of the way she handled this difficult decision, her response was to feel "victimized." Indeed, she kept referring to herself as "battered." This response troubled me for it seemed to bespeak a contradiction many women experience in positions of power. Though we may like the status of a power position and wielding power, we may still want to see ourselves as "victims" in the process, especially if we must act in ways that "good girls, dutiful daughters" have been taught are "bad."

I suggested to the women I interviewed that they had chosen particular careers that involved "playing hard ball" yet they seemed to be undermining the value of their choices and the excellence of their work by complaining that they had to get their hands dirty and suffer some bruises. I shared with them my sense that if you choose to pay hardball then you should be prepared for the bruises and not be devastated when they occur. In some ways it seemed to me these black women wanted to be "equals" in a man's world while they simultaneously wanted to be treated like fragile "ladies." Had they been able to assume full responsibility for their career choices, they would have enjoyed their work more and been able to reward themselves for jobs well done. In some cases it seemed that the individuals were addicted to being martyrs. They wanted to control everything, to be the person "in power" but also resented the position. These individuals. . . . seemed not to know when to set boundaries or that work duties could be shared. They frequently over-extended themselves. When we over-extend ourselves in work settings, pushing ourselves to the breaking point, we rarely feel positive about tasks even if we are performing them well.

Since many people rely on powerful black women in jobs (unwittingly turning us into "mammies" who will bear all the burdens—and there are certainly those among us who take pride in this role), we can easily become tragically over-extended. I noticed that a number of us (myself included) talk about starting off in careers that we really "loved" but over-working to the point of "burnout" so that the pleasure we initially found dissipated. I remember finding a self-help book that listed twelve symptoms of "burn-out," encouraging readers to go down the list and check those that described their experience. At the end, it said, "If you checked three or more of these boxes, chances are you are probably suffering from burn-out." I found I had checked all twelve! That let me know it was time for a change. Yet changing was not easy. When you do something and you do it well, it is hard to take a break, or to confront the reality that I had to face, which was that I really didn't want to be doing the job I was doing even though I did it well. In retrospect it occurred to me that it takes a lot more energy to do a job well when you really do not want to be doing it. This work is often more tiring. And maybe that extra energy would be better spent in the search for one's true vocation or calling.

In my case, I have always wanted to be a writer. And even though I have become just that and I love this work, my obsessive fears about "not being poor" have made it difficult for me to take time away from my other career, teaching and lecturing, to "just write." Susan Jeffers' book, *Feel the Fear and Do It Anyway*, has helped me to finally reach the point in my life where I can take time to "just write." Like many black women who do not come from privileged class backgrounds, who do not have family we can rely on to help if the financial going gets rough (we in fact are usually the people who are relied on), it feels very frightening to think about letting go of financial security, even for a short time, to do work one loves but may not pay the bills. In my case, even though I had worked with a self-created financial program aimed at bringing me to a point in life when I could focus solely on writing. I still found it hard to take time away. It was then that I had to tap into my deep fears of ending up poor and counter them with messages that affirm my ability to take care of myself economically irrespective of the circumstance. These fears are not irrational (though certainly mine were a bit extreme). In the last few years, I have witnessed several family members go from working as professionals to unemployment and various degrees of homelessness. Their experiences highlighted the reality that it is risky to be without secure employment and yet they also indicated that one could survive, even start all over again if need be.

My sister V. quit a job that allowed her to use excellent skills because she had major conflicts with her immediate supervisor. She quit because the level of on-the-job stress had become hazardous to her mental well-being. She quit confident that she would find a job in a few months. When that did not happen, she was stunned. It had not occurred to her that she would find it practically impossible to find work in the area she most wanted to live in. Confronting racism, sexism, and a host of other unclear responses, months passed and she has not found another job. It has changed her whole life. While material survival has been difficult, she is learning more about what really matters to her in life. She is learning about "right livelihood." The grace and skill with which she has confronted her circumstance has been a wonderful example for me. With therapy, with the help of friends and loved ones, she is discovering the work she would really like to do and no longer feels the need to have high-paying, high-status job. And she has learned more about what it means to take risks.

In *Do What You Love, the Money Will Follow,* Sinetar cautions those of us who have not been risk-takers to go slowly, to practice, to begin by taking small risks, and to plan carefully. Because I have planned carefully, I am able to finally take a year's leave from my teaching job without pay. During this time, I want to see if I enjoy working solely as a writer and if I can support myself. I want to see if (like those old-time black folks I talk about at the start of the essay) doing solely the work I feel most "called" to do will enhance my joy in living. For the past few months, I have been "just writing" and indeed, so far, I feel it is "work that makes life sweet."

The historical legacy of black women shows that we have worked hard, long, a well, yet rarely been paid what we deserve. We rarely get the recognition we deserve. However, even in the midst of domination, individual black women have found their calling, and do the work they are best suited for. Onnie Lee Logan, the Alabama midwife who tells her story *Motherwit,* never went to high school or college, never made a lot of money in her working life, but listened to her inner voice and found her calling. Logan shares:

> I let God work the plan on my life and I am satisfied at what has happened to me in my life. The sun wasn't shinin' every time and moon wasn't either. I was in the snow and the rain at night by my lonely self. . . . There had been many dreary nights but I didn't look at em as dreary nights. I had my mind on where I was going and what I was going for.
>
> Whatever I've done, I've done as well as I could and beyond. . . . I'm satisfied at what has happened in my life. Perfectly satisfied at what my life has done for me. I was a good midwife. One of the best as they say. This book was the last thing I had planned to do until God said well done. I consider myself—in fact if I leave tomorrow—I've lived my life and I've lived it well.

The life stories of black women like Onnie Logan remind us that "right livelihood" can be found irrespective of our class position, or the level of our education.

To know the work we are "called" to do in this world, we must know ourselves. The practice of "right livelihood" invites us to become more fully aware of our reality, of the labor we do and of the way we do it. Now that I have chosen my writing more fully than at any other moment of my life, the work itself feels more joyous. I feel my whole being affirmed in the act of writing. As black women unlearn the conventional thinking about work—which views money and/or status as more important than the work we do or the way we feel about that work—we will find our way back to those moments celebrated by our ancestors, when work was a passion. We will know again that "work makes life sweet."

Endnotes

1. *Hard Times Cotton Mill Girls:* an oral history of life in southern textile mills, compiled by Victoria Byerly (b. 1949), a former mill worker.
2. *Katie Geneva Cannon:* The first black woman ordained a Presbyterian minister. She worked with Victoria Byerly, author of *Hard Times Cotton Mill Girls.*

QUESTIONS

1. What sense of community and values led southern black women in the segregationist period to value even unskilled labor? What is meant by observations such as "work makes life sweet," "it's not what you do but how you do it," and "working with integrity"?
2. What different attitudes toward work did hooks notice among younger black women on welfare whom she interviewed? What kind of work

were they seeking? What causes "pain and frustration" among many black female office workers?

3. How do hooks and Marsha Senetar define the term "right livelihood"? How does this type of work ethic relate to the Buddhist quest for enlightenment? Considering the employment market of today, does such an idealistic definition of the perfect job seem like a worthwhile objective to pursue? Why or why not?

CHAPTER 6

Censoring Extreme Speech

Introduction

The First Amendment to the U.S. Constitution prohibits Congress from passing any law "abridging the freedom of speech, or of the press, or the right of the people peaceably to assemble, and to petition the Government for a redress of grievances." Even today these guarantees related to public speech and publishing acts go far beyond those available in most democracies. Not surprisingly, our history is filled with efforts at all levels of government to get around the First Amendment prohibition on laws "abridging the freedom of speech." During the anti-slavery protests in the mid-nineteenth century, for instance, local laws were passed prohibiting public assembly, as Frederick Douglass points out in his moving speech, "A Plea for Free Speech in Boston."

Recently, attempts at censorship of free speech, assembly, and publishing have occurred frequently in schools and colleges, especially through controversial "speech codes," which civil libertarian Nat Hentoff critiques as barriers to meaningful campus dialogue on issues of controversy. Academics remain somewhat divided in their arguments on the issue; for example, law professor Richard Delgado has taken a stand against "hate speech" as harmful to open public discourse in campus communities, while Stanley Fish, a law professor and college dean, argues against an absolute right to free expression of personal beliefs in the classroom on the part of college teachers. Exercising their own constitutional freedom as members of the professional press, newspaper reporters such as Mary Beth Marklein are often supportive of the rights of students in such cases.

New arguments for and against censorship are taking place in the areas of television, of radio broadcasting, and on the Internet. Censorship of "offensive" speech and music is becoming stricter in television and radio, where "out of bounds" language is sometimes used by celebrities who have in the past been able to violate speech prohibitions because of their media prominence. Richard Goldstein points out in his essay "Celebrity Bigots" many past examples of celebrity hate speech that have disparaged gays, blacks, Jews, and other groups. Today, in cases such as that of the racially charged commentary of radio personality Don Imus and the anti-gay slurs of Isaiah Washington on *Grey's Anatomy*, the hate-speaker can be fired from a lucrative media position—or sent straight to rehab.

The "Differing Perspectives" debate in this chapter illustrates the enormous international controversy over censorship of free speech and/or hate speech on the Internet. Because the Internet is a form of communication without borders, a speech act that would be legal in America may not be considered so in another country, including our close allies Canada and Great Britain, which, along with the European Union, have less stringent anti-censorship guarantees in their constitutions than we have in this country.

FREDERICK DOUGLASS

"A Plea for Free Speech in Boston"

Frederick Douglass (1818-1895), a prominent African-American orator, author, and editor, argued for abolition and broad social reform to benefit all Americans. Born a slave, Douglass learned to read and write without formal schooling, eventually escaping to New York in 1838. After gaining his freedom, Douglass worked with abolitionists like William Lloyd Garrison, lecturing widely against slavery. After publishing his bestselling A Narrative of the Life of Frederick Douglass, an American Slave *(1845), Douglass founded a series of newspapers and continued to work for freedom and equal rights for African-Americans and women both during and after the Civil War.*

The speech "A Plea for Free Speech in Boston" was delivered and published in early December, 1860—a time of turmoil throughout the nation in regard to the issue of slavery—a month after the controversial election of Lincoln in Nov 6, 1860, and only a few months before the outbreak of the Civil War. Douglass delivered the speech, an argument for freedom of speech for unpopular causes, shortly after a mob broke up an anti-slavery rally in Boston, making it impossible for the abolitionist perspective to be heard in the community.

Boston is a great city—and Music Hall has a fame almost as extensive as that of Boston. Nowhere more than here have the principles of human freedom been expounded. But for the circumstances already mentioned, it would seem almost presumption for me to say anything here about those principles. And yet, even here, in Boston, the moral atmosphere is dark and heavy. The principles of human liberty, even if correctly apprehended, find but limited support in this hour of trial. The world moves slowly, and Boston is much like the world. We thought the principle of free speech was an accomplished fact. Here, if nowhere else, we thought the right of the people to assemble and to express their opinion was secure. Dr. Channing had defended the right, Mr. Garrison had practically asserted the right, and Theodore Parker had maintained it with steadiness and fidelity to the last.

But here we are today contending for what we thought we gained years ago. The mortifying and disgraceful fact stares us in the face, that though Faneuil Hall and Bunker Hill Monument stand, freedom of speech is struck down. No lengthy detail of facts is needed. They are already notorious; far more so than will be wished ten years hence.

The world knows that last Monday a meeting assembled to discuss the question: "How Shall Slavery Be Abolished?" The world also knows that that meeting was invaded, insulted, captured by a mob of gentlemen, and thereafter broken up and dispersed by the order of the mayor, who refused to protect it, though called upon to do so. If this had been a mere outbreak of passion and prejudice among the baser sort, maddened by rum and hounded on by some wily politician to serve some immediate purpose—a mere exceptional affair—it might be allowed to rest with what has already been said. But the leaders of the mob were gentlemen. They were men who pride themselves upon their respect for law and order.

These gentlemen brought their respect for the law with them and proclaimed it loudly while in the very act of breaking the law. Theirs was the law of slavery. The law of free speech and the law for the protection of public meetings they trampled under foot, while they greatly magnified the law of slavery.

The scene was an instructive one. Men seldom see such a blending of the gentleman with the rowdy, as was shown on that occasion. It proved that human nature is very much the same, whether in tarpaulin or broadcloth. Nevertheless, when gentlemen approach us in the character of lawless and abandoned loafers—assuming for the moment their manners and tempers—they have themselves to blame if they are estimated below their quality.

No right was deemed by the fathers of the Government more sacred than the right of speech. It was in their eyes, as in the eyes of all thoughtful men, the great moral renovator of society and government. Daniel Webster called it a homebred right, a fireside privilege. Liberty is meaningless where the right to utter one's thoughts and opinions has ceased to exist. That, of all rights, is the dread of tyrants. It is the right which they first of all strike down. They know its power. Thrones, dominions, principalities, and powers, founded in injustice and wrong, are sure to tremble, if men are allowed to reason of righteousness, temperance, and of a judgment to come in their presence. Slavery cannot tolerate free speech. Five years of its exercise would banish the auction block and break every chain in the South. They will have none of it there, for they have the power. But shall it be so here?

Even here in Boston, and among the friends of freedom, we hear two voices: one denouncing the mob that broke up our meeting on Monday as a base and cowardly outrage; and another, deprecating and regretting the holding of such a meeting, by such men, at such a time. We are told that the meeting was ill-timed, and the parties to it unwise.

Why, what is the matter with us? Are we going to palliate and excuse a palpable and flagrant outrage on the right of speech, by implying that only a particular description of persons should exercise that right? Are we, at such a time, when a great principle has been struck down, to quench the moral indignation which the deed excites, by casting reflections upon those on whose persons the outrage has been committed? After all the arguments for liberty to which Boston has listened for more than a quarter of a century, has she yet to learn that the time to assert a right is the time when the right itself is called in question, and that the men of all others to assert it are the men to whom the right has been denied?

It would be no vindication of the right of speech to prove that certain gentlemen of great distinction, eminent for their learning and ability, are allowed to freely express their opinions on all subjects—including the subject of slavery. Such a vindication would need, itself, to be vindicated. It would add insult to injury. Not even an old-fashioned abolition meeting could vindicate that right in Boston just now. There can be no right of speech where any man, however lifted up, or however humble, however young, or however old, is overawed by force, and compelled to suppress his honest sentiments.

Equally clear is the right to hear. To suppress free speech is a double wrong. It violates the rights of the hearer as well as those of the speaker. It is just as criminal to rob a man of his right to speak and hear as it would be to rob him of his money. I have no doubt that Boston will vindicate this right. But in order to do so, there must be no concessions to the enemy. When a man is allowed to speak because he is rich and powerful, it aggravates the crime of denying the right to the poor and humble.

The principle must rest upon its own proper basis. And until the right is accorded to the humblest as freely as to the most exalted citizen, the government of Boston is but an empty name, and its freedom a mockery. A man's right to speak does not depend upon where he was born or upon his color. The simple quality of manhood is the solid basis of the right—and there let it rest forever.

QUESTIONS

1. How does Douglass's first paragraph put the current issue of free speech he is addressing within the larger context of Bostonian and American history? How do his opening paragraphs show respect for Boston's traditional values while posing a challenge to its citizens and their leaders, the "gentlemen"? How would they be likely to respond to his "plea" and accusations?

2. What argument does Douglass make for the power of free speech and the right to exercise it unconditionally? Is his argument persuasive, or could you think of exceptions or limitations to this right?

3. Douglass argues that the repression of free speech is a "double wrong." Who is wronged by it? How effectively does Douglass relate the general wrongs he discusses to the events in Boston?

"'Speech Codes' on the Campus and Problems of Free Speech"

Nat Hentoff (b. 1925) holds an honorary doctorate of laws from Northeastern University and has received Fulbright and Guggenheim Fellowships. He is a jazz critic, novelist, and commentator on civil liberties issues who has written for the Village Voice, Down Beat, The Progressive, Wall Street Journal, *and* Jewish World Review. *His books on civil liberties and freedom of speech include* The First Freedom: The Tumultuous History of Free Speech in America *(1980),* Free Speech for Me—But Not for Thee *(1993), and* The War on the Bill of Rights and the Gathering Resistance *(2004). Hentoff is a controversial figure; although he is for free speech and civil liberties and against the death penalty, he has supported the war in Iraq and holds unpopular views on abortion. He refuses to moderate his seemingly contradictory values and beliefs, which he sums up in the following line: "I'm a Jewish atheist civil-libertarian pro-lifer." The following 1991 essay critiquing speech codes designed to prohibit language directed against or offensive to those of a particular minority, gender, or sexual orientation on campus exemplifies Hentoff's confrontational, no-holds-barred approach to argumentation.*

During three years of reporting on anti-free-speech tendencies in higher education, I've been at more than twenty colleges and universities—from Washington and Lee and Columbia to Mesa State in Colorado and Stanford.

On this voyage of initially reverse expectations—with liberals fiercely advocating censorship of "offensive" speech and conservatives merrily taking the moral high ground as champions of free expression—the most dismaying moment of revelation took place at Stanford.

In the course of a two-year debate on whether Stanford, like many other universities, should have a speech code punishing language that might wound minorities, women, and gays, a letter appeared in the *Stanford Daily.* Signed by the African-American Law Students Association, the Asian-American Law Student Association, and the Jewish Law Students Association, the letter called for a harsh code. It reflected the letter and the spirit of an earlier declaration by Canetta Ivy, a black leader of student government at Stanford during the period of the grand debate. "We don't put as many restrictions on freedom of speech," she said, "as we should."

Reading the letter by this rare ecumenical body of law students (so pressing was the situation that even Jews were allowed in), I thought of twenty, thirty years from now. From so bright a cadre of graduates, from so prestigious a law school would come some of the law professors, civic leaders, college presidents, and even maybe a Supreme Court Justice of the future. And many of them would have learned—like so many other university students in the land—that censorship is okay provided your motives are okay.

The debate at Stanford ended when the president, Donald Kennedy, following the prevailing winds, surrendered his previous position that once you start telling people what they can't say, you will end up telling them what they can't think. Stanford now has a speech code. This is not to say that these gags on speech—every one of them so overboard and vague that a student can violate a code without knowing he or she has done so—are invariably imposed by student demand. At most colleges, it is the administration that sets up the code. Because there have been racist or sexist or homophobic taunts, anonymous notes or graffiti, the administration feels it must do something. The cheapest, quickest way to demonstrate that it cares is to appear to suppress racist, sexist, homophobic speech.

Usually, the leading opposition among the faculty consists of conservatives—when there is opposition. An exception at Stanford was law professor Gerald Gunther, arguably the nation's leading authority on constitutional law. But Gunther did not have much support among other faculty members, conservative or liberal.

At the University of Buffalo Law School, which has a code restricting speech, I could find just one faculty member who was against it. A liberal, he spoke only on condition that I not use his name. He did not want to be categorized as a racist.

On another campus, a political science professor for whom I had great respect after meeting and talking with him years ago, has been silent—students told me—on what Justice William Brennan once called "the pall of orthodoxy" that has fallen on his campus. When I talked to him, the professor said, "It doesn't happen in my class. There's no 'politically correct' orthodoxy here. It may happen in other places at this university, but I don't know about that." He said no more.

One of the myths about the rise of P. C. (politically correct) is that, coming from the left, it is primarily intimidating conservatives on campus. Quite the contrary. At almost every college I've been, conservative students have their own newspaper, usually quite lively and fired by a muckraking glee at exposing "politically correct" follies on campus.

By and large, those most intimidated—not so much by the speech codes themselves but by the Madame Defarge-like spirit behind them—are liberal students and those who can be called politically moderate.

I've talked to many of them, and they no longer get involved in class discussions where their views would go against the grain of P. C. righteousness. Many, for instance, have questions about certain kinds of affirmative action. They are not partisans of Jesse Helms or David Duke, but they wonder whether progeny of middle-class black families should get scholarship preference. Others have a question about abortion. Most are not pro-life, but they believe that fathers should have a say in whether the fetus should be sent off into eternity.

Jeff Shesol, a recent graduate of Brown and now a Rhodes scholar at Oxford, became nationally known while at Brown because of his comic strip, "Thatch," which, not too kindly, parodied P. C. students. At a forum on free speech at Brown before he left, Shesol said he wished he could tell the new students at Brown to have no fear of speaking freely. But he couldn't tell them that, he said, advising the new students to stay clear of talking critically about affirmative action or abortion, among other things, in public.

At that forum, Shesol told me, he said that those members of the left who regard dissent from their views as racist and sexist should realize that they are discrediting their goals. "They're honorable goals," said Shesol, "and I agree with them. I'm against racism and sexism. But these people's tactics are obscuring the goals. And they've resulted in Brown no longer being an open-minded place." There were hisses from the audience.

Students at New York University Law School have also told me that they censor themselves in class. The kind of chilling atmosphere they describe was exemplified last year as a case assigned for a moot court competition became subject to denunciation when a sizable number of law students said it was too "offensive" and would hurt the feelings of gay and lesbian students. The case concerned a divorced father's attempt to gain custody of his children on the grounds that their mother had become a lesbian. It was against P. C. to represent the father.

Although some of the faculty responded by insisting that you learn to be a lawyer by dealing with all kinds of cases, including those you personally find offensive, other faculty members supported the rebellious students, praising them for their sensitivity. There was little public opposition from the other students to the attempt to suppress the case. A leading dissenter was a member of the conservative Federalist Society.

What is P. C. to white students is not necessarily P. C. to black students. Most of the latter did not get involved in the N.Y.U. protest, but throughout the country many black students do support speech codes. A vigorous exception was a black Harvard law school student during a debate on whether the law school should start punishing speech. A white student got up and said that the codes are necessary because without them, black students would be driven away from colleges and thereby deprived of the equal opportunity to get an education.

A black student rose and said that the white student had a hell of a nerve to assume that he—in the face of racist speech—would pack up his books and go home. He's been familiar with that kind of speech all his life, and he had never felt the need to run away from it. He'd handled it before and he could again. The black student then looked at his white colleague and said that it was condescending to say that blacks have to be "protected" from racist speech. "It is more racist and insulting," he emphasized, "to say that to me than to call me a nigger."

But that would appear to be a minority view among black students. Most are convinced they do need to be protected from wounding language. On the other hand, a good many black student organizations on campus do not feel that Jews have to be protected from wounding language. Though it's not much written about in reports of the language wars on campuses, there is a strong strain of anti-Semitism among some—not all, by any means—black students. They invite such speakers as Louis Farrakhan, the former Stokely Carmichael (now Kwame Toure), and such lesser but still burning bushes as Steve Cokely, the Chicago commentator who has declared that Jewish doctors inject the AIDS virus into black babies. That distinguished leader was invited to speak at the University of Michigan.

The black student organization at Columbia University brought to the campus Dr. Khalid Abdul Muhammad. He began his address by saying: "My leader, my teacher, my guide is the honorable Louis Farrakhan [leader of the Black Muslim movement at the time]. I thought that should be said at Columbia Jewniversity."

Many Jewish students have not censored themselves in reacting to this form of political correctness among some blacks. A Columbia student, Rachel Stoll, wrote a letter to the Columbia *Spectator*: "I have an idea. As a white Jewish American, I'll just stand in the middle of a circle comprising. . . . Khalid Abdul Muhammad and assorted members of the Black Students Organization and let them all hurl large stones at me. From recent events and statements made on this campus, I gather this will be a good cheap method of making these people feel good."

At UCLA, a black student magazine printed an article indicating there is considerable truth to the Protocols of the Elders of Zion. For months, the black faculty, when asked their reactions, preferred not to comment. One of them did say that the black students already considered the black faculty to be insufficiently militant, and the professors didn't want to make the gap any wider. Like white liberal faculty members on other campuses, they want to be liked—or at least not too disliked.

Along with quiet white liberal faculty members, most black professors have not opposed the speech codes. But unlike the white liberals, many honestly do believe that minority students have to be insulated from barbed language. They do not believe—as I have found out in a number of conversations—that an essential part of an education is to learn to demystify language, to strip it of its ability to demonize and stigmatize you. They do not believe that the way to deal with bigoted language is to answer it with more and better language of your own. This seems very elementary to me, but not to the defenders, black and white, of the speech codes.

Consider University of California president David Gardner. He has imposed a speech code on all the campuses in his university system. Students are to be punished—and this is characteristic of the other codes around the country—if they use "fighting words"—derogatory references to "race, sex, sexual orientation, or disability."

The term "fighting words" comes from a 1942 Supreme Court decision, Chaplinsky v. New Hampshire, which ruled that "fighting words" are not protected by the First Amendment. That decision, however, has been in disuse at the High Court for many years. But it is thriving on college campuses.

In the California code, a word becomes "fighting" if it is directly addressed to "any ordinary person" (presumably, extraordinary people are above all this). These are the kinds of words that are "inherently likely to provoke a violent reaction, whether or not they *actually* do." (Emphasis added).

Moreover, he or she who fires a fighting word at any ordinary person can be reprimanded or dismissed from the university because the perpetrator should "reasonably know" that what he or she has said will interfere with the "victim's ability to pursue effectively his or her education or otherwise participate fully in university programs and activities."

Asked Gary Murikami, chairman of the Gay and Lesbian Association at the University of California, Berkeley: "What does it mean?"

Among those—faculty, law professors, college administrators—who insist such codes are essential to the university's purpose of making students feel at home and thereby able to concentrate on their work, there has been a celebratory resort to the Fourteenth Amendment. That amendment guarantees "equal protection of the laws" to all, and that means to all students on campus. Accordingly, when the First Amendment rights of those engaging in offensive speech clash with the equality rights of their targets under the Fourteenth Amendment, the First Amendment must give way.

This is the thesis, by the way, of John Powell, legal director of the American Civil Liberties Union, even though that organization has now formally opposed all college speech codes—after a considerable civil war among and within its affiliates.

The battle of the amendments continues, and when harsher codes are called for at some campuses, you can expect the Fourteenth Amendment—which was not intended to censor speech—will rise again.

A precedent has been set at, of all places, colleges and universities, that the principle of free speech is merely situational. As college administrators change, so will the extent of free speech on campus. And invariably, permissible speech will become more and more narrowly defined. Once speech can be limited in such subjective ways, more and more expression will be included in what is forbidden.

One of the exceedingly few college presidents who speaks out on the consequences of the anti-free-speech movement is Yale University's Benno Schmidt:

> Freedom of thought must be Yale's central commitment. It is not easy to embrace. It is, indeed, the effort of a lifetime. . . . Much expression that is free may deserve our contempt. We may well be moved to exercise our own freedom to counter it or to ignore it. But universities cannot censor or suppress speech, no matter how obnoxious in content, without violating their justification for existence. . . .
>
> On some other campuses in this country, values of civility and community have been offered by some as paramount values of the university, even to the extent of superseding freedom of expression.
>
> Such a view is wrong in principle and, if extended, is disastrous to freedom of thought. . . . The chilling effects on speech of the vagueness and open-ended nature of many universities' prohibitions . . . are compounded by the fact that these codes are typically enforced by faculty and students who commonly assert that vague notions of community are more important to the academy than freedom of thought and expression. . . .

This is a flabby and uncertain time for freedom in the United States.

On the Public Broadcasting System in June, I was part of a Fred Friendly panel at Stanford University in a debate on speech codes versus freedom of expression. The three black panelists strongly supported the codes. So did the one Asian-American on the panel. But then so did Stanford law professor, Thomas Grey, who wrote the Stanford code, and Stanford president Donald Kennedy, who first opposed and then embraced the code. We have a new ecumenicism of those who would control speech for the greater good. It is hardly a new idea, but the mix of advocates is rather new.

But there are other voices. In the national board debate at the ACLU on college speech codes, the first speaker—and I think she had a lot to do with making the final vote against codes unanimous—was Gwen Thomas.

A black community college administrator from Colorado, she is a fiercely persistent exposer of racial discrimination. She started by saying, "I have always felt as a minority person that we have to protect the rights of all because if we infringe on the rights of any persons, we'll be next."

"As for providing a nonintimidating educational environment, our young people have to learn to grow up on college campuses. We have to teach them how to deal with adversarial situations. They have to learn how to survive offensive speech they find wounding and hurtful."

QUESTIONS

1. Is Hentoff's argument that free speech is an inherently valuable right which should be protected on the college campus a sound one, or do you think there should be exceptions to pure freedom of speech in educational settings? Why or why not?
2. Aside from his primary position, what arguments does Hentoff make for the ill-effects of the current speech codes on campus life and our future as a nation? Are the codes applied even-handedly? What groups have benefited from the codes, and which ones have suffered? Are the examples Hentoff provides in his critique convincing and common ones? Why or why not?
3. Contrast current student attitudes to freedom of speech, speech codes, and "political correctness" to those of the period in which Hentoff's essay was written. Does his position seem viable today, or would his ideas be dismissed as unrealistic and old-fashioned?

"Hate Speech Harms Public Discourse"

Richard Delgado, who holds a J.D. from the University of California at Berkeley Boalt Law School, is professor of law and Derrick Bell Fellow at the University of Pittsburg, where he currently teaches courses in the areas of civil rights and critical race theory. He has spoken before Congress on race-related issues and has made many presentations on television and radio. Delgado has written over a hundred journal articles and 15 books, including Understanding Words That Wound *(2004) and* Justice at War: Civil Liberties and Civil Rights during Times of Crisis *(2003). In the following article, Delgado expresses his views on controlling race- and gender-based hate speech through "speech codes," refuting several of the common arguments against limitations set by the codes.*

At the University of Wisconsin, a fraternity sponsored an annual "Fiji Island" party, as part of which it erected a 15-foot plywood caricature of a black man with a bone through his nose. At the University of California at Berkeley, fraternity members shouted obscenities and racial slurs at a group of black students; later, a campus disc jockey told black students who had requested that the station play rap music to "go back to Oakland." In Mississippi, a lesbian couple trying to establish a rural retreat was hounded by threatening messages and phone calls, and a dead chicken with an obscene note was attached to their mailbox.

These cases are not atypical. More than 300 American universities have experienced racial incidents serious enough to be reported by the media, and every year the FBI reports thousands of hate crimes and violence directed against Jews, gays and members of racial minorities. It is unlikely that the number of incidents is merely the result of increased sensitivity on the part of minority groups or better reporting, since it occurs at a time when other Western nations are reporting a wave of Holocaust revisionism and attacks on Jews and minorities.

More than 200 American universities have responded by enacting student-conduct codes penalizing face-to-face insults and epithets, while courts have developed sexual-harassment doctrine for women badgered and insulted in the workplace. Are these measures a good idea? Emphatically, yes: Racist and similar taunts convey little of value. They demean the victim while communicating to all who hear the message that equal personhood is of little value in American society. Campuses and workplaces wherein a climate of racial or sexual terror thrives are unattractive and unwelcoming for members of the victimized groups. Minority enrollment at many campuses drops in the months and years following well-publicized incidents of racial insult.

Rules against hate speech, homophobic remarks and misogyny serve both symbolic and institutional values—increasing productivity in the workplace and protecting a learning environment on campus. It has been argued that such prohibitions operate in derogation of the First Amendment's guarantee of freedom of speech, but that amendment already is subject to dozens of exceptions—libel, defamation, words of conspiracy or threat, disrespectful words uttered to a judge or police officer, irrelevant or untrue words spoken in a judicial proceeding, copyright, plagiarism, official secrets, misleading advertising and many more. The social interest in deterring vicious racial or sexual vituperation certainly seems at least as great as that underlying these other forms of speech deemed unworthy of First Amendment protection.

Some argue that speech codes are not as good a remedy to racist speech as talking back to the aggressor. According to this view, talking back will teach minorities not to rely on whites for protection while educating the utterer of a racially hurtful remark so that he or she will refrain from repeating the offense. But talking back can be futile or dangerous, especially when racist remarks are hurled, as they often are, in many-on-one situations or in cowardly fashion—a leaflet slipped under a black student's dormitory door. Talking back cannot be the sole remedy for a victim of racist hate speech.

A third argument for tolerance of offensive utterances is that they serve as a kind of pressure valve, allowing tension to release itself before reaching a dangerous level. Forcing racists (homophobes, etc.) to bottle up their emotions means that they are more likely to do or say something even more harmful later. Anti-hate-speech rules, then, would increase, not reduce, minorities' jeopardy.

This argument is simplistic. Hate speech may well make the speaker feel better, but it does not make the victim safer. Social science teaches that permitting a person to do or say something hateful to another increases, not reduces, the chance that he or she will do so again. Moreover, others may feel that they can follow suit. Human behavior is more complex than the laws of physics that describe pressure valves, tanks and other mechanical things. Instead, society uses symbols to construct a social world, one that contains categories and expectations for terms such as "black," "woman," "gang member" and "child." Once these categories are in place, they govern perception and a sense of how folks may act toward others. Allowing persons to stigmatize and revile others makes them more aggressive toward those others in the future. Once a speaker comes to think of the other as a deserved victim, his or her behavior may escalate to bullying and physical violence.

Stereotypical behavior often generalizes: Action teaches others that they may act as well. Pressure valves may be safer after letting off steam; human beings are not. The experience of Canada, England, Germany, Sweden, Italy and other European countries that have enacted laws against racial revilement shows that incidents against minorities do not increase, but decrease, in the wake of passage.

Other critics of speech codes argue that the First Amendment has been a great friend and ally of social reformers. The national president of the American Civil Liberties Union, for example, has argued that without free speech Martin Luther King, Jr. could not have moved America as he did—and so also for the environmental movement, women's rights and gay liberation. This argument is paternalistic: If minorities understood their best interest, the argument goes, they would not limit speech.

But the relationship of the First Amendment to social advance is not nearly so straightforward as some think. True, in the 1960s, King and others did use speech to kindle conscience. As often as not, however, the First Amendment, as then understood and interpreted, did not protect them. They marched, were arrested and convicted; sat-in, were arrested and convicted; rallied and sang, were arrested and convicted. Their speech was deemed too forceful, too disruptive. To be sure, their convictions sometimes would be reversed years later on appeal, at the cost of thousands of dollars and hundreds of hours of gallant lawyering. Speech may have been a useful tool for racial reformers; the free-speech clause was not.

Would hate-speech laws inevitably lead to reverse enforcement? Would authorities overlook the more serious offenses of the sort mentioned in the first paragraph of this essay, while cracking down with a vengeance on the black motorist who utters something mildly disrespectful to the cop who stops him for a routine offense? This concern is plausible, because some authorities do overcharge blacks and other minorities with various offenses, including loitering. But the American experience with hate-speech rules shows that this has not been the usual pattern. Nor has it been elsewhere. A host of Western democracies have instituted laws against hate speech and crime. Some, such as Sweden, Great Britain and Canada, have traditions of respect for free speech and inquiry rivaling ours. In none has there been a noticeable erosion of the spirit of free inquiry nor a wave of prosecutions against blacks and immigrants.

If reverse enforcement occasionally happens, it is not necessarily a bad thing. If, in fact, a black or Mexican has terrorized or harassed a fellow student who is white, gay, or Asian, universities should bring charges: Minorities need to learn to speak respectfully, too. And if the fear is that college deans and administrators are so racist that they will invent or magnify charges against minority students in order to punish or hound them off campus, this is entirely implausible. Figures from *U.S. News and World Report* show that college administrators and faculty harbor less antiblack animus than the average American, even than the average college student. Indeed, it is the very concern of college administrators about dwindling minority enrollments and a worsening campus climate for minorities that underlies enactment of most hate-speech rules.

It also has been claimed that hate speech should not be driven underground but allowed to remain out in the open, since the racist one does not know is more dangerous than the one whom one does know. This argument ignores a third alternative—the racist who is cured, or at least deterred by official rules and the fear of sanction from exhibiting the behavior he or she once did. Since most conservatives (indeed most people) believe that laws and penalties change conduct, they ought to concede that institutional guidelines against hate speech and assault would discourage those behaviors.

A final objection is that prohibitions against verbal abuse and assault encourage minorities to see themselves as victims. Instead of running to campus authorities every time something wounds their feelings, persons of color ought to learn either to confront or ignore the offensive behavior. A system of hate-speech rules proclaims that minorities are weak and in need of protection, that their lot in life is to be victimized rather than to take charge of their own destinies. Will hate-speech rules have these effects? No, because other alternatives, such as talking back, will remain. No gay or minority student is required to file charges under the rules when targeted by abuse. The rules merely provide one more avenue of recourse for those who wish to take advantage of them. Filing a complaint might, indeed, be seen as one way of taking charge of one's destiny: One is active instead of passively "lumping it" when invective strikes. It is worth noticing that we do not raise the victimization issue with other offenses we suffer, such as having a car stolen or a house burglarized, or tell the victim to "rise above it." Could it be because we secretly believe that the black targeted in this fashion has not suffered a real harm? If so, this is quite different from saying that filing a complaint increases victimization. Besides, it is quite untrue: Racial invective harms; filing a civil complaint does not.

None of the arguments against hate-speech rules, then, holds water. The rules are straightforward, wholly laudable ways of protecting values society holds dear. The right of the bigot to spew racial venom, like the right to punch someone in the nose, must yield in the face of other interests. Canada, Sweden, France, Italy and many other advanced societies have come to the same conclusion. Hate-speech rules are wholly consistent with the spirit of free inquiry. Indeed, by demoralizing the victim and excluding him or her from the human community, hate speech reduces participation and dialogue. Far from diminishing the values of the First Amendment, hate-speech rules may be necessary for their full flowering and effectuation.

QUESTIONS

1. What fact-based evidence does Delgado present in his opening paragraphs for the increasing prevalence of hate speech both on American campuses and abroad? Is his evidence convincing?

2. What false causes of the rise of hate speech does Delgado refute? How does he demonstrate that counter hate speech codes can be effective, despite arguments to the contrary, such as the need for "talking back," "reverse enforcement," "pressure valves," and the importance for minorities to stop seeing themselves as "victims"? Do these refutations seem forceful to you?

3. How does Delgado counter "First Amendment" arguments against speech codes? Does his evocation of Martin Luther King, Jr. and the civil rights movement of the 1960s seem relevant here, or is it a detour from the subject of speech code restrictions?

MARY BETH MARKLEIN

"On Campus: Free Speech for You But Not for Me?"

Mary Beth Marklein, who earned a B.A. in journalism from the University of Wisconsin at Madison in 1981 and a master's in journalism and public affairs from American University in 1988, has been a freelance writer for the

San Francisco Chronicle, *the* Baltimore Sun, *and other publications. She has reported on higher education for* USA Today *from 1997 to the present and taught journalism courses at American University from 1990–2000. In the following news article from* USA Today *2003, Marklein presents conservative critiques of college rules and campus cultures that limit freedom of speech and assembly.*

Most college presidents argue that their campuses and classrooms encourage the free exchange of ideas. Where else but here, they say, can difficult issues be debated?

But as campus officials look for ways to accommodate the growing diversity of their student bodies, an increasingly vocal number of students—most of them white and predominantly conservative or Christian—say there is little room for their opinions and beliefs.

On campuses large and small, public and private, students describe a culture in which freshmen are encouraged, if not required, to attend diversity programs that portray white males as oppressors. It's a culture in which students can be punished if their choice of words offends a classmate, and campus groups must promise they won't discriminate on the basis of religion or sexual orientation—even if theirs is a Christian club that doesn't condone homosexuality.

Colleges "seek to privilege one predominantly leftist point of view," says Thor Halvorssen of the Foundation for Individual Rights in Education (FIRE), a Philadelphia-based non-profit founded four years ago. "Universities should welcome all perspectives, no matter where on the political spectrum."

Increasingly, with financial and legal backing from a loose national network of conservative, religious and civil liberties groups, those students are fighting back.

In April, two students sued Shippensburg University in Shippensburg, Pa., arguing that several parts of the school's conduct code and diversity policies intimidated them into keeping silent about their conservative politics and beliefs. Since then, other students have sued Texas Tech University in Lubbock and a California community college. All three lawsuits are part of FIRE's campaign to abolish campus speech codes.

Where controversies have erupted:

University of California, Berkeley. In a catalog description last year for a course on the "politics and poetics of Palestinian resistance," the graduate student instructor warned that "conservative thinkers are encouraged to seek other sections." The description was rewritten, and administrators assured students they could indeed speak their minds.

University of Minnesota, Twin Cities. A student group for Christians sued the school over its requirement that student groups sign a statement that they are open to all students regardless of religion, marital status or sexual orientation.

University of Alabama, Tuscaloosa. A student was urged in June to remove a Confederate flag from a hallway in his dorm after a parent complained. Officials said the flag could violate a policy being drafted. In protest, other students displayed U.S. flags in their windows. Officials have since "tabled indefinitely" the policy, spokesman Cathy Andreen says.

University of Washington, Seattle. An "affirmative action bake sale" was cut short after drawing a crowd of about 200, some of them disruptive. The College Republican sponsors charged black students 30 cents, Latinos 35 cents and white students $1 for the same item. The Board of Regents later condemned the sale as "tasteless, divisive and hurtful." Organizers say campus police told them to shut it down; officials say the students agreed to end it.

Whittier College, Whittier, Calif. After students launched a conservative newspaper in April, they were told they needed permission from a campus board before publishing again. When they sought approval, they found that the board was inactive. The students say four other publications had not been asked to register.

Christian student groups also have gone to court on similar First Amendment grounds, the most recent case filed last month against the University of Minnesota.

On about 90 campuses, meanwhile, students have joined Students for Academic Freedom, created four months ago by leftist turned conservative activist David Horowitz. They argue that campuses are overwhelmingly liberal and demand that administrations seek a more balanced point of view among faculty and in programs such as lecture series.

On some campuses, specific incidents have prompted an uproar. A senior at California Polytechnic State University-San Luis Obispo sued campus officials in September, on a claim that he was unfairly punished after he tried to post a flier promoting a speech by a black author whose conservative ideas a group of black students found offensive. At Citrus College in California, a speech instructor offered extra credit to students if they wrote to President Bush protesting the war in Iraq.

But many students, like recent Shippensburg University graduate Ellen Wray, say they are simply frustrated by policies that dismiss or ignore conservative points of view.

"I wanted to help all the students that felt oppressed like I did," says Wray, 22, who sued the school. "All my professors were liberal except one, and he retired the first year I was there." After professors belittled her, "I finally just stopped raising my hand." She works for a Republican organization in Washington, D.C.

The issue is gaining traction beyond campus borders. Colorado lawmakers are considering a bill that would encourage colleges to ensure "intellectual diversity"—that is, that all viewpoints are represented. Nationally, nearly 20 House Republicans co-sponsored a similar bill introduced last week. A Senate education committee is looking into the subject, too.

"Dry-Cleaned" Ideas

Higher-education officials balk at the notion of lawmakers meddling with faculty or campus decisions. "For every anecdote on one side of the political spectrum, there can be found an anecdote on the other," says Jonathan Knight, a spokesman with the American Association of University Professors.

Few dispute the notion that faculty tend to be liberal as a group—certainly more liberal than many of their students. Shippensburg draws most of its student body from largely Republican central Pennsylvania. And a survey out this month by Harvard's Institute of Politics found that 38% of students identify themselves as independents, compared with 31% Republican and 27% Democrats.

Some professors stress that part of their job is to challenge students to question their beliefs. "We're in the business of helping people become critical thinkers," says Shippensburg sociology professor Debra Cornelius. Though she acknowledges her own liberal politics, she says, "We on a daily basis struggle with . . . making sure people behave in a tolerant way (without) chilling speech."

But those who see a bias in higher education say the public has a right to know what goes on inside the ivory tower.

"Legislators, taxpayers, tuition payers, and donors have no idea what their dollars are underwriting," says Luann Wright, the parent of a senior at the University of California-San Diego. So outraged was she by her son's 2001 freshman writing syllabus—"basically the whole thrust was on the toxicity of the white race," she says—that she created a non-profit Web site (noindoctrination.org) where students can anonymously post incidents of bias on their campuses.

Conservative students aren't the only ones feeling pinched. In May, Wesleyan University President Douglas Bennet banned a long-standing tradition, particularly popular among gay rights groups, of writing messages in chalk on sidewalks. Some faculty were targeted by name, and increasingly vulgar obscenities, sexual and racial slurs had spurred complaints.

But the most well-oiled attack is driven by conservative and Christian students, "who basically feel they're targets for getting their minds dry-cleaned to think the right way," says Jordan Lorence, a litigator for the Alliance Defense Fund, an Arizona Christian organization involved in several lawsuits.

Speech codes and other restrictions became popular in the late 1980s and early 1990s as campuses looked for ways to address the growing number of racial minorities on campus, along with concerns about sexual harassment. By the mid-1990s, after several courts ruled that certain campus speech bans were unconstitutional, many schools withdrew those policies.

Since then, racial slurs and other incidents have persisted. In 2001, the latest year for which statistics are available, the FBI received 987 reports of hate crimes and incidents at schools and college campuses—about 10% of all hate incidents that year.

And "the level of discourse in the outside world has become more confrontational," says Roger Williams University Provost Edward Kavanagh, whose Bristol, R.I., campus temporarily froze funding for a College Republicans newspaper this month. Kavanagh objected to its Sept. 30 edition, which featured a series of articles opposed to homosexuality, including a description of a crime in which a seventh-grade boy was raped and sodomized. He vowed to strengthen oversight of future publications.

But junior Jason Mattera, 20, an editor of the paper, says, "You're not automatically a bigot if you don't agree with (homosexuality). What they're essentially doing is silencing the only conservative voice here on campus."

The administrative response is typical, some say. Indeed, many schools, including the University of Virginia and Harvard Law School, created task forces in the past year in response to similar incidents on their campuses.

In the process, says David French, the lawyer representing the Shippensburg students, speech codes have reappeared—though often disguised as anti-harassment statements or non-discrimination policies.

Today, FIRE estimates that two-thirds of colleges have speech codes. Other experts disagree: In a recent study of 100 randomly selected institutions, George Mason University professor Jon Gould found that 30% of institutions have a policy that restricts hate speech, but less than 10% would be unconstitutional.

Campuses Say Civility is the Goal

Campus officials say their goal is not to stifle students but to promote civil discourse. "What we attempt to do is try to create a civil democracy, where everybody is respected," Shippensburg President Anthony Ceddia says.

Since 1990, he says, the campus has pledged a commitment to racial tolerance, cultural diversity and social justice, and since 2000, it has required students to take a course that meets a diversity requirement. Students also are strongly encouraged to attend university-funded "Art of Being" programs, which highlight a particular culture—Jewish, African-American and Asian-American were among those offered this semester.

Some students welcome the programs. In a column in the student newspaper, opinion editor Christopher Kirkhoff lauded Ceddia for "stressing the danger of prejudice and the administration's intolerance" for homophobia, which he said "is running rampant on this campus."

But French says that, taken together, a number of Shippensburg's campus policies, while never enforced, dampened his clients' ability to express themselves. One sentence in the conduct code, for example, suggests that student expression should not "provoke, harass, intimidate or harm" another. But "if you're part of an intellectual minority, it's difficult for your speech not to provoke," he says.

The Bush administration, too, has weighed in. Key officials notified colleges and universities in August that federal civil rights regulations "do not require or prescribe speech, conduct, or harassment codes that impair the exercise of rights protected under the First Amendment."

For now, at least, the courts appear to side with the students. A U.S. district judge ruled last year that a policy at the University of Houston unfairly gave administrators "unfettered discretion" in deciding what events could be held outside designated speech zones on campus. In June, administrators said they would drop some restrictions and pay $93,000 in attorneys' fees to settle a lawsuit by student abortion protesters.

And in September, a U.S. district judge said Shippensburg's conduct codes, though well-intentioned, "could certainly be used to truncate debate and free expression by students." He encouraged campus administrators to revise seven sentences in their policies.

The anti-speech-code crowd hopes the momentum will continue as more students join the fight. "Now they know they can win," FIRE's Halvorssen says.

But for their part, some students say they have more modest goals. "I'm not looking to pick a fight," says Joe Jones, 22, a senior at the University of North Carolina at Chapel Hill and member of a Christian group. "I want the freedom to say what I want to say."

QUESTIONS

1. Do the cases Marklein presents of what conservative, religious, white student, and professional groups believe to be incursions on their rights to assemble peacefully and speak out on issues important to them convince you that serious censorship exists on American College campuses? Why or why not?

2. Examine the membership and outlook of groups such as FIRE and the Alliance Defense Fund (see their websites). Do you think Marklein quotes too frequently from officials and lawyers for such conservative organizations, or does she provide adequate balance from moderate school officials and liberal students and groups?

3. College administrators quoted in the article argue that the real purpose of the campus rules in question is to create an atmosphere of "campus civility" and "civil democracy." From the cases presented by Marklein, do you think they are using the right strategies to achieve their ends? Why or why not?

STANLEY FISH

"Conspiracy Theories 101"

Stanley Fish (b. 1938) is a literary critic and theorist, college professor, and former dean. Currently, he is the Davidson-Kahn Distinguished University Professor of Humanities and a professor of law at Florida International University. He received his Ph.D. from Yale University and has taught at several leading American universities, including University of California at Berkeley, Johns Hopkins, and Duke. Fish writes a blog for the New York Times Editorial Section, where he expresses his views on particular cases involving free speech and other legal concerns, many in the area of higher education. His books related to legal, free speech, educational, and political issues include Doing What Comes Naturally: Change, Rhetoric, the Practice of Theory in Literary and Legal Studies (1989); Professional Correctness: Literary Studies and Political Change (1999); and The Trouble with Principle (1999). *Fish's article "Conspiracy Theories 101" is his New York Times blog entry for July 23, 2006; it reveals his position on the controversial question of how far a college teacher can pursue extreme political lines of thinking in the classroom without being rightfully terminated by the college administration.*

Kevin Barrett, a lecturer at the University of Wisconsin at Madison, has now taken his place alongside Ward Churchill of the University of Colorado as a college teacher whose views on 9/11 have led politicians and ordinary citizens to demand that he be fired.

Mr. Barrett, who has a one-semester contract to teach a course titled "Islam: Religion and Culture," acknowledged on a radio talk show that he has shared with students his strong conviction that the destruction of the World Trade Center was an inside job perpetrated by the American government. The predictable uproar ensued, and the equally predictable battle lines were drawn between those who disagree about what the doctrine of academic freedom does and does not allow.

Mr. Barrett's critics argue that academic freedom has limits and should not be invoked to justify the dissemination of lies and fantasies. Mr. Barrett's supporters (most of whom are not partisans of his conspiracy theory) insist that it is the very point of an academic institution to entertain all points of view, however unpopular. (This was the position taken by the university's provost, Patrick Farrell, when he ruled on July 10 that Mr. Barrett would be retained: "We cannot allow political pressure from critics of unpopular ideas to inhibit the free exchange of ideas.")

Both sides get it wrong. The problem is that each assumes that academic freedom is about protecting the content of a professor's speech; one side thinks that no content should be ruled out in advance; while the other would draw the line at propositions (like the denial of the Holocaust or the flatness of the world) considered by almost everyone to be crazy or dangerous.

But in fact, academic freedom has nothing to do with content. It is not a subset of the general freedom of Americans to say anything they like (so long as it is not an incitement to violence or is treasonous or libelous). Rather, academic freedom is the freedom of academics to study anything they like; the freedom, that is, to subject any body of material, however unpromising it might seem, to academic interrogation and analysis.

Academic freedom means that if I think that there may be an intellectual payoff to be had by turning an academic lens on material others consider trivial—golf tees, gourmet coffee, lingerie ads, convenience stores, street names, whatever—I should get a chance to try. If I manage to demonstrate to my peers and students that studying this material yields insights into matters of general intellectual interest, there is a new topic under the academic sun and a new subject for classroom discussion.

In short, whether something is an appropriate object of academic study is a matter not of its content—a crackpot theory may have had a history of influence that well rewards scholarly scrutiny—but of its availability to serious analysis. This point was missed by the author of a comment posted to the blog of a University of Wisconsin law professor, Ann Althouse: "When is the University of Wisconsin hiring a professor of astrology?" The question is obviously sarcastic; its intention is to equate the 9/11-inside-job theory with believing in the predictive power of astrology, and to imply that since the university wouldn't think of hiring someone to teach the one, it should have known better than to hire someone to teach the other.

But the truth is that it would not be at all outlandish for a university to hire someone to teach astrology—not to profess astrology and recommend it as the basis of decision-making (shades of Nancy Reagan), but to teach the history of its very long career. There is, after all, a good argument for saying that Shakespeare, Chaucer and Dante, among others, cannot be fully understood unless one understands astrology.

The distinction I am making—between studying astrology and proselytizing for it—is crucial and can be generalized; it shows us where the line between the responsible and irresponsible practice of academic freedom should always be drawn. Any idea can be brought into the classroom if the point is to inquire into its structure, history, influence and so forth. But no idea belongs in the classroom if the point of introducing it is to recruit your students for the political agenda it may be thought to imply.

And this is where we come back to Mr. Barrett, who, in addition to being a college lecturer, is a member of a group calling itself Scholars for 9/11 Truth, an organization with the decidedly political agenda of persuading Americans that the Bush administration "not only permitted 9/11 to happen but may even have orchestrated these events."

Is the fact of this group's growing presence on the Internet a reason for studying it in a course on 9/11? Sure. Is the instructor who discusses the group's arguments thereby endorsing them? Not at all. It is perfectly possible to teach a viewpoint without embracing it and urging it. But the moment a professor does embrace and urge it, academic study has ceased and been replaced by partisan advocacy. And that is a moment no college administration should allow to occur.

Provost Farrell doesn't quite see it that way, because he is too hung up on questions of content and balance. He thinks that the important thing is to assure a diversity of views in the classroom, and so he is reassured when Mr. Barrett promises to surround his "unconventional" ideas and "personal opinions" with readings "representing a variety of viewpoints."

But the number of viewpoints Mr. Barrett presents to his students is not the measure of his responsibility. There is, in fact, no academic requirement to include more than one view of an academic issue, although it is usually pedagogically useful to do so. The true requirement is that no matter how many (or few) views are presented to the students, they should be offered as objects of analysis rather than as candidates for allegiance.

There is a world of difference, for example, between surveying the pro and con arguments about the Iraq war, a perfectly appropriate academic assignment, and pressing students to come down on your side. Of course the instructor who presides over such a survey is likely to be a partisan of one position or the other—after all, who doesn't have an opinion on the Iraq war?—but it is part of a teacher's job to set personal conviction aside for the hour or two when a class is in session and allow the techniques and protocols of academic research full sway.

This restraint should not be too difficult to exercise. After all, we require and expect it of judges, referees and reporters. And while its exercise may not always be total, it is both important and possible to make the effort.

Thus the question Provost Farrell should put to Mr. Barrett is not "Do you hold these views?" (he can hold any views he likes) or "Do you proclaim them in public?" (he has that right no less that the rest of us) or even "Do you surround them with the views of others?"

Rather, the question should be: "Do you separate yourself from your partisan identity when you are in the employ of the citizens of Wisconsin and teach subject matter—whatever it is—rather than urge political action?" If the answer is yes, allowing Mr. Barrett to remain in the classroom is warranted. If the answer is no, (or if a yes answer is followed by classroom behavior that contradicts it) he should be shown the door. Not because he would be teaching the "wrong" things, but because he would have abandoned teaching for indoctrination.

The advantage of this way of thinking about the issue is that it outflanks the sloganeering and posturing both sides indulge in: on the one hand, faculty members who shout "academic freedom" and mean by it an instructor's right to say or advocate anything at all with impunity; on the other hand, state legislators who shout "not on our dime" and mean by it that they can tell academics what ideas they can and cannot bring into the classroom.

All you have to do is remember that academic freedom is just that: the freedom to do an academic job without external interference. It is not the freedom to do other jobs, jobs you are neither trained for nor paid to perform. While there should be no restrictions on what can be taught—no list of interdicted ideas or topics—there should be an absolute restriction on appropriating the scene of teaching for partisan political ideals. Teachers who use the classroom to indoctrinate make the enterprise of higher education vulnerable to its critics and shortchange students in the guise of showing them the true way.

QUESTIONS

1. According to Fish, in the argument over Barrett's dismissal, how did "both sides get it wrong" (i.e., supporters of the lecturer and the college administration)? Consider each side's position—do you agree that either or both "got it wrong"? Why or why not?
2. What academic freedom does Fish uphold, and what kind of faculty advocacy does he condemn? Why does he consider it inadequate to present a variety of opinions on an issue, some extreme, if the instructor admits that he or she agrees with one or more of them? Do you agree with his position here?
3. Would you consider the position that an instructor must be so careful to avoid the charge of indoctrination as to keep any expression of "partisan identity" on a controversial issue out of the classroom to be a significant abridgement of free-speech rights for faculty? As a student, would you find such limits on faculty expression objectionable? Why or why not?

RICHARD GOLDSTEIN (Researched by Julia Gayduk)

"Celebrity Bigots"

Richard Goldstein (b. 1942) is an executive editor of the Village Voice, *where he has been writing about politics, popular culture, and sexuality for over three decades. He is also a regular contributor to* The Nation *and the author of* Reporting the Counterculture *(1989),* Mine Eyes Have Seen: A First-Person

History of the Events That Shaped America *(1997), and* Homocons: The Rise of the Gay Right *(2003). Goldstein was the winner of the 2001 GLAAD (Gay and Lesbian Alliance Against Discrimination) columnist of the year award. The following article, originally written for the* Village Voice *in 2000, gives a historical and sociopolitical background to current incidents and news accounts of celebrity outbursts involving hate-filled diatribes that reveal racial, gender, and anti-gay bias.*

So John Rocker[1] played at Shea, and the fans booed him. By baiting the "hate hurler" (as Rocker was dubbed by one tab), they got to feel superior, basking in their sympathy for the huddled masses on the No. 7 line. But the morning after Rocker's drubbing, many of these same defenders of diversity tuned in to Don Imus, who never met an immigrant he didn't mock. Another hate hurler? Nah, it's just the I-Man funning.

What makes Imus a hero and Rocker a target? The answer, as with so much else about New York, is location. The I-Man is one of us, but Rocker is the ultimate outsider. He's a Southerner, part of a group every New Yorker can dis. The same tabs that bristle at his bigotry call Rocker a "redneck" without blinking. He's a perpetrator and a victim of hate speech.

Every few months, it seems, another athlete is punished for making some comment that, from the mouths of shock jocks, would sail right by. But that shouldn't come as a surprise. We live in a time of intense ambivalence about group slander. On the one hand, using hate speech in the commission of a crime can get you extra time. On the other hand, defamation is a potent form of entertainment. The old etiquette of discretion about religion and race has given way to what might be called surrogate slurring. Everything you can't say on the street is being blasted on the radio, in record stores, and all over the Internet.

Insult is a driver of ratings in a media world with so many choices that it's harder than ever to stand out. They used to say that sex sells, but in this jaded climate, it's far more profitable to combine balling and bigotry. That way, you can rile up both the Christian faithful and the politically correct. Hate speech may be horrifying, but it's irresistible to millions, much as pornography is and for similar reasons. It's a repository of fantasies that are shameful, even criminal, to act on. But these thoughts also turn a lot of us on.

Enter the celebrity bigot, a personality whose fame rests on expressing mass biases. Not talking Rocker here—he didn't set out to become a slurring superstar. But Imus knows what he's doing, and so does Eminem, the white rapper whose bloody misogynist and homophobic ravings have made him America's best-selling recording artist.

Then there's Dr. Laura, the media shrink whose antigay tirades are her stock in trade. She's bigger than Rush Limbaugh, and this fall she makes her TV debut, joining various haranguing judges in the dark vaudeville of calumny.

Not so long ago, such banter was inconceivable. We were too close to the knives of World War II to be blasé about bigotry. But as the memory of fascism fades, so does any sense that hate speech has real consequences. Mind you, there are still plenty of taboos on radio and TV, still plenty of subjects that don't lend themselves to commentary or comedy. The real question is why the line is being drawn where it is.

Insult humor is nothing new. It's been a major vein in comedy ever since "Take my wife. Please!" But Henny Youngman's quips had an edge of affection, heightened by a Jewish comic's exemption from empty pieties. Even the *tummler*'s art of insult, honed for a mass audience by comics like Don Rickles, was cast as harmless hazing. Certain members of the audience were singled out for scorn, but certainly not because of their ethnicity.

All that changed with Lenny Bruce, whose comedy confronted the hypocrisy of race relations, not to mention the absurdity of otherness in Christian America. An entertainer like Imus can trace his lineage to Bruce, with one crucial distinction: Lenny made fun of the powerful and their orthodoxies. You won't find Imus mocking WASPs on a regular basis. Instead, this rude dude focuses on groups whose status is still contested, such as blacks, immigrants, and gays.

The muckraker Philip Nobile has been tracking Imus's racist rap in a series for the webzine tompaine.com. When you take this patter out of laff-riot context, it's strikingly similar to the drollery of David Duke. Imus and his buds have called O.J.'s lead attorney "chicken wing Johnny Cochran," Sammy Davis Jr. "a one-eyed lawn jockey," Patrick Ewing "Mighty Joe Young," Defense Secretary William Cohen "the Mandingo," and his black wife "a 'ho." Speaking of reporter Gwen Ifill, he's said, "Isn't the *Times* wonderful? It lets the cleaning lady cover the White House." His sidekicks do imitations of Al Sharpton with the kind of botched grammar that would get them run out of town if they ran such shtick on whites (except for Rocker, whom Imus has called "a redneck goober").

Many libertarians seem to think this ritual slandering is constructive. It clears the air for a frank discussion of race and sexuality, or it vents the rage of threatened men. In this scenario, hate speech is right up there with military hair and big tattoos: It's a show of strength designed to compensate for lost status. By providing an arena where jungle bunnies, bitches, and fags can be insulted with impunity, Imus and Eminem make it easier for their fans to bear the real conditions of life in a multicultural society. Your boss may be a woman, your sergeant an African American, your teacher a gay man, but every time you put the earphones on, you rule. So why not think of celebrity bigots as lubricators of social change?

The answer is that resentment and rage don't necessarily dissipate when they are expressed in fantasy. On the contrary, a steady stream of invective can foster violence. The men who ran amok in Central Park didn't take their marauding orders from Eminem, but the air they breathe is part of his repertoire. As in this rockin' rhyme: "In a couple of minutes that bottle of Guinness is finished/You are now allowed to officially slap bitches/You have the right to remain violent and start wilin'."

Would the culture of male violence exist without such anthems? Please! A survey of 10 organizations that deal with defamation produced no reliable data linking hate speech and crime. What seems obvious is that some people act on these messages, just as some people model violent sexual behavior on porn. But the effect on most of us is more complex. The real issue isn't how individuals react to public slander; it's how the culture takes shape around these rituals of casual abuse. This is where the lessons of fascism are worth heeding, for the ultimate uses of bigotry are political.

Of course, celebrity bigots insist they're anything but. Imus has told *60 Minutes* he never utters the N-word (except in private conversation). Everything he says is meant in fun. That's what distinguishes him from a shock jock like Bob Grant, whose description of David Dinkins as "a washroom attendant" set him up for a fall. "I mean, if he's serious about it," Imus told CNN's Jeff Greenfield, "well, then, that is offensive."

Eminem offered a street version of this disclaimer when he told one interviewer he was merely "making fun of the world." Though he recently slugged someone for calling him a fag, Eminem has "nothing against gay people." He just thought it would be witty to rap this little ditty: "My words are like a dagger with a jagged edge/That'll stab you in the head whether you're a fag or lez/Hate fags? The answer's yes."

Those who are bothered by lines like "I was put here to put fear in faggots" or "Bleed, bitch, bleed" have no sense of humor, the worst sin of the politically correct. But behind the celebrity bigot's wink and grin lies a lusty rebel yell. "I don't apologize for offending people," Imus proclaims. "I know it's not politically correct, and I don't care." Eminem is even more trenchant: "My comical," he notes, "is really political."

So it is. Eminem and Imus draw from the same well of resentment that has nourished the Angry White Male. These stars are part of the backlash, and their reach into the mainstream shows how far this attitude has advanced. Bias is now a marketable commodity, tailored to the niches of a needy audience. Young males who feel deprived of sexual supremacy can take solace in the rapine arcadia of rap. Here, blacks and whites team up against bitches of all races. But for mature malcontents whose beef has less to do with sex than with loss of skin privilege, there's the fellowship of shock jocks. Here, whites team up against other races. Different strokes for different folks, as they say. But when you put these messages together, they add up to a powerful counterculture, a brotherhood of bigotry.

Irony is what makes this sensibility appeal to those who wouldn't be caught dead in a skinhead bar. Where there's irony, people can pretend that something other than hatred is at work. It's just a fun house; you don't confuse reality with the ride. And the more progressives protest, the more it seems like they're not in on the joke. Irony has accomplished what George Wallace never could. It's now hip to hate.

Celebrity bigots like to claim they're equal-opportunity offenders. Imus insists he's global in his jibes, but there's a pattern in his patter. His audience would dwindle dramatically if he took on Mother Teresa or the international Zionist conspiracy. There's no downside to joking about dead Haitians floating on the sea, as Imus has. The groups he picks on are the ones it's permissible to mock.

It's no coincidence that every celebrity bigot targets gays. They are the newest group to enter the multiculti fold. Gays are to America what Jews were to Europe a century ago: a newly emancipated—but far from licit—caste. No wonder politicians (like Dick Armey and Rick Lazio) can use homophobic slurs without risking their careers. The more precarious one's social status, the more one is subject to casual slander and the more people are willing to regard these insults as harmless—or even worse, reasonable.

Which brings us to Dr. Laura, another entertainer whose shtick is slamming those who stray from the straight and narrow. Aside from attacking feminism on a regular basis, she is infamous for resurrecting ideas about homosexuality that haven't been heard since the 1950s. Like certain notorious shrinks of that era, she promotes treatments the Christian right calls "reparative therapy." There isn't a shred of evidence that homosexuals can be counseled into losing their same-sex desire. But the point of this strategy is conversion, not healing. That's why most gays regard reparative therapy as a profound offense. It's no different at heart from the age-old ambition to convert the Jews.

How ironic that Dr. Laura (Schlessinger) is a convert to Orthodox Judaism, since she attacks like an old-time anti-Semite. For example, she blithely asserts that "a huge portion of the male homosexual populace is predatory on young boys"—the homophobic equivalent of the blood libel, the ancient belief that Jews killed Christian children to use their blood in making matzoh. Just as Jews were seen as powerful beyond their numbers, Dr. Laura sees gays as "deviant tyrants." Just as Jews were accused of having no culture but money, Dr. Laura says gay culture is "just about sex." Gay rights! She scoffs. "That's what I'm worried about, with all the pedophilia and the bestiality and the sadomasochism. Why does deviant sexual behavior get rights?"

In this conflation of gay people and unnatural appetites, one hears the hot breath of Imus and his friends commenting on Jim Dale's now moot case against the Boy Scouts: "His idea of being prepared is bringing condoms to Jamborees." Yet a large swath of the media seem prepared to buy Dr. Laura's claim that she is making a serious critique of the gay movement, about which reasonable people might disagree. This tolerance of false science and outright slander should seem familiar to those who remember Father Coughlin, the Depression-era priest who presented Jews as a threat to America. At his height, millions fervently followed his radio ministry. Today, Dr. Laura calls gays a menace to "the basic foundation of civilization." Fundamentalists consider her a crusader, and libertarians have added to her mystique by casting her as a test case for free speech.

Not that Dr. Laura is a friend of the First Amendment. She sued a California shop owner for calling her a liar, and tried (ultimately unsuccessfully) to legally stop cybernauts who posted nude pictures of her. She advocates censorship of the Internet and attacks the American Library Association for "sexualizing our children." Yet we're urged to suffer her opinions. Even the *New York Times'* Frank Rich has joined the chorus urging the gay community to lay off Dr. Laura. After all, the same free speech that spawns bigots like her also makes it possible for the gay community to be heard.

This is a noble standard, but it doesn't apply to the world we live in. The clash of ideas in American mass media is not a cacophony but a hierarchy of voices. The ugly truth is that some forms of bigotry are more permissible than others, and some are not acceptable at all.

Where were Rich's columns urging Jewish groups to tolerate Khalid Muhammad? Why was his calumny considered more dangerous than Dr. Laura's? (After all, Khalid never had a sit-down with the Black Congressional Caucus, but Dr. Laura has met with the Republican leadership.) Why were his ideas about Jews regarded as slander while her rants about gay people are taken as a serious, if debatable, critique? The answer goes to the heart of why some groups are more susceptible than others to hate speech.

Whatever some people may feel about Jews, you rarely find anti-Semitic epithets in the mass media. That's not because Jews own the culture, whatever Khalid might think. They are largely exempt from public slander because most people have come to terms with the tradition of anti-Semitism that culminated in the Holocaust. It's a settled issue. But race is a very different cauldron, still boiling over on the American range. When it comes to sexual equality, the jury is definitely out. And gay rights are the most precarious of all. This unsettled agenda is accurately reflected in the vulnerability of various groups to hate speech. It's a marker of one's fragile social status, and it has a real effect on people who are constantly subject to this reminder.

In some, hate speech inhibits the ability to be assertive; in others it produces a chronic anxiety that becomes part of the personality, while still others are driven to outbursts of ferocity. In any case, the leaders who emerge are hardly the sort of people to soothe the savage breast. Just as postwar liberalism fostered the rise of Martin Luther King, the backlash against civil rights has created Louis Farrakhan. This is the dialectic of bigotry many libertarians seem unwilling to face. Instead, they point out that the victims can speak out too—as if the media were willing to grant them equal time.

Yes, there are gays in sitcoms, blacks in action movies, and women in sports. But you won't find these role models trafficking in slander, if only because the punishment for such conduct would be marginalization. Farrakhan may draw a million black men to Washington, but he doesn't get a slot on Black Entertainment Television. Nor was Sistah Souljah played on MTV. We don't live in a world where words like "whiteboy" and "breeder" are the coin of the realm. Indeed, the nature of being dominant is that there aren't many epithets to describe you. When a gay shrink can become a national figure by calling heterosexuals an abomination, when a black shock jock makes a fortune mocking whites, when a female rapper can go platinum by boasting of slashing up men, then we can talk about a level playing field.

But there's a better way. You can stand up and say: Hate speech isn't hip; it's wrong. And you can fight its spread, not by demanding that the government ban bigotry but by picketing those who profit from it, flooding their companies with complaints, holding teach-ins on the culture of contempt. In the current climate, such protest is piecemeal and rarely involves a coalition like the one that built the civil rights movement. Prominent black journalists have refused to appear on Imus, but their white counterparts go on chatting with the I-Man. Self-interest has replaced the old ideal of common cause. Even worse, libertarians are chastising those who care enough to protest.

The First Amendment does not require silence in the face of outrage. On the contrary, freedom demands a constant assertion of values. We've seen what the absence of righteous anger can produce. Sixty years ago, a cadre of fascist thugs nearly destroyed our civilization. They would never have gotten so far if more people had taken their hate speech seriously from the start. Let's not make that mistake in the name of entertainment. Stop the celebrity bigots before it happens again.

1. Atlanta Braves baseball player known for making insulting remarks about New Yorkers, gays, women, blacks, and Asians.

QUESTIONS

1. What are the main points in Goldstein's argument against hate-speaking celebrities? What does he consider their motivations and how does he refute their justifications for their behavior? Why does he think they particularly target gays?

2. Goldstein seems to be a believer in full freedom of speech; however, he does make some suggestions for solutions to the problem of media hate speech that stop short of actual censorship. What are his proposals, and have any of them been tried in recent years? Do they seem effective to you? Why or why not? Can you think of alternative ideas?

3. Goldstein's essay was published in 2000—is it still possible for media celebrities on radio talk shows and other public venues to use without consequences the kind of hateful speech he critiques in his article? You might consider the recent problems of Don Imus, one of the Goldstein's primary examples of "humorous" hate speakers, in contrast to Imus's position in 2000.

Differing Perspectives: Should Internet Hate Speech be Regulated?

David Matas

"Countering Hate on the Internet: Recommendations for Action"

David Matas earned an M.A. from Princeton University and B.A.s in Jurisprudence and Civil Law from Oxford University. He is a Canadian lawyer who has worked in private practice in refugee, immigration, and human rights law since 1979 and has also been a lecturer on legal issues at McGill University and the University of Manitoba. He has been appointed to numerous international forums in areas such as immigration, antisemitism, human rights, and democracy; currently, he is Canadian legal coordinator for Amnesty International, Beyond Borders, and B'nai Brith Canada, where he serves as senior honorary counsel. His books include No More: The Battle Against Human Rights Violations *(1994),* Bloody Words: Hate and Free Speech *(2000), and* Aftershock: Anti-Zionism and Antisemitism *(2005). The essay below includes a number of tentative solutions for the problem of online hate speech.*

The advent of the internet has given a new and powerful tool to hatemongers. Hate speech, because of the internet, is circulating as it never was before. It is accessible to adults and children alike, at the click of a button.

Hate speech is not, like pornography, something that is obvious at first sight. Hate speech combines in a volatile cocktail two separate speech crimes, incitement to violence and fraud. It is insidious, devious. While one can say, at least for adults, that they can choose to click on to or not to click on to pornography, one cannot say the same for hate speech. Those susceptible to the messages of hate mongers are those with little appreciation of the danger of the messages. Hate speech on the internet cannot be ignored. It represents a threat to its targets that needs to be combated. How it should be combated requires sensitivity to the medium that is used.

Before we even start to address the problem of hate speech on the internet, we must consider the more general boon the internet has become. The internet offers a great advantage for communication of information world wide. It is quick; it is cheap; it is accurate. Marshall McLuhan over thirty years ago wrote: "After three thousand years of specialist explosion and increasing specialism and alienation in the technological extensions of our bodies, our world has become compressionable by dramatic reversal. As electronically contracted the globe is no more than a village." What was compressionable in 1964 when those words were published, has, through the internet, become compressed. The internet has made Marshall McLuhan's global village an electronic reality.

The internet has made global freedom of expression a practical mundane fact for anyone with a computer and a phone. Today, because of the internet, anyone and everyone can disseminate their thoughts, their feelings, their research, their discoveries, their analyses, their opinions, world wide to millions at virtually no cost. Even at this early stage, it is not too early to say that the internet is important for democracy. . . . The internet is an asset to democracy and the full realization of human rights. It needs to be nurtured, protected and developed.

In a general sense, human rights have to be viewed as a whole, with one overall goal, the enhancement of the dignity and worth of the individual human being. Individual human rights are the different ways in which the goal can be realized. No one human right trumps other human rights. If one human right is considered absolute, or given priority, then other human rights, necessarily, end up taking second place. One facet of human development is thwarted so that another facet can be given free rein. Or, what often happens, the rights of some are given over-lavish attention; and the rights of others are completely trampled.

The right to be free to say what you want and the right to be free from hate speech targeted against you are two fundamental human rights that must be kept in balance. Neither is an absolute. Neither must be given priority over the other. Both are essential for the preservation of humanity. If free speech is given free rein, then the right to be protected from incitement to hatred is lost. If the right to be protected from incitement to hatred is given first priority, then the right to freedom of expression will be unduly threatened.

All this is true of speech on the internet. If human rights are to be truly protected, then there must be protection from hate speech on the internet. As well, if human rights are to be truly protected, then there must be protection for freedom of expression on the internet. At the level of principle, the issue of hate speech on the internet raises no new questions. The issues of balancing of rights, of priorities and absolutism remain.

What is new with the internet is the question of technology. Given that the internet is an important new medium for freedom of expression which deserves protection and enhancement, how is it possible to ban hate speech on the internet? We do not want to throw out the medium with the message. But can we extricate the message of hate speech from the medium of the internet, so that the medium remains, but the message of hate speech is gone?

Suggesting we should try to extricate the medium from the message understates the danger of hate on internet. As Marshall McLuhan has reminded us, in many ways the medium is the message. Electronic technology is an extension of our senses. Freedom of the individual means the freedom to hear what each person wants to hear, the freedom to read what each person wants to read as much as the freedom to say what each person want to say, the freedom to write what each person wants to write.

Marshall McLuhan wrote: "Once we have surrendered our senses and nervous systems to the private manipulation of those who would benefit from taking a lease on our eyes and ears and nerves, we don't really have any rights left."

The existence of hate propaganda on the internet, rather than sapping our will, should mobilize it. Hate speech on the internet is not just an old threat in new clothes. It is a whole new monster. The internet has made hate speech accessible to those who before never would have come into contact with it. It is brought hate speech to children, to the suburbs. One can say generally that those most prone to the messages of hate speech are the marginal and the alienated. It was relatively difficult, prior to the internet, for hatemongers to seek these people out. The marginal and the alienated, by their very nature, are disconnected socially and politically. There are no organizations for the marginal, clubs for the alienated, connections amongst the disconnected. The internet allows hate mongers to reach into the privacy and isolation of people's homes, to find the vulnerable, those prone to the message of hate speech, wherever they happen to be.

There are also the sheer numbers. Before the internet, hate speech was accessible to thousands, those on the mailing lists, those who called in to telephone hate lines, those who could be pamphleteered on the street or in parking lots. Now, through the internet, hate speech is accessible to millions. The random chance that those susceptible to the siren songs of hatemongers will now hear those songs has increased exponentially because of the internet.

The internet has rapidly become the medium of choice for hatemongers because of its wide access at low cost. Norman Olson, commander of the Michigan Militia Corps, one of the many extreme right wing groups using the internet, has said "Thank God for high tech."

The rise of the internet has coincided with a rise in hate crimes, a lowering of age for the commission of hate crimes and the existence of hate crimes where they never existed before. Hate crimes have spread to suburbia, because the internet, carrying hate speech, has spread to suburbia. The 1996 League for Human Rights of B'nai Brith Audit of anti-Semitic Incidents showed that anti-Semitic incidents have increased in Ontario's smaller communities, the bedroom suburban communities of the Greater Toronto Area. The majority of hate crimes are now committed by people under the age of twenty. Isolated, opportunistic hate crimes are becoming more and more prevalent. For these crimes there are no signs of organized hate crime gangs. The only plausible explanation for these crimes is the advent of the internet.

Marshall McLuhan said: "The threat of Stalin or Hitler was external. The electric technology is within our gates, and we are numb, deaf, blind and mute" to its dangers. "I am in the position of Louis Pasteur telling doctors that their greatest enemy is quite invisible, and quite unrecognized by them. . . . The new media and technologies by which we amplify and extend ourselves constitute huge collective surgery carried out on the social body with complete disregard for antiseptics. If the operations are needed, the inevitability of infecting the whole system during the operation has to be considered." Though he was talking more generally about electronic communication, what he wrote applies eloquently to hate on the internet.

McLuhan distinguishes between hot media and cool media, hot media being those that are high definition, filled with data and cool media being those that give a meager amount of information. If we use these categories, surely the internet is a hot medium. McLuhan observes that a hot medium used in cool or nonliterate cultures has a violent effect. One can say the same about the nonliterate or semiliterate individuals whom the internet reaches even where those individuals are found within generally literate cultures. The internet can be described the way McLuhan described the radio, as a medium for frenzy.

The battle to protect against incitement to hatred often turns into a battle between free speech advocates and human rights advocates. Free speech advocates are primarily concerned with freedom of expression. Other human rights, such as the duty to protect against hate speech, are given by free speech advocates second rank. Human rights advocates, on the other hand, give equal weight to the right to freedom of expression and the right to freedom from incitement to hatred. Neither right ranks higher than the other. Free speech advocates will tell you that banning hate speech on the internet will not work, cannot work. They will go even further and argue that because the internet makes a mockery of hate speech prohibition laws, there is no point any more in having any such laws.

This is the point of view, for instance, of Adam Clayton Powell III, vice president for technology programs with Freedom Forum, a non-partisan foundation for media education; Shabbir Safdar, co-founder of Voters Telecommunication Watch, dedicated to preserving free speech on the internet; and Stanton McCandlish, program director of the San Francisco based Electronic Frontier Foundation, which also fights for free speech on the internet. They have all argued that the internet is essentially uncontrollable. Jim Carroll, who wrote the *Canadian Internet Handbook*, said "It's like passing a law that makes mosquitoes illegal, or banning winter from Canada."

My first reaction to this argument is that there is a certain disingenuousness about those who proclaim that the application of hate speech laws to the internet is doomed to ineffectiveness. When they make a point of saying that it cannot be done, they are, in reality, pursuing another agenda. The critics are opposed to banning hate speech on the internet, even if the banning is effective, for an altogether different reason, because this banning is, to the critics, an unjustifiable limitation on freedom of speech.

There is a legitimate, although, I believe ultimately incorrect, argument that banning hate propaganda is an undue limitation on freedom of speech. Ineffectiveness is not the only argument free speech advocates bring to this debate, although it is quite a common one. The core concern of free speech advocates is not effectiveness. Effectiveness is, after all, a concern in all areas of the law, not just speech laws. The concern for free speech advocates, is, obviously, freedom of speech. A charge of ineffectiveness is just a weapon that is used by free speech advocates in what they see as a battle over freedom of speech.

Although I believe that the battle free speech advocates fight against hate speech laws is a wrong headed battle and that they should be defeated, the purpose of this paper is not to engage in that battle. My purpose here is just to argue that the argument of ineffectiveness drawn from the internet that free speech advocates use in this battle is not properly used. Whatever else free speech advocates say against hate speech laws, it is wrong for them to say that the internet shows us that hate speech laws cannot work.

When I say that free speech advocates are disingenuous when they charge internet hate speech laws with ineffectiveness, I do not mean to suggest that these advocates do not believe the charge. I make only the more limited point that the adversaries of internet hate speech laws are free speech advocates, not effectiveness advocates. Effectiveness in hate speech laws would not satisfy free speech advocates. And because effectiveness would not satisfy them, they are not particularly eager to find it.

Free speech advocates seize on inability, look for ineffectiveness, point to the problems the internet poses for making hate speech laws effective. Ineffectiveness in hate speech laws is, for them, a weakness in the opposing side, something to be highlighted and targeted. Free speech advocates will insist on the ineffectiveness of hate speech laws as long as it is remotely tenable to do so. And, if it ceases to be tenable, they will simply move on to other arguments, rather than abandon their opposition to hate speech laws.

So, when free speech advocates say that laws banning hate speech on the internet are doomed to ineffectiveness, their arguments should not be ignored. But they should be taken with a grain of salt. Free speech advocates do not see the possibility of effectiveness in hate speech laws, because they do not want to see it. Their blindness is, if not willful, at least convenient. The indictment of ineffectiveness is, for them, an asset, helping them make the more general point they want to make, that there should be no hate speech laws.

It is noteworthy that the United States Supreme Court, which has been sympathetic to the free speech absolutist cause, rejected this argument of ineffectiveness. Bruce J. Ennis argued in the US Supreme Court, for a coalition of civil liberties and computer industry group, in a case challenging the constitutionality of the 1996 Communications Decency Act penalizing the display of indecent material on the internet, that the law was bound to be ineffective because over 30% of indecent material on the internet came from overseas and was beyond the reach of the law. Mr. Justice Kennedy responded from the bench: "That's a weak argument. If the United States has a public policy, it can lead the way, and maybe the rest of the world will follow."

For those who are genuinely undecided whether there should or should not be laws banning hate speech on the internet, the charge of ineffectiveness has to be taken seriously. But the conclusion of ineffectiveness by free speech advocates should not be taken as the final word on the issue. This answer to the charge of ineffectiveness levied against hate speech laws, the answer that critics of hate speech laws are disingenuous, is not a complete answer to the charge. It is just a warning to be sceptical of the charge. But sceptical or not, what is our conclusion? Is it possible to have effective hate speech prohibition laws in conjunction with the internet?

A belief that the banning of hate speech on the internet is technologically impossible, that the only way to preserve the internet is to accept hate speech with it can easily lead us astray. It leads us to conclude that we should give up trying.

In a general sense, it is wrong to say that simply because something can be done, it should be done. It is also wrong to say that simply because something cannot be done, it is not worth trying. Cannot does not imply ought not.

I would argue that hate speech laws serve a value even if they are ineffective in stopping hate speech. The Criminal Code is a statement of Canadian values, the wrongs society considers most severe, the behaviour Canada condemns outright. Because hate speech is so wrong, so dangerous, we should stand against it in the most clear cut way we can, by prohibiting it in the Criminal Code.

The reality is that in human endeavours, nothing is certain. A statement of ineffectiveness is a statement about what the future will bring. However, the future in human affairs is never a passive event that just arrives. It is something that we create. If we do try to stop hate speech on the internet through every means available, including criminal prohibitions, we may or may not succeed. Of only one thing we can be sure. If we do not try, we are bound to fail. The only way we can hope to succeed is if we try. The evil of hate speech is so acute, so dangerous, that we must direct every effort to combat it. We cannot afford to be immobilized by concerns that our efforts may fail.

Hate speech on the internet is a problem. Laws prohibiting hate speech, even in this brave new technological world, remain a solution. However, laws, here as elsewhere, are not the only, or always the best solution. There is a dangerous tendency for hate speech combatants to rely on laws as the be all and end all. There is an all too ready belief that passing a law and then enforcing it resolves the problem the law was legislated to address.

However, the law is a clumsy brute instrument to achieve any social goal. The use of the law should be a last resort, when all else fails, not a first resort. Laws are not an end in themselves, but a means to an end, the modification of behavior. Penalizing misbehaviour, which is essentially what laws do, is not necessarily the most effective way of modifying behavior. When faced with hate speech, which incites to hate crimes, there are remedies besides prohibition of the speech that can prevent the crimes. The remedies

I have in mind here are fourteen in number: posting, computer games, withdrawal of internet services, withdrawal of telephone services, codes of conduct, approaching service providers, parental supervision, institutional supervision, access provider limitations, computer blocking programs, agreements with users, agreements with access providers, address prerequisites and an international convention.

Posting to combat Holocaust denial is best exemplified by the Nizkor project led by Ken McVay. The Anti-Defamation League of B'nai Brith Canada has a site more general in nature about combating anti-Semitism.

Holocaust denial has become the lead contemporary form of hate speech against Jews. It packages together in a new guise a number of traditional anti-Semitic myths including Jewish control of the media and Jewish greed. It undercuts the most powerful contemporary arguments against Nazism and racism. Because it is fraud disguised as scholarship, it is difficult for the uninformed and the disconnected to see through it.

While Holocaust information is not the only answer to Holocaust denial, it is surely one answer. Holocaust denial on the internet can be answered by Holocaust information on the internet. That is what the Nizkor project is all about. By posting information about the Holocaust on the internet, the Nizkor project allows anyone to find out all the lies, the evasions, the distortions that permeate Holocaust denial on the internet.

A variant of internet posting is the posting of anti-hate internet games. Choices, a Winnipeg social justice coalition, has developed one such game. The game is titled "Stop the Hatred." It poses a number of questions about racism and hatred. Anti-hate answers cause a serpent on the screen to disappear piece by piece. The Canadian Human Rights Commission has posted the game on the internet.

Another form of non-legal response is withdrawal of services. Access to the internet requires an internet access provider. Internet access providers are commercial enterprises which are free to offer, or to decline to offer their services to whomever they want, provided they are non-discriminatory. An internet access provider is under no obligation to provide internet access to any person who uses the internet to disseminate hatred. While there is a fundamental human right to freedom of speech, there is no fundamental human right to an internet access account. Internet access providers can withdraw their services from those who are abusing the services to spread hatred, and cut off the access hate promoters have to the internet.

The same can be said for the telephone. No one can post anything on the internet without a telephone. Whether telephone companies are state owned or privately owned, they are commercial enterprises offering services to customers. Telephone companies are free to offer, or to decline to offer, their services to whomever they want, provided they too are non-discriminatory. Phone companies can refuse to provide phone lines to those who would use the internet to propagate hatred. There is no fundamental human right to a phone line.

It is not just internet users that need access to the telephone. So do internet access providers. There has been a tendency for internet hate promoters to gravitate to amenable providers. For instance, the internet access provider Fairview Technology Centre in the Okanagan Valley town of Oliver B.C. had at one time at least twelve different hate groups using its services. Where internet access providers insist on providing internet access to hate promoters, despite requests that they stop, telephone companies can in turn deny services to the internet access providers.

Internet access providers and phone companies can and should have codes of conduct stating up front that they will deny their services to hate promoters. They should make it clear to everyone one of their customers that he/she is liable to be cut off if the service provided is abused to propagate hatred.

One common technique for combating hate speech is approaching those who would provide a platform for hatemongers and asking them to withdraw the platform. If a university student organization invites a Holocaust denier to speak on campus, the League for Human Rights of B'nai Brith Canada might ask the organization to withdraw the invitation, explaining to them who the speaker is and why the invitation is inappropriate. If a hotel rents a meeting room to a neo-Nazi extremist group, the League might ask the hotel management to cancel the room rental arrangement, so that the meeting cannot take place.

There is no reason why similar techniques could not be employed with phone companies and internet access providers. Hate speech combatants can approach phone companies and internet access providers to ask them to withdraw their services from hatemongers abusing the services to spread hatred. Anti-hate speech advocates can point out the nature of the hate speech contested, the damages of hate speech, why corporate responsibility to the community means that the services should be withdrawn.

Something like that happened with Fairview Technology Centre. Sol Littman of the Simon Wiesenthal Centre asked Fairview to stop providing internet access to hatemongers. Bernard Klatt, the owner of Fairview, stonewalled, but the local cable TV company where Fairview had its offices told Fairview to get out.

Another non-legal answer to hate in cyberspace is parental supervision. Parental supervision is more relevant to pornography than hate speech because it may be perfectly acceptable for adults to consume pornography but totally unacceptable for children to do so. No similar distinction can be made for hate speech. The harm of incitement to hatred is not age specific. Nonetheless, because children may be more susceptible to hate speech than adults, it makes sense to ask parents to restrict their children's access to it.

Parental supervision can be done in one of two ways. One is the plain old fashioned way of keeping an eye on what children do and stopping them from doing anything that would harm themselves, including connecting through the internet to hate speech sites. That sort of parental supervision is time consuming, and for teenagers, unrealistic.

The second is computer blocking programs, programs that would block access from home computers to hate sites. There are computer programs in existence which block access to pornographic sites, with such names as Net Nanny, SurfWatch, Cyberpatrol and Cybersitter. SurfWatch blocks sites and categories its researchers consider undesirable for children. Net Nanny provides a master list of sites and categories to block, but gives parents the choice of doing the blocking. Net Nanny also has a monitoring function, to allow parents to see where children have been on the internet.

Many people have access to the internet through institutions, whether it be their work place, a place of study or a place of recreation. These institutions can supervise the use of the internet access they provide.

Institutional supervision often relies on blocking. The University of Manitoba, as far back as 1992, blocked access to pornographic sites for anyone using its computer network system. University Vice President Terry Falconer said he would make the sites available for researchers doing serious work. The public libraries in Austin Texas and Oklahoma City have used filter programs to block access to sex sites. The Boston public library has installed filters on computers in its children's rooms but not on computers in its adult areas.

Access providers do not have to provide access to everything on the internet. They can provide access to only part of what is on the internet. For instance, iStar, an Ottawa based internet access provider, in July 1996 cut off its customers' connections to thirty five child pornography news groups.

Blocking programs are, however, clumsy devices. If they block only sites with specific addresses, they have to be updated almost daily as new sites proliferate. If they block sites by using keywords or categories, they have unforeseen consequences, blocking all sorts of material that would not be considered hate speech by anyone. As well, they block the computer, or the computer network, not the person. The person has only to go to another computer outside of the network with internet access or switch to another internet access provider to circumvent the blocking device.

Disputes about what is posted on the internet can potentially be resolved by arbitration rather than by laws. Internet users would agree not to post hate speech on the internet and agree to accept the rulings of an arbitrator, should anyone complain that a posting is hate speech. Complaints would be made through the internet about postings considered to be hate speech and virtual magistrates, themselves operating on the internet, would rule on whether the system operator should delete the challenged postings. The Cyberspace Law Institute of Washington D.C. has proposed such an on line arbitration mechanism.

However, for such a system to work those posting questionable material on the internet would have to agree not to post hate speech on the internet and agree further to abide by the arbitrator's decision on whether a contested posting is hate speech. There is unlikely to be any such agreement from hard core hate propagandists.

A variation on the proposal is to insert anti-hate speech stipulations into access contracts with subscribers. Access providers would be entitled to withdraw services from a subscriber who refused to accept the ruling of the virtual magistrate.

It may be easier to persuade access providers than to provide hate propagandists of the need to accept anti-hate speech stipulations. However, for such a stipulation to be effective, it is not enough for some access providers to accept it. All must accept it. Otherwise, a hate propagandist who has his/her subscription cancelled by one provider can simply sign on with another not part of the arbitration system.

The insertion by access providers of anti-hate speech stipulations in subscriber contracts can be made a prerequisite to access to the internet. No access provider can have access to the internet for itself and its customers without an internet address. The distribution of addresses is controlled globally by a cooperative named InterNIC and consisting of three members, Network Solutions Inc., the National Science Foundation, a United States government agency, and AT&T. InterNIC could insist that every access provider insert into its subscription contract a requirement that the internet not be used for hate speech and a commitment to accept the results of arbitration when there is a complaint that a posting is hate speech.

The notion of a global contract for the provision of a service has many precedents. It exists, for example, for airline passenger service. Global airline ticket terms were agreed internationally and are to be found in the Convention for the Unification of certain Rules Relating to International Carriage by Air signed at Warsaw 12th October 1929 and amended at the Hague on 28th September 1955.

While an international convention is not essential for there to be a uniform anti-hate speech stipulation in internet subscription contracts, it is desirable. It is unlikely that InterNIC would use its powers to control who connects to the internet to do anything related to internet content without international support. It would be arguably presumptuous for InterNIC, which is essentially American, to impose content controls on the internet without that international support. International action about the internet does not necessarily have to be restricted to agreement on enforcing anti-hate speech laws for hate on the internet. It can and should include agreement about uniform anti-hate speech terms in internet access subscription contracts.

As desirable as all these remedies are, the reality is that none of them may be available or effective. We may have to turn to prohibitory laws. These laws are essentially of three types, laws directed to software, laws directed to senders, and laws directed to conveyers.

Laws affecting software are perhaps the least technically problematic. Hate propaganda on a floppy disk or a CD-ROM is little different from hate propaganda in a book or a video. Floppy disks and CD-ROMs can be seized the same way that books or videos can be, and their distributors can be prosecuted the same way book or video distributors can be.

Internet technology is not an obstacle to prohibitions imposed directly on senders of hate through the internet, as long as the sender is physically within the jurisdiction of the law. A hate promoter in Canada operating through the internet is as much within the reach of Canadian law as a hate promoter putting pamphlets on windshields of cars. Traditional Canadian anti-speech law would be applied in the traditional way against such senders.

There is a case in progress now before a Canadian Human Rights Tribunal against Ernst Zundel for sending hate through the internet. The complaint was lodged by the City of Toronto's race relations committee and by Sabina Citron, a Holocaust survivor. The website for the contested material is in California. Zundel, however, is in Canada and is allegedly supplying the material that is being distributed through the internet. The Tribunal is to begin hearing evidence against Zundel on October 14, 1997.

The Canadian Human Rights Act provides that it is a discriminatory practice for a person to communicate telephonically repeatedly any matter that is likely to expose persons to hatred or contempt by reason of the fact that those persons are identifiable on the basis of a prohibited ground of discrimination. A Human Rights Tribunal has the power to order discriminatory practices to cease. Any Human Rights Tribunal order may be made an order of the Federal Court of Canada and is enforceable in the same manner as an order of that Court. A person who ignores a finding of a Canadian Human Rights Tribunal that an internet posting is hate speech and persists in the posting can be prosecuted for contempt of court.

While having a website outside of Canada with the purveyor in Canada is a twist, it is not a completely novel twist. In another case, a Canadian using the US phone system to communicate hate speech was found to violate the Canadian Human Rights Act. A Canadian Human Rights Tribunal ordered Canadian Liberty Net, a purveyor of taped telephonic messages alleged to be inciting hatred, to cease communicating the messages. The messages could be heard by dialing a British Columbia telephone number, registered in the name of Tony McAleer. The Canadian Liberty Net attempted to get round the prohibition by communicating its taped messages from an American telephone number in Bellingham, Washington. The Washington phone number was given out on a taped message from the British Columbia phone number. The Federal Court of Appeal found Canadian Liberty Net in contempt of court for the American messages. The Court sentenced McAleer to two days in jail and $2,500 fine. The Canadian Liberty Net got a $5,000 fine.

Internet sites take two forms. They are either interactive, where anyone with access to the internet can post materials to the site for all to see. Or they are controlled by the host, who determines what will be on the site for others to see. Interactive sites, newsgroups, are less problematic than host controlled sites. Hate speech news groups tend to be overwhelmed by those condemning hate speech or attempting to disprove its malicious claims. Ken McVay has argued that these interactive sites should not be banned because the discussion that is carried on in them allows the naive to see how the claims of hatemongers can be refuted, how the fraud is perpetrated.

Hate speech host controlled sites are a different matter. Their refutation can be found only in other host controlled sites or a newsgroup. A gullible internet user may connect to a hate speech host controlled site without ever accessing its refutation.

The United States Supreme Court, when striking down the 1996 Communications Decency Act as unconstitutional because of its overbreadth, suggested more narrowly tailored legislation that might survive constitutional challenge. One suggestion was regulating some portions of the Internet such as commercial Web sites differently from others, such as chat rooms.

Where the host is outside of Canada, and the persons providing the material to the host are also outside Canada, then the law is severely limited in its reach. Germany has legislated against foreign internet material by penalizing those in Germany who knowingly provide a connection overseas to content that is illegal in Germany, where it is "technically possible and reasonable" to prevent it. The big question is whether prevention is technically possible and reasonable.

Some forms of prevention are technically possible and reasonable. For instance, someone with an internet site in Canada can link the Canadian site with a hate speech site abroad. The link is made knowingly. Removing the link is both technically possible and reasonable. A law directed to preventing connection with foreign internet hate speech material can easily get at that sort of link.

Online services such as America On-Line or Compuserve or Prodigy combine information services with access to the internet. These online services can control the information they themselves provide. However, the only way they or internet access providers can cut off access to objectionable material on the internet is to use blocking devices with all the limitations described earlier. If specific sites are blocked, new sites can spring up to take their place. Free speech absolutists make a point of doing just that, producing mirror sites to replicate blocked sites. If words or word groups are blocked, all sorts of unintended material is interrupted.

Penalizing global on line services has had an anti-competitive effect. In order to comply with German law, CompuServe in December 1995 cut off access to about 200 sites. Most CompuServe content going to customers everywhere came from computers in the United States in Ohio. At the time, CompuServe had no way of cutting off the material to Germany alone. CompuServe's four million customers around the world fell under the sway of the German ban. Customers outside of Germany of other online services or access providers had no such limitations on access to the internet.

The most effective ban on internet hate speech would be a global ban. There are already international standards obligating states to prohibit hate speech, in the International Covenant on Civil and Political Rights and the International Convention on the Elimination of All Forms of Racial Discrimination. The United States, from which over 60% of the internet sites originate, has signed and ratified the International Covenant on Civil and Political Rights.

An international convention requiring states to ban hate speech on the internet should not be too hard to achieve, since it would be only a specific application of an already accepted international standard. The Government of Canada has suggested such a convention. The Honourable Herb Gray, when he was Solicitor General, said: "One solution (to hate speech on the internet) might involve some type of international convention or agreement where countries would come together to control the use of the internet."

Because hate speech on the internet is a global problem, it is not only necessary but fitting that the solution be global in scope. Because propagation of hatred is a violation of human rights, promotion of respect for human rights should be the work of all humanity. Lest we forget, the internet reminds us that human rights are universal. The internet makes us undertake the work of human rights at the level we should be undertaking it, on the scale of the planet.

QUESTIONS

1. How does Matas define hate speech on the Internet, and why does he feel that it should be controlled, while acknowledging at the same time how important the Internet is as a tool of democracy and the struggle for freedom? Is his overall argument for the need to control Internet "free speech" convincing to you and consistent with his other arguments about the need for the Internet to carry the message of freedom? Why or why not? What is different about the Internet that makes its control so necessary?

2. Although a strong argument can be made by free-speech advocates that Internet hate-speech-control laws are "ineffective," why does Matas maintain that a) it doesn't matter if they are in some cases ineffectual and b) they could work, in many cases? What evidence or logic does he provide for his position? What main types of regulation does he propose?

3. What particular laws, organizations, and forms of arbitration would help control Internet hate speech globally? Do you think that such international controls would be effective and/or desirable, considering different standards and beliefs among various world communities?

Sandy Starr

"Why We Need Free Speech Online"

Sandy Starr is public relations officer and technology editor at the British current affairs publication Spiked Online. *He has done book reviews for the* Times Literary Supplement *and has written film and TV reviews and commentary for* The Sun. *He writes, speaks, and consults on science, technology, and culture for a wide range of publications and organizations. His essays and chapters have been published in* The Media Freedom Internet Cookbook *(2004),* From Quill to Cursor: Freedom of the Media in the Digital Era *(2003), and* The Internet: Brave New World? *(2002). His recent articles for* Spiked *include the following (2005), in which Starr argues against the effort to provide strict control internationally over online hate speech.*

The rush to find new legislation outlawing "hate speech" on the internet has become a Europe-wide project. The "Brussels Declaration" issued by the Organization for Security and Cooperation in Europe (OSCE)—which came out of the proceedings of its Conference on Tolerance and the Fight against Racism, Xenophobia and Discrimination, in which I participated in Brussels in September 2004—commits OSCE member states to "combat hate crimes, which can be fuelled by racist, xenophobic and anti-Semitic propaganda in the media and on the internet."

The chair of the European Network Against Racism, a prominent network of non-governmental organizations, argued at the same Brussels conference that "any effective instrument to fight racism" in law should criminalize "incitement to racial violence and hatred," "public insults on the ground of race," "the condoning of crimes of genocide, crimes against humanity and war crimes," "the denial or trivialization of the Holocaust," "public dissemination of racist or xenophobic material," and "directing, supporting or participating in the activities of a racist or xenophobic group." Additionally, "racist motivation in common crimes should be considered an aggravating circumstance"—as it already is in UK law.

As the idea that "hate speech" is a growing problem in need of official regulation and censorship has reached prominence across Europe, it is not surprising that the internet has emerged as a particular focus for concern. The internet poses a challenge to older forms of regulation and makes a nonsense of boundaries between jurisdictions. There have been calls for the authorities to close down websites such as Redwatch and Noncewatch—both of which are linked to the fascist organization Combat 18, and which contain hit lists of supposed Marxists and pedophiles respectively. More humorous websites, such as I Hate Hawick (now defunct)—which consisted largely of strongly-worded invective against the Scottish town of Hawick and its rugby fans—have also come under fire for preaching hate (which is ironic, given that one of the things the website took Hawick's residents to task for was their alleged racism).

But what does it mean, to attempt to outlaw "hate speech" from the internet? This discussion has disturbing implications, both for the future of the internet and society's approach to free speech more broadly.

Regulating Hate Speech on the Internet

The internet continues to be perceived as a place of unregulated and unregulable anarchy. But this impression is becoming less and less accurate, as governments seek to monitor and rein in our online activities. Initiatives to combat online hate speech threaten to neuter the internet's most progressive attribute—the fact that anyone, anywhere, who has a computer and a connection, can express themselves freely on it. In the UK, the regulator the Internet Watch Foundation (IWF) advises that if you "see racist content on the internet," then "the IWF and police will work in partnership with the hosting service provider to remove the content as soon as possible."

The presumption here is clearly in favor of censorship—the IWF adds that "if you are unsure as to whether the content is legal or not, be on the safe side and report it." Not only are the authorities increasingly seeking out and censoring internet content that they disapprove of, but those sensitive souls who are most easily offended are being enlisted in this process, and given a veto over what the rest of us can peruse online.

The Council of Europe's Additional Protocol to the Convention On Cybercrime, which seeks to prohibit "racist and xenophobic material" on the internet, defines such material as "any written material, any image or any other representation of ideas or theories, which advocates, promotes or incites hatred, discrimination or violence, against any individual or group of individuals, based on race, color, descent or national or ethnic origin, as well as religion if used as a pretext for any of these factors." Can we presume that online versions of the Bible and the Koran will be the first things to go, under this regime? Certainly, there are countless artistic and documentary works that could fall afoul of such all-encompassing regulation.

In accordance with the commonly stated aim of hate speech regulation, to avert the threat of fascism, the Additional Protocol also seeks to outlaw the "denial, gross minimization, approval or justification of genocide or crimes against humanity." According to the Council of Europe, "the drafters considered it necessary not to limit the scope of this provision only to the crimes committed by the Nazi regime during the Second World War and established as such by the Nuremberg Tribunal, but also to genocides and crimes against humanity established by other international courts set up since 1945 by relevant international legal instruments."

This is an instance in which the proponents of hate speech regulation, while ostensibly guarding against the specter of totalitarianism, are acting in a disconcertingly authoritarian manner themselves. Holocaust denial is one thing—debate over the scale and causes of later atrocities, such as those in the Sudan or the former Yugoslavia, and whether it is right to describe such conflicts in terms of genocide, is another, and there is an ongoing and legitimate debate about these issues. Yet the European authorities stand to gain new powers that will entitle them to impose upon us their definitive account of recent history, which we must accept as true on pain of prosecution.

The restrictions on free speech contained in the Additional Protocol could have been even more severe than they currently are. Apparently, "the committee drafting the Convention discussed the possibility of including other content-related offences," but "was not in a position to reach consensus on the criminalization of such conduct." Still, the Additional Protocol as it stands is a significant impediment to free speech, and an impediment to the process of contesting bigoted opinions in open debate.

As one of the Additional Protocol's more acerbic critics remarks: "Criminalizing certain forms of speech is scientifically proven to eliminate the underlying sentiment. Really, I read that on a match cover." Proof, perhaps, that you cannot believe everything that you read in the bar. The idea that censorship leads people to speak and act in the correct way is a highly dubious and contested concept. What is certainly true, though, is that once free speech is limited it ceases to be free.

Once Free Speech is Limited, It Ceases to be Free

Those who argue for the regulation of hate speech often claim that they support the principle of free speech, but that there is some kind of distinction between standing up for free speech as it has traditionally been understood, and allowing people to express hateful ideas. So when he proposed to introduce an offence of incitement to religious hatred into British law, former UK home secretary David Blunkett insisted that "people's rights to debate matters of religion and proselytise would be protected, but we cannot allow people to use religious differences to create hate".

Divvying up the principle of free speech in this way, so that especially abhorrent ideas are somehow disqualified from its protection, is a dubious exercise. After all, it's not as though free speech contains within it some sort of prescription as to what the content of that speech will consist of. Any such prescription would be contrary to the essential meaning of the word "free." The Additional Protocol to the Convention On Cybercrime invokes "the need to ensure a proper balance between freedom of expression and an effective fight against acts of a racist and xenophobic nature." But this notion of "balance" is questionable. Unless we're free to say what we believe, to experience and express whatever emotion we like (including hate), and to hate whomever we choose, then how can we be said to be free at all?

According to the European human rights tradition, rights often have to be balanced with one another and with corresponding responsibilities. Even the most prominent advocates of human rights agree that this can be a tricky exercise. At an event on freedom of expression and the internet, organized by the United Nations Educational, Scientific and Cultural Organization (UNESCO) at its Paris headquarters in February 2005, I found myself speaking alongside the barrister, sometime judge and formidable human rights theorist Geoffrey Robertson. I put it to him that the exceptions to freedom of expression that he was endorsing, in instances of incitement to racial hatred or genocide, amounted to an indefensible restriction on free speech. "Human rights law is a bugger," he replied ruefully.

The American constitutional model, however, is far less ambiguous about the need to uphold certain freedoms, freedom of speech among them, without compromise. The fact that the degree of free speech enjoyed on the internet over the past decade has, at least initially, conformed more to American standards than to European standards, has been a cause of exasperation for some. Technology commentator Bill Thompson, for instance, disparages "the USA, where any sensible discussion is crippled by the Constitution and the continued attempts to decide how many Founding Fathers can stand on the head of a pin," and where "they decide to run their part of the net according to the principles laid down 250 years ago by a bunch of renegade merchants and rebellious slave owners."

Free speech has even been subject to certain exceptions in the USA, most notably according to the principle of "clear and present danger." This exception has been used as a justification for regulating hate speech, but is in fact a very specific and narrow exception, and as originally conceived does not support the idea of hate speech at all. "Clear and present danger" was conceived by the Supreme Court Justice Oliver Wendell Holmes Jr., with reference to those exceptional circumstances where rational individuals can be said to be compelled to act in a certain way. In Holmes Jr.'s classic example—"a man falsely shouting fire in a theatre and causing a panic"— rational individuals are compelled to act by immediate fear for their safety.

In the vast majority of instances, however—including incitement to commit a hateful act—no such immediate fear exists. Rather, there is an opportunity for the individual to assess the words that they hear, and to decide whether or not to act upon them. It is therefore the individual who bears responsibility for his actions, and not some third party who incited that individual to behave in a particular way. While it's understandably disconcerting, to take one example, for Nick Ryan—who writes books and makes programs exposing the far right—to encounter a message board posting about him saying "someone should knife this cunt," such words are not in themselves a legitimate pretext for censoring internet content.

The issue is not about the right of a handful of individuals to peddle hateful content. Who really cares if they have a voice or not? But what the concern about online hate speech reveals is the level of official contempt for users of the internet. There is a fear that people reading hateful content on their computer will unwittingly take those ideas on board, and be incited to commit violent acts as a result. Therefore, it is assumed that the public needs protection from hateful ideas online in much the same way that children are protected from sites containing pornography and violence. But adult internet users are not children, and nor are they stupid or so easily influenced.

We know that the internet is host to a multitude of ideas: some good, some bad, and some that are simply unworthy of our attention. To assume that internet users are incapable of filtering these ideas for themselves shows a high level of disdain for all of us, as though we are all potentially violent criminals, who only need to view a website to make us act on our base instincts. To counter this view, we need to take a step back from the easy assumptions that the authorities make about censoring hate speech, and understand why these assumptions are wrong.

Distinguishing Speech from Action, and Prejudice from Emotion

The British academic David Miller, an advocate of hate crime legislation, complains that "advocates of free speech tend to assume that speech can be clearly separated from action." But outside of the obscurer reaches of academic postmodernism, one would be hard-pressed to dispute that there is a distinction between what people say and think on the one hand, and what they do on the other.

Certainly, it becomes difficult, in the absence of this basic distinction, to sustain an equitable system of law. If our actions are not distinct from our words and our thoughts, then there ceases to be a basis upon which we can be held responsible for those actions. Once speech and action are confused, then we can always pass the buck for our actions, no matter how grievous they are—an excuse commonly known as "the Devil made me do it."

It is not words in themselves that make things happen, but the estimation in which we hold those words. And if ideas that we disagree with are held in high estimation by others, then we're not going to remedy this situation by trying to prevent those ideas from being expressed. Rather, the only legitimate way we can tackle support for abhorrent ideas, is to seek to persuade the public of our own point of view, through political debate. When the authorities start resorting to hate speech regulation, in order to suppress ideas that they object to, this is an indication that the state of political debate is far from healthy.

As well as distinguishing between speech and action, when assessing the validity of hate speech as a regulatory category, it is also useful to make a distinction between forms of prejudice such as racism, and generic emotions. Whereas racism is a prejudice that deserves to be contested, hatred is not objectionable in itself. Hatred is merely an emotion, and it can be an entirely legitimate and appropriate emotion at that.

When the Council of Europe sets out to counter "hatred," with its Additional Protocol to the Convention On Cybercrime, it uses the word to mean "intense dislike or enmity." But are right-thinking people not entitled to feel "intense dislike or enmity"? Hate is something that most of us experience at one time or another, and is as necessary and valid an emotion as love. Even David Blunkett, the principal architect of initiatives against hate speech and hate crimes in the UK, has admitted that when he heard that the notorious serial killer Harold Shipman had committed suicide in prison, his first reaction was: "Is it too early to open a bottle?" Could he even say that, under a regime where hate speech was outlawed?

Hate speech regulation is often posited as a measure that will prevent society from succumbing to totalitarian ideologies, such as fascism. Ironically, however, the idea that we might regulate speech and prosecute crimes according to the emotions we ascribe to them, is one of the most totalitarian ideas imaginable.

Most countries already have laws that prohibit intimidation, assault, and damage to property. By creating the special categories of "hate speech" and "hate crime" to supplement these offences, and presuming to judge people's motivations for action rather than their actions alone, we come worryingly close to establishing in law what the author George Orwell called "thoughtcrime."

In Orwell's classic novel *Nineteen Eighty-Four*, thoughtcrime is the crime of thinking criminal thoughts, "the essential crime that contained all others in itself." Hatred is permitted, indeed is mandatory, in Orwell's dystopia, so long as it is directed against enemies of the state. But any heretical thought brings with it the prospect of grave punishment. Orwell demonstrates how, by policing language and by forcing people to carefully consider every aspect of their behavior, orthodoxy can be sustained and heresy ruthlessly suppressed.

The human instinct to question received wisdom and resist restrictions upon thought is, ultimately and thankfully, irrepressible. But inasmuch as this instinct can be repressed, the authorities must first encourage in the populace a form of willful ignorance that Orwell calls "crimestop"—in *Nineteen Eighty-Four*, the principal means of preventing oneself from committing thougtcrime. In Orwell's words: "Crimestop means the faculty of stopping short, as though by instinct, at the threshold of any dangerous thought. It includes the power of not grasping analogies, of failing to perceive logical errors, of misunderstanding the simplest arguments . . . and of being bored or repelled by any train of thought which is capable of leading in a heretical direction. Crimestop, in short, means protective stupidity."

Labeling speech that we disagree with "hate speech," and seeking to prohibit it instead of taking up the challenge of disputing it, points to a world in which we resort to "protective stupidity" to prevent the spread of objectionable ideas. Not only is this inimical to freedom, but it gives objectionable ideas a credibility that they often don't deserve, by entitling them to assume the righteous attitude of challenging an authoritarian status quo. This is particularly stark when applied to the internet—where so many ideas float around, and many of these deserve no credibility at all.

Putting the Internet into Perspective

The internet lends itself to lazy and hysterical thinking about social problems. Because of the enormous diversity of material available on it, people with a particular axe to grind can simply log on and discover whatever truths about society they wish to. Online, one's perspective on society is distorted. When there are so few obstacles to setting up a website, or posting on a message board, all voices appear equal. The internet is a distorted reflection of society, where minority and extreme opinion are indistinguishable from the mainstream. Methodological rigor is needed, if any useful insights into society are to be drawn from what one finds online. Such rigor is often lacking in discussions of online hate speech.

For example, the academic Tara McPherson has written about the problem of deep-South redneck websites—what she calls "the many outposts of Dixie in cyberspace." As one reads through the examples she provides of neo-Confederate eccentrics, one could be forgiven for believing that "The South Will Rise Again," as the flags and bumper stickers put it. But by that token, the world must also be under dire threat from pedophiles, Satanists, and every other crackpot to whom the internet provides a free platform.

"How could we narrate other versions of Southern history and place that are not bleached to a blinding whiteness?," asks McPherson, as though digital Dixie were a major social problem. In its present form, the internet inevitably appears to privilege the expression of marginal views, by making it so easy to express them. But the mere fact of an idea being represented online does not grant that idea any great social consequence.

Of course, the internet has made it easier for like-minded individuals on the margins to communicate and collaborate. Mark Potok, editor of the Southern Poverty Law Center's Intelligence Report—which "monitors hate groups and extremist activities"—has a point when he says: "In the 1970s and 80s the average white supremacist was isolated, shaking his fist at the sky in his front room. The net changed that." French minister of foreign affairs Michel Barnier makes a similar point more forcefully, when he says: "The internet has had a seductive influence on networks of intolerance. It has placed at their disposal its formidable power of amplification, diffusion and connection."

But to perceive this "power of amplification, diffusion and connection" as a momentous problem is to ignore its corollary—the fact that the internet also enables the rest of us to communicate and collaborate, to more positive ends. The principle of free speech benefits us all, from the mainstream to the margins, and invites us to make the case for what we see as the truth. New technologies that make it easier to communicate benefit us all in the same way, and we should concentrate on exploiting them as a platform for our beliefs, rather than trying to withdraw them as a platform for other people's beliefs.

We should always keep our wits about us, when confronted with supposed evidence that online hate speech is a massive problem. A much-cited survey

SANDY STARR

314

by the web and email filtering company SurfControl concludes that there was a 26 percent increase in "websites promoting hate against Americans, Muslims, Jews, homosexuals and African-Americans, as well as graphic violence" between January and May 2004, "nearly surpassing the growth in all of 2003." But it is far from clear how such precise quantitative statistics can be derived from subjective descriptions of the content of websites, and from a subjective emotional category like "hate."

SurfControl's survey unwittingly illustrates how any old piece of anecdotal evidence can be used to stir up a panic over internet content, claiming: "Existing sites that were already being monitored by SurfControl have expanded in shocking or curious ways. Some sites carry graphic photos of dead and mutilated human beings." If SurfControl had got in touch with me a few years ago, I could easily have found a few photos of dead and mutilated human beings on the internet for them. Maybe then, they would have tried to start the same panic a few years earlier? Or do they wheel out the same alarmist claims every year?

Certainly, it's possible to put a completely opposite spin on the amount of hate speech that exists on the internet. For example, Karin Spaink, chair of the privacy and digital rights organization Bits of Freedom, concludes that "slightly over 0.015 per cent of all web pages contain hate speech or something similar"—a far less frightening assessment.

It's also inaccurate to suggest that the kind of internet content that gets labeled as hate speech goes unchallenged. When it transpired that the anti-Semitic website Jew Watch ranked highest in the search engine Google's results for the search term "Jew," a Remove Jew Watch campaign was established, to demand that Google remove the offending website from its listings. Fortunately for the principle of free speech, Google did not capitulate to this particular demand—even though in other instances, the search engine has been guilty of purging its results, at the behest of governments and other concerned parties.

Forced to act on its own initiative, Remove Jew Watch successfully used Googlebombing—creating and managing web links in order to trick Google's search algorithms into associating particular search terms with particular results—to knock Jew Watch off the top spot. Such technical "no platform" campaigns are at least preferable to Google (further) compromising its ranking criteria. But how much better would have been a decision that Jew Watch was beneath contempt and should simply be ignored. Not every crank and extremist warrants serious attention, even if they do occasionally manage to spoof search engine rankings.

According to the *Additional Protocol to the Convention On Cybercrime*, "national and international law need to provide adequate legal responses to propaganda of a racist and xenophobic nature committed through computer systems." But legal responses are entirely inadequate for this purpose. If anything, legal responses to hateful opinions inadvertently bolster them, by removing them from public scrutiny and debate, and giving their proponents cause to pose as the champions of free speech online.

"Hate speech" is not a useful way of categorizing ideas that we find objectionable. Just about the only thing that the category does usefully convey is the attitude of policymakers, regulators and campaigners towards people who use the internet. We are accorded the status of young children, uneducated, excitable and easily-led, who need a kind of parental control system on the internet to prevent us from accessing inappropriate content. The reaction to a few cranks posting their odious thoughts online is to limit all internet users" freedom about what they write and read. In seeking to restrict a communications medium in this way, it is the regulators who really hate speech.

QUESTIONS

1. What is problematic, according to Starr, about the European Council's definition of "racist and xenophobic material"? How does the method of discovering and reporting such material also involve censorship and free-speech issues?
2. According to Starr, how would the new anti-hate speech rules limit our ability to evaluate current historical events and their gravity? How would such rules as the Council proposes upset the "balance of rights" that is believed to be important in order to protect free expression?
3. Do you agree with Starr that there is not enough hate speech and violent imagery—"racist and xenophobic material"—on the Internet for us to be unduly concerned? Compare his attitudes toward such material with those of Matas concerning anti-Semitism on the Internet.

CHAPTER 7

Blaming the Media for Youth Violence

Introduction

This chapter follows logically from the debates in the previous chapter over free speech and hate speech. The classical argument about the impact of media violence on actual youth violence is in conflict with free-speech guarantees, which have made it difficult—assuming that it is important to do so—to ban violent comic books, video games, films, and CDs. Various rating systems and labeling formats have been proposed over the years, the most stringent of which may have been the "comic-book code," enacted in the mid-1950s, that made it essentially illegal to produce or market many of the most popular comic books of the day. Essayists such as Sissela Bok, Soledad Escobar-Chaves, and Craig A. Anderson believe that there are causal relationships between the aggressive negative behavior in the unrealistic violence presented in the media and actual violence on the part of young people.

On the other hand, some authors such as Mike Males dispute the causal connection between violence and violent media, citing other social phenomena with stronger causal links to violent behavior in youth, such as violence and alcoholism in the home, social alienation, and lack of attention in schools to student's psychological needs. Critics such as Jonathan L. Freedman have also cited poor use of experimental data in case studies that attempt to show relationships between media violence and violent acting out.

Instead of trying to establish a direct causal behavior between media violence and actual antisocial violence, Bryan Cowlishaw discusses the disturbing role of media violence in military-produced video games that conceal the real consequences of violent warfare, making it more likely that such games will have their desired effect of heightening military recruitment. In contrast, Professor Henry Jenkins, speaking in response to the notorious Columbine killings, disputes the fact that young people act in direct imitation of the media violence they witness; rather, he believes they create their own imaginary worlds based on a variety of media input, and when they do act out violently, it is often a response more to emotional neglect than a direct response to the media. Jenkins proposes several solutions to the problems many youth face that could lead them to violence in rare cases.

In our final "Differing Perspectives" debate, media critics and professors George Gerbner and Todd Gitlin examine the pros and cons of trying to control television violence through ratings and the G-chip, perceiving that the deeper causes of media violence are linked to the commercial nature of the media itself and the ceaseless struggle for ratings.

SISSELA BOK

"Aggression: The Impact of Media Violence"

Sissela Bok has made a major contribution to the contemporary debate over values and ethical issues in society. Born in Sweden, she received her Ph.D. in philosophy from Harvard University in 1970 and is currently a Distinguished Fellow at the Harvard Center for Population and Development Studies. Bok's writings include Secrets: On the Ethics of Concealment and Revelation *(1983),* Common Values *(1995), and* Mayhem: Violence as Public Entertainment *(1998), which contains the following argument on the causal relationship between media violence and aggressive behavior in young people.*

Even if media violence were linked to no other debilitating effects, it would remain at the center of public debate so long as the widespread belief persists that it glamorizes aggressive conduct, removes inhibitions toward such conduct, arouses viewers, and invites imitation. It is only natural that the links of media violence to aggression should be of special concern to families and communities. Whereas increased fear, desensitization, and appetite primarily affect the viewers themselves, aggression directly injures others and represents a more clearcut violation of standards of behavior. From the point of view of public policy, therefore, curbing aggression has priority over alleviating subtler psychological and moral damage.

Public concern about a possible link between media violence and societal violence has further intensified in the past decade, as violent crime reached a peak in the early 1990s, yet has shown no sign of downturn, even after crime rates began dropping in 1992. Media coverage of violence, far from declining, has escalated since then, devoting ever more attention to celebrity homicides and copycat crimes. The latter, explicitly modeled on videos or films and sometimes carried out with meticulous fidelity to detail, are never more relentlessly covered in the media than when they are committed by children and adolescents. Undocumented claims that violent copycat crimes are mounting in number contribute further to the ominous sense of threat that these crimes generate. Their dramatic nature drains away the public's attention from other, more mundane forms of aggression that are much more commonplace, and from . . . other . . . harmful effects of media violence.

Media analyst Ken Auletta reports that, in 1992, a mother in France sued the head of a state TV channel that carried the American series *MacGyver*, claiming that her son was accidentally injured as a result of having copied MacGyver's recipe for making a bomb. At the time, Auletta predicted that similar lawsuits were bound to become a weapon against media violence in America's litigious culture. By 1996, novelist John Grisham had sparked a debate about director Oliver Stone's film *Natural Born Killers*, which is reputedly linked to more copycat assaults and murders than any other movie to date. Grisham wrote in protest against the film after learning that a friend of his, Bill Savage, had been killed by nineteen-year-old Sarah Edmondson and her boyfriend Benjamin Darras, eighteen: after repeated viewings of Stone's film on video, the two had gone on a killing spree with the film's murderous, gleeful heroes expressly in mind. Characterizing the film as "a horrific movie that glamorized casual mayhem and bloodlust," Grisham proposed legal action:

> *Think of a film as a product, something created and brought to market, not too dissimilar from breast implants. Though the law has yet to declare movies to be products, it is only a small step away.*

> *If something goes wrong with the product, either by design or defect, and injury ensues, then its makers are held responsible. . . . It will take only one large verdict against the like of Oliver Stone, and his production company, and perhaps the screenwriter, and the studio itself, and then the party will be over. The verdict will come from the heartland, far away from Southern California, in some small courtroom with no cameras. A jury will finally say enough is enough; that the demons placed in Sarah Edmondson's mind were not solely of her own making.*

As a producer of books made into lucrative movies—themselves hardly devoid of violence—and as a veteran of contract negotiations within the entertainment industry, Grisham may have become accustomed to thinking of films in industry terms as "products." As a seasoned courtroom lawyer, he may have found the analogy between such products and breast implants useful for invoking product liability to pin personal responsibility on movie producers and directors for the lethal consequences that their work might help unleash.

Oliver Stone retorted that Grisham was drawing "upon the superstition about the magical power of pictures to conjure up the undead spectre of censorship." In dismissing concerns about the "magical power of pictures" as merely superstitious, Stone sidestepped the larger question of responsibility fully as much as Grisham had sidestepped that of causation when he attributed liability to filmmakers for anything that "goes wrong" with their products so that "injury ensues."

Because aggression is the most prominent effect associated with media violence in the public's mind, it is natural that it should also remain the primary focus of scholars in the field. The "aggressor effect" has been studied both to identify the short-term, immediate impact on viewers after exposure to TV violence, and the long-term influences. . . . There is near-unanimity by now among investigators that exposure to media violence contributes to lowering barriers to aggression among some viewers. This lowering of barriers may be assisted by the failure of empathy that comes with growing desensitization, and intensified to the extent that viewers develop an appetite for violence—something that may lead to still greater desire for violent programs and, in turn, even greater desensitization.

When it comes to viewing violent pornography, levels of aggression toward women have been shown to go up among male subjects who view sexualized violence against women. "In explicit depictions of sexual violence," a report by the American Psychological Association's

Commission on Youth and Violence concludes after surveying available research data, "it is the message about violence more than the sexual nature of the materials that appears to affect the attitudes of adolescents about rape and violence toward women." Psychologist Edward Donnerstein and colleagues have shown that if investigators tell subjects that aggression is legitimate, then show them violent pornography, their aggression toward women increases. In slasher films, the speed and ease with which "one's feelings can be transformed from sensuality into viciousness may surprise even those quite conversant with the links between sexual and violent urges."

Viewers who become accustomed to seeing violence as an acceptable, common, attractive way of dealing with problems find it easier to identify with aggressors and to suppress any sense of pity or respect for victims of violence. Media violence has been found to have stronger effects of this kind when carried out by heroic, impressive, or otherwise exciting figures, especially when they are shown as invulnerable and are rewarded or not punished for what they do. The same is true when the violence is shown as justifiable, when viewers identify with the aggressors rather than with their victims, when violence is routinely resorted to, and when the programs have links to how viewers perceive their own environment.

While the consensus that such influences exist grows among investigators as research accumulates, there is no consensus whatsoever about the size of the correlations involved. Most investigators agree that it will always be difficult to disentangle the precise effects of exposure to media violence from the many other factors contributing to societal violence. No reputable scholar accepts the view expressed by 21 percent of the American public in 1995, blaming television more than any other factor for teenage violence. Such tentative estimates as have been made suggest that the media account for between 5 and 15 percent of societal violence. Even these estimates are rarely specific enough to indicate whether what is at issue is all violent crime, or such crimes along with bullying and aggression more generally.

One frequently cited investigator proposes a dramatically higher and more specific estimate than others. Psychiatrist Brandon S. Centerwall has concluded from large-scale epidemiological studies of "white homicide" in the United States, Canada, and South Africa in the period from 1945 to 1974, that it escalated in these societies within ten to fifteen years of the introduction of television, and that one can therefore deduce that television has brought a doubling of violent societal crime:

> *Of course, there are many factors other than television that influence the amount of violent crime. Every violent act is the result of a variety of forces coming together—poverty, crime, alcohol and drug abuse, stress—of which childhood TV exposure is just one. Nevertheless, the evidence indicates that if hypothetically, television technology had never been developed, there would today be 10,000 fewer homicides each year in the United States, 70,000 fewer rapes, and 700,000 fewer injurious assaults. Violent crime would be half of what it now is.*

Centerwall's study, published in 1989, includes controls for such variables as firearm possession and economic growth. But his conclusions have been criticized for not taking into account other factors, such as population changes during the time period studied, that might also play a role in changing crime rates. Shifts in policy and length of prison terms clearly affect these levels as well. By now, the decline in levels of violent crime in the United States since Centerwall's study was conducted, even though television viewing did not decline ten to fifteen years before, does not square with his extrapolations. As for "white homicide" in South Africa under apartheid, each year brings more severe challenges to official statistics from that period.

Even the lower estimates, however, of around 5 to 10 percent of violence as correlated with television exposure, point to substantial numbers of violent crimes in a population as large as America's. But if such estimates are to be used in discussions of policy decisions, more research will be needed to distinguish between the effects of television in general and those of particular types of violent programming, and to indicate specifically what sorts of images increase the aggressor effect and by what means; and throughout to be clearer about the nature of the aggressive acts studied.

Media representatives naturally request proof of such effects before they are asked to undertake substantial changes in programming. In considering possible remedies for a problem, inquiring into the reasons for claims about risks is entirely appropriate. It is clearly valid to scrutinize the research designs, sampling methods, and possible biases of studies supporting such claims, and to ask about the reasoning leading from particular research findings to conclusions. But to ask for some demonstrable pinpointing of just when and how exposure to media violence affects levels of aggression sets a dangerously high threshold for establishing risk factors.

We may never be able to trace, retrospectively, the specific set of television programs that contributed to a particular person's aggressive conduct. The same is true when it comes to the links between tobacco smoking and cancer, between drunk driving and automobile accidents, and many other risk factors presenting public health hazards. Only recently have scientists identified the specific channels through which tobacco generates its carcinogenic effects. Both precise causative mechanisms and documented occurrences in individuals remain elusive. Too often, media representatives formulate their requests in what appear to be strictly polemical terms, raising dismissive questions familiar from debates over the effects of tobacco: "How can anyone definitively pinpoint the link between media violence and acts of real-life violence? If not, how can we know if exposure to media violence constitutes a risk factor in the first place?"

Yet the difficulty in carrying out such pinpointing has not stood in the way of discussing and promoting efforts to curtail cigarette smoking and drunk driving. It is not clear, therefore, why a similar difficulty should block such efforts when it comes to media violence. The perspective of "probabilistic causation" . . . is crucial to public debate about the risk factors in media violence. The television industry has already been persuaded to curtail the glamorization of smoking and drunk driving on its programs, despite the lack of conclusive documentation of the correlation between TV viewing and higher incidence of such conduct. Why should the industry not take analogous precautions with respect to violent programming?

Americans have special reasons to inquire into the causes of societal violence. While we are in no sense uniquely violent, we need to ask about all possible reasons why our levels of violent crime are higher than in all other stable industrialized democracies. Our homicide rate would be higher still if we did not imprison more of our citizens than any society in the world, and if emergency medical care had not improved so greatly in recent decades that a larger proportion of shooting victims survive than in the past. Even so, we have seen an unprecedented rise not only in child and adolescent violence, but in levels of rape, child abuse, domestic violence, and every other form of assault.

Although America's homicide rate has declined in the 1990s, the rates for suicide, rape, and murder involving children and adolescents in many regions have too rarely followed suit. For Americans aged fifteen to thirty-five years, homicide is the second leading cause of death, and for young African Americans, fifteen to twenty-four years, it is *the* leading cause of death. In the decade following the mid-1980s, the rate of murder committed by teenagers fourteen to seventeen more than doubled. The rates of injury suffered by small children are skyrocketing, with the number of seriously injured children nearly quadrupling from 1986 to 1993; and a proportion of these injuries are inflicted by children upon one another. Even homicides by children, once next to unknown, have escalated in recent decades.

America may be the only society on earth to have experienced what has been called an "epidemic of children killing children," which is ravaging some of its communities today. As in any epidemic, it is urgent to ask what it is that makes so many capable of such violence, victimizes so many others, and causes countless more to live in fear. Whatever role the media are found to play in this respect, to be sure, is but part of the problem. Obviously, not even the total elimination of media violence would wipe out the problem of violence in the United States or any other society. The same can be said for the proliferation and easy access to guns, or for poverty, drug addiction, and other risk factors. As Dr. Deborah Prothrow-Stith puts it, "It's not an either or. It's not guns or media or parents or poverty."

We have all witnessed the four effects that I have discussed . . . — fearfulness, numbing, appetite, and aggressive impulses—in the context of many influences apart from the media. Maturing involves learning to resist the dominion that these effects can gain over us; and to strive, instead, for greater resilience, empathy, self-control, and respect for self and others. The process of maturation and growth in these respects is never completed for any of us; but it is most easily thwarted in childhood, before it has had chance to take root. Such learning calls for nurturing and education at first; then for increasing autonomy in making personal decisions about how best to confront the realities of violence.

Today, the sights and sounds of violence on the screen affect this learning process from infancy on, in many homes. The television screen is the lens through which most children learn about violence. Through the magnifying power of this lens, their everyday life becomes suffused by images of shootings, family violence, gang warfare, kidnappings, and everything else that contributes to violence in our society. It shapes their experiences long before they have had the opportunity to consent to such shaping or developed the ability to cope adequately with this knowledge. The basic nurturing and protection to prevent the impairment of this ability ought to be the birthright of every child.

QUESTIONS

1. What does Dr. Deborah Prothrow-Stith mean when she states, "It's not an either or. It's not guns or media or parents or poverty"? What conclusions does Bok believe can be drawn from this statement about causes and solutions for the "problem" of media violence?

2. Considering some alternative causes for the current outbreak of youth violence—parents who neglect their children, the decay of our educational system, the violence of war, the decay of inner cities—do you think that eliminating media violence would be sufficient to significantly reduce youth violence? Why or why not?

3. How effective is Bok's analogy about the parallel between the causal link tying smoking to cancer and the link between media exposure and youth violence? Why is the link between media and violence more difficult to prove conclusively? Does it have to be proved conclusively to "do something about it," in Bok's view? Do you agree with her reasoning here?

MIKE MALES

"Stop Blaming Kids and TV for Crime and Substance Abuse"

Mike Males (b. 1950) worked in the 1970s and 1980s with troubled youth in wilderness programs and the Youth Conservation Corps while also doing environmental lobbying and supporting himself as a newspaper reporter. He studied youth issues in the graduate school of the University of California, Irvine, where he received a Ph.D. in social ecology in 1999. Since 2001 he has taught the sociology of youth problems at the University of Santa Cruz. His articles on youth crime, drug abuse, pregnancy, and poverty have been published in professional journals as well as in the New York Times, Los Angeles Times, *and the* Washington Post. *His books include* The Scapegoat Generation: America's War on Adolescents *(1996),* Framing Youth: Ten Myths About the New Generation *(1998), and* Kids and Guns: How Politicians, Experts, and the Media Fabricate Fear of Youth *(2001). In his article "Stop Blaming Kids and TV" (1997), a causal refutation argument, Males explains his belief that the real causes for youth violence can be traced to poverty and adult violence rather than the media.*

"Children have never been very good at listening to their elders," James Baldwin wrote in *Nobody Knows My Name*. "But they have never failed to imitate them." This basic truth has all but disappeared as the public increasingly treats teenagers as a robot-like population under sway of an exploitative media. White House officials lecture film, music, Internet, fashion, and pop-culture moguls and accuse them of programming kids to smoke, drink, shoot up, have sex, and kill.

So do conservatives, led by William Bennett and Dan Quayle. Professional organizations are also into media-bashing. In its famous report on youth risks, the Carnegie Corporation devoted a full chapter to media influences. Progressives are no exception. *Mother Jones* claims it has "proof that TV makes kids violent." And the Institute for Alternative Media emphasizes, "the average American child will witness . . . 200,000 acts of [TV] violence" by the time that child graduates from high school.

None of these varied interests note that during the eighteen years between a child's birth and graduation from high school, there will be fifteen million cases of real violence in American homes grave enough to require hospital emergency treatment. These assaults will cause ten million serious injuries and 40,000 deaths to children. In October 1996, the Department of Health and Human Services reported 565,000 serious injuries that abusive parents inflicted on children and youths in 1993. The number is up four-fold since 1986.

The Department of Health report disappeared from the news in one day. It elicited virtually no comment from the White House, Republicans, or law-enforcement officials. Nor from Carnegie scholars, whose 150-page study, "Great Transitions: Preparing Adolescents for a New Century," devotes two sentences to household violence. The left press took no particular interest in the story, either.

All sides seem to agree that fictional violence, sex on the screen, Joe Camel, beer-drinking frogs, or naked bodies on the Internet pose a bigger threat to children than do actual beatings, rape, or parental addictions. This, in turn, upholds the Clinton doctrine that youth behavior is the problem, and curbing young people's rights the answer.

Claims that TV causes violence bear little relation to real behavior. Japanese and European kids behold media as graphically brutal as that which appears on American screens, but seventeen-year-olds in those countries commit murder at rates lower than those of American seventy-year-olds.

Likewise, youths in different parts of the United States are exposed to the same media but display drastically different violence levels.

TV violence does not account for the fact that the murder rate among black teens in Washington, D.C., is twenty-five times higher than that of white teens living a few Metro stops away. It doesn't explain why, nationally, murder doubled among nonwhite and Latino youth over the last decade, but declined among white Anglo teens. Furthermore, contrary to the TV brainwashing theory, Anglo sixteen-year-olds have lower violent-crime rates than black sixty-year-olds, Latino forty-year-olds, and Anglo thirty-year-olds. Men, women, whites, Latinos, blacks, Asians, teens, young adults, middle-agers, and senior citizens in Fresno County—California's poorest urban area—display murder and violent-crime rates double those of their counterparts in Ventura County, the state's richest.

Confounding every theory, America's biggest explosion in felony violent crime is not street crime among minorities or teens of any color, but domestic violence among aging, mostly white baby boomers. Should we arm Junior with a V-chip to protect him from Mom and Dad?

In practical terms, media-violence theories are not about kids, but about race and class: If TV accounts for any meaningful fraction of murder levels among poorer, nonwhite youth, why doesn't it have the same effect on white kids? Are minorities inherently programmable?

The newest target is Channel One, legitimately criticized by the Unplug Campaign—a watchdog sponsored by the Center for Commercial-Free Public Education—as a corporate marketing ploy packaged as educational TV. But then the Unplug Campaign gives credence to claims that "commercials control kids" by "harvesting minds," as Roy Fox of the University of Missouri says. These claims imply that teens are uniquely open to media brainwashing.

Other misleading claims come from Johns Hopkins University media analyst Mark Crispin Miller. In his critique of Channel One in the May edition of *Extra!*, Miller invoked such hackneyed phrases as the "inevitable rebelliousness of adolescent boys," the "hormones raging," and the "defiant boorish behavior" of "young men." Despite the popularity of these stereotypes, there is no basis in fact for such anti-youth bias.

A 1988 study in the *Journal of Youth and Adolescence* by psychology professors Grayson Holmbeck and John Hill concluded: "Adolescents are not in turmoil, not deeply disturbed, not at the mercy of their impulses, not resistant to parental values, and not rebellious."

In the November 1992 *Journal of the American Academy of Child and Adolescent Psychiatry*, Northwestern University psychiatry professor Daniel Offer reviewed 150 studies and concluded, in his article

"Debunking the Myths of Adolescence," that "the effects of pubertal hormones are neither potent nor pervasive."

If anything, Channel One and other mainstream media reinforce young people's conformity to—not defiance of—adult values. Miller's unsubstantiated claims that student consumerism, bad behaviors, and mental or biological imbalances are compelled by media ads and images could be made with equal force about the behaviors of his own age group. Binge drinking, drug abuse, and violence against children by adults over the age of thirty are rising rapidly.

The barrage of sexually seductive liquor ads, fashion images, and anti-youth rhetoric, by conventional logic, must be influencing those hormonally unstable middle-agers.

I worked for a dozen years in youth programs in Montana and California. When problems arose, they usually crossed generations. I saw violent kids with dads or uncles in jail for assault. I saw middle-schoolers molested in childhood by mom's boyfriend. I saw budding teen alcoholics hoisting forty-ouncers alongside forty-year-old sots. I also saw again and again how kids start to smoke. In countless trailers and small apartments dense with blue haze, children roamed the rugs as grownups puffed. Mom and seventh-grade daughter swapped Dorals while bemoaning the evils of men. A junior-high basketball center slept outside before a big game because a dozen elders—from her non-inhaling sixteen-year-old brother to her grandma—were all chain smokers. Two years later, she'd given up and joined the party.

As a rule, teen smoking mimicked adult smoking by gender, race, locale, era, and household. I could discern no pop-culture puppetry. My survey of 400 Los Angeles middle schoolers for a 1994 Journal of School Health article found children of smoking parents three times more likely to smoke by age fifteen than children of nonsmokers. Parents were the most influential but not the only adults kids emulated. Nor did youngsters copy elders slavishly. Youths often picked slightly different habits (like chewing tobacco, or their own brands).

In 1989, the Centers for Disease Control lamented, "75 percent of all teenage smokers come from homes where parents smoke." You don't hear such candor from today's put-politics-first health agencies. Centers for Disease Control tobacco chieftain Michael Eriksen informed me that his agency doesn't make an issue of parental smoking. Nor do anti-smoking groups. Asked Kathy Mulvey, research director of INFACT: "Why make enemies of fifty million adult smokers" when advertising creates the real "appeal of tobacco to youth?"

Do ads hook kids on cigarettes? Studies of the effects of the Joe Camel logo show only that a larger fraction of teen smokers than veteran adult smokers choose the Camel brand. When asked, some researchers admit they cannot demonstrate that advertising causes kids to smoke who would not otherwise. And that's the real issue. In fact, surveys found smoking declining among teens (especially the youngest) during Joe's advent from 1985 to 1990.

The University of California's Stanton Glantz, whose exposure of 10,000 tobacco documents enraged the industry, found corporate perfidy far shrewder than camels and cowboys.

"As the tobacco industry knows well," Glantz reported, "kids want to be like adults." An industry marketing document advises: "To reach young smokers, present the cigarette as one of the initiations into adult life . . . the basic symbols of growing up."

The biggest predictor of whether a teen will become a smoker, a drunk, or a druggie is whether or not the child grows up amid adult addicts. Three-fourths of murdered kids are killed by adults. Suicide and murder rates among white teenagers resemble those of white adults, and suicide and murder rates among black teens track those of black adults. And as far as teen pregnancy goes, for minor mothers, four-fifths of the fathers are adults over eighteen, and half are adults over twenty.

The inescapable conclusion is this: If you want to change juvenile behavior, change adult behavior. But instead of focusing on adults, almost everyone points a finger at kids—and at the TV culture that supposedly addicts them.

Groups like Mothers Against Drunk Driving charge, for instance, that Budweiser's frogs entice teens to drink. Yet the 1995 National Household Survey found teen alcohol use declining. "Youths aren't buying the cute and flashy beer images," an in-depth *USA Today* survey found. Most teens found the ads amusing, but they did not consume Bud as a result.

By squabbling over frogs, political interests can sidestep the impolitic tragedy that adults over the age of twenty-one cause 90 percent of America's 16,000 alcohol-related traffic deaths every year. Clinton and drug-policy chief Barry McCaffrey ignore federal reports that show a skyrocketing toll of booze and drug-related casualties among adults in their thirties and forties—the age group that is parenting most American teens. But both officials get favorable press attention by blaming alcohol ads and heroin chic for corrupting our kids.

Progressive reformers who insist kids are so malleable that beer frogs and Joe Camel and Ace Ventura push them to evil are not so different from those on the Christian right who claim that *Our Bodies, Ourselves* promotes teen sex and that the group Rage Against the Machine persuades pubescents to roll down Rodeo Drive with a shotgun.

America's increasingly marginalized young deserve better than grownup escapism. Millions of children and teenagers face real destitution, drug abuse, and violence in their homes. Yet these profound menaces continue to lurk in the background, even as the frogs, V-chips, and Mighty Morphins take center stage.

QUESTIONS

1. How strong a case does Males make for the contribution of adult violence in the home to the problems of youth violence? Is this citing of "other wrongs" or shifting the blame from media violence a logical fallacy or a relevant approach in this situation?

2. Aside from pointing elsewhere for culprits, Males also provides statistics comparing violence levels among children of different ethnic groups and countries to bolster his views that media violence does not necessarily lead to youth violence. Are his arguments in this area persuasive? To what extent?

3. How does Males try to demonstrate that advertisements have little or no direct influence over youth smoking and drinking? Are his arguments and evidence in this area convincing? Why or why not?

SOLEDAD LILIANA ESCOBAR-CHAVES
AND CRAIG A. ANDERSON

"Media and Risky Behaviors: Aggressive and Violent Behavior"

Soledad Liliana Escobar-Chaves received her doctorate in public health and health promotion in 2002 from the University of Texas Houston School of Public Health and is currently an assistant professor of health promotion and behavioral sciences at the University of Texas Health Science Center at Houston. She has lectured and published a number of articles on the impact of drug use and media on adolescent attitudes and behavior related to sexuality, crime, and violence. Craig A. Anderson received his Ph.D. in 1980 from Stanford University and is director of the Center for the Study of Violence and distinguished professor of liberal arts and sciences in the Department of Psychology at Iowa State University. He is a leading researcher, lecturer, and author on the impact of violent video games on children; his book on the subject, Violent Video Game Effects on Children and Adolescents: Theory,

Research, and Public Policy, *was published in 2007. In the following excerpt from a 2008 article in* The Future of Children, *Escobar-Chaves and Anderson examine the impact of the trend among U.S. youths to spend increasing amounts of time using electronic media, and the resulting negative behaviors.*

Aggressive and violent behavior is usually defined by behavioral scientists as behavior that is intended to harm another person. Common forms of aggression are physical (for example, punching), verbal (for example, saying or writing hurtful things to another person), and relational (for example, intentionally and publicly not inviting someone to a party to harm his social relationships). Violence usually is conceived as more extreme forms of physical aggression that are likely to result in physical injury. The most extreme form of violence is homicide, but any form of aggressive behavior that is likely to result in an injury serious enough to warrant medical attention is considered violence. Thus, fights involving weapons as well as fistfights by adolescents old enough to be able to inflict serious injuries are considered acts of violence.

The relation of these terms to violent "crime" requires some comment. The vast majority of media violence research focuses on aggressive and violent behavior as defined earlier. Violent crime is a much more restrictive category and is applied only in cases where someone has been arrested for a crime classified by police as a major crime against persons, such as murder, rape, and assault. There are at least two reasons for the discrepancy between the behavioral scientists' focus and the criminologists' focus. First, the criminological focus is based more heavily on the consequences of a specific action, whereas the behavioral science focus is almost exclusively based on the intention behind the action. Understanding the causes of violent behavior requires this focus on intentions rather than on whether the person succeeded in harming the individual and was subsequently caught. Second, not only is it much more difficult and expensive to do research on violent crime because it is relatively rare (thereby requiring huge sample sizes), but also certain types of research, such as experimental studies, would be unethical. For these reasons, we focus on aggressive and violent behavior, though we cite violent crime data where useful.

Violent Behavior: The Scope of the Problem

Youth violence resulting in deaths and injuries has direct and indirect costs in excess of $158 billion each year. Only accidental injury (frequently auto accidents) consistently leads homicide as the cause of death of U.S. youths between one and twenty-four years of age. For youths between the ages of ten and twenty-four, homicide is the leading cause of death for African Americans, the second leading cause for Hispanics.

Young people not only suffer but also commit a disproportionate share of violence. Although twelve- to twenty-year-olds made up about 13 percent of the U.S. population in 2005, they were responsible for some 28 percent of the single-offender and 41 percent of multiple-offender violent crimes. . . . U.S. assault rates rose dramatically from the early 1980s to the early 1990s and then, just as dramatically, fell. Other overall rates for violent crime, such as homicide, show the same pattern. One factor that likely contributed to this rise and fall was changes in the share of the U.S. population in the high-violence age range. Although rates of youth violence also increased during the late 1980s and early 1990s, they have not fallen in recent years. In fact, the youth violence indicators . . . show considerable stability over time; several appear to be increasing.

Media Exposure and Aggressive and Violent Behavior

The extent to which media violence causes youth aggression and violence has been hotly debated for more than fifty years. Despite many reports that exposure to violent media is a causal risk factor, the U.S. public remains largely unaware of these risks, and youth exposure to violent media remains extremely high. Among the public advisories that have been generally ignored are congressional hearings in 1954, U.S. surgeon general reports in 1972 and 2001, a National Institute of Mental Health report in 1982, and a Federal Trade Commission report in 2000. In addition to government studies, reports have been issued by scientific organizations such as the American Psychological Association (in 1994, 2000, and 2005), the American Academy of Pediatrics, the American Academy of Child and Adolescent Psychiatry, the American Medical Association, the American Academy of Family Physicians, and the American Psychiatric Association.

The most recent thorough review of the research on media violence, by an expert panel convened by the U.S. surgeon general, concluded, "Research on violent television and films, video games, and music reveals unequivocal evidence that media violence increases the likelihood of aggressive and violent behavior in both immediate and long-term contexts." Hundreds of original empirical studies of the link between media violence and aggression have been conducted, and numerous reviews of those studies—both narrative and statistical—have come to the same conclusion. Indeed, one analysis found clear evidence that exposure to media violence increases aggressive behavior as early as 1975.

The newest form of media violence—violent video games played on computers, video game consoles, handheld systems, the Internet, and even cell phones—also is the fastest growing. Although most youth still spend more time each week watching TV, including movies, than playing video games, the time they spend with video games is increasing rapidly, and a growing share of youth is spending many hours playing video games. For example, about 90 percent of U.S. youth aged eight to eighteen play video games, with boys averaging about nineteen hours a week. Annual surveys of college freshmen over time reveal that as twelfth graders they spend ever-increasing amounts of time playing video games. The finding is especially true for boys. . . .

We review evidence on the link between youth violence and violence on television and film and on video games. We could find no studies on the effects of violence in advertising on aggressive or violent behavior, but the effects of such violent content are likely to be similar.

Television and Movie Violence and Violent Behavior

Television and movie violence are the most extensively researched forms of media violence. Studies using all three major research designs have all reached the same conclusion—exposure to television and movie violence increases aggression and violence.

Experimental studies have shown that even a single exposure increases aggression in the immediate situation. For example, Kaj Bjorkqvist randomly assigned one group of five- to six-year-old Finnish children to watch violent movies, another to watch nonviolent ones. Raters who did not know which type of movie the children had seen then observed them playing together in a room. Children who had just watched the violent movie were rated much higher on physical assault and other types of aggression. Other experiments have shown that exposure to media violence can increase aggressive thinking, aggressive emotions, and tolerance for aggression, all known risk factors for later aggressive and violent behavior.

Many cross-sectional studies have examined whether people who view many violent TV shows and movies also tend to behave more aggressively. Such studies generally find significant positive correlations.

For example, one group of researchers studied the links between "aggressive behavioral delinquency," such as fighting and hitting, and TV violence viewing in samples of Wisconsin and Maryland high school and junior high school students. They found significant positive links between TV violence exposure and aggression for both boys and girls. Another research team reported 49 percent more violent acts in the past six months by heavy viewers of TV violence than by light viewers.

Researchers also have used longitudinal studies to investigate television violence effects, using time periods that range from less than one year to fifteen years. One research team studied a group of six- to ten-year-olds over fifteen years. They found that both boys and girls who viewed television violence committed more aggression (physical, verbal, and indirect) during young adulthood. The study found the same link when the outcome examined was outright physical violence, such as punching, beating, choking, threatening, or attacking with a knife or gun. This media violence study is one of the few to include measures of violent crime. Because it is a well-conducted longitudinal study, it lends considerable strength to the view of media violence as a causal risk factor for aggression, violence, and violent crime. Interestingly, although frequent exposure to TV violence during childhood was linked to high levels of adulthood aggression, high aggressiveness during childhood did not lead to frequent viewing of television violence in adulthood.

Violent Video Games and Violent Behavior

The most popular video games played by youth contain violence. Even children's games (as designated by the industry-sponsored Entertainment Software Ratings Board) are likely to contain violence. More than 30 percent of games rated "E" (suitable for everyone) contain a violence descriptor; more than 90 percent of "E10+" games (suitable for those ten years and older) contain a violence descriptor. About 70 percent of fourth to twelfth graders report playing "Mature"-rated games (suitable for those seventeen and older), which contain the most graphic violence of all.

Research on video game violence is less extensive than that on TV and film violence, but the findings are essentially the same. Experimental studies in field and laboratory settings generally find that brief exposure to violent video games increases aggressive thoughts, feelings, and behavior. For example, one laboratory study assigned children and college students randomly to play either a children's video game that involved shooting cartoon-like characters or a nonviolent children's video game. Later, all participants completed a standard laboratory task that measures physical aggression. Those who had played the violent children's game displayed a 40 percent higher aggression rate than those who had played a nonviolent game. The effect was the same for both elementary school children and college students. In a field experiment, children were randomly assigned to play either a violent or nonviolent video game and then were observed by trained coders during a free-play period. The children who had played the violent game displayed significantly more physical aggression than those who had played a nonviolent game.

To date, the only published longitudinal study that clearly delineates the possible influence of violent video games used a relatively short time span of six months. The researchers conducting the study assessed the media habits and aggressive tendencies of elementary school children, as well as a host of control variables, twice within a school year. The children who were heavily exposed to video game violence early in the school year became relatively more physically aggressive by the end of the year, as measured by peers, teachers, and self-reports. Cross-sectional studies have also found positive correlations between exposure to violent video games and various forms of aggression, including violent behavior and violent crimes.

All three types of studies have also linked violent video games to a host of additional aggression-related cognitive, emotional, and behavioral outcomes. Outcomes include more positive attitudes toward violence, increased use of aggressive words or solutions to hypothetical problems, quicker recognition of facial anger, increased self-perception as being aggressive, increased feelings of anger and revenge motives, decreased sensitivity to scenes and images of real violence, and changes in brain function associated with lower executive control and heightened emotion.

Violent Behavior: Summary

The research evidence shows clearly that media violence is a causal risk factor for aggressive and violent behavior. There is considerably less evidence concerning violent crimes, but the few cross-sectional and longitudinal studies that included violent crime measures also found similar links with media violence. The size of the media violence effect is as large as or larger than that of many factors commonly accepted by public policymakers and the general public as valid risk factors for violent behavior. . . . [S]everal studies have directly compared video game and TV violence using the same participants and the same measures; they generally find a somewhat larger effect for video games. Thus, we expect that the effect of violent video games on long-term violence will be larger than that of TV violence and smaller than that of gang membership. Furthermore, it is likely that overall media violence exposure has a somewhat larger effect than any individual type of media violence. In any case, [it is] . . . clear that media violence exposure has a larger effect on later violent behavior than does substance use, abusive parents, poverty, living in a broken home, or having low IQ.

QUESTIONS

1. How do the authors distinguish between violent crime and violent behavior? Why is it easier to do causal research into violent behavior than it is for violent crime?
2. What statistics do the authors use to establish that youth violence is indeed a serious social problem? How do they attempt to establish a clear causal link between the statistical rise in youth violence and aggression and violent media and video game exposure? Do you find their citation of the conclusions of previous causal studies and their analysis of particular research studies convincing in this regard?
3. How persuasive is the summary of violent behavior findings at the end of the essay? Are you convinced by the authors' findings, or do you believe that factors other than media exposure play greater roles in youth violence?

BRIAN COWLISHAW

"Playing War: Real Combat Video Games"

Brian Cowlishaw is an assistant professor of English in the College of Liberal Arts at Northeastern State University in Tahlequah, Oklahoma, where he specializes in eighteenth- and nineteenth-century British literature and cultural studies. He has published on a wide variety of literature and popular-culture subjects, including the rhetoric of Ring Lardner and ghost stories. He is an avid videogamer, whose writings and reviews on videogames have appeared in the online 'zines Intelligent Agent *and* Uplink 3:The Guerilla War Issue. *In his article below from* Magazine Americana, *Cowlishaw demonstrates how military-produced realistic-seeming video battle games have been used as effective recruitment tools for our current armed struggle in the Middle East.*

While video games have been around for some time now, they have emerged, in recent years, as a major player on the profit scene. Indeed, for the past two years, the video game market has made more money than the motion picture business. Perhaps that's why filmmakers often release video game versions of their films months before theatrical release—in order to heat up the marketplace for their film.

The latest trend in video games, such as the Medal of Honor series, the Battlefield series, and America's Army, is to be especially "realistic." Such games proudly transport the gamer into immersive, gut wrenching virtual battlefields. They persuade the gamer that, in an echo of WWII-era journalism, "You Are There"—on the beaches of Normandy, in the jungles of Vietnam, in modern military hotspots.

Upon examination, this now-common claim raises other key questions. First, and perhaps most obviously: To what degree is this claim to realism justified? In other words, are the games truly as historically accurate as their makers and players claim? Answering that question raises a series of more significant and telling questions: What do these games signify? Being war games, why are they so popular now? Who benefits from this popularity, and how?

The games that most stridently and persuasively claim to be realistic, and therefore those games on which I will focus, are first-person shooters (FPSs) which purport to recreate full-scale real-world battles. For the uninitiated, the phrase "first-person" in "first-person shooters" refers to the player's point of view: onscreen appears a pair of forearms and hands aiming a weapon forward "into" the screen. The hands are "you." That gun is "your" gun. Players use controls (keyboard, mouse, and/or game controller) to virtually look up, down, and around onscreen, and the result looks and feels like brandishing a weapon. The word "shooter" in "first-person shooter" refers to what the player does: move around a "map" (virtual battlefield) and deploy an arsenal of weapons against virtual enemies.

Unreal Tournament provides clear examples of standard FPS conventions. One key convention is that weapons, ammunition, armor, and first-aid kits regularly and frequently "spawn," that is, suddenly appear out of nowhere. Simply running over them onscreen confers their benefits immediately; there is almost no time wasted simulating using the first-aid kits, or reloading the weapons. Second, all FPS players die a lot, even when they're winning. The goal is to rack up the most "frags," or kills, so how often they die is really irrelevant. Dead players immediately respawn at a semi-random spot on the map, then get right back to killing. Finally, FPSs revel in offering ungenteel, gore-intensive gameplay. Players can be slimed, shot, sniped, razored, exploded, or chainsawed to death onscreen. Bodies hit just right, with the right weapon, fly apart into bloody chunks of flesh.

Realistic war games are recent specialized offshoots of the broader FPS genre. The first FPS was Wolfenstein; Medal of Honor, published a decade later, is probably the first realistic war game. This genealogical relationship—realistic war games' direct descent from FPSs—becomes apparent with close scrutiny. This genealogical relationship also means that while realistic war games are generally more realistic than other FPSs, they still retain significant unrealistic qualities.

One key unrealistic quality of putatively realistic war games might be called "self-assessment." Players have onscreen at all times thorough, accessible-at-a-glance information regarding their condition. They can see the status of their armor, their physical health expressed as a precise percentage, and their ammunition stores for every single weapon. Obviously, this level of self-knowledge is unavailable in real life. We may have a fairly keen sense of how healthy or unhealthy we feel, and if we have just had a blood or other test we may even be able to express this feeling with some precision. But this precision never approaches that in a FPS: we could never say, "I'm 81% healthy, and my clothes are providing 34% protection." Thus, for a simulation of war truly to be realistic, such information would have to remain vague or difficult to obtain. Yet there it is, right onscreen constantly in all of the new war games—just as in unashamedly unrealistic other FPSs.

Surprisingly, another FPS convention preserved by the realistic war games is respawning. For example, in the Medal of Honor games, when players die they are magically transported back to the beginning of the scenario, with all their original weapons and health restored, to try again. This makes sense not only from a games-history perspective, but also from an entertainment perspective: it's no fun if dying onscreen means the game is over. Players want to get right back up and fight some more. Obviously, though, real life does not work this way. Death tends to be final—but not in war video games.

Not only is death in this way banished from the games, but significantly, so is bodily dismemberment. Game makers systematically exclude it, much in the way Paul Fussell shows it was excluded from images and accounts of World War II. He observes that in such accounts, with very few exceptions, "the bodies of the dead, if inert, are intact. Bloody,

BRIAN COWLISHAW

338

sometimes, and sprawled in awkward positions, but except for the absence of life, plausible and acceptable simulacra of the people they once were. . . . American bodies (decently clothed) are occasionally in evidence, but they are notably intact." The famous photographic collection Life Goes to War, for example, shows only three dismembered bodies–specifically, heads. It is significant that they are not American but Asian heads. They are displayed as trophies of our soldiers' prowess. Always showing American bodies intact directly counters real-world facts and probabilities: as Fussell points out, it was "as likely for the man next to you to be shot through the eye, ear, testicles, or brain as (the way the cinema does it) through the shoulder. A shell is as likely to blow his whole face off as to lodge a fragment in some mentionable and unvital tissue." In fact, it was also quite common for a soldier to be wounded or killed not by a bullet or shell but by a flying body part—a foot, a skull, a ribcage.

Obviously, game makers could include such graphic details if they wanted to: Unreal Tournament, five years old at this writing, which is a dinosaur in computer time, displays gore galore. The technology for depicting dismemberment convincingly onscreen is quite capable nowadays, so clearly war game makers choose not to do it. They do in war video games what wartime journalists such as Ernie Pyle did in writing: purposely, systematically remove gory details so as to make the war more palatable—as opposed to more truly realistic. One of Pyle's best-known stories involves the return of the body of one Captain Henry T. Waskow "of Belton, Texas," to his grieving company. One of the men reportedly sat by the body for a long time, holding the captain's hand and looking into his face; then he "reached over and gently straightened the points of the captain's shirt collar, and then he sort of arranged the tattered edges of the uniform around the wound." As Fussell points out, Pyle's geographical and behavioral precision calls attention to the essential information that he glosses over:

1. What killed Captain Waskow? Bullet, shell fragments, a mine, or what?
2. Where was his wound? How large was it? He implies that it was in the traditional noble place, the chest. Was it? Was it a little hole, or was it a great red missing place? Was it perhaps in the crotch, or in the testicles, or in the belly? Were his entrails extruded, or in any way visible?
3. How much blood was there? Was the captain's uniform bloody? Did the faithful soldier wash off his hands after toying with those "tattered edges"? Were the captain's eyes open? Did his face look happy? Surprised? Satisfied? Angry?

Like wartime press reports, war video games carefully elide this most basic fact of wartime: bodily damage.

The most plainly unrealistic element of the war games is the existence of the games themselves. That is, players always remain inescapably aware of two very important facts. First, the war is never finally real. Players are not, in fact, dashing around a battlefield but rather sitting in a comfortable chair. They grip a controller, or keyboard and mouse, not a Garand rifle. There is no actual danger of being killed, or physically harmed beyond getting stiff and fat from playing video games too long. No matter how immersive or even realistic the game, one can never forget that it is "just a game." Second, players may play the game, but in an important sense the game plays them. There is always a "proper" outcome, a pre-scripted story one must complete correctly, especially when the game pits the player against the computer rather than against other flesh-and-blood players. There is always a specific task to carry out, such as to storm Normandy Beach and rout the Germans from their bunkers; the ideal for game programmers is to make such tasks challenging but possible. Players' job, then, is to find the correct solution to a puzzle someone else constructed; they are in a significant sense acted upon rather than acting. In life, of course, we can choose badly or well, but we can choose. This rat-in-a-maze aspect, together with the game's inescapable "game-ness," reminds players every moment that games fundamentally differ from real life; playing a game is inherently unrealistic.

Nevertheless, talk abounds regarding how realistic the current war video games are. Official Xbox Magazine's comments on Full Spectrum Warrior are typical of the glee with which players and critics greet the newly "realistic" war games. The magazine effuses, "Now when you send your troops into a slaughter in Full Spectrum Warrior, you'll have to look in their eyes and hear their screams." Apparently this is a good thing. OXM also raves, "with [its] 5:1 [sound] it really feels like you are in the middle of a combat zone (turn it up loud enough and your neighbors might think so as well)." One fan anticipating Battlefield: Vietnam's release on EBGames.com writes, "this will alow a more real taste of the war [sic]." Another, purporting to speak for all of us, claims, "U know how u always wanted to know what the Vietnam War was like [sic]. I think this game will show you."

There is some justification for these claims to realism. Sound is one area in which the new war games truly do reproduce wartime accurately. Sound effects are as accurate and inclusive as visual representations are sanitized and edited. The realistic war games—for example,

America's Army, the Battlefield series, and the Medal of Honor series—reproduce all of the rumbling machinery, gunfire, artillery, explosions, footsteps, splats, ricochets, shouted orders, swearing, and wounded cries one would hear in a real war. And current computer/television sound technology—now standardized at seven points in the room—reproduces all these sounds with perfect clarity at 100+ decibels.

In addition to sound, the war games also reproduce historical circumstances with comparative accuracy. The games do allow players to virtually fight in battles that really did occur—famous ones such as the Normandy invasion, Pearl Harbor, and the Tet Offensive. In-game soldiers use weapons that look and perform more or less like real weapons that real soldiers used. In-game soldiers dress, look, and speak like real soldiers did. The games may not be completely historically faithful in these elements, but they certainly are more so than other, older FPSs. The genealogical relationship makes the newer war games seem more realistic than they are.

Compare any current realistic war game, for example, with Unreal Tournament. In UT, the voices and character models ("skins") are a self-consciously over-the-top assortment of idealized macho warriors and ridiculous comic figures. In addition to the macho grunts, my copy features the downloaded voices of Fat Bastard (from the Austin Powers movies), Eric Cartman (from South Park), and Homer Simpson (from The Simpsons). Players can choose UT deathmatchers' appearances: onscreen fighters can be assigned any skin from a giant, scary lizard-man, to a stereotypical macho male (or female), to Captain America, to Dr. Frankenfurter (from The Rocky Horror Picture Show). Any voice can be assigned to any skin: one might arrange a Dr. Frankenfurter with Cartman's voice, or a skull-faced badass who talks like Homer Simpson. These zany characters' weapons similarly aim for entertaining gameplay rather than factual accuracy. UT features rocket launchers, handheld frag cannons, plasma rifles, and sludge guns. The battles in which these crazy weapons are used take place on obviously artificial, nonreferential staging grounds. That is, the in-game battle sites are not intended to reproduce historical locations. They clearly exist solely so that players can virtually blast the hell out of each other in visually interesting, strategically challenging settings—and the more fantastic, the better. References to real-world locales tend to be ironic, humorous: "Hey look, here's a map like a football field!" "Here's one set on a cruise ship!" I certainly hope real deathmatches never take place in such locales. Classic FPSs, as opposed to realistic war games, are judged by how intense a deathmatch they can produce, not by how accurately they reproduce "the real Normandy."

Overall "presentation," too, proves comparatively realistic in the new war games. "Presentation" refers to the way a game is laid out for the player in terms of menu choices, art, and sound; we might call it "atmosphere." In Medal of Honor: Frontline, for example, menu choices take the form of file folders stamped with the (now-defunct) Office of Strategic Services logo. All in-game fonts look typewritten by period typewriters. "Your" portrait in the menu file appears attached by low-tech paper clip. Selecting a menu option produces a gunshot or file-rustling sound. In the America's Army game, menu headings use terminology lifted from the real-world America's Army: "Personnel Jacket," "Training Missions," "Deployment," and so on. This kind of attention to making the presentation realistic enhances the overall impression that the game accurately recreates history. Compared to the three-ring FPS circus that is their origin, the new realistic war games appear positively photographic in their historical fidelity. Even gamers, disposed by nature to find all flaws, perceive them as faithful to what the games purport to recreate.

So far, I have discussed two fairly black-and-white categories, "realistic" and "unrealistic," so that I can make descriptions clearly. But the truth is, the issue is much more complicated than that binary choice. It's more accurate to say that the games blur the boundaries between real and virtual, or mix elements of the one in among the other, so thoroughly that players finally cannot tell where reality ends and virtual reality begins.

One telling example appears in the required marksman-training mission that begins America's Army. The player must hit a specified number of targets within a time limit. After passing the test, the player receives hearty applause from the drill sergeant: "Congratulations, soldier! You have just qualified as a marksman in the United States Army!" I must admit: the first time I passed this test, I became moderately alarmed—he did mean I virtually qualified, right? So many other kinds of transactions take place online nowadays; why not real-life recruitment and qualification?

The idea that by playing a realistic war game for a few minutes I may have inadvertently enlisted is not as outlandish as it may seem out of context. Consider: the real-world America's Army created, programmed, and distributed, for free online, the game called America's Army, specifically for the purpose of recruitment. Anyone can download it for free, right now, at americasarmy.com. The real army counts on people, mostly young men ripe for recruitment, to download the game, enjoy it, think to themselves, "Hey, you know, I should do this for real," and then go enlist. Apparently the strategy is working very effectively. In late March 2004, the CBS Evening News reported on a huge America's Army gaming tournament. Hundreds of thousands of dollars in prize money and computer equipment were at stake. Several recruiters sat in the competition room. Hundreds of players walked directly from their round of competition over to sign up with recruiters. CBS reported that since the game was released in 2002, recruitment has spiked; the video game is the most effective recruitment tool since the Uncle Sam "I Want You" posters during World War II.

This video game recruitment strategy meshes very neatly with the Army's recent advertising campaign. The Army shows images of underage kids essentially playing games—flying a remote-controlled plane in one, and actually playing a video game in another. Then the same people (presumably) are shown as young adults doing pretty much the same activities in the Army: the model plane flyer pilots a decoy drone plane, and the video gamer efficiently directs real tanks and troops around a battlefield. The clear message is: "You should join the real Army because we will pay you to play pretty much the same games you play for fun right now. You were born for this."

Full Spectrum Warrior blurs reality and gaming perhaps even more thoroughly. Like America's Army, this game was produced by the real U.S. Army. In fact, it's not entirely clear that the end result was the choice of the game's original developer, William Stahl. In an interview with Official Xbox Magazine, Stahl describes how the game got made: "Three years ago, I was pitching a . . . game for the PC. Representatives of the Army were looking for a developer to create a training simulation on a videogame console. They got ahold of those early documents and thought the concept was right in line with what they wanted to achieve. . . . This game was developed in conjunction with the Army. They were essentially our publisher, and as such, they had the final say on what they wanted in the game, how it looked, etc." This statement raises worrisome questions:

1. How did the Army get "ahold" of those early documents"?
2. How much choice of publisher did Stahl and company actually have?

In any case, the Army ultimately made two versions, one of which is being used right now by real American soldiers for training, and a very similar version being sold in stores. Real soldiers and couch bound warriors alike learn battle tactics by playing a video game. Thus, the real and the virtual become indistinguishable. The U.S. Army recruits real soldiers by appealing to them through video games and suggests that video gamers' virtual prowess and enjoyment translate directly into real-world Army suitability and success.

In one important sense, the first-person-shooter genre itself contributes to this fusion of the real and the virtual. In recent years, in-game instructions have become standard parts of all FPSs and most video games in general; James Paul Gee explains in detail, in his book What Video Games Have to Teach Us about Learning and Literacy, how they help the player learn to "read" and understand the game, to figure out what to do in the game world. So, for example, in America's Army, the sergeant character gives the player basic directions to get started. He gives commands like, "Press <G> to fix jammed weapon," "Press <T> to bring up sights," and "Press <B> to reload." In doing so, he merges the player's onscreen and real-life identities. The sergeant is onscreen, talking to the player's onscreen representation; but he's giving directions that only the real-world person can carry out. The onscreen representation doesn't have a G, T, or B button to push—it's the real-world person doing that. Similarly, in Medal of Honor: Frontline the player is to "press Select to get hints from HQ," and "press Start to review mission objectives." In-game, players are spoken to as their real-world self and their onscreen self simultaneously and without differentiation, which means those identities merge.

With the real and the virtual mingling so thoroughly in war video games, perhaps it's only natural that both players and game makers reproduce and perpetuate this fusion in the way they talk. It's not some kind of schizophrenia or delusion, it's the ordinary, proper response to the postmodern facts. For example, imagining someone playing Full Spectrum Warrior with guns blazing rather than cautiously and strategically, William Stahl predicts, "His men will die. Mothers will lose their son, wives will lose their husbands, and children will lose their fathers." OXM also warns, "Don't press [the Action] button [in this game] until you've assessed the situation and made the right plan or it'll be the last button you press." Er, they do mean in-game . . . right? Thus, it's not so outlandish for the magazine to call Full Spectrum Warrior "The Game That Captured Saddam." OXM explains, "This game was made to train the US Army infantry . . . they're the ones who dug Saddam out of his hole. So technically this game caught Saddam." Nor is it as insane as it might first appear when one gamer writes in anticipation of playing

Battlefield: Vietnam, "The Vietnam War was said to be a draw, but when this game comes out everyone will see that the U.S.A. is the best army in the world." His comment suggests that an alleged misperception of history—namely, that the U.S. did not decisively win that war—will be corrected by people's playing the game. He's epistemologically assuming, and rhetorically suggesting, that not only do video games refer to and simulate real-world battles, but because this is so, they also provide players an accurate recreative picture of history. In this understanding, war games not only borrow from history, they also teach it.

Many veterans' and historical organizations have bestowed awards on games such as the Medal of Honor series for their educational value. Medal of Honor: Frontline's official sales copy at EBGames.com boasts, "Authentic WWII content with the assistance of the Smithsonian's . . . expert Russ Lee and renowned technical consultant Capt. Dale Dye," and, "The MOH team continues to work closely with the Congressional Medal of Honor Society to ensure the ideals and integrity of this prestigious commendation." Not incidentally, that game awards the Congressional Medal of Honor for especially meritorious military action—in-game. If players complete a given mission quickly enough and safely enough, they win a virtual medal. MOH: Frontline also unlocks documentary movie clips and historical speech excerpts as rewards for good performance in the game, and it mixes game elements, such as the game's logo and menus, and historical elements, such as documentary film clips and an exhortative speech by Dwight D. Eisenhower, without any differentiation of importance or validity. They all "feel real." Current war video games have blended and blurred the real and the virtual.

Because that is so, the games' romanticizing of war becomes all the more seductive and powerful. Any truly realistic recreation of war would cast some doubt on the idea that war is cool and enjoyable, and that, as in sports, all one has to do is "step up" and become an instant hero. But the titles alone hint at how current war video games support this old myth: Call of Duty, Full Spectrum Warrior, Medal of Honor. Players can almost taste the medals, just reading the game box. In-game, it immediately becomes clear that the war effort would never get off the ground without the player's personal, constant heroics. What the U. S. Army claims in its current advertising slogan is absolutely true: the player really is "An Army of One." Never mind the Army's famous unwieldy, illogical bureaucracy made famous in works such as Catch-22 and M*A*S*H*. Never mind the fact that boot camp is famously designed to tear down the individual to replace that entity with a small cog in a giant machine. Contrary to common-sense facts, the war game player is always "An Army of One." Medal of Honor: Frontline's first mission provides a brilliant example of this. During this mission, "you" are ordered onscreen to storm the beach at Normandy under heavy machine-gun and rifle fire, provide covering fire for three soldiers widely separated along the beach, run lengthwise down the beach to an engineer then cover his run all the way back, cross a minefield, storm a machine-gun nest and take it over, mow down a wave of advancing German soldiers with that machine-gun, and finally snipe two far-off machine-gunners while still under fire. And that's just the first mission! What must the odds be that any individual would a) be present at D-Day; b) be asked to personally complete every single necessary task at that battle; and c) survive to complete them all successfully, thus winning that battle single-handedly? The whole game continues like that: the player is assigned all the work at all the key European battles, eventually bringing about V-E Day completely solo.

This begins to answer the important question, "Why would someone want to realistically recreate the experience of war? Isn't it just common sense to avoid being there?" One game magazine editor raises exactly this question when he writes, "With the new wave of games pushing the envelope of realism it begs the question: how real do we want it? Do we want games that'll simulate war to such a degree that it's possible to suffer from post-game-atic syndrome?" Judging by the state of the games now, the answer for both gamers and game makers is a resounding "No." For all their attention to accurately recreating sounds, weapons, locales, and uniforms, and for all their visual drama and flair, the new "realistic" war video games do not, in fact, reproduce the real conditions of war. They still play too much like other FPSs, and significantly, like goreless FPSs. Although players see soldiers being blown into the air by mines, riddled with machine-gun fire, and sniped from all directions, they never see blood or a flying body part, ever.

Thus, I would argue, what the new war games are is not realistic, but cinematic. They don't reproduce the real world experience of war; they do reproduce the theatrical experience of war. Games use all of the same techniques as movies for framing shots, editing, pacing, and narration. Playing one of the new war video games is very much like starring in a war movie. For example, the MOH: Frontline opening mission is a rather accurate, if condensed, version of the first thirty minutes of *Saving Private Ryan*, even down to individual camera shots: bullets whizzing along underwater past slowly sinking soldiers, and the company's seeking cover under a low hill while the engineer blows away the barbed wire barrier. Medal of Honor: Rising Sun similarly steals heavily from the much less well-made movie Pearl Harbor. H. L. Mencken once described art as "life with all the boring parts taken out." War has been described as 99 percent boredom punctuated by short bursts of abject terror. No one in their right mind would want to reproduce that, and, in recent war video games, no one does. Instead, the games are, in essence, interactive movies about war with all the boring parts taken out. But the boring parts were already pretty much taken out by the movies, so in the games, all that's left is action, action, action—the player winning a war single handedly. The war games make players heroes, in a bloodless, risk-free environment where they can show off their "mad skillz."

As it turns out, then, logical answers do exist for the question, "Why in the world would anyone want to recreate the experience of war?" First, the games don't do quite that; rather, they recreate movies about the experience of war. The additional remove is key. Playing the games provides an entertaining, cinematic experience, rather than the horrible one a true recreation would give. Even if the imagery is not pleasing, it certainly is immersive. And as Miroslaw Filiciak points out, we value the experience of immersion in itself. We intentionally overlook unconvincing elements of the experience so as to become more fully immersed: "We desire the experience of immersion, so we use our intelligence to reinforce rather than to question the reality of the experience." In short, it doesn't really matter that the war games aren't fully realistic; gamers enjoy them for what they are, interactive movies that temporarily immerse us in the games' battles. The second answer to the question, "Why would anyone want to recreate the experience of war?" is to play the hero, in a cinematically intense experience in which we can play an active part rather than just settling passively down into our couches and watching as movies force us to do. And third, we get to see ourselves onscreen playing the hero. Filiciak observes: "Contemporary people have a fascination with electronic media, something we cannot define, something that escapes our rationalizations. . . . We make the screen a fetish; we desire it, not only do we want to watch the screen but also to 'be seen' on it . . . being on the screen ennobles. All the time we have the feeling (more or less true) that others are watching us. The existence of an audience is an absolute necessity." We can see "ourselves" onscreen in any video game, but in online war games such as America's Army and Battlefield: Vietnam, we can also be seen by other players. We can show off our skills, and brag about our victories, to others who have just witnessed them. We can enact the electronic equivalent of dancing in the end zone.

The reasons for making the new war video games are even more obvious than those for playing them. Foremost, there's the money. As I mentioned at the beginning of this article, Americans now spend more money on video games than on movies. Games are huge business, and they're steadily getting huger. One key game maker, the real-world U.S. Army—and by extension, the other service branches and the federal government as a whole—reaps huge benefits from the games' popularity. Not only does the current hawkish regime gain flesh-and-blood recruits for the armed services, it also gains general credibility and support as the games work their propagandist magic. By hiding ugly realities and producing cinematic cotton candy, the games make real war seem exciting, heroic, even fun. And so hawkish political candidates seem not bellicose, but reasonable. Rapidly escalating defense costs look not wasteful, but common-sensical. Thus our two-front war rolls on and on and on.

QUESTIONS

1. How do the newer virtual combat "FPS" (first-person shooter) games differ from the games they evolved from (such as Unreal Tournament? What "unrealistic" features have been carried over? What has been deliberately "left out" of military games and reporting, and to what purpose, in Cowlishaw's view?

2. Despite the unreal qualities of the newer games, they have various technical and artistic areas where they make the player feel as if within a "real" virtual world. What are some of these elements of "virtuality" in the games, according to Cowlishaw, and how might they lead players to faulty conclusions about the war in Iraq or about modern war in general?

3. Does Cowlishaw make his point effectively that many of today's war-oriented video games constitute a kind of deceptive pro-war propaganda? Does Cowlishaw make any such causal link? If so, how? If the games are in fact propaganda, do you think that many of the players really "buy" the military's recruitment/pro-war appeal, or do they (the players) simply find the games enjoyable to play?

JONATHAN L. FREEDMAN

"Evaluating the Research on Violent Video Games"

Jonathan Freedman, a professor of psychology at the University of Toronto, argues that there is no proven relationship between violent entertainment and violent behavior. He has published many articles analyzing research studies in the field, including "Effect of Television Violence on Aggressiveness" (1984), "Television Violence and Aggression: What Psychologists Should Tell the Public" (1992), and "Violence in the Mass Media and Violence in Society: The Link Is Unproven" (1996). His book Media Violence and Its Effect on Aggression *(2002) surveys the empirical studies and experiments in this field and concludes that there is not enough evidence to prove that violent entertainment causes children or adults to act aggressively and violently in social situations. The article that follows focuses on video games and their unproven potential for arousing violence in young users.*

As human beings, we have difficulty accepting random or senseless occurrences. We want to understand why something has happened, and the strength of this desire seems to be proportional to the horror of the event. When a horrible crime occurs, we want to know why. If it was related to drugs or gangs or an armed robbery, I think we find those sufficient reasons. We do not hate the crime less, but at least we think we know why it occurred.

But consider the case of the two boys who walked into Columbine High School in Littleton Colorado and deliberately killed 12 students, a teacher and then themselves; or the case of the 14-year-old Canadian boy who walked into the WR Myers High School in Taber, Alberta and killed one student and seriously injured another. It is difficult to imagine events more terrible than our young people deliberately killing each other. What makes it even worse (if that's possible) is that these appear to have been entirely senseless acts. Oh yes, we have heard that they (and others who have committed similar acts) were outsiders, that they had not been accepted, that they were teased and so on. These reports have sometimes turned out to be false. But even if they were true, nothing that was done to these boys or that they experienced even remotely explains their horrendous crimes.

It seems likely that what happened in most of the school killings was that some random combination of events and personalities and opportunities came together to cause the crime. With tens of millions of children in school, it is perhaps not surprising that every once in a while one of them does something terrible. This is not an explanation. You have all probably gone to your doctor with some ache or pain that appeared for no apparent reason, or gone to your computer expert with a machine that suddenly ceases to function properly or that wiped out a crucial file, and been told by doctor or computer expert that "These things happen." We can accept this with minor ailments and problems, but for most of us it is not an acceptable explanation for violence. We cannot accept that, oh yes, every once in a while a young boy will take out a gun and kill a classmate. We find it hard to live with this. We want something better.

Therefore, whenever these horrible crimes occur, people search for a reason. It was the parents' fault; it was Satanism and witchcraft; it was the lack of religion in the schools and at home; it was a moral breakdown in the countries; it was the availability of guns; it was the culture.

One answer that is often proposed is that the crimes are due to exposure to media violence. Children who watch television and go to the movies see thousands of murders and countless other acts of violence. Many people believe that being exposed to all this violence causes children to be more aggressive and to commit crimes? That's an explanation people can accept and, sure enough, many people in Canada and the United States believe that media violence is a major cause of violent crime.

Recently, attention has turned toward the violence in video games. It seems reasonable to many people that if passively watching violence in movies and on television causes aggression, actively participating in violence in video games should have an even greater effect. Surely, so the argument goes, spending hours shooting images of various creatures and of human beings and watching them blow up, break apart, scream in pain, spew blood all over, and so on must have a harmful effect on those who play—it must teach them that violence is acceptable, that it is a way to deal with problems, perhaps make them insensitive to real violence, and thus cause them to be more aggressive and more violent themselves.

While this seems obvious or even self-evident to some, it is less obvious to others. In any case, we know that what seems obvious is not always correct. The role of systematic research is to help determine whether it is correct. Therefore, the work on the effect of video games on aggression is potentially very important. Accordingly, it is essential that it be done very carefully and that the results be evaluated fairly and objectively. Anderson and Bushman (2001) have recently published a meta-analysis of the research. Their analysis concludes that exposure to violent video games has a negative effect on a variety of measures. The analysis of greatest import is the one indicating that playing violent video games causes an increase in aggressive behavior. On the basis of their overall analysis and presumably especially the one regarding aggressive behavior, the authors assert that video games pose a threat to public health. This is a serious paper and a very serious assertion. What should we make of it?

To begin, it should be clear that there has not been a great deal of research relevant to this question. In their meta-analysis Anderson and Bushman identified 35 research reports that included 54 independent samples of participants. Of these, 22 were published. And of these, only nine studies dealt with aggressive behavior. In other words, conclusions about whether playing violent video games causes aggressive behavior must be based on nine published experiments. I cannot think of another important issue for which scientists have been willing to reach conclusions on such a small body of research. Even if the research had been designed and conducted perfectly, there is far too little evidence to reach any firm conclusions. And, as I shall discuss below, the research is far from perfect.

Before discussing some of the problems with the research, let me acknowledge that this is a very difficult issue to study. Only experimental research can provide a definitive answer to the question whether violent video games cause aggression. Yet, as with many issues of public concern, it is impossible to conduct the perfect experiment. To determine whether exposure to violent video games causes aggression, the ideal experiment would randomly assign children to playing or not playing video games containing violence. Some would play violent video games for a great many hours, some would play such games for less time or would play games with less violence, others would play no video games, and so on. They would continue to do this for many years, and during and after that time one would obtain measures of their aggressive behavior. If those who played violent video games engaged in more aggressive or violent behavior, it would indicate that the video games caused aggression; and if this difference did not emerge, it would provide evidence that playing violent video games did not cause aggression.

Of course, such a study is not possible. For ethical, legal, moral, and logistic reasons, one cannot assign children to play certain kinds of games for years even if one were willing to do so. Accordingly, the ideal experiment cannot be conducted and we must rely on less perfect studies in attempting to answer our question. Although it is difficult to reach firm conclusions about causality without the kind of study I just described, it is not impossible. With sufficient ingenuity, resources and time, one can collect enough evidence of an effect that most scientists will be convinced. This is the case with the research on cigarette smoking and cancer—no perfect experiment can be done, but after a vast amount of research, few people doubt that smoking causes cancer. We are nowhere near the point at which we could have the same confidence in the video game research, but we can at least try to make sense out of the work that has been done. To do so requires a careful analysis of the methodology and logic of the studies and their findings. Accordingly, let me turn to a consideration of the research.

Non-experimental studies

Most of the non-experimental work consists of relatively small-scale surveys. People are asked about their exposure to video games, to violent video games, and to various other media. They are also asked about their aggressive behavior, or occasionally others provide information on the respondents' aggressive behavior. Then the researchers conduct correlational analyses (or other similar analyses) to see if those who are exposed more to violent video games are more aggressive than those who are exposed less. Sometimes more detailed analyses are conducted to see if other factors mediate or reduce any relation that is found.

The findings of this research are similar to that of the survey research on other violent media and aggression. Despite some inconsistencies and complexities, the results seem to indicate that people who spend more time playing video games tend to be more aggressive than those who spend less time playing them; and, with less certainty, that this is especially true of playing violent video games. Because there are so few studies and the lack of representative samples, we cannot put much confidence in the size of these correlations. Nevertheless, it seems likely that the basic relation is true—those who like violent video games tend to be more aggressive than those who do not like them.

This is an important finding, because it raises the possibility that playing video games causes aggression. That is, one reason why playing violent games is related to aggressiveness could be that playing the games makes people more aggressive. However, there are other plausible explanations, such as that people with a more aggressive personality like violent video games and also engage in more aggressive behavior. Playing the games does not cause the aggression, nor does the aggression cause the preference for violent games. They are both caused by another factor—the person's personality. Other such explanations are also possible. Thus, the existence of the correlation between playing violent games and aggressiveness does not prove that one causes the other. It provides no evidence for causality. While interesting, this research is not relevant to the central question whether violent video games cause aggression. Therefore, I shall restrict my comments to the experimental research since that is the only work that is relevant to this question. (I should add that as Anderson and Bushman point out, other kinds of non-experimental research could provide some evidence for causality, but it has not been done and thus does not enter the debate.)

Experimental Research

The experimental work seems to have patterned on laboratory experiments on the effects of film and television violence. The basic design is that people are brought into a laboratory, some play a video game containing violence while others play a video game with less violence or no violence, and in some studies others do not play any video games. Then various measures are obtained that are meant to indicate the participants' level of aggression. If those who played the violent video game score higher on these measures, it is interpreted to show that the violent video game caused aggression. As noted above, there are very few such experiments but according to the review by Anderson and Bushman, overall the results indicate a significant effect of violent video games on aggression. One can question some of the decisions those authors made in the classifications in their meta-analysis, but this paper is not meant as a critique of the meta-analysis so let us assume that their statistical conclusion is justified. That is, combining all of the research, there is a small but significant effect of playing violent video games on the measures of aggression employed in the studies.

This should not end the debate. The original question whether playing violent video games causes people to be aggressive is certainly not answered yet. We must still ask what this finding means. Or, to put it in other terms, should the results of this research be interpreted as indicating that playing violent video games causes aggression. The answer to this question depends on the details of how the research was designed and conducted. If it has been done perfectly, the findings would mean that violent video games do affect aggression; but if the research is flawed or limited, the findings may be open to other interpretations.

Although there are all sorts of points that can be made about the work, let me focus on three: the comparability of the violent and non-violent games, the possibility of demand factors being present and the measures of aggression.

The Choice of Games

One of the most basic requirements of good experimentation is that the various conditions be as similar as possible except for the variable of interest. As long as the conditions differ only in terms of that variable, any differences in the dependent measure can be attributed to that variable; but if the conditions differ in other ways, any differences in the dependent measure could be due to any of the ways in the which the conditions differ. That is why great effort is usually made to equate the various experiment groups on every factor except the one of concern.

For example, imagine some researchers wanted to test the effectiveness of a new drug designed to reduce flu symptoms. The researchers design a study in which some people who have the flu get the drug three times a day while others get a placebo three times a day. Because the drug does not taste very good, it is mixed with a vitamin-rich fruit drink to make it more palatable, while the placebo is taken with water. The study shows that those who are given the drug report that their symptoms were less severe that those who were given the placebo. The researchers conclude that the drug works.

This conclusion is clearly not justified because the two conditions differ in more ways than just the presence or absence of the drug. Those who got the drug also drank the fruit drink. The difference between the conditions on the dependent variable could be due to the drug or to the fruit drink. This is so obvious that no serious scientist would make such a silly mistake. In good drug research the conditions are identical except for the drug—everyone gets the same instructions, everyone takes an identical-looking pill, takes the pill under identical circumstances, and every effort is made to have the drug-pill and the placebo-pill taste the same. In fact, as I'll discuss later, both patient and physician do not even know what condition the patients are in until after the experiment is completed. Only when all of this is done is it legitimate to attribute differences to the drug. Similarly, in any kind of experiment, only if the experimental and control conditions are identical in every respect except the variable of interest can one conclude that differences on the dependent variable are due to that variable.

This ideal level of comparability between conditions has never been realized in the research on video games, even when the experimenters tried to equate conditions. For example, Anderson and Dill (2000) compared Wolfenstein, a violent video game, with Myst. They selected these two programs with considerable care. They conducted a pilot study on several video programs and found that these two did not differ in the ratings they received on various important dimensions. In particular, there were no differences on physiological measures or on ratings of action. In other words, the authors tried to find games that were equivalent.

However, it seems obvious that their attempt was not entirely successful. In the first place, players rated Wolfenstein more exciting than Myst. But perhaps equally important, anyone familiar with the two knows that they are entirely different programs. Myst was a very popular program that sold millions—but it differs in many ways from the violent game. To begin, it is not really a game but a puzzle. The players find themselves on a strange island and must figure out what is going on. This involves finding esoteric clues, interpreting them, and then using them correctly. It is extremely difficult and requires great ingenuity to solve. Those who like the game find this interesting and fascinating. But there is no action (it is hard to imagine why it was rated similar to Wolfenstein on this dimension) and nothing that makes it similar to a game. So it is not really an appropriate comparison, since presumably the question is whether games that involve violence differ from games that do not involve violence in their effects on aggression—not whether playing games differs from engaging in problem solving. Or, to put it another way, as in any experiment, you do not compare apples and oranges, but rather two kinds of apples.

Ballard and Lindeberger, 1999 did a better job. They compared NBA Jam, an exciting sports game with three versions of Mortal Kombat that differed in the amount of violence (or at least the graphic nature of the violence). It is possible that Mortal Kombat was more exciting and had more action than the basketball game, but at least all of the programs were exciting, all were games, and it was possible to compare the three levels of Mortal Kombat to look for differences due to varying amounts of violence. Graybill et al (1987) probably did still better. They used six games that did not differ in ratings of excitement, difficulty or enjoyment but only in ratings of violence. All of them were lively, action-packed games in which players compete against the computer. Presumably it is better to have six games than to have only two since this reduces the chance that any effects are due to the specific games.

My point here is not to say that all of the studies failed to equate the games or that those that did equate them found no effect on aggression. Rather, the point is that in considering all of the research, it is important to understand that few of the experiments came close to solving and none solved perfectly the tricky problem of making the violent and non-violent games comparable on all variables other than the amount of violence. It may be that this cannot be done, but we must recognize that it is a limitation of the work and a serious limitation in some of the experiments.

The lack of comparability of the video games is not a subtle or picky criticism—it is absolutely basic to the design and interpretation of the research because it leaves open the interpretation of any difference that is found between conditions. And as in other media violence research, one obvious interpretation is that any effect is due to differences in arousal. Indeed, in their review of the research Anderson and Bushman found that exposure to violent video games increased physiological arousal. If the violent video game is more arousing than the non-violent comparison program, one would expect more aggression (or almost anything else) in the condition with higher arousal. If so, there is no reason to attribute the effect to the violence—it might be just the arousal. Since all of this research compared games with violence to games (or programs) without violence, and since the two types of games differed in many ways, it is possible any effects on aggression could be due to arousal or other factors rather than to the presence of violence. Because of this problem, one must be extremely cautious in interpreting the results of this research and especially cautious in deciding that the effects are due to the amount of violence in the games.

Demand Factor

Another basic element in almost all experiments is the problem of experimenter or situational demand producing effects. Those who design experimental research know that there is always the possibility, indeed probability, that elements of the procedure will give the subject the impression that a particular response is expected or desired or allowed, and that this will affect how the subjects behave. This problem is so well recognized that virtually all drug research is designed so that neither the participants or the experiments know the participants' experimental condition. This avoids the possibility that those getting the drug would expect to get better and would therefore feel better or report that they feel better, and also that the experimenters would expect them to get better and would judge that they had gotten better. This procedure works very well for drug research, but cannot be used in the research on video games (since obviously the participants will know what game they have played).

The problem of experimenter demand effects is especially pronounced when the behavior of interest is one that is usually not allowed or is inhibited in the experimental situation. For example, imagine that a group of psychologists want to study the effect of rap music on children's tendency to use obscene language. To do this, they design an experiment in which some children listen to rap music and others listen to equally lively, equally popular heavy metal music. Note that they have been careful to equate the music in terms of arousal, popularity and so on. The children are brought into the laboratory in small groups, the music is playing in the room, and the children are asked to wait for a while. The experiments then have a long talk with the children or let them talk among themselves and they observe how much obscene language is used.

Although this is not a bad study in some respects, it suffers from the possibility of serious demand effects. The children will notice that the experimenters have chosen to play rap music and will infer that the experiments like that music or at least approve of it. This will send the message that the language in the music is acceptable to the experimenters, or at least acceptable in the laboratory. This will give the children permission to use the language themselves, whereas without that message most of them would probably be inhibited by the formality of the situation and the presence of unknown adults.

Knowing this, careful experimenters will distance themselves from the music. That is, they will make it obvious that they did not choose the music and thus give no indication whether they approve of it or even tolerate it. They could do this in various ways. For example, the children could come first to a room some distance from the laboratory, and the music (rap or otherwise) could apparently be coming from outside the building. The children would thus be exposed to the music for a while, but there would be no suggestion and no reason to infer that the experimenters had anything to do with the music. When the children then came to the laboratory, their behavior might be affected by the music, but not through the effect of experimenter demand.

Turning now to the work on video games, when some subjects are told to play a violent game and others a non-violent game, there is the clear possibility of experimenter demand (broadly defined). When the experimenters choose a violent game, they may be giving the message that they approve of such games and might therefore approve of or even expect the subjects to behave violently or aggressively. This could be avoided by separating the experimenters from the choice of game. This is admittedly not easy, but no one ever said that designing research is simple. Only if "sponsorship" of the game is removed as a factor can any differences among conditions be unambiguously attributed to the presence of violence rather than the "permission" given to act aggressively by the choice of the game.

One of the most obvious weaknesses in much of the research on media violence and especially on video game violence is that so little attention appears to have been paid to how the study was structured for the participants. Often they were told virtually nothing about why the study was being conducted or even what they could expect to be doing. When there were cover stories, they were pretty flimsy or incomplete. Anderson and Dill (2000) provided one of the better cover stories, which was that the study concerned the learning curve—how people learn and develop a motor skill and how it affects other tasks. This is not bad, but it offers no explanation of why the particular game was chosen. Since as far as each participant knows, the experimenters are using only one game, they could infer that the experimenters liked that particular game or were interested in the learning of that game and this could affect the participants' responses. Imagine that the cover story were expanded a little and included the statement that to make their findings as general as possible they were using a large number of video games (which could be shown) and that the game each person would play is randomly selected from the group. If lots of games were shown, the participant would have no reason to infer anything from the fact that he or she was asked to play a violent game (except perhaps that the experimenters did not disapprove of these games so strongly that they excluded them). This would greatly reduce or even eliminate the possibility that the choice of game affected the participants' behavior.

Let me be clear that the possibility of demand causing the results is not unlikely or far-fetched. It is a well-known phenomenon in experimental research and a continual almost ubiquitous source of problems in interpretation. That is why so much attention is usually devoted to setting up the situation to minimize this effect. Unfortunately, those studying the impact of video games have not generally been concerned enough with this problem to deal with it effectively. This leaves almost all of the results open to the alternative and uninteresting interpretation that they are caused by demand factors rather than the variable of interest, namely the direct effect of the amount of violence in the video game.

Measures of Aggression

As noted before, very few of the studies even try to measure aggression, and many of the measures have almost nothing to do with aggression. The most distant are measures of thoughts or as they are sometimes called, aggressive cognitions. In some of the studies, if the people in the violent game condition have more thoughts of aggression than those playing the non-violent game, this is considered an indication that violent games cause aggression. This interpretation is not justified. After eating a huge meal, you probably are thinking about food—but you are less rather than more likely to want to eat. After watching a war movie, you probably have thoughts of war, but no one would suggest that you are more likely to wage war unless the movie promoted war. After *Schindler's List*, I imagine that most people thought about war and torture and violence, but I hope that most people were less likely to be aggressive rather than more likely. Whatever stimulus you are exposed to, you are more likely to have thoughts related to that stimulus, but that does not mean that your behavior has been affected. Indeed, Graybill et al. used aggressive thoughts as a manipulation check to see if the aggressive content of the game was salient, not as a measure of aggression.

Similarly, some studies measure physiological arousal and consider that an indication of aggression. Again, this makes no sense. After playing a tense game that involves shooting and being shot at, people may be physiologically aroused. But there is no reason to think that this alone makes them more likely to be aggressive. As noted above, it is an indication that the violent game differed from the non-violent one in terms of arousal, which is a problem, not a finding that supports the notion that violent video games cause aggression.

I am not arguing that this research is uninteresting. It is interesting that people have violent thoughts after playing violent games and it is interesting (though less so) that they are more aroused after a violent game. Both the thoughts and the arousal may play a role in their behavior. But there is no evidence that it makes them more likely to act violently—perhaps it does the opposite. So the studies with these measures should be given little or no weight. They tell us nothing about whether playing violent video games makes people aggressive.

Most of the behavioral measures are analogues of aggression rather than the real thing. Anderson and Dill (2000) used as their measure of aggression the intensity and duration of a loud noise that one subject gave to another. Pressing a button that delivers a short burst of loud noise is pretty remote from real aggression. Cooper and Mackie (1986) observed whether the children in their study chose to play with "aggressive" or "non-aggressive" toys. Playing with an aggressive toy is hardly the same as being aggressive. One could even argue that this measure confuses the outcome with the question which is whether playing an aggressive game (i.e., video game) causes aggression. Showing that playing one aggressive game increases the likelihood that children will play another aggressive game does not tell us anything about effects on actual aggression.

Some of the measures were somewhat better than these, but is should be clear that almost all of the research involved analogues of aggression rather than the real thing. One can and I believe should question whether these analogues have anything to do with aggression—they may sound like aggression and they have often been used by other researchers to measure aggression, but they are not aggression and there is no good evidence that they indicate anything about aggressive behavior.

Conclusions

This body of research is not only extremely limited in terms of the number of relevant studies, but also suffers from many methodological problems. Insufficient attention has been paid to choosing games that are as similar as possible except for the presence of violence; virtually no attention has been paid to eliminating or at least minimizing experimenter demand; and the measures of aggression are either remote from aggression or of questionable value.

Given these problems and limitations in this body of research, what can we reasonably conclude from the findings? 1. There is substantial, though far from overwhelming or definitive evidence that people who like and play violent video games tend to be more aggressive than those who like and play them less. This is, of course, a purely correlational finding and tells us nothing about whether playing violence video games causes aggression. 2. There is some slight evidence that immediately after playing violent video games there is an increase in aggressiveness. As discussed above, the evidence for this is minimal and is greatly weakened by limitations in the research, which provide alternative explanations of the effect. 3. There is not the slightest evidence that playing violent video games causes any long-term or lasting increase in aggressiveness or violence. There is very little relevant research, and no longitudinal studies that might show such effects. It may well be that further research will indicate that playing violent video games is harmful. For the moment, however, there is no such work and no scientific reason to believe that violent video games have bad effects on children or on adults, and certainly none to indicate that such games constitute a public health risk.

References

Anderson, C. A., & Bushman, B. J. (2001) Effects of violent video games on aggressive behavior, aggressive cognition, aggressive affect, physiological arousal, and prosocial behavior: A meta-analytic review of the scientific literature. *Psychological Science, 12,* 353–359.

Anderson, C. A., & , Dill, K. E. (2000) Video games and aggressive thoughts, feelings, and behavior in the laboratory and life. *Journal of Personality and Social Psychology, 78,* 772–790.

Cooper, J., & Mackie, D. (1986) Video games and aggression in children. *Journal of Applied Social Psychology, 16,* 726–744.

Graybill, D., Strawniak, M., Hunter, T., & O'Leary, M. (1987) Effects of playing versus observing violent versus nonviolent video games on children's aggression. *Psychology: A Quarterly Journal of Human Behavior, 24,* 1–8.

QUESTIONS

1. How does Freedman link people's desire to create a clear cause for "random" events to the blaming of media for violence in our society? Is his explanation convincing? Why or why not?

2. Why does Freedman argue that it is very difficult to study and design experiments to demonstrate video game-related aggression? What is his argument based on, other than his own beliefs? How do issues such as choice of games to study and "experimental demand" influence the outcome of video-game violence experiments, in Freedman's view?

3. What distinction does Freedman draw between experiments that note behavior in the area of "analogues of aggression" as opposed to "the real thing"? Why is this distinction important in considering the actual impact of the games upon aggressive behavior?

"Testimony on Media Violence"

Henry Jenkins III (b. 1958), professor of Humanities and co-director of the MIT Comparative Media Studies program, earned his M.A. in Communication Studies from the University of Iowa and his Ph.D. in Communication Arts from the University of Wisconsin-Madison. He views media culture as active and participatory, with a focus on what he terms "media convergence," which holds that fans/participants combine insights in a complex manner that could be termed reformative, creative, and political. He has explored these issues in his 2006 book, Fans, Bloggers, and Gamers: Exploring Participatory Culture, *as well as in his work with the Convergence Culture Consortium at MIT. The text below from Jenkins's 1999 testimony before Congress on the Littleton, Colorado school killings shares some of his ideas on the complex, participatory role of media in the culture of modern youth and argues against demonizing this culture because of recent acts of school violence.*

The shootings at Colombine High School in Littleton, Colorado several weeks ago have justly sparked a period of national soul searching. . . . So far, most of the conversation about Littleton has reflected a desire to understand what the media are doing to our children. Instead, we should be focusing our attention on understanding what our children are doing with media.

As more information becomes available to us, it is becoming increasingly clear that Eric Harris and Dylan Klebold, the two Littleton shooters, had an especially complex relationship to popular culture. Various pundits have pointed their fingers at video games, violent movies, television series, popular music, comic books, websites, youth subcultures, and fashion choices to locate the cause of their violent behavior. What have we learned so far? Harris and Klebold played video games. Not surprising—roughly 80 percent of American boys play video games. Harris and Klebold spent a great deal of time on line. According to Don Tapscott's *Growing Up Digital: The Rise of the Net Generation,* 11 percent of the world's computer users are under the age of 15. Thirty six percent of American teens use an online service at home, 49 percent at school, and 69 percent have been on-line at least once in their lifetime, compared to 40% of the total population that has been on-line. They engaged in on-line gaming. According to Jon Katz, estimates of online gamers in the United States alone run as high as 15 to 20 million people. Harris and Klebold watched a range of films, including *The Matrix,* which has been the top money earner in four of the last five weeks. They listened to various popular music groups, some relatively obscure (kmfdm), some highly successful (Marilyn Manson). They may have borrowed certain iconography from the Goth subculture, a subculture that has a history going back to the 1980s and which has rarely been associated with violence or criminal activity. They may have worn black trench coats. None of these cultural choices, taken individually or as an aggregate, differentiates Harris and Klebold from a sizable number of American teenagers who also consumed these same forms of popular culture but have not gone out and gunned down their classmates. The tangled relationship between these various forms of popular culture makes it impossible for us to determine a single cause for their [Harris and Klebold's] actions. Culture doesn't work that way.

Cultural artifacts are not simple chemical agents like carcinogens that produce predictable results upon those who consume them. They are complex bundles of often contradictory meanings that can yield an enormous range of different responses from the people who consume them.

Like the rest of us, Harris and Klebold inhabited a hypermediated culture. The range of media options available to us has expanded at a dramatic rate over the past several decades. . . . New media technologies are being introduced at an astonishing rate enabling a more participatory relationship to media culture. In such a world, each of us make choices about what kinds of media we want to consume, what kinds of culture are meaningful or emotionally rewarding to us. None of us devote our attention exclusively to only one program, only one recording star, only one network, or only one medium. People define their own media environment through their own particular choices from the huge menu of cultural artifacts and channels of communication that surround us all the time. Some teens are drawn towards the angst-ridden lyrics of industrial music; others are happily jitterbugging to neo-swing. Selling popular culture to our kids isn't quite the same thing as selling cigarettes to our kids. When it comes to popular culture, we all "roll our own." We cobble together a personal mythology of symbols, images, and stories that we have adopted from the raw materials given us by the mass media, and we invest in those symbols and stories meanings that are personal to us or that reflect our shared experiences as part of one or another subcultural community. In the case of Harris and Klebold, they drew into their world the darkest, most alienated, most brutal images available to them and they turned those images into the vehicle of their personal demons, their antisocial impulses, their psychological maladjustment, their desire to hurt those who have hurt them.

In this case, those choices and investments had lethal results.

Banning black trenchcoats or violent video games doesn't get us anywhere. The black trench coats or the song lyrics are only symbols. To be effective in changing the nature of contemporary youth culture, what we want to get at are the meanings that are associated with those symbols, the kinds of affiliations they express, and more importantly, the feelings of profound alienation and powerlessness that pushed these particular kids (and others like them) over the edge. Consuming popular culture didn't make these boys into killers; rather, the ways they consumed popular culture reflected their drive towards destruction. For most kids most of the time, these forms of popular culture provide a normal, if sometimes angst-ridden, release of frustration and tension. Sometimes, indeed most often, as the old joke goes, a cigar is only a cigar and a black trenchcoat is only a raincoat.

Symbols don't necessary have fixed or universal meanings. Symbols gain meanings through their use and circulation across a variety of contexts. Some of those meanings are shared, some of them are deeply personal and private, but once we perceive a need to express a particular feeling or idea, human beings are pretty resourceful at locating a symbol that suits their needs.

It is relatively easy to get rid of one or another symbol. Some symbols—the swastika for example—maintain power over thousands of years, although they have often radically shifted meaning over that time. But most of the time, symbols have a very limited shelf life. Half the time media activists focus their energies on combating examples of popular culture that have little or no commercial appeal to begin with. Computer games such as Custer's Revenge, Death Trap, or Postal, which have been the center of so much debate about video game violence had only limited commercial success and are far from the bread and butter of the video game industry, which is, for the most part, far more dependent on its sports-focused games than on combat games. The images found in such marginal works are certainly outrageous, but they are so outrageous that they attract few customers; they alienate their potential market and collapse of their own accord. It is much harder to get rid of the feelings that those symbols express. . . .

Sometimes one or another image from mass culture does become part of the fantasy universe of a psychotic, does seem to inspire some of their antisocial behavior, but we need to recognize that these images have also been taken out of context, that they have been ascribed with idiosyncratic meanings. Despite the mass size of the audience for some of the cultural products we are discussing, there are tremendous differences in the way various audience members respond to their influence.

It is very hard to tell what these artifacts and myths mean from a position outside the cultural community that has grown up around them. All we can see are the symbols; we can't really get at the meanings that are attached to them without opening some kind of conversation with the people who are using those symbols, who are consuming those stories, and who are deploying those media.

For methodological reasons, empirical research on "media effects" chooses not to address any of these issues, tending to bracket from consideration issues about media content, context, and form as beyond its purview. Empirical researchers can only work with simple variables. Consequently, they offer only crude insights into the actual consequences of consuming violent media within specific real world contexts. They can tell us that certain media images stimulate neural responses, creating a state of tension or arousal. They can measure certain attitude shifts after consuming media images. But, in both cases, it takes a series of interpretive leaps and speculations to move from such data to any meaningful claim that media images cause real world behavior. Most "media effects" researchers pull back from making any confident claims about the possible links between popular culture and youth violence, because decades of research on media violence still yields contradictory and confusing results.

Media effects research typically starts from the assumption that we know what we mean by "media violence," that we can identify and count violent acts when we see them, that we can choose or construct a representative example of media violence and use it as the basis for a series of controlled experiments. Under most circumstances, our children don't experience violent images abstracted from social or narrative contexts. Exposing children to such concentrated doses of decontextualized violence focuses their attention on the violent acts and changes the emotional tone which surrounds them. Storytelling depends upon the construction of conflict and in visual based media, conflict is often rendered visible by being staged through violence. Stories help to ascribe meaning to the violent acts they depict. When we hear a list of the sheer number of violent acts contained on an evening of American television, it feels overwhelming. But, each of these acts occurs in some kind of a context and we need to be attentive to the specifics of those various contexts. . . . Some works depict violence in order to challenge the culture that generates that violence; other works celebrate violence as an appropriate response to social humiliation or as a tool for restoring order in a violent and chaotic culture or as a vehicle of patriotism. Some works depict self-defense; others acts of aggression. Some make distinctions between morally justifiable and morally unjustifiable violence; some don't. We know this, of course, because we are all consumers of violent images. We read murder mysteries; we watch news reports; we enjoy war movies and westerns; we go to operas and read classic works of western literature. So many of the films, for example, which have been at the center of debates about media violence—*A Clockwork Orange, Pulp Fiction, Natural Born Killers, The Basketball Diaries*, and now *The Matrix*—are works that have provoked enormous critical debates because of their thematic and aesthetic complexity, because they seem to be trying to say something different about our contemporary social environment and they seem to be finding new images and new techniques for communicating their meanings. Depicting violence is certainly not the same thing as promoting violence. Cultural studies research tells us we need to make meaningful distinctions between different ways of representing violence, different kinds of stories about violence, and different kinds of relationships to violent imagery.

Media-effects research often makes little or no distinction between the different artistic conventions we use to represent violent acts. At its worst, media effects research makes no distinction between violent cartoons or video games that offer a fairly stylized representation of the world around us and representation of violence that are more realistic. Other researchers, however, show that children learn at an early age to make meaningful distinctions between different kinds of relationships between media images and the realm of their own lived experience. These studies suggest that children are fairly adept at dismissing works that represent fantastic, hyperbolic, or stylized violence and are more likely to be emotionally disturbed by works that represent realistic violence and especially images of violence in documentary films (predator-prey documentaries, war films) that can not be divorced from their real world referents. Such research would suggest that children are more likely to be disturbed by reports of violent crimes on the evening news than representations of violence in fictional works.

One of the most significant aspects of play is that play is divorced from real life. Play exists in a realm of fantasy that strips our actions of their everyday consequences or meanings. Classic studies of play behavior among primates, for example, suggest that apes make basic distinctions between play fighting and actual combat. In some circumstances, they seem to take pleasure wrestling and tousling with each other and in other contexts, they might rip each other apart in mortal combat. We do things in our fantasies that we would have no desire to do in real life, and this is especially true of fantasies that involve acts of violence. The pleasure of play stems at least in part from escapism. The appeal of video game violence often has more to do with feelings of empowerment than with the expression of aggressive or hurtful feelings. Our children feel put down by teachers and administrators, by kids on the playground; they feel like they occupy a very small space in the world and have very limited ability to shape reality according to their needs and desires. Playing video games allows them to play with power, to manipulate reality, to construct a world through their fantasies in which they are powerful and can exert control. The pleasure stems precisely from their recognition of the contrast between the media representations and the real world. It is not the case that media violence teaches children that real world violence has no consequence. Rather, children can take pleasure in playing with power precisely because they are occupying a fantastic space that has little or no direct relationship to their own everyday environment. Fantasy allows children to express feelings and impulses that have to be carefully held in check in their real world interactions. Such experiences can be cathartic, can enable a release of tension that allows children to better cope with their more mundane frustrations. The stylized and hyperbolic quality of most contemporary entertainment becomes one of the primary markers by which children distinguish between realistic and playful representations of violence.

Let us be clear: while I am questioning both the methodology and the conclusions employed by a central tradition of media effects research, I am not arguing that children learn nothing from the many hours they spend consuming media; I am not arguing that the content of our culture makes no difference in the shape of our thoughts and our feelings. Quite the opposite. Of course, we should be concerned about the content of our culture; we should be worried if violent images push away other kinds of representations of the world. The meanings youths weave into their culture are at least partially a product of the kinds of fantasy materials they have access to and therefore we should subject those materials to scrutiny. We should encourage children to engage critically with the materials of their culture. But, popular culture is only one influence on our children's fantasy lives. As the Littleton case suggests, the most powerful influences on children are those they experience directly, that are part of their immediate environment at school or at home. In the case of Harris and Klebold, these influences apparently included a series of social rejections and humiliations and a perception that adult authorities weren't going to step in and provide them with protection from the abuse directed against them from the "in crowd."

We can turn off a television program or shut down a video game if we find what it is showing us ugly, hurtful, or displeasing. We can't shut out the people in our immediate environment quite so easily. Many teenagers find going to school a brutalizing experience of being required to return day after day to a place where they are ridiculed and taunted and sometimes physically abused by their classmates and where school administrators are slow to respond to their distress and can offer them few strategies for making the abuse stop. Media images may have given Harris and Klebold symbols to express their rage and frustration, but the media did not create the rage or generate their alienation. What sparked the violence was not something they saw on the internet or on television, not some song lyric or some sequence from a movie, but things that really happened to them. When we listen to young people talk about the shootings, they immediately focus on the pain, suffering, and loneliness experienced by Harris and Klebold, seeing something of their own experiences in the media descriptions of these troubled youths, and struggling to understand the complex range of factors which insure that they are going to turn out okay while the Colorado adolescents ended up dead. If we want to do something about the problem, we are better off focusing our attention on negative social experiences and not the symbols we use to talk about those experiences.

Some of the experts who have stepped forward in the wake of the Littleton shootings have accused mass media of teaching our children how to perform violence—as if such a direct transferal of knowledge were possible. The metaphor of media as a teacher is a compelling but ultimately misleading one. As a teacher, I would love to be able to decide exactly what I want my students to know and transmit that information to them with sufficient skill and precision that every student in the room learned exactly what I wanted, no more and no less. But, as teachers across the country can tell you, teaching doesn't work that way. Each student pays attention to some parts of the lesson and ignores or forgets others. Each has their own motivations for learning. Whatever "instruction" occurs in the media environment is even more unpredictable. Entertainers don't typically see themselves as teaching lessons. They don't carefully plan a curriculum. They don't try to clear away other distractions. Consumers don't sit down in front of their television screens to learn a lesson. Their attention is even more fragmented; their goals in taking away information from the media are even more personal; they aren't really going to be tested on what they learn. Those are all key differences from the use of video games as a tool of military training and the use of video games for recreation. The military uses the games as part of a specific curriculum with clearly defined goals, in a context where students actively want to learn and have a clear need for the information and skills being transmitted, and there are clear consequences for not mastering those skills. None of this applies to playing these same or similar games in a domestic or arcade context.

So far, the media response to the Littleton shootings has told us a great deal more about what those symbols mean to adults than what they mean to American youth, because for the most part, it is the adults who are doing all of the talking and the youth who are being forced to listen. Three key factors have contributed to the current media fixation on the role of popular culture in the shootings . . . : our generational anxiety about the process of adolescence, our technophobic reaction about our children's greater comfort with digital technologies, and our painful discovery of aspects of our children's play and fantasy lives which have long existed but were once hidden from view. Read in this context, the materials of youth culture can look profoundly frightening, but much of what scares us is a product of our own troubled imaginations and is far removed from what these symbols mean to our children.

All of the above suggests a basic conclusion: banning specific media images will have little or no impact on the problem of youth crime, because doing so gets at symbols, not at the meanings those symbols carry and not at the social reality that gives such urgency to teens' investments in those cultural materials. . . . The best way to do that is to create opportunities for serious conversations about the nature of our children's relationships with popular culture. One project which sets a good example for such discussions is the Superhero TV Project conducted by Ellen Seiter at the University of California-San Diego. Seiter recognized the centrality of superhero cartoons, games, comics, and action heroes to preschool children and recognized the recurring concerns parents and teachers had about the place of those materials in the children's lives. Seiter and her graduate students worked with teachers to encourage classroom activities that center around these superhero myths. Students were encouraged to invent their own superheroes and to make up stories about them. Students discussed their stories in class and decided that they would collaborate in the production of a superhero play.

Through the classroom discussions about what kinds of physical actions could be represented in their play, teachers and students talked together about the place of violence in the superhero stories and what those violent images meant to them. Through such conversations, both students and teachers developed a much better understanding of the role of violent imagery in popular entertainment.

Writing for the slashdot.com website, journalist Jon Katz has described a fundamentally different reaction to popular culture in high schools across America in the wake of the Littleton shootings. Schools are shutting down student access to the net and the web. Parents are cutting their children off from access to their on-line friends or forbidding them to play computer games. Students are being suspended for coming to school displaying one or another cultural symbol (black trench coats, heavy metal T-shirts). Students are being punished or sent into therapy because they express opinions in class discussions or essays that differ from the views about the events being promoted by their teachers. Guidance counselors are drawing on checklists of symptoms of maladjustment to try to ferret out those students who are outsiders and either force them into the mainstream or punish them for their dissent. Rather than teaching students to be more tolerant of the diversity they encounter in the contemporary high school, these educators and administrators are teaching their students that difference is dangerous, that individuality should be punished, and that self expression should be curbed. In this polarized climate, it becomes impossible for young people to explain to us what their popular culture means to them without fear of repercussion and reprisals. We are pushing this culture further and further underground where it will be harder and harder for us to study and understand it. We are cutting off students at risk from the lifeline provided by their on-line support groups.

We all want to do something about the children at risk. We all want to do something about the proliferation of violent imagery in our culture. We all want to do something to make sure events like the Littleton shootings do not occur again. But repression of youth culture is doomed not only to fail but to backfire against us. Instead, we need to take the following steps:

1. We need to create contexts where students can form meaningful and supportive communities through their use of digital media. Sameer Parekh, a 24-year-old software entrepreneur, has offered one such model through his development of the High School Underground website

(*http://www.hsunderground.com*). His site invites students who feel ostracized at school to use the web as a means of communicating with each other about their concerns, as a tool of creative expression and social protest, as the basis for forming alliances that leads to an end of the feelings of loneliness and isolation. We need to have more spaces like High School Underground that provide a creative and constructive direction for children who are feeling cut off from others in their schools or communities. A number of websites have been built within the goth subculture to explain its perplexing images to newcomers, to challenge its representation in the major media, and to rally support for the victims of the shootings.

2. We also need to work on building a more accepting and accommodating climate in our schools, one which is more tolerant of difference, one which seeks to understand the cultural choices made by students rather than trying to prohibit them open expression. A core assumption behind any democratic culture is that truth is best reached through the free market of ideas, not through the repression of controversial views. Popular culture has become a central vehicle by which we debate core issues in our society. Our students need to learn how to process and evaluate those materials and reach their own judgments about what is valuable and what isn't in the array of media entering their lives. They need to do this in a context that respects their right to dignity and protects them from unreasoned and unreasonable degrees of abuse. What should have rang alarm bells for us in the aftermath of the Littleton shooting is how alone and at risk students can feel in their schools and how important it is for us to have a range of different activities, supported by caring and committed teachers, which can pull all of our students into the school community and not simply those the school values because of their good grades, good sports skills, or good conduct. All signs are that Harris and Klebold were enormously talent and created kids who never found an outlet where they could get respect for what they created from the adults in their community.

3. We need to provide more support for media education in our schools. Given the centrality of media in contemporary life, media issues need to be integrated into all aspects of our K-12 curriculum, not as a special treat, but as something central to our expectations about what children need to learn about their environment. Most contemporary media education is designed to encourage children to distance themselves from media culture. The governing logic is "just say no to Nintendo" and "turn off your television set." Instead, we need to focus

on teaching children how to be safe, critical, and creative users of media. Research suggests that when we tell students that popular culture has no place in our classroom discussions, we are also signaling to them that what they learn in school has little or nothing to say about the things that matter to them in their after school hours.

4. For this new kind of media literacy to work, our teachers and administrators need to be better informed about the nature of popular culture and their students' investments in media imagery. Such understanding cannot start from the assumption that such culture is meaningless or worthless, but has to start from the recognition that popular culture is deeply significant to those who are its most active consumers and participants. The contents of that culture shift constantly and so we need to be up to date on youth subcultures, on popular music, on popular programs.

5. We need to provide fuller information to parents about the content of media products so that they can make meaningful and informed choices about what forms of popular culture they want to allow into their homes. . . . But the ratings system for games and for television needs to be more nuanced, needs to provide more specific information. We also need to create more websites where parents respond to the games and other media products they have purchased and share their insights and reactions with other parents.

6. We need to challenge the entertainment industry to investigate more fully why violent entertainment appeals to young consumers and then to become more innovative and creative at providing alternative fantasies that satisfy their needs for empowerment, competition, and social affiliation.

QUESTIONS

1. Why, according to Jenkins, is it impossible to pin down one significant media influence, event, or symbol that motivated the Columbine killers? What is the significance of his remark that "When it comes to popular culture, we all 'roll our own'"? Is the evidence he presents to support his thesis relative to the complexity of our relationship to the "hyper-mediated culture" convincing or relevant to the case of the Columbine killers? Why or why not?

2. What objections does Jenkins have to "media-effects"-oriented media violence research that add up the number of violent acts children are exposed to in media? Why does he consider such criticism a distorting "decontextualization" of media violence? Do you agree? Why or why not?

3. What solutions does Jenkins present in the last pages of his presentation that might make schools less alienating and frightening for youth, thus reducing the kind of conditions that led the Columbine killers to massacre their classmates? Do you think the solutions presented by Jenkins are adequate, or would a different approach work better in extreme cases? Explain your position.

DIFFERING PERSPECTIVES: IS MEDIA VIOLENCE A RESULT OF THE BATTLE FOR RATINGS OR OUR OWN CULTURAL VALUES?

George Gerbner and Todd Gitlin

"Is Media Violence Free Speech?"

George Gerbner (1919–2005) earned his Ph.D. in communications at the University of Southern California in 1955. He was dean of the Annenberg School for Communication at the University of Pennsylvania (1964–1989) and became Bell Atlantic Professor of Telecommunication at Temple University in 1997. Gerbner studied the impact of media situations and stories on heavy television viewers, who came to see the real world through the distorted mirror of that medium, and conducted large research studies on the medium's impact on youth. His books include The Global Media Debate: Its Rise, Fall, and Renewal *(1993) and* Invisible Crisis: What Conglomerate Control of Media Means for America and the World *(1996). Todd Gitlin holds a Ph.D. in sociology from University of California, C. Berkeley and currently teaches in the Graduate School of Journalism at Columbia University. He has written extensively on the media in newspaper and magazine articles and in his book* Media Unlimited: How the Torrent of Images and Sounds Overwhelms Our Lives *(2002). The following article from* Wired *magazine is an exchange of ideas between Gerbner and Gitlin on whether media violence is a form of free speech, with Gerbner asserting that the media violence is "de facto censorship driven by global marketing" and deserving of no special protections and Gitlin arguing that the violence of the media reflects the violence of society.*

Gerbner starts:

Formula-driven media violence is not an expression of crime statistics, popularity, or freedom. It is de facto censorship driven by global marketing, imposed on creative people, foisted on the children of the world. Far from inciting to mayhem, media violence is an instrument of fear and social control.

Violence dominates television news and entertainment, particularly what we call "happy violence"—cool, swift, painless, and always leading to a happy ending in order to deliver the audience to the next commercial message in a receptive mood.

The Cultural Indicators Project has found that heavy viewers are more likely to overestimate their chances of involvement in violence; to believe that their neighborhoods are unsafe; to state that fear of crime is a very serious personal problem; and to assume that crime is rising, regardless of the facts. Heavy viewers express a greater sense of insecurity and mistrust than comparable groups of light viewers. They are more likely to be dependent on authority and to support repression if it is presented as enhancing their security.

Gitlin responds:

Television violence is mainly redundant, stupid, and ugly. The deepest problem with TV violence is not that it causes violence—the evidence for this is very thin. The problem is that the profiteers of television in the United States—the networks, the program suppliers, and the advertisers—are essentially subsidized (e.g., via tax write-offs) to program this formulaic stuff.

Professor Gerbner may well be right about TV watchers—the more violence they watch, the more dangerous they think the world is. They may therefore support heavy-handed, authoritarian responses to crime.

But consider the case of Japan. There is far more vile media violence—including more widely available violent pornography—in Japan than in the United States. But there is less real-world violence—particularly sexual violence—in Japan than in the United States. This is not to say that television is healthy for American society. To the contrary.

It would help to provide alternatives. We could use some government-subsidized programs devoted to something other than mindless, transitory entertainment. We could tax television sets, as in Great Britain, or subsidize public broadcasting through taxes, as in Canada, or—in a more American mode—charge fees to networks, which now avail themselves of the public airwaves, buy and sell licenses, and amass immense profits, all without charge.

Gerbner rebutts:

"The case of Japan" argument surprises me from Professor Gitlin. It is the knee-jerk retort of apologists, of whom Mr. Gitlin is certainly not one. The argument assumes that media violence is the only, or major and always decisive, influence on human social behavior—*extensio ad absurdum*. Media violence (or any other single factor) is one of many factors interacting with other influences in any culture that contribute to real-world violence.

I completely agree that the main problem behind violence is virtual commercial monopoly over the public's airways. No other democracy delivers its cultural environment to a marketing operation.

But apologists might also argue that the free-market environment delivers programming tailored to its audience. However, our studies show that violence actually depresses ratings. Instead of popularity, the mechanisms of global marketing drive televised violence. Producers for global markets look for a dramatic formula that needs no translation, speaks "action" in any language, fits every culture. That formula is violence.

The V-chip is not the solution. That technology merely protects the industry from the parents, rather than the other way around. It only facilitates business as usual. Programming needs to be diversified, not just "rated." A better government regulation is antitrust, which could create a level playing field, admitting new entries and a greater diversity of ownership, employment, and representation. That would reduce violence to its legitimate role and frequency.

Gitlin explains:

By citing the case of Japan, I mean simply to restore some balance to a discussion that, like so many other American debates, gets pinned to single-cause theories and sound-bite nostrums. TV versions of violence are egregious, coarsening, and produce a social fear and anesthesia which damage our capacity to face reality, but I think many liberals have gone overboard in thinking that if they clean up television, they have accomplished a great deal to rub out violence in the real world. To make television more discriminating, intelligent, and various would be an achievement worthy in its own right, but let's not kid ourselves: The deepest sources of murderous American violence are stupefying inequality, terrible poverty, a nihilistic drug-saturated culture, and an easy recourse to guns. TV's contribution is a target of convenience for a political culture that makes it difficult to grow up with a sense of belonging to a decent society.

I'm not against the V-chip as such, since any device that enables parents to redress the imbalance of power they suffer under the invasion of television is all to the good. Given the power of nihilistic corporations over TV programs, any reasonable off-switch is defensible. But again, let's not kid ourselves about just how easy it will be to address the problem of TV violence all by itself. The Hollywood mania for dumb-bunny action is driven—as Professor Gerbner rightly says—by the export imperative. Entertainment is America's second-largest export in dollar value. The industry is not going to go quietly.

Gerbner speaks:

The V-chip is a sideshow and a diversion. I have observed this game since the 1970s. It is called "the carrot and the stick." Legislators posture in public, shaking the stick; and then vote the carrot of multibillion dollar windfalls for the same companies they pretend to threaten. They may even extract some meaningless concessions to calm the waters, take the heat off their media clients—who are among their major bankrollers—and call it a victory.

But the industry knows better. The cover story of the 14 August 1996 issue of the trade journal Broadcasting & Cable is titled "The man who made the V-chip." Pictured on the cover is "the man," liberal House Democrat Edward J. Markey, who should know better. The cover story is titled "Why the Markey Chip Won't Hurt You." In fact, it can only help the industry. It's like the major polluters saying, "We shall continue business as usual, but don't worry, we'll also sell you gas masks to 'protect your children' and have a 'free choice!'"

There is no free market in television. Viewers are sold to the highest bidders at the lowest cost. That drives both violence and drivel on television. The giveaway of the public airways to private exploitation damages our children and swamps any effort toward democracy. Only a broad citizen movement can turn this around.

Gitlin responds:

V-chips or the like are sure to come—they are perfectly tailored to the American can-do attitude that there is a technological fix for every social problem. Though I don't regard them as pernicious—parents deserve all the technohelp they can get—I agree with Dr. Gerbner that the irresponsibility of the broadcasters is the fundamental issue. They are nihilists who spend many millions of dollars to buy a supine government. Pat Robertson's willingness to sell his "Christian" channel to Rupert Murdoch, master exploiter of brainless smirkiness and sexual innuendo, shows what kind of values are in play among the movers and shakers.

The problem of TV goes far beyond violence. The speed-up of imagery undermines the capacity to pay attention. Flashy sensation clogs up the synapses. The cheapening of violence—not so much the number of incidents as their emptiness and lightweight gruesomeness—leads to both paranoia and anesthesia. The coarsening of TV inhibits seriousness. The glut of entertainment cheers consumers on primitive levels. Whiz-bang new technologies like high-definition TV will offer sharper images of banality.

To the idea of a citizen's movement, hooray! At the least, let all who want a more vital America—and more vital arts—support antitrust action against the media oligopoly.

Gerbner's last word:

We agree: The problem goes beyond violence, ratings, or any single factor, to the heart of the system. Television is driven not by the creative people who have something to tell, but by global conglomerates that have something to sell. Citizens own the airways. We should demand that it be free and fair, and not just "rated." Besides, the current so-called rating system is fundamentally flawed: Ratings flash on during opening credits, but never again Producers rate their own programs, resulting in inconsistencies across networks Ratings designed by the industry is like letting the fox (no pun intended) guard the chicken coop.

So—don't just agonize; organize! The Cultural Environment Movement (CEM) is a nonprofit organization with members and supporters worldwide, united in working for freedom and fairness in media. For more information, email *CEM@libertynet.org.*

Gitlin's last word:

The moneymaking machines that control as much of the culture as they can get their hands on will make just as many moral-sounding reforms as they think they need to keep Congress and the FCC off their backs. They will trim an ax-murder here, insert a V-chip there, and later—when public-interest groups and the FCC have taken their attention elsewhere—throw in another ax-murder, or six. The reforms, most likely transitory, will have a pleasant ring and will gain much well-meaning support. In the meantime, for the foreseeable future, the culture—the unofficial curriculum of American children—will remain infantile, degraded, and, among other things, tolerant of and conducive to a violent nihilism. Those who have access to the Web will feel that they have broken free of the tripe, but this is at least half-fanciful. Much of what goes on the Web, however decentralized and freely chosen, is as glib, shallow, and weightless as commercial TV. The great Fun Leviathan churns on.

I have been trying to argue in these few words that we are imprisoned in a mania for easy sensation. We have more and more delivery systems for hollow toys. The virtual eclipses virtue. This year's shoddy goods displace last year's. The freedom to choose is debased into the pursuit of the next kick. The frantic search for electronic sensation does violence to the reflection and deliberation that a democracy needs. No quick fixes, no "just say no" is adequate. It would make sense to curb our own hunger for distraction, as we need to curb the reach of the moguls who now lord it over the catering business.

Is market-driven culture a reflection of the population, or a toxic side-effect of global capitalism?

QUESTIONS

1. Compare Gitlin's and Gerber's overall positions on media violence, its causes, and its likely solutions. What areas do they agree on? In what general areas do they disagree? How thoroughly and convincingly does each defend his position?
2. Why does Gerbner have no confidence in the current ratings system for TV or the "V-Chip" device? Do you agree? Why or why not?
3. What ideas for regulating the television industry do both Gitlin and Gerber present? Who is more pessimistic about such regulation, and why?

Speaking Out About Pop Music

Introduction

Today's popular music touches our lives in various ways and often inspires debate or "speaking out" similar to that seen in the previous chapters of this book, particularly in regard to censorship of lyrics mentioning or containing obscenity, hate speech, sexuality, drug-use, or gang violence. People like or dislike certain types and subjects of music; similarly, fans are likely to identify with their favorite music; to appreciate (or reject) its creative and aesthetic qualities; and to love (or despise) the lyrics, the singer, or the band itself.

The essays in this chapter take stands on many of the issues mentioned above, from Ellen Willis's essay on the rock festival and mass-mediated crowds as an emblem of freedom from social controls, to Deena Weinstein's explanation of the causal factors leading to a band's creative rise and fall, to Frank Zappa's impassioned defense of the pop lyricist's right to use any type of language he or she sees fit, regardless of how "obscene" parents and other social arbiters might find it to be.

Two essays in the chapter focus on some of the fundamental political and social issues that musicians write and sing about today, from Imani Perry's critique of the negative portrayals of women in commercial hip hop by both male and female performers, to James Cusick's analysis of the political impact of huge benefit concerts such as Live

Aid, Live8, and Live Earth, all orchestrated around fundraising and policy change in a particular area of global concern.

The final issue of the chapter is presented as a debate between the recording industry, which opposes online free peer file sharing on copyright and revenue-loss grounds and targets campus students in particular, versus those performers and users who believe that file sharing on the Internet will open public access to music and allow a wider range of musical groups to be heard.

ELLEN WILLIS

"Crowds and Freedom"

Ellen Jane Willis (1941–2006) was born in Manhattan, attended Barnard College as an undergraduate, and spent one semester at the University of California, Berkeley, studying comparative literature. Willis developed her reputation as a rock critic in the 1960s, and by the early 1970s she had become the top pop music critic for The New Yorker. *She later wrote for such publications as the* Village Voice, The Nation, Rolling Stone, Slate, *and* Salon. *Willis has also published several books of collected essays. In the following essay, she puts forward her view that the rock concert, festival, or a mass-mediated music crowd can capture a utopian moment of shared freedom.*

In the course of gathering my thoughts about this panel, I reread parts of Elias Canetti's *Crowds and Power*. It occurred to me that a book about the relationship of rock 'n' roll to its audience would have to be called *Crowds and Freedom*—which is to say that the power of rock 'n' roll as a musical and social force has always been intimately connected with the paradoxical possibilities of mass freedom or collective individuality.

For its detractors, the emergence of rock 'n' roll signaled the convergence of two nightmares—the totalitarian leveling mob, destroying all hierarchy, distinctions, and standards, and the unleashed libidinal, uncowed, and unsublimated self. Both nightmares were connected with a literal darkness, with fear of black people breaching the boundaries of the dominant white culture.

For the American marketplace—if I can metaphorically indulge in the idea of The Market as an entity with a will of its own—the profitability of rock 'n' roll as a commodity translated into an unprecedented mass-mediated dissemination of the sounds and images of freedom.

At the same time the disseminators made continued efforts to package freedom so as to make it as uniform and predictable as any other mass-produced item—efforts that I would argue were partly, but only partly, successful. For instance, the effort to limit the exposure of white suburban kids to rock 'n' roll by giving them watered-down covers of r & b hits ultimately failed. There was too much demand for franker, grittier, more rebellious music—and too much money to be made from meeting that demand.

For performers and fans, the playing out of the paradox of mass freedom has been complex and various. The pop-music crowd has embraced it at some moments and denied it at others—though in my view they never truly escape it. In the context of the whole history of rock 'n' roll, there have really been only brief moments when the possibility of mass freedom seemed fulfilled. Those are the moments from which rock has drawn its utopian reputation, and a good deal of its moral and cultural capital. Yet, for the past twenty years at least, pop music has been in rebellion against its utopian legacy and therefore in rebellion against essential aspects of its own self-definition. I'm going to focus on the formation and devolution of the rock 'n' roll crowd before that point, from the fifties to the late seventies.

When we think of "the crowd" in connection with pop music, we tend to think first of live performance, yet I would argue that historically the primary crowd, the crowd that's central to understanding the relation of music and audience, has been the mass-mediated crowd that was in the first place brought together and held together by radio, records, and the public images of pop performers introduced mainly through TV. This, and not live performance, was the day-to-day pervasive experience that reconstituted the cultural life of youth in the image of rock 'n' roll and built a community that was also in some sense a movement. I'm putting this in the past tense because it seems to me that, while fans still obviously listen to the radio and buy CDs and watch MTV and are influenced by the personae of pop stars, these experiences no longer constitute a crowd in the same way, but, rather, have generated many smaller and less powerful crowds, albeit still deeply influenced by the legacy of this primary crowd I'm talking about.

I guess it's a tribute to the power and ubiquity of cyberspace jargon that I started at one point to think of this phenomenon as the "virtual crowd"; but, when I thought about I further, I realized the term was misleading, since the mass-mediated crowd was in no sense a simulation, but was, on the contrary, the primary, underlying reality that gave live performance its context and meaning. The mass-mediated crowd embodied the paradox of mass freedom in that each of us integrated the music into our lives or our lives into the music in our own way, listened and discussed it with our friends, responded to it according to our own particular filters, and, at the same time, shared it across an enormously heterogeneous spectrum of the population. Rock was the lingua franca of a crowd that could connect without demanding the subordination of the self to the group, and the strangeness and serendipity of that connection was part of the deep, primal pleasure of the music. This was true even at the very beginning, as we all watched Elvis Presley on the Ed Sullivan show—me, my parents, my cousins in Washington, D.C., the working-class kids in my high school, all kinds of people I wouldn't meet until years larer. I don't mean that I was self-conscious about any of this at the time, yet the echo of that experience was part of my enjoyment of Elvis, and my inchoate sense of his importance.

I once read a piece about the reception of *Sgt. Pepper's Lonely Hearts Club Band*. I can't remember who wrote the piece, but it expressed very well how I felt about that album and about much of what was going on in rock 'n' roll at that point. The piece described how everywhere the writer went, someone was playing *Sgt. Pepper's*. The music came at you from everywhere. It was a communal event, and yet private at the same time. This didn't mean everyone loved the album. There were already arguments about whether all this fancy studio stuff the Beatles and every other group were getting into was going too far. Richard Goldstein notoriously panned the album in the *New York Times* and got a ton of vociferous mail. The point is, at that moment there was this electric sense of collective engagement—and in response to an album that not only wasn't being performed, but because of its technology couldn't be performed. There was the sense that everyone was connected to each other through the Beatles—from twelve-year-old girls who were turned on by Paul McCartney to musicologists who were analyzing their chord structures. I was much more of a Rolling Stones fan, but without the Beatles the Stones couldn't have been what they were or meant what they did.

If this connection is emblematic of the utopian moment of the rock 'n' roll crowd, there were also always contradictory tendencies toward fragmentation. To begin with, there was race. Despite the significance of blackness for the formation of the rock 'n' roll crowd, that crowd was never really interracial. For the most part, blacks and whites didn't listen to the same music, and, even when they did, there was never any music that was equally at the center of black and white consciousness at any given time. (And, of course, the irony is that there's more of an interracial crowd now in this era of multiple minicrowds.)

The other contradiction was that the intensity and cohesion of the crowd depended on its identity as a rebellious and insurgent crowd, and as that crowd took in more and more people and became more and more ecumenical and more and more acceptable, it also began to lose its force, its center, its reason for being, and its loyalty to itself. So that *Sgt. Pepper's* was really the beginning of the end, or maybe even the middle of the end. Actually, the beginning of the end was probably the arrival of FM rock radio, which divided the radio audience according to class, which became the vehicle for the upward mobility of rock and its integration into middle-class, middlebrow culture, and reintroduced the categories of that culture, such as "serious" and "trashy," into the discussion of pop music.

It's only in the context of this primary crowd formation and disintegration that the significance of live performance during the same period can be understood. The live crowd, and especially the arena of festival crowd, functioned largely as a confirmation of the existence of the community, and a kind of convention of the community's representatives who were empowered to act out its myths and fantasies; these events and the symbols they produced then got recycled by the media back into the collective consciousness of the crowd as a whole. It's possible to trace this function of the live crowd from the kids standing on their seats as the Paramount in the fifties all the way to Woodstock.

In other words, for the most part, live crowds did not themselves create community. There were exceptions to this. One was the Newport Folk Festival where Bob Dylan was booed for playing electric guitar, which divided the folk community and brought a whole new constituency into the pop-music crowd. Probably the early British rock groups were another, though not from the viewpoint of Americans. Definitely another was the San Francisco scene in the mid-sixties, culminating in the Monterey Pop festival. The San Francisco groups and their audience invented a version of collective individuality that was explicitly utopian and insisted on intense physical and sensory contact as the basis of community, and for once transformed the mass-mediated crowd— much more than the other way around.

Woodstock was the result of the impact of Monterey and all that it entailed on the mass-mediated crowd, which among other things raised the prospect of being able so sell this brand of utopianism, of getting the market in on the act. The festival was at one time both a very real enactment of a moment of mass freedom and a symptom of its fragility. It came about through a marketing scheme that got out of control and succeeded through the sheer will of the crowd to ignore the crisis it had created in the surrounding community, and this was a pretty good metaphor for the situation of utopianism in the outside world. The mass-mediated rock 'n' roll crowd had already begun to fragment in ways that would continue to accelerate; the counterculture was under heavy attack from outside and also vulnerable to its own upper-middle-class illusions. Altamont, when it happened, was the return of the repressed, the countermyth that could no longer be denied. In the seventies, the music and audience that came out of what was left of the counterculture increasingly seemed to be the province of rich dropouts and whiny singer-songwriters, with freedom dissolving into solipsism and any idea of collectivity disappearing altogether.

This, of course, set the stage for the antiutopian period of pop history, in its many forms. There was the divide between "populism" and "avant-gardism" that was foreshadowed by the Velvet Underground and codified in punk. In an era in which populism could not be disentangled from Reaganism, the idea of mass freedom went from being a paradox to being a simple oxymoron. This was the period when Bruce Springsteen became an icon of cultural conservatism, contrary to his own conscious intentions, while the punk definition of both freedom and solidarity was refusal and negation. Punk did from its own collectivity, as did rap and heavy metal, but all these crowds had as their basis the rejection of any sense of possibility, even as their continuing use of a musical language that had possibility at its core belied that rejection. And when "alternative" broke into the mainstream, it was ultimately so trapped in the antiutopian consensus that, despite its roots in punk, its exponents ended up sounding more like the inheritors of the whiny singer-songwriters than anything else.

We're now in a political and cultural situation in which the hegemonic common sense is that freedom and collectivity are absolutely antithetical. George Gilder, the economic libertarian and moral traditionalist, has written a futurist book, *Life After Television*, about how digital technology will replace television with the interactive computer, or "teleputer" as he calls it, and he sees this technology as eliminating the centralization of broadcasting and thereby "demassifying" culture. He looks forward to no more common culture, no lingua franca or shared images at all, only millions of individuals making their individual transactions with other individuals or their machines. In this version of history, the crowd will simply disappear. But pop music is inherently an offense to this notion, even when appearing to promote it. So long as pop music exists, so will the crowd as idea, memory, and potential.

QUESTIONS

1. How does Willis explain a rock fan's "utopian moment" of the crowd? What examples of utopian moments does she discuss? What genres of rock does she label as antiutopian and why?
2. Why does Willis think that a mass-mediated crowd of fans and a crowd of fans at a rock and roll performance still have the potential to represent a utopian moment? Why is a sense of community essential for a crowd of fans to feel free?
3. From your experience listening to music and attending live performances, does Willis's definition of a utopian moment make sense to you? From your point of view, what qualities are necessary for a crowd of fans to feel free? How do you explain the irony of finding freedom in a crowd of fans?

DEENA WEINSTEIN

"Creativity and Band Dynamics"

Deena Weinstein is a professor of sociology at DePaul University, where she teaches classes such as Sociology of Rock, Mass Media, Popular Culture, and Sociology of Celebrity. She is a rock critic and scholar who has delivered many public lectures and has written on the sociology of rock and youth culture, heavy metal, rock lyrics, and band creativity. Her books include Heavy Metal: the Music and its Culture *(2000) and* Serious Rock: The Artistic Vision of Modern Society in Pink Floyd, Rush, and Bruce Springsteen *(1985). Her article included here, "Creativity and Band Dynamics" (2004) examines the common definition of a band as a "family" and provides causal analysis and examples of why bands break up.*

They all say it.

"It's like a family," reports Lars Frederiksen about his band, Rancid. "Of course you've got your little argument, your little tiffs. Just because you fight doesn't mean that you're not family anymore." Kid Rock's drummer, Stefanie Eulinberg, tells us that the members of the Detroit rocker's band "work together like a family." "Culture Club is important to me. It's like a family," Boy George attests in a 1983 interview. "Pretty

Things are like a family, really. People come, people go, but there's a wonderful camaraderie amongst the guys. Well, not always—everyone has fights and stuff," Wally Waller reflects, explaining how difficult it was for him to decide to leave the band.

No matter what era or style of rock. They all say it.

Mick Jagger declares, in response to learning of Brian Jones's death, "Something has gone. We were like a pack, like a family, we Stones." A sentence later, he adds, "I wasn't ever really close to him." Alice Cooper drummer Neal Smith looks back on his band thus: "We were like a family—you love each other but there's always tension." "We are basically like any family—we fight like a family, we love each other like a family—but like most families, we also work things out in the end," Keith Knudsen, drummer and vocalist with the Doobie Brothers, chimes in.

"Like a family"—it's the mother of all rock clichés. Who knows if the only time the phrase is uttered is when some rock scribe is within hearing range? And if truth be told, not all musicians describe their relationships with their bandmates with that cliché. But in my research, admittedly neither thorough nor extensive, the only bands I found that didn't use the phrase "like a family" are Creedence Clearwater Revival, the Kinks, AC/DC, Dire Straits, Black Crowes, and Oasis. And, yes, there is a family resemblance among these bands, despite their different musical styles: they all feature siblings.

Regardless of the real-life exceptions, the ubiquity of the family metaphor does beg the question of its meaning. Some musicians use "like a family" to stand for the warm fuzzy feelings they have for those in their band, while for others it seems to reference that very first family, the one from which Abel was summarily purged, without the possibility of some reunion decades later. What does "like a family" mean when it includes positive or negative attitudes? Reading interviews, you'd think that bands were held together with nothing more than emotions. The metaphor seems to have a rhetorical flavor that erases the sense of a rock band as a small corporation with objectively evaluated workers.

"Groups are a very complicated thing," says Mike Campbell of Tom Petty's Heartbreakers, in one of the few more nuanced invocations of the family affair cliché. "It's like a family, it's like a business relationship, it's a very emotional thing. You care about each other, and you tug just like brothers; you're jealous, and then you love each other. It's a very complicated monster."

Rock bands are like jackalopes, amazing freaks of nature. With their full racks of antlers, you'd think the top-heavy jackrabbits would fall over and die rather than hop about the western prairies. Rock bands, of course, are not mythical monstrosities. They are all-too-familiar features of the mediascape and can't help but be sighted. Yet a sociologist has no trouble seeing that rock bands are as unstable as jackalopes, ungainly groups gluing together characteristics that are usually kept strictly segregated.

The basic strain that predisposes rock groups to crash and burn comes from the difference between a close-knit circle and a specialized impersonal organization. In the close-knit circle, members are valued simply because they belong to the group. In an organization, members are valued only for their contribution to the achievement of the group's goal.

Rock bands have characteristics from both sides. They are work groups with a specialized division of labor and goals to accomplish (although you'd never guess that from the mountains of words about them in magazines, newspapers, books, and online). Their interviews rarely if ever mention this aspect. Journalists and musicians fail to discuss the details, or even to mention what goes on in the extensive hours of rehearsal. But bands are also small groups that impose an intense intimacy on their members, through the long and odd hours spent in rehearsal and recording studios and the weeks and months spent together on tours. This leads band members toward becoming friends, if they hadn't started off as such, with all of the attendant personal strains brought on by prolonged nearness.

Work and intimacy have been combined throughout history, particularly in premodern societies but also in modern small family businesses. However, that blend has traditionally been stabilized by preordained roles (like the gendered division of labor and authority based on age) that help to reconcile the inherent tensions. In contrast, in rock bands there are no such cultural forms to balance practicality and emotion; each band must resolve the tension in its own way or break apart.

The tension between the values of community and efficiency is also intensified by the role that bands play in the contemporary business economy. The entertainment giants minimize the risks of creativity and innovation for themselves by relegating those functions to the bands, which must engage in a Darwinian struggle for survival. The need for rock groups to be creative introduces acute strains into their structure that are related to the balance of influence and power. Bands are also enveloped in the romantic myth of the authentic creative artist; a requirement dictated by a corporate economy is perceived as the demand of a cultural ideal.

Pearl Jam is a case in point. "We were hanging out a lot, Eddie and me, talking politics, life, surfing, music," notes guitarist Mike McCready. "I remember telling him we need to be very cognizant of the powers that be, because it's critical to our survival. We needed to go out and play music, and enjoy it, within this capitalist structure. To still support those causes, but to work through the established channels."

The (Romantic) Creative Ideal

It's ironic that the requirement that rock bands create their own music originated in the protest era of the 1960s. Creativity was tied to a desire to oppose the fabrications of the entertainment machine with the alternative of an authentic culture expressing genuine passions and commitments. What would immediately be co-opted by the entertainment machine for its own advantage was, at first, understood as a liberation.

Before the mid-1960s, it was only the performance that mattered. Although the audience cared about the songs, it wasn't concerned, and didn't really know, if the songs had been written by the performer (as Chuck Berry and Buddy Holly had done) or by songwriting specialists in the Tin Pan Alley tradition. The Beatles and especially Bob Dylan provided the model for genuine creativity. Initially bands like the Rolling Stones and the Who were urged by their savvy managers (Beatles manager Brian Epstein wrote the book for them) to write their own songs, given the financial benefits that accrued from songwriting royalties. As the 1960s became the cultural '60s, the value of creative sincerity (what Johnny Rotten sarcastically proclaimed a decade later–"We mean it, man") became central. It provided another and, for the audience, a major reason for bands to write their own material.

But the '60s ethos also valued the group, which privileged collective performers—the band—over solo artists. Most band names reflected an egalitarian collective, rather than individuals. Think of the Animals, the Beatles, the Byrds, and even the Monkees, in contrast to the older '50s model like Buddy Holly and the Crickets. One of the few exceptions was Crosby, Stills, Nash and Young. Stage moves and especially the posed photographs emphasized this "all for one, one for all" collectivity.

At first the discourse of genuine creativity was not centered on the unique voice of the unique person, but on "authentic" cultural traditions like African American blues and working-class folk music. That was soon to change, however, as middle-class rock musicians broke free from the "prestige from below" that had nurtured their fledgling rebellion and took their music into their own hands.

Authenticity was quickly married to a romantic ideology that harkened back to the nineteenth-century *poèts maudits* like Baudelaire. These déclassé avant-garde romantics of the middle and late nineteenth century, forerunners of 1950s-era movie roles played by James Dean and Marlon Brando and other sensitive-guy juvenile delinquents, carried on the myth that had first arisen in the 1820s of the creative individual, uncompromising in passion and bearing unique gifts. It is here that the major ideological tension present in the creative process of rock bands entered the mix; the band, which remained the creative focus, or at least was thought of as such, took on a myth adapted to a radically individual practice.

This romantic understanding and value of creativity came into rock, in part, due to the influence of British art schools. As Frith and Horne document, many of the major figures of '60s rock—Keith Richards (Rolling Stones), Pete Townshend (The Who), Eric Clapton (Cream), Syd Barrett (Pink Floyd), Ray Davies (Kinks), and Jimmy Page (Led Zeppelin)—had gone to art colleges, the destination of choice for smart and unruly British boys.

Despite heavy doses of irony, let alone postmodern influences, romantic ideology still permeates thought and discussions about rock. How many interviews have you read that included some quote about "staying true" to one's art? It places a host of destabilizing burdens on bands, beyond the transfer of an individual ideal to a collective one. The romantic aesthetic privileges novelty, in contrast to what Umberto Eco calls classical aesthetics—good versions of an ideal form. "The pleasurable repetition of an already known pattern was considered, by modern theories of art, typical of Crafts—not of Art—and of industry." Bands face the demand that a new album must show growth by going further than previous efforts. Critics praise a new release when it does so and denounce it as the "same old same old" if it is too similar to earlier recordings.

The romantic legacy also sees the values of authenticity and creativity as opposed to or even fully inimical to commerce. Selling out (note ironic references in album titles—*The Who Sell Out*—and band names—Judas Priest) became a sin just when bands were destined to be absorbed by the entertainment machine (Pink Floyd's "Welcome to the Machine"), causing innumerable battles among band members and, at times, within musicians themselves (for example, Kurt Cobain).

It is telling that so many of the bastions of rock authenticity (Dylan, the Beatles, Bruce Springsteen) have been artists supported by strong and knowledgeable managers (Albert Grossman, Brian Epstein, and Jon Landau, respectively).

Still another problem created by romantic ideas about art is that the music is generally seen by the audience to be a creative product of all of the members of the band, regardless of whether each member had a hand in creating, or even approving of, the songs. Thus each individual in the group is seen in the same light as the others, regardless of actual authorship. Finally, the creative process itself is seen not as a craft or a learned skill but as the response of suffering or mad artists. And if suffering or madness doesn't come naturally, the ever helpful nineteenth-century poets provide rock with a way into those states: drugs and alcohol. Privileging substance-induced irrationality may, either actually or because of belief, enhance one's creativity for some period of time. But living and working with a person in such a condition hardly improves a group's stability.

That creative individuals are allowed and even expected to be less than stable encourages their worst sort of social behavior. If bands survive under the domination of a "difficult" creative musician, they often have a revolving-door lineup. My favorite case in point: Ritchie Blackmore's Rainbow was a five-man band whose slots were filled by sixteen people over its seven-year life.

Spheres of Creativity

The structural and ideological strains endemic to rock bands are played out in a number of spheres in which creativity is demanded, all of which can become flash points for conflict and disaffection. Songwriting is the main focus in discussions of rock creativity, for a variety of reasons. Foremost is the fact that it is the only instance of creativity that is singled out for special payment. (Probably the best literature on rock band creativity is contained within the law suits dealing with plagiarism.) The areas beyond songwriting in which rock bands are called on to be creative—sonically, verbally, and visually—are extensive. They include everything from concert set lists, stage moves, clothing, and hairstyles to facial expressions in the posed and not fully posed photos that accompany the "stories" they give to the press.

Bands, of course, are brands. Establishing a band's identity, its name, visual image, and signature sound, is the foundational creative activity.

This crucial set of activities remains in the shadows, unacknowledged. Each of these spheres of creativity involves not merely "coming up with something" but is preceded by a more or less voiced "We need." Recognizing a lack, proposing a solution, and reacting to that solution can be—but rarely are—the province of only one person in the band. Saying, "We need an up-tempo song that can raise the energy level at the show" requires different skills than writing such a song; a suggestion that "we all ought to turn our backs to the audience when we play this song" takes no real skill to execute but can cause disagreement.

The number of creative decisions that bands confront is endless. In light of the individualistic ideology of the rock band, each is a possible bond of contention. This vulnerability to conflict is only partly alleviated by the tendency of bands to develop an authority structure and a division of labor. Such stabilizing structures are threatened not only by romantic individualism but also by the myth of a closely bonded community of equals.

Reacting to suggested solutions is so fundamental to a band's functioning that roles tend to emerge. The critic evaluates the quality of a work in a variety of ways. For example, if it's a new song, the critic may ask: "Is it a good song?" "Is it a song that fits with others on the new album or on the set list?" "Does the song violate the band's image or clash with its signature sound?" "Is it a song that sounds fresh?" In contrast, the emotional appreciator—the audience-within-the-band—provides immediate feedback: "That sounds great" or "It's good but it needs something near the end." Of course, some emotional reactors are extremely stingy with praise, more given to hisses and boos.

Creativity and Band Stabilization/Destabilization

"I have spent eight months transforming this band and our new songs into an unstoppable juggernaut, and sadly Twiggy wasn't able to make himself a part of it," said Marilyn Manson in a statement explaining the departure of his band's bassist. Twiggy Ramirez, who cowrote Manson's biggest hits, like "The Beautiful People" and "The Dope Show," had been in the band for eight years. The split, *Rolling Stone* reported, "was a result of creative differences."

Rock bands start from scratch. Most groups with which we involve ourselves—at work, at home, in recreation, religion, politics, and other pursuits—have a model for roles and authority that precedes any specific set of people. This structure serves as a blueprint that newly formed groups can more or less follow. Bands have no such models, except for genre requirements; which members sing, write the music, focus on the finances, mediate disputes, and so on is left up to each group to devise. The media's inattention to the working life of bands and, worse, their promulgation of the nearly impossible all-are-creative egalitarian model, leaves each set of young musicians to reinvent the wheel themselves, and this hasn't changed over the years. Then when they bring in outsiders to help with some of these functions, there are no expectations about which band members will be the liaisons. Indeed, there is not even an expectation about the originating point—a band can be a set of friends coming together to play music or a group of musicians previously unknown to one another who start a band and then develop emotional relationships.

Once a band has a commercial goal, various leadership roles become prominent. Writing songs is a major form of domination: "Play my song," "Play these notes in this precise tempo," "Sing these words with this emotional tone." The egalitarian myth of bands is almost always violated. Not all of the other members even serve as critics, and the reactions of some are seen as more significant that the reactions of others, causing power imbalances that call for adjustments in attitudes and expectations. And as mentioned above, in bands where one person writes almost everything, there is usually one faithful member who serves as the critical and/or emotional reactor. The creator and reactor then form a strong controlling dyad.

Some, perhaps the majority, of famous bands have two major songwriters, and it is their relationship that makes or breaks the group. The list is long. Among them are John Lennon and Paul McCartney (Beatles), Keith Richards and Mick Jagger (Rolling Stones), Joe Strummer and Mick Jones (Clash), Chris Difford and Glenn Tilbrook (Squeeze), Morrissey and Johnny Marr (Smiths), and Bob Mould and Grant Hart (Hüsker Dü). It may be a complementary relationship (for example, lyricist and music writer) in which each has crucial abilities that the other lacks, or one may be better at expressing the band's romantic side while the other is most proficient at writing the energetic or musically sophisticated songs. Together they create a body of work that attracts a far larger audience than either could alone.

Another type of songwriting pair doesn't specialize in any way but works synergistically, each providing energy and ideas to the other. In yet a third pattern, each member of the pair is, either originally or over time, capable of writing full songs alone, and does so. The relationship between the two may serve as a friendly and appreciative rivalry that spurs them on. Or it can be, or can become, nastily competitive and fraught with bitter jealousy—of the other's ability, of the other band members' or the fans' greater appreciation of his songs, or of the fact that the other's songs earn him more money, since more of them find their way onto the albums. When such a pair forms the central relationship of the band, the whole band is destabilized when that relationship becomes conflicted. "We shan't work together again" is the line ending the long-term relationship between spot-on rock-band spoof *Spinal Tap's* creatives, Nigel Tufnel and David St. Hubbins.

The relationship between the creators and the noncreators in a band rarely remains constant. The dynamic equilibrium in a band results from a variety of pushes and pulls relating to the issue of creativity. Shared backgrounds, history (especially struggles to "make it" that involve the whole band), and tastes in music promote close bonding. Then, too, musicians may want to stay in a band for reasons having nothing to do with the other members: the bond may be with the band itself, because of an appreciation for the music that the band creates; the goodies the band brings, like money, "chicks," and fame; or the sense that they have no other options in life.

Counterbalancing the stabilizing factors is a host of stressing conditions, many of them involved with issues of creativity. Musicians may change their aesthetic preferences and, thus, their appreciation for the creative elements of the band's repertoire—its sonics, its lyrical themes, and its visual presentation. Rarely do tastes change in the same direction or at the same time for all members of a band. Some members are more plugged in to a changing zeitgeist, are more sensitive to the shift in audience taste, undergo an emotional maturation, or achieve greater musical proficiency or sophistication. Thus, bands whose members were once on the same wavelength (or at least appeared to be so) develop aesthetic conflicts, aka "creative differences."

Judas Priest's leather-clad multioctave singer Rob Halford wanted to focus on newer trends in metal, to head toward a more aggro than power music and toward reality-based lyrics rather than the band's "fantasy, fictional matter." Given the band's reluctance to make these changes, he tried to channel his interests into a side project. The situation became untenable, and he left his decades-old job fronting Priest. (The Hollywood version of this, *Rock Star,* badly distorted the facts of the story.)

Creative abilities within a band also change. Those who once weren't able to write songs may learn to do so, for instance. Moreover, it's common for those who were once the creators in the band to lose their ability at some point or at least to experience its decline. The deterioration of the Beach Boys' ingenious genius, Brian Wilson, is an especially poignant example. In addition, given the romantic ideology that encourages the use of drugs and alcohol to find one's muse, as well as the psychological evidence that "creatives" are statistically more likely to be mentally ill than "noncreatives," a band's creative members are often more fragile, volatile, and difficult than the others. If not incapacitated altogether, they are a constant source of instability and crisis: the rest of the band needs the creative one, yet the latter's vagaries can destroy the group. This problem is mitigated somewhat when a band crystallizes, achieving a signature sound and becoming associated with certain themes. Then the same level of creativity is no longer required; other band members, or "ringers" from the outside, can create new songs on the basis of the established code.

When destabilizing factors increase, members of the band may resort to compromises to allow them to exist in a less favorable situation. In the past decade, especially, many alienated or unfulfilled musicians have taken up side projects in which to express their new or different tastes and release the creativity that is suppressed in the band. It's not clear whether the growing number of such side projects is a testimony to the stability of rock bands (if not their friendships or pride in their sound, then their financial rewards) or to the gradual demise of the rock group itself as a way of making music. In either case, it is usually creative differences that lead a member to undertake some extramural activity, either to try something new (like a style of music that is outside the band's signature sound) or to do something similar but with a new partner (which allows them to assume a new creative role or power position). Blink-182's singer-guitarist Tom DeLonge started an old-school punk band, Box Car Racer. As the Drive-in's front man, Cedric Bixler, and guitarist, Omar Rodriguez, put together a dub-music group, Defacto. Phil Anselmo, Pantera's front man, formed Down in 1996 with members of Corrosion of Conformity, Crowbar, and EyeHateGod. The group's releases sold well and the band has done several tours in support of them. Anselmo has, or has had, several other side projects, including Superjoint Ritual, Viking Crown, Southern Isolation, and Necrophagia. Faith No More's Mike Patton, almost as promiscuous as Anselmo, is in the cult-fave avant-metal band Mr. Bungle, and in Fantomas with Buzz Osbourne from the Melvins. "It's like having an affair without breaking up the marriage," Stevie Nicks said in 1981, when she made a chart-topping solo album while still in Fleetwood Mac.

Then there are the side projects that start off as supplementary affairs but are found to be so rewarding that the straying partner seeks a divorce and sometimes winds up destroying or badly diminishing the original band. The Allman Brothers Band guitarist Warren Haynes and bassist Allen Woody got a yen for an "improvisational power trio" at a time when the ABB "was in a stagnant state. There wasn't a lot of writing or rehearsing. We were basically going through the motions, playing the same songs all the time. Gov't Mule was all of a sudden the opposite of that," Haynes reflected. Gov't Mule did so well that the pair eventually quit their main band to devote themselves full-time to it.

At times, the remaining members of a band jealously demand the divorce. The departure of Rob Halford from Priest, noted above, is a case in point. Jason Newsted, long-time bassist for both the '80s and '90s versions of Metallica, admitted that the "band's tight control of his side projects finally caused him to leave." "I keep chasing music all the time and they kept saying, 'Don't do that! You can't do that!'" Newsted said.

Creative Differences

The rock band is a jackalope, a close-knit circle with characteristics of an impersonal organization that is dependent upon and destined to an environing corporate society. It has no cultural traditions and models to stabilize it, and it is burdened by the transfer of the myth of romantic individualism to a dynamic group. Over the years, as the specialized role of the producer has come to the fore and been publicly recognized, and band management has been rationalized, some of the uncertainties of band organization have been partially dispelled. Still, it's a wonder that rock bands survive at all. Most don't; those that do learn to mitigate the inherent tensions. Success helps, providing extramusical incentives for cooperations. (Although sometimes, of course, success can break a band, as when the creative center thinks it's all due to him and his ego swells to intolerable proportions.) More important, bands that survive either develop an authority structure that violates romantic mythology, creating a gulf between the way the band presents itself to the outside world and how it actually operates, or members reach an accord on a division of labor that all can live with, acknowledging the value of one another's contributions.

When the imbalances of creative power are not mitigated, bands crash. According to the romantic myth, the only legitimate justification for a band to break up is "creative differences." That phrase is used as an excuse for any breakup—and there can be many reasons that have nothing to do with the actual creative function. Yet the appeal to creative differences is at least one case in which mythology is often not so far off the mark—creativity is the rock band's most sensitive function, and creative differences and accords often genuinely determine whether or not a band will survive.

QUESTIONS

1. Weinstein rebuts the claim that a rock band is like a family, calling this statement "the mother of all rock clichés." What evidence does she provide for the widespread nature of this false claim, and how does she refute it in her essay? What term does she use to define what she believes is a more accurate explanation of the relationships among the members of a band? What is your opinion of her new definition?
2. Why did the romantic ideal of a band being a creative family-like group become a fundamental aspect of band dynamics in the 1960s? How did this expectation of both creativity and family-like community increase the pressures on a band? What kinds of stabilizing relationships evolve within bands to satisfy these pressures? Why are these relationships often unsuccessful?
3. How does the additional pressure of fans and recording companies to be continually changing, always producing something new, as in "side projects," often lead to the breakup of a band through what is called "creative differences"? What other reasons cause bands to break up?

FRANK ZAPPA

"Statement to the Committee"

Frank Vincent Zappa (1940–1993) was the founder of The Mothers of Invention, an eclectic rock band. He wrote musical compositions for many different genres: classical, jazz, avant-garde, rock, and doo wop. Zappa produced more than sixty albums, won several Grammy awards, and was inducted into the Rock and Roll Hall of Fame. Despite his support of capitalism and free enterprise, he was a frequent critic in his songs and essays of American education, censorship, war, and organized religion. Zappa's stated his strong opposition to music censorship in his testimony on September 1985 before the United States Senate Commerce, Technology, and Transportation committee in response to the Parents' Music Resource Center or PMRC, which had proposed a labeling system for rock records with controversial lyrics. In the speech below, Zappa argues for his opposition to music censorship.

These are my personal observations and opinions. They are addressed to the PMRC as well as this committee. I speak on behalf of no group or professional organization.

The PMRC proposal is an ill-conceived piece of nonsense which fails to deliver any real benefits to children, infringes the civil liberties of people who are not children, and promises to keep the courts busy for years, dealing with the interpretational and enforcement of problems inherent in the proposal's design.

It is my understanding that, in law, First Amendment Issues are decided with a preference for the least restrictive alternative. In this context, the PMRC's demands are the equivalent of treating dandruff by decapitation.

No one has forced Mrs. Baker or Mrs. Gore to bring Prince or Sheena Easton into their homes. Thanks to the Constitution, they are free to buy other forms of music for their children. Apparently, they insist on purchasing the works of contemporary recording artists in order to support a personal illusion of aerobic sophistication. Ladies, please be advised: The $8.98 purchase price does not entitle you to a kiss on the foot from the composer or performer in exchange for a spin on the family Victrola. Taken as a whole, the complete list of PMRC demands reads like an instruction manual for some sinister kind of "toilet training program" to house-break all composers and performers because of the lyrics of a few. Ladies, how dare you?

The ladies' shame must be shared by the bosses at the major labels who, through the RIAA, chose to bargain away the rights of composers, performers, and retailers in order to pass H.R. 2911, The Blank Tape Tax: A private tax levied by an industry on consumers for the benefit of a select group within that industry. Is this a "consumer issue"? You bet it is. PMRC spokesperson, Kandy Stroud, announced to millions of fascinated viewers on last Friday's ABC Nightline debate that Senator Gore, a man she described as "A friend of the music industry," is co-sponsor of something she referred to as "anti-piracy legislation". Is this the same tax bill with a nicer name?

The major record labels need to have H.R. 2911 whiz through a few committees before anybody smells a rat. One of them is chaired by Senator Thurmond. Is it a coincidence that Mrs. Thurmond is affiliated with the PMRC? I cannot say she's a member, because the PMRC has no members. Their secretary told me on the phone last Friday that the PMRC has no members . . . only founders. I asked how many other D.C. wives are nonmembers of an organization that raises money by mail, has a tax-exempt status, and seems intent on running the Constitution of the United States through the family paper-shredder. I asked her if it was a cult. Finally, she said she couldn't give me an answer and that she had to call their lawyer.

While the wife of the Secretary of the Treasury recites "Gonna drive my love inside you . . .", and Senator Gore's wife talks about "Bondage!" and "oral sex at gunpoint," on the CBS Evening News, people in high places work on a tax bill that is so ridiculous, the only way to sneak it through is to keep the public's mind on something else: 'Porn rock'.

The PMRC practices a curious double standard with these fervent recitations. Thanks to them, helpless young children all over America get to hear about oral sex at gunpoint on network TV several nights a week. Is there a secret FCC dispensation here? What sort of end justifies THESE means? PTA parents should keep an eye on these ladies if that's their idea of 'good taste'.

Is the basic issue morality? Is it mental health? Is it an issue at all? The PMRC has created a lot of confusion with improper comparisons between song lyrics, videos, record packaging, radio broadcasting, and live performances. These are all different mediums, and the people who work in them have the right to conduct their business without trade-restraining legislation, whipped up like an instant pudding by The Wives of Big Brother.

Is it proper that the husband of a PMRC nonmember/founder/person sits on any committee considering business pertaining to the Blank Tape Tax or his wife's lobbying organization? Can any committee thus constituted 'find facts' in a fair and unbiased manner? This committee has three. A minor conflict of interest?

The PMRC promotes their program as a harmless type of consumer information service providing 'guidelines' which will assist baffled parents in the determination of the 'suitability' of records listened to by 'very young children'. The methods they propose have several unfortunately [sic] side effects, not the least of which is the reduction of all American Music, recorded and live, to the intellectual level of a Saturday morning cartoon show.

Teenagers with $8.98 in their pocket might go into a record store alone, but 'very young children' do not. Usually there is a parent in attendance. The $8.98 is in the parent's pocket. The parent can always suggest that the $8.98 be spent on a book.

If the parent is afraid to let the child read a book, perhaps the $8.98 can be spent on recordings of instrumental music. Why not bring jazz or classical music into your home instead of Blackie Lawless or Madonna? Great music with no words at all is available to anyone with sense enough to look beyond this week's platinum-selling fashion plate.

Children in the 'vulnerable' age bracket have a natural love for music. If, as a parent, you believe they should be exposed to something more uplifting than sugar walls, support Music Appreciation programs in schools. Why haven't you considered your child's need for consumer information? Music Appreciation costs very little compared to sports expenditures. Your children have a right to know that something besides pop music exists.

It is unfortunate that the PMRC would rather dispense governmentally sanitized Heavy Metal Music, than something more 'uplifting'. Is this an indication of PMRC's personal taste, or just another manifestation of the low priority this administration has placed on education for The Arts in America? The answer, of course, is neither. You cannot distract people from thinking about an unfair tax by talking about Music Appreciation. For that you need sex ... and lots of it.

Because of the subjective nature of the PMRC ratings, it is impossible to guarantee that some sort of 'despised concept' won't sneak through, tucked away in new slang or the overstressed pronunciation of an otherwise innocent word. If the goal here is total verbal/moral safety, there is only one way to achieve it; watch no TV, read no books, see no movies, listen to only instrumental music, or buy no music at all.

The establishment of a rating system, voluntary or otherwise, opens the door to an endless parade of Moral Quality Control Programs based on "Things Certain Christians Don't Like". What if the next bunch of Washington Wives demands a large yellow "J" on all material written or performed by Jews, in order to save helpless children from exposure to 'concealed Zionist doctrine'?

Record ratings are frequently compared to film ratings. Apart from the quantitative difference, there is another that is more important: People who act in films are hired to 'pretend'. No matter how the film is rated, it won't hurt them personally. Since many musicians write and perform their own material and stand by it as their art (whether you like it or not), an imposed rating will stigmatize them as individuals. How long before composers and performers are told to wear a festive little PMRC arm band with their Scarlet Letter on it?

The PMRC rating system restrains trade in one specific musical field: Rock. No ratings have been requested for Comedy records or Country Music. Is there anyone in the PMRC who can differentiate infallibly between Rock and Country Music? Artists in both fields cross stylistic lines. Some artists include comedy material. If an album is part Rock, part Country, part Comedy, what sort of label would it get? Shouldn't the ladies be warning everyone that inside those Country albums with the American Flags, the big trucks, and the atomic pompadours there lurks a fascinating variety of songs about sex, violence, alcohol, and the devil, recorded in a way that lets you hear every word, sung for you by people who have been to prison and are proud of it.

If enacted, the PMRC program would have the effect of protectionist legislation for the Country Music Industry, providing more security for cowboys than it does for children. One major retail outlet has already informed the Capitol Records sales staff that it would not purchase or display an album with any kind of sticker on it.

Another chain with outlets in shopping malls has been told by the landlord that if it racked "hard-rated albums" they would lose their lease. That opens up an awful lot of shelf space for somebody. Could it be that a certain Senatorial husband and wife team from Tennessee sees this as an 'affirmative action program' to benefit the suffering multitudes in Nashville?

Is the PMRC attempting to save future generations from SEX ITSELF? The type, the amount, and the timing of sexual information given to a child should be determined by the parents, not by people who are involved in a tax scheme cover-up.

The PMRC has concocted a Mythical Beast, and compounds the chicanery by demanding 'consumer guidelines' to keep it from inviting your children inside its sugar walls. Is the next step the adoption of a "PMRC National Legal Age for Comprehension of Vaginal Arousal"? Many people in this room would gladly support such legislation, but, before they start drafting their bill, I urge them to consider these facts:

1. There is no conclusive scientific evidence to support the claim that exposure to any form of music will cause the listener to commit a crime or damn his soul to hell.

2. Masturbation is not illegal. If it is not illegal to do it, why should it be illegal to sing about it?

3. No medical evidence of hairy palms, warts, or blindness has been linked to masturbation or vaginal arousal, nor has it been proven that hearing references to either topic automatically turns the listener into a social liability.

4. Enforcement of anti-masturbatory legislation could prove costly and time consuming.
5. There is not enough prison space to hold all the children who do it.

The PMRC's proposal is most offensive in its "moral tone". It seems to enforce a set of implied religious values on its victims. Iran has a religious government. Good for them. I like having the capitol of the United States in Washington, DC, in spite of recent efforts to move it to Lynchburg, VA.

Fundamentalism is not a state religion. The PMRC's request for labels regarding sexually explicit lyrics, violence, drugs, alcohol, and especially occult content reads like a catalog of phenomena abhorrent to practitioners of that faith. How a person worships is a private matter, and should not be inflicted upon or exploited by others. Understanding the Fundamentalist leanings of this organization, I think it is fair to wonder if their rating system will eventually be extended to inform parents as to whether a musical group has homosexuals in it. Will the PMRC permit musical groups to exist, but only if gay members don't sing, and are not depicted on the album cover?

The PMRC has demanded that record companies "re-evaluate" the contracts of those groups who do things on stage that THEY find offensive. I remind the PMRC that groups are comprised of individuals. If one guy wiggles too much, does the whole band get an "X"? If the group gets dropped from the label as a result of this 're-evaluation' process, do the other guys in the group who weren't wiggling get to sue the guy who wiggled because he ruined their careers? Do the founders of the tax-exempt organization with no members plan to indemnify record companies for any losses incurred from unfavorably decided breach of contract suits, or is there a PMRC secret agent in the Justice Department?

Should individual musicians be rated? If so, who is qualified to determine if the guitar player is an "X", the vocalist is a "D/A" or the drummer is a "V". If the bass player (or his Senator) belongs to a religious group that dances around with poisonous snakes, does he get an "O"? What if he has an earring in one ear, wears an Italian Horn around his neck, sings about his astrological sign, practices yoga, reads the Quaballah, or owns a rosary? Will his "occult content" rating go into an old CoIntelPro computer, emerging later as a "fact", to determine if he qualifies for a home-owner loan? Will they tell you this is necessary to protect the folks next door from the possibility of 'devil-worship' lyrics creeping through the wall?

What hazards await the unfortunate retailer who accidentally [sic] sells an "O" rated record to somebody's little Johnny? Nobody in Washington seemed to care when Christian Terrorists bombed abortion clinics in the name of Jesus. Will you care when the "Friends of the wives of big brother" blow up the shopping mall?

The PMRC wants ratings to start as of the date of their enactment. That leaves the current crop of 'objectionable material' untouched. What will be the status of recordings from that Golden Era to censorship? Do they become collector's items . . . or will another "fair and unbiased committee" order them destroyed in a public ceremony?

Bad facts make bad law, and people who write bad laws are, in my opinion, more dangerous than songwriters who celebrate sexuality. Freedom of Speech, Freedom of Religious Thought [sic], and the Right to Due Process for composers, performers and retailers are imperiled if the PMRC and the major label consummate this nasty bargain. Are we expected to give up Article One so the big guys can collect an extra dollar on every blank tape and 10 to 25% on tape recorders? What's going on here? Do WE get to vote on this tax? There's an awful lot of smoke pouring out of the legislative machinery used by the PMRC to inflate this issue. Try not to inhale it. Those responsible for the vandalism should pay for the damage by voluntarily rating themselves. If they refuse, perhaps the voters could assist in awarding the Congressional "X", the Congressional "D/A", the Congressional "V", and the Congressional "O". Just like the ladies say: these ratings are necessary to protect our children. I hope it's not too late to put them where they really belong.

QUESTIONS

1. Zappa's statement uses an informal and often sarcastic tone with explicit language. Does Zappa's argumentative strategy, given that his audience is U.S. Senators, seem appropriate or effective? Do you think that Zappa's true intended audience was music fans rather than the committee? Or was he trying to capture the attention of both on the issue of music censorship?

2. What main arguments does Zappa use to discredit the PMRC plan for record labeling? How do the logical fallacies that he uses impact the persuasive effect of his argument? Do you think that the Senators took his argument seriously?

3. The ideas and policies applied to censorship of music have changed over the years. Compare today's pop music censorship policies to those in effect in 1985. Would you say that music today is more or less censored and controlled now than it was then? Explain your response.

IMANI PERRY

"The Venus Hip Hop and the Pink Ghetto"

Imani Perry earned a B.A. from Yale University in Literature and American Studies, a Ph.D. in the History of American Civilization from Harvard, and a J.D. from Harvard Law School. Since 2002 she has taught at Rutgers Law School, offering classes in law and critical race theory, as well as pursuing her scholarly issues in law and popular culture studies, with a special focus on ways that black-produced media "re-envision images of blackness on aesthetic and political levels." She has published many articles in law and cultural studies journals as well as in anthologies such as Gender, Race, and Class in Media: A Text Reader *(2003). Perry's book on hip hop as a black cultural and political form,* Prophets of the Hood: Politics and Poetics in Hip Hop *(2004), includes the following article, which argues in protest of the distorted images of women projected by male and female hip hop performers.*

It seemed to happen suddenly. Every time one turned on BET (Black Entertainment Television) or MTV, one encountered a disturbing music video: Black men rapped surrounded by dozens of black and Latina women dressed in bathing suits, or scantily clad in some other fashion. Video after video proved the same, each one more objectifying than the former. Some took place in strip clubs, some at the pool, at the beach, or in hotel rooms, but the recurrent theme was dozens of half-naked women. The confluence of cultural trends leading to this moment merits more extended scholarly attention than it will receive here, but, in short, it occurred as pornography became increasingly mainstreamed and alluded to in objectifying shows such as *Baywatch,* as the tech boom gave rise to a celebration of consumption and widespread wealth, and as hip hop continued its pattern of shifting dominant foci—from political consciousness to social realism to gangsterism to humor to in this moment, a hedonist conspicuous consumption previously largely associated with Miami Bass music.

The sexist message embraced here proves complex. Its attack on black female identity is multifaceted. First, and most obviously, the women are commodified. They appear in the videos quite explicitly as property, not unlike the luxury cars, Rolex watches, and platinum and diamond medallions also featured. The male stars of the videos do not have access to these legions of women because of charisma or sexual prowess, but rather because they are able to "buy" them due to their wealth. The message is not, "I am a Don Juan," but instead, "I am rich and these are my spoils." Not only are the women commodified, but sex as a whole is.

Moreover the women are often presented as vacuous, doing nothing in the videos but swaying around seductively. Often, they avert their eyes from the camera, allowing the viewer to have a voyeuristic relationship to them. Or they look at the camera, eyes fixed in seductive invitation, mouth slightly open. Any signs of thought, humor, irony, intelligence, anger, or any other emotion, prove extremely rare. Even the manner in which the women dance signals cultural destruction. Black American dance is discursive in that sexuality is usually combined with humor, and that the body is used to converse with other moving bodies. Yet the women who appear in these videos usually dance in a two-dimensional fashion, in a derivative but nonintellectual version of black dance more reminiscent of symbols of pornographic male sexual fantasy than the ritual, conversational, and sexual traditions of black dance. Despite all the gyrations of the video models, their uninterested, wet-lipped languor stands in sharp contrast to (for example) the highly sexualized booty dancing of the Deep South, which features polyrhythmic rear end movement, innuendo, and sexual bravado.

This use of black women in the music videos of male hip hop artists often makes very clear reference to the culture of strip clubs and pornography. Women dance around poles, and porn actresses and exotic dancers are often the stars of the videos, bringing the movement-based symbols of their trades with them. The introduction of porn symbols into music videos is consistent with a larger movement that began in the late 1990s, in which pornographic imagery, discourses, and themes began to enter American popular culture. Powerful examples may be found in the *Howard Stern Show*, E! Entertainment Television, and daytime talk shows. Porn film stars attain mainstream celebrity, exotic dancers are routine talk show guests, and the public face of lesbianism becomes not a matter of the sexual preference of women, but of the sexual consumption and fantasy life of men. The videos discussed here make for an appropriate companion piece to this wider trend. While the music videos are male-centered in that they assume a heterosexual male viewer who will appreciate the images of sexually available young women, it is clear that young women watch them as well. The messages such videos send to young women are instructions on how to be sexy and how to look in order to capture the attention of men with wealth and charisma. Magazines geared toward young women have given instructions on how women should participate in their own objectification for decades, but never before has a genre completely centralized black women in this process.

The beauty ideal for black women presented in these videos is as impossible to achieve as the waif-thin models in *Vogue* magazine are for white women. There is a preference for lighter-complexioned women of color, with long and straight or loosely curled hair. Hair that hangs slick against the head when wet as the model emerges out of a swimming pool (a common video image) is at a premium too. Neither natural tightly curled hair nor most coarse relaxed hair becomes slick, shining, and smooth when wet. It is a beauty ideal that contrasts sharply to the real hair of most black women. When brown-skinned or dark-skinned women appear in the videos, they always have hair that falls well below shoulder length, despite the fact that the average length of black women's natural hair in the United States today is four to six inches, according to Barry Fletcher.

Camera shots linger on very specific types of bodies. The videos have assimilated the African American ideal of a large rotund behind, but the video ideal also features a very small waist, large breasts, and slim shapely legs and arms. Often, while the camera features the faces of lighter-complexioned women, it will linger on the behinds of darker women, implying the same thing as the early 1990s refrain from Sir Mix-A-Lot's "Baby Got Back," "L.A. face with an Oakland booty." That is, the ideal features a "high-status" face combined with a highly sexualized body read by the viewer as the body of a poor or working-class woman. Color is aligned with class, and women are created or valued by how many fantasy elements have been pieced together in their bodies.

While one might argue that the celebration of the rotund behind signals an appreciation of black women's bodies, the image taken as a whole indicates how difficult a beauty ideal this proves to attain for anyone. A small percentage of women, even black women, have such Jessica Rabbit proportions. As journalist Tomika Anderson wrote for *Essence* magazine, "In movies, rap songs and on television, we're told that the attractive, desirable and sexy ladies are the ones with 'junk in their trunks.' And even though this might seem ridiculous, some of us actually listen to (and care about) these obviously misogynistic subliminal messages—just as we are affected by racialized issues like hair texture and skin tone."

Americans have reacted with surprise to abundant social scientific data showing that black girls comprise the social group that scores highest on self-esteem assessments and that they tend to have much better body images that white girls. While these differences in esteem and body image are to a large extent attributable to cultural differences, with black girls having been socialized to see beauty in strong personality characteristics and grooming rather than in particular body types, I believe the media plays a role as well. White girls find themselves inundated with images of beauty impossible for most to attain: sheets of blond hair, waif-thin bodies, large breasts, no cellulite, small but round features, and high cheekbones. Over the years, black women have remained relatively absent from public images of beauty, an exclusion which may have saved black girls from aspiring to impossible ideals. But with the recent explosion of objectified and highly idealized images of black women in music videos, it is quite possible that the body images and even self-esteem of black girls will begin to drop, particularly as they move into adolescence and their bodies come under scrutiny. Many of the music videos feature neighborhood scenes including children. In them, little black girls are beautiful. They laugh, smile, play double Dutch, and more. They are full of personality, and they emerge as cultural celebrations with their hair plaited, twisted, or curled and adorned with colorful ribbons to match their outfits in characteristic black girl grooming style. And yet the adult women generally remain two-dimensional and robbed of personality. Is this what puberty is supposed to hold for these girls?

A Feminist Repsonse?

In such troubling moments, we should all look for a gender-critical voice—in the world, in ourselves. Where do we find a response to this phenomenon that will compellingly argue against such characterizations of black women, where do we find a hip hop feminism? Hip hop has seen a feminist presence since the 1980s in such figures as Salt-N-Pepa, Queen Latifah, and MC Lyte, and hip hop feminism continues to exist despite the widespread objectification of black female bodies. We can find numerous examples of feminist and antisexist songs in hip hop and hip hop soul. Mary J. Blige, Lauryn Hill, Destiny's Child, Missy Elliot, Erykah Badu, and others each have their individual manner of representing black female identity and self-definition.

Alicia Keys, one of the crop of singer-songwriters who fit into the hip hop nation, presents an images that contrasts sharply with the video models. The classically trained pianist who has claimed Biggie Smalls and Jay-Z among her music influences appeared in her first music video for the song "Fallin'" in a manner both stylish and sexy but decidedly not self-exploiting. Her hair in cornrows, wearing a leather jacket and fedora, she sings with visible bluesy emotion. She describes repeatedly falling in love with a man who is not good for her. In the music video, Keys travels by bus to visit the man in prison. This element figures as an important signifier of hip hop sensibilities, as rap music is the one art form that consistently engages with the crisis of black imprisonment and considers imprisoned people as part of its community. As Keys rides in the bus, she gazes at women prisoners working in a field outside the window. They sing the refrain to the song, "I keep on fallin', in and out, of love with you/I never loved someone the way I love you." The women on the bus riding to visit men in prison mirror the women outside of the bus, who are prison laborers. This visual duality comments on the often overlooked problem of black female imprisonment in conversations about the rise of American imprisonment and black imprisonment in particular. It makes reference to two issues facing black women. One is that many black women are the mates of imprisoned men. The second is that many black women wind up in prison because they unwittingly or naively became involved with men participating in illegal activities. The video poignantly alludes to these social ills with a close-up of a stone-faced women in prison clothing with a single tear rolling down her cheek. Although, like Badu, Keys frequently appeared on her first albums to be narratively enmeshed in a "stand by your man" ethos that propped up male-centered heteronormativity, both of their voices and images offer dramatic feminist moments notable for their departure from objectifying and exploitative depictions.

Singer-songwriter India Arie offers another critical example of a black feminist space in the hip hop world. A young brown-skinned and dread-locked woman, she burst on the music scene with her song and companion music video "Video" which criticize the image of women in videos. In the refrain she sings, "I'm not your average girl from a video/My body's not built like a supermodel but/I've learned to love myself unconditionally/because I am a queen."

Similar lyrics assert that value is found in intelligence and integrity rather than expensive clothes, liquor, and firearms. The video celebrates Arie who smiles and dances and pokes fun at the process of selecting girls for music videos. She rides her bicycle into the sunshine with her guitar strapped across her shoulder. Arie refuses to condemn artists who present a sexy image but has stated that she will not wear a skirt above calf length on stage and that she will do nothing that will embarrass her family. Musically, while her sound is folksy soul, she does understand her work as being related to hip hop. "I'm trying to blend acoustic and hip-hop elements," she explains. "I used the most acoustic-sounding drum samples, to have something loud enough to compete with other records, but to keep the realistic, softer feel." Arie understands her work as inflected with hip hop sensibilities, more than with the music's compositional elements. She says: "I don't define hip-hop the way a record company would. The thread that runs though both my music and hip-hop is that it's a very precise expression of my way of life. It's like blues; it's very real and honest output of emotion into a song. Because of that legacy, my generation now has an opportunity to candidly state our opinions. That's what my album is about. I just wanna be me."

Arie's definition of hip hop as honest self-expression is true to the ideology at the heart of the genre at its beginnings, a concept that multitudes of hip hop artists continue to profess to. Yet that element of hip hop stands in tension with the process of celebrity creation. The "honest" words in hip hop exist in a swamp of image making. It does not suffice to examine the clear and simple feminist presences in hip hop; we must consider the murkier ones as well. When it comes to feminist messages, often the words and language of a hip hop song may have feminist content, but the visual image may be implicated in the subjugation of black women. Unlike the individualistic and expressive visuals we have of Arie, Keys, Jill Scott, or Missy Elliot, other artists are often marketed in a manner quite similar to the way in which objectified video models are presented.

Tensions Between Texts

Wholesome young stars like Arie and Keys present both strong and respectable images of black womanhood, yet those women who are "sexy" in particular have a much more difficult time carving out a feminist space for themselves. In an earlier piece, "It's My Thang and I'll Swing It the Way that I Feel: Sexual Subjectivity and Black Women Rappers," I argued for the existence of a feminist space in hip hop in which women articulated sexual subjectivity and desire. While I still do believe this is possible, I find it more difficult to achieve now. When the women articulating subjectivity are increasingly presented in visual media as objects rather than subjects, as they are now, their statement to the world is ambiguous at best, and, at worst, the feminist message of their work will become undermined. Joan Morgan reflects on the tension that this presents in her work, which details the conflicts facing a woman with a feminist identity and the erotics of a hip hop market culture: "Am I no longer down for the cause if I admit that while total gender equality is an interesting intellectual concept, it doesn't do a damn thing for me erotically. That, truth be told, men with too many feminist sensibilities have never made my panties wet, at least not like that reformed thug nigga who can make even the most chauvinistic 'wassup baby' feel like a sweet wet tongue darting in and out of your ear." The question is whether the appeal to the erotics of male desire proves too strong to still make the sexy female MC a voice "for the cause."

A musical artist occupies a multitextual space in popular culture. Lyrics, interviews, music, and videos together create a collage, often finely planned, from which an audience is supposed to form impressions. But the texts may conflict with one another. Lil' Kim, the much discussed, critiqued, and condemned nasty-talking bad girl of hip hop, is a master of shock appeal. Her outfits often expose her breasts, her nipples covered by sequined pasties color-coordinated with the rest of her attire. Despite Kim's visual and lyrical vulgarity, many of her critics admit to finding her endearing. Her interviewers know her as sweet-natured and generous. But Lil' Kim stands as a contradiction because while she interviews as a vulnerable and sweet woman, she raps with the hardness adored by her fans. She has an impressive aggressive sexual presence, and she has often articulated a sexual subjectivity through words, along with an in-your-face camera presence. However, as Kim has developed as an entertainer, it has become clear that her image is complicit in the oppressive language of American cinematography in regard to women's sexuality. She has adopted a Pamela-Anderson-in-brown-skin aesthetic, calling on pornographic tropes but losing the subversiveness sometimes apparent in her early career. Andre Leon Talley of *Vogue* magazine noted her transformation from an "around the way girl" with a flat chest, big behind a and jet black (or green, or blue) weave to the celebrity Kim who shows off breast implants and shakes her long blond hair. In her videos, the camera angles exploit her sexuality. In the video for the song "How Many Licks," she appears as a Barbie-type doll, her body parts welded together in a factory. The video stands as an apt metaphor for her self-commodification and use of white female beauty ideals. The video closes off its own possibilities. The doll factory image might have operated as a tongue-in-cheek criticism of image making or white female beauty ideals, but, instead the video functions as a serious vehicle for Kim to be constructed as beautiful and seductive with blond hair and blue eyes. To be a doll in American popular culture is to be perfect, and she will satisfy many male fantasies as many times as she is replicated. Over several years, Kim has become defined more by her participation in codes of pornographic descriptions of women than by her challenging of concepts of respectability or her explicit sexuality.

It is a delicate balance, but it is important to distinguish between sexual explicitness and internalized sexism. While many who have debated the image of female sexuality have put "explicit" and "self-objectifying" on one side and "respectable" and "covered-up" on the other, I find this a flawed means of categorization. The nature of sexual explicitness proves important to consider, and will become more so as more nuanced images will emerge. There is a creative possibility for liberatory explicitness because it may expand the confines of what women are allowed to say and do. We just need to refer to the history of blues music—one full of raunchy, irreverent, and transgressive women artists—for examples. Yet the overwhelming prevalence of the Madonna/whore dichotomy in American culture means that any woman who uses explicit language or images in her creative expression is in danger of being symbolically cast into the role of whore regardless of what liberatory intentions she may have, particularly if she does not have complete control over her image.

Let us turn to other examples to further explore the tensions between text and visual image in women's hip hop. Eve has emerged as one of the strongest feminist voices in hip hop today. She rhymes against domestic violence and for women's self-definition and self-reliance. She encourages women to hold men in their lives accountable for disrespectful or less-than-loving behavior. Yet the politics of Eve's image are conflicted. She has appeared in music videos for songs on which she has collaborated with male hip hop artists, videos filled with the stock legions of objectified video models. On the one hand, Eve's provocative dress validates the idea of attractiveness exemplified by the models. But the rapper is also distinguished from these women because she is the star. She appears dignified and expressive, while they do not. Her distinction from the other women supports their objectification. She is the exception that makes the rule, and it is her exceptionalism that allows her to have a voice. Similar dynamics have appeared in videos featuring hip hop singer Lil' Mo. In fact, a number of women hip hop artists who claim to be the only woman in their crews, to be the only one who can hang with the fellas, through their exceptionalism make arguments that justify the subjugation of other women, even the majority of women.

Moreover, both Eve and Lil' Kim often speak of the sexual power they have as deriving from their physical attractiveness to men. It is therefore a power granted by male desire, rather than a statement of the power of female sexual desire. While neither artist has completely abandoned the language of empowering female subjectivity in her music, any emphasis on power granted through conventional attractiveness in this media language limits the feminist potential of the music. In one of the songs in which Eve most explicitly expresses desire, "Gotta Man," the desire is rooted in the man's ability to dominate. She describes him as "the only thug in the hood who is wild enough to tame me," and therefore she is "the shrew," willingly stripped of her defiant power by a sexual union. Instead of using her aggressive tongue to challenge prevailing sexist sexual paradigms, she affirms them by saying that she simply needs a man stronger than most, stronger than she, to bring everything back to normal.

The tensions present in hip hop through the interplay of the visual and the linguistic, and the intertextuality of each medium, are various. Even Lauryn Hill, often seen as the redeemer of hip hop due to her dignified, intellectually challenging, and spiritual lyricism has a complicated image. As a member of the Fugees, she often dressed casually in baggy yet interesting clothes thoroughly rooted in hip hop style. It seems no accident that she became a celebrity, gracing the covers of British GQ, Harper's Bazaar, and numerous other magazines, when her sartorial presentation changed. Her skirts got shorter and tighter, her cleavage more pronounced, and her dreadlocks longer. When she began to sport an alternative style that nevertheless garnered mainstream acceptability, she was courted by high-end designers like Armani. As Lauryn's image became more easily absorbable into the language of American beauty culture, her celebrity grew. She even appeared on the cover of Sophisticates Black Hair Magazine, a black beauty guide that usually relegates natural hair to a couple of small pictures of women with curly afros or afro weaves, while the vast majority of its photos show women with long straight weaves and relaxers. The hip hop artist was certainly one of the few Sophisticates cover models ever to have natural hair, and the only with locks. (Interestingly, the silhouette of the locks was molded into the shape of shoulder-length relaxed hair.) In the issue of British GQ that featured Lauryn as a cover model, journalist Sanjiv writes, "She could be every woman in a way Chaka Khan could only sing about—the decade's biggest new soul arrival with the looks of a supermodel and Hollywood knocking at her door."

In September of 1999, Lauryn appeared on the cover of *Harper's Bazaar*. The article inside discussed her community service projects, and the cover celebrated her model-like beauty. Of course, the cover had something subversive to it. Dark-skinned and kinky-haired Lauryn Hill was beautiful, and the image was ironic. Her locks were styled into the shape of a Farah Fawcett flip, a tongue-in-cheek hybridization at once referencing the seventies heyday of unprocessed afro hair and that era's symbol of white female beauty, Farah Fawcett. The hybrid cover proves analogous to the diverse elements used in the creation of the new in hip hop. Nevertheless, it is important to note that Lauryn became widely attractive when her silhouette—thin body and big hair—matched that of mainstream beauty. So even as the artist has been treated as the symbol of black women's dignity and intelligence in hip hop (and rightfully so given her brilliant lyricism), she too found herself pulled into the sexist world of image making. Although she has made some public appearances since cutting off her long hair, getting rid of the makeup, and returning to baggy clothes, publicity about her has noticeably dropped.

In contrast to Lauryn Hill, Erykah Badu has remained unapologetically committed to the drama of her neo-Afrocentric stylings in her image making, and she therefore has only achieved limited mainstream beauty acceptance. After she shaved her head, doffed her enormous head wrap, and wore a dress shaped like a ball gown (although in reality it was a deconstructed, rough textured "warrior princess," as she called it, work of art), Joan Rivers named her the best-dressed attendee at the 2000 Grammy Awards. Yet she also, rather than simply complimenting her dress or style, said that this was the best Badu had ever looked and that she was an extremely beautiful woman. Rivers appeared to insinuate that the singer was receiving recognition for coming closer to looking "as beautiful as she really is," not for truly being the best dressed. A 2001 *Vogue* article discussed Badu in the context of how ugliness could prove beautiful and how fine the line between the beauty and ugliness was, making reference to her unusual attire, again a sign of how disturbing the beauty industry finds her unwillingness to fit into standard paradigms of female presentation, even as her large hazel eyes and high cheekbones undeniably appeal to individuals in that industry.

I used the examples of Lil' Kim, Eve, Lauryn Hill, and Erykah Badu—all very distinct artists—to draw attention to the kinds of tensions that might exist between a feminist conent in hip hop lyrics and the visual image of the artist. I hope these examples encourage readers, as viewers and listeners of popular culture, to become attuned to the multitextual character of the music world and to read as many layers of the media as possible.

The Colonizer and Colonized

In her essay "Language and the Writer," novelist and cultural critic Toni Cade Bambara reminds us that "the creative imagination has been colonized. The global screen has been colonized. And the audience—readers and viewers—is in bondage to an industry. It has the money, the will, the muscle, and the propaganda machine oiled up to keep us all locked up in a delusional system—as to even what America is." Musical artists are cultural actors, but those backed by record labels are hardly independent actors. In music videos and photo layouts, they exist within what Cade Bambara has described as a colonized space, particularly in regard to race and gender. In a context in which a short, tight dress and a camera rolling up the body, lingering on behinds and breasts, holds particular power with regard to gender and personal value, we must ask how powerful words can be that intend to contradict such objectification. How subversive are revolutionary words in a colonized visual world full of traditional gender messages?

QUESTIONS

1. What reasons does Perry give for the exploitation and sexual objectification of black women in the hip hop and rap scenes? Why is the "sexist message embraced"? How do music videos of the songs deepen the stereotyping of black women?
2. According to Perry, which black women singers present themselves as people with self-respect and self-esteem rather than as stereotypes? What impact have these musicians had on the mainstream image of black women and musicians?
3. Do you agree with Perry's conclusions about the prevalence of degradation and exploitation of black women in hip hop and rap music? If so, what solutions might be offered to this serious problem? You might decide to debate the roots of this issue as well as possible solutions with your classmates.

JAMES CUSICK

"Politicians Might Hear, But Does Popular Culture Have the Power to Make Them Act?"

James Cusick is the Westminister reporter for the Sunday Herald Tribune, *a Scottish independent newspaper. Cusick's writing frequently focuses on political and governmental issues such as Britain's role in the war in Iraq, conflicts within the government, election fraud, and race-hate legislation. In the following article from the* Tribune, *he argues about the ability of large political rock concerts like the Live8 concert in the summer of 2005 to change politicians' minds and to convince them to act on global problems such as AIDS, starvation, and genocide.*

"KEEP your eyes wide. The chance won't come again."

The time is 1963. The voice is Bob Dylan. The wider message is stark and threatening for politicians who aren't listening to a new generation that thinks it knows the answers and warns those who don't not to "stand in the doorway" or block up the hall.

Four decades on our politicians are again being warned not to get in the way; warned to listen . . . or else. Four decades on we still prefer to put our faith in the simple gospels of pop star missionaries like Bob Geldof or Bono. We applaud basic questions such as, "How many ears do we need before we can hear people cry?", rather than bother ourselves with the market obstacles that need to be overcome in implementing a successful economic growth model for Africa. We prefer our would-be saints and stars to be raw, youthful and accessible, rather than elected and stuffed with shirt and stripped club tie.

Put Geldof on a platform alongside an establishment politician and its obvious which is which. Geldof is the deliberate antithesis of city smart. He looks as though he's borrowed Dylan's worried hair—and much else; his message is the same, only the poetry is of a lower caliber. Last week, Dylan's final "chance" had changed into a "unique opportunity"—to permanently end poverty in Africa. So twenty years after Live Aid there will be a rerun, Live8, to coincide with next month's G8 summit.

We elect the politicians who will travel to Gleneagles and tell us Africa's problems are complex. But we'll follow, and we prefer to believe, Geldof: the pop star who tells us to "just do it." Why? What place is occupied in our collective psyche by the Dylan's, the Joan Baez's and the latter-day pop puppeteers? And can they actually change the world?

Dylan, almost by accident, found himself the emblem of the fight against Washington's political elite. He was a rag-tag jean-clad youth: a slight figure that looked incapable of finding his next meal on the streets of New York's Greenwich Village, never mind creating unease among powerful senators and congressmen. But he had what the establishment didn't have—and still don't. He possessed what today's pop prophets and campaigners have inherited and continue to use: youthful energy and rawness and the confidence not to rely on pretence. When pop prophets speak, followers believe they "speak to me," and so they are listened to.

Marshal McLuhan, the early guru of media culture, said The Beatles' secret was that they spoke with Liverpool accents and flaunted their low-rent, working-class roots.

American writer and social commentator Tom Wolfe thought The Beatles brought stardom down to the level of their lowliest audience. There was no longer a class barrier, no air of superiority. The illusionary show of wealth and elegance had gone. And in its place? Youth and a willingness to abandon the safety of all rules.

Geldof's "Give us your f**king money" is his badge of authority and energy, his ditching of the rules. It makes him sound like he's made sense of the world—on our terms.

Those at the rock industry's epicenter aren't surprised that people trust pop stars more than politicians. "With pop stars, at least you know who's paying them and what their sins are," argues Joe Levy, deputy managing editor of *Rolling Stone* magazine in New York. "There's less false morality and they are less beholden to special interest groups." For Levy, it doesn't even come down to preferring a pop idol over a politician. "Wouldn't we rather have individuals making these decisions rather than massive corporations?" Levy believes pop stars hold a kind of unique democratic office. "They stand for election every time they put out a single, rather than every four years. I think it's better to trust people who haven't made a career out of getting elected. Pop stars have nothing to fear from speaking from their hearts." For Levy, there is a complexity about the solutions offered by politicians: questions about who they need to keep onside; who they might offend; who they trade with.

"Bono doesn't worry about this stuff. He can operate from a more humanistic perspective." Although Live8 is a complex business, for people like Bono "it will be less subject to compromise." In fact, argues Levy, "their clarity comes from a lack of compromise: so they pay attention to the real lives that are on the line here." Here in Britain, Richard Holloway, retired Anglican bishop of Edinburgh and chair of the Scottish Arts

Council, offers an alternative, almost religious, perspective on why pop apostles command our trust. He believes simple "recognition and celebrity" helps us listen and believe. "John Lennon once said he thought The Beatles were more popular than Jesus. He had put his finger on something, because The Beatles carried more clout in the world than religious figures—and that continues today." Holloway doesn't seem overly concerned that today's preachers might be packaged, not in sacred vestments or clerical collars, but in jeans and wrap-round dark sunglasses. Bono and others simply have "high recognition" combined with openness and a seeming lack of self-regard. This pits them against politicians who are regarded with suspicion because they lack either quality.

But there's a caveat for Holloway. "What pop stars have is celebrity, not power." But don't our pop choirmasters hold the illusion of power: the notion that things can be changed, that the officially impossible can become possible?

Ted Honderich, Emeritus Professor of Mind and Logic at University College London, argues that judgments about what can and can't be changed "are a matter of the greatest importance," and what is conceivable, possible and even necessary, needs a lot more reflection. Honderich believes there is a "paralyzing ideology" of what we can't do, more influenced by governments than by pop stars.

He thinks we have accepted that there are limitations on what is possible, almost as a matter of convention. "The convention is owes more to fundamental distributions of political power and influence in a society." Politicians, he says, have more power than pop stars, and so does the media. The ultimately optimistic Honderich argues that the matter of what will happen is more open than we think.

Honderich is "delighted" that a million people have been invited to demonstrate in Edinburgh, but seems unsure of what they will achieve. "They may be making a move, a start in the right direction, but then there's what happens after that. What happens at the World Bank over the next 10 years? What happens when Tony Blair actually faces paying a price for things he's talked about?" But it is governments that worry about the long term. Pop prophets want action now. And "now" is easier to understand and battle for than a distant future.

Nicholas Bayne, of the London School of Economics' International Trade Policy Unit, identifies a relationship between what pop stars bring to the table, and what politicians learn from their campaigns. "The great merit of involving celebrities . . . is that they bring these issues to the attention of a far wider circle than governments can reach. Their involvement can help governments judge how far their aid and development policies have popular support—or whether they should do more."

Bayne, whose new book on recent G8 summits is published later this month, accepts that popular campaigns like Geldof's can oversimplify the issues or back proposals that would do more harm than good. But if the pop prophets are engaged in the business of blue-skies dreaming, Bayne thinks it then becomes the job of governments to point out the flaws, to effectively deal with the dangers of a short-term focus on what might essentially be a long-term problem.

The pop apostle as economic sounding board seems a nice idea. But it can't explain our continuing belief in pop-driven protest. So if we've lost faith in politicians and prefer the short-term passion offered by rock stars, how do we recognize where simple trust should end and hard-faced pragmatism should kick in?

Here, Holloway thinks we are guided by an almost natural antenna of trust:

"When a pop star says something, they may be right or they may be wrong. But it is their opinion; it's not an official line." Geldof, Bono and other informed pop apostles are characterized by what Holloway dubs "raw passion," linked to a deeper understanding of what they are trying to do and what grand gestures are required to achieve it. Geldof is what Holloway calls a "technical authority" that is still seen as a "tortured soul" and therefore capable of generating empathy with his cause. Geldof and Bono belong to a tradition that goes back to Pete Seeger, Joan Baez and the anti-war protest singers of the 1960s whose genuine moral passion came through in their songs. Holloway is romantic, quasi-religious even, about such connectivity. "It is a kind of apostolic succession—a DNA handed down." He seems to be saying that the Geldofs and Bonos will retain our faith and belief as long as they remain off to one side of formal power, "as long as they don't get sucked into too many dinners at Downing Street." Yet that is precisely what Bono and Geldof have done. They have gone to the enemy, the lion's den, but refused to be eaten; they haven't been turned to the dark side.

At last year's Labor conference in Brighton, Bono even joked to the audience about the irony of the place in which he found himself. "Listen, I know what this looks like, a rock star standing up here, shouting imperatives others have to fulfill. But that's what we do, rock stars. Rock stars get to wave flags, shout at the barricades, and escape to the south of France. We're unaccountable. We behave accordingly. But not you. You can't. We're counting on you."

Geldof is different from Bono. And he's different from Dylan. As a pop star he had no poetry to offer. As an activist he lacks subtlety. Instead he offers anger and impatience—two things we all recognize, because we deal with anger, we live with impatience.

Twenty years after Live Aid, it strikes Geldof as "morally repulsive and intellectually absurd that people die of want in a world of surplus." He was a driving force in getting Blair to set up and deliver the recently published Commission for Africa report. It recommended debt cancellation, increased aid and fairer trade laws. But having dined at Downing Street to get the report, Saint Bob said it was "gathering dust on the shelf." Now he wants the public pressure generated from the Live8 concerts to get it off the shelf and implemented.

The consistency of Geldof's passion to solve Africa's economic problems has given him, according to Stirling University's film and media professor, Simon Frith, "a stronger moral voice on Africa than the Archbishop of Canterbury." But Frith is wary about seeing all would-be pop apostles in the same light as Geldof; wary about the assumption that we place our faith in anything a pop preacher says or does. "We only put our trust in some pop stars." So Geldof might be a one-off, a pop missionary who we recognize as achieving huge success, even though his success is measured by "media achievement" and not by the reality of his impact on Africa. Geldof, claims Frith, understands the media and works it to his advantage. If that sounds intentionally manipulative, it is.

Geldof knows that the culture of the pop world is all about the ability to mobilize large crowds—and that's what he's done. Music didn't drive the success of Live Aid in 1985; big crowds and known names did. The same strategy is driving Live8. Live Aid highlighted the potential global reach of music to the television industry. Live8 simply builds on the audiences that have grown up, and grown with, MTV and the hybrid music/TV culture born since the mid-1980s.

But having created the stage, and the audience: what to do with it? Politicians today—unlike those of the late 19th or early 20th century—are incapable of sustaining lengthy moral rhetoric to mass audiences. During the general election, Blair not only avoided large crowds, he avoided meeting anyone who hadn't first been vetted by his party organizers.

Filling the vacuum left by politicians, unable or unwilling to address crowds in the way Martin Luther King did in the 1960s, are crusading pop stars. For Frith a better personal comparison for Geldof's appealing and clear moral rhetoric is the last pope. "The pope offered a moral certainty and perhaps simple-mindedness in his objectives. But he did it on the world's largest stages. The same is true for Geldof. And there is no point in criticizing his moral voice—because that is the only voice he has," says Frith.

So Geldof's nickname of Saint Bob is appropriate. However, for the NGOs (non governmental organizations) who have to deliver the aid, and the sweat, where it counts, after the Blessed Bob has banged the table for cash or demanded a march to Edinburgh's castle mount, it matters little. Their troubled job is getting people to listen and pop apostles—with a stage and audience—are able to do what they can't.

John Coventry at War on Want says the NGOs have to "bang on and on. Then a pop star or celebrity comes along, says something and everyone listens. They don't usually look to them for a political steer, it's usually a cultural steer they're after. And it seems amazing that here are these famous people giving up time, energy and money to help this great cause." The fact rock stars don't normally "bang on" about aid and power is what gives them their power.

"Bob speaks and everyone listens—fantastic." But what of the detractors? What of those who believe we've put our faith in the wrong place, the wrong people; that the problems are too complex, too important to be left to the pop apostles?

Clare Short, the former international development secretary, who used to have responsibility for Africa, expressed concern last week that Live8 would end in disillusionment and cynicism. "My fear is there will be all these people wearing the wrist bands [Make Poverty History] and thinking they are helping, when nothing is agreed to stop the killing on the ground, and Africa goes on getting poorer." Short was in Blair's government in 2001 when he said: "Africa is a scar on the conscience of the world. But if the world as a community focused on it, we could heal it. And if we don't it will become deeper and angrier." Richard Holloway thinks the reason we believe Geldof when he says much the same thing, is that professional politicians' "narcissism and self-righteousness" get in the way. "People just don't respond to their pleas in the same way." Dylan had advice for the dissenters. It still stands. "Don't criticize what you can't understand." So for Geldof and perhaps those who come after him, we have to at least hope that the times are changing.

QUESTIONS

1. Do you think that people are more inclined to listen to rock celebrities speaking on behalf of a social cause than they are to a politician's speech? How much of an impact have these musicians had? Can you quantify the impact of the protests of musicians?

2. To what extent, if at all, does Cusick think that politicians believe that concerts like Live Aid and Live8 can effectively change people's views on a public issue? Why do you think most people attend such concerts: for the music, to support a cause, or for social reasons?

3. Argue your own point of view on the power of large social-issue concerts to bring about social change as compared to the ordinary political process. Take into account the reservations expressed by the people Cusick quotes in his essay, such as Nicholas Bayne and Clare Short.

DIFFERING PERSPECTIVES: SHOULD COLLEGE STUDENTS ON CAMPUS BE THE TARGET OF RECORDING INDUSTRY CRACKDOWNS ON ILLEGAL DOWNLOADING?

Kenneth C. Green

"The Music Industry's 'Spring Offensive'"

Kenneth Green attended New College in Sarasota, Florida, completed his master's degree at Ohio State University, and earned his Ph.D. from the University of California, Los Angeles. He went on to become the founding director of the Campus Computing Project, the largest national project to study the role of information technology in higher education. A prolific writer and a popular speaker, he attends many academic and professional conferences every year and consults with major technology corporations such as Apple, Dell, Google, and Oracle. Green's knowledge, energy, and intelligence earned him the first EDUCAUSE Award for Leadership in Public Policy and Practice (2002), which recognized his "prominence in the arena of national and international technology agendas, and the linking of higher education to those agendas." In the article that follows, originally published in Inside Higher Education *(a leading online publication widely read by college faculty and administrators) in March of 2007, Green critiques the* Recording Industry Association of America's *recent threats of legal action against illegal downloading on campus. Visit the URL http://www.insidehighered.com/views/2007/03/08/green for links to related sites and commentary.*

This afternoon, in a Congressional office building, Rep. Howard Berman (D-Calif.), chairman of the House of Representatives Judiciary Subcommittee on the Courts, the Internet, and Intellectual Property, will convene a public hearing about digital piracy on college and university networks. Berman is Hollywood's man in Congress—literally! His Los Angeles Congressional district is home to many major movie and music studios.

Today's hearing is the latest in a continuing Congressional review of digital piracy—both on and off college networks. Digital piracy—be it copy shops in Asia churning out thousands of counterfeit copies of CDs, DVDs, and computer software, or individuals downloading music, movies and software from the Internet—involves big bucks. A recent report by the Los Angeles Economic Development Corporation suggests that all forms of digital piracy and counterfeiting (including counterfeit clothing) cost Los Angeles area companies some $5.2 billion in lost revenue in 2005, and state and local governments $483 million in lost tax revenue. The development corporation reports that digital piracy and product counterfeiting cost Los Angeles 106,000 jobs in 2005.

There can be no posturing about the core issue: Copyright is a good thing. Copyright protects the rights of individuals and organizations that create and distribute music, movies, and other kinds of digital content and resources. Piracy is theft. Piracy is bad. Piracy is illegal.

That said, while there is no question that digital piracy—by copy shops or college students—is wrong, so too is the underlying assumption of today's hearing: that college students are the primary source of digital piracy affecting the music and movie industries, and that campus officials are implicitly complicit in the illegal downloading done by college students.

Late last month, Cary Sherman, president of the Recording Industry Association of America and point person in the entertainment industry's campaign to stem the tide of digital piracy, particularly among college students, sent a letter to some 2,000 college and university presidents, delivered via e-mail by David Ward, president of the American Council on Education. Sherman offered a pro forma acknowledgement that there has been some progress regarding "illegal file trafficking of copyrighted content on peer-to-peer (P2P) systems," stating that the RIAA and others in the entertainment industry are "grateful for the proactive work of many institutions." But Sherman's letter also stated clearly that because "the piracy problem on campuses remains extensive and unacceptable," the RIAA felt "compelled to escalate [its] deterrence" efforts, as reflected in a new wave of lawsuits under the Digital Millennium Copyright Act, announced earlier in February.

(Meanwhile, there's also some back room speculation around Washington that Mr. Sherman and others in the entertainment industry would like Congress to deal with digital piracy in the long-delayed reauthorization of the Higher Education Act. Who knows: Perhaps violations of copyright law will join drug convictions as cause for students to be ineligible to participate in government financial aid programs?)

The RIAA's February lawsuits and Sherman's February 28 letter to college presidents appears to be the first phase of a spring offensive targeting college students and coercing campus officials. The firm but polite language of Sherman's letter outlines "a reasonable role that college administrators can play" in stemming P2P downloading. The last page of Sherman's four-page letter identifies four "ways to prevent/ reduce student exposure to lawsuits and DMCA notices."

The RIAA wants colleges and universities to (1) implement a technical network solution; (2) offer an online music service to students; (3) take disciplinary action against students; and (4) provide user education programs about copyright and downloading. Additionally, in his cover letter Sherman suggests that campus officials can "facilitate the [RIAA's] new deterrence program by forwarding pre-lawsuit letters" to students and others with access the campus network to settle legal claims ahead of RIAA lawsuits

All this smacks of extortion. The RIAA's proposed "remedies" represent an easily inferred threat to campus officials: Do as we "suggest" or we will sue your institution and hold you liable for the activities of your students.

The RIAA cites data that "college students, the most avid music fans, get more of their music from illegal peer-to-peer downloading than the rest of the population: 25 percent vs. 16 percent (percentage of total music acquisition from peer-to-peer downloading)." The RIAA claims that "more than half of college students download music and movies illegally."

Some of this is simply a numbers game for press releases. The term "college student" generically applies to some 17 million Americans, ages 16–67, who take college courses. In this context, only a small proportion of the nation's 17 million "college students" depend on campus networks for Internet access, and a far smaller number are downloading digital content. Yes, the downloading may be illegal, but the RIAA's numbers don't document some 8.5 million students engaged in illegal P2P activity.

While traditional college students who depend on campus networks for Internet access may, as the RIAA claims, get more of their music from P2P downloading than the general population, the size of the denominator of this college student population—perhaps some 2 to 2.5 million full-time undergraduates who reside in college dorms and who depend on campus networks for Internet access—pales when compared to the tens of millions of consumers who purchase broadband services from cable and telecommunications companies such as AT&T, Comcast, Earthlink, TimeWarner and Verizon.

The real numbers suggest that the RIAA has lost sight of the hemor-rhaging of digital content via consumer broadband services as it focuses its legal campaign and PR efforts on college students. (In 2005, concurrent with the Supreme Court's *Grokster* decision, a billboard in Los Angeles promoting SBC/Yahoo's DSL service used the tag line "faster downloading of music, movies and stuff." Of course the billboard did not say anything about how to pay for "this stuff.")

Additionally, the RIAA's numbers on "John Doe" lawsuits filed in 2004 and 2005, culled from its own press releases, indicate that college students accounted for just 4 percent (329) of the more than 8,400 "John Does" targeted in RIAA filings. In other words, "consumer piracy" represents a far greater threat to the music industry than does the admittedly inappropriate and illegal downloading and file sharing activity of college students on campus networks. Moreover, while the RIAA's February 28 news release asserts that "college students are the most avid music fans," the RIAA's 2005 *Consumer Profile* reveals that college students (ages 18–24) account for approximately a sixth (roughly 15–17 percent) of the music buying population; in contrast, consumers aged 25 and older purchase two-thirds (66.9 percent) of all recorded music.

Sherman asserts that while "many schools have worked with [the RIAA] to recognize the [P2P] problem and address it effectively ... a far greater number of schools ... have done little or nothing at all." Not so! Data from the fall 2006 *Campus Computing Survey* indicate that the vast majority of colleges and universities have acceptable use policies to address copyright issues and digital piracy. A small but growing number of institutions are following the Cornell model of requiring network users—students, faculty, and staff—to complete an online user education tutorial about copyright, P2P, and acceptable use policies before they gain access to their campus e-mail accounts and the university network.

And many institutions punish students for inappropriate and illegal P2P activity. Poking fun at campus officials and students, a 2003 "Doonesbury" cartoon highlighted the efforts of campus officials to pursue "digital down-loaders." More importantly, this past week the Educause CIO online discussion list has had an active conversation among campus officials about sanctions their institutions impose for DMCA violations. In contrast, consumer ISPs provide no active user education on the P2P issue and do little or nothing to address digital piracy.

These numbers notwithstanding, the RIAA has not pursued consumer broadband providers on the copyright/downloading issue. When I raised this issue with an RIAA official in fall 2004, I was told, in essence, that the consumer broadband providers view litigation as a cost of doing business, while, in contrast, the RIAA knows that colleges and universities, when presented with the threat of litigation, will "jump."

The RIAA's continuing—and seemingly exclusive, if not myopic—focus on college students as the primary source of digital piracy stands in stark contrast to the activities of its European affiliate. On January 17, the London-based International Federation of the Phonographic Industries threatened action against consumer broadband Internet Service Providers (ISPs) if they failed to move against users who illegally download digital content. Yes, the RIAA has sued individuals who used consumer broadband services to download or distribute digital content illegally. However, even as the illegal downloading and distribution on consumer networks presents a greater threat to digital content than the inappropriate P2P activity occurring over campus networks, the RIAA seems to focus its major PR (and Congressional) efforts on college students.

The campus community has been largely silent in response to the RIAA's continuing PR assault. Yes, we in the campus community do care about copyright: the Association of Governing Boards of Colleges and Universities' list of "Top 10 Public Policy Issues for Higher Education in 2005-6" cites intellectual property as a key policy issue for campus officials, noting that "respect for intellectual property—created as part of faculty research and teaching or provided as commercial content by the information and entertainment industries—will help institutions maximize and protect their own resources." And yes, sadly, an occasional campus official has offered up unfortunate (if not just plain dumb) public comments about P2P on campus networks, saying that they don't consider it a top campus IT priority.

Of course, no college president condones piracy. Still, it is discouraging, but not surprising, that college presidents have not been willing to challenge the RIAA's PR campaign. Several have offered up their names and the prestige of their institutions to support the RIAA's PR efforts. To date, however, none have stepped forward to state firmly that while their institutions are addressing digital piracy via user education and student sanctions, they also will not submit to the bullying tactics of RIAA officials.

Let's be clear: I'm not condoning digital piracy. I'm on record in a variety of forums and published articles, spanning two decades that copyright matters. Campuses and college students are an admittedly easy target for the music and movie industries concerned about digital piracy. But we are the wrong target. We in the campus community are doing more about P2P and digital piracy—and doing it far better—than the consumer broadband ISPs that provide Internet service to more than 45 percent of American households (more than 35 million homes and small businesses).

The RIAA's single-minded focus on college students—and easily inferred threats to campus officials—misses the larger issue: Digital piracy is a consumer market problem, not simply a campus issue.

QUESTIONS

1. What important background on the downloading issue does Green's opening paragraph provide? How does Green acknowledge the position of the RIAA in the opening of his article? Does he indicate their position accurately (see the essay by RIAA executives below)?

2. What are Green's strongest criticisms of the RIAA's position as regards suing students on college campuses for downloading? Do you agree with his arguments? Why or why not?

3. Interview your classmates or friends in your dorm to learn more about their position on P2P downloading. Also try to interview an administrator at your college to learn about his or her thoughts on illegal trafficking of music. How do you think that the illegal downloading of music will affect the future of music and student life?

Mitch Bainwol and Cary Sherman

"Explaining the Crackdown on Student Downloading"

Mitch Bainwol (b. 1959) earned his B.A. at Georgetown University and received an MBA from Rice University. After working in Washington as a lobbyist, he became chairman and CEO of the Recording Industry Association of America (RIAA) in 2003. Cary H. Sherman graduated from Cornell University in 1968 and Harvard Law School in 1971. He has worked with many organizations that protect the intellectual property rights of musicians and artists, as well as computer corporations, and is currently the president and chief counsel of the Recording Industry Association of America. In the following article, Bainwol and Sherman present the RIAA's rationale for imposing downloading prosecution and fines for students living in college dorms. The essay also responds to some points raised by Greene's essay above.

As many in the higher education community are well aware from news coverage here and elsewhere, the Recording Industry Association of America (RIAA), on behalf of its member labels, recently initiated a new process for lawsuits against computer users who engage in illegal file-trafficking of copyrighted content on peer-to-peer (P2P) systems. In the new round of lawsuits, 400 of these legal actions were directed at college and university students around the country. The inclusion of so many students was unprecedented. Unfortunately, it was also necessary.

In the three and a half years since we first began suing individuals for illegal file-trafficking, we have witnessed an immense growth in national awareness of this problem. Today, virtually no one, particularly technology savvy students, can claim not to know that the online "sharing" of copyrighted music, movies, software and other works is illegal. By now, there is broad understanding of the impact from this activity, including billions of dollars in lost revenue, millions of dollars in lost taxes, thousands of lost jobs, and entire industries struggling to grow viable legitimate online market places that benefit consumers against a backdrop of massive theft.

We have made great progress—both in holding responsible the illicit businesses profiting from copyright infringement and in deterring many individuals from engaging in illegal downloading behavior. Nevertheless, illegal file-trafficking remains a significant and disproportionate problem on college campuses. A recent survey by *Student Monitor* from spring 2006 found that more than half of college students download music and movies illegally, and according to the market research firm NPD, college students alone accounted for more than 1.3 billion illegal music downloads in 2006.

We know some in the university community believe these figures overstate the contribution of college students to the illegal file-trafficking problem today. Yet new data confirms that students are more prone to engaging in this illegal activity than the population at large. While college students represented only 10 percent of the sample in the online NPD study, they accounted for 26 percent of all music downloading on P2P networks and 21 percent of all P2P users in 2006. Furthermore, college students surveyed by NPD reported that more than two-thirds of all the music they acquired was obtained illegally.

Moreover, our focus on university students is not detracting from our continuing enforcement efforts against individuals using commercial Internet Service Provider (ISP) accounts to engage in this same behavior. Indeed, we have asked ISPs to participate in the same new process that we have implemented for university network users.

Yet this is about far more than the size of a particular slice of the pie. This is about a generation of music fans. College students used to be the music industry's best customers. Now, finding a record store still in business anywhere near a campus is a difficult assignment at best. It's not just the loss of current sales that concerns us, but the habits formed in college that will stay with these students for a lifetime. This is a teachable moment—an opportunity to educate these particular students about the importance of music in their lives and the importance of respecting and valuing music as intellectual property.

The prevalence of this activity on our college campuses should be as unacceptable to universities as it is to us. These networks are intended for educational and research purposes. These are the environments where students receive the guidance necessary to become responsible citizens. Institutions of higher education, of all places, are where people should learn about the value of intellectual property and the importance of protecting it.

The fact that students continue to engage in this behavior is particularly egregious given the extraordinary lengths to which we have gone to address the problem. Our approach always has been and continues to be collaborative—partnering with and appealing to the higher motives of universities. We have met personally with university administrators. We have provided both instructional material and educational resources, including an orientation video to help deter illegal downloading. We have worked productively through organizations like the Joint Committee of the Higher Education and Entertainment Communities. We have participated in Congressional hearings.

We have informed schools of effective network technologies to inhibit illegal activity. We have licensed legitimate music services at steeply discounted rates for college students and helped to arrange partnership opportunities between universities and legitimate services. We have stepped up our notice program to alert schools and students of infringing activity. And, of course, we have as a last resort brought suit against individual file-traffickers.

With this latest round of lawsuits, we have initiated a new prelawsuit settlement program intended to allow students to voluntarily settle claims before a suit is actually filed. We have asked for school administrations' assistance in passing our letters on to students in order to give them the opportunity to settle a claim at a discounted rate and before a public record is created. This is a program initiated in part as a response to defendants who told us they would like this opportunity, and we are encouraged by the swift response of so many schools. Lawsuits are by no means our desired course of action. But when the problem continues to persist, year after year, we are left with no choice.

An op-ed writer recently published in this forum [Kenneth C. Greene] described this approach as bullying. There is a big difference between using "bullying tactics" and using a "bully pulpit" to make an important point. Should we ignore this problem and stand silent as entire generations of students learn to steal? Should we not point out that administrators are brushing off responsibility, choosing not to exercise their moral leadership on this issue? This problem is anything but ours and ours alone. If music is stolen with such impunity, what makes term papers any different? Yet we know university administrators very aggressively pursue plagiarism. Why would universities—so prolific in the creation of intellectual capital themselves—not apply the same high standards to intellectual property of all kinds? This is, after all, a segment of our economy responsible for more than 6 percent of our nation's GDP.

Furthermore, a Business Software Alliance study conducted last year found that 86 percent of managers say that the file-sharing attitudes and behaviors of applicants affect on their hiring decisions. Don't administrators have an obligation to prepare students for the real world, where theft is simply not tolerated? Our strategy is not to bully but to point out that the self-interest of universities lies remarkably close to the interests of the entertainment industries whose products are being looted. And, most importantly, we have sought to do so in a collaborative way.

It doesn't have to be like this. We take this opportunity to once again ask schools to be proactive, to step up and accept responsibility for the activity of their students on their network—not legal responsibility, but moral responsibility, as educators, as organizations transmitting values. Turning a blind eye will not make the problem go away; it will further ingrain in students the belief that a costly and illegal pastime is sanctioned, and even facilitated, by school administrations.

The necessary steps are simple. First, implement a network technical solution. Products like Red Lambda's cGrid are promising as effective and comprehensive solutions that maintain the integrity, security, and legal use of school computing systems without threatening student privacy. Some schools have used these products to block the use of P2P entirely, realizing that the overwhelming, if not sole, use of these applications on campus is to illegally download and distribute copyrighted works. For schools that do not wish to prohibit entirely access to P2P applications, products such as Audible Magic's Copy Sense can be used to filter illegal P2P traffic, again, without impinging on student privacy.

Second, offer a legal online service to give students an inexpensive alternative to stealing. One such service, Ruckus, is funded through advertising and is completely free to users. When schools increasingly provide their students with amenities like cable TV, there is simply no reason not to offer them cheap or free legal access to the music they crave.

Third, take appropriate and consistent disciplinary action when students are found to be engaging in infringing conduct online. This includes stopping and punishing such activity in dorms and on all Local Area Networks throughout a school's computing system.

Some administrations have embraced these solutions, engaged in productive dialogue with us to address this problem, and begun to see positive results. We thank these schools and commend them for their responsible actions.

Yet the vast majority of institutions still have not come to grips with the need to take appropriate action. As we continue our necessary enforcement measures—including our notices and pre-lawsuit settlement initiative—and as Congress continues to monitor this issue with a watchful eye, we hope these schools will fully realize the harm their inaction causes them and their students. We call upon them to do their part to address this continuing, mutual problem.

QUESTIONS

1. How do the RIAA executives use statistics to build an argument that supports their point of view? How do they justify particularly targeting on-campus students for not following the copyright laws that condemn peer file sharing (P2P)? Why does the RIAA avoid presenting the opposing position, other than accusing Kenneth Greene of calling them bullies?

2. Why do you think that students and administrators are not all willing to stop illegal peer file sharing? What are the RIAA's proposals for solutions to the illegal use of file sharing, both from the student side and from that of the administration? Which of their points seem most realistic?

3. Compare and contrast the two positions presented in the debate on the impact of illegal downloading. Which side has the most compelling argument, and why?

Spying and Privacy

Introduction

Although it is not formally a part of the Constitution, there is presumed in the United States to be a kind of inherent "right to privacy," a right that was first traced through legal history and argued for in Samuel Warren and Lewis Brandeis's famous essay by the same name and strengthened through several subsequent Supreme Court decisions. At times, the right to privacy comes in conflict with other rights, such as the right of free speech and freedom of the press, as well as the responsibility of government to be watchful for criminal or terrorist activity; these rights and responsibilities take precedence over the right to privacy in some cases, but dispute over such conflicting rights is a subject of intense social argumentation and litigation.

Other developments that infringe on the right to privacy and result in considerable debate include the development of technological breakthroughs that make privacy almost impossible to maintain on a consistent basis. Ted Koppel and David Brin discuss some of the electronic devices that can be found in modern automobiles, such as electronic tracking devices that ensure that people you know—and many others you probably don't want to know—are aware of your whereabouts (or that of your car) at all times. Electronic tracking and spying devices are found commonly in computers, in the sky (satellite conveyance), and on and in the body (implanted chips, miniature cameras, and biometric scanners). David Brin argues that such devices will soon be available to the general public, enabling everyone to invade anyone else's privacy at any time, which will remove some of the government's power to have a monopoly on spying.

Communitarian thinkers like Amitai Etzioni have argued that the concern over privacy can be excessive, a separating demand, decreasing the unity of the social network as well as a making it more difficult for police to catch criminals and illegal immigrants. However, security expert Bruce Schneier, in his article in this chapter, refutes positions such as those of Brin and Etzioni by pointing out the high position of power held by governmental officials that have spying technology and the legal right to use it in relation to members of the public, who may be the victims of such relatively low-tech spying devices as security cameras or wire taps. This power imbalance can only be corrected by changes in the legal status of the spied-upon versus the spies.

Taking a similar position to Schneier's in regard to personal intrusion through "social network" sites such as MySpace, the International Working Group on Data Protection in Telecommunications presents in "The Rome Memorandum" a series of solutions for self-regulation, legal regulation, and personal cautions for users of such sites, where new paradoxes of behavior have emerged among users of MySpace and Facebook who may reveal themselves to possible "friends" in open and possibly dangerous ways.

Finally, as our "Differing Perspectives" authors in this chapter argue, with the attacks of 9/11 and the passage of the Patriot Act, we have come to a place where government intrusion has become an anti-terror mandate, despite the fact that innocent individuals may get caught up in the web of spy hunting, as libertarian writer James Bovard points out.

TED KOPPEL

"Take My Privacy, Please!"

Edward James "Ted" Koppel (b. 1940), who holds an M.A. in mass communications research and political science from Stanford University, worked for forty-two years for ABC News and was anchor of the acclaimed news analysis program Nightline *from 1989–1995. The winner of every broadcasting award, in 1995 he retired from ABC and now manages the Discovery Channel, writes Op-Ed columns for the* New York Times, *and appears on news specials on television and public radio. His books include* In the National Interest *(1977) and* Off Camera: Private Thoughts Made Public *(2000). His* New York Times *article "Take my Privacy, Please!" (2005) presents a satirical argument about recent electronic inventions that show a willingness (or obliviousness) on the part of Americans to go along with invasions of their privacy that promise to make their lives more convenient.*

The Patriot Act-brilliant! Its critics would have preferred a less stirring title, perhaps something along the lines of the Enhanced Snooping, Library and Hospital Database Seizure Act. But then who, even right after 9/11, would have voted for that?

Precisely. He who names it and frames it, claims it. The Patriot Act, however, may turn out to be among the lesser threats to our individual and collective privacy.

There is no end to what we will endure, support, pay for and promote if only it makes our lives easier, promises to save us money, appears to enhance our security and comes to us in a warm, cuddly and altogether nonthreatening package. To wit: OnStar, the subscription vehicle tracking and assistance system. Part of its mission statement, as found on the OnStar Web site, is the creation of "safety, security and peace of mind for drivers and passengers with thoughtful wireless services that are always there, always ready." You've surely seen or heard their commercials, one of which goes like this:

> Announcer: *The following is an OnStar conversation. (Ring)*
> OnStar: *OnStar emergency, this is Dwight.*
> Driver (crying): *Yes, yes??!*
> OnStar: *Are there any injuries, ma'am?*
> Driver: *My leg hurts, my arm hurts.*
> OnStar: *O.K. I do understand. I will be contacting emergency services.*
> Announcer: *If your airbags deploy, OnStar receives a signal and calls to check on you.*
> *(Ring)*
> Emergency Services Police.
> OnStar: *This is Dwight with OnStar. I'd like to report a vehicle crash with airbag deployment on West 106th Street.*
> Emergency Services: *We'll send police and E.M.S. out there.*
> Driver (crying): *I'm so scared!*
> OnStar: *O.K., I'm here with you, ma'am; you needn't be scared.*

Well, maybe just a little scared. Tell us again how Dwight knows just where the accident took place. Oh, right! It's those thoughtful wireless services that are always there. Always, as in any time a driver gets into an OnStar-equipped vehicle. OnStar insists that it would disclose the whereabouts of a subscriber's vehicle only after being presented with a criminal court order or after the vehicle has been reported stolen. That's certainly a relief. I wouldn't want to think that anyone but Dwight knows where I am whenever I'm traveling in my car.

Of course, E-ZPass and most other toll-collecting systems already know whenever a customer passes through one of their scanners. That's because of radio frequency identification technology. In return for the convenience of zipping through toll booths, you need to have in your car a wireless device. This tag contains information about your account, permitting E-ZPass to deduct the necessary toll—and to note when your car whisked through that particular toll booth. They wouldn't share that information with anyone, either; that is, unless they had to.

The State Department plans to use radio frequency identification technology in all new American passports by the end of 2005. The department wants to be sure that we all move through immigration quickly and efficiently when we return from overseas. Privacy advocates have suggested that hackers could tap into the information stored on these tags, or that terrorists might be able to use them to pinpoint American tourists in a crowd. The State Department assures us that both concerns are unfounded, and that it will allow privacy advocates to review test results this summer.

Radio frequency identification technology has been used for about 15 years now to reunite lost pets with their owners. Applied Digital Solutions, for example, manufactures the VeriChip, a tiny, implantable device that holds a small amount of data. Animal shelters can scan the chip for the name and phone number of the lost pet's owner. The product is now referred to as the HomeAgain Microchip Identification System.

Useful? Sure. Indeed, it's not much of a leap to suggest that one day, the VeriChip might be routinely implanted under the skin of, let's say, an Alzheimer's patient. The Food and Drug Administration approved the VeriChip for use in people last October. An Applied Digital Solutions spokesman estimates that about 1,000 people have already had a VeriChip implanted, usually in the right triceps. At the moment, it doesn't carry much information, just an identification number that health care providers can use to tap into a patient's medical history. A Barcelona nightclub also uses it to admit customers with a qualifying code to enter a V.I.P. room where drinks are automatically put on their bill. Possible variations on the theme are staggering.

And how about all the information collected by popular devices like TiVo, the digital video recorder that enables you to watch and store an entire season's worth of favorite programs at your own convenience?

It also lets you electronically mark the programs you favor, allowing TiVo to suggest similar programs for your viewing pleasure. In February, TiVo announced the most frequently played and replayed commercial moment during the Super Bowl (it involves a wardrobe malfunction, but believe me, you don't want to know), drawing on aggregated data from a sample of 10,000 anonymous TiVo households. No one is suggesting that TiVo tracks what each subscriber records and replays. But could they, if they needed to? That's unclear, although TiVo does have a privacy policy. "Your privacy," it says in part, "is very important to us. Due to factors beyond our control, however, we cannot fully ensure that your user information will not be disclosed to third parties."

Unexpected and unfortunate things happen, of course, even to the most reputable and best-run organizations. Only last February, the Bank of America Corporation notified federal investigators that it had lost computer backup tapes containing personal information about 1.2 million federal government employees, including some senators. In April, LexisNexis unintentionally gave outsiders access to the personal files (addresses, Social Security numbers, drivers license information) of as many as 310,000 people. In May, Time Warner revealed that an outside storage company had misplaced data stored on computer backup tapes on 600,000 current and former employees. That same month, United Parcel Service picked up a box of computer tapes in New Jersey from CitiFinancial, the consumer finance subsidiary of Citigroup, that contained the names, addresses, Social Security numbers, account numbers, payment histories and other details on small personal loans made to an estimated 3.9 million customers. The box is still missing.

Whoops!

CitiFinancial correctly informed its own customers and, inevitably, the rest of the world about the security breach. Would they have done so entirely on their own? That is less clear. In July 2003, California started requiring companies to inform customers living in the state of any breach in security that compromises personally identifiable information. Six other states have passed similar legislation.

No such legislation exists on the federal stage, however—only discretionary guidelines for financial institutions about whether and how they should inform their customers with respect to breaches in the security of their personal information.

Both the House and Senate are now considering federal legislation similar to the California law. It's a start but not nearly enough. We need mandatory clarity and transparency; not just with regard to the services that these miracles of microchip and satellite technology offer but also the degree to which companies share and exchange their harvest of private data.

We cannot even begin to control the growing army of businesses and industries that monitor what we buy, what we watch on television, where we drive, the debts we pay or fail to pay, our marriages and divorces, our litigations, our health and tax records and all else that may or may not yet exist on some computer tape, if we don't fully understand everything we're signing up for when we avail ourselves of one of these services.

QUESTIONS

1. Why does Koppel begin his essay with a statement about the Patriot Act as a "lesser threat" to our privacy? Is this an effective set-up for the essay's real subject?

2. How does Koppel's inclusion of a dialogue from an On-Star ad help us both to understand the operation of and to feel some concern about the invasiveness of the product? How well does his subsequent explanation supply a convincing "clincher" of his point? Does the long list of other acts by businesses he provides succeed in making the reader feel fearful and alert to the dangers he implies?

3. What conclusions about possible legislation and the need for heightened awareness does Koppel present in his final paragraphs? Do his conclusions seem reasonable and potentially helpful to you? Why or why not?

AMITAI ETZIONI

"Less Privacy Is Good for Us (and You)"

Amitiai Etzioni was born in Cologne, Germany in 1929 and received his Ph.D. from the University of California, Berkeley (1958). He began his teaching career at Columbia University and taught at George Washington University (1980–1987). He is the editor of The Responsive Community: Rights and Responsibilities, *a communitarian quarterly, and is the author of twenty-one books, including* The New Golden Rule: Community and Morality in an a Democratic Society *(1996) and* Next: the Road to the Good Society *(2001). In the following selection from* The Privacy Journal *(1999), Etzioni argues for some particular cases in which privacy rights need to be abridged.*

Despite the fact that privacy is not so much as mentioned in the Constitution and that it was only shoehorned in some thirty-four years ago, it is viewed by most Americans as a profound, inalienable right.

The media is loaded with horror stories about the ways privacy is not so much nibbled away as it is stripped away by bosses who read your e-mail, neighbors who listen in on your cell phones, and E-Z passes that allow tollbooth operators to keep track of your movements. A typical headline decries the "End of Privacy" (Richard A. Spinello, in an issue of *America*, a Catholic weekly) or "The Death of Privacy" (Joshua Quittner, in *Time*).

It is time to pay attention to the other half of the equation that defines a good society: concerns for public health and safety that entail some rather justifiable diminution of privacy.

Take the HIV testing of infants. New medical data—for instance, evidence recently published by the prestigious *New England Journal of Medicine*—show that a significant proportion of children born to mothers who have HIV can ward off this horrible disease but only on two conditions: that their mothers not breast-feed them and that they immediately be given AZT. For this to happen, mothers must be informed that they have HIV. An estimated two-thirds of infected mothers are unaware. However, various civil libertarians and some gay activists vehemently oppose such disclosure on the grounds that when infants are tested for HIV, in effect one finds out if the mother is a carrier, and thus her privacy is violated. While New York State in 1996, after a very acrimonious debate, enacted a law that requires infant testing and disclosure of the findings to the mother, most other states have so far avoided dealing with this issue.

Congress passed the buck by asking the Institute of Medicine (IOM) to conduct a study of the matter. The IOM committee, dominated by politically correct people, just reported its recommendations. It suggested that all pregnant women be asked to consent to HIV testing as part of routine prenatal care. There is little wrong with such a recommendation other than it does not deal with many of the mothers who are drug addicts or otherwise live at society's margins. Many of these women do not show up for prenatal care, and they are particularly prone to HIV, according to a study published in the American Health Association's *Journal of School Health*. To save the lives of their children, they must be tested at delivery and treated even if this entails a violation of mothers' privacy.

Recently a suggestion to use driver's licenses to curb illegal immigration has sent the Coalition for Constitutional Liberties, a large group of libertarians, civil libertarians, and privacy advocates, into higher orbit than John Glenn ever traversed. The coalition wrote:

> This plan pushes us to the brink of tyranny, where citizens will not be allowed to travel, open bank accounts, obtain health care, get a job, or purchase firearms without first presenting the proper government papers.
>
> The authorizing section of the law . . . is reminiscent of the totalitarian dictates by Politburo members in the former Soviet Union, not the Congress of the United States of America.

Meanwhile, Wells Fargo is introducing a new device that allows a person to cash checks at its ATM machines because the machines recognize faces. Rapidly coming is a whole new industry of so-called biometrics that uses natural features such as voice, hand design, and eye pattern to recognize a person with the same extremely high reliability provided by the new DNA tests.

It's true that as biometrics catches on, it will practically strip Americans of anonymity, an important part of privacy. In the near future, a person who acquired a poor reputation in one part of the country will find it much more difficult to move to another part, change his name, and gain a whole fresh start. Biometrics see right through such assumed identities. One may hope that future communities will become more tolerant of such people, especially if they openly acknowledge the mistakes of their past and truly seek to lead a more prosocial life. But they will no longer be able to hide their pasts.

Above all, while biometrics clearly undermines privacy, the social benefits it promises are very substantial. Specifically, each year at least half a million criminals become fugitives, avoiding trial, incarceration, or serving their full sentences, often committing additional crimes while on the lam. People who fraudulently file for multiple income tax refunds using fake identities and multiple Social Security numbers cost the nation between $1 billion and $5 billion per year. Numerous divorced parents escape their financial obligations to their children by avoiding detection when they move or change jobs. (The sums owed to children are variously estimated as running between $18 billion to $23 billion a year.) Professional and amateur criminals, employing fraudulent identification documentation to make phony credit card purchases, cost credit card companies and retail businesses an indeterminate number of billions of dollars each year. The United States loses an estimated $18 billion a year to benefit fraud committed by illegal aliens using false IDs. A 1998 General Accounting Office report estimates identity fraud to cost $10 billion annually in entitlement programs alone.

People hired to work in child care centers, kindergartens, and schools cannot be effectively screened to keep out child abusers and sex offenders, largely because when background checks are conducted, convicted criminals escape detection by using false identification and aliases. Biometrics would sharply curtail all these crimes, although far from wipe them out singlehandedly.

The courts have recognized that privacy much be weighed against considerations of public interest but have tended to privilege privacy and make claims for public health or safety clear several high hurdles. In recent years these barriers have been somewhat lowered as courts have become more concerned with public safety and health. Given that these often are matters of state law and that neither legislatures nor courts act in unison, the details are complex and far from all pointing in one direction. But, by and large, courts have allowed mandatory drug testing of those who directly have the lives of others in their hands, including pilots, train engineers, drivers of school buses, and air traffic controllers, even though such testing violates their privacy. In case after case, the courts have disregarded objections to such tests by civil libertarians who argue that such tests constitute "suspicionless" searches, grossly violate privacy, and—as the ACLU puts it—"condition Americans to a police state."

All this points to a need to recast privacy in our civic culture, public policies, and legal doctrines. We should cease to treat it as unmitigated good, a sacred right (the way Warren and Brandeis referred to it in their famous article and many since) or one that courts automatically privilege.

Instead, privacy should rely squarely on the Fourth Amendment, the only one that has a balance built right into its text. It recognizes both searches that wantonly violate privacy ("unreasonable" ones) and those that enhance the common good to such an extent that they are justified, even if they intrude into one's privacy. Moreover, it provides a mechanism to sort out which searches are in the public interest and which violate privacy without sufficient cause, by introducing the concept of warrants issued by a "neutral magistrate" presented with "probable cause." Warrants also limit the invasion of privacy "by specification of the person to be seized, the place to be searched, and the evidence to be sought." The Fourth may have become the Constitutional Foundation of privacy a long time ago if it was not for the fact that *Roe v. Wade* is construed as a privacy right, and touching it provokes fierce opposition. The good news, though, is that even the advocates of choice in this area are now looking to base their position on some other legal grounds, especially the Fourteenth Amendment.

We might be ready to treat privacy for what it is: one very important right but not one that trumps most other considerations, especially of public safety and health.

QUESTIONS

1. Why does Etzioni believe that privacy issues should be examined under the Fourth Amendment (concerned with searches in the public interest)? Do you agree or disagree with his point of view? Is the distinction he makes here relevant?

2. Clearly there is a gap between lawmakers and lawyers who understand the complex applications of the First and Fourth amendments and the typical American whose basic knowledge of law is minimal. What can be done to help people to understand and make more reasoned decisions?

3. Analyze the problems and contradictions in one of the new privacy issues that Etzioni brings up in his article, such as biometrics and use of driver's licenses to curb illegal immigration. Does he seem to oversimplify or minimize the concerns of those who object to the privacy infringements involved in this particular change? Why or why not?

DAVID BRIN

"Three Cheers for the Surveillance Society!"

David Brin (b.1950) started his career as a scientist, writing on science-related and research issues and technology. He soon began writing award-winning science fiction as well as nonfiction essays about privacy and the future and began speaking on a variety of subjects. Brin holds a Ph.D. in space physics from the University of California at San Diego and has done post-doctorate work at the California Space Institute at UCSD and the Jet Propulsion Laboratory. His 1998 nonfiction book, The Transparent Society: Will Technology Force Us to Choose Between Freedom and Privacy? *(winner of the Freedom of Speech Prize from the American Library Association) examines technology and the future of privacy, which Brin believes will continue to be greatly challenged and redefined. The following article, developed from the ideas in* The Transparent Society, *was published in* Salon Magazine *in 2004.*

Ten centuries ago, at the previous millennium, a Viking lord commanded the rising tide to retreat. No deluded fool, King Canute aimed in this way to teach flatterers a lesson—that even sovereign rulers cannot halt inexorable change.

A thousand years later, we face tides of technology-driven transformation that seem bound only to accelerate. Waves of innovation may liberate human civilization, or disrupt it, more than anything since glass lenses and movable type. Critical decisions during the next few years—about research, investment, law and lifestyle—may determine what kind of civilization our children inherit. Especially problematic are many information-related technologies that loom on the near horizon—technologies that may foster tyranny, or else empower citizenship in a true global village.

Typically we are told, often and passionately, that Big Brother may abuse these new powers. Or else our privacy and rights will be violated by some other group. Perhaps a commercial, aristocratic, bureaucratic, intellectual, foreign, criminal or technological elite. (Pick your favorite bogeyman.) Because one or more of these centers of power might use the new tools to see better, we're told that we should all be very afraid. Indeed, our only hope may be to squelch or fiercely control the onslaught of change. For the sake of safety and liberty, we are offered one prescription: We must limit the power of others to see.

Half a century ago, amid an era of despair, George Orwell created one of the most oppressive metaphors in literature with the telescreen system used to surveil and control the people in his novel "1984." We have been raised to a high degree of sensitivity by Orwell's *self-preventing* prophecy, and others like it. Attuned to wariness, today's activists preach that any growth in the state's ability to see will take us down a path of no return, toward the endless hell of Big Brother.

But consider. The worst aspect of Orwell's telescreen—the trait guaranteeing tyranny—was not that agents of the state could use it to see. The one thing that despots truly need is to avoid accountability. In *1984,* this is achieved by keeping the telescreen aimed in just one direction! By preventing the people from looking back. While a flood of new discoveries may seem daunting, they should not undermine the core values of a calm and knowledgeable citizenry. Quite the opposite: While privacy may have to be redefined, the new technologies of surveillance should and will be the primary countervailing force against tyranny.

In any event, none of those who denounce the new technologies have shown how it will be possible to stop this rising tide.

Consider a few examples:

Radio frequency identification (RFID) technology will soon replace the simple, passive bar codes on packaged goods, substituting inexpensive chips that respond to microwave interrogation, making every box of toothpaste or razor blades part of a vast, automatic inventory accounting system. Wal-Mart announced in 2003 that it will require its top 100 suppliers to use RFID on all large cartons, for purposes of warehouse inventory keeping. But that is only the beginning. Inevitably as prices fall, RFID chips will be incorporated into most products and packaging. Supermarket checkout will become a breeze, when you simply push your cart past a scanner and grab a printout receipt, with every purchase automatically debited from your account.

Does that sound simultaneously creepy and useful? Well, it goes much further. Under development are smart washers that will read the tags on clothing and adjust their cycles accordingly, and smart medicine cabinets that track tagged prescriptions, in order to warn which ones have expired or need refilling. Cars and desks and computers will adjust to your preferred settings as you approach. Paramedics may download your health status—including allergies and dangerous drug-conflicts—even if you are unconscious or unable to speak.

There's a downside. A wonderful 1960s paranoia satire, "The President's Analyst," offered prophetic warning against implanted devices, inserted into people, that would allow them to be tracked by big business and government. But who needs implantation when your clothing and innocuous possessions will carry cheap tags of their own that can be associated with their owners? Already some schools—especially in Asia—are experimenting with RFID systems that will locate all students, at all times.

Oh, there will be fun to be had, for a while, in fooling these systems with minor acts of irreverent rebellion. Picture kids swapping clothes and possessions, furtively, in order to leave muddled trails. Still, such measures will not accomplish much over extended periods. Tracking on vast scales, national and worldwide, will emerge in rapid order. And if we try to stop it with legislation, the chief effect will only be to drive the surveillance into secret networks that are just as pervasive.

Only they will operate at levels we cannot supervise, study, discuss or understand.

Wait, there's more. For example, a new Internet protocol (IPv6) will vastly expand available address space in the virtual world.

The present IP, offering 32-bit data labels, can now offer every living human a unique online address, limiting direct access to something like 10 billion Web pages or specific computers. In contrast, IPv6 will use 128 bits. This will allow the virtual tagging of every cubic centimeter of the earth's surface, from sea level to mountaintop, spreading a multidimensional data overlay across the planet. Every tagged or manmade object may participate, from your wristwatch to a nearby lamppost, vending machine or trash can—even most of the discarded contents of the trash can.

Every interest group will find some kind of opportunity in this new world. Want to protect forests? Each and every tree on earth might have a chip fired into its bark from the air, alerting a network if furtive loggers start transporting stolen hardwoods. Or the same method could track whoever steals your morning paper. Not long after this, teens and children will purchase rolls of ultra-cheap digital eyes and casually stick them onto walls. Millions of those "penny cams" will join in the fun, contributing to the vast IPv6 datasphere.

Oh, this new Internet protocol will offer many benefits—for example, embedded systems for data tracking and verification. In the short term, expanded powers of vision *may* embolden tyrants. But over the long run, these systems could help to empower citizens and enhance mutual trust.

In the mid-'90s, when I began writing "The Transparent Society," it seemed dismaying to note that Great Britain had almost 150,000 CCD police cameras scanning public streets. Today, they number in the millions.

In the United States, a similar proliferation, though just as rapid, has been somewhat masked by a different national tradition—that of dispersed ownership. As pointed out by UC-San Diego researcher Mohan Trivedi, American constabularies have few cameras of their own. Instead, they rely on vast numbers of security monitors operated by small and large companies, banks, markets and private individuals, who scan ever larger swaths of urban landscape. Nearly all of the footage that helped solve the Oklahoma City bombing and the D.C. sniper episode—as well as documenting the events of 9/11—came from unofficial sources.

This unique system can be both effective and inexpensive for state agencies, especially when the public is inclined to cooperate, as in searches for missing children. Still, there are many irksome drawbacks to officials who may want more pervasive and direct surveillance. For one thing, the present method relies upon high levels of mutual trust and goodwill between authorities and the owners of those cameras—whether they be convenience-store corporations or videocam-equipped private citizens. Moreover, while many crimes are solved with help from private cameras, more police are also held accountable for well-documented lapses in professional behavior.

This tattletale trend began with the infamous beating of Rodney King, more than a decade ago, and has continued at an accelerating pace. Among recently exposed events were those that aroused disgust (the tormenting of live birds in the Pilgrim's Pride slaughterhouse) and shook America's stature in the world (the prisoner abuse by jailers at Abu Ghraib prison in Iraq). Each time the lesson is the same one: that professionals should attend to their professionalism, or else the citizens and consumers who pay their wages will find out and—eventually—hold them accountable.

(Those wishing to promote the trend might look into Project Witness, which supplies cameras to underdogs around the world.)

Will American authorities decide to abandon this quaint social bargain of shared access to sensors under dispersed ownership? As the price of electronic gear plummets, it will become easy and cheap for our professional protectors to purchase their own dedicated systems of surveillance, like those already operating in Britain, Singapore and elsewhere. Systems that "look down from above" (surveillance) without any irksome public involvement.

Or might authorities simply use our networks without asking? A decade ago, the U.S. government fought activist groups such as the Electronic Frontier Foundation, claiming a need to unlock commercial-level encryption codes at will, for the sake of law enforcement and national defense. Both sides won apparent victories. High-level commercial encryption became widely available. And the government came to realize that it doesn't matter. It never did.

Shall I go on?

Driven partly by security demands, a multitude of biometric technologies will identify individuals by scanning physical attributes, from fingerprints, iris patterns, faces and voices to brainwaves and possibly unique chemical signatures. Starting with those now entering and leaving the United States, whole classes of people will grow accustomed to routine identification in this way. Indeed, citizens may start to demand more extensive use of biometric identification, as a safety measure against identity theft. When your car recognizes your face, and all the stores can verify your fingerprint, what need will you have for keys or a credit card?

Naturally, this is yet another trend that has put privacy activists in a lather. They worry—with some justification—about civil liberties implications when the police or FBI might scan multitudes (say, at a sporting event) in search of fugitives or suspects. Automatic software agents will recognize individuals who pass through one camera view, then perform a smooth handoff to the next camera, and the next, planting a "tail" on dozens, hundreds, or tens of thousands of people at a time.

And yes, without a doubt this method could become a potent tool for some future Big Brother.

So? Should that legitimate and plausible fear be addressed by reflexively blaming technology and seeking ways to restrict its use? Or by finding ways that technology may work for us, instead of against us?

Suppose you could ban or limit a particular identification technique. (Mind you, I've seen no evidence that it can be done.) The sheer number of different, overlapping biometric approaches will make that whole approach fruitless. In fact, human beings fizz and froth with unique traits that can be spotted at a glance, even with our old-fashioned senses. Our ancestors relied on this fact, building and correlating lists of people who merited trust or worry, from among the few thousands that they met in person. In a global village of 10 billion souls, machines will do the same thing for us by prosthetically amplifying vision and augmenting memory.

With so many identification methodologies working independently and in parallel, our children may find the word "anonymous" impossibly quaint, perhaps even incomprehensible. But that needn't mean an end to freedom—or even privacy. Although it will undoubtedly mean a redefinition of what we think privacy means.

But onward with our scan of panopticonic technologies. Beyond RFID, IPv6 and biometrics there are smart cards, smart highways, smart airports, smart automobiles, smart televisions, smart homes and so on.

The shared adjective may be premature. These systems will provide improved service long before anything like actual "artificial intelligence" comes online. Yet machinery needn't be strictly intelligent in order to transform our lives. Moreover, distributed "smart" units will also gather information, joining together in cross-correlating networks that recognize travelers, perform security checks, negotiate micro-transactions, detect criminal activity, warn of potential danger and anticipate desires. When these parts fully interlink, the emerging entity may not be self-aware, but it will certainly know the whereabouts of its myriad parts.

Location awareness will pervade the electronic world, thanks to ever more sophisticated radio transceivers, GPS chips, and government-backed emergency location initiatives like Enhanced-911 in the United States and Enhanced-112 in Europe. Cellphones, computers and cars will report position and unique identity in real time, with (or possibly without) owner consent. Lives will be saved, property recovered, and missing children found. But these benefits aren't the real reason that location awareness and reporting will spread to nearly every device. As described by science fiction author Vernor Vinge, it is going to happen because the capability will cost next to nothing as an integrated part of wireless technology. In the future, you can assume that almost any electronic device will be trackable, though citizens still have time to debate who may do the tracking.

The flood of information has to go someplace. Already databases fill with information about private individuals, from tax and medical records to credit ratings; from travel habits and retail purchases to which movies they recently downloaded on their TiVo personal video recorder. Yahoo's HotJobs recently began selling "self" background checks, offering job seekers a chance to vet their own personal, financial and legal data—the same information that companies might use to judge them. (True, a dating service that already screens for felons, recently expanded its partnership with database provider Rapsheets to review public records and verify a user's single status.) Data aggregators like Acxiom Corp., of Arkansas, or ChoicePoint, of Georgia, go even further, listing your car loans, outstanding liens and judgments, any professional or pilot or gun licenses, credit checks, and real estate you might own—all of it gathered from legal and open sources.

On the plus side, you'll be able to find and counter those rumors and slanderous untruths that can slash from the dark. The ability of others to harm you with lies may decline drastically. On the other hand, it will be simple for almost anybody using these methods to appraise the background of anyone else, including all sorts of unpleasant things that are inconveniently true. In other words, the rest of us will be able to do what elites (define them as you wish, from government to aristocrats to criminal masterminds) already can.

Some perceive this trend as ultimately empowering, while others see it as inherently oppressive. For example, activist groups from the ACLU to the Electronic Privacy Information Center call for European-style legislation aiming to seal the data behind perfect firewalls into separate, isolated clusters that cannot cross-link or overlap. And in the short term, such efforts may prove beneficial. New database filters may help users find information they legitimately need while protecting personal privacy . . . for a while, buying us time to innovate for the long term.

But we mustn't fool ourselves. No firewall, program or machine has ever been perfect, or perfectly implemented by fallible human beings. Whether the law officially allows it or not, can any effort by mere mortals prevent data from leaking? (And just one brief leak can spill a giant database into public knowledge, forever.) Cross-correlation will swiftly draw conclusions that are far more significant than the mere sum of the parts, adding up to a profoundly detailed picture of every citizen, down to details of personal taste.

Here's a related tidbit from the *Washington Post:* Minnesota entrepreneur Larry Colson has developed WebVoter, a program that lets Republican activists in the state report their neighbors' political views into a central database that the Bush-Cheney campaign can use to send them targeted campaign literature. The Bush campaign has a similar program on its Web site. And here's Colson's response to anyone who feels a privacy qualm or two about this program: "[It's] not as if we're asking for Social Security number and make and model and serial number of car. We're asking for party preference . . . Party preference is not something that is such a personal piece of data."

That statement may be somewhat true in today's America. We tend to shrug over each other's harmless or opinionated eccentricities. But can that trait last very long when powerful groups scrutinize us, without being scrutinized back? In the long run, tolerance depends on the ability of any tolerated minority to enforce its right to be left alone. This is achieved assertively, not by hiding. And assertiveness is empowered by knowledge.

The picture so far may seem daunting enough. Only now add a flood of new sensors. We have already seen the swift and inexpensive transformation of mere cellphones into a much more general, portable, electronic tool by adding the capabilities of a digital camera, audio recorder and PDA. But have we fully grasped the implications, when any well-equipped pedestrian might swiftly transform into an ad hoc photojournalist—or peeping Tom—depending on opportunity or inclination?

On the near horizon are wearable multimedia devices, with displays that blend into your sunglasses, along with computational, data-storage and communications capabilities woven into the very clothes you wear. The term "augmented reality" will apply when these tools overlay your subjective view of the world with digitally supplied facts, directions or commentary. You will expect—and rely on—rapid answers to queries about any person or object in sight. In essence, this will be no different than querying your neuron-based memories about people in the village where you grew up. Only we had a million years to get used to tracking reputations that way. The new prosthetics that expand memory will prove awkward at first.

Today we worry about drivers who use cellphones at the wheel. Tomorrow will it be distracted pedestrians, muttering to no one as they walk? Will we grunt and babble while strolling along, like village idiots of yore?

Maybe not. Having detected nerve signals near the larynx that are preparatory to forming words, scientists at NASA Ames Research Center lately proposed *subvocal speech systems*—like those forecast in my 1989 novel "Earth"—that will accept commands without audible sounds. They would be potentially useful in spacesuits, noisy environments and to reduce the inevitable babble when we are all linked by wireless all the time.

Taking this trend in more general terms, *volition sensing* may pick up an even wider variety of cues, empowering you to converse, give commands, or participate in faraway events without speaking aloud or showing superficial signs.

Is this the pre-dawn of tech-mediated telepathy? It may be closer than you think. Advertising agencies are already funding research groups that use PET scans and fMRI to study the immediate reactions of test subjects to marketing techniques and images. "We are crossing the chasm" said Adam Koval, chief operating officer of Thought Sciences, a division of Bright House, an Atlanta advertising and consulting firm whose clients include Home Depot, Delta Airlines and Coca-Cola, "and bringing a new paradigm in analytic rigor to the world of marketing and advertising." Those who decry such studies face a tough burden, since all of the test subjects are paid volunteers. But how about when these methods leave the laboratory and hit the street? It is eerie to imagine a future when sensitive devices might scan your very thoughts when you pass by. Clearly there must be limits, only how? Will you be better able to protect yourself if these technologies are banned (and thus driven underground) or *regulated,* with a free market that might offer us all pocket detectors, to catch scanners in the act?

Microsoft recently unveiled Sensecam, a camera disguisable as jewelry that automatically records scores of images per hour from the wearer's point of view, digitally documenting an ongoing daily photodiary. Such "Boswell machinery" may go far beyond egomania. For example, what good will your wallet do to a mugger when images of the crime are automatically broadcast across the Web? Soon, cyber-witnessing of public events, business deals, crimes and accidents will be routine. In movie parlance, you will have to assume that everybody you meet is carrying a "wire."

Meanwhile, you can be sure that military technologies will continue spinning off civilian versions, as happened with infrared night vision. Take "sniffers" designed to warn of environmental or chemical dangers on the battlefield. Soon, cheap and plentiful sensors will find their way into neighborhood storm drains, onto lampposts, or even your home faucet, giving rapid warnings of local pollution. Neighborhood or activist groups that create detector networks will have autonomous access to data rivaling that of local governments. Of course, a better-informed citizenry is sure to be more effective . . .

. . . and far more noisy.

The same spinoff effect has emerged from military development of inexpensive UAV battlefield reconnaissance drones. Some of the "toys" offered by Draganfly Innovations can cruise independently for more than an hour along a GPS-guided path, transmit 2.4 GHz digital video, then return automatically to the hobbyist owner. In other companies and laboratories, the aim is toward miniaturization, developing micro-flyers that can assist an infantry squad in an urban skirmish or carry eavesdropping equipment into the lair of a suspected terrorist. Again, civilian models are already starting to emerge. There may already be some in your neighborhood.

Cheap, innumerable eyes in the sky. One might envision dozens of potentially harmful uses . . . hundreds of beneficial ones . . . and millions of others in between ranging from irksome to innocuous . . . all leading toward a fundamental change in the way each of us relates to the horizon that so cruelly constrained the imagination of our ancestors. Just as baby boomers grew accustomed to viewing faraway places through the magical—though professionally mediated—channel of network television, so the next generation will simply assume that there is always another independent way to glimpse real-time events, either far away or just above the streets where they live.

Should we push for yet another unenforceable law to guard our backyards against peeping Toms and their drone planes? Or perhaps we'd be better off simply insisting that the companies that make the little robot spies give us the means to trace them back to their nosy pilots. In other words, looking back may be a more effective way to protect privacy.

One might aim for reciprocal transparency using new technology. For example, Swiss researcher Marc Langheinrich's personal digital assistant application detects nearby sensors and then lists what kind of information they're collecting. At a more radical and polemical level, there is the *sousveillance* movement, led by University of Toronto professor Steve Mann. Playing off "surveillance" (overlooking from above), Mann's coined term suggests that we should all get in the habit of looking from below, proving that we are sovereign and alert citizens down here, not helpless sheep. Mann contends that private individuals will be empowered to do this by new senses, dramatically augmented by wearable electronic devices.

We have skimmed over a wide range of new technologies, from RFID chips and stick-on penny cameras to new Internet address protocols and numerous means of biometric identification. From database mining and aggregation to sensors that detect chemical pollution or the volition to speak or act before your muscles get a chance to move. From omni-surveillance to universal localization. From eyes in the sky to those that may invade your personal space.

Note a common theme. Every device or function that's been described here serves to enhance some human sensory capability, from sight and hearing to memory. And while some may fret and fume, there is no historical precedent for a civilization refusing such prosthetics when they become available.

Such trends cannot be boiled down to a simple matter of good news or bad. While technologies of distributed vision may soon empower common folk in dramatic ways, giving a boost to participatory democracy by highly informed citizens, you will not hear that side of the message from most pundits, who habitually portray the very same technologies in a darker light, predicting that machines are about to destroy privacy, undermine values and ultimately enslave us.

In fact, the next century will be much too demanding for fixed perspectives. (Or rigid us-vs.-them ideologies.) Agility will be far more useful, plus a little healthy contrariness. When in the company of reflexive pessimists—or knee-jerk optimists—the wise among us will be those saying . . . "Yes, but . . ."

Which way will the pendulum of good and bad news finally swing?

We are frequently told that there is a fundamental choice to be made in a tragic trade-off between safety and freedom. While agents of the state, like Attorney General John Ashcroft, demand new powers of surveillance—purportedly the better to protect us—champions of civil liberties such as the ACLU warn against surrendering traditional constraints upon what the government is allowed to see. For example, they decry provisions of the PATRIOT Act that open broader channels of inspection, detection, search and data collection, predicting that such steps take us on the road toward Big Brother.

While they are right to fear such an outcome, they could not be more wrong about the specifics. As I discuss in greater detail elsewhere, the very idea of a *trade-off* between security and freedom is one of the most insidious and dismal notions I have ever heard—a perfect example of a devil's dichotomy. We modern citizens are living proof that people can and should have both. Freedom and safety, in fact, work together, not in opposition. Furthermore, I refuse to let anybody tell me that I must choose between liberty for my children and their safety! I refuse, and so should you.

As we've seen throughout this article, and a myriad other possible examples, there is no way that we will ever succeed in limiting the power of the elites to see and know. If our freedom depends on blinding the mighty, then we haven't a prayer.

Fortunately, that isn't what really matters after all. . . . By far the most worrisome and dangerous parts of the PATRIOT Act are those that remove the tools of supervision, allowing agents of the state to act secretly, without checks or accountability. (Ironically, these are the very portions that the ACLU and other groups have most neglected.) In comparison, a few controversial alterations of procedure for search warrants are pretty minor. After all, appropriate levels of surveillance may shift as society and technology experience changes in a new century. (The Founders never heard of a wiretap, for example.)

But our need to watch the watchers will only grow.

It is a monopoly of vision that we need to fear above all else. So long as most of the eyes are owned by the citizens themselves, there will remain a chance for us to keep arguing knowledgeably among ourselves, debating and bickering, as sovereign, educated citizens should.

It will not be a convenient or anonymous world. Privacy may have to be redefined much closer to home. There will be a lot of noise.

But we will not drown under a rising tide of overwhelming technology. Keeping our heads, we will remain free to guide our ships across these rising waters—to choose a destiny of our own.

QUESTIONS

1. According to Brin, why is it impossible to stop the "rising tide of technology" that leads to losses in traditional privacy? What possibilities of counter-attack and security does the new technology bring to the public, in contrast to the passive world of the citizens depicted in Orwell's *1984*? Are the examples Brin presents convincing?
2. Why is it useless, in Brin's opinion, to ban certain kinds of identification techniques that seem to infringe too much on our privacy? Do you agree with Brin's view of the inevitable failure of laws such as those proposed by the ACLU designed to protect against electronic snooping?
3. Brin ends his article by assuring us that we have little to fear from the Patriot Act except for government agent secrecy, as opposed to the common argument that the Act is overly intrusive into the privacy of individual citizens and their associations. Do you agree with his argument here and the evidence he provides to support it? Why or why not?

BRUCE SCHNEIER

"The Myth of the 'Transparent Society'"

Bruce Schneier (b. 1963) received an M.S. in computer science from American University and a B.S. in physics from the University of Rochester. He is an author and security technologist and the founder and head of Counterpane Internet Security, which provides security services for organizations around the world. Schneier served on the board of directors of the International Association for Cryptologic Research and is an advisory board member for the Electronic Privacy Information Center. His books include Applied Cryptography *(1996),* Secrets & Lies: Digital Security in a Networked World *(2000), and* Beyond Fear: Thinking Sensibly about Security in an Uncertain World *(2003). Schneier presents papers at international conferences and publishes in many periodicals on computer security and privacy issues. The short essay that follows on the power imbalance between citizen computer users and governmental agencies in terms of privacy concerns is a*

When I write and speak about privacy, I am regularly confronted with the mutual disclosure argument. Explained in books like David Brin's *The Transparent Society*, the argument goes something like this: In a world of ubiquitous surveillance, you'll know all about me, but I will also know all about you. The government will be watching us, but we'll also be watching the government. This is different than before, but it's not automatically worse. And because I know your secrets, you can't use my secrets as a weapon against me.

This might not be everybody's idea of utopia—and it certainly doesn't address the inherent value of privacy—but this theory has a glossy appeal, and could easily be mistaken for a way out of the problem of technology's continuing erosion of privacy. Except it doesn't work, because it ignores the crucial dissimilarity of power.

You cannot evaluate the value of privacy and disclosure unless you account for the relative power levels of the discloser and the disclosee.

If I disclose information to you, your power with respect to me increases. One way to address this power imbalance is for you to similarly disclose information to me. We both have less privacy, but the balance of power is maintained. But this mechanism fails utterly if you and I have different power levels to begin with.

An example will make this clearer. You're stopped by a police officer, who demands to see identification. Divulging your identity will give the officer enormous power over you: He or she can search police databases using the information on your ID; he or she can create a police record attached to your name; he or she can put you on this or that secret terrorist watch list. Asking to see the officer's ID in return gives you no comparable power over him or her. The power imbalance is too great, and mutual disclosure does not make it OK.

You can think of your existing power as the exponent in an equation that determines the value, to you, of more information. The more power you have, the more additional power you derive from the new data.

Another example: When your doctor says "take off your clothes," it makes no sense for you to say, "You first, doc." The two of you are not engaging in an interaction of equals.

This is the principle that should guide decision-makers when they consider installing surveillance cameras or launching data-mining programs. It's not enough to open the efforts to public scrutiny. All aspects of government work best when the relative power between the governors and the governed remains as small as possible—when liberty is high and control is low. Forced openness in government reduces the relative power differential between the two, and is generally good. Forced openness in laypeople increases the relative power, and is generally bad.

Seventeen-year-old Erik Crespo was arrested in 2005 in connection with a shooting in a New York City elevator. There's no question that he committed the shooting; it was captured on surveillance-camera videotape. But he claimed that while being interrogated, Detective Christopher Perino tried to talk him out of getting a lawyer, and told him that he had to sign a confession before he could see a judge.

Perino denied, under oath, that he ever questioned Crespo. But Crespo had received an MP3 player as a Christmas gift, and surreptitiously recorded the questioning. The defense brought a transcript and CD into evidence. Shortly thereafter, the prosecution offered Crespo a better deal than originally proffered (seven years rather than 15). Crespo took the deal, and Perino was separately indicted on charges of perjury.

Without that recording, it was the detective's word against Crespo's. And who would believe a murder suspect over a New York City detective? That power imbalance was reduced only because Crespo was smart enough to press the "record" button on his MP3 player. Why aren't all interrogations recorded? Why don't defendants have the right to those recordings, just as they have the right to an attorney? Police routinely record traffic stops from their squad cars for their own protection; that video record shouldn't stop once the suspect is no longer a threat.

Cameras make sense when trained on police, and in offices where lawmakers meet with lobbyists, and wherever government officials wield power over the people. Open-government laws, giving the public access to government records and meetings of governmental bodies, also make sense. These all foster liberty.

Ubiquitous surveillance programs that affect everyone without probable cause or warrant, like the National Security Agency's warrantless eavesdropping programs or various proposals to monitor everything on the internet, foster control. And no one is safer in a political system of control.

QUESTIONS

1. Do you agree with Schneier's refutation of the "mutual disclosure argument" put forth by writers like David Brin, or does he oversimplify Brin's argument as presented in his essay "Three Cheers for the Surveillance Society!"?

2. Schneier makes extensive use of hypothetical examples and the specific case of Erik Crespo, a tech-savy murder suspect who recorded his own police interrogation and got a reduced sentence. Do Schneier's examples really make the case for a power imbalance between "discloser and the disclosee"? What other examples or statistics might he have used?

3. Schneier presents solutions that will "foster liberty" through heightened privacy, contrasting his proposals to those which "foster control." Do you think his ideas are adequate to reduce the power imbalance he describes in his essay? Do you feel that stronger proposals or laws should be put forth? If so, provide examples.

INTERNATIONAL WORKING GROUP ON DATA PROTECTION IN TELECOMMUNICATIONS

"Rome Memorandum: Report and Guidance on Privacy in Social Network Services"

Founded in 1983 as part of the International Conference of Data Protection and Privacy Commissioners at the initiative of the Berlin Commissioner for Data Protection, the International Working Group has adopted many recommendations ("Common Positions" and "Working Papers") aimed at improving personal privacy in telecommunications. Membership of the Group includes representatives from Data Protection Authorities and other bodies of national public administrations and international organizations, as well as scientists from around the world. For the past two decades the Group has focused on issues related to protection of privacy on the Internet. The following "Report and Guidance" (2008), addressed to both users and providers of "social network services" such as Facebook and MySpace, sets forth reasons for, examples of, and ways of avoiding potential dangerous privacy infringements on the sites.

Background

"A social network service focuses on the building and verifying of on-line social networks for communities of people who share interests and activities, or who are interested in exploring the interests and activities of others, and which necessitates the use of software. Most services are primarily web based and provide a collection of various ways for users to interact [. . .]" (Wikipedia). Specifically, many popular sites offer means to interact with other subscribers (based on self-generated personal profiles).

The advent and ever increasing popularity of social network services heralds a sea change in the way personal data of large populations of citizens all over the world become more or less publicly available. These services have become incredibly popular in the past years especially with young people. But increasingly such services are also being offered for professionals and the elderly.

The challenges posed by social network services are on the one hand yet another flavor of the fundamental changes that the introduction of the Internet in the 90s of the past century has brought with it, by—*inter alia*—abolishing time and space in publishing information and real-time communication, and by blurring the line between service providers (authors) on the one hand and users/consumers (readers) on the other.

At the same time, social networking services seem to be pushing at the boundaries of what societies see as a person's individual space: Personal data about individuals become publicly (and globally) available in an unprecedented way and quantity, especially including huge quantities of digital pictures and videos.

With respect to privacy, one of the most fundamental challenges may be seen in the fact that most of the personal information published in social network services is being published at the initiative of the users and based on their consent. While "traditional" privacy regulation is concerned with defining rules to protect citizens against unfair or unproportional processing of personal data by the public administration (including law enforcement and secret services), and businesses, there are only very few rules governing the publication of personal data at the initiative of private individuals, partly because this had not been a major issue in the "offline world", and neither on the Internet before social network services came into being. Furthermore, the processing of personal data from public sources has traditionally been privileged in data protection and privacy legislation.

At the same time, a new generation of users has arrived: The first generation that has been growing up while the Internet already existed. These "digital natives" have developed their own ways of using Internet services, and of what they see to be private and what belongs to the public sphere. Furthermore they—most of them being in their teens—may be more ready to take privacy risks than the older "digital immigrants". In general, it seems that younger people are more comfortable with publishing (sometimes intimate) details of their lives on the Internet.

Legislators, Data Protection Authorities as well as social network service providers are faced with a situation that has no visible example in the past. While social network services offer a new range of opportunities for communication and real-time exchange of any kind of information, the use of such services can also lead to putting the privacy of its users (and of other citizens not even subscribed to a social network service) at risk.

Risks for Privacy and Security

The surge of social network services has only just begun. While it is possible to identify some risks associated to the provision and use of such services already now, it is very likely that we are at present only looking at the tip of the iceberg, and that new uses—and accordingly new risks—will continue to emerge in the future. Specifically, new uses for the personal data contained in user profiles will be invented by public authorities (including law enforcement and secret services) and by the private sector.

The following list of risks can only represent a snapshot which may need to be revised and updated as social network services develop. Risks associated to the use of social network services identified up to now include the following:

1. No oblivion on the Internet: The notion of oblivion does not exist on the Internet. Data, once published, may stay there literally forever—even when the data subject has deleted them from the "original" site, there may be copies with third parties (including archive services and the "cache" function provided by a well-known search engine provider). Additionally, some service providers refuse to speedily comply (or even to comply at all) with user requests to have data, and especially complete profiles, deleted.

2. The misleading notion of "community": Many service providers claim that they are bringing communication structures from the "real" world into cyberspace. A common claim is that it is safe to publish (personal) data on those platforms, as it would just resemble sharing information with friends as it used to be face-to-face. However, a closer look at some features in some services reveals that this parallel has some weaknesses, including that the notion of "friends" in cyberspace may in many cases substantially differ from the more traditional

idea of friendship, and that a community may be very big. If users are not openly informed about how their profile information is shared and what they can do to control how it is shared, they may by the notion of "community" as set out above be lured into thoughtlessly sharing their personal data they would not otherwise. The very name of some of these platforms (e.g. "MySpace") creates the illusion of intimacy on the web.

3. "Free of charge" may in fact not be "for free", when users of many social network services in fact "pay" through secondary use of their personal profile data by the service providers, e.g. for (targeted) marketing.

4. Traffic data collection by social network service providers, who are technically capable of recording every single move a user makes on their site; eventually sharing of personal (traffic) data (including users' IP-addresses which can in some cases also resemble location data) with third parties (e.g. for advertising or even targeted advertising). Note that in many jurisdictions these data will also have to be disclosed to law enforcement and/or (national) secret services upon request, including maybe also foreign entities under existing rules on international cooperation.

5. The growing need to refinance services and to make profits may further spur the collection, processing and use of user data, when they are the only real asset of social network providers. Social network sites are not—while the term "social" may suggest otherwise—public utilities. At the same time, Web 2.0 as a whole is "growing up", and there is a shift from startups sometimes run by groups of students with less financial interests to major international players entering the market. This has partially changed the rules of the game, as many of these companies noted on national stock markets are under extreme pressure from their investors to create and maximize profits. As for many providers of social networks user profile data and the number of unique users (combined with frequency of use) is the only real asset these companies have, this may create additional risks for unproportional collection, processing and use of users' personal data. Note that at present, many providers of social network services follow the concept of externalization of privacy costs to users.

6. Giving away more personal information than you think you do: For example, photos may become universal biometric identifiers within a network and even across networks. Face recognition software has been dramatically improved over the past years, and will continue

to reap even "better" results in the future. Note that once a name can be attached to a picture, this can also endanger the privacy and security of other, possibly pseudonymous or even anonymous user profiles (e.g. dating profiles, which normally have a picture and profile information, but not the real name of the data subject published). Additionally, the European Network and Information Security Agency points to an emerging technology called "content based image retrieval" (CBIR), which creates additional possibilities for locating users by matching identifying features of a location (e.g. a painting in a room, or a building depicted) to location data in a database. Furthermore, "social graph" functionalities popular with many social network services do reveal data about the relationships between different users.

7. Misuse of profile data by third parties: This is probably the most important threat potential for personal data contained in user profiles of social network services. Depending on available privacy (default) settings and whether and how users use them, and as well on the technical security of a social network service, profile information, including pictures (which may depict the data subject, but also other people) are made available to—in the worst case—the entire user community. At the same time, very little protection exists at present against copying any kind of data from profiles, and using them for building personal profiles, and/or re-publishing them outside of the social network service. But even "normal" uses of (user) profile data uses can encroach upon users' informational self-determination and, for example, also severely limit their career prospects: One example that has gained public attention is personnel managers of companies crawling user profiles of job applicants and/or employees, which seems to emerge as a steady feature: According to press reports, already today one third of human resources managers admit to use data from social network services for their work, e.g. to verify and/or complete data of job applicants. Law enforcement agencies and secret services (including from less democratic countries with low privacy standards) are other entities likely to capitalize on these sources. In addition, some social network service providers make available user data to third parties via application programming interfaces, which are then under control of these third parties.

8. The Working Group is especially concerned about further increased risks of identity theft fostered by the wide availability of

personal data in user profiles, and by possible hijacking of profiles by unauthorized third parties.

9. Use of a notoriously insecure infrastructure: Much has been written over the (lack of) security of information systems and networks, including web services. Recent incidents include well-known service providers like Facebook, flickr, MySpace, Orkut and the German provider "StudiVZ". While service providers have taken measures to strengthen the security of their systems, there is still room for improvement. At the same time, it is likely that new security leaks will keep emerging in the future, and is unlikely that 100% security will ever be realized at all given the complexity of software applications at all levels of Internet services.

10. Existing unsolved security problems of Internet services add to risk of using social network services and may also in some cases raise the level of risk, or develop "flavors" specific to social network services. A recent position paper by the European Network and Information Security Agency (ENISA) interalia lists SPAM, cross site scripting, viruses and worms, spear-phishing and social network-specific phishing, infiltration of networks, profile-squatting and reputation slander through ID theft, stalking, bullying, and corporate espionage (i.e. social engineering attacks using social network services). According to ENISA, "social network aggregators" pose an additional security threat.

11. The introduction of interoperability standards and application programming interfaces (API; e.g. "open social" introduced by Google in November 2007) to make different social network services technically interoperable entails additional new risks: They allow for automatic evaluation of all social networks websites implementing this standard. The API delivers literally the entire functionality for automatic evaluation implemented in the web interface. Possible applications with potential repercussions on user privacy (and possibly also on the privacy of non-users whose data are part of a user profile) may include: Global analysis of (professional and private) user relationships, which may well cross "borders" between different networks where user act in different roles (e.g. professionally oriented vs. more leisure-oriented networks). Interoperability may also further foster download and third-party re-use of profile information and photos, and creation of profiles about change histories of user profiles (including making available of information a user has deleted from his profile).

Guidance

Based on the above said, the Working Group makes the following (preliminary) recommendations to regulators, providers and users of social network services:

Regulators

1. Introduce the option of a right to pseudonymous use—i.e. to act in a social network service under a pseudonym—where not already part of the regulatory framework.
2. Ensure that service providers are honest and clear about what information is required for the basic service so that users can make an informed choice whether to take up the service, and that users can refuse any secondary uses (at least through opt-out), specifically for (targeted) marketing. Note that specific problems exist with consent of minors.
3. Introduction of an obligation to data breach notification for social network services. Users will only be able to deal especially with the growing risks of identity theft if they are notified of any data breach. At the same time, such a measure would help to get a better picture of how well companies secure user data, and provide a further incentive to further optimize their security measures.
4. Re-thinking the current regulatory framework with respect to controllership of (specifically third party) personal data published on social networking sites, with a view to possibly attributing more responsibility for personal data content on social networking sites to social network service providers.
5. Improve integration of privacy issues into the educational system. As giving away personal data online becomes part of the daily life especially of young people, privacy and tools for informational self-protection must become part of school curricula.

Providers of social network services

Providers must have a vital self-interest in preserving security and privacy of personal data of their users. A failure to make swift progress in this field may result in loss of user confidence (which is already now considerably shaken by recent security and privacy incidents), and may well result in an economic backlash comparable to the crisis that hit the digital economy in the late 1990s.

1. Transparent and open information of users is one of the most important elements of any fair processing and use of personal information. While the need for such a mechanism is recognized in most national, regional and international regulatory instruments for privacy, the present form in which many service providers inform their users may need to be revisited: At present—and in many cases in line with existing regulatory frameworks—privacy information form a part of sometimes complex and lengthy "terms and conditions" of a service provider. In addition, a privacy policy may be provided. Some service providers suggest that the percentage of users actually downloading this information is very low. Even if this information is displayed on the screen when a user signs up to a service, and can also be accessed later if the user so wishes, the goal to inform users about potential consequences of their actions during the use of a service (e.g. when changing privacy settings for a collection of—say—pictures) may be better served by built-in, context-sensitive features, that would deliver the appropriate information based on user actions. User information should specifically comprise information about the jurisdiction under which the service provider operates, about users' rights (e.g. to access, correction and deletion) with respect to their own personal data, and the business model applied for financing the service. Information must be tailored to the specific needs of the targeted audience (especially for minors) to allow them to make informed decisions.

Information of users should also refer to third party data: Providers of social network services should—on top of informing their users about the way they treat their (the users') personal data, also inform them about the do's and don'ts of how they (the users) may handle third party information contained in their profiles (e.g. when to obtain the data subjects' consent before publication, and about possible consequences of breaking the rules). Especially the huge quantities of photos in user profiles showing other people (in many cases even tagged with name and/or link to the other persons' user profile) are an issue in this context, as current practices are in many cases not in line with existing legal frameworks governing the right to control one's own image.

Candid information should also be given about remaining security risks, and possible consequences of publishing personal data in a profile, as well as about possible legal access by third parties (including also e.g. law enforcement, secret services).

2. Introduce the creation and use of pseudonymous profiles as an option, and encourage its use.

3. Living up to promises made to users: A *conditio sine qua non* for fostering and maintaining user trust is clear and unambiguous information about how their information will be treated by the service provider, specifically when it comes to sharing personal data with third parties. However, with some service providers there are at present ambiguities with respect to those promises. The most prominent example is the popular statement "we will never share your personal information with third parties" in relation to targeted advertising. While this statement may be formally correct in the eyes of the service provider, some providers fail to clearly communicate the fact that for displaying advertisements in the browser window of a user, the IP address of these users may be transmitted to another service provider delivering the content of the advertisement, in some cases based on information processed by the social network service provider from a users' profile. While the profile information itself may indeed not be transmitted to the advertisement provider, the users' IP address will (if the social network provider does not use a proxy mechanism to hide the user IP address from the provider of the advertisement). The problem is that some providers of social network services erroneously assume that IP addresses are not personal data, while in most jurisdictions they in fact often are. Such ambiguities may mislead users and may spur an erosion of trust when users learn about what happens in reality, which is neither in the interest of the users, nor in the interest of the service provider. Similar problems exist regarding the use of cookies.

4. Privacy-friendly default settings play a key role in protecting user privacy: It is known that only a minority of users signing up to a service will make any changes to default settings—including privacy settings. The challenge for service providers here is to choose settings that offer high degree of privacy by default without making the service unusable. At the same time, usability of setting features is key to encourage users to make their own changes. In any case, non-indexibility of profiles by search engines should be a default.

5. Improve user control over use of profile data:

■ Within the community; e.g. allow restriction of visibility of entire profiles, and of data contained in profiles, as well as restriction of visibility in community search functions. Tagging of photos (i.e. the addition of links to an existing user profile or the naming of depicted persons) should be bound to the data subject's prior consent.

- Create means allowing for user control over third party use of profile data—vital to especially address risks of ID theft. However, there are at present only limited means to control nformation once it is published. The experience of the movie and music industries with digital rights management technologies suggests that possibilities may in this respect stay limited. Nevertheless, services providers should strengthen research activities in this domain: Existing and maybe promising approaches include research on the "semantic" or "policy-aware web", encrypting user profiles, decentralize storage of user profiles (e.g. with users themselves), the use of watermarking technologies for photos, the use of graphics instead of text for displaying information, and the introduction of an expiration date to be set by users for their own profile data. Service providers should also strive to discourage secondary use especially of pictures by offering a function allowing users to pseudonymise or even anonymize pictures. They should also take effective measures to prevent spidering, bulk downloads (or bulk harvesting) of profile data. Specifically, user data should only crawled by (external) search engines if a user has given his explicit, prior and informed consent.

- Allow for user control over secondary use of profile and traffic data; e.g. for marketing purposes, as a minimum: opt-out for general profile data, opt-in for sensitive profile data (e.g. political opinion, sexual orientation) and traffic data. Many existing legal frameworks contain binding rules on secondary uses for marketing purposes, which must be observed by providers of social network services. Consider letting users decide for themselves, which of their profile data (if any) they would like to be used for targeted marketing. In addition, the introduction of a fee should be considered as an additional option at the choice of the user for financing the service instead of use of profile data for marketing.

- Comply with user rights recognized in national, regional and international privacy frameworks; including the right of data subjects to have data—which may well be entire profiles—erased in a timely manner.

- Address the issues that may arise in cases of a takeover or merger of a social network service company: Introduce guarantees for users that new owner will maintain present privacy (and security) standard.

6. Appropriate complaint handling mechanisms should be introduced (e.g. to "freeze" contested information, or pictures), where they do not already exist, for users of social networks, but also with respect to third party personal data. Timely response to data subjects is important. Measures may also include a penalty mechanism for abusive behavior with respect to profile data of other users and third party personal data (incl. removing users from site as appropriate).

7. Improve and maintain security of information systems. Use recognized best practices in planning, developing, and running social network service applications, including independent certification.

8. Devise and/or further improve measures against illegal activities, such as spamming, and ID theft.

9. Offer encrypted connections for maintaining user profiles, including secured log-in.

10. Social network providers acting in different countries or even globally should respect the privacy standards of the countries where they operate their services.

Users of social networks

1. Be careful. Think twice before publishing personal data (specifically name, address, or telephone number) in a social network profile. Think also about whether you would like to be confronted with information or pictures in a job application situation. Maintain your profile information. Learn from CEOs of big companies: These people know about the value of their personal information and control it. This is why you will not find a lot of personal information about them on the web.

2. Think twice before using your real name in a profile. Use a pseudonym instead. Note that even then you have only limited control over who can identify you, as third parties may be able to lift a pseudonym, especially based on pictures. Think of using different pseudonyms on different platforms.

3. Respect the privacy of others. Be especially careful with publishing personal information about others (including pictures or even tagged pictures), without that other person's consent. Note that illegal publication especially of pictures is a crime in many jurisdictions.

4. Be informed: Who operates the service? Under which jurisdiction? Is there an adequate regulatory framework for protecting privacy? Is there an independent oversight mechanism (like a Privacy

Commissioner) that you can turn to in case of problems? Which guarantees does the service provider give with respect to handling your personal data? Has the service been certified by independent and trustworthy entities for good quality of privacy, and security? Use the web to educate yourself about other people's experience with the privacy and security practices of a service provider you do not know. Use existing information material from providers of social network services, but also from independent sources like Data Protection Agencies, and security companies.

5. Use privacy friendly settings. Restrict availability of information as much as possible, especially with respect to indexing by search engines.
6. Use different identification data (e.g. login and password) than those you use on other web-sites you visit (e.g. for your e-mail or bank account).
7. Use opportunities to control how a service provider uses your personal (profile and traffic) data. For example, opt out of use for targeted marketing.
8. Pay attention to the activity of your children in the Internet, especially on social network web-sites.

Closing remark

The Working Party calls upon Consumer and Privacy Protection Organizations to take appropriate measures to raise awareness with regulators, service providers, the general public, and notably young people about privacy risks regarding the use of social networks and responsible behavior with respect to one's own personal data, as well as those of others.

The Working Group will closely monitor future developments with respect to the protection of privacy in social network services and revise and update this Guidance as necessary.

QUESTIONS

1. According to the Working Group, what are some of the risks to privacy and security to users of such sites as MySpace and Facebook? Do you consider these risks truly disturbing, as compared to many other sorts of Internet sites, or does the Working Group seem to unfairly target such popular social networking sites?
2. What ideas or solutions does the Working Group provide for potential external regulators? Do you think they provide enough such regulations,

considering the severity of the problem they define, or do they provide too many? What other type of regulations could be offered?

3. Consider the Working Group's suggestions for self-regulation by social networking sites and users. How effective would these ideas be for lowering the risk factors of identity theft, reputation damage, or other interference with the privacy of users? Would many users and sites be willing to follow these suggestions? Why or why not?

DIFFERING PERSPECTIVES: HAS THE PATRIOT ACT MADE US FEEL SAFER AT THE COST OF OUR PRIVACY?

Ramesh Ponnuru

RAMESH PONNURU

"1984 in 2003?: Fears About the Patriot Act Are Misguided"

Ramesh Ponnuru, a senior editor for National Review, *graduated summa cum laude from Princeton with a B.A. in history. He has published in newspapers and journals such as the* New York Times, *the* Washington Post, *the* Wall Street Journal, The New Republic, *and* Reason, *and published the book* The Party of Death: The Democrats, the Media, the Courts, and the Disregard for Human Life *(2006). A fellow at the Institute of Economic Affairs in London and a media fellow at Stanford University's Hoover Institution, Ponnuru has appeared on many television news programs, including Fox News, CNN's Inside Politics, and PBS's The News Hour with Jim Lehrer. In the following article, first published in the* National Review *(2003), Ponnuru attempts to refute some of the criticisms levied by civil libertarians against the Patriot Act, particularly in the area of privacy rights.*

Has the war on terrorism become a war on Americans' civil liberties? A coalition of left- and right-wing groups fears so, and has been working hard to restrain the law-and-order impulses of the Bush administration. It's a coalition that includes the ACLU and the American Conservative Union, Nat Hentoff and William Safire, John Conyers and Dick Armey.

The coalition started to form in 1996, when Congress passed an anti-terrorism bill. But it really took off after September 11. Members of the coalition believe that Washington's legislative response—called, rather ludicrously, the "USA Patriot Act," an acronym for "Uniting and Strengthening America by Providing Appropriate Tools to Intercept and Obstruct Terrorism"—was a too-hastily conceived, excessive reaction to the atrocities.

Since then, the coalition has regularly found new cause for alarm. It has protested the administration's plans for military tribunals, the president's designation of "enemy combatants," and the Pentagon's attempts to consolidate data under a program called "Total Information Awareness." This spring, the civil libertarians of left and right worked together again to block

Sen. Orrin Hatch's attempt to make permanent those provisions of the Patriot Act which are set to expire next year. They have organized, as well, against the possibility that the Justice Department will propose another dangerous anti-terror bill ("Patriot II").

The civil libertarians have had some success. They forced modifications in the Patriot Act before its enactment. They have inspired some cities to pass resolutions banning their employees from cooperating with federal authorities to implement provisions of the act that violate the Constitution. (Officials in other cities are, presumably, free to violate the Constitution at will.) They imposed legislative restrictions on Total Information Awareness. They have inhibited the administration from proposing anti-terror measures that would generate adverse publicity.

They themselves have gotten favorable publicity. It's an irresistible story for the press: the lion and the lamb lying down together. The press has tended to marvel at the mere existence of the coalition. They have not been quick to note that there is a larger bipartisan coalition on the other side, which is why the civil libertarians have been losing most of the battles. The Patriot Act passed 357-66 in the House and 98-1 in the Senate. In early May, the Senate voted 90-4 to approve another anti-terror provision—making it easier to investigate "lone wolf" terrorists with no proven connection to larger organizations—that the civil libertarians oppose.

More important, the press has not adequately scrutinized the civil libertarians' claims. This has kept the debate mired in platitudes about liberty and security. It has also reduced the incentive for the civil libertarians to do their homework, which has in turn made their case both weaker and more hysterical than it might otherwise have been.

Take the attack on TIPS, the Terrorist Information and Prevention System. This abortive plan would have encouraged truckers, deliverymen, and the like to report suspicious behavior they observed in the course of their work. How effective this idea would have been is open to question. Most of the criticism, however, echoed former Republican congressman Bob Barr, who said that TIPS "smacks of the very type of fascist or communist government we fought so hard to eradicate in other countries in decades past."

But of all the measures the administration has adopted, it's the Patriot Act (along with the possible Patriot II) that has inspired the most overheated criticisms. When it was passed, the Electronic Frontier Foundation wrote that "the civil liberties of ordinary Americans have taken a tremendous blow with this law." The ACLU says the law "gives the Executive Branch sweeping new powers that undermine the Bill of Rights." But most of the concerns about Patriot are misguided or based on premises that are just plain wrong.

Roving wiretaps. Thanks to the Patriot Act, terrorism investigations can use roving wiretaps. Instead of having to get new judicial authorization for each phone number tapped, investigators can tap any phone their target uses. This is important when fighting terrorists whose MO includes frequently switching hotel rooms and cell phones. It's a commonsense measure. It's also nothing new: Congress authorized roving wiretaps in ordinary criminal cases back in 1986. It's hard to see Patriot as a blow to civil liberties on this score.

Internet surveillance. Libertarians have been particularly exercised about Patriot's green light for "spying on the Web browsers of people who are not even criminal suspects"—to quote *Reason* editor Nick Gillespie. This is a misunderstanding of Patriot, as George Washington University law professor Orin Kerr has demonstrated in a law-review article. Before Patriot, it wasn't clear that any statute limited the government's, or even a private party's, ability to obtain basic information about electronic communications (e.g., to whom you're sending e-mails). Patriot required a court order to get that information, and made it a federal crime to get it without one.

Kerr believes that the bar for getting a court order should be raised. But he notes that Patriot made the privacy protections for the Internet as strong as those for phone calls and stronger than for mail. Patriot's Internet provisions, he concludes, "updated the surveillance laws without substantially shifting the balance between privacy and security."

James Bovard traffics in another Patriot myth in a recent cover story for *The American Conservative:* that it "empowers federal agents to cannibalize Americans' e-mail with Carnivore wiretaps." Carnivore is an Internet surveillance tool designed by the FBI. Don't be scared by the name. The FBI's previous tool was dubbed "Omnivore," and this new one was so named because it would be more selective in acquiring information, getting only what was covered by a court order and leaving other information private. But even if Carnivore is a menace, it's not the fault of Patriot. As Kerr points out, "The only provisions of the Patriot Act that directly address Carnivore are pro-privacy provisions that actually restrict the use of Carnivore."

Hacking. Also in *Reason*, Jesse Walker writes that Patriot "expands the definition of terrorist to include such non-lethal acts as computer hacking." That's misleading. Pre-Patriot, an al-Qaeda member who hacked the electric company's computers to take out the grid could not be judged guilty of terrorism, even if he would be so judged if he accomplished the same result with a bomb. Hacking per se isn't terrorism, and Patriot doesn't treat it as such.

Sneak and peek. The ACLU is running ads that say that Patriot lets the government "secretly enter your home while you're away . . . rifle through your personal belongings . . . download your computer files . . . and seize any items at will." Worst of all, "you may never know what the government has done." Reality check: You will be notified if a sneak-and-peek search has been done, just after the fact—usually within a few days. The feds had the authority to conduct these searches before Patriot. A federal judge has to authorize such a search warrant, and the warrant has to specify what's to be seized.

Library records. Bovard is appalled that Patriot allows "federal agents to commandeer library records," and the American Library Association shares his sentiment. Patriot doesn't mention libraries specifically, but does authorize terrorism investigators to collect tangible records generally. Law enforcement has, however, traditionally been able to obtain library records with a subpoena. Prof. Kerr suggests that because of Patriot, the privacy of library records may be better protected in terrorism investigations than it is in ordinary criminal ones.

The civil libertarians deserve some credit. Their objections helped to rid Patriot of some provisions—such as a crackdown on Internet gambling—that didn't belong in an anti-terrorism bill. Armey added the Carnivore protections to the bill. The law, as finally enacted, places limits on how much officials may disclose of the information they gain from Internet and phone surveillance. Moreover, the civil libertarians make a reasonable demand when they ask that Patriot be subject to periodic re-authorizations, so that Congress can regularly consider making modifications.

The civil libertarians rarely acknowledge the costs of legal laxity: Restrictions on intelligence gathering may well have impeded the investigation of Zacarias Moussaoui, the "twentieth hijacker," before 9/11. David Cole, one of the movement's favorite law professors, goes so far as to lament that U.S. law makes "mere membership in a terrorist group grounds for exclusion and deportation."

And while civil libertarians may scant the value of Patriot, terrorists do not. Jeffrey Battle, an accused member of a terrorist cell in Portland, complained about Patriot in a recorded phone call that was recently released in court. People were less willing to provide financial support, he said, now that they were more likely to be punished for it.

Speaking of the administration's civil-liberties record, Al Gore said last year that President Bush has "taken the most fateful step in the direction of [a] Big Brother nightmare that any president has ever allowed to occur." Dick Armey worries about "the lust for power that these people in the Department of Justice have." The civil-liberties debate could use a lot less rhetoric of this sort—and a lot more attention to detail.

A calm look at the Patriot Act shows that it's less of a threat to civil liberties than, say, campaign-finance reform. A lot of the controversy is the result of confusion. Opponents of the Patriot Act are fond of complaining that few people have bothered to read it. No kidding.

QUESTIONS

1. In the first paragraphs of his essay, Ponnuru names and describes the coalition of groups opposed to the Patriot Act's provisions relating to privacy. How does he try to discredit these groups in his initial description of their activities and in the language he uses relative to their accomplishments? Is he successful at raising doubts about their motives and understanding of the Act?

2. In the main part of the essay, what five types of activities of the Patriot Act does Ponnuru defend that the civil libertarian groups find objectionable? What kind of evidence does he present to buttress his refutation of their claims? Does he ever actually quote the language of the Act itself? Would this have been helpful? Why or why not?

3. Although Ponnuru does concede that the civil libertarians "deserve some credit," his final paragraphs make some more direct attacks on the wisdom and consequences of their actions, such as the potential for making it harder to catch terrorists. Are these final criticisms justified by the evidence he presents?

James Bovard

"Surveillance State"

James Bovard is a libertarian writer and policy advisor. He has received the Thomas Szasz Award for Civil Liberties, the Mencken Award, and similar recognition for his writings in the area of government power and intrusion into the privacy and freedoms of citizens. His articles have appeared in American Spectator, *the* Wall Street Journal, *the* New York Times, The New Republic, *the* Washington Post, *and* Newsweek. *He has written nine books, including* Freedom in Chains: The Rise of the State and The Demise of the Citizen *(1999),* Terrorism and Tyranny *(2003), and* The Bush Betrayal *(2004). His writings have denounced both democratic and republican regimes; the* Wall Street Journal *has termed him "the roving inspector general of the modern state." The following article, which first appeared in* The American Conservative *in 2003, presents Bovard's critique of the Patriot Acts (both I and II) as infringements on civil liberties.*

Perhaps you've visited your local library to keep speed with the War on Terror: borrowed a few books on Islamic fundamentalism or did web research on biochemical weapons. Beware.

Last January, an FBI agent entered a branch of the St. Louis Public Library and requested a list of all the sign-up sheets showing names of people who used library computers on Dec. 28, 2002. Even though the FBI agent did not have a warrant or subpoena, the library quickly surrendered the list of all users. The FBI acted because someone phoned in a tip that they "smelled something strange" about a library patron of Middle Eastern descent.

Welcome to America under the Patriot Act. One person claims to "smell something," and the feds can round up everyone's records. From books you check out to credit card purchases, money transfers to medications, your activities are now subject to federal surveillance. Uncle Sam now has a blank check to search and pry—all in the name of security.

Last October, then House Majority Leader Dick Armey branded our own Justice Department "the biggest threat to personal liberty in the country." And while that characterization of a Republican Justice Department makes many conservatives cringe, the DOJ has been working overtime to expand its power—and the biggest danger may be yet to come.

When John Ashcroft was in the U.S. Senate, he was a leader in the fight to protect Americans' privacy. In an August 1997 op-ed, Ashcroft declared, "This is no reason to hand Big Brother the keys to unlock our e-mail diaries, open our ATM records, read our medical records, or translate our international communications." His early days as attorney general showed a keen appreciation for the Bill of Rights' constraints. That changed on 9/11.

Within days of the Twin Towers' collapse, Ashcroft began strong-arming Congress to enact sweeping anti-terrorism legislation—and Americans seemed ready to trade a measure of liberty to restore their shaken security. The month of the attacks, an NBC/Wall Street Journal poll found 78 percent willing to have Internet activity monitored. The administration took this as free rein, moving swiftly to enact the Patriot (Provide Appropriate Tools Required to Intercept and Obstruct Terrorism) Act. Some of its provisions were simply updates to existing law. As. Sen. Russell Feingold (D-Wis.), the only senator to vote against the act observed, "It made sense to stiffen penalties and lengthen or eliminate statutes of limitation for certain terrorist crimes." But the Patriot Act goes far beyond "good government" amendments.

It empowers federal agents to cannibalize Americans' e-mail with Carnivore wiretaps, allows federal agents to commandeer library records, and requires banks to surrender personal account information. It also authorizes federal agents to confiscate bulk cash from travelers who fail to fill out Customs Service forms disclosing how much money they are taking out of or into the U.S. and allows the attorney general to order long-term detentions if he has "reasonable grounds to believe that the alien is engaged in any activity that endangers the national security of the United States." Last year alone, Ashcroft personally issued 170 emergency domestic spying warrants, permitting agents to carry out wiretaps and search homes and offices for up to 72 hours before requesting a search warrant from the Foreign Intelligence Surveillance Court.

When privacy-minded legislators question these new powers, the Justice Department stonewalls. House Judiciary Chairman James Sensenbrenner (R-Wis.) threatened to subpoena the DOJ last summer to get information to which his committee is specifically entitled. Justice eventually divulged a few fragments of information but has refused to reveal the number of secret searches, the number of libraries whose records have been seized, and how often Carnivore e-mail wiretaps have been used. Freedom has apparently become so fragile that citizens can no longer be permitted to know how often their government invades their privacy.

Some intrusive provisions of the Patriot Act were temporary—set to expire in 2005 absent Congressional reauthorization. But Sen. Orrin Hatch (R-Utah), chairman of the Senate Judiciary Committee, recently proposed making the federal prying powers permanent.

The Wrong Response

The Patriot Act was rushed into law before any effort was made to understand why the feds failed to stop the 9/11 attacks. The government could have done a better job of tracking the terrorist suspects, but the feds had all the relevant information to detect and block the conspiracy to hijack four airplanes. The Joint House-Senate Intelligence Committee observed that the FBI's negligence "contributed to the United States becoming, in effect, a sanctuary for radical terrorists." Its investigation concluded, "It is at least a possibility that increased analysis, sharing and focus would have drawn greater attention to the growing potential for a major terrorist attack in the United States involving the aviation industry."

But the administration rewarded failure by the FBI and intelligence agencies with bigger budgets, more power, and presidential commendations. There is nothing in the Patriot Act that can solve the problem of FBI agents who do not understand the Foreign Intelligence Surveillance Act or solve the shortage of CIA and National Security Agency employees who can read intercepted messages in the languages of prime terrorist threats. Neither does the legislation compensate for lackadaisical federal agents who failed to add promptly the names of al-Qaeda members to terrorism watch-lists or of analysts who ignored the cascading warnings of terrorists using stolen airplanes as flying bombs. The success of the 9/11 hijackers was due far more to a lack of government competence than to a shortfall in government power. Yet the Bush administration has successfully suppressed investigations and revelations of federal failures, thereby permitting Ashcroft and others to portray new government powers as the key to national safety.

The Justice Department isn't the only agency taking aim at American liberties. The Department of Transportation has compiled secret "no fly" lists of passengers suspected of terrorist ties—or at least those critical of the administration. In one instance, two dozen members of a peace group, students chaperoned by a priest and nun, were detained en route to a teach-in thus missing their flight.

The Department of Defense is piling on with its Total Information Awareness program. TIA's goal is to stockpile as much information as possible about everyone on Earth—thereby allowing government to protect everyone from everything. New York Times columnist William Safire warned, "Every purchase you make with a credit card, every magazine subscription you buy and medical prescription you fill, every Web site you visit and e-mail you send or receive, every academic grade you receive, every bank deposit you make, every trip you book and every event you attend—all these transactions and communications will go into what the Defense Department describes as 'a virtual, centralized grand database.'" Columnist Ted Rall noted that the feds will even scan "veterinary records. The TIA believes that knowing if and when Fluffy got spayed—and whether your son stopped torturing Fluffy after you put him on Ritalin—will help the military stop terrorists before they strike."

Congress passed a law seeking to rein in TIA. The Pentagon, however, is barging forward, and the congressional provision specifies that if Bush formally certifies that TIA is necessary for national security, the law is null and void.

Coming Soon: Patriot II

In February, the Center for Public Integrity obtained and released an 86-page draft version of the Domestic Security Enhancement Act—quickly dubbed Patriot II. Notations on the Justice Department document—stamped "Confidential—Not for Distribution" on every page—showed that it had already been sent to Vice President Cheney and House Speaker Dennis Hastert (R-Ill.). Justice Department spokesman Mark Corallo dismisses DSEA as a benign sequel, "filling in the holes" in the Patriot Act.

Section 101 of the proposed bill, titled "Individual Terrorists as Foreign Powers," would revise the Foreign Intelligence Surveillance Act (FISA) to permit the U.S. government to label individuals who are suspected terrorists—including American citizens—as "foreign powers" for the purpose of conducting total surveillance of their activities. This alteration nullifies all Fourth Amendment rights of the target, allowing the government to tap phones, search computers, and read e-mail—even when there is no evidence that a citizen is violating any statute. If Section 101 becomes law, the more people the feds wrongfully accuse of being terrorists, the more power federal agents will receive.

Americans suspected of gathering information for a foreign power could be subject to FISA surveillance even though they were violating no law and the information gathered did not pertain to national security. The administration's confidential explanation of proposed Section 102 notes, "Requiring the additional showing that the intelligence gathering violates the laws of the United States is both unnecessary and counterproductive, as such activities threaten the national security regardless of whether they are illegal." But, as the ACLU noted, "This amendment would permit electronic surveillance of a local activist who was preparing a report on human rights for London-based Amnesty International, a 'foreign political organization,' even if the activist was not engaged in any violation of law."

While some parts of the new bill would overturn federal court decisions, Section 106 is more visionary, seeking to negate principles established in the Nuremberg trials: that following orders is no excuse for violating the law. As proposed, it would permit federal agents illegally to wiretap and surveil and leak damaging personal information on Americans—as long as they are following orders from the president or the attorney general. The Senate COINTELPRO investigation revealed how President Johnson and top Nixon aides personally ordered federal agents to conduct illegal surveillance of political opponents and others, though neither the FBI nor LBJ was ever held accountable. This proposal is a further attempt to make federal agents legally untouchable and could encourage law-breaking at every level of the federal government.

Section 129, entitled "Strengthening Access to and Use of Information in National Security Investigations," would empower federal agents to issue "national security letters" that compel businesses and other institutions to surrender confidential or proprietary information without a court order. Anyone hit with such a letter will be obliged to remain forever silent on the demand with disclosure punishable by up to five years in prison. The ACLU noted that this provision would "reduce judicial oversight of terrorism investigations by relegating the role of the judge to considering challenges to orders already issued, rather than ensuring such orders are drawn with due regard for the privacy and other interests of the target." This turns the Fourth Amendment on its head by creating a presumption that the government is entitled to personal or confidential information unless the citizen or business can prove to a federal judge that the "national security letter" should not be enforced against them. But few Americans can afford the cost of litigating against the world's largest law firm—the U.S. Justice Department—to preserve their privacy.

Secret mass arrests could be the result of Section 201. The provision notes, "Although existing Freedom of Information Act (FOIA) exemptions . . . permit the government to protect information relating to detainees, defending this interpretation through litigation requires extensive Department of Justice resources, which would be better spent detecting and incapacitate [sic] terrorists." In the wake of 9/11, the feds locked up over 1,200 "special interest" detainees and continually insisted that none of their names or details of their cases could be disclosed without endangering national survival, though federal courts denounced the secret arrests as "odious to democracy" or "profoundly undemocratic." To save the Justice Department the bother of having to defend secret round-ups, the Bush administration now seeks to amend the federal statute book to imitate repressive dictatorships around the globe.

Section 312, "Appropriate Remedies with Respect to Law Enforcement Surveillance Activities," would unleash local law enforcement to spy on Americans, nullifying almost all federal, state, and local court "consent decrees" that restrict the power of local and state police. The administration complains that such decrees result in police lacking "the ability to use the full range of investigative techniques that are lawful under the Constitution, and that are available to the FBI." But, in every case, consent decrees were imposed after gross abuses of citizens' rights by the police. The administration draft bill explanation declares, "All surviving decrees would have to be necessary to correct a current and ongoing violation of a Federal right, extend no further than necessary to correct the violation of the Federal right, and be narrowly drawn and the least intrusive means to correct the violation." Historically, the Supreme Court has required the federal government to use the "least intrusive means" to achieve some policy in cases involving the First Amendment, in order to prevent any unnecessary restriction of freedom of speech. The administration now demands the "least intrusive" restrictions on government intrusions.

Section 402 would permit U.S. attorneys to prosecute Americans for aiding terrorist organizations even if they made donations to organizations that the U.S. government did not publicly label as terrorist groups. Yale Law School professor Jack Balkin said, "Give a few dollars to a Muslim charity Ashcroft thinks is a terrorist organization and you could be on the next plane out of this country." Robert Higgs of the Independent Institution warns that the feds "can categorize the most innocent action"—such as "signing a petition"—as an act of terrorism.

Users of Pretty Good Privacy and other common encryption software could face greater perils from Section 404, which creates "a new, separate crime of using encryption technology that could add five years or more to any sentence for crimes committed with a computer," the ACLU notes. Encryption software is routinely included on new computers and is commonly used for business transactions. The Justice Department thus seeks to treat use of encryption software the same way that the federal government treats gun possession—something sinister enough to justify routinely doubling or tripling prison sentences for people who violate other federal statutes, regardless of whether the gun was actually used.

Critics label Section 501 of the bill the "citizenship death penalty." Under existing law, an American must state his intent to relinquish his citizenship in order to lose it. Under this provision, intent "need not be manifested in words but can be inferred from conduct," thus empowering the Justice Department to strip Americans of their citizenship if the feds accuse them of supporting terrorism—either domestic or international. The American Immigration Lawyers Association cautions that, under this provision, "targeted [U.S. citizens] potentially could find themselves consigned to indefinite detention as undocumented immigrants in their own country."

Shortly after the text of Patriot II surfaced, the attorney general was asked at a press conference about this expansion of federal power. He refused to confirm plans formally to propose Patriot II but did declare, "Every day we are asking each other, what can we do to be more successful in securing the freedoms of America and sustaining the liberty, the tolerance, the human dignity that America represents, and how can we do a better job in defeating the threat of terrorism."

Despite Ashcroft's reassurances, resistance is building. Eighty-nine cities have passed resolutions condemning the Patriot Act, and a coalition is stretching across ideological lines to oppose it. Recently the ACLU drafted a letter to Congress and found 67 organizations from the conservative Gun Owners of America to the liberal La Raza eager to sign on. They accuse Patriot II of "new and sweeping law enforcement and intelligence gathering powers, many of which are not related to terrorism, that would severely dilute, if not undermine, basic constitutional rights."

Three months after 9/11, Ashcroft announced, "To those who scare peace-loving people with phantoms of lost liberty, my message is this, your tactics only aid terrorists for they erode our national unity and . . . give ammunition to American's enemies." Ashcroft is wrong to portray any criticism of Bush administration civil liberties policies as aiding and abetting terrorism. America is overdue for a searching examination of the powers the Bush administration has seized and the powers it is seeking.

QUESTIONS

1. Bovard devotes considerable space in his article to attacking former Attorney General John Ashcroft and the Justice Department for its aggressive implementation of the Patriot Act, accusing Ashcroft of flip-flopping from his earlier position on civil liberties while a U.S. Senator. Does this seem like a fair criticism of Ashcroft's tenure? Do some research into Ashcroft's record on civil liberties and that of his successor, Alberto Gonzales.

2. In the "Wrong Response" section of his essay and elsewhere, Bovard details some of the extreme potential violations of privacy and other freedoms under the Patriot Act. How common have such violations actually been in the years since the passage of the bill, and how many have been either speculative on the part of Bovard's sources or relatively atypical?

3. Compare Bovard's approach and arguments on the Patriot Act with those of the previous essay by Ponnuru. Which writer uses a more fact-based approach to the subject, and which relies more on arguing from general principles? Which author is more effective, and why?

Changing Nature

Introduction

Our final chapter concerns issues relating to the environment. It is difficult to argue for environmental rights and protections from a Constitutional perspective, since no bill of rights has been written for plants, animals, or the earth itself, all of which have commonly been viewed as commodities designed for human use. However, the environmental movement recently has shifted its attention to the phenomenon of global warming, which is the focus of most of the essays in this chapter. Travel writer Daniel Glick and MIT professor Richard S. Lindzen take different positions on the issue, with Glick presenting evidence and interviews related to climate change and Lindzen maintaining that the evidence for long-term trends in global warming is essentially unfounded, a matter of hype and panic rather than established scientific fact.

Despite the voices of doubters like Lindzen, the movement to reverse the effects of global warming or at least to slow down the process continues to gather strength. In his speech, "Policy Address on Global Warming," Al Gore shares some possible solutions for global warming, using a number of ideas rather than a single "silver bullet" approach. Gore's speech is followed by an essay from Good Jobs First researcher Phil Mattera, who presents a definition argument on the topic of "greenwashing." He discusses the origins of the term as a way of critiquing corporate efforts to give the impression through advertising language and images that a business is doing a great deal to alleviate ecological concerns such as global warming when in fact it is doing little or nothing—or trying to cover up its own egregious polluting.

Carbon offsets, one of Gore's suggested strategies to combat global warming, is debated in an essay by Dara Colwell. Colwell takes the position of the European "Carbon Watch" group, which criticizes carbon offsets for being more a matter of distraction and celebrity/corporate public relations than genuine environmental concern and conscience.

The "Differing Perspectives" debate in this chapter focuses on environmental issues that involve changing nature in a significant way through genetically engineered seeds and crops. The emotional side of the argument can be seen in the language describing these now products as "frankenfoods"; however, authors Jeremy Rifkin and Jonathan Rauch also provide strong causal reasoning to demonstrate the environmental advantages and disadvantages of creating new plant species in the laboratory.

DANIEL GLICK

"GeoSigns: The Big Thaw"

Daniel Glick traveled and taught English in Japan and Tibet for several years before receiving a master's in journalism from the University of California at Berkeley. Glick was awarded a prestigious Knight Fellowship in journalism in 2006 and a Ted Scripps Fellowship at the University of Colorado for his journalism, which currently focuses on travel and nature. Glick's stories have appeared in many national magazines, including National Geographic, Smithsonian, *the* New York Times Magazine, *and* Wilderness. *His books include* Powder Burn *(2001) and* Monkey Dancing *(2003). In his article "The Big Thaw" (National Geographic 2004), Glick creates a factual, descriptive narrative argument that illustrates the effects global warming has had in melting glaciers and transforming natural habitats and landscapes around the planet.*

"If we don't have it, we don't need it," pronounces Daniel Fagre as we throw on our backpacks. We're armed with crampons, ice axes, rope, GPS receivers, and bear spray to ward off grizzlies, and we're trudging toward Sperry Glacier in Glacier National Park, Montana. I fall in step with Fagre and two other research scientists from the U.S. Geological Survey Global Change Research Program. They're doing what they've been doing for more than a decade: measuring how the park's storied glaciers are melting.

So far, the results have been positively chilling. When President Taft created Glacier National Park in 1910, it was home to an estimated 150 glaciers. Since then the number has decreased to fewer than 30, and most of those remaining have shrunk in area by two-thirds. Fagre predicts that within 30 years most if not all of the park's namesake glaciers will disappear.

"Things that normally happen in geologic time are happening during the span of a human lifetime," says Fagre. "It's like watching the Statue of Liberty melt."

Scientists who assess the planet's health see indisputable evidence that Earth has been getting warmer, in some cases rapidly. Most believe that human activity, in particular the burning of fossil fuels and the resulting buildup of greenhouse gases in the atmosphere, have influenced this warming trend. In the past decade scientists have documented record-high average annual surface temperatures and have been observing other signs of change all over the planet: in the distribution of ice, and in the salinity, levels, and temperatures of the oceans.

"This glacier used to be closer," Fagre declares as we crest a steep section, his glasses fogged from exertion. He's only half joking. A trailside sign notes that since 1901, Sperry Glacier has shrunk from more than 800 acres to 300 acres (324 hectares to 121 hectares). "That's out of date," Fagre says, stopping to catch his breath. "It's now less than 250 acres."

Everywhere on Earth ice is changing. The famed snows of Kilimanjaro have melted more than 80 percent since 1912. Glaciers in the Garhwal Himalaya in India are retreating so fast that researchers believe that most central and eastern Himalayan glaciers could virtually disappear by 2035. Arctic sea ice has thinned significantly over the past half century, and its extent has declined by about 10 percent in the past 30 years. NASA's repeated laser altimeter readings show the edges of Greenland's ice sheet shrinking. Spring freshwater ice breakup in the Northern Hemisphere now occurs nine days earlier than it did 150 years ago, and autumn freeze-up ten days later. Thawing permafrost has caused the ground to subside more than 15 feet (4.6 meters) in parts of Alaska. From the Arctic to Peru, from Switzerland to the equatorial glaciers of Irian Jaya in Indonesia, massive ice fields, monstrous glaciers, and sea ice are disappearing, fast.

When temperatures rise and ice melts, more water flows to the seas from glaciers and ice caps, and ocean water warms and expands in volume. This combination of effects has played the major role in raising average global sea level between four and eight inches (10 and 20 centimeters) in the past hundred years, according to the Intergovernmental Panel on Climate Change (IPCC).

Scientists point out that sea levels have risen and fallen substantially over Earth's 4.6-billion-year history. But the recent rate of global sea level rise has departed from the average rate of the past two to three thousand years and is rising more rapidly—about one-tenth of an inch (about one-fourth of a centimeter) a year. A continuation or acceleration of that trend has the potential to cause striking changes in the world's coastlines.

Driving around Louisiana's Gulf Coast, Windell Curole can see the future, and it looks pretty wet. In southern Louisiana coasts are literally sinking by about three feet (about one meter) a century, a process called subsidence. A sinking coastline and a rising ocean combine to yield powerful effects. It's like taking the global sea-level-rise problem and moving it along at fast-forward.

The seventh-generation Cajun and manager of the South Lafourche Levee District navigates his truck down an unpaved mound of dirt that separates civilization from inundation, dry land from a swampy horizon. With his French-tinged lilt, Curole points to places where these bayous, swamps, and fishing villages portend a warmer world: his high school girlfriend's house partly submerged, a cemetery with water lapping against the white tombs, his grandfather's former hunting camp now afloat in a stand of skeleton oak snags. "We live in a place of almost land, almost water," says the 52-year-old Curole.

Rising sea level, sinking land, eroding coasts, and temperamental storms are a fact of life for Curole. Even relatively small storm surges in the past two decades have overwhelmed the system of dikes, levees, and pump stations that he manages, upgraded in the 1990s to forestall the Gulf of Mexico's relentless creep. "I've probably ordered more evacuations than any other person in the country," Curole says.

The current trend is consequential not only in coastal Louisiana but around the world. Never before have so many humans lived so close to the coasts: More than a hundred million people worldwide live within three feet of mean sea level. Vulnerable to sea-level rise, Tuvalu, a small country in the South Pacific, has already begun formulating evacuation plans. Megacities where human populations have concentrated near coastal plains or river deltas—Shanghai, Bangkok, Jakarta, Tokyo, and New York—are at risk. The projected economic and humanitarian impacts on low-lying, densely populated, and desperately poor countries like Bangladesh are potentially catastrophic. The scenarios are disturbing even in wealthy countries like the Netherlands, with nearly half its landmass already at or below sea level.

Rising sea level produces a cascade of effects. Bruce Douglas, a coastal researcher at Florida International University, calculates that every inch of sea-level rise could result in eight feet of horizontal retreat of sandy beach shorelines due to erosion. Furthermore, when salt water intrudes into freshwater aquifers, it threatens sources of drinking water and makes raising crops problematic. In the Nile Delta, where many of Egypt's crops are cultivated, widespread erosion and saltwater intrusion would be disastrous—since the country contains little other arable land.

In some places marvels of human engineering worsen effects from rising seas in a warming world. The system of channels and levees along the Mississippi effectively stopped the millenniaold natural process of rebuilding the river delta with rich sediment deposits. In the 1930s, oil and gas companies began to dredge shipping and exploratory canals, tearing up the marshland buffers that helped dissipate tidal surges. Energy drilling removed vast quantities of subsurface liquid, which studies suggest increased the rate at which the land is sinking. Now Louisiana is losing approximately 25 square miles (65 square kilometers) of wetlands every year, and the state is lobbying for federal money to help replace the upstream sediments that are the delta's lifeblood.

Local projects like that might not do much good in the very long run, though, depending on the course of change elsewhere on the planet. Part of Antarctica's Larsen Ice Shelf broke apart in early 2002. Although floating ice does not change sea level when it melts (any more than a glass of water will overflow when the ice cubes in it melt), scientists became concerned that the collapse could foreshadow the breakup of other ice shelves in Antarctica and allow increased glacial discharge into the sea from ice sheets on the continent. If the West Antarctic ice sheet were to break up, which scientists consider very unlikely this century, it alone contains enough ice to raise sea level by nearly 20 feet (6 meters).

Even without such a major event, the IPCC projected in its 2001 report that sea level will rise anywhere between 4 and 35 inches (10 and 89 centimeters) by the end of the century. The high end of that projection—nearly three feet (0.9 meters)—would be "an unmitigated disaster," according to Douglas.

Down on the bayou, all of those predictions make Windell Curole shudder. "We're the guinea pigs," he says, surveying his aqueous world from the relatively lofty vantage point of a 12-foot-high (3.7 meter) earthen berm. "I don't think anybody down here looks at the sea-level-rise problem and puts their heads in the sand." That's because soon there may not be much sand left.

Rising sea level is not the only change Earth's oceans are undergoing. The ten-year-long World Ocean Circulation Experiment, launched in 1990, has helped researchers to better understand what is now called the ocean conveyor belt.

Oceans, in effect, mimic some functions of the human circulatory system. Just as arteries carry oxygenated blood from the heart to the extremities, and veins return blood to be replenished with oxygen, oceans provide life-sustaining circulation to the planet. Propelled mainly by prevailing winds and differences in water density, which changes with the temperature and salinity of the seawater, ocean currents are critical in cooling, warming, and watering the planet's terrestrial surfaces—and in transferring heat from the Equator to the Poles.

The engine running the conveyor belt is the density-driven thermohaline circulation ("thermo" for heat and "haline" for salt). Warm, salty water flows from the tropical Atlantic north toward the Pole in surface currents like the Gulf Stream. This saline water loses heat to the air as it is carried to the far reaches of the North Atlantic. The coldness and high salinity together make the water more dense, and it sinks deep into the ocean. Surface water moves in to replace it. The deep, cold water flows into the South Atlantic, Indian, and Pacific Oceans, eventually mixing again with warm water and rising back to the surface.

Changes in water temperature and salinity, depending on how drastic they are, might have considerable effects on the ocean conveyor belt. Ocean temperatures are rising in all ocean basins and at much deeper depths than previously thought, say scientists at the National Oceanic and Atmospheric Administration (NOAA). Arguably, the largest oceanic change ever measured in the era of modern instruments is in the declining salinity of the subpolar seas bordering the North Atlantic.

Robert Gagosian, president and director of the Woods Hole Oceanographic Institution, believes that oceans hold the key to potential dramatic shifts in the Earth's climate. He warns that too much change in ocean temperature and salinity could disrupt the North

Atlantic thermohaline circulation enough to slow down or possibly halt the conveyor belt—causing drastic climate changes in time spans as short as a decade.

The future breakdown of the thermohaline circulation remains a disturbing, if remote, possibility. But the link between changing atmospheric chemistry and the changing oceans is indisputable, says Nicholas Bates, a principal investigator for the Bermuda Atlantic Time-series Study station, which monitors the temperature, chemical composition, and salinity of deep-ocean water in the Sargasso Sea southeast of the Bermuda Triangle.

Oceans are important sinks, or absorption centers, for carbon dioxide, and take up about a third of human-generated CO_2. Data from the Bermuda monitoring programs show that CO_2 levels at the ocean surface are rising at about the same rate as atmospheric CO_2. But it is in the deeper levels where Bates has observed even greater change. In the waters between 250 and 450 meters (820 and 1,476 feet) deep, CO_2 levels are rising at nearly twice the rate as in the surface waters. "It's not a belief system; it's an observable scientific fact," Bates says. "And it shouldn't be doing that unless something fundamental has changed in this part of the ocean."

While scientists like Bates monitor changes in the oceans, others evaluate CO_2 levels in the atmosphere. In Vestmannaeyjar, Iceland, a lighthouse attendant opens a large silver suitcase that looks like something out of a James Bond movie, telescopes out an attached 15-foot (4.6 meter) rod, and flips a switch, activating a computer that controls several motors, valves, and stopcocks. Two two-and-a-half-liter (5.3 pint) flasks in the suitcase fill with ambient air. In North Africa, an Algerian monk at Assekrem does the same. Around the world, collectors like these are monitoring the cocoon of gases that compose our atmosphere and permit life as we know it to persist.

When the weekly collection is done, all the flasks are sent to Boulder, Colorado. There, Pieter Tans, a Dutch-born atmospheric scientist with NOAA's Climate Monitoring and Diagnostics Laboratory, oversees a slew of sensitive instruments that test the air in the flasks for its chemical composition. In this way Tans helps assess the state of the world's atmosphere.

By all accounts it has changed significantly in the past 150 years.

Walking through the various labs filled with cylinders of standardized gas mixtures, absolute manometers, and gas chromatographs, Tans offers up a short history of atmospheric monitoring. In the late 1950s a researcher named Charles Keeling began measuring CO_2 in the atmosphere above Hawaii's 13,679-foot (4,169 meter) Mauna Loa. The first thing that caught Keeling's eye was how CO_2 level rose and fell seasonally. That made sense since, during spring and summer, plants take in CO_2 during photosynthesis and produce oxygen in the atmosphere. In the fall and winter, when plants decay, they release greater quantities of CO_2 through respiration and decay. Keeling's vacillating seasonal curve became famous as a visual representation of the Earth "breathing."

Something else about the way the Earth was breathing attracted Keeling's attention. He watched as CO_2 level not only fluctuated seasonally, but also rose year after year. Carbon dioxide level has climbed from about 315 parts per million (ppm) from Keeling's first readings in 1958 to more than 375 ppm today. A primary source for this rise is indisputable: humans' prodigious burning of carbon-laden fossil fuels for their factories, homes, and cars.

Tans shows me a graph depicting levels of three key greenhouse gases—CO_2, methane, and nitrous oxide—from the year 1000 to the present. The three gases together help keep Earth, which would otherwise be an inhospitably cold orbiting rock, temperate by orchestrating an intricate dance between the radiation of heat from Earth back to space (cooling the planet) and the absorption of radiation in the atmosphere (trapping it near the surface and thus warming the planet).

Tans and most other scientists believe that greenhouse gases are at the root of our changing climate. "These gases are a climate-change driver," says Tans, poking his graph definitively with his index finger. The three lines on the graph follow almost identical patterns: basically flat until the mid-1800s, then all three move upward in a trend that turns even more sharply upward after 1950. "This is what we did," says Tans, pointing to the parallel spikes. "We have very significantly changed the atmospheric concentration of these gases. We know their radiative properties," he says. "It is inconceivable to me that the increase would not have a significant effect on climate."

Exactly how large that effect might be on the planet's health and respiratory system will continue to be a subject of great scientific and political debate—especially if the lines on the graph continue their upward trajectory.

Eugene Brower, an Inupiat Eskimo and president of the Barrow Whaling Captains' Association, doesn't need fancy parts-per-million measurements of CO_2 concentrations or long-term sea-level gauges to tell him that his world is changing.

"It's happening as we speak," the 56-year-old Brower says as we drive around his home in Barrow, Alaska—the United States' northernmost city—on a late August day. In his fire chief's truck, Brower takes me to his family's traditional ice cellars, painstakingly dug into the permafrost, and points out how his stores of muktuk—whale skin and blubber—recently began spoiling in the fall because melting water drips down to his food stores. Our next stop is the old Bureau of Indian Affairs school building. The once impenetrable permafrost that kept the foundation solid has bucked and heaved so much that walking through the school is almost like walking down the halls of an amusement park fun house. We head to the eroding beach and gaze out over open water. "Normally by now the ice would be coming in," Brower says, scrunching up his eyes and scanning the blue horizon.

We continue our tour. Barrow looks like a coastal community under siege. The ramshackle conglomeration of weather-beaten houses along the seaside gravel road stands protected from fall storm surges by miles-long berms of gravel and mud that block views of migrating gray whales. Yellow bulldozers and graders patrol the coast like sentries.

The Inupiat language has words that describe many kinds of ice. Piqaluyak is salt-free multiyear sea ice. Ivuniq is a pressure ridge. Sarri is the word for pack ice, tuvaqtaq is bottom-fast ice, and shore-fast ice is tuvaq. For Brower, these words are the currency of hunters who must know and follow ice patterns to track bearded seals, walruses, and bowhead whales.

There are no words, though, to describe how much, and how fast, the ice is changing. Researchers long ago predicted that the most visible impacts from a globally warmer world would occur first at high latitudes: rising air and sea temperatures, earlier snowmelt, later ice freeze-up, reductions in sea ice, thawing permafrost, more erosion, increases in storm intensity. Now all those impacts have been documented in Alaska. "The changes observed here provide an early warning system for the rest of the planet," says Amanda Lynch, an Australian researcher who is the principal investigator on a project that works with Barrow's residents to help them incorporate scientific data into management decisions for the city's threatened infrastructure.

Before leaving the Arctic, I drive to Point Barrow alone. There, at the tip of Alaska, roughshod hunting shacks dot the spit of land that marks the dividing line between the Chukchi and Beaufort Seas. Next to one shack someone has planted three eight-foot ... sticks of white driftwood in the sand, then crisscrossed their tops with whale baleen, a horny substance that whales of the same name use to filter life-sustaining plankton out of seawater. The baleen, curiously, looks like palm fronds.

So there, on the North Slope of Alaska, stand three makeshift palm trees. Perhaps they are no more than an elaborate Inupiat joke, but these Arctic palms seem an enigmatic metaphor for the Earth's future.

QUESTIONS

1. How does Glick establish Daniel Fagre as an authority on nature and global warming before quoting him? What other authorities or "guides" are introduced in the essay? What key facts about the effects of global warming do they share, and how are these facts arranged to drive home Glick's point about the problem?

2. Are Glick's attempts to reveal the diverse and interrelated effects of global warming by moving back and forth between different geographic places and changing landscapes effective or confusing? Explain your response.

3. How does the detail in the essay, particularly the two paragraphs descriptive of Point Barrow that end the essay, provide an effective and disturbing tone? What ambiguity is conveyed by the final detail, the "makeshift palm trees"?

RICHARD S. LINDZEN

"Don't Believe the Hype"

Richard Lindzen received his Ph.D. in 1964 from Harvard University. He is currently the Alfred P. Sloan Professor of Meteorology in the Department of Earth, Atmospheric and Planetary Sciences at MIT. A specialist in dynamical meterology, his research background is in temperature shifts, climate instability, and glaciation cycles. He is on the NRC Board on Atmospheric Sciences and Climate and is a consultant to the Global Modeling and Simulation Group at NASA's Goddard Space Flight Center. The following article from The Wall Street Journal *(2006) critiques Al Gore's film* An Inconvenient Truth, *arguing that its thesis of a global emergency due to the threat of global warming is neither based on solid scientific fact nor supported by a consensus of scientific opinion.*

According to Al Gore's new film "An Inconvenient Truth," we're in for a planetary emergency: melting ice sheets, huge increases in sea levels, more and stronger hurricanes, and invasions of tropical disease, among other cataclysms—unless we change the way we live now.

Bill Clinton has become the latest evangelist for Mr. Gore's gospel, proclaiming that current weather events show that he and Mr. Gore were right about global warming, and we are all suffering the consequences of President Bush's obtuseness on the matter. And why not? Mr. Gore assures us that "the debate in the scientific community is over."

That statement, which Mr. Gore made in an interview with George Stephanopoulos on ABC, ought to have been followed by an asterisk. What exactly is this debate that Mr. Gore is referring to? Is there really a scientific community that is debating all these issues and then somehow agreeing in unison? Far from such a thing being over, it has never been clear to me what this "debate" actually is in the first place.

The media rarely help, of course. When *Newsweek* featured global warming in a 1988 issue, it was claimed that all scientists agreed. Periodically thereafter it was revealed that although there had been lingering doubts beforehand, now all scientists did indeed agree. Even Mr. Gore qualified his statement on ABC only a few minutes after he made it, clarifying things in an important way. When Mr. Stephanopoulos confronted Mr. Gore with the fact that the best estimates of rising sea levels are far less dire than he suggests in his movie, Mr. Gore defended his claims by noting that scientists "don't have any models that give them a high level of confidence" one way or the other and went on to claim—in his defense—that scientists "don't know . . . . They just don't know."

So, presumably, those scientists do not belong to the "consensus." Yet their research is forced, whether the evidence supports it or not, into Mr. Gore's preferred global-warming template—namely, shrill alarmism. To believe it requires that one ignore the truly inconvenient facts. To take the issue of rising sea levels, these include: that the Arctic was as warm or warmer in 1940; that icebergs have been known since time immemorial; that the evidence so far suggests that the Greenland ice sheet is actually growing on average. A likely result of all this is increased pressure pushing ice off the coastal perimeter of that country, which is depicted so ominously in Mr. Gore's movie. In the absence of factual context, these images are perhaps dire or alarming.

They are less so otherwise. Alpine glaciers have been retreating since the early 19th century, and were advancing for several centuries before that. Since about 1970, many of the glaciers have stopped retreating and some are now advancing again. And, frankly, we don't know why.

The other elements of the global-warming scare scenario are predicated on similar oversights. Malaria, claimed as a byproduct of warming, was once common in Michigan and Siberia and remains common in Siberia—mosquitoes don't require tropical warmth. Hurricanes, too, vary on multidecadal time scales; sea-surface temperature is likely to be an important factor. This temperature, itself, varies on multidecadal time scales. However, questions concerning the origin of the relevant sea-surface temperatures and the nature of trends in hurricane intensity are being hotly argued within the profession.

Even among those arguing, there is general agreement that we can't attribute any particular hurricane to global warming. To be sure, there is one exception, Greg Holland of the National Center for Atmospheric Research in Boulder, Colo., who argues that it must be global warming because he can't think of anything else. While arguments like these, based on lassitude, are becoming rather common in climate assessments, such claims, given the primitive state of weather and climate science, are hardly compelling.

A general characteristic of Mr. Gore's approach is to assiduously ignore the fact that the earth and its climate are dynamic; they are always changing even without any external forcing. To treat all change as something to fear is bad enough; to do so in order to exploit that fear is much worse. Regardless, these items are clearly not issues over which debate is ended—at least not in terms of the actual science.

A clearer claim as to what debate has ended is provided by the environmental journalist Gregg Easterbrook. He concludes that the scientific community now agrees that significant warming is occurring, and that there is clear evidence of human influences on the climate system. This is still a most peculiar claim. At some level, it has never been widely contested. Most of the climate community has agreed since 1988 that global mean temperatures have increased on the order of one degree Fahrenheit over the past century, having risen significantly from about 1919 to 1940, decreased between 1940 and the early '70s, increased again until the '90s, and remaining essentially flat since 1998.

There is also little disagreement that levels of carbon dioxide in the atmosphere have risen from about 280 parts per million by volume in the 19th century to about 387 ppmv today. Finally, there has been no question whatever that carbon dioxide is an infrared absorber (i.e., a greenhouse gas—albeit a minor one), and its increase should theoretically contribute to warming. Indeed, if all else were kept equal, the increase in carbon dioxide should have led to somewhat more warming than has been observed, assuming that the small observed increase was in fact due to increasing carbon dioxide rather than a natural fluctuation in the climate system. Although no cause for alarm rests on this issue, there has been an intense effort to claim that the theoretically expected contribution from additional carbon dioxide has actually been detected.

Given that we do not understand the natural internal variability of climate change, this task is currently impossible. Nevertheless there has been a persistent effort to suggest otherwise, and with surprising impact. Thus, although the conflicted state of the affair was accurately presented in the 1996 text of the Intergovernmental Panel on Climate Change, the infamous "summary for policy makers" reported ambiguously that "The balance of evidence suggests a discernible human influence on global climate." This sufficed as the smoking gun for Kyoto.

The next IPCC report again described the problems surrounding what has become known as the attribution issue: that is, to explain what mechanisms are responsible for observed changes in climate. Some deployed the lassitude argument—e.g., we can't think of an alternative—to support human attribution. But the "summary for policy makers" claimed in a manner largely unrelated to the actual text of the report that "In the light of new evidence and taking into account the remaining uncertainties, most of the observed warming over the last 50 years is likely to have been due to the increase in greenhouse gas concentrations."

In a similar vein, the National Academy of Sciences issued a brief (15-page) report responding to questions from the White House. It again enumerated the difficulties with attribution, but again the report was preceded by a front end that ambiguously claimed that "The changes observed over the last several decades are likely mostly due to human activities, but we cannot rule out that some significant part of these changes is also a reflection of natural variability." This was sufficient for CNN's Michelle Mitchell to presciently declare that the report represented a "unanimous decision that global warming is real, is getting worse and is due to man. There is no wiggle room." Well, no.

More recently, a study in the journal *Science* by the social scientist Nancy Oreskes claimed that a search of the ISI Web of Knowledge Database for the years 1993 to 2003 under the key words "global climate change" produced 928 articles, all of whose abstracts supported what she referred to as the consensus view. A British social scientist, Benny Peiser, checked her procedure and found that only 913 of the 928 articles had abstracts at all, and that only 13 of the remaining 913 explicitly endorsed the so-called consensus view. Several actually opposed it.

Even more recently, the Climate Change Science Program, the Bush administration's coordinating agency for global-warming research, declared it had found "clear evidence of human influences on the climate system." This, for Mr. Easterbrook, meant: "Case closed." What exactly was this evidence? The models imply that greenhouse warming should impact atmospheric temperatures more than surface temperatures, and yet satellite data showed no warming in the atmosphere since 1979. The report showed that selective corrections to the atmospheric data could lead to some warming, thus reducing the conflict between observations and models descriptions of what greenhouse warming should look like. That, to me, means the case is still very much open.

So what, then, is one to make of this alleged debate? I would suggest at least three points.

First, nonscientists generally do not want to bother with understanding the science. Claims of consensus relieve policy types, environmental advocates and politicians of any need to do so. Such claims also serve to intimidate the public and even scientists—especially those outside the area of climate dynamics. Secondly, given that the question of human attribution largely cannot be resolved, its use in promoting visions of disaster constitutes nothing so much as a bait-and-switch scam. That is an inauspicious beginning to what Mr. Gore claims is not a political issue but a "moral" crusade.

Lastly, there is a clear attempt to establish truth not by scientific methods but by perpetual repetition. An earlier attempt at this was accompanied by tragedy. Perhaps Marx was right. This time around we may have farce—if we're lucky.

QUESTIONS

1. One of Lindzen's key arguments is that there is no "consensus" among scientists over the existence of global warming. Do some outside research on whether there is a consensus on this issue. What are your conclusions?

2. Discuss the emotionally charged language Lindzen uses in this article to describe the proponents of the global warming thesis such as Al Gore, Bill Clinton, and members of the media, all of whom Lindzen accuses of being involved in a "bait and switch scam." Do you think Lindzen's

disparaging language use is inappropriate for a scientific essay, or does the audience and controversial nature of the subject demand such a rhetorical style?

3. What are the three points that Lindzen wishes to make about the presumed inaccuracies in the debate over global warming? Are these points presented convincingly? Why or why not?

AL GORE

"Policy Address on Global Warming"

Al Gore (b. 1948) graduated from Harvard University with a degree in government and was elected to the US. Senate in 1984 and 1988. In 1993 he became the 45th vice-president of the United States. After his narrow defeat by George W. Bush in a contested election for the presidency, Gore has pursued interests in technological developments such as educational television, computing, and the Internet, as well as speaking internationally on environmental issues. He developed and starred in a film on global warming, An Inconvenient Truth, *for which he received an Academy Award in 2007, and won the Nobel Peace Prize in that same year. His books include* Earth in the Balance: Forging a New Common Purpose *(1992),* An Inconvenient Truth: The Planetary Emergency of Global Warming and What We Can Do About it *(2006), and* The Assault on Reason *(2007). The following speech, "Policy Address on Global Warming" (2006), outlines some possible long-term solutions for the problems of environmental pollution and global warming.*

Ladies and Gentlemen:

Thank you Paul and Jim for those kind introductions. I would especially like to thank our host, New York University and the President of the College John Sexton and the Dean of the Law School Richard Revesz. I am also grateful to our co-sponsors, the World Resources Institute and Set America Free.

A few days ago, scientists announced alarming new evidence of the rapid melting of the perennial ice of the north polar cap, continuing a trend of the past several years that now confronts us with the prospect that human activities, if unchecked in the next decade, could destroy one of the earth's principle mechanisms for cooling itself. Another group of scientists presented evidence that human activities are responsible for the dramatic warming of sea surface temperatures in the areas of the ocean where hurricanes form. A few weeks earlier, new information from yet another team showed dramatic increases in the burning of forests throughout the American West, a trend that has increased decade by decade, as warmer temperatures have dried out soils and vegetation. All these findings come at the end of a summer with record breaking temperatures and the hottest twelve month period ever measured in the U.S., with persistent drought in vast areas of our country. *Scientific American* introduces the lead article in its special issue this month with the following sentence: "The debate on global warming is over."

Many scientists are now warning that we are moving closer to several "tipping points" that could—within as little as 10 years—make it impossible for us to avoid irretrievable damage to the planet's habitability for human civilization. In this regard, just a few weeks ago, another group of scientists reported on the unexpectedly rapid increases in the release of carbon and methane emissions from frozen tundra in Siberia, now beginning to thaw because of human caused increases in global temperature. The scientists tell us that the tundra in danger of thawing contains an amount of additional global warming pollution that is equal to the total amount that is already in the earth's atmosphere. Similarly, earlier this year, yet another team of scientists reported that the previous twelve months saw 32 glacial earthquakes on Greenland between 4.6 and 5.1 on the Richter scale— a disturbing sign that a massive destabilization may now be underway deep within the second largest accumulation of ice on the planet, enough ice to raise sea level 20 feet worldwide if it broke up and slipped into the sea. Each passing day brings yet more evidence that we are now facing a planetary emergency—a climate crisis that demands immediate action to sharply reduce carbon dioxide emissions worldwide in order to turn down the earth's thermostat and avert catastrophe.

The serious debate over the climate crisis has now moved on to the question of how we can craft emergency solutions in order to avoid this catastrophic damage.

This debate over solutions has been slow to start in earnest not only because some of our leaders still find it more convenient to deny the reality of the crisis, but also because the hard truth for the rest of us is that the maximum that seems politically feasible still falls far short of the minimum that would be effective in solving the crisis. This no-man's land—or no politician zone—falling between the farthest reaches of political feasibility and the first beginnings of truly effective change is the area that I would like to explore in my speech today.

T. S. Eliot once wrote: "Between the idea and the reality,/Between the motion and the act Falls the Shadow. . . . Between the conception and the creation, Between the emotion and the response Falls the Shadow."

My purpose is not to present a comprehensive and detailed blueprint—for that is a task for our democracy as a whole—but rather to try to shine some light on a pathway through this terra incognita that lies between where we are and where we need to go. Because, if we acknowledge candidly that what we need to do is beyond the limits of our current political capacities, that really is just another way of saying that we have to urgently expand the limits of what is politically possible.

I have no doubt that we can do precisely that, because having served almost three decades in elected office, I believe I know one thing about America's political system that some of the pessimists do not: it shares something in common with the climate system; it can appear to move only at a slow pace, but it can also cross a tipping point beyond which it can move with lightning speed. Just as a single tumbling rock can trigger a massive landslide, America has sometimes experienced sudden avalanches of political change that had their beginnings with what first seemed like small changes.

Two weeks ago, Democrats and Republicans joined together in our largest state, California, to pass legally binding sharp reductions in CO_2 emissions. Two hundred ninety-five American cities have now independently "ratified" and embraced CO_2 reductions called for in the Kyoto Treaty. Eighty-five conservative evangelical ministers publicly broke with the Bush-Cheney administration to call for bold action to solve the climate crisis. Business leaders in both political parties have taken significant steps to position their companies as leaders in this struggle and have adopted a policy that not only reduces CO_2 but makes their companies zero carbon companies. Many of them have discovered a way to increase profits and productivity by eliminating their contributions to global warming pollution.

Many Americans are now seeing a bright light shining from the far side of this no-man's land that illuminates not sacrifice and danger, but instead a vision of a bright future that is better for our country in every way—a future with better jobs, a cleaner environment, a more secure nation, and a safer world.

After all, many Americans are tired of borrowing huge amounts of money from China to buy huge amounts of oil from the Persian Gulf to make huge amounts of pollution that destroys the planet's climate. Increasingly, Americans believe that we have to change every part of that pattern.

When I visit port cities like Seattle, New Orleans, or Baltimore, I find massive ships, running low in the water, heavily burdened with foreign cargo or foreign oil arriving by the thousands. These same cargo ships and tankers depart riding high with only ballast water to keep them from rolling over.

One-way trade is destructive to our economic future. We send money, electronically, in the opposite direction. But, we can change this by inventing and manufacturing new solutions to stop global warming right here in America. I still believe in good old-fashioned American ingenuity. We need to fill those ships with new products and technologies that we create to turn down the global thermostat. Working together, we can create jobs and stop global warming. But we must begin by winning the first key battle—against inertia and the fear of change.

In order to conquer our fear and walk boldly forward on the path that lies before us, we have to insist on a higher level of honesty in America's political dialogue. When we make big mistakes in America, it is usually because the people have not been given an honest accounting of the choices before us. It also is often because too many members of both parties who knew better did not have the courage to do better.

Our children have a right to hold us to a higher standard when their future—indeed the future of all human civilization—is hanging in the balance. They deserve better than the spectacle of censorship of the best scientific evidence about the truth of our situation and harassment of honest scientists who are trying to warn us about the looming catastrophe. They deserve better than politicians who sit on their hands and do nothing to confront the greatest challenge that humankind has ever faced—even as the danger bears down on us.

We in the United States of America have a particularly important responsibility, after all, because the world still regards us—in spite of our recent moral lapses—as the natural leader of the community of nations. Simply put, in order for the world to respond urgently to the climate crisis, the United States must lead the way. No other nation can.

Developing countries like China and India have gained their own understanding of how threatening the climate crisis is to them, but they will never find the political will to make the necessary changes in their growing economies unless and until the United States leads the way. Our natural role is to be the pace car in the race to stop global warming.

So, what would a responsible approach to the climate crisis look like if we had one in America?

Well, first of all, we should start by immediately freezing CO_2 emissions and then beginning sharp reductions. Merely engaging in high-minded debates about theoretical future reductions while continuing to steadily increase emissions represents a self-delusional and reckless approach. In some ways, that approach is worse than doing nothing at all, because it lulls the gullible into thinking that something is actually being done when in fact it is not.

An immediate freeze has the virtue of being clear, simple, and easy to understand. It can attract support across partisan lines as a logical starting point for the more difficult work that lies ahead. I remember a quarter century ago when I was the author of a complex nuclear arms control plan to deal with the then rampant arms race between our country and the former Soviet Union. At the time, I was strongly opposed to the nuclear freeze movement, which I saw as simplistic and naive. But, three-fourths of the American people supported it—and as I look back on those years I see more clearly now that the outpouring of public support for that very simple and clear mandate changed the political landscape and made it possible for more detailed and sophisticated proposals to eventually be adopted.

When the politicians are paralyzed in the face of a great threat, our nation needs a popular movement, a rallying cry, a standard, a mandate that is broadly supported on a bipartisan basis.

A responsible approach to solving this crisis would also involve joining the rest of the global economy in playing by the rules of the world treaty that reduces global warming pollution by authorizing the trading of emissions within a global cap.

At present, the global system for carbon emissions trading is embodied in the Kyoto Treaty. It drives reductions in CO_2 and helps many countries that are a part of the treaty to find the most efficient ways to meet their targets for reductions. It is true that not all countries are yet on track to meet their targets, but the first targets don't have to be met until 2008 and the largest and most important reductions typically take longer than the near term in any case.

The absence of the United States from the treaty means that 25% of the world economy is now missing. It is like filling a bucket with a large hole in the bottom. When the United States eventually joins the rest of the world community in making this system operate well, the global market for carbon emissions will become a highly efficient closed system and every corporate board of directors on earth will have a fiduciary duty to manage and reduce CO_2 emissions in order to protect shareholder value.

Many American businesses that operate in other countries already have to abide by the Kyoto Treaty anyway, and unsurprisingly, they are the companies that have been most eager to adopt these new principles here at home as well. The United States and Australia are the only two countries in the developed world that have not yet ratified the Kyoto Treaty. Since the Treaty has been so demonized in America's internal debate, it is difficult to imagine the current Senate finding a way to ratify it. But the United States should immediately join the discussion that is now underway on the new tougher treaty that will soon be completed. We should plan to accelerate its adoption and phase it in more quickly than is presently planned.

Third, a responsible approach to solutions would avoid the mistake of trying to find a single magic "silver bullet" and recognize that the answer will involve what Bill McKibben has called "silver-buckshot"— numerous important solutions, all of which are hard, but no one of which is by itself the full answer for our problem.

One of the most productive approaches to the "multiple solutions" needed is a road-map designed by two Princeton professors, Rob Socolow and Steven Pacala, which breaks down the overall problem into more manageable parts. Socolow and Pacala have identified 15 or 20 building blocks (or "wedges") that can be used to solve our problem effectively—even if we only use 7 or 8 of them. I am among the many who have found this approach useful as a way to structure a discussion of the choices before us.

Over the next year, I intend to convene an ongoing broad-based discussion of solutions that will involve leaders from government, science, business, labor, agriculture, grass-roots activists, faith communities and others.

I am convinced that it is possible to build an effective consensus in the United States and in the world at large on the most effective approaches to solve the climate crisis. Many of those solutions will be found in the building blocks that currently structure so many discussions. But I am also certain that some of the most powerful solutions will lie beyond our current categories of building blocks and "wedges."

Our secret strength in America has always been our capacity for vision. "Make no little plans," one of our most famous architects said over a century ago, "they have no magic to stir men's blood."

I look forward to the deep discussion and debate that lies ahead. But there are already some solutions that seem to stand out as particularly promising:

First, dramatic improvements in the efficiency with which we generate, transport and use energy will almost certainly prove to be the single biggest source of sharp reductions in global warming pollution. Because pollution has been systematically ignored in the old rules of America's marketplace, there are lots of relatively easy ways to use new and more efficient options to cheaply eliminate it. Since pollution is, after all, waste, business and industry usually become more productive and efficient when they systematically go about reducing pollution. After all, many of the technologies on which we depend are actually so old that they are inherently far less efficient than newer technologies that we haven't started using. One of the best examples is the internal combustion engine. When scientists calculate the energy content in BTUs of each gallon of gasoline used in a typical car, and then measure the amounts wasted in the car's routine operation, they find that an incredible 90% of that energy is completely wasted. One engineer, Amory Lovins, has gone farther and calculated the amount of energy that is actually used to move the passenger (excluding the amount of energy used to move the several tons of metal surrounding the passenger) and has found that only 1% of the energy is actually used to move the person. This is more than an arcane calculation, or a parlor trick with arithmetic. These numbers actually illuminate the single biggest opportunity to make our economy more efficient and competitive while sharply reducing global warming pollution.

To take another example, many older factories use obsolete processes that generate prodigious amounts of waste heat that actually has tremendous economic value. By redesigning their processes and capturing all of that waste, they can eliminate huge amounts of global warming pollution while saving billions of dollars at the same time.

When we introduce the right incentives for eliminating pollution and becoming more efficient, many businesses will begin to make greater use of computers and advanced monitoring systems to identify even more opportunities for savings. This is what happened in the computer chip industry when more powerful chips led to better computers, which in turn made it possible to design even more powerful chips, in a virtuous cycle of steady improvement that became known as "Moore's Law." We may well see the emergence of a new version of "Moore's Law" producing steadily higher levels of energy efficiency at steadily lower cost.

There is yet another lesson we can learn from America's success in the information revolution. When the Internet was invented—and I assure you I intend to choose my words carefully here—it was because defense planners in the Pentagon forty years ago were searching for a way to protect America's command and communication infrastructure from being disrupted in a nuclear attack. The network they created—known as ARPANET—was based on "distributed communication" that allowed it to continue functioning even if part of it was destroyed.

Today, our nation faces threats very different from those we countered during the Cold War. We worry today that terrorists might try to inflict great damage on America's energy infrastructure by attacking a single vulnerable part of the oil distribution or electricity distribution network. So, taking a page from the early pioneers of ARPANET, we should develop a distributed electricity and liquid fuels distribution network that is less dependent on large coal-fired generating plants and vulnerable oil ports and refineries.

Small windmills and photovoltaic solar cells distributed widely throughout the electricity grid would sharply reduce CO_2 emissions and at the same time increase our energy security. Likewise, widely dispersed ethanol and biodiesel production facilities would shift our transportation fuel stocks to renewable forms of energy while making us less dependent on and vulnerable to disruptions in the supply of expensive crude oil from the Persian Gulf, Venezuela and Nigeria, all of which are extremely unreliable sources upon which to base our future economic vitality. It would also make us less vulnerable to the impact of a category 5 hurricane hitting coastal refineries or to a terrorist attack on ports or key parts of our current energy infrastructure.

Just as a robust information economy was triggered by the introduction of the Internet, a dynamic new renewable energy economy can be stimulated by the development of an "electranet," or smart grid, that allows individual homeowners and business-owners anywhere in America to use their own renewable sources of energy to sell electricity into the grid when they have a surplus and purchase it from the grid when they don't. The same electranet could give homeowners and business-owners accurate and powerful tools with which to precisely measure how much energy they are using where and when, and identify opportunities for eliminating unnecessary costs and wasteful usage patterns.

A second group of building blocks to solve the climate crisis involves America's transportation infrastructure. We could further increase the value and efficiency of a distributed energy network by retooling our failing auto giants—GM and Ford—to require and assist them in switching to the manufacture of flex-fuel, plug-in, hybrid vehicles. The owners of such vehicles would have the ability to use electricity as a principle source of power and to supplement it by switching from gasoline to ethanol or biodiesel. This flexibility would give them incredible power in the marketplace for energy to push the entire system to much higher levels of efficiency and in the process sharply reduce global warming pollution.

This shift would also offer the hope of saving tens of thousands of good jobs in American companies that are presently fighting a losing battle selling cars and trucks that are less efficient than the ones made by their competitors in countries where they were forced to reduce their pollution and thus become more efficient.

It is, in other words, time for a national oil change. That is apparent to anyone who has looked at our national dipstick.

Our current ridiculous dependence on oil endangers not only our national security, but also our economic security. Anyone who believes that the international market for oil is a "free market" is seriously deluded. It has many characteristics of a free market, but it is also subject to periodic manipulation by the small group of nations controlling the largest recoverable reserves, sometimes in concert with companies that have great influence over the global production, refining, and distribution network.

It is extremely important for us to be clear among ourselves that these periodic efforts to manipulate price and supply have not one but two objectives. They naturally seek to maximize profits. But even more significantly, they seek to manipulate our political will. Every time we come close to recognizing the wisdom of developing our own independent sources of renewable fuels, they seek to dissipate our sense of urgency and derail our effort to become less dependent. That is what is happening at this very moment.

Shifting to a greater reliance on ethanol, cellulosic ethanol, butanol, and green diesel fuels will not only reduce global warming pollution and enhance our national and economic security, it will also reverse the steady loss of jobs and income in rural America. Several important building blocks for America's role in solving the climate crisis can be found in new approaches to agriculture. As pointed out by the "25 by 25" movement (aimed at securing 25% of America's power and transportation fuels from agricultural sources by the year 2025) we can revitalize the farm economy by shifting its mission from a focus on food, feed and fiber to a focus on food, feed, fiber, fuel, and ecosystem services. We can restore the health of depleted soils by encouraging and rewarding the growing of fuel source crops like switchgrass and sawgrass, using no till cultivation, and scientific crop rotation. We should also reward farmers for planting more trees and sequestering more carbon, and recognize the economic value of their stewardship of resources that are important to the health of our ecosystems.

Similarly, we should take bold steps to stop deforestation and extend the harvest cycle on timber to optimize the carbon sequestration that is most powerful and most efficient with older trees. On a worldwide basis, two and one-half trillion tons of the 10 trillion tons of CO_2 emitted each year come from burning forests. So, better management of forests is one of the single most important strategies for solving the climate crisis.

Biomass—whether in the form of trees, switchgrass, or other sources—is one of the most important forms of renewable energy. And renewable sources make up one of the most promising building blocks for reducing carbon pollution.

Wind energy is already fully competitive as a mainstream source of electricity and will continue to grow in prominence and profitability.

Solar photovoltaic energy is—according to researchers—much closer than it has ever been to a cost-competitive breakthrough, as new nanotechnologies are being applied to dramatically enhance the efficiency with which solar cells produce electricity from sunlight–and as clever new designs for concentrating solar energy are used with new approaches such as Stirling engines that can bring costs sharply down.

Buildings—both commercial and residential—represent a larger source of global warming pollution than cars and trucks. But new architecture and design techniques are creating dramatic new opportunities for huge savings in energy use and global warming pollution. As an example of their potential, the American Institute of Architecture and the National Conference of Mayors have endorsed the "2030 Challenge," asking the global architecture and building community to immediately transform building design to require that all new buildings and developments be designed to use one half the fossil fuel energy they would typically consume for each building type, and that all new buildings be carbon neutral by 2030, using zero fossil fuels to operate. A newly constructed building at Oberlin College is producing 30 percent less energy than it consumes. Some other countries have actually required a standard calling for zero carbon based energy inputs for new buildings.

The rapid urbanization of the world's population is leading to the prospective development of more new urban buildings in the next 35 years than have been constructed in all previous human history. This startling trend represents a tremendous opportunity for sharp reductions in global warming pollution through the use of intelligent architecture and design and stringent standards.

Here in the US the extra cost of efficiency improvements such as thicker insulation and more efficient window coatings have traditionally been shunned by builders and homebuyers alike because they add to the initial purchase price—even though these investments typically pay for themselves by reducing heating and cooling costs and then produce additional savings each month for the lifetime of the building. It should be possible to remove the purchase price barrier for such improvements through the use of innovative mortgage finance instruments that eliminate any additional increase in the purchase price by capturing the future income from the expected savings. We should create a Carbon Neutral Mortgage Association to market these new financial instruments and stimulate their use in the private sector by utilities, banks and homebuilders. This new "Connie Mae" (CNMA) could be a valuable instrument for reducing the pollution from new buildings.

Many believe that a responsible approach to sharply reducing global warming pollution would involve a significant increase in the use of nuclear power plants as a substitute for coal-fired generators. While I am not opposed to nuclear power and expect to see some modest increased use of nuclear reactors, I doubt that they will play a significant role in most countries as a new source of electricity. The main reason for my skepticism about nuclear power playing a much larger role in the world's energy future is not the problem of waste disposal or the danger of reactor operator error, or the vulnerability to terrorist attack. Let's assume for the moment that all three of these problems can be solved. That still leaves two serious issues that are more difficult constraints. The first is economics; the current generation of reactors is expensive, take a long time to build, and only come in one size—extra large.

In a time of great uncertainty over energy prices, utilities must count on great uncertainty in electricity demand—and that uncertainty causes them to strongly prefer smaller incremental additions to their generating capacity that are each less expensive and quicker to build than are large 1000 megawatt light water reactors. Newer, more scalable and affordable reactor designs may eventually become available, but not soon. Secondly, if the world as a whole chose nuclear power as the option of choice to replace coal-fired generating plants, we would face a dramatic increase in the likelihood of nuclear weapons proliferation. During my 8 years in the White House, every nuclear weapons proliferation issue we dealt with was connected to a nuclear reactor program. Today, the dangerous weapons programs in both Iran and North Korea are linked to their civilian reactor programs. Moreover, proposals to separate the ownership of reactors from the ownership of the fuel supply process have met with stiff resistance from developing countries who want reactors. As a result of all these problems, I believe that nuclear reactors will only play a limited role.

The most important set of problems that must be solved in charting solutions for the climate crisis have to do with coal, one of the dirtiest sources of energy that produces far more CO_2 for each unit of energy output than oil or gas. Yet, coal is found in abundance in the United States, China, and many other places. Because the pollution from the burning of coal is currently excluded from the market calculations of what it costs, coal is presently the cheapest source of abundant energy. And its relative role is growing rapidly day by day.

Fortunately, there may be a way to capture the CO_2 produced as coal is burned and sequester it safely to prevent it from adding to the climate crisis. It is not easy. This technique, known as carbon capture and sequestration (CCS) is expensive and most users of coal have resisted the investments necessary to use it. However, when the cost of not using it is calculated, it becomes obvious that CCS will play a significant and growing role as one of the major building blocks of a solution to the climate crisis.

Interestingly, the most advanced and environmentally responsible project for capturing and sequestering CO_2 is in one of the most forbidding locations for energy production anywhere in the world—in the Norwegian portions of the North Sea. Norway, as it turns out, has hefty CO_2 taxes; and, even though there are many exceptions and exemptions, oil production is not one of them. As a result, the oil producers have found it quite economical and profitable to develop and use advanced CCS technologies in order to avoid the tax they would otherwise pay for the CO_2 they would otherwise emit. The use of similar techniques could be required for coal-fired generating plants, and can be used in combination with advanced approaches like integrated gasification combined cycle (IGCC). Even with the most advanced techniques, however, the economics of carbon capture and sequestration will depend upon the availability of and proximity to safe deep storage reservoirs. Nevertheless, it is time to recognize that the phrase "clean coal technology" is devoid of meaning unless it means "zero carbon emissions" technology.

CCS is only one of many new technological approaches that require a significant increase by governments and business in advanced research and development to speed the availability of more effective technologies that can help us solve the climate crisis more quickly. But it is important to emphasize that even without brand new technologies, we already have everything we need to get started on a solution to this crisis.

In a market economy like ours, however, every one of the solutions that I have discussed will be more effective and much easier to implement if we place a price on the CO_2 pollution that is recognized in the marketplace. We need to summon the courage to use the right tools for this job.

For the last fourteen years, I have advocated the elimination of all payroll taxes—including those for social security and unemployment compensation—and the replacement of that revenue in the form of pollution taxes—principally on CO_2. The overall level of taxation would remain exactly the same. It would be, in other words, a revenue neutral tax swap. But, instead of discouraging businesses from hiring more employees, it would discourage business from producing more pollution.

Global warming pollution, indeed all pollution, is now described by economists as an "externality." This absurd label means, in essence: we don't to keep track of this stuff so let's pretend it doesn't exist.

And sure enough, when it's not recognized in the marketplace, it does make it much easier for government, business, and all the rest of us to pretend that it doesn't exist. But what we're pretending doesn't exist is the stuff that is destroying the habitability of the planet. We put 70 million tons of it into the atmosphere every 24 hours and the amount is increasing day by day. Penalizing pollution instead of penalizing employment will work to reduce that pollution.

When we place a more accurate value on the consequences of the choices we make, our choices get better. At present, when business has to pay more taxes in order to hire more people, it is discouraged from hiring more people. If we change that and discourage them from creating more pollution they will reduce their pollution. Our market economy can help us solve this problem if we send it the right signals and tell ourselves the truth about the economic impact of pollution.

Many of our leading businesses are already making dramatic changes to reduce their global warming pollution. General Electric, Dupont, Cinergy, Caterpillar, and Wal-Mart are among the many who are providing leadership for the business community in helping us devise a solution for this crisis.

Leaders among unions—particularly the steel workers—have also added momentum to this growing movement.

Hunters and fishermen are also now adding their voices to the call for a solution to the crisis. In a recent poll, 86% of licensed hunters and anglers said that we have a moral obligation to stop global warming to protect our children's future.

And, young people—as they did during the Civil Rights Revolution—are confronting their elders with insistent questions about the morality of not moving swiftly to make these needed changes.

Moreover, the American religious community—including a group of 85 conservative evangelicals and especially the US Conference of Catholic Bishops—has made an extraordinary contribution to this entire enterprise. To the insights of science and technology, it has added the perspectives of faith and values, of prophetic imagination, spiritual motivation, and moral passion without which all our plans, no matter how reasonable, simply will not prevail. Individual faith groups have offered their own distinctive views. And yet—uniquely in religious life at this moment and even historically—they have established common ground and resolve across tenacious differences. In addition to reaching millions of people in the pews, they have demonstrated the real possibility of what we all now need to accomplish: how to be ourselves, together and how to discover, in this process, a sense of vivid, living spirit and purpose that elevates the entire human enterprise.

Individual Americans of all ages are becoming a part of a movement, asking what they can do as individuals and what they can do as consumers and as citizens and voters. Many individuals and businesses have decided to take an approach known as "Zero Carbon." They are reducing their CO_2 as much as possible and then offsetting the rest with reductions elsewhere including by the planting of trees. At least one entire community—Ballard, a city of 18,000 people in Washington State—is embarking on a goal of making the entire community zero carbon.

This is not a political issue. This is a moral issue. It affects the survival of human civilization. It is not a question of left vs. right; it is a question of right vs. wrong. Put simply, it is wrong to destroy the habitability of our planet and ruin the prospects of every generation that follows ours.

What is motivating millions of Americans to think differently about solutions to the climate crisis is the growing realization that this challenge is bringing us unprecedented opportunity. I have spoken before about the way the Chinese express the concept of crisis. They use two symbols, the first of which—by itself—means danger. The second, in isolation, means opportunity. Put them together, and you get "crisis." Our single word conveys the danger but doesn't always communicate the presence of opportunity in every crisis. In this case, the opportunity presented by the climate crisis is not only the opportunity for new and better jobs, new technologies, new opportunities for profit, and a higher quality of life. It gives us an opportunity to experience something that few generations ever have the privilege of knowing: a common moral purpose compelling enough to lift us above our limitations and motivate us to set aside some of the bickering to which we as human beings are naturally vulnerable. America's so-called "greatest generation" found such a purpose when they confronted the crisis of global fascism and won a war in Europe and in the Pacific simultaneously. In the process of achieving their historic victory, they found that they had gained new moral authority and a new capacity for vision. They created the Marshall Plan and lifted their recently defeated adversaries from their knees and assisted them to a future of dignity and self-determination. They created the United Nations and the other global institutions that made possible many decades of prosperity, progress and relative peace. In recent years we have squandered that moral authority and it is high time to renew it by taking on the highest challenge of our generation. In rising to meet this challenge, we too will find self-renewal and transcendence and a new capacity for vision to see other crises in our time that cry out for solutions: 20 million HIV/AIDs orphans in Africa alone, civil wars fought by children, genocides and famines, the rape and pillage of our oceans and forests, an extinction crisis that threatens the web of life, and tens of millions of our fellow humans dying every year from easily preventable diseases. And, by rising to meet the climate crisis, we will find the vision and moral authority to see them not as political problems but as moral imperatives.

This is an opportunity for bipartisanship and transcendence, an opportunity to find our better selves and in rising to meet this challenge, create a better brighter future—a future worthy of the generations who come after us and who have a right to be able to depend on us.

QUESTIONS

1. Gore uses the expression "tipping point" at the beginning of his speech and at the point that he begins to introduce some possible solutions to global warming. Is his use of this term clear? Are the examples of the "tipping points" he believes to be near clear and convincing? Why or why not?

2. Why does Gore reject the term "silver bullet" in relation to a solution for the global warming crisis, preferring instead Bill McKibben's phrase, "silver buckshot"? What is the distinction between these two analogies, and what examples does Gore provide of "buckshot"? Which of his suggested solutions seem most promising?

3. What "unprecedented opportunity" does Gore believe the crisis in global warming is opening for the United States? Do the examples he presents of new opportunities seem convincing and realistic? Why or why not?

PHIL MATTERA

"Is Corporate Greenwashing Headed for a Fall?"

Phil Mattera, a former writer for Fortune Magazine, *is research director of* Good Jobs First, *"a national policy resource center for grassroots groups and public officials, promoting corporate and government accountability in economic development." He is head of Good Job's Corporate Research Project, which assists labor and environmental organizations through "identifying the information activists can use as leverage to get business to behave in a socially responsible manner." Mattera has contributed many articles to Alternet and is the author of* Off the Books: The Rise of the Underground Economy *(1985),* Prosperity Lost *(1991), and, with Greg LeRoy,* The Jobs are Back in Town: Urban Smart Growth and Construction Employment *(2003).*

In the following article, written for the Corporate Research Project, Mattera defines and traces the increasing public disillusion with the process of "greenwashing," which involves corporate efforts to convince consumers that businesses are doing great things to improve environmental conditions and combat global warming—when in fact the opposite may be true.

Imagine you are a communication technician on a planet in another solar system that is facing an ecological disaster and is looking for new solutions. One day you suddenly pick up broadcast signals from Earth that happen to include a man talking to a group of children sitting beside a hulking vehicle he is describing as a "vegetarian" because it uses a fuel called ethanol. The segment ends with the statement: "Chevy: from gas-friendly to gas-free. That's an American revolution."

Then you get a transmission from something called BP that is talking about going beyond—beyond darkness, beyond fear, beyond petroleum. Another from Toyota shows a vehicle being put together like a grass hut and then disintegrating back into nature without a trace. The messages keep coming—from General Electric ("eco-imagination"), Chevron (celebrating the miraculous power of "human energy") and so on.

As you receive more of these signals, you rush to your superiors and announce the good news: Planet Earth has wonderful entities called corporations that can solve all our environmental problems.

Residents of our planet may be tempted to jump to the same conclusion. These days we are bombarded with advertisements that want us to believe that major oil companies, automakers and other large corporations are solving the environmental and energy problems facing the earth. Fear not global warming, peak oil, polluted air and water—big business will take care of everything.

In the late 1990s we saw a hyped-up dot com boom that came crashing down. In the past year or so, we have seen a hyped real estate boom turn into a credit crunch and an unprecedented number of home foreclosures. Are we now seeing a green business boom that will also turn out to be nothing more than hot air?

The "Green Con"

Today's surge of corporate environmentalism is not the first time business has sought to align itself with public concerns about the fate of the Earth. Two decades ago, marketers began to recognize the benefits of appealing to green consumers. This revelation first took hold in countries such as Britain and Canada. For example, in early 1989 the giant British supermarket chain Tesco launched a campaign to promote the products on its shelves that were deemed "environmentally friendly." That same year, Canadian mining giant Inco Ltd. began running ads promoting its effort to reduce sulfur emissions from its smelters, conveniently failing to mention it was doing so under government orders.

In 1990 the green business wave spread to the United States in time to coincide with the 20th annual Earth Day celebration. Large U.S. companies such as DuPont began touting their environmental initiatives and staged their own Earth Tech environmental technology fair on the National Mall. General Motors ran ads emphasizing its supposed concern about the environment, despite its continuing resistance to significant increases in fuel efficiency requirements.

Such exercises in corporate image-burnishing did not have a great deal of impact. For one thing, environmental groups wasted no time debunking the ads. In 1989 Friends of the Earth in Britain gave "Green Con" awards to those companies that made the most exaggerated and unsubstantiated environmental claims about their products. First prize went to British National Fuels for promoting nuclear power as friendly to the environment.

Greenpeace USA staged a protest at the 1990 corporate Earth Tech fair, denouncing companies such as DuPont for trying to whitewash their poor environmental record with green claims. Greenpeace's invented term for this practice—greenwashing—immediately caught on, and to this day is a succinct way of undermining dubious corporate claims about the environment.

The general public was also not taken in by the corporate environmental push of 1989–1990. It was just a bit too obvious that these initiatives were meant to deflect attention away from recent environmental disasters such as the Exxon Valdez oil spill in Alaska and Union Carbide's deadly Bhopal chemical leak. It also didn't help that many of the claims about green products turned out to be misleading or meaningless.

"Little Green Lies"

The question today is whether people have become more receptive to corporate environmental hype. One thing business has going for it in the United States is that the Bush Administration has pursued environmental policies so retrograde that even the most superficial green measures by the private sector shine in comparison. Another is that some environmental groups have switched from an outside adversarial strategy to a more collaborative approach that often involves forming partnerships with companies. Such relationships serve to legitimize business initiatives while turning those groups into cheerleaders for their corporate partners. Former Sierra Club president Adam Werbach took it a step further and joined the payroll of Wal-Mart.

On the other hand, the use of the term "greenwashing" is enjoying a resurgence and has entered the mainstream. A search of the Nexis news archive turns up more than 700 mentions of the term in the past six months alone. Even that bible of the marketing world—*Advertising Age*—recently published a list titled "The Green and the Greenwashed: Ten Who Get It and 10 Who Talk a Good Game." Among the latter were General Motors, Toyota, ExxonMobil, Chevron, Wal-Mart, General Electric and Ikea, though Toyota, Wal-Mart and Ikea were also put on the green list for other reasons.

Other business publications have also been taking a more critical approach to green claims. Last September, the *Wall Street Journal* looked behind GE's eco-imagination campaign and found all was not well. For one thing, there was significant resistance even within GE's managerial ranks and among many of the conglomerate's major industrial customers. Then there was the fact that GE was still pushing big-ticket products such as coal-fired steam turbines that were significant contributors to global warming. Finally, the paper pointed out that the campaign was motivated in substantial part by a desire to increase sales of existing GE products such as wind turbines that could be promoted as eco-friendly.

In October, *Business Week* published a cover story titled "Little Green Lies." It began with the declaration: "The sweet notion that making a company environmentally friendly can be not just cost-effective but profitable is going up in smoke." The piece featured Auden Schendler of Aspen Skiing Company, a pioneer in adopting environmentally friendly practices. After showing off his company's energy-efficient facilities, he was described as having turned to the *Business Week* reporter and said: "Who are we kidding?" He then acknowledged that the growth of the company necessarily means burning more power, including the ever-increasing energy needed to create artificial snow during warmer winters. "How do you really green your company? It's almost f------ impossible."

The Six Sins

Another factor working against corporate hype is that critics are becoming more systematic in their critique of greenwashing. In November, a marketing firm called TerraChoice did an analysis of more than 1,000 products bearing environmental claims. After finding that all but one of those claims were false or misleading in some respect, TerraChoice issued a paper called *The Six Sins of Greenwashing* that analyzed the various forms of deception.

The most common shortcoming found by TerraChoice is the "sin of the hidden trade-off," in which a single positive attribute of a product is promoted while ignoring the detrimental environmental impact of the whole manufacturing process. For example, paper that has some recycled content but is produced in a way that causes serious air and water pollution as well as entailing a large amount of greenhouse gas emissions. The other sins listed by TerraChoice are no proof, vagueness, irrelevance, lesser of two evils and fibbing.

Do-it-yourself greenwashing criticism is now possible through a *website* recently launched by EnviroMedia Social Marketing. Its Greenwashing Index site allows users to post ads—usually video footage taken from YouTube—and rate them on a scale of one (good ad) to five (total greenwashing).

More troubling, from the corporate perspective, are signs that government regulators and industry-established watchdog groups are giving more scrutiny to green claims. Last month, the UK's Advertising Standards Authority found that a series of television ads being run around the world by the Malaysian Palm Oil Council contained misleading statements about the environmental benefits of its product. Several months ago, government regulators in Norway banned automobile ads from stating that any cars are environmentally friendly, given their contribution to global warming.

Even in the United States there are signs that regulators may be getting concerned about greenwashing. The Federal Trade Commission, which in 1992 issued national guidelines for environmental marketing claims but has done little on the subject since then, announced in November that it was beginning a review of its guidelines.

Unclean Hands and Excessive Size

Corporations, no doubt, will not give up their environmental claims without a fight. Perhaps the hardest nut to crack will be Wal-Mart. For the past couple of years, the giant retailer has depicted itself as being on a crusade to address global warming and other environmental issues—a crusade it wants its suppliers, its workers and its customers to join. In October 2005 CEO Lee Scott gave a speech in which he embraced sweeping goals to reduce greenhouse gas emissions and raise energy efficiency. Last month he gave another speech that reaffirmed those goals and upped the ante by envisioning a future in which Wal-Mart customers would drive to the store in electric cars that could be recharged in the parking lot using power generated by wind turbines and solar panels.

Wal-Mart's greenwashing involves sins beyond those listed by TerraChoice. First there is the sin of unclean hands. It is difficult to avoid thinking that the company is using its environmental initiatives to draw attention away from its widely criticized labor practices—both in its own stores and in the factories of its low-wage suppliers abroad. Until the company provides decent working conditions, respects the right of its employees to unionize and ceases to sell goods made by sweatshop labor, Wal-Mart cannot expect to be a paradigm of social responsibility.

Then there's the sin of size. A company as large as Wal-Mart will inevitably have a negative effect on the countries from which it obtains its goods, the agricultural areas from which it gets it food products, and the communities where it locates its big-box stores. There's a growing sense that true sustainability entails a substantial degree of localism and moderate-size enterprise. That rules out Wal-Mart, no matter what its CEO professes.

Wal-Mart's problem may be the problem of big business as a whole. As hard as they try to convince us, huge profit-maximizing transnational corporations may never be true friends of the environment. Let's hope this message also gets through to those listening in distant worlds.

QUESTIONS

1. Why is the opening series of paragraphs in Mattera's essay set on another planet that listens to transmissions from ads from Earth? Is this fanciful approach an effective way to begin this essay on greenwashing? Why or why not?
2. What are the "Six Sins of Greenwashing" as written and distributed by the ecological marketing firm TerraChoice? Do you think such publications and/or magazine exposés would be effective in the effort to combat greenwashing-style advertising campaigns? Why or why not?

3. How do Wal-Mart and other international mega-corporations go beyond the original six sins of greenwashing? Does Mattera see any hope for such organizations as "true friends of the environment"? Do you agree with his skeptical perspective?

DARA COLWELL

"Carbon Offsets: Buying Your Way Out of Responsibility"

Dara Colwell, a freelance writer based in Amsterdam, earned her M.A. in journalism at UC Berkeley's Graduate School of Journalism in 1999. She has contributed many articles to alternet.org, where she publishes on environmental, work-related, economic, and lifestyle issues. She has written for Metroactive.com, Scholastic Inc., the Village Voice, Details Magazine, *and* Breathe Magazine. *A contributing writer at* Amsterdam Weekly, *an English-language arts and entertainment journal, Colwell recently published a travel book:* The Q Guide to Amsterdam *(2007). In the following Alternet article, she defines and critiques carbon offsets as a form of self-publicity for wealthy individuals, groups, and corporations, pointing out that they may be a way of staving off the need for higher "green taxes" and stricter governmental regulation of environmental pollution standards.*

Presidential hopefuls do it, celebrities do it, educated CEOs and even Swedes do it—it's carbon offsets, the market-based solution to global warming that's currently grabbing column inches and investment bankers' lips. A booming multimillion-dollar market that's expected to more than quadruple within the next three years, the industry has garnered as much criticism as feel-good hype. Its detractors, mainly in Europe, remain unconvinced the system actually works, claiming its impact is unclear at best, and that it creates loopholes that lets polluters do business as usual.

"It's buying your way out of responsibility," says Kevin Smith, a researcher with Carbon Trade Watch, a project of the Transnational Institute, an academic think tank based in Amsterdam, Netherlands. Smith, who also co-authored "The Carbon Neutral Myth," believes that free-market environmentalism is a gimmick that appeals to an increasingly carbon-conscious public. "It's a technological quick fix that's deeply flawed and used more as a means to absolve climate sins rather than tackle the actual issue," he says.

Carbon offset credits is essentially a market that helps consumers or corporations reduce or neutralize the impact of their net carbon dioxide emissions—from flights, commuting, hefty utility bills or shipping online purchases—through cost-effective alternatives. The system is based on carbon emissions trading, aimed at governments, industries and corporations that cannot meet emission targets set by the Kyoto Protocol, and in turn, buy or trade credit from those that beat theirs. In both cases, the polluter pays.

Since Kyoto came into force in 2005, the nascent, and potentially highly lucrative, emissions market has steadily increased. In America, which has refused to sign on to the Kyoto Protocol, much growth has been geared instead towards the voluntary offsets market. One such example is the Chicago Climate Exchange, the world's first greenhouse gas reduction trading system, which was established in 2003.

More recently, forerunners in the consumer market such as Terra-Pass, Native Energy and DriveNeutral have become high-profile, thanks to Al Gore, the Oscars and celebrity spin. Europe also boasts its share of offset companies. Germany's AtmosFair, Oxford-based Climate Care and the Dutch GreenSeat have joined the ranks of the carbon revolution.

Much of the criticism aimed at the voluntary market is what opponents claim is its seductive sales pitch: Just buy back your pollution and click, and the provider takes care of the rest, whether it's buying emission trading credits, planting a tree—meant to absorb carbon from the atmosphere and by far the most popular, if controversial offset method—or investing in renewable energy sources.

But there's a huge, immediate glitch: the current offsets market, an industry that has mushroomed only in the last several years, is unregulated and no universal carbon-offset standard exists. As carbon is an intangible commodity, companies can sell what they want, claiming it's carbon neutral; and "carbon calculators" and costs fluctuate widely, making what consumers are buying unclear.

"It's selling hot air and susceptible to fraud," says Oscar Reyes, Transnational Institute's communications officer, who cautions that all trading schemes are "ineffective as a means to stimulate cuts in carbon emissions."

"There is a lot of scope for 'cowboys' to cash in, and the supposed climate benefits are impossible to measure," says Smith, noting that offsets don't actually remove the tons of carbon dioxide currently in the atmosphere, and trying to guess how it will involves so many variables that working it out is almost impossible.

While Smith believes many people genuinely buy offsets out of concern for climate change, he sees businesses using them in a more cynical and calculating way. "It gives them a sophisticated veneer of environmental sensitivity they don't deserve," he says, referring to British Airways, one of many airlines that now encourage customers to buy carbon offsets for their flights.

The airline industry is a huge polluter, however. According to the Tufts University Climate Initiative, a round trip flight from America to Europe adds 3–4 tons of CO_2 to the atmosphere, the equivalent of the carbon emissions from 20 Bangladeshis over the course of a year. Worse, in addition to carbon dioxide and other pollutants released during flight, airplanes also trail water vapor, which has a significant heat-trapping effect.

"British Airways is continuing to aggressively expand in the face of a known threat, and yet they're using these offset schemes to gain environmental legitimacy in the eyes of the public and the media," says Smith, who notes that since BA has been partnered with offset provider Climate Care, it has shown a 20 percent increase in pretax profits and launched a budget airline for commuter flights. "They're 'greenwashing' themselves, marketing themselves as being eco-friendly when they've done nothing to change the underlying reality, and the consumer is paying for it."

Climate Care actually highlights another issue—the strange corporate partnerships many offset companies have formed to do business. Climate Care recently announced a comprehensive offset program in the United Kingdom with Land Rover, whose parent company Ford has the worst fuel efficiency and highest average vehicle greenhouse gas emissions of major U.S. automakers, according to a 2004 report from the Union of Concerned Scientists.

Ford is also partnered with Terrapass, of recent Oscar hype, and which has been cutely dubbed by the *L.A.Times* as "Kyoto for commuters." This begs the question is this really tackling the issue (such as reducing emissions from fossil fuels by using, er, less fossil fuel) or peddling positive publicity?

But one of the most important points for environmentalists is the north/south exploitation that the offsets industry embodies. A crucial element of the Kyoto Protocol is the Clean Development Mechanism (CDM), which allows heavily industrialized northern countries to invest in carbon saving projects in the global south as an alternative to reducing their own emissions. There are many reasons for this, the first quite obvious: It's cheaper. The same goes for many offset projects, which choose to invest in projects in Latin America, Africa and Asia. But, as environmentalists are quick to point out, it's not cheap for the locals who suffer the impact.

A case in point is the band Coldplay, which offset recording its "A Rush of Blood" album with 10,000 mango saplings in Karnataka, India. The band urged fans to join in and offset trees with Carbon Neutral Co., the United Kingdom's largest offset provider, also used by Al Gore. According to various media reports, nearly 40 percent of the saplings died, mostly because the dry, rocky village didn't have an adequate water supply and there was no financial infrastructure in place to support it. And while the companies involved in the project got paid, the local peasants who maintained the trees did not.

Or there's Mount Elgon National Park in east Uganda, where the Dutch FACE Foundation has been planting carbon offset trees since 1994. FACE is partnered on this project with offset provider GreenSeat, whose clients include Amnesty International, the British Council and the Body Shop. According to a report by World Rainforest Movement, a Uruguay-based nonprofit, villagers living along the park's boundary have been beaten and shot at, seen their livestock confiscated by armed park rangers guarding the "carbon trees," and largely made homeless, forced to sleep in either neighboring town mosques or caves.

"CDM is being used as a way of legitimizing industries that continue to damage the local environment," says Reyes of Transnational Institute. While Reyes is speaking more broadly of government carbon trading schemes, similar conditions apply to offset companies, which create projects that are actively opposed by local communities.

For example, according to Reyes, in Raigarh city (in the Indian state of Chhattisgarh), sponge iron plants that pollute water from rivers and irrigation channels are being rebranded as CDM projects; in West Bengal, many firms that use the heat from kilns to generate electricity are now being paid carbon credits for their efforts, even though they continue to pollute groundwater supplies and the local atmosphere.

But those who work in the voluntary offsets industry say the market's still young and don't disagree that major kinks need to be ironed out. "I understand the criticism. I always think criticism is an important message the system's not working good enough," says Sascha Bloemhoff, marketing and sales director at New Values, an online emission rights trading service based in Amsterdam. Geared towards businesses rather than individuals, New Values works rather like eBay, where companies can counter bid on emission rights, or pay for credits on the spot. Bloemhoff, who has worked in development aid her entire career, admits that while she sees many hurdles ahead, she also remains positive.

"Considering how rapidly the market has taken off, I'd say it has been a huge success. That doesn't mean it is working as it should, but we're only in the first phase. If we do nothing at all, there will be no change," she says, adding, "It's easy to say business is creating the problem, but it's our consumption, or consumer demand, that's creating climate change. We're buying it."

This is a point where environmentalists would agree. If the offset industry has created a situation much like this: deck chairs, Titanic, reshuffle—then environmentalists believe it's important to seek alternatives. "There's a danger that offsets will absorb all the public's attention because they're easy, convenient and cheap. But they're stymieing collective action and debate, and encouraging complacency," says Smith. "There are hundreds of things people can do to address climate change. Offsets are not the only solution."

What can people do? Smith launches rapid fire into a list: Lobby to cut the $200 billion per year global subsidies for coal and oil power; reduce the supply of fossil fuels by supporting communities resisting their development, address over consumption, put pressure on the government to create systematic change, and so forth. For example, before Kyoto went into effect, in the 1990s Denmark introduced a variety of "green taxes," including an energy tax, recycling the revenues into subsidies for energy-saving projects.

While environmentalists seek alternatives to emissions trading, Mark Trexler, president of Trexler Climate + Energy Services, Inc., an energy and environmental policy consulting firm in Portland, Ore., feels they are having at least one positive impact: educating the public. "Certainly no one should be arguing offsets are the answer, but they're a step in the right direction if used to start to building constituencies for future public policy," he says. "Whether it's emissions trading, new technology or carbon taxes, each has a role to play in what is a very large jigsaw puzzle."

Trexler believes the voluntary markets are no substitute for government policy. "This [is] by far the hardest environmental issue we have ever tried to tackle, and unfortunately, there's no silver bullet solution," he says. "It will take lots of work and experimentation."

Only it's anybody's guess how much time we have to experiment.

QUESTIONS

1. What is Colwell's definition and general attitude towards carbon offset credits? Is she clear in explaining how they actually work?
2. Colwell gives several examples of unsuccessful carbon offset programs. How well do these cases help to support her central argument on the issue? Do they seem like typical examples, or are they chosen more for their shock value?
3. Coldwell's primary interviewee is Kevin Smith, author of "The Carbon-Neutral Myth," who is quoted repeatedly in her essay. Would you consider Smith as an objective source? Do his alternatives to carbon offsets seem realistic at this point? Would they be likely to be accepted in the United States?

DIFFERING PERSPECTIVES: WILL GENETICALLY ENGINEERED CROPS AND ORGANISMS HELP US SURVIVE CLIMATE CHANGE OR FURTHER UPSET THE BALANCE OF NATURE?

Jeremy Rifkin

"Biotech Century: Playing Russian Roulette with Mother Nature's Designs"

Jeremy Rifkin (b. 1945) earned degrees in economics from the Wharton School of the University of Pennsylvania and in international affairs from the Fletcher School of Law and Diplomacy at Tufts University. As president of the Foundation on Economic Trends (FOET), Rifkin speaks frequently to American CEOs and before congressional committees and files lawsuits that attempt to make government policies and programs more responsible in a number of areas. He has advised the European Union and its leaders on biotechnological and environmental issues, and his writings appear often in European journals. Rifkin's books focus mainly on the impact of scientific change and technology on citizens and the environment; his recent works include The Hydrogen Economy *(2002) and* The European Dream: How Europe's Vision of the Future Is Quietly Eclipsing the American Dream *(2004). The following article, adapted from his 1998 book* Biotech Century, *introduces a new term, "genetic pollution", and argues that this new type of biotechnological pollution represents a major threat to the future of our planet.*

We are in the midst of a great historic transition into the Biotech Age. The ability to isolate, identify and recombine genes is making the gene pool available, for the first time, as the primary raw resource for future economic activity on Earth. After thousands of years of fusing, melting, soldering, forging and burning inanimate matter to create useful things, we are now splicing, recombining, inserting and stitching living material for our own economic interests. Lord Ritchie-Calder, the British science writer, cast the biological revolution in the proper historical perspective when he observed that "just as we have manipulated plastics and metals, we are now manufacturing living materials."

The Nobel Prize-winning chemist Robert F. Curl of Rice University spoke for many of his colleagues in science when he proclaimed that the 20th century was "the century of physics and chemistry. But it is clear that the next century will be the century of biology."

Global "life-science" companies promise an economic renaissance in the coming Biotech Century—they offer a door to a new era of history where the genetic blueprints of evolution itself become subject to human authorship. Critics worry that the re-seeding of the Earth with a laboratory-conceived second Genesis could lead to a far different future—a biological Tower of Babel and the spread of chaos throughout the biological world, drowning out the ancient language of creation.

A Second Genesis

Human beings have been remaking the Earth for as long as we have had a history. Up to now, however, our ability to create our own second Genesis has been tempered by the restraints imposed by species boundaries. We have been forced to work narrowly, continually crossing close relatives in the plant or animal kingdoms to create new varieties, strains and breeds. Through a long, historical process of tinkering and trial and error, we have redrawn the biological map, creating new agricultural products, new sources of energy, more durable building materials, and life-saving pharmaceuticals. Still, in all this time, nature dictated the terms of engagement.

But the new technologies of the Genetic Age allow scientists, corporations and governments to manipulate the natural world at the most fundamental level—the genetic one. Imagine the wholesale transfer of genes between totally unrelated species and across all biological boundaries—plant, animal and human—creating thousands of novel life forms in a brief moment of evolutionary time. Then, with clonal propagation, mass-producing countless replicas of these new creations, releasing them into the biosphere to propagate, mutate, proliferate and migrate. This is, in fact, the radical scientific and commercial experiment now underway.

Global Powers at Play

Typical of new biotech trends is the bold decision by the Monsanto Corporation, long a world leader in chemical products, to sell off its entire chemical division in 1997 and anchor its research, development and marketing in biotech-based technologies and products. Global conglomerates are rapidly buying up biotech start-up companies, seed companies, agribusiness and agrochemical concerns, pharmaceutical, medical and health businesses, and food and drink companies, creating giant life-science complexes from which to fashion a bio-industrial world. The concentration of power is impressive. The top 10 agrochemical companies control 81 percent of the $29 billion per year global agrochemical market. Ten life science companies control 37 percent of the $15 billion per year global seed market. Meanwhile, pharmaceutical companies spent more than $3.5 billion in 1995 buying up biotech firms. Novartis, a giant new firm resulting from the $27 billion merger of Sandoz and Ciba-Geigy, is now the world's largest agrochemical company, the second-largest seed company and the second-largest pharmaceutical company.

Global life-science companies are expected to introduce thousands of new genetically engineered organisms into the environment in the coming century. In just the past 18 months, genetically engineered corn, soy and cotton have been planted over millions of acres of U.S. farmland. Genetically engineered insects, fish and domesticated animals have also been introduced.

Virtually every genetically engineered organism released into the environment poses a potential threat to the ecosystem. To appreciate why this is so, we need to understand why the pollution generated by genetically modified organisms is so different from the pollution resulting from the release of petrochemical products into the environment.

Because they are alive, genetically engineered organisms are inherently more unpredictable than petrochemicals in the way they interact with other living things in the environment. Consequently, it is much more difficult to assess all of the potential impacts that a genetically engineered organism might have on the Earth's ecosystems.

Genetically engineered products also reproduce. They grow and they migrate. Unlike petrochemical products, it is difficult to constrain them within a given geographical locale. Finally, once released, it is virtually impossible to recall genetically engineered organisms back to the laboratory, especially those organisms that are microscopic in nature.

The risks in releasing novel, genetically engineered organisms into the biosphere are similar to those we've encountered in introducing exotic organisms into the North American habitat. Over the past several hundred years, thousands of non-native organisms have been brought to America from other regions of the world. While many of these creatures have adapted to the North American ecosystems without severe dislocations, a small percentage of them have run wild, wreaking havoc on the flora and fauna of the continent. Gypsy moth, Kudzu vine, Dutch elm disease, chestnut blight, starlings and Mediterranean fruit flies come easily to mind.

Whenever a genetically engineered organism is released, there is always a small chance that it, too, will run amok because, like nonindigenous species, it has been artificially introduced into a complex environment that has developed a web of highly integrated relationships over long periods of evolutionary history. Each new synthetic introduction is tantamount to playing ecological roulette. That is, while there is only a small chance of it triggering an environmental explosion, if it does, the consequences could be significant and irreversible.

Spreading Genetic Pollution

Nowhere are the alarm bells going off faster than in agricultural biotechnology. The life-science companies are introducing biotech crops containing novel genetic traits from other plants, viruses, bacteria and animals. The new genetically engineered crops are designed to perform in ways that have eluded scientists working with classical breeding techniques. Many of the new gene-spliced crops emanating from laboratories seem more like creations from the world of science fiction. Scientists have inserted "antifreeze" protein genes from flounder into the genetic code of tomatoes to protect the fruit from frost damage. Chicken genes have been inserted into potatoes to increase disease resistance. Firefly genes have been injected into the biological code of corn plants. Chinese hamster genes have been inserted into the genome of tobacco plants to increase sterol production.

Ecologists are unsure of the impacts of bypassing natural species boundaries by introducing genes into crops from wholly unrelated plant and animal species. The fact is, there is no precedent in history for this kind of "shotgun" experimentation. For more than 10,000 years, classical breeding techniques have been limited to the transference of genes between closely related plants or animals that can sexually interbreed, limiting the number of possible genetic combinations. Natural evolution appears to be similarly circumscribed. By contrast, the new gene-splicing technologies allow us to bypass all previous biological boundaries in nature, creating life forms that have never before existed. For example, consider the ambitious plans to engineer transgenic plants to serve as pharmaceutical factories for the production of chemicals and drugs. Foraging animals, seed-eating birds and soil insects will be exposed to a range of genetically engineered drugs, vaccines, industrial enzymes, plastics and hundreds of other foreign substances for the first time, with untold consequences. The notion of large numbers of species consuming plants and plant debris containing a wide assortment of chemicals that they would normally never be exposed to is an unsettling prospect.

Much of the current effort in agricultural biotechnology is centered on the creation of herbicide-tolerant, pest-resistant and virus-resistant plants. Herbicide-tolerant crops are a favorite of companies like Monsanto and Novartis that are anxious to corner the lucrative worldwide market for their herbicide products. More than 600 million pounds of poisonous herbicides are dumped on U.S. farm land each year, most sprayed on corn, cotton and soybean crops. Chemical companies gross more than $4 billion per year in U.S. herbicide sales alone.

To increase their share of the growing global market for herbicides, life-science companies have created transgenic crops that tolerate their own herbicides (see "Say It Ain't Soy," *In Brief*, March/April,1997). The idea is to sell farmers patented seeds that are resistant to a particular brand of herbicide in the hope of increasing a company's share of both the seed and herbicide markets. Monsanto's new "Roundup Ready" patented seeds, for example, are resistant to its best-selling chemical herbicide, Roundup.

The chemical companies hope to convince farmers that the new herbicide-tolerant crops will allow for a more efficient eradication of weeds. Farmers will be able to spray at any time during the growing season, killing weeds without killing their crops. Critics warn that with new herbicide-tolerant crops planted in the fields, farmers are likely to use even greater quantities of herbicides to control weeds, as there will be less fear of damaging their crops in the process of spraying. The increased use of herbicides, in turn, raises the possibility of weeds developing resistance, forcing an even greater use of herbicides to control the more resistant strains.

The potential deleterious impacts on soil fertility, water quality and beneficial insects that result from the increased use of poisonous herbicides, like Monsanto's Roundup, are a disquieting reminder of the escalating environmental bill that is likely to accompany the introduction of herbicide-tolerant crops.

The new pest-resistant transgenic crops pose similar environmental problems. Life-science companies are readying transgenic crops that produce insecticide in every cell of each plant. Several crops, including Ciba Geigy's pest-resistant "maximizer corn" and Rohm and Haas's pest-resistant tobacco are already available on the commercial market. A growing body of scientific evidence points to the likelihood of creating "super bugs" resistant to the effects of the new pesticide-producing genetic crops.

The new generation of virus-resistant transgenic crops pose the equally dangerous possibility of creating new viruses that have never before existed in nature. Concerns are surfacing among scientists and in scientific literature over the possibility that the protein genes could recombine with genes in related viruses that find their way naturally into the transgenic plant, creating a recombinant virus with novel features.

A growing number of ecologists warn that the biggest danger might lie in what is called "gene flow"—the transfer of genes from altered crops to weedy relatives by way of cross-pollination. Researchers are concerned that manufactured genes for herbicide tolerance, and pest and viral resistance, might escape and, through cross pollination, insert themselves into the genetic makeup of weedy relatives, creating weeds that are resistant to herbicides, pests and viruses. Fears over the possibility of transgenic genes jumping to wild weedy relatives heightened in 1996 when a Danish research team, working under the auspices of Denmark's Environmental Science and Technology Department, observed the transfer of a gene from a transgenic crop to a wild weedy relative—something critics of deliberate-release experiments have warned of for years and biotech companies have dismissed as a remote or nonexistent possibility.

Transnational life-science companies project that within 10 to 15 years, all of the major crops grown in the world will be genetically engineered to include herbicide-, pest-, virus-, bacterial-, fungus- and stress-resistant genes. Millions of acres of agricultural land and commercial forest will be transformed in the most daring experiment ever undertaken to remake the biological world. Proponents of the new science, armed with powerful gene-splicing tools and precious little data on potential impacts, are charging into this new world of agricultural biotechnology, giddy over the potential benefits and confident that the risks are minimum or non-existent. They may be right. But, what if they are wrong?

Insuring Disaster

The insurance industry quietly let it be known several years ago that it would not insure the release of genetically engineered organisms into the environment against the possibility of catastrophic environmental damage, because the industry lacks a risk-assessment science—a predictive ecology—with which to judge the risk of any given introduction. In short, the insurance industry clearly understands the Kafka-esque implications of a government regime claiming to regulate a technology in the absence of clear scientific knowledge.

Increasingly nervous over the insurance question, one of the biotech trade associations attempted early on to raise an insurance pool among its member organizations, but gave up when it failed to raise sufficient funds to make the pool operable. Some observers worried, at the time, and continue to worry—albeit privately—over what might happen to the biotech industry if a large-scale commercial release of a genetically altered organism were to result in a catastrophic environmental event. For example, the introduction and spread of a new weed or pest comparable to Kudzu vine, Dutch elm disease or gypsy moth, might inflict costly damage to flora and fauna over extended ranges.

Corporate assurances aside, one or more significant environmental mishaps are an inevitability in the years ahead. When that happens, every nation is going to be forced to address the issue of liability. Farmers, landowners, consumers and the public at large are going to demand to know how it could have happened and who is liable for the damages inflicted. When the day arrives—and it's likely to come sooner rather than later— "genetic pollution" will take its place alongside petrochemical and nuclear pollution as a grave threat to the Earth's already beleaguered environment.

Allergic to Technology?

The introduction of new genetically engineered organisms also raises a number of serious human health issues that have yet to be resolved. Health professionals and consumer organizations are most concerned about the potential allergenic effects of genetically engineered foods. The Food and Drug Administration (FDA) announced in 1992 that special labeling for genetically engineered foods would not be required, touching off protest among food professionals, including the nation's leading chefs and many wholesalers and retailers.

With two percent of adults and eight percent of children having allergic responses to commonly eaten foods, consumer advocates argue that all gene-spliced foods need to be properly labeled so that consumers can avoid health risks. Their concerns were heightened in 1996 when *The New England Journal of Medicine* published a study showing genetically engineered soybeans containing a gene from a Brazil nut could create an allergic reaction in people who were allergic to the nuts. The test result was unwelcome news for Pioneer Hi-Bred International, the Iowa-based seed company that hoped to market the new genetically engineered soy. Though the FDA said it would label any genetically engineered foods containing genes from common allergenic organisms, the agency fell well short of requiring across-the-board labeling, leaving *The New England Journal of Medicine* editors to ask what protection consumers would have against genes from organisms that have never before been part of the human diet and that might be potential allergens. Concerned over the agency's seeming disregard for human health, the Journal editors concluded that FDA policy "would appear to favor industry over consumer protection."

Depleting the Gene Pool

Ironically, all of the many efforts to reseed the biosphere with a laboratory-conceived second Genesis may eventually come to naught because of a massive catch-22 that lies at the heart of the new technology revolution. On the one hand, the success of the biotech revolution is wholly dependent on access to a rich reservoir of genes to create new characteristics and properties in crops and animals grown for food, fiber and energy, and products used for pharmaceutical and medical purposes. Genes containing beneficial traits that can be manipulated, transformed and inserted into organisms destined for the commercial market come from either the wild or from traditional crops and animal breeds (and from human beings). Notwithstanding its awesome ability to transform nature into commercially marketable commodities, the biotech industry still remains utterly dependent upon nature's seed stock—germplasm—for its raw resources. At present, it is impossible to create a "useful" new gene in the laboratory. In this sense, biotechnology remains an extractive industry. It can rearrange genetic material, but cannot create it. On the other hand, the very practice of biotechnology—including cloning, tissue culturing and gene splicing—is likely to result in increasing genetic uniformity, a narrowing of the gene pool, and loss of the very genetic diversity that is so essential to guaranteeing the success of the biotech industry in the future.

In his book *The Last Harvest*, Paul Raeburn, the science editor for *Business Week*, penetrates to the heart of the problem. He writes, "Scientists can accomplish remarkable feats in manipulating molecules and cells, but they are utterly incapable of re-creating even the simplest forms of life in test tubes. Germplasm provides our lifeline into the future. No breakthrough in fundamental research can compensate for the loss of the genetic material crop breeders depend upon."

Agricultural biotechnology greatly increases the uniformity of agricultural practices as did the Green Revolution when it was introduced more than 30 years ago. Like its predecessor, the goal is to create superior varieties that can be planted as monocultures in agricultural regions all over the world. A handful of life-science companies are staking out the new biotech turf, each aggressively marketing their own patented brands of "super seeds"—and soon "super" farm animals as well. The new transgenic crops and animals are designed to grow faster, produce greater yields, and withstand more varied environmental and weather-related stresses. Their cost effectiveness, in the short run, is likely to guarantee them a robust market. In an industry where profit margins are notoriously low, farmers will likely jump at the opportunity of saving a few dollars per acre and a few cents per pound by shifting quickly to the new transgenic crops and animals.

However, the switch to a handful of patented transgenic seeds and livestock animals will likely further erode the genetic pool as farmers abandon the growing of traditional varieties and breeds in favor of the commercially more competitive patented products. By focusing on short-term market priorities, the biotech industry threatens to destroy the very genetic heirlooms that might one day be worth their weight in gold as a line of defense against new resistant diseases or superbugs.

Most molecular biologists and the biotechnology industry, at large, have all but dismissed the growing criticism of ecologists, whose recent studies suggest that the biotech revolution will likely be accompanied by the proliferation and spread of genetic pollution and the wholesale loss of genetic diversity. Nonetheless, the uncontrollable spread of super weeds, the buildup of resistant strains of bacteria and new super insects, the creation of novel viruses, the destabilization of whole ecosystems, the genetic contamination of food, and the steady depletion of the gene pool are no longer minor considerations, the mere grumbling of a few disgruntled critics. To ignore the warnings is to place the biosphere and civilization in harm's way in the coming years. Pestilence, famine, and the spread of new kinds of diseases throughout the world might yet turn out to be the final act in the script being prepared for the biotech century.

QUESTIONS

1. How effectively does Rifkin define key terms for his argument, such as "the ancient language of creation," "genetic pollution," "genetic heirlooms," "super weeds," and "super bugs"? To what extent do these

unusual phrases seem designed to evoke strong emotions rather than
to clarify the effects of genetically modified seeds?

2. How much hard evidence does Rifkin present to prove that genetically
   engineered seeds and crops might lead to "pestilence, famine . . . new
   diseases"? What kind of scientific case studies might have been
   convincing or might be tried in the future?

3. Why does Rifkin believe that many molecular biologists have "all but
   dismissed the growing criticism of ecologists" relative to bioengineering
   hazards? Could you think of other possible reasons than the ones he
   suggests for this negligence?

Jonathan Rauch

"Will Frankenfood Save the Planet?"

*Jonathan Rauch graduated Summa Cum Laude with a B.A. in history from Yale Uni-
versity in 1982; since then he has been a contributing editor at the National Journal
and writer in residence at the Brookings Institution. He has appeared often on television and has written for publications such as the* Economist, Atlantic Monthly,
Reason, *and* The New Republic. *His books include* Kindly Inquisitors: The New
Attacks On Free Thought *(1993); and* Gay Marriage: Why It Is Good for Gays,
Good for Straights, and Good for America *(2004). The following article by Rauch
from the October 2003* Atlantic Monthly *argues for the need for genetically altered
foods in a period when the nature of our climate is changing, producing new stresses
on agricultural crops and the environments in which they are grown and harvested.*

That genetic engineering may be the most environmentally beneficial
technology to have emerged in decades, or possibly centuries, is not
immediately obvious. Certainly, at least, it is not obvious to the many U.S.
and foreign environmental groups that regard biotechnology as a bête
noire. Nor is it necessarily obvious to people who grew up in cities, and
who have only an inkling of what happens on a modern farm. Being agri-
culturally illiterate myself, I set out to look at what may be, if the planet is
fortunate, the farming of the future.

It was baking hot that April day. I traveled with two Virginia state soil-
and-water-conservation officers and an agricultural-extension agent to an
area not far from Richmond. The farmers there are national (and therefore
world) leaders in the application of what is known as continuous no-till farming. In plain English, they don't plough. For thousands of years, since the
dawn of the agricultural revolution, farmers have ploughed, often several
times a year; and with ploughing has come runoff that pollutes rivers and
blights aquatic habitat, erosion that wears away the land, and the release into
the atmosphere of greenhouse gases stored in the soil. Today, at last, farmers
are working out methods that have begun to make ploughing obsolete.

At about one-thirty we arrived at a 200-acre patch of farmland known as the Good Luck Tract. No one seemed to know the provenance of the name, but the best guess was that somebody had said something like "You intend to farm this? Good luck!" The land was rolling, rather than flat, and its slopes came together to form natural troughs for rainwater. Ordinarily this highly erodible land would be suitable for cows, not crops. Yet it was dense with wheat—wheat yielding almost twice what could normally be expected, and in soil that had grown richer in organic matter, and thus more nourishing to crops, even as the land was farmed. Perhaps most striking was the almost complete absence of any chemical or soil runoff. Even the beating administered in 1999 by Hurricane Floyd, which lashed the ground with nineteen inches of rain in less than twenty-four hours, produced no significant runoff or erosion. The land simply absorbed the sheets of water before they could course downhill.

At another site, a few miles away, I saw why. On land planted in corn whose shoots had only just broken the surface, Paul Davis, the extension agent, wedged a shovel into the ground and dislodged about eight inches of topsoil. Then he reached down and picked up a clump. Ploughed soil, having been stirred up and turned over again and again, becomes lifeless and homogeneous, but the clump that Davis held out was alive. I immediately noticed three squirming earthworms, one grub, and quantities of tiny white insects that looked very busy. As if in greeting, a worm defecated. "Plant-available food!" a delighted Davis exclaimed.

This soil, like that of the Good Luck Tract, had not been ploughed for years, allowing the underground ecosystem to return. Insects and roots and microorganisms had given the soil an elaborate architecture, which held the earth in place and made it a sponge for water. That was why erosion and runoff had been reduced to practically nil. Crops thrived because worms were doing the ploughing. Crop residue that was left on the ground, rather than ploughed under as usual, provided nourishment for the soil's biota and, as it decayed, enriched the soil. The farmer saved the fuel he would have used driving back and forth with a heavy plough. That saved money, and of course it also saved energy and reduced pollution. On top of all that, crop yields were better than with conventional methods.

The conservation people in Virginia were full of excitement over no-till farming. Their job was to clean up the James and York Rivers and the rest of the Chesapeake Bay watershed. Most of the sediment that clogs and clouds the rivers, and most of the fertilizer runoff that causes the algae blooms that kill fish, comes from farmland. By all but eliminating agricultural erosion and runoff—so Brian Noyes, the local conservation-district manager, told me—continuous no-till could "revolutionize" the area's water quality.

Even granting that Noyes is an enthusiast, from an environmental point of view no-till farming looks like a dramatic advance. The rub—if it is a rub—is that the widespread elimination of the plough depends on genetically modified crops.

It is only a modest exaggeration to say that as goes agriculture, so goes the planet. Of all the human activities that shape the environment, agriculture is the single most important, and it is well ahead of whatever comes second. Today about 38 percent of the earth's land area is cropland or pasture—a total that has crept upward over the past few decades as global population has grown. The increase has been gradual, only about 0.3 percent a year; but that still translates into an additional Greece or Nicaragua cultivated or grazed every year.

Farming does not go easy on the earth, and never has. To farm is to make war upon millions of plants (weeds, so-called) and animals (pests, so-called) that in the ordinary course of things would crowd out or eat or infest whatever it is a farmer is growing. Crop monocultures, as whole fields of only wheat or corn or any other single plant are called, make poor habitat and are vulnerable to disease and disaster. Although fertilizer runs off and pollutes water, farming without fertilizer will deplete and eventually exhaust the soil. Pesticides can harm the health of human beings and kill desirable or harmless bugs along with pests. Irrigation leaves behind trace elements that can accumulate and poison the soil. And on and on.

The trade-offs are fundamental. Organic farming, for example, uses no artificial fertilizer, but it does use a lot of manure, which can pollute water and contaminate food. Traditional farmers may use less herbicide, but they also do more ploughing, with all the ensuing environmental complications. Low-input agriculture uses fewer chemicals but more land. The point is not that farming is an environmental crime—it is not—but that there is no escaping the pressure it puts on the planet.

In the next half century the pressure will intensify. The United Nations, in its midrange projections, estimates that the earth's human population will grow by more than 40 percent, from 6.3 billion people today to 8.9 billion in 2050. Feeding all those people, and feeding their billion or so hungry pets (a dog or a cat is one of the first things people want once they move beyond a subsistence lifestyle), and providing the increasingly protein-rich diets that an increasingly wealthy world will expect—doing all of that will require food output to at least double, and possibly triple.

But then the story will change. According to the UN's midrange projections (which may, if anything, err somewhat on the high side), around 2050 the world's population will more or less level off. Even if the growth does not stop, it will slow. The crunch will be over. In fact, if in 2050 crop yields are still increasing, if most of the world is economically developed, and if population pressures are declining or even reversing—all of which seems reasonably likely—then the human species may at long last be able to feed itself, year in and year out, without putting any additional net stress on the environment. We might even be able to grow everything we need while reducing our agricultural footprint: returning cropland to wilderness, repairing damaged soils, restoring ecosystems, and so on. In other words, human agriculture might be placed on a sustainable footing forever: a breathtaking prospect.

The great problem, then, is to get through the next four or five decades with as little environmental damage as possible. That is where biotechnology comes in.

One day recently I drove down to southern Virginia to visit Dennis Avery and his son, Alex. The older Avery, a man in late middle age with a chinstrap beard, droopy eyes, and an intent, scholarly manner, lives on ninety-seven acres that he shares with horses, chickens, fish, cats, dogs, bluebirds, ducks, transient geese, and assorted other creatures. He is the director of global food issues at the Hudson Institute, a conservative think tank; Alex works with him, and is trained as a plant physiologist. We sat in a sunroom at the back of the house, our afternoon conversation punctuated every so often by dog snores and rooster crows. We talked for a little while about the Green Revolution, a dramatic advance in farm productivity that fed the world's burgeoning population over the past four decades, and then I asked if the challenge of the next four decades could be met.

"Well," Dennis replied, "we have tripled the world's farm output since 1960. And we're feeding twice as many people from the same land. That was a heroic achievement. But we have to do what some think is an even more difficult thing in this next forty years, because the Green Revolution had more land per person and more water per person—"

"—and more potential for increases," Alex added, "because the base that we were starting from was so much lower."

"By and large," Dennis went on, "the world's civilizations have been built around its best farmland. And we have used most of the world's good farmland. Most of the good land is already heavily fertilized. Most of the good land is already being planted with high-yield seeds. [Africa is the important exception.] Most of the good irrigation sites are used. We can't triple yields again with the technologies we're already using. And we might be lucky to get a fifty percent yield increase if we froze our technology short of biotech."

"Biotech" can refer to a number of things, but the relevant application here is genetic modification: the selective transfer of genes from one organism to another. Ordinary breeding can cross related varieties, but it cannot take a gene from a bacterium, for instance, and transfer it to a wheat plant. The organisms resulting from gene transfers are called "transgenic" by scientists—and "Frankenfood" by many greens.

Gene transfer poses risks, unquestionably. So, for that matter, does traditional crossbreeding. But many people worry that transgenic organisms might prove more unpredictable. One possibility is that transgenic crops would spread from fields into forests or other wild lands and there become environmental nuisances, or worse. A further risk is that transgenic plants might cross-pollinate with neighboring wild plants, producing "superweeds" or other invasive or destructive varieties in the wild. Those risks are real enough that even most biotech enthusiasts—including Dennis Avery, for example—favor some government regulation of transgenic crops.

What is much less widely appreciated is biotech's potential to do the environment good. Take as an example continuous no-till farming, which really works best with the help of transgenic crops. Human beings have been ploughing for so long that we tend to forget why we started doing it in the first place. The short answer: weed control. Turning over the soil between plantings smothers weeds and their seeds. If you don't plough, your land becomes a weed garden—unless you use herbicides to kill the weeds. Herbicides, however, are expensive, and can be complicated to apply. And they tend to kill the good with the bad.

In the mid-1990s the agricultural-products company Monsanto introduced a transgenic soybean variety called Roundup Ready. As the name implies, these soybeans tolerate Roundup, an herbicide (also made by Monsanto) that kills many kinds of weeds and then quickly breaks down into harmless ingredients. Equipped with Roundup Ready crops, farmers found that they could retire their ploughs and control weeds with just a few applications of a single, relatively benign herbicide—instead of many applications of a complex and expensive menu of chemicals. More than a third of all U.S. soybeans are now grown without ploughing, mostly owing to the introduction of Roundup Ready varieties. Ploughless cotton farming has likewise received a big boost from the advent of bioengineered varieties. No-till farming without biotech is possible, but it's more difficult and expensive, which is why no-till and biotech are advancing in tandem.

In 2001 a group of scientists announced that they had engineered a transgenic tomato plant able to thrive on salty water—water, in fact, almost half as salty as seawater, and fifty times as salty as tomatoes can ordinarily abide. One of the researchers was quoted as saying, "I've already transformed tomato, tobacco, and canola. I believe I can transform any crop with this gene"—just the sort of Frankenstein hubris that makes environmentalists shudder. But consider the environmental implications. Irrigation has for millennia been a cornerstone of agriculture, but it comes at a price. As irrigation water evaporates, it leaves behind traces of salt, which accumulate in the soil and gradually render it infertile. (As any Roman legion knows, to destroy a nation's agricultural base you salt the soil.) Every year the world loses about 25 million acres—an area equivalent to a fifth of California—to salinity; 40 percent of the world's irrigated land, and 25 percent of America's, has been hurt to some degree. For decades traditional plant breeders tried to create salt-tolerant crop plants, and for decades they failed.

Salt-tolerant crops might bring millions of acres of wounded or crippled land back into production. "And it gets better," Alex Avery told me. The transgenic tomato plants take up and sequester in their leaves as much as six or seven percent of their weight in sodium. "Theoretically," Alex said, "you could reclaim a salt-contaminated field by growing enough of these crops to remove the salts from the soil."

His father chimed in: "We've worried about being able to keep these salt-contaminated fields going even for decades. We can now think about centuries."

One of the first biotech crops to reach the market, in the mid-1990s, was a cotton plant that makes its own pesticide. Scientists incorporated into the plant a toxin-producing gene from a soil bacterium known as Bacillus thuringiensis. With Bt cotton, as it is called, farmers can spray much less, and the poison contained in the plant is delivered only to bugs that actually eat the crop. As any environmentalist can tell you, insecticide is not very nice stuff—especially if you breathe it, which many Third World farmers do as they walk through their fields with backpack sprayers.

Transgenic cotton reduced pesticide use by more than two million pounds in the United States from 1996 to 2000, and it has reduced pesticide sprayings in parts of China by more than half. Earlier this year the Environmental Protection Agency approved a genetically modified corn that resists a beetle larva known as rootworm. Because rootworm is American corn's most voracious enemy, this new variety has the potential to reduce annual pesticide use in America by more than 14 million pounds. It could reduce or eliminate the spraying of pesticide on 23 million acres of U.S. land.

All of that is the beginning, not the end. Bioengineers are also working, for instance, on crops that tolerate aluminum, another major contaminant of soil, especially in the tropics. Return an acre of farmland to productivity, or double yields on an already productive acre, and, other things being equal, you reduce by an acre the amount of virgin forest or savannah that will be stripped and cultivated. That may be the most important benefit of all.

Of the many people I have interviewed in my twenty years as a journalist, Norman Borlaug must be the one who has saved the most lives. Today he is an unprepossessing eighty-nine-year-old man of middling height, with crystal-bright blue eyes and thinning white hair. He still loves to talk about plant breeding, the discipline that won him the 1970 Nobel Peace Prize: Borlaug led efforts to breed the staples of the Green Revolution. Yet the renowned plant breeder is quick to mention that he began his career, in the 1930s, in forestry, and that forest conservation has never been far from his thoughts. In the 1960s, while he was working to improve crop yields in India and Pakistan, he made a mental connection. He would create tables detailing acres under cultivation and average yields—and then, in another column, he would estimate how much land had been saved by higher farm productivity. Later, in the 1980s and 1990s, he and others began paying increased attention to what some agricultural economists now call the Borlaug hypothesis: that the Green Revolution has saved not only many human lives but, by improving the productivity of existing farmland, also millions of acres of tropical forest and other habitat—and so has saved countless animal lives.

From the 1960s through the 1980s, for example, Green Revolution advances saved more than 100 million acres of wild lands in India. More recently, higher yields in rice, coffee, vegetables, and other crops have reduced or in some cases stopped forest-clearing in Honduras, the Philippines, and elsewhere. Dennis Avery estimates that if farming techniques and yields had not improved since 1950, the world would have lost an additional 20 million or so square miles of wildlife habitat, most of it forest. About 16 million square miles of forest exists today. "What I'm saying," Avery said, in response to my puzzled expression, "is that we have saved every square mile of forest on the planet."

Habitat destruction remains a serious environmental problem; in some respects it is the most serious. The savannahs and tropical forests of Central and South America, Asia, and Africa by and large make poor farmland, but they are the earth's storehouses of biodiversity, and the forests are the earth's lungs. Since 1972 about 200,000 square miles of Amazon rain forest have been cleared for crops and pasture; from 1966 to 1994 all but three of the Central American countries cleared more forest than they left standing. Mexico is losing more than 4,000 square miles of forest a year to peasant farms; sub-Saharan Africa is losing more than 19,000.

That is why the great challenge of the next four or five decades is not to feed an additional three billion people (and their pets) but to do so without converting much of the world's prime habitat into second- or third-rate farmland. Now, most agronomists agree that some substantial yield improvements are still to be had from advances in conventional breeding, fertilizers, herbicides, and other Green Revolution standbys. But it seems pretty clear that biotechnology holds more promise—probably much more. Recall that world food output will need to at least double and possibly triple over the next several decades. Even if production could be increased that much using conventional technology, which is doubtful, the required amounts of pesticide and fertilizer and other polluting chemicals would be immense. If properly developed, disseminated, and used, genetically modified crops might well be the best hope the planet has got.

If properly developed, disseminated, and used. That tripartite qualification turns out to be important, and it brings the environmental community squarely, and at the moment rather jarringly, into the picture.

Not long ago I went to see David Sandalow in his office at the World Wildlife Fund, in Washington, D.C. Sandalow, the organization's executive vice-president in charge of conservation programs, is a tall, affable, polished, and slightly reticent man in his forties who holds degrees from Yale and the University of Michigan Law School.

Some weeks earlier, over lunch, I had mentioned Dennis Avery's claim that genetic modification had great environmental potential. I was surprised when Sandalow told me he agreed. Later, in our interview in his office, I asked him to elaborate. "With biotechnology," he said, "there are no simple answers. Biotechnology has huge potential benefits and huge risks, and we need to address both as we move forward. The huge potential benefits include increased productivity of arable land, which could relieve pressure on forests. They include decreased pesticide usage. But the huge risks include severe ecological disruptions—from gene flow and from enhanced invasiveness, which is a very antiseptic word for some very scary stuff."

I asked if he thought that, absent biotechnology, the world could feed everybody over the next forty or fifty years without ploughing down the rain forests. Instead of answering directly he said, "Biotechnology could be part of our arsenal if we can overcome some of the barriers. It will never be a panacea or a magic bullet. But nor should we remove it from our tool kit."

Sandalow is unusual. Very few credentialed greens talk the way he does about biotechnology, at least publicly. They would readily agree with him about the huge risks, but they wouldn't be caught dead speaking of huge potential benefits—a point I will come back to. From an ecological point of view, a very great deal depends on other environmentalists' coming to think more the way Sandalow does.

Biotech companies are in business to make money. That is fitting and proper. But developing and testing new transgenic crops is expensive and commercially risky, to say nothing of politically controversial. When they decide how to invest their research-and-development money, biotech companies will naturally seek products for which farmers and consumers will pay top dollar. Roundup Ready products, for instance, are well suited to U.S. farming, with its high levels of capital spending on such things as herbicides and automated sprayers. Poor farmers in the developing world, of course, have much less buying power. Creating, say, salt-tolerant cassava suitable for growing on hardscrabble African farms might save habitat as well as lives—but commercial enterprises are not likely to fall over one another in a rush to do it.

If earth-friendly transgenics are developed, the next problem is disseminating them. As a number of the farmers and experts I talked to were quick to mention, switching to an unfamiliar new technology—something like no-till—is not easy. It requires capital investment in new seed and equipment, mastery of new skills and methods, a fragile transition period as farmer and ecology readjust, and an often considerable amount of trial and error to find out what works best on any given field. Such problems are only magnified in the Third World, where the learning curve is steeper and capital cushions are thin to nonexistent. Just handing a peasant farmer a bag of newfangled seed is not enough. In many cases peasant farmers will need one-on-one attention. Many will need help to pay for the seed, too.

Finally there is the matter of using biotech in a way that actually benefits the environment. Often the technological blade can cut either way, especially in the short run. A salt-tolerant or drought-resistant rice that allowed farmers to keep land in production might also induce them to plough up virgin land that previously was too salty or too dry to farm. If the effect of improved seed is to make farming more profitable, farmers may respond, at least temporarily, by bringing more land into production. If a farm becomes more productive, it may require fewer workers; and if local labor markets cannot provide jobs for them, displaced workers may move to a nearby patch of rain forest and burn it down to make way for subsistence farming. Such transition problems are solvable, but they need money and attention.

In short, realizing the great—probably unique—environmental potential of biotech will require stewardship. "It's a tool," Sara Scherr, an agricultural economist with the conservation group Forest Trends, told me, "but it's absolutely not going to happen automatically."

So now ask a question: Who is the natural constituency for earth-friendly biotechnology? Who cares enough to lobby governments to underwrite research—frequently unprofitable research—on transgenic crops that might restore soils or cut down on pesticides in poor countries? Who cares enough to teach Asian or African farmers, one by one, how to farm without ploughing? Who cares enough to help poor farmers afford high-tech, earth-friendly seed? Who cares enough to agitate for programs and reforms that might steer displaced peasants and profit-seeking farmers away from sensitive lands? Not politicians, for the most part. Not farmers. Not corporations. Not consumers.

At the World Resources Institute, an environmental think tank in Washington, the molecular biologist Don Doering envisions transgenic crops designed specifically to solve environmental problems: crops that might fertilize the soil, crops that could clean water, crops tailored to remedy the ecological problems of specific places. "Suddenly you might find yourself with a virtually chemical-free agriculture, where your cropland itself is filtering the water, it's protecting the watershed, it's providing habitat," Doering told me. "There is still so little investment in what I call design-for-environment." The natural constituency for such investment is, of course, environmentalists.

But environmentalists are not acting as such a constituency today. They are doing the opposite. For example, Greenpeace declares on its Web site: "The introduction of genetically engineered (GE) organisms into the complex ecosystems of our environment is a dangerous global experiment with nature and evolution . . . GE organisms must not be released into the environment. They pose unacceptable risks to ecosystems, and have the potential to threaten biodiversity, wildlife and sustainable forms of agriculture."

Other groups argue for what they call the Precautionary Principle, under which no transgenic crop could be used until proven benign in virtually all respects. The Sierra Club says on its Web site,

> *In accordance with this Precautionary Principle, we call for a moratorium on the planting of all genetically engineered crops and the release of all GEOs [genetically engineered organisms] into the environment, including those now approved. Releases should be delayed until extensive, rigorous research is done which determines the long-term environmental and health impacts of*

each GEO and there is public debate to ascertain the need for the use of each GEO intended for release into the environment.

Under this policy the cleaner water and healthier soil that continuous no-till farming has already brought to the Chesapeake Bay watershed would be undone, and countless tons of polluted runoff and eroded topsoil would accumulate in Virginia rivers and streams while debaters debated and researchers researched. Recall David Sandalow: "Biotechnology has huge potential benefits and huge risks, and we need to address both as we move forward." A lot of environmentalists would say instead, "before we move forward." That is an important difference, particularly because the big population squeeze will happen not in the distant future but over the next several decades.

For reasons having more to do with politics than with logic, the modern environmental movement was to a large extent founded on suspicion of markets and artificial substances. Markets exploit the earth; chemicals poison it. Biotech touches both hot buttons. It is being pushed forward by greedy corporations, and it seems to be the very epitome of the unnatural.

Still, I hereby hazard a prediction. In ten years or less, most American environmentalists (European ones are more dogmatic) will regard genetic modification as one of their most powerful tools. In only the past ten years or so, after all, environmentalists have reversed field and embraced market mechanisms—tradable emissions permits and the like—as useful in the fight against pollution. The environmental logic of biotechnology is, if anything, even more compelling. The potential upside of genetic modification is simply too large to ignore—and therefore environmentalists will not ignore it. Biotechnology will transform agriculture, and in doing so will transform American environmentalism.

QUESTIONS

1. Rauch takes a very different approach from that of Rifkin in studying the benefits of genetically modified seeds and crops. Where does he go to find evidence of the success of the new plants? What environmental problems does he believe they are solving today?

2. Compare Rauch's definitions of key terms in biotechnology to those of Rifkin. Give examples where Rauch's explanations of key processes and effects were interesting and clear, as well as places where he might have allowed for more detailed accounts.

3. Rauch concludes his essay with several paragraphs that contrast his position with those of ecologists and the Sierra Club, which he believes demand too much time to introduce new genetically seeds and crops that can reverse past ecological and pollution damage. What would Rifkin's response be to Rauch's argument here? What would yours be?

credits

Mitch Bainwol and Cary Sherman, "Explaining the Crackdown on Student Downloading" from *Inside Higher Ed,* March 15, 2007. Reprinted by permission of the authors.

Brita Belli, "Cleaner, Greener U" from *E Magazine,* March/April 2008, Vol. XIX, No. 2. Reprinted by permission of Featurewell .com.

David C. Berliner and Sharon L. Nichols, "High Stakes Testing Is Putting the Nation at Risk," *Education Week,* March 12, 2007. Reprinted by permission of David Berliner.

Sissela Bok, from *Mayhem: Violence as Public Entertainment.* Copyright © Sissela Bok. Reprinted by permission of Da Capo Press, a member of the Perseus Books Group.

Alain de Botton, "Workers of the World, Relax," *The New York Times* OP-ED, September 6, 2004. Copyright © 2004, The New York Times. Reprinted by permission.

James Bovard, "Surveillance State" from *The American Conservative,* May 19, 2003. Reprinted by permission of The American Conservative.

David Brin, "Three Cheers for the Surveillance Society!" from *Salon.com,* August 4, 2004. Reprinted by permission of the author.

Dacia Charlesworth, speech "Which Number Will You Be?" delivered at the National Society of Collegiate Scholars Induction Ceremony, Robert Morris University, September 19, 2004. Reprinted by permission of the author.

Linda Chavez, "Hispanics and the American Dream," *Imprimis,* November 1996, Vol. 24, No. 12. Reprinted by permission from *Imprimis,* a publication of Hillsdale College.

Dara Colwell, "Carbon Offsets: Buying Your Way Out of Responsibility" posted April 11, 2007 on AlterNet. http://www.alternet. org/story/50077/ Reprinted by permission of AlterNet.

index